A
LIFETIME
OF
*R*ELATIONSHIPS

A LIFETIME OF RELATIONSHIPS

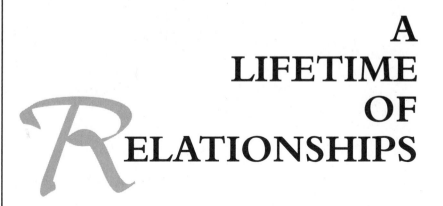

Nelly Vanzetti
Private Practice
Tulsa, Oklahoma

Steve Duck
University of Iowa

Brooks/Cole Publishing Company

I(T)P™ An International Thomson Publishing Company

Pacific Grove • Albany • Bonn • Boston • Cincinnati • Detroit • London • Madrid • Melbourne
Mexico City • New York • Paris • San Francisco • Singapore • Tokyo • Toronto • Washington

Sponsoring Editor: *Marianne Taflinger*
Marketing Team: *Jean Thompson and Carolyn Crockett*
Editorial Assistant: *Laura Donahue*
Production Coordinator: *Fiorella Ljunggren*
Production: *Jane Hoover, Lifland et al., Bookmakers*
Manuscript Editor: *Denise Throckmorton*
Permissions Editor: *Cathleen S. Collins*

Interior Design: *Quica Ostrander*
Cover Design: *Cheryl Carrington*
Cover Photo: © *The Henry Moore Foundation*
Photo Researcher: *Quica Ostrander*
Typesetting: *University Graphics, Inc.*
Cover Printing: *Phoenix Color Corporation, Inc.*
Printing and Binding: *Quebecor/Fairfield*

For more information, contact:

BROOKS/COLE PUBLISHING COMPANY
511 Forest Lodge Road
Pacific Grove, CA 93950
USA

International Thomson Publishing Europe
Berkshire House 168–173
High Holborn
London WC1V 7AA
England

Thomas Nelson Australia
102 Dodds Street
South Melbourne, 3205
Victoria, Australia

Nelson Canada
1120 Birchmount Road
Scarborough, Ontario
Canada M1K 5G4

International Thomas Editores
Campos Eliseos 385, Piso 7
Col. Polanco
11560 México D. F. México

International Thomson Publishing GmbH
Königswinterer Strasse 418
53227 Bonn
Germany

International Thomson Publishing Asia
221 Henderson Road
#05-10 Henderson Building
Singapore 0315

International Thomson Publishing Japan
Hirakawacho Kyowa Building, 3F
2-2-1 Hirakawacho
Chiyoda-ku, Tokyo 102
Japan

Printed in the United States of America

10 9 8 7 6 5 4 3 2 1

Library of Congress Cataloging-in-Publication Data
A lifetime of relationships / Nelly Vanzetti, Steve Duck [editors].
    p.   cm.
    Includes bibliographical references and index.
    ISBN 0-534-20628-X (pbk.)
    1. Interpersonal relations.   I. Vanzetti, Nelly.   II. Duck, Steve.
HM132.L535   1996
302—dc20   95-794
                                                  CIP

To Rachel Who is just beginning her journey through a lifetime
of relationships

Contents

6 *Pathways to Interpersonal Competence: Parenting and Children's Peer Relations*   125
Gregory S. Pettit and Mellisa A. Clawson

7 *Peer Relations during Middle Childhood*   155
Doran C. French and Marion K. Underwood

10 *Courtship and Marriage: Choosing a Primary Relationship*   *243*
Tamara Goldman Sher

11 *Marriage: Will I Be Happy or Will I Be Sad?*   *265*
Clifford I. Notarius

15 *Adults and Their Midlife Parents*   *364*
Robert A. Lewis and Li-Wen Lin

16 *Forty-Forever Years? Primary Relationships and Senior Citizens*   *383*
Judy C. Pearson

Part Three   THE NEXT MILLENNIUM   485

20   *The Future of Interpersonal Relationships*   487
Nelly Vanzetti and Steve Duck

Preface

Few among us would dispute the important role that personal relationships play in shaping our life experiences, our outcomes, our happiness or unhappiness, perhaps even our personalities and destinies. In the last decade the academic world has witnessed a surge of interest in the study of interpersonal relationships. This book reflects this surge of academic interest, as well as the interest that has always bubbled beneath the surface in the lay community, as a cursory examination of popular movies, books, and television programs indicates. This convergence of scientific and lay interest in relationships has resulted in both the rapid emergence and the ready popularity of college courses on the subject. Our goal in creating *A Lifetime of Relationships* is to make a contribution to an important arena where scholarly and lay interests overlap: the undergraduate classroom.

An excellent index of the expanded academic interest in personal relationships is the rapid growth of membership in the International Network on Personal Relationships. In just seven years this network has grown from a handful of members to over a thousand, representing disciplines as diverse as anthropology, biology, child development, clinical psychology, communication, counseling, education, family studies, gerontology, health studies, home economics, leisure studies, life-span studies, management studies, medicine, personality studies, philosophy, psychiatry, social psychology, sociology, statistics, and women's studies.

Another indication of increased academic interest is that the *Journal of Social and Personal Relationships*, created in 1984, now ranks among the top ten journals in the fields of social psychology, family studies, developmental studies, communication, applied psychology, sociology, clinical psychology, and social issues, according to impact figures from the *Social Sciences Citation Index*.

A third index of growth in this field is the number of books on personal relationships published each year. Between 1960 and 1975 only about five books with "personal relationships" or "social relationships" in the title were published. Since 1981 at least 47 such titles have appeared on the academic market, including a 1988 handbook of personal relationships that is already being issued in a second edition. These numbers attest in part to the interdisciplinary appeal of the subject matter and in part to the ubiquity of relational processes in the subject matter of the social sciences and humanities.

To provide a sense of how relationships develop over time, our book follows close relationships across the life span. This approach has several advantages, including a more contextualized and integrated view of the person within any given relationship. *A Lifetime of Relationships* is the first text to follow this developmental approach. Each chapter of *A Lifetime of Relationships* is written by an expert in the topic discussed. This is a classroom textbook that presents authoritative material catering to the growing demand for relationships courses in a large number of schools and within a variety of disciplines. This feature, as well as the book's unique consideration of an individual's relationships through life, gives the book wide appeal across a range of disciplines, since students will be able to relate the material more easily to their own disciplines and extend their comprehension to other related work.

A Lifetime of Relationships discusses the specific needs and the specific influences that each relationship exerts on a person at each stage of life. Theory and empirical work in each area are used to highlight the issues important to each type of relationship. In addition to addressing the developmental nature of the functions of relationships, the idea of a lifetime of relationships encourages consideration of the diverse influences—such as cultural, ethnic, gender, and social influences—that help create an individual's experience of any given relationship. For example, students will get a clear sense that the process and outcome of a personal relationship—whether friendship, dating, or marriage—do not occur in a vacuum; the person's social, socioeconomic, and relational history influence those relationships, as do social contexts and cultural factors.

Part One of the text is an introduction to some basic interpersonal processes. The first two chapters discuss the functions of interpersonal relationships and introduce some of the processes that operate in every relationship. Chapter 3 defines and describes social support.

Part Two traces the individual's significant relationships from infancy through old age. Chapter 4 offers a look at the infant-parent relationship, including infant temperament and parental characteristics as factors in infant-parent attachments. Relationships with siblings and their influences on well-being and adjustment, social understanding, and individual development are explored in Chapter 5. The direct and indirect effects of parents on children's social experiences, particularly from the point of view of development of social competence in relating to peers, are considered in Chapter 6. Chapter 7 discusses relationships in middle childhood, as the individual becomes involved in networks and acquires a peer social status.

The next three chapters focus on adolescence and young adulthood. Chapter 8 presents the special concerns of the adolescent agenda and the place of friendship in adolescent life—a life often incorrectly thought to be based on peer pressures. Chapter 9 explores the development of adolescent sexuality and the management of puberty with its accompanying experiences and responsibilities. Chapter 10 considers the processes of selecting a primary relationship for later life, one based on romantic attachment.

The next several chapters explore adulthood. Chapter 11 describes the lifetime search for intimacy, represented for most people by some form of exclusive sexual relationship—usually marriage. Chapter 12 considers the effects of the presence of children on these forms of stable, exclusive relationships between adults. Chapter 13 discusses the nature of "the family" and the individual's place within it, and Chapter 14 looks outside the family at friendship patterns between mid-life adults. Finally, Chapter 15 considers the relationships between mid-life adults and their parents.

The next four chapters are devoted to the elderly years, beginning with Chapter 16, which discusses the challenges and satisfactions of primary relationships of senior citizens. Chapter 17 explores friendships in old age and includes a discussion of different solutions to some of the problems of old age. Chapter 18 looks carefully at the relationships of older persons in multi-generational families, and Chapter 19 explores the implications of the caregiver role for family interaction.

With Chapter 20, in Part Three, the book closes with an imaginative look forward at the changes taking place as technology, humans' increased life expectancy, the increase in the average age of the population, and the health risks associated with sexual behavior exercise an increasing effect on people's relational activities.

The subject matter of *A Lifetime of Relationships* is intuitively appealing to students. They will recognize themselves in the material and be interested in learning how their relationships work. Properly described and reported, the empirical work in this area often provides guidelines for relational skills, which students find interesting and useful. Consistent with the goals of a broad liberal arts education, the interdisciplinary nature of the material promotes students' awareness of the diversity of influences on individuals and emphasizes the desirability of considering diverse viewpoints when examining an issue.

The affordable softcover format of the book makes it appropriate for use either as a primary text for courses that adopt a life-span approach to the study of personal relationships or as a supplementary volume for courses that use a different framework but touch on some of the topics covered. Although *A Lifetime of Relationships* is written in a style and at a level that are accessible to beginning undergraduate students, each chapter includes a list of additional readings that could be used to supplement the text for more advanced classes. Class discussion topics and homework assignments provide pedagogical tools for maximizing learning. We feel that the life-span approach, the diversity of backgrounds represented by the chapter contributors, and the attention to the multitude of influences each person encounters in shaping her or his relational world combine to make *A Lifetime of Relationships* a unique and valuable addition to any course that deals with relationships. We hope you agree.

Acknowledgments

Naturally, we could not have completed this book without the efficiency, dedication, and open-minded helpfulness of the contributors, all of whom reacted thoughtfully to our suggestions and even responded to our demands! We would like to thank each of them, as well as the reviewers, who, without exception, provided insightful and valuable comments on earlier drafts of the manuscript. The reviewers are Victoria Bedford, University of Indianapolis; Rodney Cate, Iowa State University; Susan Coady, Ohio State University; Mark Fine, University of Missouri; Warren Jones, The University of Tennessee, Knoxville; Douglas Leber, University of Denver; William Todd Mancillas, California State University-Chico; Terri Orbuch, University of Michigan; Roger Rubin, The University of Maryland; Phillip R. Shaver, University of California-Davis; Susan Sprecher, Illinois State University; Ellen Strommen, Michigan State University; Ann Weber, University of North Carolina at Asheville; and Ladd Wheeler, University of Rochester. We are also very grateful to Ladonna Gardner and Donna Smith for their help in preparing the final manuscript and handling the mountainous correspondence that an enterprise such as this generates.

Nelly Vanzetti
Steve Duck

Part One

Fundamentals of Human Relationships

1 An Introduction to Personal Relationships

Steve Duck
University of Iowa

Nelly Vanzetti
Private Practice, Tulsa

This chapter introduces you to some of the fundamental reasons why relationships throughout one's lifetime are not only pleasant but also necessary for both physical and psychological health. The chapter presents some thought-provoking questions about relationships and their nature. You will find out that although everyone has relationships and knows intuitively how they work, it is easy to overlook some of the important things that relationships do for us. You will also learn something about different perspectives on relationships and how you can start to think about them in new and more expert ways.

NV & SD

Chapter Outline

- What Is a "Personal Relationship"?
- Why Do We Have Relationships at All?
The Functions of Personal Relationships
- Summary

We all take part in all sorts of relationships virtually every day of our lives. We are sons or daughters, brothers or sisters, friends, acquaintances, colleagues, lovers, husbands or wives, mothers or fathers. Yet it has proved no easy thing to define a personal relationship or to indicate the elements that are necessary before something can be called "a relationship." What makes a relationship fundamentally different from an unconnected series of interactions? What qualities of interactions distinguish "a personal relationship" from "an acquaintance" or the activities of strangers thrown together? What aspects of behavior or feelings are essential to relationships? This chapter will present several perspectives on personal relationships and explore the functions of relationships, the "ideal" features of personal relationships, and the behaviors that characterize personal relationships.

WHAT IS A "PERSONAL RELATIONSHIP"?

Over the years, many perspectives on personal relationships have been proposed by researchers working in this area. This section will review a few of the more important perspectives, or models, that have been developed. Bear in mind, however, that these are based on the Western culture in which most of the research has been done and that not all cultures share the same assumptions about relationships (see Box 1).

A General Model: Prototypical Features of Relationships

The research on **prototypical features** (essential elements) of personal relationships has concentrated on adults' beliefs about the characteristics of a friend. We know that people expect different things from a relationship partner at different stages in their lives. For example, infants need to be fed, children need playmates, adolescents seek groups to join, and adults look for sexual partners and companions. Some important similarities underlie these differences, however. These will be sketched out in this chapter, and the general discussion of the prototypical features of relationships presented here will focus on adults' beliefs. Chapters 4 through 19 are devoted to discussion of the specific beliefs associated with each developmental stage.

Keith Davis and Michael Todd published a report in 1985 that showed that there are distinctive adult ways of defining the prototypical friend. These investigators used a technique called **Paradigm Case Formulation,** which generates the classic features of a particular phenomenon. In principle, these features should distinguish a generic case of the phenomenon from other closely allied but different phenomena. For example, suppose the key features of a friendship are identified as "participating in the relationship as equals," "spending a lot of time together," "doing things for each other," "enjoying each other's company," "accepting each other as each really is," "respecting each other," and so forth. The procedure then goes on to see what happens when a given feature is deleted. For example, does a relationship cease to be friendship if the two people cannot spend a lot of time together or cannot do things for each other? Using this latter example, Davis and Todd were able to distinguish "dormant friendships" from "active friendships," but to determine that both still count as friendships.

As another example, if trust is important in friendship, does it matter what the trust applies to, and does the nature of the relationship change if there are restrictions on trust? For example, Juanita may trust Sophie as a friend who would help her whenever she needs help, but she might be wary of telling Sophie too much about Grover because she knows that Sophie finds him attractive, too. Are they still friends, or must the trust of friends be unconditional and unlimited? From adolescence on, people's definitions of the ideal friendship change very little. (Many of the features

---

Box 1

Relationship Ideas in Other Cultures

According to June Ock Yum (1988), one of the main differences between Eastern and Western relationships is the Western emphasis on individualism and individual choice versus the Eastern emphasis on proper social relationships and group solidarity. In brief, Western cultures celebrate the individual and his or her freedom to join or leave groups more or less at will; Eastern cultures, on the other hand, glorify the bonds between people. (For example, Confucianism, an important Eastern philosophy, has Five Codes of Ethics: loyalty between king and subject, closeness between father and son, duty of husband and wife to one another, obedience by younger people to their elders, and mutual faith between friends.) A Westerner might be proud to be an individual who resists group or family pressure, but an Easterner would perhaps see this behavior as thoughtless and disruptive selfishness. Whereas a Westerner might see a person who obeyed the group's or family's desires as a subservient conformist, an Easterner might praise the family devotion or constructive loyalty of such a person. In Western cultures, friends and partners have a duty to be fair to one another but can leave the relationship when things get out of balance (see Chapter 2). In Eastern cultures, friends and partners have an eternal obligation to one another that goes beyond a mercenary calculation of advantages at a particular moment in time.

Compared to Western cultures, Eastern cultures make much stronger distinctions between "in-group" members, with whom there is a long-lasting, mutually involving obligation, and "out-group" members, with whom there is not. Forms of address and style of language, for instance, are quite different when talking to in-group members and out-group members. Westerners might greet just about anyone with "Good morning" (if the person is known well or is a superior) or "Hi" (if the person is an acquaintance or not a superior). In contrast, Ogino, Misono, & Fukushima (1985) report that there are 210 different word forms that can be used in Japan to address a person, making distinctions between 8 different greeting situations and 20 different categories of relationship!

Finally, a Western account of a relationship might stress the importance of a particular cause ("I was attracted because of his looks," "I liked her personality," "We're friends because we like the same things"), but an Eastern account might emphasize the coming together of several things (the time was right for the meeting, the conjunction of circumstances and personal "karma," or destiny, made the relationship happen).

Yelsma and Athappilly (1986) specifically compared marriages in the United States and India, noting that Indian marriages are often arranged by parents, rather than by the marriage partners themselves.

If love (as we understand the term in the West) occurs at all between husband and wife, it is expected to develop after marriage rather than before marriage, and it may take the form of something Westerners might be more inclined to call "dutiful respect and loyalty." Along with differences in the beginning of marital relationships in the two cultures, however, there are also differences in endings: The divorce rate in the West is about 50%; in India it is more like 1%. (See also the Class Discussion topics.)

such as trust and loyalty have been endorsed as central to friendship throughout history.) The same features tend to be listed by most adults (Weiss & Lowenthal, 1975),[1] even though people recognize that the ideal is not fully encountered in real-life relationships at all times. The ideal is composed of affection/enjoyment, confiding/self-disclosure (see Chapter 2), equality, giving assistance, receiving assistance, reliability/loyalty/trust, respect/acceptance, satisfaction, and understanding. At different stages in the life-cycle there may be greater or lesser emphasis on any given feature, but, in general, these same characteristics have been reported for many years by different studies of friendship across the life-cycle (Davis & Todd, 1985).

Although the above discussion is focused specifically on friendship, Paradigm Case Formulation can be used equally well with other relationships. You could use this technique to analyze romantic relationships, for example, or the concept of love [as Beverley Fehr did in a chapter that she published recently (Fehr, 1993)]. You could use it to distinguish the changes in features of, and expectations for, a relationship that occurs when a friendship crosses over into a romance or a dating relationship becomes "serious."

[1] Note: Throughout this book, we will use the academic convention of referring to sources of information by using the surnames of the author(s) and the date when the work was published. The reference list at the end of each chapter gives the details of each source in case you wish to look it up in the library. The term "et al." that you will encounter from time to time in the text (for example, Ogino et al., 1985) is used as a space saver and means "and other authors." In each reference list, the surnames of these authors will be given in full (in the example, the full list of names would be given as Ogino, Misono, & Fukushima, 1985).

Behavior in Relationships

In addition to evaluating relationships against relational ideals, we can also assess them by observing individuals' behavior in relationships. For example, are they holding hands? Do they smile or frown at each other when they speak? Do they talk to each other or sit silently facing away from each other? By observing two people together, we can often form strong opinions as to the degree of their relationship; likewise, we display our own feelings and assess partners' feelings through behavior. Indeed, when you think about it, the whole notion of scientific research on relationships is obviously based on the premise that such judgments by outside observers (that is, scientists) are both possible and meaningful. If scientists could not observe relational behavior as a guide to the nature of a relationship, then relationships could not be studied at all. Robert Hinde (1981), a distinguished animal ethologist, has proposed some ways in which relationships between humans can be described and differentiated. He uses eight categories of judgment to make the distinctions, and he believes that in everyday experience we make similar distinctions on the basis of these categories, just as we can do more formally in research.

Content of Interactions   The fact that we can distinguish a mother-child relationship, for example, from a doctor-patient relationship is at least in part due to the sorts of things that the two partners do with each other in each case. Within a particular culture there are certain regularities about the ways in which a mother and child respond to each other and a doctor and patient behave toward each other that make those relationships different and identifiable. These regularities differ across cultural and ethnic groups as well as varying over time within groups. The kind of relationship an Asian mother has with her child is different in important ways from the relationship an American mother and child have. Similarly, the relationship an African-American mother has with her child in the 1990s is probably different from the relationship in an African-American mother-child dyad in the 1890s. Nevertheless, members of a given culture and historical period could easily recognize the differences between a mother-child relationship and a doctor-patient relationship (even if the child's mother and doctor were both female). The same is true of successful and unsuccessful relationships of a particular type. For instance, a "good" romantic relationship is characterized by affectionate interactions, expressions of love, instances of caring for one another, and satisfactory resolution of conflicts, whereas a "bad" romantic relationship might be full of interactions that are quarrelsome or stressful.

Diversity of Interactions   We can differentiate relationships by the diversity or restrictiveness of the interactions that occur in them. Some types of relationships involve limited sorts of interactions, whereas others are diverse. For example, parents do many different things with their children, from nurturing them, teaching them, admonishing them, and protecting them to playing with them and buying them presents. Drinking buddies probably just get together to drink and chat. A professor-student relationship is likely to focus mainly on teaching and learning rather than on a variety of social experiences; indeed, most universities have rules that explicitly and directly restrict the range of interactions between professors and students (for example, by declaring sexual interactions between them unethical).

Qualities of Interactions Another important dimension of interactions that helps us to distinguish relationships is to be found in the *ways* in which the partners do what they do together—that is, in the qualities of their interactions. An intimate relationship is one in which the partners sit close to each other, feel comfortable whispering together privately, joke with each other, and speak to each other in terms of endearment. A quarrelsome relationship is evidenced when the partners shout at each other rather than whisper, put each other down rather than support each other, and show negative feeling, or **negative affect,** toward each other. The quality of interaction can also be demonstrated by the subtle nature of the verbal interactions partners have: For example, a teenager who asks, "May I please borrow the car tonight?" probably has a different sort of relationship with a parent than one who says, "I'm taking the car tonight, OK?"

Relative Frequency and Patterning of Interactions The quality of the relationship can also be detected from certain other features of the overall pattern of interaction. For instance, if a caregiver picks up an infant only when the child cries, the relationship is subtly different from one in which the parent picks up the child only when it is *not* crying. A couple who have sex only when both partners desire it differs from a couple who have sex whenever either partner desires it. As Woody Allen so aptly showed in the movie *Annie Hall,* perceptions of frequency and patterning relative to partner desire are quite varied and amount to a judgment about the quality of relationship: One partner may say, "We have sex all the time—about three times a week," while the other says, "We hardly have sex at all—only about three times a week."

Reciprocity versus Complementarity Sometimes partners adapt their behavior to each other in a way that merely repeats or reflects what the other does, using a similar form ("Hi! How are you?" and "Fine! How are you?"). When each person "pays back in kind," or does exactly the same thing in return (for example, when one person borrows some CDs from another person and then later the other person borrows some CDs from the first person), that is referred to as **reciprocity,** or reciprocal behavior, and it may indicate a reciprocal relationship. Alternatively, the intercon-

---

| Box 2 | **Tie Signs** |

The existence of a relationship, and sometimes its type and strength, can be indicated by recognizable symbols, or signs. For instance, people who are in love tend to sit closer to each other than do people who just like one another; and people who like each other sit closer together than people who do not. There are other formal signs of relationship with which we are all familiar. For example, a wedding ring indicates the existence of a certain type of relationship and is different in shape and style from an engagement ring, which signals a relationship of a type that is clearly different from marriage.

Goffman (1959) referred to such symbols as "tie signs"—signs that indicate a tie between two people or among members of a group. Other examples of tie signs for relationships are the uniforms that members of some organizations wear (for example, those in the armed forces or service personnel on the same airline), holding hands while walking down the street, and wearing similar clothing (as, for example, some parents encourage twins to do and as some romantic partners do). Teenage gangs usually have some indicators of membership that involve a dress code as a tie sign. Followers of popular groups often sport particular clothing, emblems, hats, hair styles, or other badges of loyalty that denote their tie to the group and their allegiance to its music.

Take a look around you as you sit in class and see if you can see other examples of tie signs that indicate relationships among groups of people and between pairs of people. Don't overlook the fact that even the way people speak can indicate a tie between them, as can the things they carry around with them, the places they go, and the material they read.

---

nection may be more extensive and developed; the behavior of one person may differ from but complement that of the other. For example, when one person reacts to a partner's dominant move by making a submissive move, or one person responds to the partner's expression of needs by fulfilling those needs, then the behavior is not repayment in kind but is complementary. Such interconnected action is referred to as **complementarity,** or complementary behavior. It may indicate a complementary relationship, one that researchers have recognized as more complicated than a reciprocal relationship and more likely to require thoughtful awareness of a partner's needs. In a complementary relationship, the partners' behaviors are not identical but instead fit together well. Most personal relationships involve behavioral complementarity rather than simple reciprocity, and the measure of a relationship's closeness can be gauged in part by the amount of complementarity relative to reciprocity. The more the partners feel a relationship is merely reciprocal, the less likely they are to be really noticing and engaging one another, and so the less personal the relationship is. The deeper a relationship becomes, the more the partners will act complementarily—that is, will recognize and respond to each other's needs and respect each other's beliefs.

Knowledge of other

Intimacy   As a relationship becomes closer, the partners will know more about one another, they will have better access to each other's thoughts, and they will share more intimate information. **Intimacy** is derived from the Latin for "innermost," and the whole concept involves access to things that nonintimate partners do not gain access to. Usually this notion applies to the information that one knows about someone else, but it can also apply to behavior with that person. People who know one another well are inclined to stand or sit closer together when they talk, for example, and they may use codewords, or **personal idioms,** that only the two of them (or members of their family) understand. Use of such idioms helps the partners to convey messages to each other in public yet be confident that other people will not guess what is being indicated. For example, a pair of friends might use "Zoom!" to mean "That went right over my head and I have no idea what it meant. I think this guy is an idiot!" Or, at a party, one member of a couple might say, "Let's go eat some pancakes," meaning "Let's go home and have sex." Such messages exclude other people and so signal the intimacy, solidarity, and personalness of the relationship, whether it is a dating relationship or a friendship (Bell & Healey, 1992; Hopper, Knapp, & Scott, 1981).

Interpersonal Perception   The degree of relationship between two people is indicated in many cases by the extent to which one understands the other or can predict his or her feelings and thoughts (Duck, 1994). The development of relationships is sometimes defined in terms of the ability of the partners to understand each other or in terms of the knowledge that they have about each other. Adult friends, family members, and romantic partners are usually somewhat similar to each other and so can understand what their partners mean, how they value things, what their preferences and dislikes are, and so on. People in such relationships can also usually make intelligent predictions about how their partners will react to certain situations—indeed, there are TV shows that challenge relational partners to predict one another's responses to unusual situations. Partners in really close relationships usually know a lot about each other's psychological makeup and can even make subtle distinctions such as between the other person's true views of self and those things that the person would like to be true about self (the ideal self).

Commitment   Commitment is a measure of the degree to which a person feels permanently involved and attached to a relationship. However, it

feeling of permanency of heart invited.

takes at least two forms: personal commitment and social commitment (Johnson, 1982). A **personal commitment** to a relationship or to some other individual is a choice that is based on a person's feelings for her or his partner. Personal commitment can be based on liking or amount of effort and time invested in a relationship. A **social commitment** is represented by the sorts of constraints that are imposed by membership in a community, inclusion in a larger network beyond a particular dyad, or involvement in broader circumstances. For example, a person may stay committed to a marriage not because of personal desire to remain in it but because of what his or her family might think, what might become of the children, or the fact that his or her job is at a corporation that strongly disapproves of divorce. These restraints derive from social commitments, or from the person's attention to forces outside of himself or herself.

A Research Definition

In the early 1980s, a group of researchers (Kelley et al., 1983) interested in close relationships proposed an operational definition of what constitutes a close interpersonal relationship. An **operational definition** of a close interpersonal relationship is a definition that different researchers agree captures the essential elements of a close relationship and use in studying these relationships. Such a definition would provide a common framework for discussion and investigation of close relationships.

This group proposed that a "close relationship is one of strong, frequent, and diverse interdependence that lasts over a considerable period of time" (Kelley et al., 1983, p. 38). There are several important parts to this definition, the first of which is the notion of interdependence. **Interdependence** is the extent to which one person's actions, feelings, wishes, and thoughts have an effect on the other person in the relationship. For example, if your next-door neighbor got a job in another state, you probably would not move to that state because he or she was moving. Your neighbor's move would not affect your life to that degree, indicating a lack of interdependence. If your spouse accepted a job in another state, however, you probably would move. Thus, your spouse's actions have a direct effect on your actions; there is interdependence between the two of you. The term *inter*dependence highlights the two-way nature of the influence: Your partner's actions affect your life, and your actions affect your partner's life. According to this definition, then, the first essential element for a relationship to qualify as a close relationship is interdependence.

But interdependence alone is not enough. There might be situations in which interdependence is a function of circumstances, not closeness. If your college roommate decided to move off campus after the first week of school, you might have to move, too, but this would not necessarily indicate a close relationship. Since interdependence can exist without closeness, Kelley and his colleagues identified four qualities of interdependence that must be present before a relationship can be considered close.

The first of these qualities is *frequency*. In order for a relationship to be considered close, the individuals must have frequent impact on each other—that is, they must interact often in a meaningful way. Second, the effect of these interactions must be *strong*—the partners must really feel the force of each other's thoughts, actions, and feelings. Third, interactions between close individuals must be *diverse*—they must include a variety of activities. Finally, the interdependence characterized by frequency, strength, and diversity must last "a considerable period of time" (Kelley et al., 1983, p. 38). Exactly what qualifies as a considerable period of time is not precisely defined by these authors.

Taken together, the elements of this definition suggest that a close interpersonal relationship cannot exist between two people who have just met or who engage in only one activity together or who see each other rarely. This view is quite different from many widely held conceptions of what can constitute a close relationship—for instance, the popular belief in instant intimacy (the "I just met you, but I feel like I've known you all my life" syndrome) and the belief that individuals can have close relationships with people they rarely see (for example, a childhood friend who lives in another state but is still considered a close friend).

Voluntariness and Interdependence

In some cases, we have little choice about the relationships in which we find ourselves. Infants are born into a relationship with parents and have a relationship with caregivers that is both very special and unavoidable. In the early days of life, infants are dependent on caregivers for the maintenance of their very lives. Although this physical dependence may diminish with time and be replaced by emotional attachment, parents and children do not choose each other except in adoptions and even then not in the way in which people choose friends or romantic partners. Yet one of the features we most often associate with personal relationships is **voluntariness**—we believe that we have choices about our partners and that a relationship lasts for as long as both partners want it to last.

Obviously, not all relationships are like this. We do not really have direct control over who our boss is—even though, in theory, we could leave and take another job. We cannot choose which professors teach our courses, but we can pick our courses, within certain limits. We cannot pick our parents, but when we become adults we have a certain amount of control over how frequently we see them. In other ways it may be that even these freedoms are illusory. We can choose bosses by changing jobs, but we can do so only if there is a range of acceptable jobs where we happen to want to live; most of us do not have the freedom to take no job at all. Although we can choose romantic partners, we might live in a small

We do not always have the choice of which relationships we are in and cannot always leave when we feel like it.

town where the selection is restricted or we might never meet the kinds of people we like the most. Or we might fall in love with someone in unfavorable circumstances (for example, she or he is just about to leave to spend three years in a foreign country or his or her parents strongly object to the relationship). Despite these difficulties with the idea that we have unlimited freedom to choose relationships, it is usually taken for granted in the discussion of most forms of relationships that the persons in them have at least some freedom of choice—perhaps balanced at most ages by a set of obligations and duties such as loyalty and commitment. These obligations are essentially freely entered into in particular cases, and the fact that there is such freedom means that throughout life we must actively attract others into relationships with us. Attraction and rejection represent messages from others about us as people; rejection in childhood, whether by parents or peers, is a powerful influence on the **self-esteem** that we carry with us right through life. Thus, the notion of freedom of choice about relationships immediately connects to the issue that relationships have implications for self-worth and self-esteem, throughout the life-cycle.

Another strong element of most relationships was discussed above—the interdependence of the partners; the idea that each partner has an effect on the other and is affected by the other. Our notions of fairness in a relationship are tied to the idea that each person does as much as the other (see Chapter 2), though this equality is more obvious in some cases than in others. Obviously, children do not do as much physically for parents as parents do for them, although they clearly can provide large rewards in other ways—through verbal and nonverbal responsiveness to parents, through embodiment of parental genetic continuity, and a host of other means. Also, we often hear parents express the view that the care bestowed on a child when she or he is a helpless infant will be owed to the parents when they are less able-bodied in old age. Of course, although relationships work best when they are balanced and equitable, like the notion of voluntariness, this is something of an ideal. But interdependence also refers to the fact that one person's behavior has consequences for the other person. Partners in a relationship are behaviorally interconnected—actually may see themselves as a unit (for example, as "a couple")—and act in ways that recognize and take account of each other's behavior, desires, and needs and that benefit each other. The expectations of such reciprocations alter through the life-cycle (see Chapter 2), but a fundamental interconnection of relational partners is a basic idea that makes "a relationship." Both of these elements—voluntariness and interdependence—may be present in a relationship or they may not; nonetheless, the elements focus our attention on what happens once a relationship has started rather than on why people find voluntary relationships attractive in the first place or why they want to exercise their freedom of choice in order to develop these interdependencies and intricate connections.

Some Restraints on Relationships

Although it makes a lot of sense to analyze relationships in terms of the features of their interactions, as described above, it is also important to note that relationships occur in the context of the whole of people's lives and are influenced by features other than individual desires. Each relationship between two people occurs within a set of other relationships, and occasionally the desires of the two partners may be thwarted by the activities of other people. For example, Romeo and Juliet loved each other but were not permitted to get married because their families objected. We often experience such influences of other people in our everyday lives. Even today, parents sometimes disagree quite strongly with their children's choice of romantic partner. At school, children occasionally experience peer pressure that encourages them to avoid someone they really like. An adolescent may be strongly discouraged by his or her own friends from getting into a relationship with someone from another social group or a rival gang. As a final example, parents can influence children's social relationships directly and indirectly, whether by the choice of neighborhood in which they live or the kinds of playmates they invite into the home and those they discourage from visiting. Thus, although we might think that choices of and interactions within friendships and other relationships are under the control of the partners themselves, this is only a part of the story.

WHY DO WE HAVE RELATIONSHIPS AT ALL? THE FUNCTIONS OF PERSONAL RELATIONSHIPS

Robert Weiss (1974) suggested that there are seven basic benefits, functions, or **provisions of relationships** that draw us into them. As later chapters of the book will show, the emphasis on each of these provisions changes somewhat with age, but at least one of them is relevant to a person of any age in any sort of relationship.

Weiss's Provisions of Relationships

Assistance and Physical Support   Relationships offer us support or help with tasks that are too difficult for us to perform on our own. Obviously, this can be true in the case of physical tasks such as lifting large ob-

Our relational partners often provide physical assistance as well as emotional support.

jects or changing residence, but it is also true of some activities that require advice or guidance. Various forms of help with routine daily tasks are provided by friends and relatives. The division of labor has been shown to be one of the major features of a romantic relationship's progressive development, and it often extends into division of leisure activities as well as distribution of responsibility for household tasks (Huston, Surra, Fitzgerald, & Cate, 1981).

Belonging and a Sense of Reliable Alliance Relationships offer us a sense of membership, acceptance, and availability of others to whom we can turn in an emergency—they offer us a **reliable alliance.** A person who can be trusted to be a friend when you are in need is a friend indeed. One of the most powerful elements of loneliness is the loss of a sense of membership and inclusion. Even the U.S. Constitution recognizes the importance of this factor when it defines treason as "adhering to the enemies [of the United States] or giving them aid or comfort" (Article iii, section 3). This definition recognizes that including others in our community and giving them physical assistance or emotional support is a good measure of relationship to them; we should help and support those who are our friends, but we should not give such aid or comfort to our enemies.

Emotional Integration Relationships offer us a sounding board for our opinions and emotional reactions. By using these sounding boards, we can assess the appropriateness of our responses and our reactions to events and experiences of the world. Although we are all members of a culture that conducts itself in particular ways (for example, members of the Western European culture wear black to funerals, but members of many other cultures consider white the color of mourning), relationships are minicultures in which people agree about the ways in which things should be done. Partners in a relationship develop their own ways of reacting to events and their own beliefs about what sorts of things matter and should be attended to.

Communication about Self Relationships offer us a place in which to express ourselves and voice our opinions and values or else disclose and "ventilate" about things that concern us. One of the frequent comments people make about their close personal relationships is that they feel they can say what they really think and still be understood and accepted by the partner.

Reassurance of Worth Relationships offer us a chance to see how much other people care about us and hold us in esteem. In voluntary relationships, we are valued for who we are. And in Western cultures, the

Box 3

Self-Disclosure

In many relationships, it is usual to find the partners disclosing themselves to each other emotionally and, in some cases, physically. As romantic relationships develop in intimacy, for example, partners typically achieve access to each other's bodies to a greater extent than is true of nonromantic partners. For example, you can put your arm around your lover but not around a stranger. In all close personal relationships, partners typically inform one another about personal feelings, private ideas, self-revealing thoughts, worries or concerns, and intimate evaluations of life and other people. Such self-disclosure of personal information is a normal part of intimacy and is so typical of many sorts of relationships that it is often discussed in the popular media.

At early points in a relationship's life-cycle, self-disclosure can serve purposes other than intimacy development. Recent evidence suggests that self-disclosure is a much more complex process than media depictions have suggested. For instance, Spencer (1994) has shown that adolescents are often taught by self-disclosure from parents, who might say, for example, "When I was your age, I was very shy too, and I dealt with it by . . . ." The revelation of shyness on the parent's part is a self-disclosure, as typically defined, and the purpose of the disclosure by the parent is to pass on advice to the adolescent, not just to reveal intimate information for its own sake or for the purpose of developing intimacy. Self-disclosure can show caring as well as a desire for intimacy. The importance and frequency of self-disclosure as a component of relationships is just as strong in old age as it is at younger ages, with the proviso that older people are more willing than younger people to disclose negative feelings and experiences (Dickson-Markman, 1986).

number of friends a person has is sometimes taken as an index of her or his worth. Some people are inclined to exaggerate the number of friends they have, doing such things as name dropping and playing up their connections to other people. When we do these things, we are trying to send a signal that other people really like and trust us—and so we must be worthwhile persons. One of the notable features of people with depression is that they seem to have lost their sense of self-worth and come to see themselves as people who do not count—whether in someone else's eyes or in their own.

Opportunities to Help Others (and Feel Good about Self)   Relationships provide us with many opportunities to be of use to other people and to feel good by doing good things for others. A person can increase his or her sense of worth and value by feeling that he or she has been good to others, been useful, provided a service that other people could not provide, or just "made a difference." Obviously, if no one is around to be helped, then a person cannot experience this particular form of feeling good.

Personality Support   Relationships offer validation and support for the ways in which we do things and the ways in which we understand and interpret experience. We all have the occasional doubt about how we deal with the world and need to be assured from time to time that our view of things is correct. Since we all have complex ways of viewing reality that are formed into our personality, supporting our ways of dealing with the world is one way friends support our personality.

SUMMARY

The chapter has indicated some basic needs that people have for relationships. Whether relationships help us feel good about ourselves or merely offer us physical support or assistance, they serve important functions throughout our lives. We have looked at some ways to classify and distinguish different sorts of relationships and have explored some of the main elements of relating to others.

Class Discussion Questions

1. What cues do we use to assess the degree of relationship between two people? How can you tell whether two people are in a relationship and how strong it is? Describe the cues for different sorts of relationships, not just friendship or a romantic relationship.
2. Carry out a Paradigm Case Formulation exercise on friendship, romance, and love. In other words, try to establish the key characteristics of those relationships and find out what distinguishes one from the other in terms of the features that people see as central to one type and different from the other types. Do the men and the women in your class have different ideas about what goes into each category?
3. Do the models and definitions presented in the chapter help you to understand "bad" relationships (for example, abusive romantic relationships, one-way friendships, and exploitative doctor-patient or therapist-client relationships)? In what ways do these sorts of relationships not fit the "molds" described? In what ways do they fit? Can you identify other concepts that would help you understand these types of relationships better?
4. Is there anything we get out of relationships that is not covered in the section on the functions of relationships? It might help you to think

about your own relationships (both good and bad) in answering this question.

5. Consider the ways in which your romantic relationships are "arranged" for you (see the discussion of arranged marriages in India in Box 1). For example, is your partner from the same race, intelligence level, socio-economic group, educational background? Did you live in the same town, neighborhood, or residence before you became romantically involved? Were you introduced by mutual friends? Do your parents know about and approve of your relationship? How about your friends? Are you going out with someone whom all of your friends dislike?

Homework Assignments

1. a. Make a list of all of the people with whom you have a personal relationship. Then rate each relationship as high, medium, or low on each of the following characteristics described in the chapter: voluntariness, intimacy, interdependence, affection/enjoyment, confiding/self-disclosure, equality, giving assistance, receiving assistance, reliability/loyalty/trust, respect/acceptance, satisfaction, understanding, diversity of interactions, frequency of interactions, reciprocity, complementarity, commitment, constraints.

    b. As you examine your list and ratings, answer the following questions: Are there recognizable patterns of differences between relationships with friends, family members, romantic partners, or others? Which type of relationship best fits the ideal? Which type of relationship fits the ideal worst?

2. Ask five people you know to define a "personal relationship." Make a special effort to ask people from different age groups or cultures. Write down their definitions, and compare them to the definitions in the chapter. Which of the definitions presented in the text are most like the definitions you collected? Which are the least like the definitions you collected? Are there concepts in the text that are not represented in the definitions you gathered (such as voluntariness)? If these were omitted from the definitions you got, do you think that the people you asked do not believe these concepts are important in personal relationships? If your respondents represented different age groups, cultures, and/or backgrounds, can you see contrasts in their definitions that might reflect their different life experiences?

Additional Readings

Duck, S. W. (1991). *Understanding relationships*. New York: Guilford.

Davis, K. E., & Todd, M. J. (1985). Assessing friendship: Prototypes, paradigm cases and relationship description. In S. W. Duck & D. Perlman (Eds.), *Understanding personal relationships* (pp. 17–38). London: Sage.

Erwin, P. (1993). *Children's friendships*. Chichester, England: Wiley.

Hinde, R. A. (1981). The bases of a science of interpersonal relationships. In S. W. Duck & R. Gilmour (Eds.), *Personal relationships 1: Studying personal relationships* (pp. 1–22). London: Academic Press.

Kelley, H. H., Berscheid, E., Christensen, A., Harvey, J., Huston, T. L., Levinger, G., McClintock, D., Peplau, L. A., & Peterson, D. (1983). *Close relationships*. San Francisco: Freeman.

References

Bell, R. A., & Healey, J. G. (1992). Idiomatic communication and interpersonal solidarity in friends' relational cultures. *Human Communication Research, 18,* 307–335.

Davis, K. E., & Todd, M. J. (1985). Assessing friendship: Prototypes, paradigm cases and relationship description. In S. W. Duck & D. Perlman (Eds.), *Understanding personal relationships* (pp. 17–38). London: Sage.

Dickson-Markman, F. (1986). Self-disclosure with friends across the life-cycle. *Journal of Social and Personal Relationships, 3,* 259–264.

Duck, S. W. (1994). *Meaningful relationships: Talking, sense, and relating*. Thousand Oaks, CA: Sage.

Fehr, B. (1993). How do I love thee? . . . let me consult my prototype. In S. W. Duck (Ed.), *Individuals in relationships* [*Understanding relationship processes 1*] (pp. 87–120). Thousand Oaks, CA: Sage.

Goffman, E. (1959). *Behavior in public places*. Harmondsworth, England: Penguin.

Hinde, R. A. (1981). The bases of a science of interpersonal relationships. In S. W. Duck & R. Gilmour (Eds.), *Personal relationships 1: Studying personal relationships* (pp. 1–22) London: Academic Press.

Hopper, R., Knapp, M. L., & Scott, L. (1981). Couples' personal idioms: Exploring intimate talk. *Journal of Communication, 31,* 23–33.

Huston, T. L., Surra, C. A., Fitzgerald, N. M., & Cate, R. M. (1981). From courtship to marriage: Mate selection as an interpersonal process. In S. W. Duck & R. Gilmour (Eds.), *Personal relationships 2: Developing personal relationships* (pp. 53–88). London: Academic Press.

Johnson, M. P. (1982). Social and cognitive features of dissolving commitment to relationships. In S. W. Duck (Ed.), *Personal relationships 4: Dissolving personal relationships* (pp. 51–74). London: Academic Press.

Kelley, H. H., Berscheid, E., Christensen, A., Harvey, J., Huston, T. L., Levinger, G., McClintock, D., Peplau, L. A., & Peterson, D. (1983). *Close relationships*. San Francisco: Freeman.

Ogino, T., Misono, Y., & Fukushima, C. (1985). Diversity of honorific usage in Tokyo: A sociolinguistic approach based on a field survey. *Journal of the Sociology of Language, 55,* 23–39.

Spencer, E. (1994). Transforming relationships through ordinary talk. In S. W. Duck (Ed.), *Dynamics of relationships* [*Understanding relationship processes 4*]. Thousand Oaks, CA: Sage.

Weiss, L., & Lowenthal, M. F. (1975). Life-course perspectives on friendship. In M. F. Lowenthal, M. Thurner, & D. Chiriboga (Eds.), *Four stages of life*. San Francisco: Jossey-Bass.

Weiss, R. S. (1974). The provisions of social relationships. In Z. Rubin (Ed.), *Doing unto others*. Englewood Cliffs, NJ: Prentice-Hall.

Yelsma, P., & Athappilly, K. (1986, November). Comparisons among Indian and American couples' communication practices and marital satisfaction. Paper presented to the Speech Communication Association, Chicago, IL.

Yum, J. O. (1988). The impact of Confucianism on interpersonal relationships and communication patterns in East Asia. *Communication Monographs, 55,* 374–388.

Glossary

Complementarity   A matching up of one behavior to another in such a way that one behavior makes up for or fits the other (for example, submissive behavior in response to dominant behavior). (*See also* Reciprocity.)

Interdependence   The behavioral or psychological connectedness of two people, such that the actions of one person have an intricate connection with or effect on those of the other person

Intimacy   Personal feelings of closeness, expressed in behavior, thought, or speech

Negative affect   Negative feelings about something

Operational definition   A definition of a concept that allows easy measurement of the concept for research or other purposes—for example, an operational definition of *fever* might be "a temperature of 99 degrees or higher"

Paradigm Case Formulation   A technique used for generating the classic features of the phenomenon of interest

Personal commitment   A commitment to another person that derives from one's own choice and feelings, not from social pressure. (*See* Social commitment.)

Personal idioms   Special forms of speech (e.g., nicknames, codewords, phrases with special meaning) used to communicate specifically with one's partner and prevent other people from understanding the remarks

Prototypical features   Those elements of something (in this case, of relationships) that represent the essential characteristics that must be present before the relationship label is properly applied

Provisions of relationships   The benefits or opportunities that are provided by being a partner in a relationship

Reciprocity   A matching up of one behavior to another in such a way that one behavior reflects, mimics, or repeats the other (as, for example, when one person says "Hi" and the other says "Hi" back). (*See also* Complementarity.)

Reliable alliance   The sense that another person in a relationship will always "be there" for you

Self-esteem   A person's private view of his or her own value and worth

Social commitment   Those social or other forces that seem to compel a person to stay in a relationship (such as others' expectations and opinions, legal requirements, or felt obligations). (*See* Personal commitment.)

Voluntariness   The sense that relationships may be started or finished, entered or left, by one's own choice

2 Some Interpersonal Processes of Relationships

Steve Duck
University of Iowa

Although we all participate in all sorts of relationships throughout our lives, we often do not notice what makes our relationships work in the ways that they do—the nuts and bolts of relationships. Just as real iron and steel hardware holds objects together, these metaphorical nuts and bolts hold relationships together and make them run smoothly, from parent-child relationships to boss-worker relationships and everything in between. For many people, understanding and successfully managing these processes can mean the difference between relational health and relational distress. This chapter deals with some of these processes across the life span, and it explores the function of talk, the importance of fairness, the role of power, the handling of conflict, and the management of intimacy. The chapter also implicitly makes two other important points about processes of relationships: (1) The processes are important to individuals throughout the life cycle, and individual development does not stop at adolescence. We are learning about these processes all the time and adapting to them in our present life circumstances. (2) The processes happen not only to individuals but also to relational systems—thus as one person in a relationship changes, so too must the other people in it. Relationship processes are never just about individuals.

NV & SD

Chapter Outline

- Talk
- Fairness
- Power
- Conflict
- Intimacy Management
- Summary

We continually learn about relationships throughout life. In childhood we begin to understand the nature of cooperation (as distinct from achieving only our own selfish goals). In adolescence we learn about membership in groups and about romantic partnerships. As adults we enter new relationship forms, such as lifelong loving and exclusive relationships, perhaps becoming parents, becoming members of work teams, and becoming active in our communities, and gradually moving toward relationships that include roles of supervision rather than subordination. During old age we experience a whole range of possible new relationship processes to do with loss, death of loved ones, and retirement. Through all of this we experience not only the pleasures and rewards of relationships but almost certainly their painful side too. More than half of us will get divorced (at least in Western cultures), and almost everyone will experience a painful relationship loss as well as the more frequent binds and obligations of relationships that match the enjoyable benefits of them.

This continuous learning makes it all the more important for us to know about the basic processes that occur in most types of relationships. As indicated in Chapter 1, human beings typically think about relationships at any point in life beyond early childhood in ways that recognize the centrality of trust, loyalty, and intimacy. But many other processes are so familiar to us that we do not really think about them very much. For example, some kind of power structure is present in most relationships, but we do not always notice it working. The creation and the management of meaning occur in all interactions, yet we can easily overlook the fundamental sharing of meanings that creates a basis for relationships. Talk—even trivial, everyday conversation—continually reinforces and sustains a relationship. **Self-disclosure** occurs in most developing relationships and does not necessarily stop as a relationship becomes stable and intimate—indeed, partners are likely to become more familiar with each other over time, so they recognize a self-disclosing statement more easily. Various unconscious *intimacy* processes are active in relationships, such as coordination of **nonverbal behaviors** and synchronicity of thought or empathic understanding. Finally, though we might become sharply aware of an imbalance or inequity of effort or rewards in a relationship, we rarely focus on whether every single action in a relationship is "fair." But fairness is nonetheless a powerful factor in relationships.

From these and all the other processes that occur in relationships, I have selected talk, fairness, power, and conflict to discuss because of their centrality to almost all forms of relationship. Later chapters will follow up on this discussion and will also deal with other important processes that are not specifically covered here. This chapter will not explore the effects of knowledge about relationships (Andersen, 1993), the discovery of similarity (Duck, 1994), the influence of gender (Wood, 1993) or of social structural forces (Allan, 1993), the social consequences of cognitive development (Miller, 1993), or the influence of previous history of relation-

Box 1

The Interconnectedness of Relationship Processes and Experiences

Putallaz, Costanzo, and Klein (1993) considered the degrees to which one set of relational experiences has an influence on other relational experiences. They explored the degree to which a mother's experiences of childhood had an effect on the experiences that she provided to her children. If a parent has the sort of power over a child discussed in the chapter, then one of the important consequences of such power is likely to be the ability to transmit one's beliefs, attitudes, values, and concepts to the child. Since socialization is the process whereby a social ideology is transmitted to a member of a new generation, the parent plays a unique role in communicating an ideology of relationships and connectedness. Putallaz et al. (1993) show that the ways in which a mother recalls her own parent-child relationship strongly affect the ways in which she approaches the task of bringing up a child. These researchers believe that the nature of social relationships is transmitted intergenerationally by this means and that such models of social relationships are carried through life. Repetitive intergenerational communicative cycles of negative social behavior (such as abuse) are not simple products of imitation of parental behavior but are instead based on the ways in which parents teach their children to understand the nature of social relationships.

ships (Putallaz, Costanzo, & Klein, 1993; see Box 1). These forces are important—for example, our very understanding of the quality and strength of a relationship may depend on what our society defines as important elements of relationships—but such issues are given coverage in other chapters. If you wish to explore them all, please consult the later chapters and the additional readings listed at the end of this chapter.

Note that none of the four processes I plan to discuss happens in isolation. Just as we should not ignore the fact that individuals carry experiences from childhood through to other relationships in later life, we should not overlook the fact that relationships involve more than one person. A child may be developing relationship skills, but the parents too are learning—to be parents or to cope with the child's new skills, demands, and needs. An adolescent may be developing new relationship ideas and skills, but these changes also affect the family as a whole. Parents learn not only to adopt new focuses for relationships as children leave home but also to fill new roles as, for instance, they become grandparents. Therefore in reading this chapter it should be clear that a lifetime of relationships *perpetually* demands change, adjustment, and awareness of others. Development and change occur not only within young individuals but within individuals of all ages and in relationship systems.

TALK

Whatever else occurs in relationships of any type, one obvious element is communication. Communication has a number of important features that are crucial to relationships at any point in life (see Box 2). For instance, you cannot take it back; you can only try to excuse, explain, or modify what was said. (An old Arab proverb says "Two things cannot be called back: the speeding arrow and the spoken word.") Also, some scholars say "you cannot *not* communicate" (Watzlawick, Beavin, & Jackson, 1967); even silence can communicate anger, indifference, stubbornness, or hostility, for example. Third, communication is interdependent and reciprocal, not just linear—I answer you because your communication was phrased as a question; my messages respond to your messages; my talk follows the topic of your talk and vice versa. Fourth, every message has both content elements (*what* is said) and relationship elements (indicated by the *way* it is said). Fifth, communication is a process of adjustment whereby partners learn to understand and deal with each other's idiosyncratic signals. One of the bad things that often happens in conflicts is that partners adjust their communication so that it becomes reciprocal rather than complementary. They try to answer each accusation with another ("*You* did *this*," "Well, *you* did *that,* so there"). Nagging is reciprocated by nagging, reproaches by reproaches, criticism by criticism (see Chapter 11).

Communication is central to relationships—indeed, there are scholars who have drawn attention to the way in which communication *is* a relationship (Duck & Pond, 1989—ain't that great?). Obviously, communication in relationships takes many forms, but the most common form is talk (although some strong relationships are built and sustained by letters [Mamali, 1993] and even by "conversation" over computer-based electronic mail systems [Lea & Spears, 1995]). Much research has focused on the quality of this communication, and **quality of communication** is obviously an important factor in both pulling relationships together and sustaining satisfaction with them. However, the mere occurrence of talk is important. Duck, Rutt, Hurst, and Strejc (1991) showed that across a range of different types of relationships, the mere occurrence of everyday conversation was enough to sustain a person's confidence that the relationship was still in existence and was staying on track. Though

Simply talking together does a lot to sustain and continue relationships.

Box 2

Some Features of Communication in Relationships

You cannot take it back. Once a communication has been made it cannot be unsaid. What has been written has been written. Lawyers make a great deal of this in a courtroom, where a witness is supposed to tell a consistent story and not change even the smallest detail of evidence from one occasion to the next. Politicians do the same in their dealings with members of the other party. No politician ever directly admits to a change of mind without a *very* good reason, or it will be derided by the other side as a "U-turn," "waffling," "indecisiveness," or a "failure to keep promises." Once you have said something, you are committed to it. A promise is a promise.

You cannot not communicate. Even a silent student sitting at the back of the room half asleep is communicating something, whether boredom, disagreement, an implied criticism of the teacher, or discourtesy. All behavior (or the absence of behavior) is open to interpretation by others. If interpretation is "communication," then all behavior is communicative.

Communication is interdependent and reciprocal. In discussing communication in a relationship it is not always easy to decide what is a stimulus and what is a response. If a child jumps up and down and screams and the parent responds harshly, did the parent respond to the child's stomping or did the child respond to the parent's refusing to buy something he or she wanted? The child is likely to remember that it all started with a parental refusal. The parent is likely to regard the refusal as straightforward and taken for granted and to see the child's tantrum as unreasonable and an obvious stimulus for a harsh response. In the parent's view, a tantrum is a direct challenge to parental authority (relational element), not just an expression of feeling (content element) (see below).

Messages have a content element and a relationship element. Consider a situation in which a cold breeze is blowing through an open door into a classroom and a communicator needs to have the door shut. Which of the two possible communicators—a student and the teacher—is likely to say to the person sitting next to the door "Shut the door!" and which to say "Could you possibly shut the door?" Although the content is really the same in both cases and serves to get the door shut, the structure of the messages conveys different sorts of power relationship between the speaker and the door-closer. One conveys the power to command, and the other conveys a deferential request. Some important work on communication has looked at the question of whether men's and women's speech is typically structured to imply different forms of relationships between speaker and listener (Dindia, 1987, 1994; Lakoff, 1973; Mulac, Wiemann, Widenmann, & Gibson, 1988). You might like to think about that and discuss it in class.

Communication is a process of continual adjustment to one another. Over time the partners in a relationship learn more about one another's styles of communication and one another's meaning patterns or thought processes. As relationships develop and become more intimate, just as each person in a pair of communicators adjusts her or his messages to those produced by the other person (see above), so partners learn to understand and adjust to one another's idiosyncratic signals and messages. In conflict situations such adjustment to one another is often missed, and messages intended to convey good will or caring are sometimes misinterpreted as making a fuss or as signs of overintrusiveness.

such a small thing as everyday conversation is a force in relationship maintenance, the more important element is likely to be the quality of communication (Montgomery, 1988). Acitelli (1993) shows that the process of talking about a relationship essentially helps each person to focus on the relationship and the patterns, comparisons, and contrasts between the self and the other partner in the relationship. **Relationship awareness** is an important source of good communication in relationships (Acitelli, 1988).

Good communication is often extolled as the key to a relationship's success, whatever type of relationship we are thinking about. The notion frequently appears in popular books and magazines and is defined differently by different writers. However, good communication clearly has two distinct sides to it—expression and listening—and combines them to involve the following three elements:

1. The ability to understand one another's verbal utterances as they were intended; it is not merely about the expression of our own feelings and needs, but involves an important base of mutual understanding.
2. The ability to take account of the other person and his or her needs and goals; naturally, this depends on our ability to use listening skills (Notarius & Herrick, 1988)—the ability to really *hear* what the other person is saying.
3. The ability to speak openly and directly about our feelings and needs without humiliating the other person and so to assist understanding while minimizing the risks of conflict.

Such aspects of relationships have long been regarded as important but not always as important as they now are seen to be. Studies of advice about relationships contained in popular magazines have mapped out the changing ways in which the different aspects have been seen in these publications (see Box 3). Kidd (1975) showed that the advice to "communicate" had become one of the most popular forms of advice to couples in romantic relationships by the mid-1970s. In the 1950s and early 1960s the popular advice suggested that there was only one "right" way to deal with each problematic issue in marital relationships (and a way upon which all experts would agree, based on the "correct" views of men's and women's respective roles in marriage). In the late 1960s and early 1970s this advice was gradually supplanted by the notion that specific couples should resolve their relational problems in their own ways through "good communication." More recent research (Prusank, Duran, & DeLillo, 1993) shows that this view is still widely held today and has been extended to romantic relationships other than marriage (see Box 3). One of the elements in the new advice about relationships is a vision of equality and fairness in relationships.

FAIRNESS

One of the major concepts used to explain successful relationships and relationship satisfaction has been the notion of **exchange,** or, using an economic analogy, people's attempt to balance out **rewards** and **costs.** The basic idea (Homans, 1950) suggests that a person is happiest when the costs (that is, the efforts put in to maintain a relationship) balance out the rewards (the love, respect, or services obtained from the relationship)—that is, when the **outcome** is that the rewards "offset" the costs. There have been several variations and developments of this old idea, and, although scholars still debate whether a reward-cost analysis explains the operation of truly intimate relationships, the theoretical orientation is still widely and strongly held, at least with regard to young adults' voluntary relationships. Interestingly, the economic analogy is used hardly at all to explain children's relationships (which are more often accounted for in terms of the age-related changes that occur in children's cognitive abilities), adolescent relationships (which are accounted for in terms of social processes and group factors), or older persons' relationships (which are often accounted for in terms of social structural factors and prevailing life circumstances).

One early development of the concept of exchange was proposed by Thibaut & Kelley (1959), who suggested that a person's absolute level of rewards and costs was less important than the level of outcomes relative to two other benchmarks: (1) the person's usual level of outcomes and (2) the person's likely outcomes in alternative relationships. **Comparison Level (CL)** is the baseline level of reward-cost outcomes that a person has come to expect in life as a whole, a kind of average composite expectation based on past experience in a variety of types of relationships. **Comparison Level for Alternatives (CL_{alt})** is the level of reward-cost outcomes that a person expects in alternative relationships (that is, the level that a person

Box 3

Popular Magazines and Their Changing Advice about Relationships

In 1975 Virginia Kidd analyzed the advice given about relationships in popular magazines. She found that there were essentially two "visions" of relationships.

Vision I (1950s to mid-1960s) essentially supposed that there is an ideal form of relationship that is based on conforming to an established set of processes and norms that lead to relational bliss. Such processes involve avoidance of conflict and restriction of communication to issues about which partners can agree or else a clearly differentiated hierarchical role for each partner (thus, this view hold that wives should in general defer to husbands, except in the case of topics that are the good wife's responsibility, such as cooking). This belief in hierarchy and norms of course explains the consistency, stability, and rigidity of relationships and definitions of relationship success.

Vision II (late 1960s to 1970s) stressed the increasingly changing nature of relationships and the fact that partners needed to sort out things for themselves. This vision explored the importance to relationships of self-orientation and self-awareness, open discussion of conflict issues, and a creative, uniquely tailored focus. The emphasis was on honestly expressing one's own needs and views, "being yourself," and self-fulfillment. This vision also emphasized the chaotic unpredictability of relationships and the fact that success depended on individuals seeking their own goals in the context of the relationship.

Recently, Prusank, Duran, and DeLillo (1993) extended Kidd's work to see what had happened to such advice. They concluded that recent magazines contain a new vision of relationship success, based on the view that relationships have phases and stages that are predictable, even if individual partners go through change ("all romantic relationships go through rocky patches"). This vision emphasizes that relationships go through a stable sequence in which individuals' characteristics may change, after which the relationship can regain equilibrium.

The new vision uncovered in magazines by Prusank et al. (1993) also emphasizes equality, equity, and balance, as these reflect a struggle for the stability and health of the relationship. In this vision it is less important that both partners do the same amount of work than that the two partners negotiate things in a way that is seen to be fair by each of them. Also, although partners should "know themselves," they are not so strongly advised to fulfill themselves if this works to the detriment of the partnership. This new vision symbolizes the unity between the partners by focusing on the relationship as a process or system, not only on the relationship partners as individuals. As Acitelli (1993) has indicated, in this new vision it is the process of talking about the relationship that helps the partners to differentiate themselves and establish relationship awareness.

believes she or he could obtain in relationships other than the present one). Thus, if I am unhappy in my present dating relationship but my CL_{alt} tells me that I have always been even worse off in other dating relationships, I will choose to stay put, even though I am dissatisfied with my present outcomes.

A development of this approach has been labeled Equity Theory (Adams, 1964; Walster, Walster, & Berscheid, 1978). Equity Theory proposes that a person's level of satisfaction is determined not just by reflecting on his or her own reward-cost outcomes but by looking at them *relative to effort,* as compared to the partner's reward-cost outcomes *relative to effort.* Thus, if I feel that I am working harder on the relationship than my partner is, yet we both obtain the same level of outcome (if the proportions of outcomes to efforts are unequal), then I will feel dissatisfaction (probably in the form of anger), irrespective of the absolute level of reward-cost outcome. On the other hand, if I am lazy or inattentive and do very little for the relationship yet receive high rewards, and I see my partner working hard on the relationship and also getting high rewards, then I might also feel dissatisfaction—in the form of guilt—despite the fact that I am obtaining high rewards myself.

These two basic forms of **fairness**—exchange and equity—represent only a couple of ways in which fairness can be calculated by relational partners (La Gaipa, 1977). When all partners receive equal outcomes, **parity,** one partner could object that this takes no account of effort. In the case in which outcome reflects the degree of effort, **equity,** a person could object that this takes no account of valued resources (such as status, wealth, or beauty) that a person brings to the relationship. A **Marxist justice** view of fairness, however, is based on the idea that a person should *contribute* according to his or her resources and *receive* according to his or her needs, irrespective of the total amount of effort or reward.

Although not based explicitly on the Marxist justice view, a proposal by Mills and Clark (1982) focused on "communal relationships," or those in which partners are motivated more by an understanding of one another's needs than by a desire to maximize their own outcomes. Mills and Clark have presented considerable evidence over a number of years that a defining characteristic of truly intimate personal relationships between young adults is the fact that the two persons do not calculate rewards and costs so much as attend to and take account of each other's needs, at least as long as doing so will not seriously spoil their own rewards.

POWER

Many of the exchange approaches to analyzing relationships also provide an account of power in relationships (Huston, 1983). The person in a relationship who can control the other person's resources and outcomes obviously has power over that person. There are, however, different sorts of power, and in the course of a lifetime of relationships, the type of power in a given relationship may change. As long ago as 1959, French and Raven differentiated five types of power:

Reward power, based on the ability to provide resources and incentives

Coercive power, based on the ability to punish, constrain, coerce, or make life unpleasant

Legitimate power, based on the position to which a person has been legitimately elected or appointed (for example, a group leader, the chair of a committee, or the Student Union president)

Expert power, based on the skills and knowledge that a person, such as a doctor, lawyer, or car mechanic, possesses

Referent power, based on the fact that a person may have indirect influence on individuals or groups of individuals, as pop stars and film idols have.

Each of these categories of power can be applied in different ways to persons in relationships. For example, the object of an adolescent crush has referent power; a toddler's caregivers have reward and coercive powers; a boss at work has legitimate power, may have expert power, and probably also has reward and coercive powers.

However, as Kelvin (1977) first pointed out, these five types of power reduce to two when you take into account their relationship base. Reward and coercive powers depend on the same idea, namely, *compliance.* That is to say, they both depend on the subject's willingness to accept the other person's authority just in order to make life more acceptable, whether or not the subject really thinks the other person is right. The other three depend on another idea: *acceptance*—that is, the observer's willingness to accept the power as valid. An expert ceases to be powerful as soon as the audience loses faith in her or his expertise, and one partner ceases to have much influence over the other partner as soon as the other partner decides to leave the relationship. So, although relationships can be explored in terms of power concepts (Huston, 1983), such analyses frequently miss the important point that power is not an absolute characteristic of a person, but rather a relational construct involving acceptance by the person over whom power is exercised. Let me illustrate this in the context of parent–child relationships.

It is normally taken for granted that in a parent–child relationship the parent has power over the child because the parent controls many resources that the child requires, such as food. However, parents also have power over the child in the allotment of such resources as love, which may be withheld or expressed as a means of controlling the child to produce behavior desired by the parent. The withdrawal of love is a powerful influence against the performance of certain behaviors by the child, just as is physical punishment or control (Mills & Grusec, 1988). The parent is also likely to exercise power more intentionally and purposefully than the child, especially when the child is young and is being explicitly socialized by the parent. As noted in Chapter 6, this socialization can continue in both direct and indirect ways throughout childhood and adolescence. Parents often coach children about relationships (Pettit & Mize, 1993), not only directly, by instructing them on how to deal with social situations ("Go play with Tracy—and be nice!"), but also indirectly, by modeling relationship behavior through their own behavior with friends and with each other. Furthermore, parents have the power to accept or refuse certain playmates or to select the schools and groups in which the children obtain social experience and friendships or associations. They also provide stylistic family experiences that influence their children's social lives (by explicitly discouraging competition, for example, or by teaching the child to be assertive). Ladd, LeSieur, and Profilet (1993) show that parents can take different roles:

1. *Designers,* when they actively seek to influence their child's social environment (for example, deciding to send the child to a particular preschool; taking the child to parks and places where there are other kids to play with)
2. *Mediators,* when they select specific playmates, regulate the child's choices of partners, arrange particular play dates, or initiate particular peer contacts
3. *Supervisors,* when they oversee or regulate ongoing interaction with peers and playmates, or when they intervene, take part in play, or monitor what is going on
4. *Consultants,* when they give advice about how to handle situations (for example, how to deal with bullies), solve interpersonal problems, or react (or not) to provocation in the school playground

Children obviously recognize that parents have direct power to extract compliance to rules and prohibitions. The general view is that the acquiescence to such power eventually becomes *internalized*—that is, it becomes part of the way in which the child thinks about self and other aspects of life. It is also natural for us to think of power as a unidirectional force in the parent-child relationship; the parent is in control, and the child either accepts this or else experiences the conflict that results from not acquiescing. All the same, this thinking is far too simple. It has been increasingly observed that children often have power over parents, and the directionality of power is now better understood as interactional and bidirectional, even if asymmetrical. For instance, children can make their parents do things, too! At the very least, consider that parents do react to squawking children, and very often the parents' responses to their children's distress calls are immediate and extensive. Put simply, some parents will do almost anything to stop a child crying.

Often parents are powerless and their children have power over them, even though we typically think of the parent as the power figure in the parent-child relationship.

Given this observation, recent research on power and influence in the parent-child relationship has explored the complex ways in which parents and children are interdependent. Children evidently prefer their parents to exercise some authority over them, although they have views about the acceptability of some forms of control as compared to others. Tisak (1986) showed that children are less likely to resent parental authority exerted with respect to a moral transgression (for example, if the child is caught stealing) than they are to resent a rebuke for failing to carry out some family convention (for example, if the child fails to complete a chore) or for breaking some rule of personal behavior (if the child is caught playing with a forbidden friend).

The fact that children and adolescents can respond negatively to exertion of parental authority illustrates the idea that power is essentially a relational construct and depends not just on the powerful person but also on the person over whom the power is exerted (Kelvin, 1977). Interpersonal power works because another person accepts it as a legitimate exercising of control (or else sees there is no choice, which is effectively the same thing). In the case of adult friendships and romantic relationships, the nature of power is subtly affected by this critical point: A person in a relationship has power over his or her partner for as long as, and to the extent that, the partner permits the power to be exercised. Once the partner decides to "call" the person, then the power ceases until a resolution is worked out. In voluntary relationships either person usually has the power to end the relationship and so undercut the other person's power to control the relationship—a point first explored by Simmel (1950 edition) nearly 100 years ago. Of course, there are some very important cases in which this power is illusory up to a point. Married partners are usually less willing and able to just walk out of the marriage than friends or dates to walk out of their relationship. Obviously, this is because married partners often have to consider a host of factors, such as the presence of children; the fear of negative evaluation by the neighbors, friends, or in-laws; financial responsibilities; and even such practicalities as the trouble of finding somewhere else to live. However, none of these things is in theory a final barrier to the ending of the relationship, although many of them obviously present severe psychological constraints. The crucial factor is the importance of such things relative to the problems that exist in the relationship: If it is more trouble to leave, then partners will stay; if it is more trouble to stay, then they will go.

Obviously, people make their own decisions about these things, and these decisions will be based on their particular motivations. In reviewing studies of the relationship between power and heterosexual relationships among adults, McAdams (1988) notes that those relationships in which the male has a strong power motivation are more likely to run into serious problems than those in which the male has a low power motivation. For instance, men with high power motivation are more likely to be "womanizers," to end up getting divorced, and to experience greater marital dissatisfaction. They even draw pictures of women that are frightening and bizarre and show exaggerated sexual characteristics. Such pictures are thought to demonstrate a negative attitude toward women and to indicate that a motivation to control the "evil forces" will characterize much of their dealings with women, even in close personal relationships.

In the case of friendship, by contrast, an orientation toward power seems to express itself as an **agentic style** (a style of behavior that values self-expression, self-expansion, and self-display). This style is not associated with difficulties in friendship. An agentic style places emphasis on *doing things* and is one that brings friends together to execute tasks jointly. Such behavior would also manifest itself in a desire to do things for the partner and to be helpful by assisting him or her to complete tasks—characteristics that, as we saw in Chapter 1, are basic to success in adult friendships. Thus, in this case, the orientation toward power and agency can contribute to the success of relationships because it happens to align with the features desired in that particular sort of relationship.

Such findings suggest that in relationships in which agency brings about joint completion of tasks, an orientation to power will be helpful; but in relationships in which labor is more likely to be explicitly divided or shared between the two parties, the agentic partner is likely to end up in conflict with the other person about completion of (or failure to complete) tasks.

CONFLICT

Cahn (1992, p. 2) defines conflict as what occurs whenever there is disagreement, difference, or incompatibility in a relationship. It can arise from a specific disagreement, a problem-solving discussion, or stormy interactions in unhappy, dysfunctional, or dissolving relationships. Given this broad approach, conflict is an almost inevitable consequence of being in a relationship with another person who has goals, needs, desires, and intentions that may be different from our own. For example, especially in childhood, one person may be struggling to assert individual or selfish needs, and others may oppose such expression. Apart from the kinds of conflict that arise from contesting parental power during early socialization, as discussed earlier, there are two major types of conflict in the early part of the life cycle:

1. The conflicts arising in the school playground as the child moves out of the home and into the social world of peers. These are often good opportunities for learning about the importance of cooperation, competition, alliances, and loyalty—as well as about experiences to be avoided, such as bullying and rejection (Smith, Bowers, Binney, & Cowie, 1993).

2. The conflicts between adolescents and parents. These are fundamentally related to the tasks of adolescence that revolve around development of an identity that will serve in later life (Rawlins & Holl, 1988).

In later life, conflicts can arise in any sort of relationship, most obviously those in which interaction occurs most often, such as romantic relationships or relationships at work. Even at earlier points in the life span, however, conflicts most certainly occur. Anyone who has ever seen a two-year-old toddler beginning to test the limits of behavior and the extent of parental tolerance can tell you that conflict is usually first experienced in the parent-child relationship.

Conflict and Conflict Strategies

Conflict in close relationships has many possible outcomes, one of which is *increased* intensity of affection (yes, you read it right!). Braiker and Kelley (1979) indicated that many couples experience paradoxical outcomes from conflict—whether about their respective roles in the relationship or "who does what" sorts of disputes—during the development of their romantic relationship. The resolution of those conflicts very often (but not always) leaves the partners feeling closer and more intimate with one another. The process of dealing with conflict in a constructive manner can be one that results in the couple's feeling much better about themselves and one another (see Box 4). On the other hand, conflict is more familiar as something that leads to minimization of the problem through avoidance or silence or leads to blame or brute force or even violent death. We have only to pick up a newspaper to see stories of the violent outcome of conflicts. In fact, some statistics show that a person is much more likely to be murdered or attacked by a family member than by a perfect stranger, and several studies have shown that conflict increases as relationships develop (Straus, 1990). Other possible outcomes of conflict include the following:

Domination, whereby one party establishes power and control over the other

Compromise, whereby the two parties agree to a resolution of the conflict that satisfies both of them, even though they do not both get everything that they wanted

Box 4

Conflict Resolution Strategies

There are many strategies for resolving conflicts constructively, but there are also some very basic guides to doing it right, whatever sort of conflict or type of relationship we are considering at any point in the life cycle. Unfortunately, not all conflicts can be resolved in a way that appeals to both parties; however, these basic steps probably create the best chances for handling the conflict well.

1. *Define the problem clearly.* Be sure that the parties agree on the issue that has provoked the conflict and have put it in the proper context.
2. *Identify unmet needs.* Have each person spell out the needs that are not met by the way things are right now.
3. *Fix a time to discuss the problem, after some cooling-off period.* Agree on a time to discuss the issue after each person is less angry and the parties have had a chance to reflect on the conflict constructively.
4. *Have each person describe his or her needs and problems while the other listens without interruption.* Ensure that each person spells out her or his position in a constructive way while the other listens and saves questions until the end.
5. *Check back to ensure that each person understands what the other is complaining about.* Have each person ask questions only after both parties have laid out their own positions.
6. *Define a list of possible solutions.* Begin to identify an assortment of ways in which the conflict could be solved, but without reaching agreement on the answers yet.
7. *Evaluate the alternative solutions.* Consider the advantages and disadvantages of the different solutions.
8. *Decide on the solution that works best for everyone.* Consider which solution has the fewest drawbacks and the greatest advantages, given that few solutions will have only advantages and no drawbacks.
9. *Check later that the decision really does work best for everyone.* Give the solution some time to work, and then have a reevaluation session to confirm that it is working well for everyone.

Relational change, whereby the two parties agree to some new relational arrangement, such as separation, or that they will be friends not lovers, or that they will move in together instead of just dating

This range of outcomes is incomplete, and you can probably think of others.

INTIMACY MANAGEMENT

Intimacy, like several of the other processes discussed in this chapter, used to be thought of as a characteristic of relationships—that is, a relationship itself either was or was not an intimate one. So a friendship was considered "intimate" and a relationship with a salesperson or a stranger was "not intimate." Thus, the authors of even some classic works on relationships write about "intimate relationships," such as marriage, as if they are all intimate at all times (Kelley et al., 1983). More recent thinking has made clear that **intimacy** is something that can be a characteristic of a person's style of relating (Prager, 1991) and yet can also vary across time in the same relationship (Acitelli & Duck, 1987; Reis & Shaver, 1988). Like power, intimacy is better thought of as a variable *interpersonal process* rather than a fixed relationship characteristic—although it also has a strong individualistic component, as some people have a higher capacity for intimacy than others (Prager, 1991).

Think about the relationships that you have had and the ways in which they could be characterized in terms of intimacy. Think of two elements of intimacy: physical intimacy and psychological intimacy. It is likely that your relationship with your parents when you were a child was less intimate in some ways and more intimate in others than it is now. For example, when you were a child your parents had the right to touch you anywhere on your body, especially when you were a baby and needed your diaper changed. Once you grew up and matured, limits were established and extended with respect to touch. On the other hand, it is likely that your relationship with your parents became more psychologically intimate as you developed through middle childhood and acquired more adult ways of thinking about human problems—and yet, as you went through adolescence, you may have confided less in parents than in friends. Just from this simple example we can see that the way we characterize intimacy in a relationship depends on the way we classify intimacy itself (physical or psychological), the age of the person concerned, and the other things that are going on in his or her life at the time (such as whether there was a wider range of possible partners for some expressions of intimacy, like confiding).

All the same, broadly speaking, relationships can be differentiated according to the sorts of physical and psychological intimacy that occur in them. Sisters and brothers typically have more access to one another's bodies than do strangers (for example, it is acceptable for them to kiss one another on the face, whereas that would be inappropriate for a stranger to do), and lovers have more access to each other than does anyone else, except maybe a physician. People are more likely to confide in friends or acquaintances than in parents, although it might depend on what we are confiding. (For instance, many gays and lesbians are more willing to tell friends than their parents about their romances.)

Besides these aspects of intimacy, Acitelli and Duck (1987) and Reis and Shaver (1988) have shown that intimacy is developed through a process of adjustment, just like communication is. In the course of interactions, partners "read" one another and then adjust their behavior, partly as a result of their own feelings and needs, partly as a result of beliefs about the other person's feelings and needs, and partly because of knowledge about the situation (formal or informal) and social rules guiding how intimacy can be expressed (in public or private settings).

Thus, intimacy is a complex topic and not, as used to be thought, easily categorized as associated with one sort of relationship or another in absolute terms. It also changes in character throughout life, as you will see in later chapters.

SUMMARY

In this chapter we have looked at processes of relating that have important effects on the operation and smooth running of relationships. Talk, fairness, power, and conflict all operate in various influential ways in different sorts of relationships throughout life and all influence the management of intimacy. All are present at almost any point in life, having strong but sometimes unnoticed effects on the ways we feel toward people.

Class Discussion Questions

1. Discuss the notes that you have gathered in carrying out the homework assignments.
2. Form discussion groups, and split each into halves—one half has the task of disagreeing strongly with everything the other members say; the other half has the task of attempting to minimize conflict by any means possible. After about 15 minutes, revert to discussing the nature of conflict in light of what you have learned from this exercise.
3. Discuss the main features of intimacy in different types of relationships. Is intimacy the same thing in all types of relationships, so that the relationships are distinguished by different *amounts* of intimacy? Or are there different kinds of intimacy in different sorts of relationships? Try to find out whether men and women see intimacy differently. For example, do the women tend to regard talking as intimate, whereas the men regard doing things together as intimate? How about flirting? Do men and women see that the same way?

Homework Assignments

1. To tie the notions of power and talk to relationships, tell your friends that you now wish to be known as Mr. _____ or Ms. _____ and conduct your friendships with them on those terms for an hour or so. The point

of this exercise is to notice a) what it does to the way the relationship is conducted and b) how it feels to you as you do it. Make notes on the differences in your relationships, and bring them to class for discussion.

2. Each time your friends do something for you, you should give them a direct and immediate reward of some kind, whether a statement of respect, a small gift, or a favor in return. The point is to notice the effect this rewarding has on the relationship if you do it immediately. Again, make notes on the results, and bring them to class for discussion.

3. Make some notes on the ways in which you ordinarily talk to friends and to other people that you meet. Write down some of the differences in the nature of the language: Is it formal or informal? How do topics of conversation differ in each case, and what might account for the differences? How does the physical location of the conversation affect the structure of the talk and the feelings that you have about the interaction? Do men and women typically speak differently (see Box 2)? Bring your notes to class.

4. Watch a TV show that depicts some conflict, and describe the resolution strategies employed by the characters as well as the outcome that is depicted. If you have time, watch two shows—one dealing with a domestic situation and one with a situation from the workplace. Compare the types of conflict and the resolution strategies, and bring your notes to class for discussion.

Additional Readings

Allan, G. (1989). *Friendship*. Hemel Hempstead: Harvester Wheatsheaf.

Brehm, S. S. (1992). *Intimate relationships* (2nd ed.). New York: Random House.

Duck, S. W. (1988). *Relating to others*. London: Open University Press; Monterey, CA: Brooks/Cole/Wadsworth.

Duck, S. W. (Ed.) (1993). *Individuals in relationships* [*Understanding relationship processes 1*]. Newbury Park, CA: Sage.

Duck, S. W. (Ed.) (1993). *Learning about relationships* [*Understanding relationship processes 2*]. Newbury Park, CA: Sage.

Duck, S. W. (Ed.) (1993). *Social contexts of relationships* [*Understanding relationship processes 3*]. Newbury Park, CA: Sage.

Duck, S. W. (Ed.) (1994). *Dynamics of relationships* [*Understanding relationship processes 4*]. Newbury Park, CA: Sage.

Stafford, L., & Bayer, C. L. (1993). *Interaction between parents and children*. Newbury Park, CA: Sage.

References

Acitelli, L. K. (1988). When spouses talk to each other about their relationship. *Journal of Social and Personal Relationships, 5,* 185–199.

Acitelli, L. K. (1993). You, me, and us: Perspectives on relationship awareness. In S. W. Duck (Ed.), *Understanding relationship processes 1: Individuals in relationships*. Newbury Park, CA: Sage.

Acitelli, L. K., & Duck, S. W. (1987). Intimacy as the proverbial elephant. In D. Perlman & S. W. Duck (Eds.), *Intimate relationships: Development, dynamics, and deterioration* (pp. 297–308). Beverly Hills, CA: Sage.

Adams, J. S. (1964). Inequity on social exchange. In L. Berkowitz (Ed.), *Advances in experimental social psychology* (Vol. 2). London: Academic Press.

Allan, G. (1993). Social structure and relationships. In S. W. Duck (Ed.), *Understanding relationship processes 3: Social contexts of relationships*. Newbury Park, CA: Sage.

Andersen, P. A. (1993). Cognitive schemata in personal relationships. In S. W. Duck (Ed.), *Understanding relationship processes 1: Individuals in relationships*. Newbury Park, CA: Sage.

Braiker, H. B., & Kelley, H. H. (1979). Conflict in the development of close relationships. In R. L. Burgess & T. L. Huston (Eds.), *Social exchange in developing relationships* (pp. 135–168). New York: Academic Press.

Cahn, D. (1992). *Conflict in close relationships*. New York: Guilford Press.

Dindia, K. (1987). The effects of sex of subject and sex of partner on interruptions. *Human Communication Research, 13,* 345–371.

Dindia, K. (1994). The intrapersonal-interpersonal dialectical process of self-disclosure. In S. W. Duck (Ed.), *Understanding relationship processes 4: Dynamics of relationships*. Newbury Park, CA: Sage.

Duck, S. W. (1994). *Meaningful relationships: Talking, sense and relating*. Newbury Park, CA: Sage.

Duck, S. W., & Pond, K. (1989). Friends, Romans, countrymen, lend me your retrospections: Rhetoric and reality in personal relationships. In C. Hendrick (Ed.), *Close relationships* (pp. 17–38). Newbury Park, CA: Sage.

Duck, S. W., Rutt, D. J., Hurst, M., & Strejc, H. (1991). Some evident truths about conversation in everyday relationships: All communications are not created equal. *Human Communication Research, 18,* 228–267.

French, J. R. P., & Raven, B. (1959). The bases of social power. In D. Cartwright (Ed.), *Studies in social power*. Ann Arbor: ISR.

Homans, G. C. (1950). *The human group*. New York: Routledge.

Huston, T. L. (1983). Power. In H. H. Kelley, E. Berscheid, A. Christensen, J. Harvey, T. L. Huston, G. Levinger, D. McClintock, L. A. Peplau, & D. Peterson, *Close relationships* (pp. 169–219). San Francisco: Freeman.

Kelley, H. H., Berscheid, E., Christensen, A., Harvey, J., Huston, T. L., Levinger, G., McClintock, D., Peplau, L. A., & Peterson, D. (1983). *Close relationships*. San Francisco: Freeman.

Kelvin, P. (1977). Predictability, power and vulnerability in interpersonal attraction. In S. W. Duck (Ed.), *Theory and practice in interpersonal attraction* (pp. 355–378). London: Academic Press.

Kidd, V. (1975). Happily ever after and other relationship styles: Advice on inter-personal relations in popular magazines, 1951–1972. *Quarterly Journal of Speech, 61,* 31–39.

La Gaipa, J. J. (1977). Interpersonal attraction and social exchange. In S. W. Duck (Ed.), *Theory and practice in interpersonal attraction* (pp. 129–164). London: Academic Press.

Ladd, G. W., LeSieur, K., & Profilet, S. (1993). Direct parental influences on young children's peer relations. In S. W. Duck (Ed.), *Understanding relationship processes 2: Learning about relationships.* London: Sage.

Lakoff, R. (1973). Language and women's place. *Language in Society, 2,* 45–79.

Lea, M., & Spears, R. (1995). Relationships over electronic mail. In J. T. Wood & S. W. Duck (Eds.), *Understanding relationship processes 6: Understudied relation-ships: Off the beaten track.* Newbury Park, CA: Sage.

Mamali, C. (1993). *Interknowledge.* Unpublished manuscript, University of Iowa.

McAdams, D. (1988). Personal needs and personal relationships. In S. W. Duck, D. F. Hay, S. E. Hobfoll, W. Ickes, & B. Montgomery (Eds.), *Handbook of per-sonal relationships* (pp. 7–22). Chichester, England: Wiley.

Miller, J. B. (1993). Learning from early relationship experience. In S. W. Duck (Ed.), *Understanding relationship processes 2: Learning about relationships.* Newbury Park, CA: Sage.

Mills, J., & Clark, M. S. (1982). Communal and exchange relationships. In L. Wheeler (Ed.), *Review of personality and social psychology* (Vol. 3) (pp. 121–144). Beverly Hills, CA: Sage.

Mills, R. S. L., & Grusec, J. E. (1988). Socialization from the perspective of the parent-child relationship. In S. W. Duck, D. F. Hay, S. E. Hobfoll, W. Ickes, & B. Montgomery (Eds.), *Handbook of personal relationships* (pp. 177–191). Chich-ester, England: Wiley.

Montgomery, B. M. (1988). Quality communication in personal relationships. In S. W. Duck, D. F. Hay, S. E. Hobfoll, W. Ickes, & B. Montgomery (Eds.), *Handbook of personal relationships* (pp. 343–362). Chichester, England: Wiley.

Mulac, A., Wiemann, J., Widenmann, S. J., & Gibson, T. W. (1988). Male/fe-male language differences and effects in same-sex and mixed-sex dyads: The gen-der-lined language effect. *Communication Monographs 55,* 314–335.

Notarius, C. I., & Herrick, L. R. (1988). Listener response strategies to a dis-tressed other. *Journal of Social and Personal Relationships, 5,* 97–108.

Pettit, G. S., & Mize, J. (1993). Substance and style: Understanding the ways in which parents teach children about social relationships. In S. W. Duck (Ed.), *Understanding relationship processes 2: Learning about relationships.* Newbury Park, CA: Sage.

Prager, K. (1991). Intimacy status and couple conflict resolution. *Journal of Social and Personal Relationships, 8,* 505–526.

Prusank, D. T., Duran, R. L., & DeLillo, D. A. (1993). Interpersonal relation-ships in women's magazines: Dating and relating in the 1970s and 1980s. *Journal of Social and Personal Relationships, 10,* 307–320.

Putallaz, M., Costanzo, P. R., & Klein, T. P. (1993). Parental childhood social experiences and their effects on children's relationships. In S. W. Duck (Ed.), *Understanding relationship processes 2: Learning about relationships*. Newbury Park, CA: Sage.

Rawlins, W., & Holl, M. (1988). Adolescents' interaction with parents and friends: Dialectics of temporal perspective and evaluation. *Journal of Social and Personal Relationships, 5,* 27–46.

Reis, H. T., & Shaver, P. R. (1988). Intimacy as an interpersonal process. In S. W. Duck, D. F. Hay, S. E. Hobfoll, W. Ickes, & B. M. Montgomery (Eds.), *Handbook of personal relationships* (pp. 367–390). Chichester, England: Wiley.

Simmel, G. (1950). *The sociology of Georg Simmel* (K. Wolff, Trans.). New York: Free Press.

Smith, P. K., Bowers, L., Binney, V., & Cowie, H. (1993). Relationships of children involved in bully/victim problems at school. In S. W. Duck (Ed.), *Understanding relationship processes 2: Learning about relationships*. London: Sage.

Straus, M. A. (1990). Injury and frequency of assaults and the 'representative sample fallacy' in measuring wife beating and child abuse. In M. A. Straus & R. J. Gelles (Eds.), *Physical violence in American families: Risk factors and adaptations in 8145 families*. New Brunswick, NJ: Transaction Books.

Thibaut, J. W., & Kelley, H. H. (1959). *The social psychology of groups*. New York: Wiley.

Tisak, M. S. (1986). Children's conception of parental authority. *Child Development, 57,* 166–176.

Walster, E., Walster, G. W., & Berscheid, E. (1978). *Equity theory and research*. Boston: Allyn & Bacon.

Watzlawick, P., Beavin, J., & Jackson, D. (1967). *Pragmatics of human communication: A study of interactional patterns, pathologies and paradoxes*. New York: Norton.

Wood, J. T. (1993). Engendered relations: Interaction, caring, power and responsibility in intimacy. In S. W. Duck (Ed.), *Understanding relationship processes 3: Social contexts of relationships*. Newbury Park, CA: Sage.

Glossary

Agentic style   A style of behavior focused on agency, or *doing*

Comparison Level (CL)   The baseline level of reward-cost outcomes that a person typically receives in relationships as a whole

Comparison Level for Alternatives (CL_{alt})   The baseline level of reward-cost outcomes that a person typically receives in other relationships of a particular type as compared with the relationship the person is in at the moment

Costs   The disadvantages, or negative effects, of a behavior. (*See* Rewards.)

Equity   A balance of outcomes and the efforts expended to achieve them

Exchange   The activity of transacting rewards and costs

Fairness   A just outcome of a transaction, whether viewed as parity, as equity, or as Marxist justice

Intimacy   Physical or psychological closeness

Marxist justice   An outcome in which those with the greatest need receive the most, and those with the most resources give the most

Nonverbal behaviors   Movements of the eyes, face, or body that involve no speech yet communicate emotion or serve to regulate speech

Outcome   The results of a transaction involving rewards and costs

Parity   A relationship in which all persons receive exactly equal outcomes, with no regard to effort or other factors

Power   A generic term used to refer to the influence of one person over another; five types of power are defined in the text

Quality of communication   An assessment of the extent to which communication has the hallmarks of "good communication"

Relationship awareness   A person's thinking about interaction patterns, comparisons, or contrasts between self and a partner in the relationship

Rewards   The advantages, or positive effects, of a behavior. (*See* Costs.)

Self-disclosure   The exposure of one's secrets, fears, or innermost thoughts and feelings

3

Social Support: Will You Be There When I Need You?

Stevan E. Hobfoll
Kent State University

In addition to the interpersonal processes described in the preceding chapter, social support is an important aspect of many of our interpersonal relationships and one that we will use to help us understand the types of relationships we will examine throughout the text. This chapter defines different types of social support, discusses exactly how social support helps people deal with problems or challenges, and examines factors that make support networks work better—or less well—for individuals in their times of need.

NV & SD

Chapter Outline

- What Is Social Support?
- How Social Support Affects Us
- Social Support Fit
- Negative Effects of Social Support
- Personal Characteristics and Social Support
- Summary

Social support refers to the extent to which a person receives help from others and also to a person's sense of belonging to a family, group, or organization. Social support is an important resource provided by personal relationships throughout the life span. Social support is especially helpful during stressful conditions. Those who receive such support when experiencing **stress** are less likely to develop psychological or physical health problems than those who do not receive such support. Even during non-stressful periods, however, social support has been found to be related to better physical health and psychological well-being. It is important to consider who receives social support and who does not. We need to learn much more about what kinds of social support are most beneficial and about cultural differences in the giving and receiving of social support.

47

In the 1960s psychologists and sociologists began to look for a link between stress and well-being. This research proceeded in two directions. One direction concerned how stress affects **psychological well-being**. Some early studies, for example, found that the more numerous the **stressful events** people had experienced over the past year, the more likely they were to become depressed (Billings & Moos, 1984; Brown & Harris, 1978). Perhaps these researchers were just finding what you and I already know—that stress can get you down or give you the blues. Nevertheless, this was an important finding, because the traditional psychiatric literature attributed psychological disorders such as depression mainly to childhood experiences. The fact that stress in adult life causes depression and anxiety was newsworthy for mental health professionals.

Research in the other direction found that when people experience life stress, they are more vulnerable to physical illness (Selye, 1976). The more life stress individuals underwent, the more likely they were to experience consequences as diverse as heart attacks and common colds. Again, this finding may seem to support common wisdom. Disease, however, is generally considered to be caused by *pathogens* such as viruses and bacteria or by such factors as overexhaustion or injury. That stress makes people more susceptible to these pathogens, more vulnerable to overexhaustion, and more likely to have accidents illuminated the role stress plays in the disease process.

What was perhaps more surprising, however, than finding a link between stress and depression or stress and illness was the fact that these relationships were not as consistent or as strong as researchers had expected. True, stress was linked to both psychological and physical distress, but the sizes of the relationships were very modest. How was it that people survived (and even survived well) after experiencing such events as war, natural and technological disasters, loss of loved ones, rape, and other major stressful events? This presented a troubling puzzle for those who believed that stress should affect all people equally deeply. Equally puzzling was the fact that when the stressor was a challenge rather than a terrible event, some people even thrived on the stress. Other people, in contrast, buckled under the threat of such challenges. Challenging events could include such circumstances as facing an examination or hearing about a reshuffling at one's place of employment. One attorney might enjoy the stress of a difficult court fight, for example, whereas another attorney might find such altercations too stressful to handle.

The lack of uniform stress reactions and the fact that many people survive even major stressors at least reasonably well led to a new area of investigation. Researchers began to ask the question, Why isn't stress having as negative an effect on people as we expected? The area they turned to for a possible answer was *social support*. This chapter will explore what social support is, how it helps people, and why some individuals are able to obtain more social support than others. We will also consider why social support backfires in some instances and can actually be harmful to people.

As we think about stress and social support, it is important that we consider a life-span approach. For a child, stress and social support are likely to be familial or to pertain to the child's environment at school or in the immediate neighborhood. Among adults, stress and social support are usually heavily influenced by both family and work factors. As people become older, failing health and the imminence of death become increasingly important factors in stress. Many of an elderly individual's social supporters may have already died, and younger potential supporters may be separated from the elderly individual because of his or her institutionalization or the general mobility of modern society. This chapter will focus mainly on young adults and adults, but the principles you will learn apply to both younger and older people as well.

WHAT IS SOCIAL SUPPORT?

Social support is similar to many of the concepts introduced in this book in that it is not simple to define, even though we have some good ideas about what we mean when we talk about social support. You probably have many of your own ideas about supportive and unsupportive relationships in your own life. What makes the supportive ones supportive, and what are the central defining characteristics of interpersonal aid and helping? Let's consider some of the major definitions that have been suggested.

Support as Assistance in Mastering Problems: Mastery Support

Gerald Caplan (1974), a pioneer in community psychiatry, considered social support to be **mastery support**—the help we receive that assists us in mastering life problems. Working both in Israel and at Harvard in the United States, Caplan was one of the first researchers concerned with how stress affects people. He saw life crises as critically important in shaping people's mental health and thought that psychiatrists and psychologists were focusing too much attention on early life experiences alone.

Perhaps Caplan's experiences as a psychiatrist in the fledgling state of Israel exposed him to an important lesson: Amidst stressful conditions, people can accomplish much more together than they can alone. From this premise he developed the idea that when we are confronted with stress, we often rely on others to do two main things: (1) help us *feel* that we can master the challenge and (2) help us actually *master* the challenge.

Caplan's concept of social support can be simply illustrated, using your imagination. You are standing next to a table that you have to move into your new apartment, and you have only 10 minutes before a big date. You can physically lift the table, but it is too awkward to move up the stairs. A friend is there, and she tells you that she is confident you can make your date on time, which gives you the feeling of **mastery**. She also provides the solution—she will lift one end of the table and guide it through the corridors. Her supportive idea and effort allow you to master the problem. Clearly this is a small problem, but the same principles apply to the mastery involved in successfully facing a major examination or adjusting to a lost love. Significant others can supply support by enhancing our feeling of mastery and providing help that allows us to master the task.

Social Support as Information

Cobb (1976) saw social support more as information that is provided by significant others. In this vein, when people give us advice, encouragement, love, and affection, they are providing information about us or about our situation. Since we are social animals, what others think about us is very important. If others hold us in esteem, then we are likely to feel good about ourselves. If others believe that we can accomplish a task, then we are more likely to believe that we can. Even when others help us with a simple task and offer no verbal support, the fact that they are expending time and effort in our behalf gives us information about how they think about us.

Not all personal relationships provide such positive messages, however. Think about your own close relationships; some are likely to be more supportive than others. Is your mom or dad the kind of person who points out your strengths and emphasizes how well you are doing, or does she or he point out your weaknesses and emphasize that you could do better? In either case, this is what Cobb called **informational support**. Does your best friend provide helpful advice when you are in a jam? This too is informational support.

Social support can help us complete difficult tasks.

Social Support as Action Help

House (1981) and Shumaker and Brownell (1984) suggest more action-oriented definitions of social support. According to this definition, social support is the exchange between at least two individuals in which one or both feel that the *intent* of the action is to be helpful. So, if my intent is to help you and I actually do something about that intent, I am providing social support.

Note that what is emphasized here is the intent, not the outcome. Your sister might try to console you after your boyfriend has left you for another woman. She may be warm, comforting, and genuine. Still, her attempts at social support may not help. Nevertheless, we would call this social support according to action definitions, even if it did not have its desired effect.

When social support is defined as action help, or **action-oriented support**, it is common to subdivide it into five kinds of action support, as follows:

1. **Emotional support** is support aimed at making us feel better emotionally. Example: "I love you and know you can beat this problem."
2. **Advice support** is the provision of suggestions and advice.
3. **Task support** is help with completing specific tasks. Example: Help with grocery shopping or babysitting
4. **Companionship support** is just being with someone during a difficult period.
5. **Material support** is the provision of material goods. Example: A loan of cash or a car to use when yours breaks down

Social Support as a Sense of Belonging

Other theorists suggest that social support is a **sense of belonging** and being supported by others. Irwin and Barbara Sarason have done much work on this idea (Sarason, Sarason, & Pierce, 1990). These theorists are really saying two things about social support. First, they are saying that social support is a sense of belonging, or **intimacy**, that we gain from the actions and behaviors of others who are close to us. Box 1 features some questions asked in a Social Support Questionnaire. These questions deal with the intimate kinds of support provided by others, such as accepting you no matter what and being there for you when you really need them. You can take this test and see how you score.

But there is something deeper to the Sarasons's message. If social support is a feeling of being supported, then it does not come only from the environment and it does not come only from others. Social support is also a sense we carry inside us that we are loved and cared for and part of a community. Some people have this sense of being supported more than others. Research by the Sarasons indicates that even though two individuals receive the same level of social support, they may have a very different sense of being supported. According to their research, this sense of being supported is related to how much love, affection, and positive regard people receive as children. Those who received plenty of love, whose families provided them with a sense that they could be successful, and who were made to feel that they had stable relationships on which to rely, developed a strong, internalized sense of social support. Moreover, those who have this strong sense of social support are likely to be able to use the support they receive more effectively than those who lack a good support base.

How might childhood experiences in receiving support affect us? Consider a child who does not have his father's backing at critical times.

Box 1   **Intimate Support**

Receiving support from even a few intimate others is critical. This test will give an idea of your level of intimate support. If you find yourself lacking in intimate support, you might consider making friends, joining a church or synagogue group, or finding some other ways to develop close ties with others.

Answer each of the following questions using a number from 1 to 5. Then add up your score.

1 = Very much disagree
2 = Disagree
3 = Neither agree nor disagree
4 = Agree
5 = Very much agree

1. I have a friend or family member with whom I can   1   2   3   4   5
   really speak freely about what is important to me.
2. I have a friend or family member with whom I can   1   2   3   4   5
   share my personal feelings.
3. I have a friend or family member who provides me   1   2   3   4   5
   affection and warmth.
4. I have a friend or family member who appreciates me   1   2   3   4   5
   as I am.

What does your score mean? Scores 18 or above indicate excellent intimate support. Scores from 15 to 17 indicate good intimate support. Scores from 12 to 15 indicate some weak areas of intimate support. Scores below 12 indicate that you may be feeling unsupported.

What do you do if you scored low?

Invest in making friends.

Be a good "feeling sharer" and "feeling listener"; open up more to others and be open to them.

Reach out to others when they need help.

Reach out to others when you need help.

If you feel particularly lonely or socially isolated, talk to a counselor or psychologist. He or she is equipped to help you address this concern.

His dad lives elsewhere and seldom visits. This absence may be especially influential when the boy feels he needs his dad, such as times when other boys' dads are around. From this experience he may learn the lesson that you cannot depend on people. This feeling becomes internalized (that is, it becomes part of the child's internal belief system, or personality). Later, as a grown man, he may continue to hold this belief and prefer not to rely on others for help. Even when others help him, he may discredit the aid because he believes "help is just never there when you need it." In a sense, this belief, acquired early in life, is stronger for him than the reality he experiences as an adult.

Social Support as the Structure, or Social Network, of How People Are Connected

A very different way of looking at support is by analyzing the structure of people's associations with others who are close to them. This view of social support emphasizes the structure of the ties between people—what has been called people's **social network**. For example, how many people you feel close to, the extent they have relationships with one another, and the context of those relationships (for example, professional or personal) are aspects of your social network. Key indicators of support, according to the social network view, include the following:

1. *Number of intimate supporters:* the number of people you can turn to for help in a time of trouble
2. *Breadth of support interactions:* determined by whether individuals discuss only one or two specific topics with their supporters (a narrow support relationship) or discuss many topics (a broad support relationship). Broad-based relationships sound better and usually are because they provide support for many kinds of problems. But a narrow-based relationship may provide important support in a key area of need, so which is better actually depends on the question "Better for what?"
3. *Support density:* the extent to which your supporters are in relationships with each other—the more interpersonal ties there are among the supporters, the denser the support system is said to be
4. *Border density:* the extent to which your supporters from different life domains (work, school, friends, family) have relationships with each other. If your work and home lives are completely separate, the border density would be very low. If your colleagues at work are also your close friends, then border density would be quite high. In other words, think about the divisions between work and home and friends and family as borders and the number of relationships that cross these borders as a measure of border density. Dense borders help form communication across life domains. However, dense borders may also mean that problems at home are leaked at work and vice versa. There are advantages to both high and low border density.
5. *Ratio of kith and kin:* the ratio of friends (kith) to family (kin) within a support system. If you have many friends and few family in your support system, you have a high ratio. If you have few

friends and many family supporters, you have a low ratio. In general, a good balance (scores near 1) indicates that both friends and family are available for support.

Completing the diagram in Box 2 can help you learn more about the structure of social support and the kind of social network that you have.

Support as a Meta-Construct

With all these definitions of social support, how do you know which one is the true definition? Some would say that they all are. Alan Vaux (1988) has argued that social support is a **meta-construct**—in other words, a bridge that links together a series of **constructs**, or concepts. No one definition is necessarily more correct than another. Indeed, to fully understand social support, we need to look at what each definition has to offer. What is important, however, is that researchers studying social support make clear which aspect of support that they are studying, because the different kinds of social support will have differing influences on well-being and coping.

Do different kinds of social support have differing influences in your life? They probably do, although most of us do not usually pick apart the various kinds of support we receive. Some friends may provide all kinds of social support, including being emotionally supportive, offering quiet companionship, and giving physical help (in, say, moving furniture). Other close friends may never offer outright emotional support but are always there when you need them. Social support covers all of these rather varied kinds of aid, which is why we refer to it as a meta-construct.

How Social Support Affects Us

"With a Little Help from My Friends," "Bridge over Troubled Water," "Lean on Me," "Stand by Your Man"—these are not just titles from popular songs, they are descriptions of the importance of social support in coping with stress. We often turn to and rely on others during difficult times in our lives.

For young children, parents usually perform the primary social support role. In fact, this support is so critical that children who cannot rely on such family support tend to have major difficulties forming relationships and developing trust throughout their lives (Bowlby, 1969). In their teen years, young people lean on their friends and romantic partners for help and assistance. The teen years can be seen as a time when young people begin to apply the support lessons they learned in their families to the relationships they form outside of the family. At work, people must often depend on colleagues to provide both technical assistance in completing a task and esteem-building support aimed at keeping morale high.

Box 2

Support Structure

Here is a way to learn about your support system, your social network. This test was used in a study of support systems among women who had cancer (Hobfoll & Walfisch, 1984). Refer to Figure 3-1. For each item below, place the initials of each person in the quadrant where that relationship was *first* established.

1. Think about the people who are most likely to provide you with social support. If they are among the very closest people to you, place their initials in the innermost circle.
2. Now think about the people who are close to you, but not as close as the people in the innermost circle. Place their initials in the second circle.
3. Now think about the people who sometimes provide you support, but with whom you do not have a very close relationship. Place their initials inside the outermost of the three circles.
4. Now, draw lines between those people in any of the circles who have a relationship with each other.

The total number of initials is one measure of the *size* of your support system. You can also tabulate the size at each *level* of support by calculating the number of people within each circle. The number of lines drawn between people is a measure of *network density*. The number of lines drawn across borders between work, school, home, and family is a measure of *border density*.

Figure 3-1

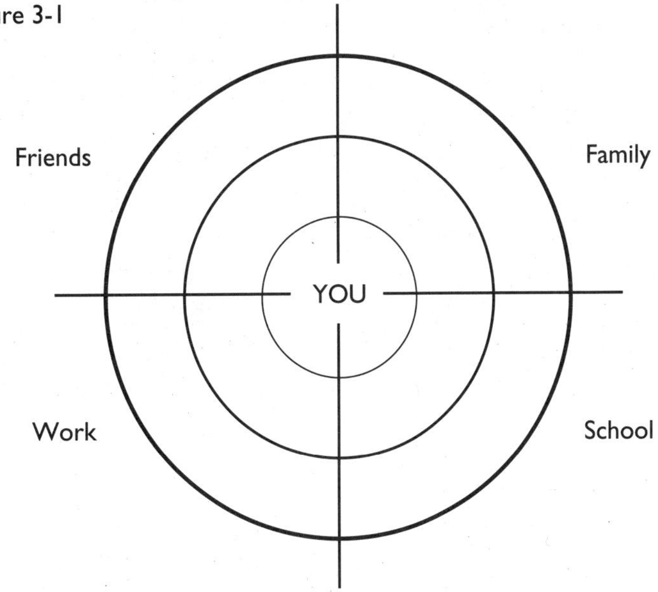

Box 3   **Communal Orientation**

Do some ethnic groups have a stronger orientation toward social support than others? This important question has been explored in the work of Triandis and his colleagues (Triandis, McCusker, & Hui, 1990), cross-cultural social psychologists, and by African-American theorists concerned with culture, such as Myers (1987). These investigators have studied what have been called Afrocentric and Asiacentric world-views, which differ in many ways from the Eurocentric worldview. Afrocentric and Asiacentric worldviews are similar in that great emphasis is placed on the family and social unit; this emphasis has been called a communal orientation, or communal-mindedness. Eurocentric culture (the culture originating in Europe) is oriented more toward the individual.

Those who are communally minded are more likely to feel a strong connection with their family and social group, to have strong "in-group" versus "out-group" ways of viewing their social surroundings, and to depend more on social support—but only from members of the in-group. The African-American extended family often includes aunts, uncles, cousins, siblings, and friends who are considered family. This communal orientation may translate to a great cultural advantage for social support. For example, care for children, the elderly, and the sick is the responsibility of the entire family, and a move to a nursing home or reliance on just one member of the family is less likely to occur. There are many advantages to a communally oriented culture because of the shared sense of responsibility. One possible disadvantage is that, because of the same intense social connections, individual advancement may be blocked if it is not in the best interest of the group. We are only beginning to learn about how cultural and ethnic differences affect social support, and this will be a key area for future investigation.

Social support is found worldwide, but it is expressed differently in different cultures. For example, it is common for Japanese workers to have dinner and spend the evening with colleagues from work each day, returning home at midnight only to sleep. This is one indication of the deep level of social support in the Japanese workplace. You might imagine that social support between husband and wife might suffer in the balance, and this is currently an important area of concern in Japan. In some cultures support is more obligatory than in others, and some cultures depend more on family than on friends. Still, there is no culture in which social support is not a critical part of society.

Stress-Buffering and Direct Effects of Social Support

Researchers have explored two major hypotheses explaining how social support affects people. These have been called the *stress-buffering* and *direct-effect hypotheses* of social support. Let's look at each of them in turn.

The **stress-buffering hypothesis** predicts that social support has a stress-limiting, or buffering, effect during stressful life circumstances. When individuals are experiencing high stress, social support may act to buffer the negative impact that stress would otherwise have on psychological or physical well-being. Like the pillows that children hold under their shirts when fighting with their brothers and sisters, social support helps to absorb the impact of life's punches. For example, in a classic study, Nuckolls, Cassel, and Kaplan (1972) found that women who had experienced high levels of stressful life events during and prior to pregnancy and who had low levels of social support had very high rates of pregnancy complications. They were more likely to deliver prematurely, experience prolonged labor, and have such problems as high blood pressure. In contrast, women who underwent similarly high levels of stress but had high levels of social support were unlikely to have medical complications during pregnancy. In fact, women who had high stress and low social support had four times the rate of pregnancy complications of those who had high stress and high social support. This was one of the pioneer studies of social support, and its findings have been replicated in more recent research.

The stress-buffering effect is illustrated graphically in Figure 3-2. The top graph shows that as stress increases along the *x*-axis (horizontal axis), physical or psychological complications increase along the *y*-axis (vertical axis), but only for the low social support group. Now follow the trend for the high social support group; for them, as stress increases there is little or no increase in medical complications of pregnancy. This stress-buffering effect seems to hold for both physical and psychological outcomes.

To put it another way, the stress-buffering effect of social support suggests that social support is effective under high stress conditions. But under low stress conditions there is little difference between those who have social support and those who do not. Perhaps if you are not stressed by examinations, are not experiencing financial problems, and have no problems with your love life, you do not need to rely on others for support. In contrast, when trouble strikes, emotional and task support from friends, family, and colleagues can be vital to preserving well-being.

The **direct-effect hypothesis**, on the other hand, argues that social support has a beneficial influence *whether or not* individuals are experiencing stressful circumstances. According to this model of social support, social support plays a positive role for both individuals who are under high stress and those who are not currently experiencing stressful circumstances.

Figure 3-2
The Stress-Buffering
and Direct Effects of
Social Support

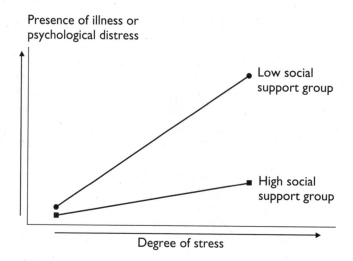

Presence of illness or
psychological distress

Low social
support group

High social
support group

Degree of stress

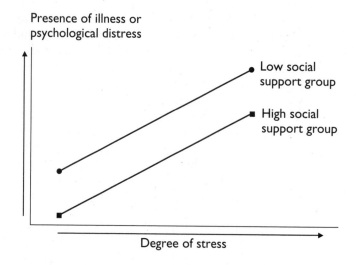

Presence of illness or
psychological distress

Low social
support group

High social
support group

Degree of stress

Williams, Ware, and Donald (1981) conducted a particularly well-designed study of social support that illustrates the direct-effect hypothesis. Williams and colleagues gathered data from 2234 persons living in Seattle, Washington. The study sample was generally representative of Seattle residents. Questionnaires were sent to participants on two occasions, approximately 1 year apart. Questionnaires were self-administered, and about 90% of all participants returned their questionnaires. Stress, social support, and general mental health were measured. The results of this study are illustrated in the lower graph in Figure 3-2. As the graph shows, people who had more social support had better mental health, and those who had less had worse mental health. However, the positive effect of social support was about the same under high stress and low stress conditions. In other words, there was no *added* positive effect of social support under high stress conditions when compared to low stress conditions.

If the stress-buffering hypothesis had held, then we would have seen that the effect of social support was greater under high stress than under low stress. The line for the high social support group would be flat, whereas the line for the low support group would be steep (as in the upper graph in Figure 3-2). The parallel lines in the lower graph are indicative of the direct-effect hypothesis.

Direct Versus Stress-Buffering Effect: Which Is It?

During the 1980s there was much discussion among social support and stress researchers as to whether the stress-buffering hypothesis or the direct-effect hypothesis represented the real, or true, effect of social support. Cohen and Wills (1985) reviewed the extensive literature on this topic available at that time. They suggested that **perceived support**—a person's sense that he or she is supported—is more likely to have a stress-buffering effect. In contrast, they argued, when measures of support tap *social embeddedness* (the extent to which someone is in social contact with others), direct effects of social support will be observed. This distinction, however, is an imperfect one. Indeed, in some studies the same measure of social support had a stress-buffering effect on one outcome variable and a direct effect on a second outcome variable.

Today most experts on social support would probably say that both direct and stress-buffering effects occur simultaneously and all that can be said is that one type of effect is more prominent in a given instance than the other (Cohen & Wills, 1985). This process can be illustrated with an example of soldiers in combat. Faced with the harsh realities of combat, soldiers learn to rely on their comrades and often develop very close personal relationships on the battlefield. Social support in this arena may take the form of both encouragement and help with survival, and both kinds of support are vitally necessary. Under battle conditions, the support of high troop morale and close personal ties can be critical in keeping a soldier alive and psychologically healthy. Those who lack social support—who are in units with poor morale—are more likely to be wounded or killed, to develop malaria in swamp environments, to develop frostbite in cold conditions, and to experience psychiatric breakdown than those who have a high level of support from comrades. Few soldiers, however, experience these negative outcomes under the lower stress conditions outside of combat. That bad outcomes are more likely under the conditions of high stress and low support is illustrative of the stress-buffering effect. However, if we measure another negative outcome, loneliness, we find that so-

A good social support network helps us during good times as well as bad times.

cial support in the unit keeps soldiers from becoming lonely and becoming depressed and from dwelling on thoughts of home and lost opportunities. As these positive influences of social support occur under relatively low stress, non-combat conditions, they reflect the direct effect of social support.

SOCIAL SUPPORT FIT

Rather than focusing on whether the direct or the stress-buffering hypothesis more truly depicts the process of social support, we can examine what may be a better concept for understanding how social support works: the concept of **social support fit**. People receive different kinds of social support and find themselves in different kinds of stressful situations. Cohen and McKay (1984) suggest that when social support fits the demands of the particular stressful situation, then the support is most likely to be beneficial. But social support does not always fit situational demands, and in these cases we cannot expect that it will have a positive influence. For instance, if you were mourning the death of a loved one, the support that might best fit that situation is the close companionship of someone else you also love. That person might need only to be with you, to talk about how you both feel, and perhaps to recall past experiences you shared with the deceased. If, on the other hand, you lost a job, the support that fit best might include contacts with many people with whom you have only loose social ties but who might provide you with good job leads. Now imagine that you received the support suited to the first situation when you lost the job or, conversely, received the casual, informational support needed in the second situation when you were mourning a deep loss. The fit in these circumstances would be poor and unhelpful, even though both kinds of support are beneficial when they fit the situational demands.

Often the factor that determines whether social support fits a situational demand is timing. After a person sustains a heart attack, initial support might be companionship and emotional support. Following initial adjustment, the best fit of support might be encouragement to get back to work and once again become socially active. Acquaintances might provide excellent support in relating how they overcame difficulties following their heart attacks, and they might provide information and ideas for rehabilitation. Sometimes sexual dysfunction accompanies post-coronary recovery. If this occurs, only support from the most intimate other will fit the demands of the problem. In fact, social support might prove inadequate; professional support might be the best remedy for this serious life challenge. As you can see, the kinds of support that best fit the demands of a situation change over time. "Fit" is not a static concept: support fit should be seen as a moving film, not a single-frame photograph.

Recently, attempts have been made to develop a schema for predicting when social support will match stressful circumstances. Cutrona and Russell (1990) suggest that stressful events that are beyond a person's control require emotional kinds of support, such as encouragement, shared affection, and esteem-building support. Controllable events, in contrast, require support that fosters problem solving. Examples of support that fosters problem solving include advice, information, feedback on plans of action, tangible assistance, and emotional support that engenders a greater sense of competence. These researchers further suggest that if what is lost can be directly *replaced* by social support, then this kind of support will benefit the recipient. For example, if someone were to suffer a financial loss, a loan of money might be the best fit.

There is some evidence supporting Cutrona and Russell's model of optimal matching, but they also recognize the problem of timing that was discussed earlier. So, although an event may not be controllable, some aspects of the solution may be, as in the case of someone who experiences a job layoff because of a plant closing. Losing her job may not have been under her control, but finding a new job may very well be under her control. Marital problems that develop due to economic hardship may, in turn, be partially within her control, but they are partially under her spouse's control too. Hence, it is difficult to apply the model of optimal matching, even though it makes sense and has proven helpful when the kind of stress is clear and not of the more mixed variety that life often offers people.

NEGATIVE EFFECTS OF SOCIAL SUPPORT

Another important question regarding social support is whether social support has a uniformly positive effect. Until now in this chapter we have been assuming that the influence of social support is always positive. In fact, the literature on social support in the 1970s and early 1980s assumed that if an interaction could be defined as social support it must be positive. However, it has become increasingly obvious that not all social support is positive, or at least not under all circumstances. In some situations, social support can even backfire and negatively affect the recipient.

Conflicted Relationships

We may sometimes forget that the same relationship that offers social support might also create social conflicts. Karen Rook (1984) studied the effects of both social support and social conflict. Her work concentrated on the elderly. She found that when social support and **social conflict** were both part of a relationship, the negative influence of social conflict was stronger than the positive influence of social support.

Often, however, the conflicted part of the relationship is not obvious. For example, a man may appear to be offering social support to his wife by encouraging her to work and be more independent. However, he may be undermining that support with messages that imply she is incompetent and she should feel guilty about leaving her homemaker role and by complaining when the house is not as clean as it was when she was at home full time. A marriage counselor would surely want to uncover both the superficial messages of support and the underlying messages of guilt and anger that are being communicated. From Rook's research on the relative influence of support and conflict, we would expect the negative messages to outweigh the positive ones.

Inappropriate or Ill-Timed Support

Even when social support is intended to be positive and is a kind of behavior that usually is supportive, it may nevertheless have a negative influence. This backfiring of social support occurs when support is particularly ill-timed or inappropriate for the situation. Alan Vaux, a leading social support researcher, makes this point with a bit of dark humor: "Imagine that you offer a drowning man emotional support from the river's edge, and the next day offer his mourning wife a rope" (Vaux, personal communication, 1991). The support efforts would have been excellent had they been applied in the opposite order—otherwise the results are dreadful.

Social support may also have a negative effect if it increases stress levels. This can happen when supporters share their miseries or feel the troubles of others to be a heavy burden.

Researchers found these paradoxical, negative effects of social support in work conducted during war in Israel. They studied women whose loved ones were called up for service during the Israel-Lebanon War in 1982 (Hobfoll & London, 1986). Men had been called from their beds during the night, and information about their whereabouts, their well-being, and the battles being fought was not forthcoming to those left at home. Women were left not only with these worries, but also with family and work burdens created by the men's absence. Naturally, women shared their concerns and offered support to each other. Rather than alleviating stress, however, talking about their worries often resulted in what the researchers called a "pressure cooker" effect. When the women shared their concerns it was like turning up the heat under a pressure cooker. All the women could talk about was the war, and rumors about battles and casu-

Box 4   **Support Etiquette**

Is there an etiquette of social support? Well, not exactly, but we are learning more about what constitutes helpful and unhelpful social interactions. For example, researchers have found that people generally should not try to minimize a tragedy or compare themselves to another person as if they know exactly how the other feels (Lehman, Ellard, & Wortman, 1986). Statements like, "It's not so bad that you lost the baby, you can always get pregnant again," or "I know just how you feel" may be offered with a positive intent but may produce anger or loneliness instead of positive feelings. Johnson, Hobfoll, and Zalcberg-Linetzy (1993) developed a measure of social support knowledge that they found to be related to the development of intimacy. Items from the test are presented below. Take the test, and see how high you score.

Social Support Knowledge

Imagine that you are with a close family member or friend who is going through a difficult crisis (failure at work, marital difficulty, serious illness, or the like), and you wish to help him or her.

Following are a number of things that might or might not help a person in distress. Indicate next to each item whether the behavior would most likely be helpful or not helpful, in your opinion. Scoring is described at the end of the test.

Helpful	Not helpful	
_____	_____	1. Show concern.
_____	_____	2. Let her openly express her feelings (to cry, to be angry, to yell).
_____	_____	3. Encourage him to stand up to the problem and "pull himself up by his own bootstraps."
_____	_____	4. Give her the message not to make such a big deal out of this: "It could be worse." "It's not so bad."
_____	_____	5. Act cheerful, even if you have to force it.
_____	_____	6. Provide a philosophical reason or meaning for the event ("It's just fate").
_____	_____	7. Provide religious meaning for the event ("It's God's will").
_____	_____	8. Show interest.
_____	_____	9. Show willingness to invest time and attention.
_____	_____	10. Steer the conversation to a happier topic.
_____	_____	11. Show that you understand his feelings ("I know how you feel").
_____	_____	12. Listen.

Box 4 continues

Box 4
(continued)

_____ _____ 13. Provide support by physical closeness.
_____ _____ 14. Share your experience (in a similar situation).
_____ _____ 15. Encourage her to forget and "open a new page" in her life.
_____ _____ 16. Free up time for him.
_____ _____ 17. Show affection.

Scoring: Give yourself 1 point for items 1, 2, 8, 9, 11, 12, 13, 16, and 17 if you indicated that the behavior would likely be helpful. Give yourself 1 point for items 3, 4, 5, 6, 7, 10, 14, and 15 if you indicated that the behavior would likely be unhelpful. Total up your points.

What does your score mean? If you score 15 or above, you know a lot about social support. If you score 12 to 14, you are in a mid-range group, but you probably usually know when and how to provide support. If you score below 12, you may experience difficulty offering support to others.

What do you do if you scored low? The simplest things to do to be a better support provider are to ask what the support recipient needs and simply to express that you care and want to help. Don't try to know all the answers. That is the first support mistake.

alties abounded. The more social support they reported, the higher became their feelings of depression and anxiety.

Perhaps an example of this from your own experience would clarify the pressure cooker phenomenon. Before an examination, would listening to other students' anxiety about the test serve to calm you or to increase your own anxiety? Others might be looking for your support and encouragement, but you may be ready for the test and wish just to stay calm and go over your notes. Stress can be contagious, and the very interactions that provide social support at some times might increase your worry, concern, and anxiety. If the support provider and the support recipient have the same problem or crisis, then they may both benefit and both suffer from a support exchange.

PERSONAL CHARACTERISTICS AND SOCIAL SUPPORT

We have seen that social support can be a powerful coping resource; that it may aid people's **stress resistance** and generally contribute to their well-being. We have also seen that the effects of social support are not uniform and may even backfire and increase stress reactions. Overall, however, research on this topic indicates that social support is an important tool for coping and that those who have support are better able to withstand the negative impact of life stress. Furthermore, they enjoy better mental and physical health.

Social support does not fall from the sky, however. Nevertheless, research on social support during the 1970s and early 1980s ignored this fact and failed to study how social support was obtained. Investigators did not consider such questions as "Who receives social support?" and "How do they do so?" They merely studied the effects of having or lacking social support on adjustment to stressful circumstances. In retrospect, we can see that they were ignoring the general study of personal relationships, which is the focus of this book (Duck, 1990). Research since about 1985 has increasingly recognized the importance of learning how social support is obtained and how it is best used.

Four important factors contribute to the development, maintenance, and receipt of social support. They are:

1. Gender
2. Personality
3. Coping style
4. Network characteristics

We will examine each of these.

Gender

Women tend to both provide and receive more social support than men do. Of course, this is not true of all women and all men, but this trend is nevertheless a strong and fairly consistent one. Women tend to consider more people as intimate supporters, are turned to more often for social support, and are more strongly affected by the give and take of social support (Kessler, McLeod, & Wethington, 1985). When asked who they would mainly turn to for support, both men and women tend to choose a woman (Reis, Senchak, & Solomon, 1985).

In recent research, young African-American inner-city women were asked to nominate a support person who could tell the researchers about them. Virtually everyone who did not have a steady romantic partner indicated that a female filled this role. Brothers, fathers, and male friends were not included on this most intimate level of support. Instead, the role was filled by mothers, sisters, aunts, and female friends. Men were not included in this particular study, and researchers need to learn more about the support preferences of African-American men.

There are a number of reasons women may be more involved in the commerce of social support than men. First, young girls may be socialized to disclose more personal information about themselves to friends, whereas boys may be encouraged to be more physically active in their play. Second, it may be more acceptable for women to express emotions. Men, in contrast, may tend to feel that it is feminine to express emotions ("big boys don't cry!"). The one emotion that men may express more of than women is anger, and anger tends to drive others away, not attract supporters (Lane & Hobfoll, 1992). Finally, women's social role as family nurturer may contribute to our learning that we should turn to mom for emotional support when the going gets rough. After we learn this in early life, we may simply continue to use what worked for us as children. To the extent that women enter the paid workplace and more fathers provide nurturant support at home, these gender differences may very well change.

Personality Characteristics

Personality characteristics are related to obtaining and using social support. Some people have a strong sense of control over their lives, and this has been seen as an important aspect of people's personalities. People who are high on this sense of control have been found in a number of studies to use social support better (Kobasa & Puccetti, 1983; Sandler & Lakey, 1982). This trait may stem from two factors: First, they may attract more positive social support because they tend to be open about both giving and receiving help from others, and, second, when they need support, their high sense of control helps them use it appropriately.

For example, a college student who has a strong sense of control over her future does not call on support to study for an exam for which she knows she can competently prepare on her own. However, when she hears that her grandmother, with whom she has always been close, is quite ill, she feels comfortable turning to her best friend for a shoulder to cry on and a heartfelt conversation about grandmothers. Another student, who does not feel in control of her future, behaves quite differently. She feels inadequate in the face of an exam and repeatedly seeks help, disregarding others' needs to study and the fact that she would more profitably spend the time applying herself to study. So, when she hears about an illness at home, she has already exhausted her social support during exam time and has no one to whom she can turn.

Self-esteem, another central aspect of personality, has also been found to be related to social support. **Self-esteem** is the extent to which individuals feel a positive sense of self-worth. Researchers found that women who were higher in self-esteem were more satisfied with social support than were women who lacked self-esteem (Hobfoll, Nadler, & Leiberman, 1986). Those who were low in self-esteem may actually have found using social support to be an additional source of stress. How might this occur? Perhaps when people already feel in a "one-down" position—when they feel insecure about themselves or less valued—asking for help makes them feel even worse. It appears that people find it easier to ask for help when they feel good about themselves than when they have negative feelings about themselves. After all, when you ask for help, you are admitting that you need others, and someone whose self-esteem is low may feel threatened to admit such needs.

Coping Style

Coping style is one's manner of behaving in stressful situations. How people cope with stress may positively or negatively influence social support. For example, when people become depressed they may need a great deal of support, but their coping style may push others away. Jim Coyne's (1976) research on this topic has been especially insightful. He found that depressed people elicit negative feelings in others that alienate these potential supporters rather than making them want to help. He attributes this to depressed people's coping style—depressed people may act hostile toward their friends and family, thus pushing them further away. Depressed people may also fail to respond to help when it is offered. Consequently, friends and family may think that their help is unwanted. Depression can close the door on social support. This is truly a paradox, because depressed people often very much want affection and contact even though they seem to send the opposite message as they try to cope with their depression. As one person put it: "My sadness is like a wall. I want to reach over it for help, but it's too high. In the end, the wall keeps everyone away, and that makes me even sadder."

Another way coping style influences social support is in terms of how comfortable people feel using social support to help them cope. Researchers have studied this phenomenon of *discomfort seeking social support.* How comfortable are you seeking social support? Actually, few people are completely comfortable asking others for help. So, researchers talk about "relative discomfort." If you are relatively comfortable seeking help, you are likely to be more able to ask for social support when you need it (Hobfoll & Lerman, 1989). Another question that you might ask yourself is whether you encourage friends and family to seek help from you. Since social support is a reciprocal process, giving social support is one of the best ways to get social support.

Discomfort asking for help is important because people will often not ask for help unless they are encouraged to do so. In Japan there is a tradition that you must offer many times before your friend can accept your offer of help. He or she wishes to be sure not to burden you. Also, in Japanese society, once you accept help, you incur an obligation to reciprocate. This obligation is neither easily taken on nor easily relinquished once accepted. This tradition ritualizes helping, and one must understand the culture intimately to avoid making a *faux pas* that may cause one's friend to lose all-important honor.

Box 5

Social Support Guidelines

What should you do to be able to receive social support? In workshops on social support, people are taught the following guidelines. They might help you as well. Although they are all simple to understand, they involve complex social skills that you will learn about throughout this book.

1. Ask clearly for help when needed, and offer it when you think others need it.
2. Provide feedback to supporters about their efforts, including asking for more, less, or different kinds of support.
3. Express appreciation clearly when you receive help.
4. Share your positive plans. Supporters want to hear how you plan to do better now that you have their help.
5. Plan positive (mastery) steps toward minimizing problems and share these positive plans with supporters.
6. Listen carefully to advice once you have asked for it. Many people reject advice with a lot of "Yes, but . . ." statements—this alienates support.
7. Remember the importance of having an advocate outside of the family. This is especially important if you wish to do something that the family feels threatened by.
8. Think about how you can provide support to others, even when you are the one receiving support. This will enhance your sense of mastery, while showing that you, too, care.

Network Characteristics

Network characteristics, which we defined at the beginning of this chapter, affect people's receipt of social support (Hirsch, 1980; Vaux, 1988). If your friends know each other, they might spread the word about your support needs. If, however, your friends do not know each other, even if one friend knows you are having trouble, he or she might not have the means or opportunity to share that knowledge with others. The breadth or narrowness of relationships, another social network characteristic discussed earlier, also affects social support. Breadth or narrowness here refers to the number of issues that are discussed between you and your friends. If you discuss only practical matters of business with a friend at work (a narrow relationship), then you both may feel uncomfortable being supportive of each other in more personal areas. If, on the other hand, you discuss personal concerns, sexuality, work, and family, then many more topics could be comfortably broached.

Our social networks are built over long periods of time, and they tend to develop to meet a certain pattern of personal and social needs. When needs fall outside of this pattern, the structure of a person's social network may not be well suited to meeting them.

SUMMARY

Overall, social support is a valuable social commodity. Social support has been defined in many ways. It includes help on an emotional level and help on a more task-oriented level aimed at accomplishing a specific goal. Some theorists see social support as information that tells recipients they are accepted, loved, and part of a community that cares. Other theorists emphasize that social support enhances people's sense that they can master the environment. All these definitions tell us something special about social support, and no one definition is right or wrong.

Social support has been found to have both direct and stress-buffering effects on stress reactions. Those with social support have been found to have better psychological and physical health outcomes when faced with stress (the stress-buffering hypothesis), and those with social support tend to have better psychological and physical well-being, independent of their stress level (the direct-effect hypothesis).

Social support is not always beneficial, however. When social support fits situational demands, it tends to have its most positive effects. When matching of social support with the task is optimal, people derive the most positive results. When social support does not fit the circumstances well, it may have a limited effect. Some research even indicates that social support can have a negative effect, if the fit with circumstances is especially poor.

It is also important to remember that social conflict may be a part of the same relationship that provides social support. Social conflict may result in more negative effects than social support can offset. In fact, if social conflict is high, it may overwhelm any positive effect of social support.

We also examined the factors that may affect the receipt of social support. Gender, personality, coping style, and social network characteristics all influence the commerce and quality of social support. Women tend to be more comfortable with social support, and certain personality and coping styles are more conducive to obtaining social support than others. If a person's social network has never provided a certain type of support, it might not be well-suited for providing that particular type.

These are important topics of study, and future research on social support is likely to help us learn much more about its provision and receipt. Researchers today are also especially interested in the topic of social support fit and optimal matching. Research during the next 10 years will probably pay a lot of attention to developing a better understanding of how and why social support fits some circumstances better than others.

Investigators are also beginning to look at new areas, not covered in this chapter, such as the ways social support affects us on a biological level and the ways community factors such as supportive schools and workplaces affect their constituencies. The study of social support has helped us understand much more clearly how stress affects people and whether they are better or worse off after surviving stress.

Class Discussion Questions

1. Complete the support structure diagram in Box 2 and then come prepared for class discussion. How do the networks look? What do you and your classmates feel are strengths of your networks? How might you improve your networks? Were there any surprises for you when you completed this task?
2. Discuss what messages your families gave you about seeking support. Is it something one does or shuns? Is support sought only within the family or more broadly?
3. Do your family's "rules" (see question 2 above) make sense in terms of your ethnic background? (Yes, Anglo-Saxon is an ethnic background, and it is largely characterized by rugged individualism, which tends to downplay seeking support, even among intergenerational family members.)
4. Discuss gender differences in support. Do men and women seek support differently? Where and how were these learned?
5. Discuss incidents when social support was very helpful. Were there any incidents in which social support backfired on the giver and had negative effects?

Homework Assignments

1. Have your friends and family complete the support structure diagram (Box 2), being sure to note the subject's gender. With the rest of the class, check for differences by gender. Are the findings in the chapter confirmed?
2. Break into groups to construct a measure of social support specific for college students. See whether you can construct additional items for ethnic minority students. You may need to discuss with ethnic minority students any special challenges that they face. Write an explanation of how this exercise has helped you understand how a seemingly neutral test can be culturally biased if it does not consider ethnic minority concerns.
3. Complete the Intimacy Scale in Box 1. Score your own test, and on a separate sheet of paper, indicate your gender, ethnic origin, and GPA along with your test score. Pass these sheets forward; your instructor will display the information. Look for trends.
4. Interview four people at different stages of life (child, teenager, young adult, older adult), focusing on whom they turn to for help when they

need it and what kind of help they feel they need. Then either write a paper or use the material for class discussion.

5. Get three or four people you know fairly well (not in the class) to fill out the support structure diagram (Box 2). Then write a statement about (1) the similarities and differences between respondents' diagrams; (2) whether you can see differences in the respondents' personalities or lives that co-vary with the variations in the diagrams (for example, perhaps the person who had the fewest social supporters gets sick a lot or is depressed); (3) what conclusions you might draw based on this sample. Be sure that you ask the respondent's permission to use the diagram and that you do not disclose information that might allow others to know the respondent's identity. (This will help you learn more about the ethics of personal relationships research.)

Additional Readings

Duck, S. W. (Ed.) with Silver, R.C. (1990). *Personal relationships and social support.* London, CA: Sage.

Hobfoll, S. E. (1989). *The ecology of stress.* Washington, DC: Hemisphere.

Lerner, H. G. (1989). *The dance of intimacy: A woman's guide to courageous acts of change in key relationships.* New York: Harper & Row.

Sarason, B. R., Sarason, I. G., & Pierce, G. R. (Eds.). (1990). *Social support: An interactional view.* New York: John Wiley & Sons.

References

Billings, A. G., & Moos, R. H. (1984). Coping, stress, and social support resources among adults with unipolar depression. *Journal of Personality and Social Psychology, 46,* 877–891.

Bowlby, J. (1969). *Attachment and loss (vol. 1): Attachment.* London: Hogarth Press.

Brown, G. W., & Harris, T. (1978). *The social origins of depression: The study of psychiatric disorder in women.* New York: Free Press.

Caplan, G. (1974). *Support systems and community mental health: Lectures on concept development.* New York: Behavioral Publications.

Cobb, S. (1976). Social support as a moderator of life stress. *Psychosomatic Medicine, 3,* 300–314.

Cohen, S., & McKay, G. (1984). Interpersonal relationships as buffers of the impact of psychological stress on health. In A. Baum, J. E. Singer, & S. E. Taylor (Eds.), *Handbook of psychology and health* (Vol. 4, pp. 253–267). Hillsdale, NJ: Lawrence Erlbaum.

Cohen, S., & Wills, T. A. (1985). Stress, social support, and the buffering hypothesis. *Psychological Bulletin, 98,* 310–357.

Coyne, J. C. (1976). Toward an interactional description of depression. *Psychiatry, 39,* 28–40.

Cutrona, C. E., & Russell, D. W. (1990). Type of social support and specific stress: Toward a theory of optimal matching. In B. R. Sarason, I. G. Sarason, & G. R. Pierce (Eds.), *Social support: An interactional view* (pp. 319–366). New York: Wiley.

Duck, S. W. (Ed.) with Silver, R. C. (1990). *Personal relationships and social support.* London, CA: Sage.

Hirsch, B. J. (1980). *Behavior-genetics analysis.* New York: McGraw-Hill.

Hobfoll, S. E., & Lerman, M. (1989). Predicting receipt of social support: A longitudinal study of parents' reactions to their child's illness. *Health Psychology, 8,* 61–77.

Hobfoll, S. E., & London, P. (1986). The relationship of self-concept and social support to emotional distress among women during war. *Journal of Social and Clinical Psychology, 12,* 87–100.

Hobfoll, S. E., Nadler, A., & Leiberman, J. (1986). Satisfaction with social support during crisis: Intimacy and self-esteem as critical determinants. *Journal of Personality and Social Psychology, 51,* 296–304.

Hobfoll, S. E., & Walfisch, S. (1984). Coping with a threat to life: A longitudinal study of self-concept, social support and psychological distress. *American Journal of Community Psychology, 12,* 87–100.

House, J. S. (1981). *Work, stress, and social support.* Reading, MA: Addison-Wesley.

Johnson, R., Hobfoll, S. E., & Zalcberg-Linetzy, A. (1993). Social support knowledge and behavior and relational intimacy: A dyadic study. *Journal of Family Psychology, 6,* 1–12.

Kessler, R. C., McLeod, J. D., & Wethington, E. (1985). The costs of caring: A perspective on the relationship between sex and psychological distress. In I. G. Sarason & B. R. Sarason (Eds.), *Social support: Theory, research, and applications* (pp. 491–506). The Hague, The Netherlands: Martinus Nijhoff.

Kobasa, S. C., & Puccetti, M. C. (1983). Personality and social resources in stress resistance. *Journal of Personality and Social Psychology, 45,* 839–850.

Lane, C., & Hobfoll, S. E. (1992). How loss affects anger and alienates potential supporters. *Journal of Consulting and Clinical Psychology, 60,* 935–942.

Lehman, D. R., Ellard, J. H., & Wortman, C. B. (1986). Social support for the bereaved: Recipients' and providers' perspectives on what is helpful. *Journal of Consulting and Clinical Psychology, 54,* 438–446.

Myers, L. (1987). The deep structure of culture: Relevance of traditional African culture in contemporary life. *Journal of Black Studies, 18*(1), 72–85.

Nuckolls, K. G., Cassel, J., & Kaplan, B. H. (1972). Psychosocial assets, life crisis and the prognosis of pregnancy. *American Journal of Epidemiology, 95,* 431–441.

Reis, H. T., Senchak, M., & Solomon, B. (1985). Sex differences in the intimacy of social interaction: Further examination of potential explanations. *Journal of Personality and Social Psychology, 48,* 1204–1217.

Rook, K. S. (1984). The negative side of social interaction: Impact on psychological well-being. *Journal of Personality and Social Psychology, 46,* 1097–1108.

Sandler, I. N., & Lakey, B. (1982). Locus of control as a stress moderator: The role of control perceptions and social support. *American Journal of Community Psychology, 10,* 65–80.

Sarason, B. R., Sarason, I. G., & Pierce, G. R. (1990). Traditional views of social support and their impact on assessment. In B. R. Sarason, I. G. Sarason, & G. R. Pierce (Eds.), *Social support: An interactional view* (pp. 7–25). New York: Wiley.

Selye, H. (1976). *Stress in health and disease.* Boston: Butterworth.

Shumaker, S. A., & Brownell, A. (1984). Toward a theory of social support: Closing the conceptual gaps. *Journal of Social Issues, 40,* 55–76.

Triandis, H. C., McCusker, C., & Hui, C. H. (1990). Multimethod probes of individualism and collectivism. *Journal of Personality and Social Psychology, 59*(5), 1006–1020.

Vaux, A. (1988). *Social support: Theory, research, and intervention.* New York: Praeger.

Vaux, A. (1991). Personal communication.

Williams, A. W., Ware, J. E., & Donald, C. A. (1981). A model of mental health, life events, and social supports applicable to general populations. *Journal of Health and Social Behavior, 22,* 324–336.

Glossary

Action-oriented support   Exchange between at least two people in which one or both feel the intent was to be helpful

Advice support   Giving of advice in the hope of helping or providing aid

Border density   The extent to which supporters who come from different kinds of settings (such as family or work) have relationships with one another

Companionship support   The support offered by just being with someone during his or her time of need

Construct   A concept or abstract idea that is usually hypothesized to play a role in some phenomenon of interest. For example, the construct of psychological well-being is thought to be related to an individual's level of social support.

Coping style   The kinds of behaviors people employ to meet stressful demands

Direct-effect hypothesis   The prediction that social support will provide equal benefit under high and low stress conditions

Emotional support   Support directed at helping people with their feelings or emotions

Informational support   Provision of helpful information

Intimacy   The sense of emotional closeness with another

Mastery   The sense that one can effectively combat stress and successfully influence one's future

Mastery support   Help that is intended to raise the recipient's sense that she or he can be successful and positively influence his or her environment

Material support   The provision of objects, goods, or money for the purpose of helping

Meta-construct   A general construct that is an umbrella for smaller constructs

Perceived support   The perception or sense that one is supported by others

Psychological well-being   The state of being psychologically healthy, or free of psychological dysfunction

Ratio of kith and kin   The ratio of number of friends to number of family members in a person's social network

Self-esteem   A person's sense of positive regard for himself or herself and feeling that he or she is of worth; can be high or low

Sense of belonging   The feeling that one is an esteemed member of a family, group, or organization

Social conflict   The presence of disagreement or tension between members of a family or social group

Social network   The connections or ties among people who interact with one another

Social support   A general (or meta) construct that encompasses both the extent to which one receives help from others and the sense of belonging to a family, group, or organization

Social support fit   The extent to which social support meets the needs experienced by the individual

Stress   (1) The degree to which a person loses or is under threat of losing what he or she values; (2) the state of having lost or been threatened with the loss of what is valued; (3) the state in which situational demands overtax coping resources

Stress-buffering hypothesis   The prediction that social support will be more effective under high stress conditions than low stress conditions

Stress resistance   The combatting of stressful circumstances

Stressful events   Events that cause stress; usually negative events that threaten or cause loss of valued things or states

Support density   The degree of attachment among individuals in a social network

Task support   Help aimed at executing a specific physical task (such as moving, buying groceries)

Part Two

Relationships Across the Life Span

4 Infant-Parent Relationships

Douglas M. Teti
University of Maryland, Baltimore County

Laureen O. Teti
University of Maryland, Baltimore County

*S*o far we have examined some fundamentals of personal relationships. Beginning with this chapter we will look at the important relationships we have throughout our lifetimes, starting from when we are born and ending with our relationships in old age. This chapter focuses on our first—and, some have argued, our most formative—relationships: those between infants and primary caregivers, usually parents. The chapter examines critical factors believed to shape those relationships, including infant temperament, "goodness of fit" between parent and infant, and an influential school of thought known as attachment theory.

NV & SD

Chapter Outline

- Emotions and Communication in Infancy
- Infant Temperament, Parental Characteristics, and "Goodness of Fit"
- Infant-Parent Attachments
- Conclusions
- Summary

Clarisse and Frank are new parents of an infant daughter, Julia, born five months ago. Clarisse and Frank never realized how much fun parenting would be. Although the pregnancy and delivery were somewhat difficult (Clarisse suffered intermittent bouts of nausea and morning sickness during the pregnancy and a forceps delivery), Julia was born a healthy 7-pound, 9-ounce infant who seemed unusually alert for a newborn and ready to meet the world. Julia took to breast feeding immediately and without any difficulty. Despite the typical and normal adjustments that take place during the transition to parenthood, Clarisse, Frank, and Julia settled nicely into a routine only two weeks after Julia came home from the birthing center. Julia was a fairly vocal baby and let her parents know very clearly when she was hungry or tired, and it became evident very early to Clarisse when Julia would be ready for a feeding or nap and when she would wake up. After about three months, Clarisse became quite adept at recognizing and differentiating Julia's vocalizations, knowing which ones indicated hunger, fatigue, and so on. Amazingly, Julia began sleeping through the night at about 2 months of age, and she would regularly wake up at about 6:00 A.M. Although Clarisse did most of the routine caregiving for Julia during these early months, Frank often stepped in to lend a hand. Julia was a strong crier, but by 3 months of age she was smiling regularly at any and all adults who would pay attention to her—especially at her parents. She was, in all respects, an alert, happy baby who seemed to take pleasure in the world around her. Her parents, in turn, took great pleasure in her, and relatives and visitors would frequently comment on what a "good" baby Julia was, and what wonderful parents Clarisse and Frank seemed be.

Josephine gave birth to her son Stefan about five months ago. Josephine, and especially her husband Gerald, were ambivalent about having a child even before Stefan was born. The couple was financially strapped, Josephine was prone to anxiety and depression, and Gerald would frequently withdraw from his wife emotionally. Within a week after Stefan's birth, Josephine lapsed into a deep postpartum depression, and caring for Stefan required a good deal of effort. Stefan also seemed to be a fussy baby, and his mother frequently seemed at a loss to know how to calm him. Josephine's difficulties in parenting Stefan were made worse by her sadness and anxiety, which sometimes led her to respond to Stefan in ineffective, inappropriate ways. In the meantime, Gerald became more and more absorbed in his job, leaving almost all of the care of Stefan to Josephine. Within a month after his birth, Stefan seemed to be getting more irritable and would cry during the day and at night without any apparent cause. This, and Gerald's withdrawal of emotional support and unwillingness to help with Stefan's care, in turn worsened Josephine's depression. Although she loved Stefan a great deal, her interactions with him were frequently characterized by frustration and loss of temper, and she would leave him alone in his crib for long stretches of time. When Stefan reached 5 months of age, Josephine's mother noted the difficulty that Josephine and Gerald were having with him and how unhappy Josephine was and recommended that they seek counseling.

These two very different family scenarios are all too common and indicate that differences in children's development and the parent-child relationship can be seen as early as infancy. The developmental prognosis for Julia and for Stefan, both of whom were healthy, full-term newborns, could not be more different. As a result of her easy disposition and her parents' joint devotion to her and to each other, Julia seems to be off on the right track. One can easily see the development of a healthy, secure attachment between Julia and her parents and the development in Julia of a positive and emotionally healthy orientation to the world around her. For Stefan, unfortunately, this does not seem to be so. His fussy temperament and the problems his parents are having as a couple as well as with him suggest difficulties down the road in his attachments to his parents and in his view of himself and the world around him. Fortunately, these trends can be altered if Josephine and Gerald take heed of their situation and do something about it.

In this chapter we discuss the relationships that infants form with their parents and, in particular, the premise that not only are infants and parents predisposed to form relationships but these relationships serve as the framework for later social competence within and outside the family. This topic, like all topics in developmental psychology, relates directly to the issue of **nature** versus **nurture.** We will explore the roles of nature— one's genetic endowment and constitutional makeup—and nurture— one's history of experiences—in determining infants' developing relationships with their parents. As you will see, infants appear to be preadapted to form relationships with others, although experience plays a crucial role in shaping the quality of these exchanges.

Lamb and Bornstein (1987) distinguish between two biologically based tendencies: species-specific influences and heritable influences. Species-specific influences are those characteristic of a species as a whole. For humans these might include biological preadaptations to prefer novel to familiar stimuli (Fantz, 1964) and newborns' ability to distinguish various human speech sounds (Aslin, Pisoni, & Jusczyk, 1983). Heritable influences, by contrast, are those genetically based tendencies that are unique to an individual, such as emotional expressivity, daily sleep and wake rhythms, and sensitivity to external stimulation. Both types of influences are related in important ways to infant-parent relationships, and both are explored in this chapter.

We begin with a discussion of the emotional life of infants—in particular, infants' biologically based abilities to perceive and express emotions and the ways emotions work to establish and maintain infant-parent relationships. This is followed by a discussion of individual differences in infants' abilities to use emotional signals effectively and in parents' abilities to read and respond appropriately to their infants' signals. We will examine how these competencies relate, theoretically, to infants' and parents' feelings of efficacy or to parents' feelings of competence in the parental role. We then explore the construct of infant temperament and how variations in temperamental characteristics affect parent-child interactions and children's developmental outcomes during the preschool and school years. Finally, the ways infants develop specific attachments to their parents are examined, with the discussion focused not only on species-specific tendencies to attach but also on the ways parent-child interactions and infant temperamental characteristics shape the quality of infant-parent attachments. Throughout the chapter we relate these discussions not only to "low-risk" infant-parent **dyads** (that is, pairs) but also to infants and parents who, because of environmental and/or constitutional stressors, experience special challenges in the parent-child relationship.

EMOTIONS AND COMMUNICATIONS IN INFANCY

All human relationships are built on the foundation of ability to communicate. Adults usually think of communication in terms of sentences and words, either spoken or written. Yet all people unwittingly communicate much more than their ideas; their facial expressions as well as their vocal quality often tell the world how they feel about things. In this sense emotions are communications from one individual to another. This is the language infants use to communicate with the world: the language of emotion.

In order for parents and infants to communicate emotionally, infants must not only be able to communicate their feelings to adults but also be able to perceive and understand the emotional expressions of adults. Research indicates that infants appear to be predisposed to perceive and react to the facial expressions of others (Haviland & Lelwica, 1987). In a study by Haviland and Lelwica (1987), infants as young as 10 weeks responded differently to presentations of happy, sad, and angry facial expressions by their mothers. Additionally, infants appear to expect their mothers to display emotions and become distressed when mothers suppress emotional displays. Field, Vega-Lahr, Seafidi, and Goldstein (1986) found that 4-month-old infants became more distressed when mothers inhibited emotional expression than when they were physically separated from their mothers. Cohn and Tronick (1983) found that 3- to 4-month-old infants responded negatively when their mothers acted and made facial expressions as if they were depressed, and the infants' negative displays continued even after their mothers returned to normal emotional displays. Three- to six-month-old infants of depressed mothers were found to display more general negative emotion and behavior toward both strangers and their mothers than infants of nondepressed mothers (Field et al., 1988). Malatesta and Haviland (1982) observed that when mothers' styles of emotional expressiveness led them to use particular parts of their faces and make certain expressions often, their infants were likely also to use the same parts of their faces and make expressions similar to their mothers' expressions. This relation be-

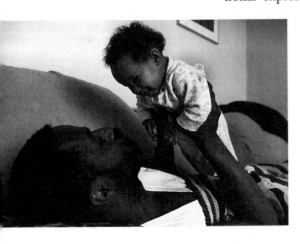

Babies learn to read emotions and express them from a very early age.

tween maternal emotional expression and infant emotional expression became stronger over time. These studies indicate that infants respond differently to different emotional expressions and that infants appear to expect their parents to be emotionally responsive to them. These findings also suggest that maternal emotional style can affect the development of emotional expressiveness in infants.

INFANT TEMPERAMENT, PARENTAL CHARACTERISTICS, AND "GOODNESS OF FIT"

Infants appear to have a rich emotional life, and their expressed emotions and the emotions they perceive from others appear to serve a major function in communication. As we shall see, however, not all infants are capable of effective emotional signaling, and the parents of those who are not may find it especially challenging to establish harmonious relationships with them.

In an important paper, Goldberg (1977) has argued that "competent" infant-parent dyads are created by infants who use clear, unambiguous emotional signals (such as distress cries and smiling) in interactions with parents. Clear and readable infant signals foster **parental self-efficacy,** or parental perceptions that they are good at understanding what their infants need and want and at responding appropriately to meet those needs. For example, a mother who understands from her infant's clearly signaled cries that the infant is hungry, tired, hurt, or afraid is more likely to be successful in calming the infant. In turn, such a mother stands a good chance of feeling competent (or self-efficacious) in the parental role. By contrast, the mother of an infant who signals poorly—perhaps because it was premature (Field, 1987), because it was exposed to toxins prenatally (Lester et al., 1991), or simply because it is highly active and irritable—may be less successful understanding her infant's needs and, as a consequence, may respond incorrectly or inappropriately. This mother would be more likely than the mother of a "readable" baby to feel ineffective in the parental role.

Goldberg (1977) also argues that contingently responsive parenting (parenting that is appropriately responsive to infant social signals such as crying and bids for play) fosters infants' feelings of efficacy—that is, their perception that their behavior has an impact on the environment. Such feelings of efficacy in infants appear to be associated with positive affect and also may be related to infants' motivation to explore and master their environment. Watson (1972), for example, found that when infants (some as young as 8 weeks old) were given the opportunity to perceive that they were the cause of an environmental event (in this case, to see that a mobile suspended overhead moved whenever they moved their heads on their pillows), they not only increased the amount of the causative action (head turning), but also smiled and cooed more. It was as if the infants enjoyed the sense of being in control of their environment, leading Watson to speculate that one of the reasons parents (or caregivers) become important to infants is because parents are the ones who typically respond to infant distress calls, cries to be fed, and bids to interact and play. Thus "competent" infant-parent dyads are those in which infants signal their needs clearly and parents easily read and respond to these infant signals. Under such conditions, feelings of effectiveness may be fostered in both parent and child.

Although all infants use emotions as communicative devices, much individual variation exists in the abilities of infants to have a predictable effect on their environment. One of the most widely discussed factors in infant development is **infant temperament,** which can be defined broadly as a biologically based set of emotional and behavioral predispositions. Infant temperament influences how infants affect their caregiving environment and may figure prominently in individual variations in personality development. Although there is disagreement among the experts about exactly what dimensions comprise infant temperament, you can get a good intuitive sense of what temperament is by simply asking anyone who is the parent of two or more children whether they perceive their children to be different, how they are different, and how early in life these differences were apparent. (Those of you with siblings might want to try this out with your parents—you might be surprised at what you learn!) Indeed, it is not unusual for parents to comment on how different from one another their children are and on how early these differences emerged. In some cases, differences were noted as early as the first few weeks of life along such dimensions as soothability, activity, sociability, ease of eating and going to sleep (and predictability of both), intensity of response to new situations, and general fussiness.

Perhaps the most well-known study of infant temperament and its effects was the New York Longitudinal Study (NYLS), conducted in the 1950s by Alexander Thomas and Stella Chess (1977). Through it Thomas and Chess identified nine behavioral dimensions on which infants as young as 2 months differed: activity level, rhythmicity, approach/withdrawal, adaptability, intensity of reaction, attention span and persistence, distractibility, quality of mood, and threshold of responsiveness. Patterns of differences across these nine dimensions led to the identification of four temperamental types: "easy" babies (40% of the sample), "difficult" babies (10% of the sample), "slow-to-warm-up" babies (15% of the sample), and "average" babies (35% of the sample). Thomas and Chess regarded these types as a reflection of individual differences in infant behavioral styles of responding. Easy babies were so identified by their adaptability and rhythmic bodily functions, positive mood, general "approach" response to new situations, and low intensity of response. Difficult babies, by contrast, were characterized by negativity in mood, unadaptability, general withdrawal in response to novelty, and high intensity of response. Slow-to-warm-up babies likewise generally withdrew from new situations and had negative moods, but they also were low in activity and had low-to-moderate response intensity. Finally, babies in the average category were rated as moderate on all dimensions.

Of these four temperamental types, the most positive outcomes (in terms of parent-child relationships, school problems, and relationships with peers) were associated with children who had earlier been identified as "easy," whereas the most adverse outcomes were associated with children identified in babyhood as "difficult." Indeed, 70% of the difficult babies later showed behavioral difficulties in their interactions with parents, with peers, or in school, suggesting that their particular set of temperamental characteristics predisposed these children to having a negative impact on their parents and subsequently on their wider social world. Just as important, however, was the finding that the remaining 30% of children labeled "difficult" in infancy had positive outcomes. This finding prompted Thomas and Chess to examine closely how the parents of difficult children adapted to their children's negativity and unadaptability. Indeed, the parents of difficult children with more positive developmental outcomes differed from the parents of difficult children with negative outcomes in that they responded with consistency, firmness, and patience to their children's negative moods, and they did not feel undue anxiety and self-blame over their children's difficult temperaments. Thus although parents found it hard to cope with and adapt to difficult children, their children's later social and instrumental competence was positive when their difficult temperament was matched with a parental style characterized by responsivity, consistent limit setting, and confidence that the children's early problems were not of the parents' making.

That infant temperament appeared to interact with style of parenting prompted Thomas and Chess to discuss more broadly the importance of **goodness of fit** between child and parent characteristics in predicting not only parent-child outcomes but also how well children will move into the wider world. A broader array of parental characteristics may "fit" well with easy infants, whose adaptability and positive moods may be minimally taxing to parents and may regularly elicit more positive responses from parents. Easy babies should be associated with high feelings of parental efficacy, given the ease with which parents can read and respond to the babies' emotional signals and bodily rhythms. By contrast, difficult infants may best fit with parents who are already confident in their parenting skills and/or who correctly see their children's negativity as constitutional rather than a product of their own behavior. Such parents may be emotionally equipped to optimize both their relationships with their difficult children and their children's development over the long term.

Of course, it should be noted that even easy babies may suffer poor developmental outcomes under conditions of parental neglect and/or abuse, and so there clearly are limits to the degree to which an easy temperament leads to a good parent-infant fit.

INFANT-PARENT ATTACHMENTS

Attachment theory and research have provided some useful formulations about how infant emotionality and temperament and parental behavior collectively contribute to the formation of infants' attachments to their parents. An **attachment** can be thought of as a strong, intimate, affectional tie between one person and another that persists across time and space (Ainsworth, Blehar, Waters, & Wall, 1978; Bowlby, 1969). Attachments are thus selective, not random, occurring between specific individuals at specific times. Human beings' first attachments occur in infancy— toward their parents. However, as we all know, many different attachments can be formed over the life span, be they between lovers, friends, or siblings. We should also make a distinction between an infant's attachment to her or his parents, which appears to develop gradually over the first eight to ten months of life, and **mother–infant bonding,** which refers to Klaus and Kennell's (1976) controversial hypothesis that mothers develop strong emotional attachments to their infants if given access to them during the first few hours after birth (see Box 1).

Recent thinking on infant-parent attachments owes much to the seminal work of Harry Harlow, a comparative psychologist who worked extensively with monkeys, and John Bowlby, a psychoanalyst who was frustrated with conceptualizations of attachment that involved associative conditioning. The theory of associative conditioning, formally known as **secondary drive theory,** states that it is through repeated associations of the infant's caregiver with the gratification of the infant's primary drive for food that the caregiver becomes the focus of a secondary drive, which leads the infant to seek out and interact with the caregiver even in the absence of food. Secondary drive theory held sway for some 40 years, primarily because of its acceptability to both learning theorists and psychoanalytic theorists. Harlow's work on attachments among monkeys (Harlow, 1958; Harlow & Zimmerman, 1959), however, shed new light on the nature of attachment bonds and suggested that feeding was only incidental to the process of attachment formation. Specifically, Harlow designed a study in which monkeys were separated from their mothers in the first day of life and reared for about four months with two "surrogate," or substitute, mothers—one constructed of wire, the other constructed of foam rubber and terrycloth, which was comfortable to the touch. Half of the monkeys were fed consistently by the wire mother (via a tube protruding from the "chest"), and the remaining half were similarly fed by the cloth monkey. Harlow was particularly interested in determining which "mother" the babies would turn to when apprehensive or frightened by novel objects or

Box 1

Early Bonding: Critical or Not?

Early emotional bonding between a parent and infant, if it can be shown to exist, may be a species-specific behavior that promotes parental care for the young and in doing so enhances the survival of the human species. Researchers over the last 20 years have raised many questions about early bonding between parents and infants. One question that researchers have focused on is, Does early emotional bonding between parents and infants actually occur? Initial research on bonding by Klaus and Kennell (1976) suggested a way in which this might happen. These researchers found that mothers who had had skin-to-skin contact with their infants within 3 hours of birth, as well as extended hours of nursing and cuddling with their infants while still in the hospital, soothed and cuddled their infants more both at one month and one year after birth (Klaus & Kennell, 1976). In interpreting these data, Klaus and Kennell (1982) concluded that the early skin-to-skin contact between mother and infant was largely responsible for these differences. They suggested that the first 6 to 12 hours after birth are a sensitive period for emotional bonding between parent and infant; this implies that parents who have skin-to-skin contact with their infants during this time will have stronger affection for their infants than those who do not.

In response to Klaus and Kennell's hypothesis, many hospitals altered their visitation schedules to allow more contact between newborns and parents and began allowing fathers to be present at the birth of their children. But later attempts to replicate the results of Klaus and Kennell's early work were largely unsuccessful (Goldberg, 1983). Most of the studies found that when early skin-to-skin contact had occurred shortly after birth there were some differences in the amount and quality of contact between mother and infant during the first week of the infant's life, but these differences were no longer present at one month, one year, or three years after birth (Carlsson et al., 1979; Schaller, Carlsson, & Larsson, 1979). Thus skin-to-skin contact between parent and infant during the first hours of life does not appear to have any long-term influence on the emotional bonds that parents develop with their children.

This is happy news for the many parents who cannot have early contact with their children, including parents of premature or ill infants and parents who adopt; it suggests that they are just as likely to have close emotional ties with their children as parents who are able to have early contact. The emotional bond between infant and parent, like an emotional bond between any two individuals, is more likely based on their shared interactions and experiences. Early infant-parent contact may indeed be desirable in terms of providing the opportunity for families to share in the experience of the birth of a new family member, a decidedly emotional event. Klaus and Kennell's (1976) work thus affected hospital practices in a positive way by deemphasizing the use of delivery rooms (except in the case of high-risk pregnancies) in favor of more comfortable, family-oriented birthing rooms where family members could be together during the birth. However, parents who are deprived of early contact with their newborns are not at any disadvantage in establishing strong emotional ties with them.

toys (for example, wooden spiders) introduced into their cages. Secondary drive theory would predict that each monkey would prefer the mother that fed it—that is, monkeys fed by the wire mother would run to the wire mother when alarmed; monkeys fed by the cloth mother would run to the cloth mother. The results of this study, however, clearly indicated that all of the baby monkeys, regardless of which surrogate fed them, preferred the cloth monkey when distressed, running and clinging to it when the frightening objects were first introduced and then actually managing to explore the previously frightening object "under the protective gaze of their mothers" (Harlow & Zimmerman, 1959, p. 423). Even when they were not exposed to frightening stimuli, the monkeys fed by the wire mother spent much more of their time holding onto the cloth mother (over 12 hours per day) than to the wire mother (only about 1 hour per day, typically during feedings). This study suggests that the provision of contact comfort, which was clearly associated with the cloth rather than the wire mother, is an important ingredient in the development of infant-mother attachment bonds and clearly more important than feeding per se.

Using the data from Harlow's laboratory and data provided by other comparative psychologists, ethologists, and psychodynamic theorists, John Bowlby (1969) proposed what is commonly known as **ethological attachment theory.** Bowlby's theory has today become the dominant social developmental theory accounting for the formation and significance of social relationships in infancy and early childhood. In brief, ethological attachment theory states that human infants have an innate, or biologically based, need for social interaction. Through the evolutionary process of natural selection, human infants have acquired a repertoire of attachment behaviors—the **attachment behavioral system**—that is geared specifically to attaining and maintaining proximity to others of the same species, especially adults. Included in this repertoire are such behaviors as crying, looking, smiling, reaching, and following, all of which reliably lead to adult responses. Also through the process of natural selection, adults are equipped with a repertoire of caregiving behaviors that complement the proximity-seeking behaviors of the infant. Adults are predisposed, for example, to respond to a crying infant with behaviors designed to soothe the infant, such as picking the baby up, holding the baby upright, and rocking it gently. Adults also find infant smiling quite engaging and frequently respond to infant smiles with smiles of their own, accompanied by "baby talk." Thus human infants and adults are preadapted to respond to each other in mutually complementary ways that function jointly to promote not only the survival of the infant but also, in an evolutionary sense, the species. Indeed, without such attachment mechanisms, species that have a limited number of offspring and who have relatively long developmental periods before maturity would very likely die out.

Bowlby saw the attachment system during the first six months of life as goal-directed: that is, its goal is to maintain the proximity of the attachment figure through signaling behaviors that reliably elicit the attention and approach of the caregiver. This goal is particularly important before the onset of locomotion (that is, crawling or walking), when infants are not yet able to approach the caregiver themselves. With the onset of locomotion and the attainment of certain cognitive milestones by the second half of the first year, however, the responsibility for proximity maintenance shifts gradually from parent to infant. By 8 to 10 months of age, most infants have begun crawling and most have also developed a rudimentary sense of "person permanence," or the knowledge that the caregiver is an entity who exists even when out of the infant's sight. These milestones presage a shift in the attachment behavioral system from being goal-directed to goal-corrected, in which infants' attempts to remain close to the caregiver depend on a variety of circumstances that can be exogenous (related to changes in the environment) or endogenous (related to

Children typically seek out their attachment figures in response to the approach of a stranger.

changes in the infant). Exogenous factors that predispose proximity-maintenance behaviors include being separated from the caregiver, the approach of someone unfamiliar (especially an adult), or being exposed to novel and ambiguous stimuli (as were the baby monkeys in Harlow's studies). "Separation anxiety" and "stranger anxiety," which typically appear by the second half of the first year in human infants, are associated with attempts on the infant's part to gain access to and seek the protection of the attachment figure. However, an infant's attachment system may not be activated to as high a degree under less stressful circumstances. For example, an infant in her or his home environment would be expected to withstand separations from the caregiver of a much larger distance and perhaps even to remain calm with the approach of a stranger. Thus by the end of the second year the attachment behavioral system is goal-corrected, in that the goal of proximity maintenance depends on whether the infant perceives the immediate situation as "dangerous." Endogenous factors that have an impact on the attachment system include factors within the baby such as illness, pain, hunger, or fatigue, all of which predispose an infant to seek the proximity of the attachment figure and elicit caregiving behavior.

Other innate infant behavioral systems were also discussed in Bowlby's theory. In particular, the **exploratory behavioral system** works in conjunction with but opposite to the attachment system by orienting the infant away from the caregiver and toward novelty in the environment. It is quite natural for infants to be fascinated by novel, unfamiliar stimuli and to explore novel objects in the absence of fear-producing circumstances, which send the infant back toward the attachment figure. Bowlby saw the exploratory and attachment behavioral systems to be in dynamic interplay, especially by the end of the first year, when infants' abilities to locomote are well developed. The balance of the attachment-exploratory systems can thus tip in one direction or the other, depending on the particular exogenous and endogenous factors that are present. As we shall see, the balance of the attachment-exploratory behavioral systems became the central focus of attachment researchers interested in studying individual differences in the quality of attachments.

Bowlby (1969) proposed four basic stages in the development of attachments. The first, "orientation and signals without discrimination of figure" (the "pre-attachment" phase, as Ainsworth et al., 1978, call it), occurs from birth to about 2 months of age and is characterized by the infant's tendency to be nondiscriminating about the adults toward whom he or she displays attachment behavior. Babies' needs in this early phase can be satisfied by any adult, because babies under 2 months of age, although they do distinguish caregivers from strangers, do not yet have the ability to produce preferential behaviors. The eventual exhibition of such behaviors depends on maturation and experience as well as on linkages between cognitive and motor systems that will only occur in the next phase. The second phase, "orientation and signals directed toward one (or more) discriminated figures" (the "attachment in the making" phase, Ainsworth et al., 1978), takes place between approximately 2 and 8 months of age and is characterized by an increasing preference for familiar caretakers over unfamiliar ones. Thus infants in this phase calm more rapidly with and respond more playfully to the social bids of familiar adults than those of unfamiliar adults. However, although this phase witnesses infants' growing preference for familiar over unfamiliar adults, this orientation is not yet so strong that infants reject unfamiliar adults completely. The third phase, "maintenance of proximity to discriminated figures by means of locomotion and signals" (the "clear-cut attachment" phase, Ainsworth et al., 1978), occurs between 7 months and about 2 years and is the stage in which true goal-corrected attachment is seen. True attachment to one or perhaps a few familiar caregivers is shown by the development of separa-

[handwritten margin notes: sep anxiety; dev. of locomotion; sense of person permanence; goal-corrected partnership 3–4 years; awareness of needs of others; goal corrected attachment; sfill exists; look for attach figure when frightened or hurt]

tion anxiety, characterized by infants growing upset and fearful when separated from their caregivers, and stranger anxiety, in which infants show fear of strangers. As we mentioned earlier, this phase coincides with the development of locomotion and a rudimentary sense of person permanence (the infant's awareness that the caregiver can be out of sight and still exist). We use the word *rudimentary* because the final emergence of person and object permanence awaits the end of the second year of life (Piaget, 1952). The fourth and final of Bowlby's proposed attachment phases, "goal-corrected partnership," begins at about 3 or 4 years of age and witnesses the development of children's abilities to see that others (such as their parents) have wants and needs and that the wants and needs of both parties should be accounted for in some fashion during social interactions. Goal-corrected attachment behavior still exists in this stage; preschool-aged children still seek out their attachment figures when frightened or hurt. However, by 4 years of age children have more advanced social and cognitive abilities and much more experience dealing with separations and strange adults than do children at earlier stages. As a result, children in the goal-corrected phase are likely to make use of questioning, dialogue, and negotiation with their attachment figures to help them understand and manage their distress.

Quality of Infant-Parent Attachments

Although Bowlby (1969) saw the attachment and exploratory behavioral systems as innate systems that predispose infants to form attachments, he also acknowledged that the quality of the caregiving environment is related in an important way to the quality of attachments. Many current concepts of attachment quality can be credited to Mary Ainsworth, whose work in Uganda (Ainsworth, 1967) and later at Johns Hopkins University (Ainsworth et al., 1978) identified particular attachment patterns among infants that have been found to relate to caregiving behavior in the home and to later developmental outcomes. Ainsworth was particularly concerned with the attachment-exploration balance in infants in the goal-corrected, clear-cut attachment phase (Bowlby's third phase), specifically, the ability of infants in this phase to use their attachment figures as "secure bases" from which to explore the environment. Ainsworth believed that the ways in which infants organize their behavior around their attachment figures following a brief and moderately stressful separation in a strange environment reveal a great deal (and much more than infants' emotional reactions to the separation itself) about whether infants are securely or insecurely attached to their parents.

Most of Ainsworth's findings were based on a procedure she developed called the Strange Situation, an 8-episode, 22- to 24-minute laboratory observation involving the infant, the attachment figure (typically the mother), and an adult female stranger (see Box 2). This procedure, used in conjunction with coding schemes developed by Ainsworth et al. (1978)

Box 2   **The Strange Situation Laboratory Observation**

The Strange Situation procedure developed by Mary Ainsworth (Ainsworth et al., 1978) has been used by researchers to assess the quality of infants' attachments to their parents. Infants in this procedure experience a series of separations and reunions involving the caregiver and a stranger in a small playroom. The intent is to assess how infants organize their attachment and exploratory behavior around the caregiver. Each episode lasts 3 minutes, or less if the infant becomes distressed. The eight episodes, in sequence, are as follows:

Episode	Participants in the playroom
1	Infant, caregiver, and observer
2	Infant and caregiver
3	Infant, caregiver, and stranger
4	Infant and stranger
5	Infant and caregiver
6	Infant alone
7	Infant and stranger
8	Infant and caregiver

Particular attention is given to the ways infants pattern their behavior during reunions with the caregiver. Secure infants (type B) demonstrate appropriate secure-base behavior by investigating unfamiliar territory comfortably in their caregivers' presence, with occasional checks on, and positive social interactive bids to, their caregivers. If distressed, secure infants will reliably seek the proximity of their caregivers for comfort, and then ease back into an exploratory mode characterized by periodic checks on their caregivers. Insecure infants, by contrast, do not use their caregivers as a secure base. Avoidant (type A) infants explore unfamiliar territory with an almost exclusive, seemingly compulsive focus on the toys and objects in the room, checking back on caregivers' whereabouts only infrequently. It is not uncommon for avoidant infants to "snub" their mothers on reunion, showing either no greeting or a delayed greeting, to play with their backs to their mothers, and to ignore their mothers' social bids. Resistant (type C) babies are characterized by their repeated expressions of anger, incessant crying, pouting, whining, and the like, behaviors that are especially prevalent during infant-mother reunions. These infants appears to be negatively preoccupied with their caregivers, are difficult to calm when distressed, and are not very successful at easing back into toy play in their mothers' presence after separation. Disorganized/disoriented (type D) babies, identified by Main and Solomon (1990) appear to be undecided as to whether, or how, to interact with their attachment figures. Instead of showing a clear avoidant, secure, or resistant pattern, or "strategy," disorganized/disoriented babies appear fearful, confused or dazed, or conflicted—for example, some may approach their mothers, but with their heads strongly turned away.

and Main and Solomon (1990), identified four attachment types: avoidant (type A), secure (type B), resistant (type C), and disorganized/disoriented (type D). As Teti and Nakagawa (1990) have noted, the validity of Ainsworth's classification system is supported by the wide variety of studies finding that secure infants (type B) are the products of sensitive, responsive caretaking during the first year (that is, parenting characterized by prompt and consistent responses to infant distress signals, infant bids for social interaction, and the like), whereas insecure infants (types A, C, and D) are associated with suboptimal, insensitive caregiving. In addition, secure attachment in infancy has been associated with more adaptive developmental outcomes in later childhood, such as better relationships with peers and cooperativeness with parents (Teti & Nakagawa, 1990).

Nonetheless, the Strange Situation classifications have aroused some controversy. Some researchers (such as Clarke-Stewart & Fein, 1983) have suggested that Ainsworth's attachment classifications are meaningful only under certain rearing circumstances—for example, when infants are raised at home with their mothers. Indeed, it is precisely because Ainsworth's attachment classifications have become so popular among researchers on early attachment that controversies have sprung up about how attachments should be assessed in alternative rearing environments such as day care (see Box 3).

Infant Temperament and Early Attachment

One of the most daunting controversies in the field of early social development has been how infant constitutional characteristics, specifically infant temperamental dispositions, figure into the development of early attachments. Infant temperament is highly individualistic. Intuitively, one might expect infants to contribute to their own attachments to their parents. Whether this contribution is direct or indirect, however, has been a subject of much debate.

Kagan (1984) has taken the "nature" side of this debate and argues that individual variation seen in separation-reunion procedures like the Strange Situation are the direct product of individual variation in infant temperament. He proposes that infants who are easily predisposed to distress are likely to be classified as resistant (type C) simply because they are more difficult to soothe during reunions. By contrast, children who are temperamentally very sociable and "easy" (using the terms of Thomas & Chess, 1977), even if distressed by separations and the approach of strangers, will likely be classified as secure (type B) because of their propensity to greet mothers on reunions and calm quickly. Finally, shy, introverted children who are not prone to distress and who are not easily aroused by separations and who give their mothers rather nonchalant greetings on reunion may be erroneously designated as "avoidant."

Box 3

Is Day Care Bad for Babies?

The topic of whether infant day care is bad for babies has never been more sharply debated than in the past five years. As ever-increasing numbers of mothers of small children enter the workforce, greater numbers of infants are being placed in day care than ever before (U.S. Bureau of the Census, 1986).

To a great extent, the current controversy about infant day care has resulted from the new ways of looking at early attachment offered by Ainsworth and her colleagues, which involve examining how infants organize their behavior in response to their parents following brief separations. In his review of the day-care literature, Jay Belsky, a prominent developmental psychologist, has argued that placing infants in day care for 20 hours or more per week in their first year may place them at risk of becoming insecurely attached to their mothers (Belsky, 1986; Belsky & Rovine, 1988). Significantly higher levels of insecure attachments and, in particular, avoidant attachments were associated with infants who were in day care for 20 or more hours per week when compared to infants with less than 20 hours of day care per week. Belsky and others (Barglow, Vaughn, & Molitor, 1987) also noted that infants who were in day care for 20 hours or more per week were more likely to show behavior disturbances later in childhood (for example, higher levels of aggressive behavior toward peers). The risk associated with infant day care, it was argued, was due to repeated separations of infants from their parents, which disrupted the developing attachment relationship.

These reports created a firestorm among behavioral scientists and parents alike. Critics argued that Belsky's reports ignored day care *quality* in predicting children's developmental outcome. Since infant day care was an economic necessity for a great many families, social scientists could better spend their time studying how the quality of infant day care could be improved to benefit the lives of infants (Clarke-Stewart & Fein, 1983; Phillips, McCartney, Scarr, & Howes, 1987). Clarke-Stewart and Fein (1983) further argued that what is labeled as avoidant behavior in the Strange Situation procedure could actually be viewed as independence, not insecurity. Infants placed in day care in their first year of life would become accustomed to repeated separations from and reunions with their mothers and would thus show very little separation distress and perhaps exhibit a nonchalant response to parents during reunions. This raises an important concern about whether infants' experiences of separations from and reunions with mothers is different for babies in day care versus infants raised at home. If this experience is different for day-care versus home-care babies, do Strange Situation classifications derived for day-care babies have the same meaning as they do for babies reared at home?

Box 3 continues

Box 3
(continued)

> It is very likely that infant day care is here to stay, and it is reasonable to expect that the quality of both the home and the day-care environment will have an impact on infants' relationships with their parents and on infant development. More attention needs to be given to what parents should look for when choosing day care for their infants and to how parents and day care providers can best work together to optimize the development of children in their care.

Thus Kagan hypothesizes that infants' temperaments are directly responsible for their behavior in the Strange Situation. However, most of the data addressing this question do not support this view. For example, infants frequently do not show the same attachment pattern to mothers as to fathers (Sroufe, 1985). If temperament were playing a direct role in the patterning of attachment behavior, one would expect the attachment patterns shown to different parents to be nearly the same. Different patterns, however, would indicate differences in the quality of the interactions infants have with different parents. Second, infant attachment patterns are significantly related to the quality of infants' rearing environments. It is typical to find approximately two-thirds of the infants in a sample of "low-risk" families (families showing no indications of parental abuse, parental psychopathology, or other problems) to be secure and to find two-thirds (or more) of infants in "high-risk" families to be insecure (Teti & Nakagawa, 1990). It is hard to imagine that such differences are only a reflection of infants' genetic makeup (that is, of infants' temperamental predispositions) rather than of, at least to some degree, the quality of parenting. Third, infants' attachments are not static. Several studies attest to the fact that attachment classifications can change over a 6- to 7-month period and are especially prone to do so when the life circumstances in the family are changing (Egeland & Farber, 1984; Thompson, Lamb, & Estes, 1982). If attachment behavior were a straightforward function of temperamental dispositions, one might expect more stability in attachment classifications despite changes in family life conditions. Finally, Vaughn, LeFever, Seifer, and Barglow (1989) reported that whereas dimensions of infant temperament are significantly related to infants' behavior in Strange Situations during separations from mothers, they bear no relation to infants' behavior during the reunions, which, as we discussed, form the basis for Ainsworth's Strange Situation classifications.

These data collectively do not support Kagan's (1984) hypothesis of a direct influence of infant temperament on infant attachment. Many experts agree, however, that variations in infant temperament can influence attachment formation indirectly, perhaps by affecting how parents interact

Box 4

Nonorganic Failure-to-Thrive Infants: Relationships at Risk

Non-organic failure to thrive (NOFTT), a disorder usually diagnosed in infants of 18 months or younger, accounts for 5% of pediatric hospital admissions (O'Brien, Repp, Williams, & Christopherson, 1991). Infants are diagnosed as having NOFTT if their weight at birth is within norms for their gestational age yet from the time of their birth both their weight and their rate of weight gain decrease to below the fifth percentile, based on National Center for Health Statistics norms, and no organic cause can be found.

Caloric depletion is the immediate cause of NOFTT, but the causes of this caloric depletion are difficult to determine (O'Brien et al., 1991). One possible cause of NOFTT is feeding problems (Drotar, 1991). Early studies examining problems with feeding found that parents of NOFTT infants reported significantly more problems with the infant during feeding (such as nipple rejection, food refusal, vomiting, or falling asleep) (Kotelchuck & Newberger, 1983). Mothers whose infants engage in these behaviors often misread the signals from the infant and assume the infant has had enough food, resulting in lower food intake. Poorly educated mothers sometimes attempt to feed their infants age-inappropriate foods, again leading to insufficient caloric intake by the infants.

However, NOFTT can also occur in the absence of feeding problems. Although researchers have identified numerous risk factors associated with NOFTT, specific causes have been elusive. For example, observational studies have found mothers of NOFTT infants to be less responsive, less accepting, more negative, and less organized in their caregiving than mothers of physically healthy infants from comparable socioeconomic environments (Drotar, 1991). Mothers of NOFTT infants often have lower IQs than average (Drotar & Sturm, 1989) and frequently suffer from adjustment disorder with depressed mood (Phelps, 1991; Polan et al., 1991). Furthermore, many of these mothers also report inadequate nurturance in their own upbringing (Drotar, 1991), which may in turn affect their own parenting ability (Fraiberg, 1980). Infant temperament may also play a role in NOFTT. Casey (1983) found behaviors such as being difficult to soothe, poor signalling, and deficiencies in responding to stimulation were frequently observed in NOFTT infants. NOFTT infants are often less socially responsive, are more irritable, show higher reactivity and distractibility to extraneous stimuli, and show less distress upon separation from their caregiver (Phelps, 1991). More broadly, the family context and related ecological risk factors have also been linked to NOFTT. NOFTT is associated with poverty (Bruenlin, Desai, Stone, & Swilley,

Box 4 continues

Box 4
(continued)

1983) and family dysfunction (Drotar, 1991; Phelps, 1991), which can place limits on family members' ability to avail themselves of community resources and may contribute to maladaptive caretaking patterns, including the inability to recognize early signs of growth deficiency and make necessary adjustments (Hertzler, 1983).

The complexity of NOFTT's causes highlights the complexity of infant-parent relationships in general. A myriad of factors determine the quality of infant-parent interaction; when many of these factors are not optimal, NOFTT may be one result. An infant-parent relationship in which NOFTT is present is a relationship at risk.

with their children and shaping the quality of these interactions during the first year. Cranky, irritable, difficult babies, for example, may be prone to insecure attachments if parents are unable to adapt successfully to their babies' negativity (see Goldsmith & Alansky, 1987; Sroufe, 1985). Indeed, Mangelsdorf, Gunnar, Kestenbaum, Lang, and Andreas (1990) argue that it is not infant temperament per se that directly relates to attachment classifications, but how well caregivers adapt to the specific temperamental dispositions of their children. When the fit between caregiver and infant characteristics is especially poor, it may even compromise an infant's physical health, as exemplified by failure-to-thrive infants, whose growth rates during the first year of life fall far below the norm. Caregivers who can deal with infants' negative moods and unadaptability with sensitivity, flexibility, patience, and perhaps some degree of appropriate limit setting are more likely to shape secure attachments than are caregivers who have difficulty coping with their infants' difficult behavior and, as a result, parent inconsistently.

You may have noticed the similarity between the proposition that early attachment patterns are shaped by how well parents adjust to the temperamental dispositions of their infants, rather than by just infant temperament, and the goodness-of-fit hypothesis advanced by Thomas and Chess (1977) almost two decades ago. Recall that 30% of the difficult children in their sample had favorable outcomes by the time they reached preschool and school age and that these researchers credited parents' success in adjusting to their children's problematic dispositions with shaping their children's development. In addition to infant temperament, there are probably many factors that contribute to parent-child goodness-of-fit, including the parents' own developmental histories (Eiden, Teti, & Corns, in press), marital harmony and social supports (Crockenberg, 1981; Goldberg & Easterbrooks, 1984), life stress (Crnic, Greenberg, Ragozin, Robinson, & Basham, 1983), psychiatric symptoms such as depression

(Gelfand & Teti, 1990), and parental age and experience with childrearing (Lamb & Elster, 1986). Clearly the equation is complex, and the importance of each of these factors in predicting attachment may vary according to the individual infant-parent dyad.

CONCLUSIONS

Infant-parent relationships evolve in a complex arena. Theory and research evidence indicates that both members of the infant-parent dyad have species-specific preadaptations to form relationships and that the need for social interaction may be just as primary as the need for food. At the same time, both infants and parents bring their own sets of heritable and experiential attributes to bear upon the relationship, and how well these fit has a great deal to do with the health of the infant-parent dyad. From a developmental perspective, establishing harmonious parent-child interactions and a secure attachment may be important to dealing effectively with (and resolving) developmental tasks as a toddler. Erikson (1963) and Sroufe (1979) argue that successful resolution of earlier developmental tasks paves the way for successful resolution of later tasks. For example, being securely attached in infancy (establishing a sense of trust in the world, in Erikson's terms) may assist children in the move toward more individual functioning as toddlers. This theory is supported by the findings, discussed earlier in this chapter, that toddlers and preschoolers designated as secure in infancy are found to be more sociable, compliant, and independent than same-aged children who were earlier designated as insecure.

Equally important to note, however, is that the quality of the infant-parent relationship does not necessarily determine the child's ability to function in later life, as traditional psychoanalytic theory would have us believe (Freud, 1940). Several studies, for example, have found insecure infant attachments related to psychopathology at the age of 6 only in families in which other high-risk factors were present, such as very low socioeconomic status and/or high levels of life stress (Bates & Bayles, 1988; Fagot & Kavanagh, 1990; Lewis, Feiring, McGoffog, & Jaskir, 1984). Development is a highly dynamic process, and even healthy parent-infant relationships may go awry if family circumstances in later childhood become difficult to cope with—for example, if the parents divorce (Hetherington, Cox, & Cox, 1982). It is clearly desirable for parents and infants to get off to a good start. However, infant-parent dyads with more problematic beginnings (such as dyads involving low-birthweight or preterm infants) will likely have many opportunities to self-correct and steer toward a healthier path. This ability to compensate for early relational difficulties is yet another example of a species-specific preadaptation.

SUMMARY

This chapter has examined species-specific, heritable, and environmental factors that predispose infants and parents to form relationships and that underlie individual differences in infant-parent interactions. Infants come preadapted to perceive and express emotions, an ability that is fine tuned by learning and that figures importantly in infant-parent communicative exchanges. Contributing to the quality of these exchanges are differences in infants' temperamental characteristics (that is, biologically based differences in activity level, fussiness, mood, sociability, and the like), which interact with parental personality to determine parent-child goodness-of-fit. The attachment of infants to their parents relates directly to the contact comfort and interaction provided by parents, rather than to a "secondary drive" based on associating parents with the provision of food. Attachment security in infancy appears to relate to the quality of parent-child interaction. Although some theorists maintain that infant attachments are indirect measures of infant temperament (rather than measures of the infant-parent relationship), others argue that temperament plays a role in infant-parent attachment only to the extent that it affects the quality of parental behavior. Theoretically, the infant-parent relationship is critical to the developing child's ability to resolve, by the end of the second year, the developmental task of establishing a sense of trust in the world and a sense of himself or herself as effective and valued. At the same time, the flexibility that characterizes the human species indicates that a poor start does not necessarily lead to a poor developmental outcome later in life.

Class Discussion Questions

1. If you have siblings, how would your parents say you are different, temperamentally speaking, from one of your brothers or sisters? Was one of you easier to feed, bathe, or calm down if distressed? How early in your lives were these differences first noticed? If you do not have any brothers or sisters, you could ask your parents about how early in your life they were able to figure out when you were ready to go to sleep, wake up, eat, and such, and if they considered you easy, difficult, or in between.

2. Why do you think some species have developed elaborate mechanisms for establishing attachment between infants and their mothers, whereas others (such as snakes, some species of fish, or insects) have not? (Think of this question in terms of how different reproductive strategies foster survival of the species.)

3. Which baby do you think would be at higher risk of relationship problems with its mother during the first year of life: A 2-month-old premature baby whose mother feels competent in the mothering role, or a 2-month-old premature baby whose mother is depressed and doubtful

about her mothering abilities? Justify your opinion with information from the chapter.

4. True or False: An extremely difficult baby is probably going to show behavior problems toward parents and peers during preschool. Justify your answer.

5. Make a list of events that you believe will reliably activate the attachment behavioral system in infants and predispose infants to seek out their caregivers. Justify your choices.

Homework Assignments

1. Obtain permission to observe a mother and her infant in the home. The infant should be between 2 months and 12 months old (be sure to record the infant's age). In the home, ask the mother to play with her baby as she normally does, while you sit in the background and observe. Record the number and kinds of emotions expressed by the baby toward the mother. Write a brief, two-paragraph summary of what you saw, paying particular attention to the emotions expressed by the baby and what the mother did to elicit these emotions (based on chapter information). Be prepared to discuss what you saw and to compare what you saw in your infant with what others saw in infants of different ages.

2. Obtain permission to visit a mother and her 1- to 2-year-old baby, in the home, with a friend of yours whom the baby does not know. Once the baby is playing contentedly with toys, ask the mother to move out of the baby's sight (just to the next room will suffice). Make sure you tell the mother beforehand what you are going to do. Have your friend approach the baby in a friendly way and try to play with the baby for about 30 seconds to 1 minute (or less, if the baby gets very distressed). Take notes on how the baby reacts. Write a summary of what the baby did when the stranger approached, and answer the following questions:
   a. Does what you saw the baby do constitute stranger anxiety? Why or why not?
   b. More generally, what reasons might there be for individual differences among babies in the amount of stranger anxiety they show?

Additional Readings

Ainsworth, M. D. S., Blehar, M. C., Waters, E., & Wall, S. (1978). *Patterns of attachment: A psychological study of the Strange Situation*. Hillsdale, NJ: Erlbaum.

Belsky, J. (1990). Parental and nonparental child care and children's socioemotional development: A decade in review. *Journal of Marriage and the Family, 52,* 885–903.

Karen, R. (1990, February). Becoming attached. *The Atlantic Monthly,* pp. 35–70.

Thomas, A., Chess, S., & Birch, H. (1970). The origin of personality. *Scientific American, 223,* 102–109.

References

Ainsworth, M. D. S. (1967). *Infancy in Uganda: Infant care and the growth of love.* Baltimore: Johns Hopkins University Press.

Ainsworth, M. D. S., Blehar, M. C., Waters, E., & Wall, S. (1978). *Patterns of attachment: A psychological study of the Strange Situation.* Hillsdale, NJ: Erlbaum.

Aslin, R. N., Pisoni, D. B., & Jusczyk, P. W. (1983). Auditory development and speech perception in infancy. In P. Mussen (Ed.), *Handbook of child psychology* (Vol. 2) (pp. 573–687). New York: Wiley.

Barglow, P., Vaughn, B., & Molitor, N. (1987). Effects of maternal absence due to employment on the quality of infant-mother attachment in a low-risk sample. *Child Development, 58,* 945–954.

Bates, J. E., & Bayles, K. (1988). Attachment and the development of behavior problems. In J. Belsky & T. Nezworski (Eds.), *Clinical implications of attachment* (pp. 253–299). Hillsdale, NJ: Erlbaum.

Belsky, J. (1986). Infant day care: A cause for concern? *Zero to Three: Bulletin of the National Center for Clinical Infant Programs, 6,* 1–7.

Belsky, J., & Rovine, M. (1988). Nonmaternal care in the first year of life and the security of infant-parent attachment. *Child Development, 59,* 157–167.

Bowlby. J. (1969). *Attachment and loss. Vol. 1: Attachment.* New York: Basic Books.

Bruenlin, D. C., Desai, V. J., Stone, M. E., & Swilley, J. (1983). Failure to thrive with no organic etiology: A critical review. *International Journal of Eating Disorders, 2,* 25–49.

Carlsson, S. G., Fagerberg, H., Horneman, G., Hwang, C., Larsson, K., Rodholm, M., Schaller, J., Danielsson, B., & Gundewall, C. (1976). Effects of various amounts of contact between mother and child on the mother's nursing behavior: A follow-up study. *Infant Behavior and Development, 2,* 209–214.

Casey, P. H. (1983). Failure to thrive: A reconceptualization. *Journal of Developmental and Behavioral Pediatrics, 4,* 63–66.

Clarke-Stewart, K. A., & Fein, G. G. (1983). Early childhood programs. In P. H. Mussen (Ed.), *Handbook of child psychology* (Vol. 2) (pp. 917–999). New York: Wiley.

Cohn, J. F., & Tronick, E. Z. (1983). Three-month-old infants' reaction to simulated maternal depression. *Child Development, 54,* 185–193.

Crnic, K. A., Greenberg, M. T., Ragozin, A. S., Robinson, N. M., & Basham, R. (1983). Effects of stress and social support on mothers and premature and full-term infants. *Child Development, 54,* 209–217.

Crockenberg, S. B. (1981). Infant irritability, mother responsiveness, and social support influences on the security of infant-mother attachment. *Child Development, 52,* 857–865.

Drotar, D. (1991). The family context of nonorganic failure to thrive. *American Journal of Orthopsychiatry, 61,* 23–34.

Drotar, D., & Sturm, L. (1989). Influences on the home environment of preschool children with early histories of nonorganic failure to thrive. *Journal of Developmental and Behavioral Pediatrics, 10,* 229–235.

Egeland, B., & Farber, E. A. (1984). Infant-mother attachment: Factors related to its development and changes over time. *Child Development, 55,* 753–771.

Eiden, R. D., Teti, D. M., & Corns, K. M. (in press). Maternal working models of attachment, marital adjustment, and the parent-child relationship. *Child Development.*

Erikson, E. (1963). *Childhood and society* (2nd ed.). New York: W. W. Norton.

Fagot, B. I., & Kavanagh, K. (1990). The prediction of antisocial behavior from avoidant attachment classifications. *Child Development, 61,* 864–873.

Fantz, R. L. (1964). Visual experience in infants: Decreased attention to familiar patterns relative to novel ones. *Science, 146,* 668–670.

Field, T. M. (1987). Affective and interactive disturbances in infants. In J. D. Osofsky (Ed.), *Handbook of infant development* (2nd ed.). New York: Wiley.

Field, T., Healy, B., Goldstein, S., Perry, S., Bendell, D., Schanberg, S., Zimmerman, E. A., & Kuhn, C. (1988). Infants of depressed mothers show "depressed" behavior even with nondepressed adults. *Child Development, 59,* 1569–1579.

Field, T., Vega-Lahr, N., Scafidi, F., & Goldstein, S. (1986). Effects of maternal unavailability on mother-infant interactions. *Infant Behavior and Development, 9,* 473–478.

Fraiberg, S. (1980). *Clinical studies in infant mental health: The first year of life.* New York: Basic.

Freud, S. (1940). *An outline of psychoanalysis.* New York: Norton.

Gelfand, D. M., & Teti, D. M. (1990). The effects of maternal depression on children. *Clinical Psychology Review, 10,* 329–353.

Goldberg, S. (1977). Social competence in infancy: A model of parent-infant interaction. *Merrill-Palmer Quarterly, 23,* 163–177.

Goldberg, S. (1983). Parent-infant bonding: Another look. *Child Development, 54,* 1355–1382.

Goldberg, W., & Easterbrooks, M. A. (1984). Role of marital quality in toddler development. *Developmental Psychology, 10,* 504–514.

Goldsmith, H. H., & Alansky, J. A. (1987). Maternal and infant temperamental predictors of attachment: A meta-analytic review. *Journal of Consulting and Clinical Psychology, 55,* 805–816.

Harlow, H. F. (1958). The nature of love. *American Psychologist, 13,* 673–685.

Harlow, H. F., & Zimmerman, R. R. (1959). Affectional responses in the infant monkey. *Science, 130,* 421–432.

Haviland, J. M., & Lelwica, M. (1987). The induced affect response: Ten-week-old infants' responses to three emotions. *Developmental Psychology, 23,* 97–104.

Hertzler, A. A. (1983). Children's food patterns: A review. II. Family and group behavior. *Journal of the American Dietetic Association, 83,* 555–560.

Hetherington, E. M., Cox, M., & Cox, R. (1982). Effects of divorce on parents and children. In M. E. Lamb (Ed.), *Nontraditional families* (pp. 233–288). Hillsdale, NJ: Erlbaum.

Kagan, J. (1984). *The nature of the child.* New York: Basic Books.

Klaus, M. H., & Kennell J. H. (1976). *Maternal-infant bonding.* St. Louis: Mosby.

Klaus, M. H., & Kennell J. H. (1982). *Parent-infant bonding.* St. Louis: Mosby.

Kotelchuck, M., & Newberger, E. H. (1983). Failure to thrive: A controlled study of family characteristics. *Journal of the American Academy of Child Psychiatry, 22,* 322–328.

Lamb, M. E., & Bornstein, M. H. (1987). *Development in infancy* (2nd ed.). Hillsdale, NJ: Erlbaum.

Lamb, M. E., & Elster, A. B. (1986). Parental behavior of adolescent mothers and fathers. In A. B. Elster & M. E. Lamb (Eds.), *Adolescent fatherhood* (pp. 89–106). Hillsdale, NJ: Erlbaum.

Lester, B. M., Corwin, M. J., Sepkoski, C., Seifer, R., Peucker, M., McLaughlin, S., & Golub, H. L. (1991). Neurobehavioral syndrome in cocaine-exposed newborn infants. *Child Development, 62,* 694–705.

Lewis, M., Feiring, C., McGuffog, C., & Jaskir, J. (1984). Predicting psychopathology in six-year-olds from early social relations. *Child Development, 55,* 123–136.

Main, M., & Solomon, J. (1990). Procedures for identifying infants as disorganized/disoriented during the Ainsworth Strange Situation. In M. T. Greenberg, D. Cicchetti, & E. M. Cummings (Eds.), *Attachment in the preschool years: Theory, research, and intervention* (pp. 121–160). Chicago: University of Chicago Press.

Malatesta, C. Z., & Haviland, J. M. (1982). Learning display rules: The socialization of emotion expression in infancy. *Child Development, 53,* 991–1003.

Mangelsdorf, S., Gunnar, M., Kestenbaum, R., Lang, S., & Andreas, D. (1990). Infant proneness-to-distress temperament, maternal personality, and mother-infant attachment: Associations and goodness of fit. *Child Development, 61,* 820–831.

O'Brien, S., Repp, A. C., Williams, G. E., & Christopherson, E. R. (1991). Pediatric feeding disorders. Special issue: Current perspectives in the diagnosis, assessment, and treatment of child and adolescent disorders. *Behavior Modification, 15,* 394–418.

Phelps, L. (1991). Nonorganic failure to thrive: Origins and psychoeducational implications. *School Psychology Review, 20,* 417–427.

Phillips, D., McCartney, K., Scarr, S., & Howes, C. (1987). Selective review of infant day care research: A cause for concern! *Zero to Three: Bulletin of the National Center for Clinical Infant Programs, 7,* 18–21.

Piaget, J. (1952). *The origins of intelligence in children.* (M. Cook, Trans.). New York: International Universities Press.

Polan, H. J., Kaplan, M. D., Kessler, D. B., Shindledecker, R., Newmark, M., & Stern, D. N. (1991). Psychopathology in mothers of children with failure to thrive. *Infant Mental Health Journal, 12,* 55–64.

Schaller, J., Carlsson, S. G., & Larsson, K. (1979). Effects of extended post-partum mother-child contact on the mother's behavior during nursing. *Infant Behavior and Development, 2,* 319–324.

Sroufe, L. A. (1979). The coherence of early development: Early care, attachment, and subsequent developmental issues. *American Psychologist, 34,* 834–841.

Sroufe. L. A. (1985). Attachment classification from the perspective of infant-caregiver relationships and infant temperament. *Child Development, 56,* 1–14.

Teti, D. M., & Nakagawa, M. (1990). Assessing attachment in infancy: The Strange Situation and alternate systems. In E. D. Gibbs & D. M. Teti (Eds.), *Interdisciplinary assessment of infants: A guide for early intervention professionals* (pp. 191–214). Baltimore: Paul H. Brookes.

Thomas, A., & Chess, S. (1977). *Temperament and development.* New York: Brunner/Mazel.

Thompson, R. A., Lamb, M. E., & Estes, D. (1982). Stability of infant-mother attachment and its relationship to changing life circumstances in an unselected middle class sample. *Child Development, 53,* 144–148.

U. S. Bureau of the Census. (1986). *Fertility of American women.* Washington, DC: Author.

Vaughn, B. E., LeFever, G. B., Seifer, R., & Barglow, P. (1989). Attachment behavior, attachment security, and temperament during infancy. *Child Development, 60,* 728–737.

Watson, J. S. (1972). Smiling, cooing, and "the game." *Merrill-Palmer Quarterly, 18,* 323–340.

Glossary

Attachment   A strong, intimate, affectional tie between one person and another that persists across time and space

Attachment behavioral system   A repertoire of behaviors, present at birth and fine tuned by learning experiences, that are geared specifically to gain and maintain proximity to an attachment figure

Dyad   A pair of individuals who have a significant emotional or social relationship to each other

Ethological attachment theory   John Bowlby's theory of how attachments form and function, based on material drawn and synthesized from ethology, psychoanalysis, and control systems theory

Exploratory behavioral system   A repertoire of behaviors, present at birth and fine tuned by learning experiences, that orient one away from one's attachment figure and toward the novel and unfamiliar

Goodness of fit   The degree to which infant temperamental characteristics "fit" with parental characteristics to facilitate the infant-parent relationship

Infant temperament   An inherited set of behavioral predispositions relating to infants' activity levels, reactivity to stimuli, general emotional tone, and sociability with others

Mother-infant bonding   Klaus and Kennell's (1976) controversial hypothesis that mothers who are given access to their infants during the first few hours after birth will develop stronger emotional attachments to their infants than will mothers who do not have this access

Nature versus nurture   The issue of the roles of nature, or one's genetic endowment and constitutional makeup, and nurture, or one's history of experiences, in determining the development of particular behaviors, traits, or predispositions

Non-organic failure to thrive (NOFTT)   A medical diagnosis made when an infant's weight at birth is within prescribed norms for her or his gestational age, yet from the time of birth both weight and rate of weight gain decrease to below the fifth percentile, based on National Center for Health Statistics norms; NOFFT has no known biological cause

Parental self-efficacy   Parental perceptions of how good they are at understanding what their children need and want and how good they are at responding appropriately to meet those needs

Secondary drive theory   Theory of attachment formation that proposes that an infant forms attachments to the caregiver through repeated associations of the caregiver with the provision of food, thus associating the caregiver with the gratification of a primary drive; the caregiver then becomes the focus of a secondary drive, which leads the infant to seek out and interact with the caregiver even in the absence of food.

5

Siblings: The First Society

Judy Dunn
Penn State University

Although an infant's first attachment is to an adult caregiver (often a parent), his or her first experience of being in a social group is likely to be with brothers and sisters, or siblings. Children not only gain some understanding of power and conflict from these relationships but also learn vicariously about their own worth and esteem in comparison to their siblings, by observing the treatment of siblings by their parents and others. This chapter explores the important influence of sibling relationships on the growing child.

NV & SD

Chapter Outline

- Growing Up with a Sibling: Influences on Children's Development
- Siblings and Children's Well-Being and Adjustment
- Siblings and Social Understanding
- Influences on Differences in Sibling Relationships
- Siblings in Different Cultural Context

Young siblings fight and play, tease and mock each other, join in games of wild excitement, and share a pretend world of make-believe of absorbing interest. For some children, it is a relationship of happy friendship and support. Here is what Sally, age 6, says about her sister Anny, age 3: "She's nice. . . . It's good to have a sister because you can play with her. . . . That's the only part of my life that I like, when I'm playing with her. . . . I do have lots of friends but my best friend is Anny." For other children, the relationship is continuous warfare: "I HATE my brother!" says Kate, also age 6. "He's disgusting!"

Most of us grow up with siblings, and these relationships influence us in a variety of important ways.

How does growing up with a friendly, supportive sibling like Sally or a hostile one like Kate affect the way children develop? Why do some siblings get along and others fight and quarrel with such hostility? Is it an important relationship for kids' development?

In commonsense terms it seems likely to be so. Most children grow up with siblings (80% in the United States), and, in their early years, they spend more time interacting with each other than they do with their parents. In many cultures children are brought up by their siblings: From the age of 1 or 2 they are fed, carried, disciplined, and played with by a brother or sister only three or four years older than they are. What is more, it is a relationship that lasts a lifetime; it is longer than the relationship between husband and wife or between parent and child. And many psychologists argue that what children learn from other children can dramatically influence their development (Hartup, 1983; Piaget, 1932; Sullivan, 1953). Because they are more similar in age and status than children and adults, because they share more **reciprocal and symmetrical relationships**—it is argued—children are likely to pay attention to and understand the feelings and viewpoints of other children in a way they don't with adults; they are more likely to understand how people who are children like themselves think about or see things. In this chapter we'll be looking first at the question of how experiences with brothers and sisters in the early years influence children—their adjustment and well-being, the way they think about themselves, and what they learn from each other. Then we will look at the issue of why some brothers and sisters get on well and others don't—the influences on their relationship.

GROWING UP WITH A SIBLING: INFLUENCES ON CHILDREN'S DEVELOPMENT

In the last decade there has been a wealth of research on siblings, and we have learned much about the key characteristics of sibling relationships and about the influences of brothers and sisters—particularly in relation to their adjustment to and their understanding of other people. The key characteristics include the familiarity of the two children, the emotional nature of their interactions, the fact that they share parents—and thus potentially compete for parental love and attention—and the great range of individual differences in the friendliness or hostility of the relationship. For many siblings, it is an **ambivalent relationship:** They feel affection and sympathy as well as irritation, rivalry, and hostility toward their sibling. How do these characteristics affect siblings' influence on each other's development?

Siblings and Children's Well-Being and Adjustment

The presence of a sibling can have both direct effects on children—as we'll see in looking at aggression and social understanding—and indirect effects, by influencing their relationships with their parents. In Box 1 there is an example of indirect effects on children's adjustment and relationships: the impact of the birth of a sibling on firstborn children.

Aggression

If you have a brother or sister, you'll know all too well what an uninhibited relationship it can be. If your sibling feels irritated or mad at you, he or she probably doesn't bother to hide it. And young siblings express any irritation, anger, or jealousy very freely—it is a no-holds-barred relationship. For some kids, that means growing up with someone who hits you on the head when you try to join in play, who takes your toys, and who calls you names and teases you endlessly. Not surprisingly, studies of aggressive behavior within the family show that these experiences have a role in shaping children's aggressive behavior. Studies of children from the second year of life through middle childhood consistently report that aggressive behavior from one sibling correlates with aggression by the other. Research that follows the same families over time shows that these patterns develop as the children grow up together. If one child is very aggressive to a sibling at one time, the sibling is likely to become more aggressive as time goes by. What is more, children who are very aggressive with their siblings are likely to be rejected by their peers when they go to school. And research that follows children over time also finds that those who have poor sibling relationships in early childhood are particularly likely to be disturbed later on (Richman, Stevenson, & Graham, 1982).

Many of these studies show that the links between the siblings' interactions and other behavior problems are correlational. This means that although researchers know there is a tendency for behavioral problems to occur in the families in which the siblings are aggressive, they cannot conclude that the siblings *caused* the later problems. It could be that some other factor—such as the children's difficult **temperamental characteristics,** or behavioral problems early on, or disturbed parent-child relationships—actually lies behind both the aggression toward the sibling and the later disturbed behavior. But studies that look very carefully at how children react to aggressive acts from their siblings do show that these interactions actually *foster* further aggression (Patterson, 1986).

Box 1 **The Arrival of a Sibling**

How do firstborn children react to the arrival of a sibling? Studies in the United States, Canada, and Britain describe the following changes:

Increases in aggression toward mother and peers

Increases in unhappy, moody behavior

Increases in "deliberate naughtiness" and contrariness

Increases in withdrawal

Disturbances in sleeping, feeding, and toilet training

Positive changes in children's behavior are also described:

Increases in independent behavior (for instance, dressing self, going to the toilet alone, playing alone)

Noticeable advances in language development

To what could these changes be due?

When a new sibling arrives, there are changes in firstborn children's relationships with their mothers and fathers. There is a decline in positive interactions and parental attention to the firstborn; mothers are frequently very tired and stressed. There are a host of changes in children's daily lives, and toddlers and preschoolers are often deeply affected by such changes in routine and predictable daily patterns. Children also witness their parents' loving attention to the new baby. Any or all of these changes in their lives may contribute to the disturbed behavior children show. These changes can explain the negative impact of the new sibling on the firstborn. Could some of them also contribute to positive changes in the firstborns' behavior?

Worrying, Anxiety, and Poor Self-Esteem

Box 1 showed that the arrival of a sibling is linked, for some firstborn children, to an increase in worrying and unhappiness. What about later-born siblings? Can the experience of growing up with an unfriendly older brother or sister influence a child's well-being?

The answer is yes. Unfriendly behavior from a sibling in the early years is linked to **internalizing behavior** (worrying, anxious, depressed behavior seven years later—and this is especially true for secondborn children whose older siblings were distant or unfriendly when they were preschoolers. Furthermore, children's self-esteem in middle childhood and early adolescence is related to how friendly or hostile their siblings had been to them years before. This should not surprise us when we realize how much children compare themselves with their siblings and how frequently their parents—often unwittingly—draw their attention to the ways in which they don't "match up" to their siblings' successes. Just how early children become aware of differences between themselves and their siblings is illustrated by the incident in Box 2, drawn from an observational study (Dunn, 1988).

The Significance of Differential Parental Treatment

Andy, the 2-year-old described in Box 2, was clearly monitoring what happened between his mother and his sister. Children's sensitivity to **differential parental treatment** turns out to be a major influence on how they relate to their siblings and also on their adjustment. This is another example of the indirect impact of a sibling on children. In a study of 90 firstborn children, internalizing behavior and **externalizing behavior** (aggressive, undercontrolled behavior) problems were found to be associated with the extent of maternal differential treatment: Children whose mothers showed them less affection than their sibling, or disciplined them more, had more problems than those whose mothers treated them and their siblings similarly (Dunn, Stocker, & Plomin, 1990).

Siblings as Sources of Support

So far we've looked at the bleaker aspects of how siblings affect one another's well-being and adjustment. But it is not all a sad story. Siblings can also be real sources of comfort and support for one another in times of stress. For instance, children growing up in disharmonious homes have fewer problems if they have a good sibling relationship (Jenkins, 1992). They appear to benefit from both offering comfort to and receiving comfort from their siblings. One study found that confiding in a sibling was much more commonly reported as a way of coping with the stress of growing up in a family with quarreling parents than was confiding in a friend (Jenkins, 1992). And one line of clinical research that highlights the importance of sibling support is the study of siblings as therapists for children with eating disorders (Van Eyken & van Vrecken, 1992). Children can—and do—really help their siblings who are disturbed in this way.

Siblings also frequently offer effective support to one another in the daily troubles that so many children face. In a follow-up study of siblings over seven years, from early childhood to early adolescence (Dunn, 1993), researchers found that many of the children described ways in which their siblings provided support—when they had problems at school, when they were in trouble with their parents, when they couldn't do their homework, when they were ill or had accidents.

Box 2

Comparing Yourself to Your Sibling Begins Very Early

Consider the following incident, drawn from an observational study of young siblings (Dunn, 1988). Andy, a child of 30 months, is watching his mother and his younger sister Susie, who is 14 months old. Andy is a cautious, anxious, and sensitive child, whereas Susie is an ebullient and assertive girl. Susie has been repeatedly forbidden to try to get something from the table. She persists in trying and finally succeeds in getting the forbidden object. Andy listens as his mother makes a proud comment to his sister:

Mother: *(To Susie, warmly)* Susie, you *are* a determined little devil!
Andy: *(To mother, sadly)* I'm not a determined little devil.
Mother: *(Laughing)* No you're not! What are you? A poor old boy!

It is usually assumed that children don't begin to make evaluative comparisons between themselves and others until they are 7 or 8 years old. Yet Andy at only 30 months, in the emotional circumstances of the family, notices his mother's affectionate attention to his sister and makes a muted but accurate comment on himself in comparison. Studies of older siblings show that children continue to compare themselves with their siblings and are very sensitive to parental comparisons.

SIBLINGS AND SOCIAL UNDERSTANDING

The idea that what happens between young children plays a special part in the development of children's **social understanding** and moral understanding is one that has had wide acceptance among psychologists—Piaget (1932) and Sullivan (1953), for instance. Siblings spend much time together and become very familiar with one another, so it seems likely that if peers can be important in influencing developments in these domains, siblings can too. And now we have evidence that they do.

Before we look at that evidence, it is important to note that when children are playing and arguing with their siblings, they often show particularly mature, sophisticated behavior. Sometimes it is so mature that it challenges the accepted view of what children *can* do in early childhood—as you saw in the case of Andy in Box 2. Comforting (shown to siblings early in the second year) and teasing are two examples. Consider the following incidents (Dunn, 1988):

1. Eric wants to play with the magnetic letters that his older sister Laura has. After gently saying no several times, Laura finally takes the letters on a tray to a high table that Eric cannot reach. He is furious, runs straight to the settee where Laura's comfort objects—a rag doll and a pacifier—are lying. He takes the doll and clutches it tight, looking at Laura. She for the first time gets very upset, starts crying, and runs to retrieve her doll.
2. Andrew overhears his mother saying that his older sister is afraid of spiders, that there's even a toy spider she doesn't like. Andrew promptly runs to the next room, searches through the toy box, finds the toy spider, and thrusts it under his sister's nose. She immediately gets upset.

Andrew and Eric in these examples behave in a way that suggests they understand how to irritate their older siblings. They seem to know what will annoy these particular persons. Yet they are, respectively, only 14 and 16 months old, an age at which psychologists have assumed that children have very little grasp of the feelings and wishes of other people. How is it that children are able to comfort or to annoy a brother and sister well before they are 2, when more "formal" tests of understanding other people seem to show such understanding only begins when children are 4 or 5? Here are some possible explanations, all of which may well be important:

1. Children are very familiar with their siblings, whose reactions and actions they watch daily.
2. What excites and upsets a sibling frequently has the same effect on the child himself or herself; the sources of joy, fear, disgust, and pleasure are similar for them both.
3. The emotional setting of sibling interaction is important: The depth of conflict, jealousy, or affection between siblings means that it matters very much to young children that they understand what their siblings are feeling or are intending to do.

Just as Andy in Box 2 showed very grown-up behavior in the emotional circumstances of watching his mother enjoying his sister's personality, so here we see that when children are angry or frustrated by their siblings, they can show strikingly sophisticated understanding of that sibling.

Now let's consider some examples of sibling influence on social understanding.

Evidence for Sibling Influence on Social Understanding: Three Examples

Pretend Play   Observational studies that follow toddlers and preschool-aged siblings over time show that children who grow up with an older sibling who welcomes them into make-believe games and shared pretend play develop the ability to understand pretend play and to participate in it

Box 3	**The Sophistication of a Toddler Playing with an Older Sibling**

Katy, aged 24 months, is playing with her older sister Maggie. In the course of a long game of make-believe, they pretend to go to bed, and Katy addresses her sister as "Mummy"—a new move in the fantasy. Katy responds to her "Mummy's" sighs with concern, talks about having cold hands, and later, when instructed to "eat" by her "Mummy," comments that she likes the food (a pencil).

Maggie: We got to leave it there to go to sleep. *(Leans back, sighs, shuts eyes.)* You sleep with me! *(Sighs and whispers.)*
Katy: *(To the observer)* We're going to bed!
      (Maggie sighs.)
Katy: What's the matter, Mummy?
Maggie: *(Whispers.)* Go to sleep.
Katy: Mummy? Mummy?
Maggie: Yes. Go to sleep.
Katy: Mummy?
Maggie: Yes?
Katy: Come here.
Maggie: *(Cuddles Katy.)* Yes. Have you got cold hands?
Katy: Yes!
Maggie: Ooh, rub it up that cold hands! ... Do you want some dinner?
Katy: Want some dinner.
Maggie: Have that dinner. *(Gives Katy a pencil.)*
Katy: *(Pretends to eat the pencil, with enthusiasm.)* Yum yum! I like it! I like it!

In the study in which Katy and Maggie were observed (Dunn, 1988), 32 of the 40 secondborn children who were studied were observed to engage in pretend play with their siblings, and each explicitly announced her or his pretend identity as *driver, daddy, mummy,* or *baby,* or as a character in a favorite story. Although these games were usually set up and organized by the older siblings, the 24-month-olds and 30-month-olds often also made innovative contributions—as Maggie did in the example above.

very early indeed—long before it used to be thought they could do so (see Box 3). More generally, children whose older siblings are kind, helpful, and caring to them develop more caring, cooperative behavior toward their siblings than children who haven't had these experiences with their older siblings (Dunn & Munn, 1986b).

What makes this shared pretend play with a sibling so interesting and developmentally important is that to share a make-believe world not only involves understanding what the other child is thinking and planning but also provides a key setting in which children begin to explore their social world—what is allowed and expected, what happens in the world of school and work, how mothers and fathers relate. Matters of life and death, drama and excitement, travels to the moon or to the bottom of the sea as well as to the local shops—all are discussed and *played with*.

Conflict Management   A second example of sibling influence on social understanding comes from a close look at how children argue and fight. Consider the differences in how these three 4-year-old children (from different families) are arguing with their siblings. In each case the dispute is about who should have a coveted crown when the kids are playing at being kings and queens.

> Sib A: (*To his brother*) I want it! Give it to me!
> Sib B: (*To her sister*) I want it! And I should have it because it looks pretty on me. It looks ugly on you—it doesn't match your dress!
> Sib C: (*To his brother, who is desperate to wear the crown*) I know—we'll both be princes—you can have this crown, and I'll wear this. We'll be like the princes in the tower in that story.

Both Sibling B and Sibling C are doing more than just yelling about what they want: They are giving reasons—justifications for what they suggest in the course of the dispute. And their suggestions are quite sophisticated for 4-year-olds. It is clear that although she is only 4, Sibling B already knows that looking ugly will matter to her sister. She is using sophisticated argument—even though in this case it is to pursue her own interests rather than to resolve the dispute amicably. Sibling C, in contrast, is offering a resolution that takes his brother's wishes into account and negotiates a harmonious end to the dispute. Again, this is sophisticated behavior for a 4-year-old. And it is clearly an important achievement—as anyone who spends time with small children will agree! When researchers look at differences between children in how they "manage" disputes with their siblings, they find that one source of influence is how children's siblings have argued with them in earlier months. If an older sibling frequently offers conciliation and negotiation, over time the younger sibling becomes more likely to do so. (These skills of resolving disputes don't always show up in the same child's other relationships, unfortunately!)

Success on Tests of Understanding   A third example of sibling influence comes from studies that test children's understanding of how other people feel or think. There are lots of different sources of influence on children's understanding of others' emotions, but one that turns out to be important is the experience of growing up with a friendly, responsive sibling (Dunn, Brown, Slomkowski, Tesla, & Youngblade, 1991). Children who have had such a relationship with their older siblings perform better on tests of understanding "other minds" and of understanding emotions.

Summary: Teaching and Learning from Siblings   From early in the first year, children watch and imitate their siblings, and older siblings teach their younger siblings physical skills, how to use toys, and how to play games. Are they good teachers—and do children actually *learn* from these direct "teaching" experiences? Experimental studies show that by 7 years of age siblings can certainly be effective teachers (Cicirelli, 1972, 1976). Research comparing what children learn from their siblings and from their peers has shown that children are more likely to watch, imitate, and learn effectively from their siblings than from an older peer and that older siblings give more explanations, positive feedback, and more control than do older peers (Azmitia & Hesser, 1993).

DIFFERENCES IN SIBLING RELATIONSHIPS

The birth of a younger sibling can raise many different feelings for the older child in the family.

Some siblings fight and quarrel endlessly; other siblings enjoy each other's company. These differences are evident with preschoolers and toddlers, with school-aged siblings, and even with adolescents. Sibling relationships are a great source of worry to parents, who often feel responsible for the hostility between their children—many parenting books lay the blame for jealousy and quarrels squarely on the parents. And with the evidence that the quality of the sibling relationship does influence children's adjustment and development, the question of *why* siblings differ in their levels of affection, hostility, and interest toward one another takes on special significance.

It is often said that each child's position in the family, the age differences between siblings, and their gender all influence how well they get along. How much evidence is there to support this view? And what about the children's personalities? We'll look first at the individual characteristics of the children themselves (birth order, temperament, age gap, gender), then at links between the parents' relationships and the sibling relationship, and finally at the impact of life events and family size on the children's relationship.

Birth Order

It will come as no surprise to any parent with more than one child that firstborn children tend to feel more hostility and ambivalence toward their siblings than do later-born children. They are, after all, the ones who have been displaced. Here is what one 5-year-old girl in the classic study done by Helen

Koch (1960) said when asked if she would like to change places with her sibling:

> Yes, I would like to change places with my baby brother.
> Then I could yell my head off and my mommy would take care
> of nobody but me.

Firstborns are seen by both first- and later-born children as bossier and more dominant than later-born children, and their power tactics in dealing with their siblings differ. Here is a firstborn boy describing how he got his sister to do what he wanted:

> I told her to get out of my room. And I kept shouting at her
> and she wouldn't go. And I started hitting her and she still
> wouldn't go. So I just picked her up and threw her out.

(Does this sound familiar?)

But whether firstborn children do feel (and show) hostility to their younger siblings is very strongly affected by a factor that can contribute to differences: the children's temperaments.

Temperament

The personality or temperament of both siblings in a pair is important in determining the amount of conflict between them. Children who are active, intense, or unadaptable in temperament have more conflicted relationships with their siblings (Brody & Stoneman, 1987; Stocker, Dunn, & Plomin, 1989). And the match of temperament between the two is also important (Munn & Dunn, 1988). Siblings who differ widely in personality get along less well than those who are similar.

Age Gap

There is surprisingly little evidence to support the idea that the age gap between siblings has an important effect on how affectionate or quarrelsome they are. With the arrival of a sibling, the form of disturbed behavior shown by firstborn children differs according to their age, but in general terms the affection and hostility that siblings feel for one another is not explained by the age gap between them. Siblings who are close in age obviously do more together, since they are more likely to have similar interests, than siblings with a gap of five or six years between them. But they don't necessarily like each other more.

Sex

The impact of sex of the siblings on the quality of their relationship is less clear than the impact of temperament. The results of studies of siblings during early childhood show few links between sex and sibling relationships or are inconsistent (for a review, see Dunn, 1988). But recent studies of siblings in middle childhood and early adolescence show that sex begins to influence the relationship at these ages, with older sisters being more intimate and affectionate to their younger siblings than older brothers are (Buhrmester, 1992; Dunn, Slomkowski, & Beardsall, 1993).

Links Between Parent-Child Relationships and Sibling Relationships

The idea that parent-child relationships have an important influence on sibling relationships has a long history. How good is the evidence for such links, and what kinds of processes might underlie the connections? Four themes have been emphasized by those studying families.

The first is the idea that the security of the attachment between parent and child affects the quality of the child's relationship with her or his siblings. The prediction is that children who have insecure relationships with their parents will be more hostile to their siblings, as they "re-enact aspects of the non-nurturant caregiver role" in their interactions with each other (Teti & Ablard, 1989, p. 1520). The evidence for these links consists of correlations, and, as noted earlier, we have to be very careful about concluding that the quality of the parent-child relationship *causes* the differences in the sibling relationships. It is possible, for instance, that the correlations reflect a third factor that underlies both attachment quality and sibling relationship quality—such as differences in children's temperaments.

The second theme in research on this topic is the issue of the importance of differential parental treatment. There is a striking consistency in recent studies that find that differential maternal treatment is associated with more difficult, hostile sibling relationships (see Dunn, 1992, for a review). The link between differential parental treatment and poor sibling relationships seems to be particularly strong in families under stress. The connection has been reported, for example, in studies of siblings following parental divorce (Hetherington, 1988), of siblings of cancer patients (Cairns, Clark, Smith, & Lansky, 1979), and of children whose siblings have disabilities (McHale & Harris, 1992). Again, the link is correlational, and we cannot assume a simple cause-and-effect connection between differential treatment and poor sibling relationships. If one child is repeatedly mistreated by his or her sibling, for instance, it might be that this influences the mother to pay special attention to him or her rather than the sibling.

The third theme is the issue of parental involvment in sibling conflict. It is widely assumed that when parents become involved in their children's quarrels, conflict between the siblings is likely to increase. Two ideas lie behind this assumption. One is that siblings quarrel chiefly because they are jealous of each other's relationship with the parents and they hope to gain parental attention by quarreling. The argument goes that if parents "reward" the children by intervening and paying attention to them, the children will quarrel more frequently. The other idea is that if children's quarrels are "sorted out" by their parents, then the children will not have the opportunity to learn how to resolve conflict themselves (Brody & Stoneman, 1987). But what is the evidence in support of these two ideas? Correlational studies do show that the frequency of sibling conflict is related to the frequency of parental involvement (Brody & Stoneman, 1987; Dunn & Munn, 1986a). However, it is not clear that parental involvement leads to the frequent conflict; it could just as easily be the case that parents become involved in sibling conflicts *as a result of* the intense and frequent conflicts. To answer questions about what leads to what, we need intervention studies to test the idea that if parents stay out of fights, fights become less frequent. To date we don't have good evidence from such studies on a reasonably large scale.

The final theme in the study of links between parent-child and sibling-sibling relationships concerns the effects of the birth of a sibling. As Box 1 illustrated, the birth of a sibling is accompanied by sharp changes in the parent-child relationship, and these changes are linked to the kind of relationship that develops between the siblings.

Life Events and Long-Term Patterns

Recent research on the impact of **life events** on family relationships provides interesting information on individual differences in sibling relationships. Research on divorce, for instance, shows that after divorce the presence of a stepfather is linked with poor sibling relationships (Hetherington, 1988) and that the quality of the relationship between the two ex-spouses contributes to how well the siblings themselves get along (McKinnon, 1989). Conflict between parents, too, appears to be associated with more conflict between siblings (Jenkins, 1992), although as noted earlier, having a good sibling relationship appears to provide some support for children in disharmonious homes.

Research on other kinds of life events, however, tells a rather different story. In a longitudinal study that followed siblings over a period of seven to eight years, researchers found that following events that had a negative impact—for example, having problems at school, changing residence or schools, or the mother entering the hospital—the siblings tended to draw closer together and to be particularly friendly. They provided significant support for one another (Dunn, Slomkowski, & Beardsall, 1993).

How long term are the patterns of sibling relationships that have been described, which begin in early childhood? The answer is that we do not know. No one has followed siblings beyond adolescence. Interviews with adults, however, suggest that toward the end of the life span, siblings become very important to one another, and they refer to their early years together as key to how they get along as older adults (Ross & Milgram, 1982). Completing the questionnaire in Box 4 will give you an idea of some patterns in your relationships with your own siblings.

Box 4	**Sibling Inventory of Differential Experience (SIDE): Interactions with Your Sibling**

This questionnaire is designed to examine your interactions with your sibling. Compare yourself to your sibling (or one of your siblings) when you were growing up and living at home. Scoring instructions and comparison scores are provided at the end of the questionnaire.

1 = My sibling has been much more this way than I have.

2 = My sibling has been a bit more this way than I have.

3 = My sibling and I have been the same in this way.

4 = I have been a bit more this way than my sibling.

5 = I have been much more this way than my sibling.

	1	2	3	4	5
1. In general, who started fights more often?	1	2	3	4	5
2. In general, who showed more trust for the other?	1	2	3	4	5
3. In general, who showed more concern and interest for the other?	1	2	3	4	5
4. In general, who was more willing to help the other succeed?	1	2	3	4	5
5. In general, who liked spending time with the other more?	1	2	3	4	5
6. In general, who was more likely to take responsibility for the other?	1	2	3	4	5
7. In general, who was more stubborn with the other?	1	2	3	4	5
8. In general, who showed more confidence in the other?	1	2	3	4	5
9. In general, who acted more bitter toward the other?	1	2	3	4	5
10. In general, who compared himself or herself with the other more?	1	2	3	4	5
11. In general, who was more likely to show feelings of anger to the other?	1	2	3	4	5
12. In general, who was more likely to feel superior over the other?	1	2	3	4	5
13. In general, who showed more understanding for the other?	1	2	3	4	5
14. In general, who was more likely to get jealous of the other?	1	2	3	4	5
15. In general, who acted more kindly toward the other?	1	2	3	4	5
16. In general, who was more likely to let the other down?	1	2	3	4	5

Box 4 continues

Box 4
(continued)

17. In general, who showed more affection toward the
    other?   1   2   3   4   5
18. In general, who was more likely to deceive the
    other?   1   2   3   4   5
19. In general, who was more bossy toward the other?   1   2   3   4   5
20. In general, who was more likely to want to get
    along well with the other?   1   2   3   4   5
21. In general, who was more supportive of the other?   1   2   3   4   5
22. In general, who tried to outdo the other more?   1   2   3   4   5
23. In general, who admired the other more?   1   2   3   4   5
24. In general, who felt inferior more often?   1   2   3   4   5

Scoring: Four scales are scored—caretaking, jealousy, closeness, and antagonism:

> *Caretaking*: Add your responses to items 3, 4, 6, 12, 19, and 21, and divide by 6.
>
> *Jealousy*: Add your responses to items 5, 10, 14, 22, 23, and 24, and divide by 6.
>
> *Closeness*: Add your responses to items 2, 8, and 17, and divide by 3.
>
> For *antagonism*, your responses to items 13, 15, and 20 need to be "reversed," because a high score on these items implies *less* antagonism. To reverse items, if you entered a 3, leave it as a 3. If you reported 1, change it to 5. Similarly, if you reported 2, change it to 4, change 4 to 2 and change 5 to 1. Once you have reversed the scores for items 13, 15, and 20, add your responses to items 1, 7, 9, 11, 13, 15, 16, 18, and 20, and divide by 9.
>
> Siblings in a large study yielded the following average scores for the four scales, which you can compare to your scores.

Caretaking:	2.6
Jealousy:	3.0
Closeness:	3.1
Antagonism:	2.9

The extent to which your scores are below or above these averages indicates the degree to which you view your sibling relationship as *different* for the two of you.

SIBLINGS IN DIFFERENT CULTURAL CONTEXTS

Much of the research described so far has been done on siblings in Europe and North America, and much of it has focused on white families. But now there are studies of siblings in a far wider range of cultural worlds: in Hawaii, Melanesia, Senegal, Mexico, India, and a number of Southeast Asian cultures

(Nuckolls, 1993; Zukow, 1989). Those who have studied children growing up in other contexts stress that sibling relationships in these cultures can be even more central to children's lives than they are in North America and Europe—for instance, in many cultures children play key roles as caregivers for their younger siblings. But the patterns of influence will of course differ in different cultures. Here is how one anthropologist (Wiesner, 1989) who has studied siblings in many different cultures sees it:

> Siblings *matter*. How siblings should relate to each other, what to call them, and what resources they are to have and share is important to all cultures. . . . Siblings usually live with at least some of their brothers and sisters for much of their childhood, and very often on into adulthood. The particular beliefs regarding family roles and responsibilities of siblings can vary widely across cultures: how and when siblings inherit wealth varies widely; the structure of their relationships to their full siblings and cousins, aunts and uncles differs . . . and the same variation exists for many other customs. The universal cultural concern betrays the pan-human significance of the sibling relationship. (p. 14)

Class Discussion Questions

1. Why do some siblings get along well and others fight continually?
2. Could brothers and sisters be *learning* anything through their arguments and quarrels? How would you test whether this was so?
3. How do relationships between siblings differ from those between friends? How are they similar?
4. In what ways are the strong emotions in sibling relationships important for individual development?

Homework Assignments

1. Watch four different TV sitcoms that involve families with siblings, and describe the portrayal of the siblings' relationship. How does each portrayal compare with the patterns of the relationships of young siblings described in the chapter? How does each fit with your own experience of being a sibling or with experiences of siblings in other families that you know well?
2. Complete the self-report questionnaire in Box 4 about differences between you and your siblings. Collate and compare the completed questionnaires of at least ten students in your class. How similar are the members of the class to their siblings?

Additional Readings

Boer, F., & Dunn, J. (1992). *Children's sibling relationships: Developmental and clinical issues.* Hillsdale, NJ: Erlbaum. (A summary of the most recent research on siblings, with a special emphasis on clinical issues)

Dunn, J., & Plomin, R. (1990). *Separate lives: Why siblings are so different.* New York: Basic Books. (A discussion of why siblings growing up in the same family are so different from one another)

Zukow, P. G. (1989). *Sibling interaction across cultures.* Berlin: Springer-Verlag. (A series of studies of siblings in different cultures, written by both anthropologists and psychologists)

References

Azmitia, M., & Hesser, J. (1993). Why siblings are important agents of cognitive development: A comparison of siblings and peers. *Child Development, 64,* 430–444.

Brody, G. H., & Stoneman, Z. (1987). Sibling conflict: Contributions of the siblings themselves, the parent-sibling relationship, and the broader family system. *Journal of Children in Contemporary Society, 19,* 39–53.

Buhrmester, D. (1992). The developmental courses of sibling and peer relationships. In F. Boer & J. Dunn (Eds.), *Children's sibling relationships: Developmental and clinical issues* (pp. 19–40). Hillsdale, NJ: Erlbaum.

Cairns, N., Clark, G., Smith, S., & Lansky, S. (1979). Adaptation of siblings to childhood malignancy. *Journal of Pediatrics, 95,* 484–487.

Cicirelli, V. G. (1972). The effect of sibling relationships on concept learning of young children taught by child teachers. *Child Development, 43,* 282-287.

Cicirelli, V. G. (1976). Mother-child and sibling-sibling interactions on a problem-solving task. *Child Development, 47,* 588–596.

Dunn, J. (1988). *The beginnings of social understanding.* Cambridge, MA: Harvard University Press.

Dunn, J. (1992). Sisters and brothers: Current issues in developmental research. In F. Boer & J. Dunn (Eds.), *Children's sibling relationships: Developmental and clinical issues* (pp. 1–17). Hillsdale, NJ: Erlbaum.

Dunn, J. (1993). Sibling relationships and perceived self-competence: Patterns of stability between childhood and early adolescence. In A. Sameroff & M. Haith (Eds.), *Reason and responsibility: The passage through childhood.* Chicago: University of Chicago Press.

Dunn, J., Brown, J. R., Slomkowski, C., Tesla, C., & Youngblade, L. (1991). Young children's understanding of other people's feelings and beliefs: Individual differences and their antecedents. *Child Development, 62,* 1352–1366.

Dunn, J., & Munn, P. (1986a). Sibling quarrels and maternal intervention: Individual differences in understanding and aggression. *Journal of Child Psychology and Psychiatry, 27,* 583–595.

Dunn, J., & Munn, P. (1986b). Siblings and prosocial development. *International Journal of Behavioral Development, 9,* 265–284.

Dunn, J., Slomkowski, C., & Beardsall, L. (1993). Sibling relationships from the preschool period through middle childhood and early adolescence. *Developmental Psychology, 30,* 315–324.

Dunn, J., Stocker, C., & Plomin, R. (1990). Nonshared experiences within the family: Correlates of behavioral problems in middle childhood. *Development and Psychopathology, 2,* 113–126.

Hartup, W. W. (1983). Peer relations. In P. H. Mussen (Ed.), *Handbook of child psychology:* Vol. 4. *Socialization, personality, and social development* (pp. 103–196). New York: John Wiley & Sons.

Hetherington, E. M. (1988). Parents, children, and siblings: Six years after divorce. In R. A. Hinde & J. Stevenson-Hinde (Eds.), *Relationships within families: Mutual influences* (pp. 311–331). Oxford, England: Oxford University Press.

Jenkins, J. (1992). Sibling relationships in disharmonious homes: Potential difficulties and protective effects. In F. Boer & J. Dunn (Eds.), *Children's sibling relationships: Developmental and clinical issues* (pp. 125–138). Hillsdale, NJ: Erlbaum.

Koch, H. L. (1960). The relation of certain formal attributes of siblings to attitudes held toward each other and toward their parents. *Monographs of the Society for Research in Child Development.* Chicago: Chicago University Press.

McHale, S. M., & Harris, V. S. (1992). Children's experiences with disabled and nondisabled siblings: Links with personal adjustment and relationship evaluations. In F. Boer & J. Dunn (Eds.), *Children's sibling relationships: Developmental and clinical issues* (pp. 83–100). Hillsdale, NJ: Erlbaum.

McKinnon, C. E. (1989). An observational investigation of sibling interactions in married and divorced families. *Developmental Psychology, 25,* 36–44.

Munn, P., & Dunn, J. (1988). Temperament and the developing relationship between siblings. *International Journal of Behavioral Development, 12,* 433–451.

Nuckolls, C. W. (Ed.). (1993). *Siblings in South Asia.* New York: Guilford Press.

Patterson, G. R. (1986). The contribution of siblings to training for fighting: A microsocial analysis. In D. Olweus, J. Block, & M. Radke-Yarrow (Eds.), *Development of antisocial and prosocial behavior: Research, theories, and issues* (pp. 235–261). New York: Academic Press.

Piaget, J. (1932). *The moral judgment of the child.* London: Routledge and Kegan Paul.

Richman, N., Stevenson, J. E., & Graham, P. (1982). *Preschool to school: A behavioral study.* London: Academic Press.

Ross, H. G., & Milgram, J. I. (1982). Important variables in adult sibling relationships: A qualitative study. In M. E. Lamb & B. Sutton-Smith (Eds.), *Sibling relationships: Their nature and significance across the lifespan* (pp. 225–250). Hillsdale, NJ: Erlbaum.

Stocker, C., Dunn, J., & Plomin, R. (1989). Sibling relationships: Links with child temperament, maternal behavior, and family structure. *Child Development, 60,* 715–727.

Sullivan, H. S. (1953). *The interpersonal theory of psychology.* New York: Norton.

Teti, D. M., & Ablard, K. E. (1989). Security of attachment and infant-sibling relationships: A laboratory study. *Child Development, 60,* 1519–1528.

Van Eyken, W. S., & van Vrecken, E. (1992). Siblings as co-patients and co-therapists in eating disorders. In F. Boer & J. Dunn (Eds.), *Children's sibling relationships: Developmental and clinical issues* (pp. 109–124). Hillsdale, NJ: Erlbaum.

Wiesner, T. S. (1989). Comparing sibling interaction across cultures. In P. G. Zukow (Ed.), *Sibling interaction across cultures* (pp. 11–25). New York: Springer-Verlag.

Zukow, P. G. (Ed.). (1989). *Sibling interaction across cultures: Theoretical and methodological issues*. New York: Springer-Verlag.

Glossary

Ambivalent relationship   A relationship in which emotions are a mixture of both positive and negative

Correlational   A term that indicates that two measures vary together—for example, when one measure increases, so does the other

Differential parental treatment   Differences in the behavior of a parent toward his or her various children—for example, in affection shown or discipline meted out to siblings

Externalizing behavior   Aggressive, undercontrolled behavior

Internalizing behavior   Worrying, anxious, depressed behavior

Life events   Life changes with potential impact on health or adjustment; usually refers to potentially stressful events with negative impact

Reciprocal and symmetrical relationships   Relationships in which the participants show similar behavior, either simultaneously or alternately

Social understanding   Understanding of others' emotions, thoughts, and beliefs, as well as social rules, practices, and expectations

Temperamental characteristics   A person's personality or behavioral style, such as levels of activity, sociability, emotionality, and adaptability

6

Pathways to Interpersonal Competence: Parenting and Children's Peer Relations

Gregory S. Pettit
Auburn University

Mellisa A. Clawson
Auburn University

The authors wish to express appreciation to Jacquelyn Mize and Robert Zundel for their helpful comments on an earlier version of this chapter.

A *child's first experience of extrafamilial relations with peers reresents a milestone in his or her relational life. What you will see repeatedly throughout this text, however, is that none of our relationships is completely independent of our previous relational experiences. In this chapter, we will explore the ways that parents influence their children's early peer relationships as well as their children's social skills. In addition, the characteristics and consequences of children's early peer relationships will be examined.*

NV & SD

Chapter Outline

• Characteristics and Consequences of Children's
Relationships with Peers
• Social Competence in Peer Relations
• Parenting and Children's Social Skills: Multiple Pathways

Four-year-old Annalisa looks forward to being dropped off at nursery school by her parents. She has a few playmates with whom she spends most of her time, and together they endlessly pretend to be their favorite cartoon characters, construct whole villages from an assortment of blocks and plastic figurines, and work on joint arts-and-crafts projects. Even though Annalisa prefers playing with her friends, she has a good bit of contact with several other children in the class and usually is welcomed into these other playgroups because she is known as a fun person to play with. In short, Annalisa is highly regarded by her peers; she has a few close companions who seek her out, and she has developed some social skills that make playing with other children a mutually exciting adventure. This brief portrait of Annalisa illustrates three important themes of emerging social relationships in the preschool-age period. First, Annalisa displays well-developed play skills, especially the ability to engage peers in coordi-

nated and sustained bouts of exciting, playful interacti[...]
lisa clearly enjoys a positive reputation among her pe[...]
other children's positive responses to her and their inte[...]
become a part of their playgroups. Third, Annalisa is beg[...]
friendships, which at this age mainly center on commo[...]
like to play Batman"), physical proximity ("She sits next[...]
ordination of actions, and the maximization of exciten[...]
hints of these relationship attributes at even earlier ages[...]
children can and do engage in a variety of play activities, an... ...ey do have
preferences regarding playmates. In the preschool years and beyond, however, these relationship themes are worked out more fully as the peer
group becomes ever more prominent in children's social lives.

Not all children master the age-appropriate tasks of successful peer relationships as well as Annalisa, however. Some children find these tasks
formidable. Perhaps they lack the play skills that would enable them to
have fun-filled interactions with peers; or perhaps they are not receptive
to the intimacy of a special friendship; or perhaps they behave in generally
disagreeable ways when they are around other children, with the result
that they are shunned by their peers.

Why is it that some children are resourceful and competent in their
interactions with peers, whereas other children find such situations to be
stressful and difficult? There are several possible reasons, including the
child's own **temperament** (Lamb & Nash, 1989), the presence of siblings
(see Chapter 5), and the frequency and quality of early social networks
(Sinclair, Pettit, Harrist, Dodge, & Bates, in press). However, because parents typically serve as the primary agents of **socialization** in early childhood, parenting practices are widely viewed as critical determinants of
children's current and later successes with peers. Evidence of connections
between parents' childrearing practices and their children's social behavior
is well documented, with Diana Baumrind's (1967) pioneering work on
authoritative parenting (described below) perhaps providing the best
known (and most widely cited) example. More recently, researchers have
tried to clarify the means by which children's experiences with parents
pave the way for future encounters with peers (for example, Cohn, Patterson, & Christopoulos, 1991; Parke & Ladd, 1992).

In this chapter we examine in detail the ways parents may promote or
inhibit their children's development of social competence. The chapter is
organized to first provide you with an appreciation of the complexities and
significance of peer relationships. We then turn our attention to the major
questions of interest: What role(s) do parents play in children's acquisition of
peer interaction skills? Do parents intentionally set out to assist their children
in acquiring these skills, and if so, how do they go about it? Similarly, what
is the impact of being reared by warm and supportive (or cold and indifferent) parents on children's social skills development? Most importantly, what
exactly is it that children learn from their parents that is then carried forward

[handwritten margin notes:]
Differences in children's interactions w/ other children.
resourceful & competent — stressful & difficult
Depend on:
• child's own temperament
• presence of siblings
• frequency & quality of early social networks

Parents' Practices — early agent of socialization

into relationships with peers? We attempt to answer these questions by carefully considering the multiple pathways through which social skills, knowledge, and expectations are transmitted from parent to child.

CHARACTERISTICS AND CONSEQUENCES OF CHILDREN'S RELATIONSHIPS WITH PEERS

Throughout the early childhood years, children show increasing interest in interacting with peers. Moreover, as children develop, peer relationships take on new meaning, and children become more selective about whom they want to play with and whom they choose as friends. But, as we shall see, even in early childhood, peer relationships play important roles in social development.

Developmental Trends in Peer Relationships

As infants, most children are curious and sociable with their peers. By the end of the first year infants use several peer-directed social signals—for example, they imitate the activities of other children and direct smiles and vocalizations to peers (Brownell & Brown, 1992). However, peer interaction at this young age often is limited to parallel play (playing side-by-side with the same materials), which includes little intentional social exchange. Compared with infants, toddlers are considerably more interested in, and motivated to play with, peers. Toddlers demonstrate high rates of engagement and positive affect during play (Adamson & Bakeman, 1985), which suggests they recognize that playing with other children yields more enjoyment than playing alone. Indeed, early childhood peer relationships often center on fun, excitement, and mutual enjoyment (Parker & Gottman, 1989), as was shown in the description of Annalisa.

• Friendship, a special form of peer relationships, begins to emerge during the preschool period. Among younger preschoolers, friendships may be based on common activities (Parker & Gottman, 1989) or simply on whom they are playing with at a particular time (Rubin, 1980). For example, two 3-year-old children wear bandannas and play "Ninja Turtles" for a day or two, and for that short period of time they appear to be best friends—at least until one of the children becomes interested in playing "Terminator" with another child. Younger preschoolers also use "friendship" to serve other types of functions, such as initiating contact with another child ("Will you be my friend?") or bargaining ("I'll be your friend if you let me play with the Barbie doll").

Older preschoolers often form longer-lasting friendships, perhaps because they have developed greater self-control in managing their emotions and behavior or because they are beginning to recognize that friendship is an enduring relationship, rather than a momentary playmate (Parker & Gottman, 1989). Preschool children consider a friend to be "someone who plays a lot"

[handwritten margin note: Preschool friendships—serve to initiate contact with another child. based on who I'm playing with at a specific time, common activities, bargaining.]

77

or "someone who is fun to play with." Even though young children describe a friend as one with whom they play or share toys, the interpersonal significance of these descriptions should not be underestimated. Young children's interactions with friends are qualitatively different than those with mere acquaintances (Parker & Gottman, 1989), and friends (more than acquaintances) serve as sources of support and are missed when they are absent (Berndt, 1986). Thus children's descriptions of friends may reflect immature verbal skills and self-awareness rather than a real superficiality of relationships.

Consequences of Children's Peer Relationships

In the short term, peer relationships provide children with opportunities for exciting, fun-filled play. Peer relationships have more significant consequences over the long term, however, in that they make important, unique contributions to children's overall social development (Berndt, 1989) and provide a means by which children become capable of independent social functioning in broader social contexts.

Peer relationships differ from the parent-child relationship in that the peers have an equal power base (Hartup, 1989). Within peer relationships, children expand their social knowledge and skills concerning particular relationship dynamics, such as reciprocity, cooperation, competition, and conflict (Hartup, 1989). For example, if preschool children want to play together with a tricycle, they must grapple with issues such as order (that is, who gets to go first), turn-taking, and the length of each child's turn. Peer relationships also provide a setting in which children can play (Parker & Gottman, 1989) and develop their own self-worth (Furman & Buhrmester, 1985). When two children pretend to be monsters, for example, they are coordinating a high level of play. Moreover, they are working through their individual fears and validating their own competencies in coping with fears.

It is apparent that peers play important roles in children's social development during early childhood. However, not all children develop satisfying peer relationships. Individual differences in the quality of children's peer relationships are evident during preschool years and remain stable well into the early elementary years (Ladd & Price, 1987). Thus some children (like Annalisa) may be well liked and popular. Other children may be ignored or disliked by their peers. Such children are more likely to report feelings of loneliness (Cassidy & Asher, 1992) and to have greater difficulty in making the transition to kindergarten (Ladd & Price, 1987). Moreover, active dislike by peers over time may result in severe negative consequences for some children. In fact, being able to get along with others in childhood is one of the single best predictors of later life adjustment, including school success. Several studies (summarized in Kupersmidt & Coie, 1990) have shown that children who are rejected by their peers are at greater risk for dropping out of school and developing deviant behavioral profiles (including being violence prone) that result in their having contacts with police and other adult authorities.

Box 1

Identifying Children Who Are Experiencing Difficulties in Their Peer Relationships

When thinking about children's peer relationships, it is not difficult to imagine the different experiences of individual children. You may know a child like Annalisa, for example, who enjoys popularity among her peers and who has several close peer relationships, or friendships. No doubt there are other children, however, who are not as highly regarded by their peers. The shy, reserved boy who tries not to draw attention to himself may not be disliked, just "overlooked," compared to more outgoing or showy children. Another child may be actively disliked by her peers, at least in part because she hits them or disrupts their play activities. Still other children may not be class "stars" but enjoy a few close relationships and can play well enough with peers.

The best known method for assessing individual differences in children's peer status is **sociometric assessment,** which involves measuring the attraction between members in a group (or in a classroom). Sociometric assessments include nomination and rating scale measures (Asher & Hymel, 1981). In the nomination procedure, each child is asked to nominate a certain number of classmates according to a particular criterion—for example, "Tell me the three kids you like to play with the most" and "Tell me the three kids you don't like to play with." The number of times each child is nominated for each of the two roles is then tabulated. Popular children receive many "like" votes and few "don't like" votes; rejected children receive the opposite. With a rating scale measure, children rate how much they like to play with (or work with) each classmate—for example, "Do you like to play with Tyrone a lot, a little bit, or not at all?" These ratings are then averaged across all children in the class.

Although these two types of sociometric assessments are similar, the conclusions that can be drawn from them are not necessarily the same. For example, one child may not receive any nominations as most liked or least liked but may nonetheless be generally well regarded by his peers, as shown by above-average ratings (Asher & Hymel, 1981). Another child may receive several nominations for most liked but not be especially popular among her peers as a whole (that is, she may be highly regarded by a select few but not particularly well liked by the majority of the class). Some low-visibility children (the "overlooked" ones) may receive few or no positive nominations yet be rated as someone who most children like to play with a good bit. For these reasons, rating scales and nomination procedures often are used in conjunction with one another.

Other types of assessments also have been used in order to provide more comprehensive evaluations of children's peer status. Teachers may provide descriptions of children's behavior with peers, rate children's peer acceptance, or describe friendship patterns. Alternatively, researchers may observe children on the playground and in the classroom to assess the quality of their peer relationships. Sometimes researchers arrange special situations to observe children's behavior with peers in important interpersonal contexts, such as when a child attempts to join a group of children already at play (Asher & Hymel, 1981).

Sociometric and observational methods also have been used to study children's friendships. A simple definition of "friend" might be those children who nominate one another for positive roles in a sociometric interview (Asher & Hymel, 1981). One might also observe children to see who affiliates with whom. Presumably children who frequently seek each other out as playmates would consider one another to be friends. Yet another approach to identifying which children are friends is simply to ask children who their friends are.

As we think about the complex world of peer relationships during childhood, it becomes readily apparent that children differ substantially in their levels of skill in establishing and maintaining close interpersonal ties. Recognition that such skills are critical spurred an interest in their origins and the role of early family experiences in their development. Let us now examine what is currently known about these skills and their function in peer relations.

SOCIAL COMPETENCE IN PEER RELATIONS

How might socially skillful behavior be described? Are there things that some children do that make their interactions interesting and enjoyable for all participants? Research suggests that successful social encounters among children and their peers have three general properties. First, the behavioral style of **socially competent** children is both *positive and agreeable*. A long history of research (summarized in Cohn et al., 1991) has shown consistently that a positive outlook and an open and congenial style of relating characterizes the social behavior of well-liked, competent individuals from preschool age through adulthood. One way in which positiveness may be manifested in early childhood is when children engage in prosocial acts, such as when they spontaneously offer assistance or help. Of course, positive, agreeable children also refrain from inappropriate, interpersonal **aggression**—that is, they get angry at others less often, and they are unlikely to bully others to get their way. As it turns out, relatively high levels of **prosocial behavior** and low levels of aggression are associated with peer acceptance throughout childhood (Coie, Dodge, &

The rewards of social competence include pleasant, cooperative interactions with peers.

Kupersmidt, 1990). At a general level, then, an agreeable and positive social orientation would seem to underlie most satisfying and productive interpersonal exchanges throughout the childhood years and beyond.

Second, socially competent children are *circumspect* in making use of contextual and social cues to guide behavior (Pettit & Harrist, 1993). To say that someone lacks **circumspection** is to say that she or he behaves without regard to the demands of the particular social context, that she or he displays poor judgment, that she or he seems insensitive, if not oblivious, to other people. A substantial body of observational research findings supports the view that competent children of all ages are circumspect—that is, they are "tuned in" to social and environmental cues and are able to adjust their own behavior to that of their partners (Mize, in press; Pettit & Harrist, 1993). These findings suggest that children who are preferred as playmates better understand the contextual demands of the social settings in which they find themselves (for instance, that other children are more likely to want to play a game with them during recess than during classroom quiet time), and they are better able to adjust their behavior so that it fits in with what their peers are doing.

The third important characteristic of socially competent children is that they demonstrate positive *synchrony,* in that they sensitively and responsively "mesh" their behavior with that of their play partners (Mize, in press; Pettit & Harrist, 1993). Positive **synchrony** in behavior means that a child's behavior is connected in relevant and meaningful ways to that of his or her peers. Children as young as age 2 show responsivity during conversation by making relevant comments and smiling at appropriate times (Miller, Lechner, & Rugs, 1985), and positively synchronous play in toddlerhood often takes the form of reciprocal, turn-taking games such as run-and-chase (Howes, 1988). Positively synchronous behavior also characterizes the interactions of socially competent preschool children (Mize, in press). For example, well-liked preschoolers are more likely than their disliked peers to acknowledge and respond contingently to the play leads of other children (Hazen & Black, 1989). Disliked children, on the other hand, more often are disengaged, disconnected, or otherwise "tuned-out" to those around them. Unfortunately, these children appear to be unable to participate in synchronous, reciprocal exchanges unless they are engaged in negative and conflictual interactions with peers, such as arguments or fights

(Asaranow, 1983; Pettit & Harrist, 1993). These out-of-step and antagonistic behaviors, of course, usually are disruptive of peers' activities and frequently are ignored or scorned by peers (Dodge, Coie, Pettit, & Price, 1990).

Successful adaptation to the peer group, then, requires more of a child than just limiting aggression and behaving in generally positive ways; it requires careful attention to contextual detail (such as what the other children are saying and doing) and skill in blending her or his behavior with that of others, so that ongoing activities with peers—especially enjoyable and stimulating activities—flow smoothly and easily.

Social Cognition and Social Competence: The Role of Knowledge, Beliefs, and Perceptions

In the past couple of decades, child-development researchers have become increasingly interested in the connection between children's thoughts and feelings—what are referred to as social cognitions—and children's behavior with peers (Dodge, Pettit, McClaskey, & Brown, 1986; Mize & Ladd, 1990). The general notion guiding research in this area is that individual differences in children's skill in social behavior may be a function (at least in part) of underlying social-cognitive abilities and orientations. That is, whether a child behaves in a friendly manner with a peer may depend on how the child feels about the peer (Is this someone who is fun to play with?) and how knowledgeable the child is about how to initiate a friendly interaction (How can I get her to play a game with me?).

Pettit and Mize (1993) have developed a conceptual model that summarizes three interrelated facets of social-cognitive functioning in early childhood. The model borrows from existing theoretical frameworks (for example, Crick & Ladd, 1990; Dodge et al., 1986) but is geared to the **social-cognitive processes** that appear to be most salient for preschoolers' social behavior. According to Pettit and Mize, children's ability to achieve positive, synchronous peer interaction hinges on a set of social-cognitive processes that may serve as guides for the behaviors that children are likely to perform.

The first process involves social knowledge. Socially competent children, compared to less skilled children, have repertoires of social knowledge that are richer and more relevant to the social problems they face (Pettit, Dodge, & Brown, 1988), "friendlier" (Mize & Ladd, 1988), and more effective (Asher & Renshaw, 1981). In other words, when confronted with a social task, such as working through a conflict with a peer over possession of a toy or joining a group of children already at play, competent children are more likely to meet with success than less skilled children because they have more behavioral options available to them. For example, a child is presented with the problem of getting a peer to give her a turn on a swing: "Suppose that Juanita has been swinging for a long time, and you've been waiting for your turn. What could you say or do so that Juanita would give you a turn?" A socially competent child might suggest several options: "Will you tell me when you're finished so I can get on the swing next?" or "I'll push you now if you'll push me later." A less competent child, on the other hand, might simply respond with "I'd push her out" or "I'd go tell the teacher."

The second process is reading social cues. Socially competent children are skilled at attending to and discriminating relevant social cues (Dodge et al., 1986; Meese, Mize, & Pettit, 1993); that is, they attend to important interpersonal signals and interpret them realistically and constructively. Children who are lacking in social perception skills often appear to lack good judgment because they overlook important social signals (such as their partner's looking bored or irritated), attend exclusively to one type of signal (such as signs of hostility or rejection), or misconstrue a peer's actions (such as a child's assuming that a peer's accidental bump was intentional and malicious). From this perspective, social perception skills entail attending to relevant social and contextual cues, observing the reactions of others to one's behavior, and interpreting others' behavior in nonbiased, constructive ways (Mize, in press).

The model's third social-cognitive process is children's relationship views and expectations. Competent children differ from less competent children in their general approach to and expectations for relationships, including their tendency to view relationships with others as rewarding (Ladd & Crick, 1989) and to view themselves as capable and confident in producing positive peer outcomes (Perry, Perry, & Rasmussen, 1986). The net result is that socially effective children are more likely to seek out the company of peers and to expect that peers will seek them out. Moreover, competent children anticipate that such encounters will be positive and enjoyable.

A Question of Origins

As you have seen, the formation of friendships and establishment of ties with peers in early childhood serve important developmental functions. The early years appear to be critical for development of the behavioral and social-cognitive skills that enable children to navigate the complex world of the peer group successfully. Because individual differences in social skills appear early and are relatively stable (Howes, 1987), researchers have sought to identify their origins and have focused on the role of parents as the primary social agents during the early childhood years.

PARENTING AND CHILDREN'S SOCIAL SKILLS: MULTIPLE PATHWAYS

In this section we will examine the ways parents may influence their children's development of peer interaction skills. We will be concerned not only with *what* parents do, but also with the processes that explain *how* parents transmit social skills and social knowledge to their children.

It is fairly easy to identify some of the more obvious things that parents do to promote their children's development of social skills, such as when they enroll their children in socially oriented preschool programs or arrange family outings and special events (like birthday parties) to ensure that their children are exposed to a variety of peers in safe and supportive contexts (Parke, MacDonald, Beitel, & Bhavnagri, 1988; Rubin & Sloman, 1984). Other parental actions, however, may have more subtle effects on children's social behavior and skillfulness in peer interaction. The following vignette, although hypothetical, is based on researchers' experiences and observations and highlights some of the themes that will be explored below.

Four-year-old Joseph and his father are enjoying their routine after-breakfast game of finger wrestling (Joseph uses his thumb; his father uses his little finger). Joseph's mother gently interrupts the fun to remind them that today is Joseph's first day at the new preschool. Joseph takes advantage of the distraction and bends his father's finger back a little too far, eliciting a "Yow!" and a mock frown from his father. Joseph grins but says "Sorry" and then takes a quick swing on his father's arm before the two of them leave for school. Upon arrival, Joseph is escorted into his new classroom by his father. Joseph reacts by hanging back, shyly peering around his father. After they enter the room, Joseph's father waits a moment until the teacher finishes getting some children involved in block play before introducing her to Joseph. The father and the teacher have an amiable chat, and the father draws Joseph into the conversation by commenting that the teacher knows some of the other children in Joseph's neighborhood. The teacher talks with Joseph for a minute and then asks him if he would like to play with some of the other children. When Joseph seems a bit reluctant, his father smiles at him and gently leads him to the block area, where together they begin building a block tower. Joseph notices another child picking up some plastic farm animals nearby, and his father suggests that the other child might want some help. Joseph slowly approaches the child and within a few minutes they are happily engaged in fantasy farm play.

In this scene we see several elements of potential parental influence. Joseph and his father seem to have a satisfying personal relationship, as evidenced by the smiling and playful behavior. Part of this playfulness is of a physical nature, as shown in the daily finger-wrestling game. Within this game Joseph may be learning to read emotional cues and to recognize when he may have gone too far in his efforts to engage his father in a physically playful activity. Joseph's father models positive social skills in the timing of his initial approach to the preschool teacher. Finally, his father provides Joseph with explicit social guidance by making a concrete suggestion as to how he might initiate interaction with a classmate.

It is clear that parental influences on children's peer relations and friendships can take various forms. The nature of these influences is not always straightforward, however. Part of the problem is that it often is difficult to judge parents' motives for behaving in certain ways with their children. For example, when we observe a parent giving a child advice on making friends, are we to conclude that the parent's actions stem from a desire to foster the child's continuing development of relationship skills or from concern that the child may be socially underdeveloped? Understanding what motivates a parent to provide advice and guidance may require a consideration of the parent's values ("Social skills are important for my child") and beliefs ("My actions make a difference in my child's behavior with peers"), as well as the child's level of actual (and parent-perceived) social skillfulness.

Our understanding of parental influences on children's social skills development is further complicated by the fact that parents sometimes give out mixed messages about how relationships work and how one should behave in social situations. In the example of Joseph and his father each aspect of parental influence is positive, in the sense that it might be expected to promote effective social skills and a healthy social orientation. But parental actions are not always so uniformly consistent; sometimes there is a discrepancy between what a parent says ("Just be nice and the other children will want to be your friend") and how she or he says it (the tone of voice conveys, "You better be nice or you'll be in trouble, mister!"). How do children make sense of such communications? How do they translate these messages into social behavior?

These and related questions have intrigued researchers and theorists interested in the interconnections among parent-child and child-peer relationships. Generally, three sets of issues have guided research and thinking in this area. First, researchers have sought to map out the major types of parental influences. These influences have been explored primarily in terms of parents' roles as interactive partners, as educators and advisors, and as managers of their children's peer relationships (Parke & Ladd, 1992). Second, researchers have searched for the possible determinants or causes of parents' behavior, in an effort to understand what might motivate parents to become more (or less) active in their children's social lives (Ladd, Profilet, & Hart, 1992; Mize, Pettit, & Brown, 1993). Third, a considerable amount of attention has been aimed at providing more precise explanations of how the social transmission process actually works. **Social transmission** is the process by which parents convey messages to their children about what to expect and how to behave in interpersonal relationships. This latter issue is perhaps the most crucial, because it lies at the very heart of the parent-to-peers developmental transition. Somehow children acquire something that they carry forward from their relationships with parents to their relationships with their peers. Better understanding of what is acquired and how it generalizes to new relationships may provide the key to unlocking one of the fundamental mysteries of the socialization process.

Types of Parental Influence: What Matters?

Parent-Child Interaction   Researchers have had a longstanding interest in the role of family socialization processes in children's development of interpersonal competencies. Many of the classic studies of children's social development were conducted to explore this issue. These early studies focused primarily on aspects of parent-child interaction such as parents' effectiveness in disciplining their children, the emotional tone of the interactions (for example, affectionate and warm versus hostile or uncaring), and the quality of parents' communication with their children. Diana Baumrind's (1967, 1973) pioneering work in this field is probably best known. Baumrind reported that an **authoritative** style of parenting—characterized by a blending of firm and consistent control, affection, and respect—was associated with socially competent behavior (that is, confident, assertive, and socially responsible) by children with their preschool peers. Baumrind also identified two less optimal patterns of childrearing, which she described as **authoritarian** (overcontrolling and emotionally hostile or distant) and **permissive** (undercontrolling and indulgent), which were associated with children's aggressiveness and social anxiety (Baumrind, 1967). A fourth childrearing pattern, termed **neglectful** (indifferent and undemanding), has been linked to poor social-developmental outcomes in childhood (Maccoby & Martin, 1983). The social competence–promoting character of an authoritative style (in contrast to the competence-inhibiting character of authoritarian, permissive, and neglectful styles) has been documented by an impressive array of research studies conducted over the past 25 years (see Cohn et al., 1991; Putallaz & Heflin, 1990). Clearly, children being raised by authoritative parents have acquired a positive social orientation that pays dividends in subsequent encounters with peers.

The effectiveness and style of parental discipline also has been linked to children's peer competence. In general, the research conducted on American children suggests that socially competent children are likely to have parents who refrain from using harsh and punitive methods of control and instead use inductive methods, such as offering reasons for measures taken and encouraging verbal give-and-take (Hart, DeWolf, & Burts, 1993). On the other end of the continuum, extreme cases of parental punitiveness—such as abuse—have been found to be associated with undesirable child outcomes, including aggressive behavior and peer rejection (Dodge, Bates, & Pettit, 1990; Weiss, Dodge, Bates, & Pettit, 1992). It has been argued that exposure to inept and aversive parental discipline eventually trains children to use similar kinds of styles in their interactions with family members and with peers (Patterson, 1982), although the precise operation of these socialization influences is as yet not fully understood (Wahler, 1993).

Other studies have highlighted the importance of positive and agreeable parent-child interaction in children's development of social competence (see Cohn et al., 1991). For example, Putallaz (1987) found that the mothers of children who received high sociometric assessment ratings from their first-grade peers were congenial and likely to focus on others' feelings. Moreover, mothers who engaged their children in positive and agreeable ways had children who displayed similar styles in their interactions with peers.

Even when children are experiencing peer relationship problems, the quality of their relationships with their parents can help to offset some of the potential adverse effects of peer rejection. Patterson, Cohn, and Kao (1989) identified a group of elementary-aged children who were rejected by their peers in sociometric assessments. They found that later problem behaviors (such as aggressiveness) were evident only in those children whose mothers were cold and rejecting (versus warm and accepting). In other words, the presence of maternal warmth seemed to serve as a **protective factor** in preventing the development of behavior problems.

Although warmth, disciplinary effectiveness, and having an authoritative style are important parenting characteristics, other qualities of the parent-child relationship may also be consequential for children's developing social competencies. Pettit and his colleagues (Pettit & Harrist, 1993; Pettit, Harrist, Bates, & Dodge, 1991; Pettit & Mize, 1993) have suggested that children's later success with peers hinges in part on the degree to which parent-child interactions are synchronous. As we discussed in the description of peer-interaction skills, synchrony refers to how responsive partners are to one another's cues and the extent to which they engage in smooth and reciprocated behavioral exchanges. Just as synchrony appears to be a key feature of competent interaction among children, it is also an indicator of the quality of the parent-child relationship. Synchronous parent-child exchanges have been found to be associated with children's social perception skills and playground behavior and competence with peers (Pettit et al., 1991; Pettit & Harrist, 1993).

The importance of parent-child synchrony is perhaps nowhere better illustrated than in studies of infant-parent attachment. **Attachment** refers to the close and significant emotional bond between the infant and caregivers that typically emerges in the latter half of the first year of life (see Chapter 4). Isabella and Belsky (1991) have shown that sensitive, responsive parenting and harmonious infant-parent exchanges early in the first year forecast the quality of attachment at age 12 months. Securely attached infants had previously experienced infant-parent interactions that were positively synchronous (harmonious and sensitively connected). In contrast, the earlier interactions of insecurely attached infants were characterized by a lack of synchrony, as manifested in inconsistent, insensitive, and intrusive patterns of maternal involvement (Isabella & Belsky, 1991). Attachment security, in turn, is associated with children's later interpersonal competence with peers (Elicker, Englund, & Sroufe, 1992).

Parents as Play Partners   So far we have identified different aspects of parenting style that seem to influence children's general social orientations (such as whether children tend to be agreeable, responsive social partners). It also is the case, however, that children must somehow acquire specific play skills that they can employ in order to join ongoing playgroups, initiate friendships, and create play themes with which to entice their peers. Some investigators have recently begun to wonder whether children first acquire play skills in the context of their play interactions with parents (Carson, Burks, & Parke, 1993; Lindsey, Mize, & Pettit, 1993). Think for a moment about the scene involving Joseph and his father, described earlier: Was Joseph learning some important lessons about being a play partner during the finger-wrestling episode? Skilled play in early childhood requires that children learn to take turns and alternate roles of leader and follower. Moreover, children must learn just how far they can go in the pursuit of excitement and thrills. In Joseph's case, when he crossed the line, his father voiced displeasure with his behavior, but in a gentle way.

The role of parent-child play in children's social development is only beginning to receive systematic research attention (MacDonald, 1993), but already there is some intriguing evidence that aspects of children's play skills are initially acquired, and subsequently practiced, during playful parent-child interactions. Because fathers typically engage in proportionally more playful interactions with their children than do mothers (Russell & Russell, 1987), father-child play has been the target of several investigations.

Good early studies of this type were conducted by MacDonald and Parke (1984) and by MacDonald (1987), who wondered whether children's styles of interacting with peers might have parallels in the kinds of interactions that the children experienced in playful contexts with their parents. Parents (especially fathers) who more frequently engaged their children in physical play that was accompanied by positive affect had children who engaged in higher levels of harmonious interactions and lower levels of abrasive interactions with peers. The fathers of popular boys were physically playful and elicited positive affect during play; the play of the fathers of unpopular boys was either less emotionally arousing or it was "over the top," in that the boys became angry and upset (MacDonald, 1987).

A more precise specification of the connection between father-child play attributes and children's play interaction skills was undertaken by Lindsey et al. (1993). This study found that play leads and **turnabouts** (whereby one partner either accepts or redirects the other's play suggestion) in the context of father-child play were predictors of children's play leads and responses in actual peer interaction. Moreover, sociometrically popular children are more likely to use leads and turnabouts in peer interaction than are less popular children (Hazen & Black, 1989).

Do children acquire these skills while playin w/parents?

Enjoyable physical play with a father may contribute to a child's popularity with peers.

children-peers children parents are there any parallels?

| $\mathcal{B}ox\ 2$ | **Do Children Learn Different Things about Relationships from Mothers and from Fathers?** |

Because fathers have been observed to engage in proportionally more physical play with their children compared with mothers (MacDonald & Parke, 1984; Russell & Russell, 1987), and because the frequency of parents' active, physical play has been found to be associated with children's peer competence (Carson et al., 1993), it has been speculated that mothers and fathers play distinct roles in developing their children's social skills (Lindsey et al., 1993). For example, it may be that father-child play serves special functions in helping children learn how to regulate their emotional arousal in exciting and stimulating social encounters, whereas mothers' calmer but more emotionally expressive styles enhance children's interpersonal awareness and sensitivity.

Of course, *some* fathers eschew physical contact, and *some* mothers are emotionally distant. It is probably less important which parent provides the child with these kinds of experiences than it is that *someone* provides them, which probably explains why most children growing up in single-parent families develop adequate social skills: The single parent assumes both parenting roles and/or other significant adults assume some of the socializing role of the absent parent (Patterson, Kupersmidt, & Vaden, 1990).

Current knowledge suggests that general stylistic qualities of parent-child interaction, including the playful styles of interaction that tend to characterize fathers' interactions with their preschool-aged children, may be significant influences on children's social skills development and relationships with peers. These interactive styles therefore represent one important pathway through which parents transmit social skills and knowledge to their children. An alternative pathway, however, focuses on parental behaviors that are more deliberate and intentional efforts to promote children's peer relationships. These parenting strategies are discussed in the next section.

Parents as Managers, Educators, and Advisors   As was mentioned earlier, there are a number of ways in which parents may serve as social architects of their children's peer relationships. By deciding that the family will live in a neighborhood rich with opportunities for peer contact or by choosing a preschool program that promises to encourage the development of peer interaction skills, parents take an active role in promoting their children's peer relationships (Rubin & Sloman, 1984). Of course, many parents use even more hands-on strategies—for example, advising children on how to get other children to be their friends, teaching children how to pay attention to others' feelings, or managing children's social schedules and inviting peers over for a party. Because most of the research conducted on parents' deliberate and intentional efforts to promote social skills development has been concerned with such strategies, they are the focus of this section.

When describing parental management practices it is useful to distinguish between parents' **orchestration** (that is, specific attempts to arrange and manage children's peer activities) and parental guidance (instruction and advice about peer issues). With respect to the former, a series of investigations by Ladd (summarized in Ladd, LeSieur, & Profilet, 1993) has shown that parents not only take on an active role in initiating and organizing peer contacts for their children, they also employ strategies in these efforts that are associated with children's peer competence. Ladd and Golter (1988) examined parents' initiation and monitoring of their preschoolers' peer contacts. Parents were trained to keep detailed daily diaries regarding their children's peer contacts (outside of school) and whether the contact had been initiated by the parent or by the child. Parents also recorded whether they monitored these contacts directly (by making sure they stayed near where the children were playing) or indirectly (by checking in occasionally to make sure play was proceeding smoothly). Children whose parents actively arranged contacts and relied on indirect monitoring were better liked by peers and were rated as more socially competent by teachers.

Why might direct (and presumably conspicuous) parental supervision be associated with lower levels of peer competence? Ladd et al. (1993) offer two possible explanations. First, they note that parents who rely extensively on direct forms of supervision may inhibit their children's development of important social skills. This makes sense if you consider that social skills develop partly through practice: If the parent oversees the vast majority of the child's peer contacts, the child doesn't get the necessary practice, so the skills relevant to initiating and maintaining interaction may develop more slowly (Mize & Ladd, 1990). An alternative explanation is that parents' management styles are a reflection of their children's competence; therefore, low levels of skillfulness with peers, as perceived by parents, elicit more overt forms of supervision (Mills & Rubin, 1992).

Researchers also have wondered whether children play together more skillfully when their parents are present and provide assistance. Parke and Bhavnagri (1989) observed toddler pairs interacting with and without mothers' help and found that the quality of the toddlers' interactions with one another improved when the mothers helped the children play. In a later study, Bhavnagri and Parke (1991) found that parents' interventions were associated with improved play quality for younger children (toddlers) but not for older children (preschoolers). This suggests that hands-on supervision may be especially important when children are just beginning to acquire social skills, but that more indirect supervision strategies work best with children who already have basic skill repertoires.

As one would expect, the quality of assistance that parents offer also is important. Finnie and Russell (1988) examined the specific information communicated by mothers to their preschool children during initial play encounters with unfamiliar peers. Mothers of popular children gave better quality advice than did mothers of less popular children. Specifically, mothers of popular children were more likely than other mothers to help their children understand the group's frame of reference and make relevant group-oriented statements (such as commenting on the game the other children were playing). Mothers of less popular children, in contrast, were more likely to urge their children to do things that focused the group's attention on themselves ("Tell them that *you* know how to play that game") or that disrupted the group activity. In a follow-up study, Russell and Finnie (1990) showed that mothers of popular children also were more skilled in "prepping" their children for a subsequent peer encounter (for example, by providing useful suggestions on how to approach the group).

Most of what is known about the peer-relations teaching and advice that parents provide their children has been learned from observing families under somewhat artificial conditions. In a typical study a parent (usually the mother) and a child are placed in a playroom with other children, and the parent is asked to assist the child in playing with the peers. Pettit and Mize (1993) termed this approach "prompted coaching" and have pointed out that although use of such procedures sheds light on the strategies parents use when they have been explicitly asked to perform, they tell us little about what parents may do under more natural circumstances, where they are freer to choose when and how to respond to their children.

Pettit and Mize (1993) have addressed this issue by observing parents and their preschool-aged children in both a "natural" supervision situation and a prompted-coaching situation. For the more natural situation, the children and their parents were observed in a comfortably furnished, homelike playroom. After a warm-up period, the children were introduced to a same-age, same-sex peer, and the parent was told simply to do whatever he or she normally would at home, were the children playing together for the first time. The frequency and quality of parent involvement in facilitating play was recorded, and these scores were related to the measures of the children's competence and peer acceptance in their classrooms. Surprisingly, parental supervision in the natural situation was *not* associated with children's actual classroom competence. Rather, whether a parent was more or less active in helping the children play together was more a function of how the parent perceived her or his child (Mize, Pettit, & Brown, 1993). That is, parents who viewed their children as socially skilled (based on the parents' responses to a questionnaire) were more likely to take a hands-off stance and allow the children to work things out on their own. Parents who considered their children to be skills deficient, on the other hand, were more active and involved in assisting the children in their play.

Pettit and Mize (1993) also observed parents who had been asked to discuss with their children a series of videotaped vignettes in which child actors depicted several common peer relationship problems (such as conflicts about possessions and trying to find someone to play with). The parents were asked to help their children understand what happened in each story and to make suggestions to their children about how they might respond in similar situations. This was referred to as **coaching**. The children of parents who suggested more constructive strategies and who encouraged a resilient, bounce-back attitude received higher peer competence scores in their classrooms (Mize, Pettit, Lindsey, & Laird, 1993). Parent perceptions played a lesser role in how parents responded in the coaching situation. In this kind of prompted task, parents who were more knowledgeable about children's development and who believed that children's social skills are teachable (as opposed to innate) were more likely to provide good quality coaching.

Mize, Pettit, Lindsey, and Laird (1993) also examined the issue of mixed messages that we raised earlier. That is, these researchers wondered whether a positive, synchronous parent-child relationship enhanced the effectiveness of parental management practices and, conversely, whether a nonsynchronous parent-child relationship undermined the effectiveness of parents' guidance and supervision. Stylistic aspects of parent-child interaction had been coded during both coaching situations. The mothers of the most socially competent children were more positively and synchronously involved with their children and also provided them with good coaching content. Moreover, when parent-child interaction style was below average in quality, coaching content assumed even greater importance in predicting children's peer competence. Perhaps, then, being a good coach and supervisor of peer relations can help to compensate for a less-than-optimal parent-child relationship (Parke, 1992).

Parents' Beliefs and Values as Determinants of Parental Behavior

The Mize, Pettit, Lindsey, and Laird (1993) findings suggest that different aspects of parental behavior are motivated by different factors. A considerable amount of attention has been devoted to understanding the psychological determinants of parenting (Belsky, 1984), but relatively little research has focused specifically on parents' management practices (Ladd et al., 1992). In general, however, it appears that parents are more active in managing and supervising their children's peer relations when they consider social skills to be important and teachable (Cohen & Woody, 1991), when they have the skills and social knowledge needed to guide their children's behavior (Ladd et al., 1993), and when they view their children as lacking in important social skills (Mize, Pettit, & Brown, in press).

There also is some recent evidence that parents' recollections of their own peer relationships in childhood influence their socialization strategies (Cohen & Woody, 1991; Putallaz, Costanzo, & Klein, 1993). (See Box 3.) A parent may seek to ensure that the child acquires the skills necessary to overcome obstacles that the parent perceives as having limited his or her own relationships with peers.

Active parental involvement in children's peer relationships appears to be another pathway by which parents transmit social skills to their children. Parents' skillfulness in structuring peer contacts and the quality of the advice that parents provide about peer issues have been linked with children's peer competence. Moreover, as shown by Pettit and Mize (1993), parents' efforts to promote peer relationship skills and parents' general style of interacting with the child are somewhat independent processes. The most competent children, it would seem, are most likely to have parents who are both good teachers, or "coaches," and good interactive partners.

So far we have touched only very generally on the ways in which these pathways of influence may operate. Now we examine in greater detail what children may be learning from parents that is then carried over into peer relationships.

Mechanisms of Transmission: What Are Children Really Learning from Their Parents?

We conclude this chapter by delving into one of the thorniest issues in the study of children's social development: How do children translate the messages transmitted by their parents (intentionally or unintentionally) into the specific social skills that they can then use in interactions with peers? Different theoretical perspectives offer distinct points of view on this issue. Some perspectives stress learning principles, whereby exposure to a particular kind of parenting is thought to "train" children to behave in similar sorts of ways (Patterson, 1982). Other theorists place greater emphasis on underlying social–cognitive processes as mediators of behavior. From the point of view of **cognitive-social learning theory** (Bandura, 1986), children acquire social orientations as a consequence of parental modeling. Attachment theorists have stressed the internalization of beliefs and expectations as a way of explaining the connection between socializing experiences and later social orientations (Bretherton, 1985). As a by-product of attachment relationships, an infant presumably develops an **internal working model** of self and others that serves to guide her or his behavior in new social situations.

A growing body of evidence suggests that social-cognitive factors like those described earlier serve as a link between children's experiences with parents and their later styles of interacting with peers (Hart et al., 1993; Pettit, Dodge, & Brown, 1988; Pettit, Harrist, Bates, & Dodge, 1991). For example, warm, responsive parenting is associated with children's positive beliefs about their own competence and the outcomes they expect in

Box 3

Memories of Childhood: Do Parents' Recollections Influence Their Socialization Strategies?

Putallaz et al. (1993) highlight a number of studies indicating that memories of early social experiences may carry over into later intimate relationships. Putallaz, Costanzo, and Smith (1991) conducted their own study of this issue by having mothers of preschoolers recall a particular childhood encounter that they felt characterized their peer experience. (Too few fathers participated to permit analysis.) Three themes emerged in the recollections. The largest group of mothers recalled positive experiences, and they described themselves as being nurturant with their children and viewed their children as being socially competent. The second group recalled negative childhood experiences, and they described themselves as less nurturant and their children as less competent. The third group of mothers recalled anxious, lonely peer experiences, and they described themselves as nurturant and as highly active in providing their children with skills-promoting social experiences (for example, enrolling their children in many activities). The children of mothers in the anxious-lonely group were more socially competent at school (based on teacher and peer reports) than the children of the mothers who described positive or negative recollections.

Putallaz et al. (1991) offer two explanations to account for the higher social competence of the children of the anxious-recollection mothers.

1. The anxious-recollection mothers showed more evidence of an internal locus of control, in that they often attributed their loneliness to their own social inadequacy. They may have become actively involved in their children's social lives in order to empower them with a sense of control or efficacy in peer relationships.
2. The anxious-recollection mothers provided their children with models of emotional openness and sensitivity. As Putallaz et al. (1993) note, "Mothers not only model behavior and actively create environments for their children but also communicate interpretations of the meaning of social behaviors and context" (p. 85). By being honest and forthcoming about the sources of their insecurity, the anxious-recollection mothers may help their children to become more sensitive social partners and thus more attractive as playmates.

social interaction (Pettit et al., 1991). Harsh, punitive parenting, on the other hand, predicts children's tendencies to make misattributions about others' behavior (Dodge et al., 1990) and to display poor interpersonal problem-solving skills (Pettit et al., 1988).

No study has yet linked parents' management practices with children's social-cognitive skills. However, Pettit and Mize (1993) have speculated on the ways in which styles of parent-child interaction and the quality of parents' teaching and advice giving may each contribute to a set of cognitive-affective processes that in turn are associated with peer competence. This model of social transmission is outlined below.

Pettit and Mize (1993) have hypothesized that the style of parent-child interaction and parent coaching skill each contribute in both direct and indirect ways to children's social competence with peers. *Direct* indicates that there are no intervening processes; the experience in the parent-child context generalizes readily and without conscious thought to experiences with peers. For instance, being in a positive, responsive relationship with a parent (or parents) may contribute to the development of a warm, outgoing interpersonal style that transfers easily to relationships with peers. *Indirect* contributions, on the other hand, are those that are mediated by children's social-cognitive skills. That is, parenting practices lead to variations in children's knowledge, beliefs, and perceptions, which in turn lead to individual differences in peer relationship skills. This type of influence might be seen when a parent explicitly instructs the child in the use of a particular skill (such as sharing a toy with a new acquaintance) and explicitly reinforces the child's belief that such an action will lead to a positive outcome (such as having a new friend).

Summary ⟶ What kinds of parenting practices might have direct links to children's social competence? Our earlier discussion suggested that parent-child synchrony and parent-child physical play may enhance children's development of important interpersonal skills. Early parent-child interactions, when synchronous, probably provide a key context for learning and practicing the fundamental relationship skills of turn taking and reciprocity, necessary ingredients for sustained and enjoyable play with peers (Pettit & Harrist, 1993). Parent-child physical play, on the other hand, helps children to acquire more specific skills that can be used during peer play, such as initiating (leading) games and activities and responding positively to (supporting) others' initiations (Lindsey et al., 1993).

However, it also is likely that interaction style and parent-child physical play contribute indirectly to children's peer interaction skills through distinct social-cognitive processes. By participating in warm, synchronous interactions with parents, children may learn to expect that relationships with others will be rewarding. Moreover, positively synchronous relationships may encourage attentiveness and sensitivity to social cues, which in turn allow children to better coordinate their behavior with that of peers. This interpersonal sensitivity is in part a product of having many opportunities to practice reading the cues of caregivers and mesh behavior with that of a sensitive partner (Pettit & Mize, 1993). Similarly, parent-child physical play provides the child with experience in detecting the emotional signals of an interactive partner in an emotionally charged, exciting context (Carson et al., 1993). Moreover, parent-child play may enlarge the child's knowledge base with respect to fun and exciting play themes and activities. In other words, because of their experiences playing with parents, children may learn new games and new play techniques that they can then use with peers.

Parenting style and parent-child play may not provide children with all of the skills they will need to meet the challenges of peer interaction. Sometimes children require concrete advice about how to deal with specific issues, such as how to make friends in a new neighborhood or how to defend their property without becoming involved in a conflict. Parent advice giving and coaching may play key roles in this regard. Some parents may regularly teach social perception skills by pointing out how others are feeling and helping the child to notice important background cues in a peer's behavior (Pettit & Mize, 1993). It also is likely that parental discussions about peer relationships affect the size and quality of children's repertoires of social strategies. The relation between parental coaching and advice giving and children's actual behavioral competence with peers, therefore, is likely to be mediated through the children's social knowledge and social perception skills.

Since these studies were conducted in the United States and the subjects were American, the reader should keep in mind that these results might not hold true in all cultures or for all families in American culture. Given that caution, we can conclude that there appear to be multiple paths to peer competence, and children learn different lessons about relationships from different kinds of parental behavior. Some of these lessons may not be intended, but their impact on children's views of relationships and on their skillfulness in peer interaction may nonetheless be substantial.

Class Discussion Questions

1. Think about your own relationships with peers during early childhood, later childhood, and as a young adult. Compare your experiences with the information that you have read in this chapter.
   a. Who were the peers you had relationships with when you were younger? What were these relationships like (that is, what were they based on—playing together, talking with each other, common activities)? How have your relationships with peers changed over time in terms of their influence on you and their overall importance?
   b. Now, think specifically about your friendships. Who was your best friend when you were a young child? Why was this person your friend? Think of the other special friendships you experienced as you got older. Looking back, what were the bases of these friendships (that is, common activities, provision of support, someone to talk to)? How have your expectations for your friends changed as you have matured?

2. Consider the role your parents had in your peer relationships. Again, compare your experience with the material presented in this chapter.
   a. What kinds of things did your mother do when you were younger that facilitated your peer relationships (for instance, host birthday parties, invite other children to lunch, play baseball with you and your friends)? What did your father do?
   b. What do you think you have learned about peer relationships from each of your parents? If you are from a single-parent family, what other adults in your childhood were influential in regard to your peer relationships? How has the role of your parents in your peer relationships changed over time?

Homework Assignment

1. Arrange to spend several hours with parents and young children. The setting may be a neighborhood park or playground on a Saturday afternoon, or it may be early in the morning at a day care center, when parents are dropping off their children. Quietly observe the interactions of parents and children for several minutes. Observe several children and their families. You should spend at least 10 minutes watching each family. During your observations, record the following for each child and his or her family:
   a. In what kinds of activities do the parents and child participate (for example, physical play, pretend play)?
   b. What kinds of things do the parents do to help their child interact with other children (for example, do the parents talk to other children, do the parents start a game in which other children can participate)?
   c. What type of parenting style (authoritative, authoritarian, permissive, neglectful) do you think the parents are exhibiting? What might the child be learning from the parents' style?

Additional Readings

Duck, S. W. (Ed.). (1993). *Learning about relationships* [*Understanding relationship processes 2*]. Newbury Park, CA: Sage.

Ladd, G. W. (1991). Introduction: Family-peer relations during childhood: Pathways to competence and pathology? [Special issue]. *Journal of Social and Personal Relationships, 8,* 307–314.

MacDonald, K. (Ed.). (1993). *Parent-child play: Descriptions and implications.* Albany: State University of New York Press.

Parke, R. D., & Ladd, G. W. (1992). *Family-peer relationships: Modes of linkage.* Hillsdale, NJ: Erlbaum.

References

Adamson, L., & Bakeman, R. (1985). Affect and attention: Infants observed with mothers and peers. *Child Development, 56,* 582–593.

Asaranow, J. (1983). Children with peer adjustment problems: Sequential and non-sequential analyses of school behavior. *Journal of Consulting and Clinical Psychology, 51,* 709–717.

Asher, S. R., & Hymel, S. (1981). Children's social competence in peer relations: Sociometric and behavioral assessment. In J. D. Wine & M. D. Smye (Eds.), *Social competence* (pp. 125–157). New York: Guilford.

Asher, S. R., & Renshaw, P. D. (1981). Children without friends: Social knowledge and social skill training. In S. R. Asher & J. M. Gottman (Eds.), *The development of children's friendships* (pp. 273–296). New York: Cambridge University Press.

Bandura, A. (1986). *Social foundations of thought and action: A social cognitive theory.* Englewood Cliffs, NJ: Prentice-Hall.

Baumrind, D. (1967). Child care practices anteceding three patterns of preschool behavior. *Genetic Psychology Monographs, 75,* 43–88.

Baumrind, D. (1973). The development of instrumental competence through socialization. In A. Pick (Ed.), *Minnesota symposia on child psychology* (Vol. 7, pp. 3–46). Minneapolis: University of Minnesota Press.

Belsky, J. (1984). The determinants of parenting: A process model. *Child Development, 55,* 83–96.

Berndt, T. J. (1986). Children's comments about their friendships. In M. Perlmutter (Ed.), *Cognitive perspectives on children's social and behavioral development: Minnesota symposia on child psychology* (Vol. 18, pp. 189–212). Hillsdale, NJ: Erlbaum.

Berndt, T. J. (1989). Contributions of peer relationships to children's development. In T. J. Berndt & G. W. Ladd (Eds.), *Peer relationships in child development* (pp. 407–416). New York: Wiley.

Bhavnagri, N. P., & Parke, R. D. (1991). Parents as direct facilitators of children's peer relationships: Effects of age of child and sex of parent. *Journal of Social and Personal Relationships, 8,* 423–440.

Bretherton, I. (1985). Attachment theory: Retrospect and prospect. In I. Bretherton & E. Waters (Eds.), Growing points of attachment theory and research. *Monographs of the Society for Research in Child Development, 50* (Serial No. 209).

Brownell, C. A., & Brown, E. (1992). Peers and play in infants and toddlers. In V. Van Hasselt & M. Hersen (Eds.), *Handbook of social development: A lifespan perspective* (pp. 183–200). New York: Plenum.

Carson, J., Burks, V., & Parke, R. D. (1993). Parent-child physical play: Determinants and consequences. In K. MacDonald (Ed.), *Parent–child play: Descriptions and implications* (pp. 197–220). New York: State University Press.

Cassidy, J., & Asher, S. R. (1992). Loneliness and peer relations in young children. *Child Development, 63,* 350–365.

Cohen, J. S., & Woody, E. (1991, April). *Maternal involvement in children's peer relationships: The contributions of mothers' experiences, values, and beliefs.* Paper presented at the Biennial Meeting of the Society for Research in Child Development, Seattle.

Cohn, D. A., Patterson, C. J., & Christopoulos, C. (1991). The family and children's peer relations. *Journal of Social and Personal Relationships, 8,* 347–362.

Coie, J. D., Dodge, K. A., & Kupersmidt, J. (1990). Peer group behavior and social status. In S. R. Asher & J. D. Coie (Eds.), *Peer rejection in childhood* (pp. 17–59). New York: Cambridge University Press.

Crick, N. R., & Ladd, G. W. (1990). Children's perceptions of the outcomes of social strategies: Do the ends justify being mean? *Developmental Psychology, 26,* 612–620.

Dodge, K. A., Bates, J. E., & Pettit, G. S. (1990). Mechanisms in the cycle of violence. *Science, 250,* 1678–1683.

Dodge, K. A., Coie, J. D., Pettit, G. S., & Price, J. M. (1990). Peer status and aggression in boys' groups: Developmental-contextual analyses. *Child Development, 61,* 1289–1309.

Dodge, K. A., Pettit, G. S., McClaskey, C. L., & Brown, M. M. (1986). Social competence in children. *Monographs of the Society for Research in Child Development, 51* (2, Serial No. 213).

Elicker, J., Englund, M., & Sroufe, L. A. (1992). Predicting peer competence and peer relationships in childhood from early parent-child relationships. In R. D. Parke & G. W. Ladd (Eds.), *Family-peer relations: Modes of linkage* (pp. 77–106). Hillsdale, NJ: Lawrence Erlbaum.

Finnie, V., & Russell, A. (1988). Preschool children's social status and their mothers' behavior and knowledge in the supervisory role. *Developmental Psychology, 24,* 789–801.

Furman, W., & Buhrmester, D. (1985). Children's perceptions of the personal relationships in their social networks. *Developmental Psychology, 21,* 1016–1024.

Hart, C. H., DeWolf, M., & Burts, D. C. (1993). Parental disciplinary strategies and preschoolers' play behavior in playground settings. In C. H. Hart (Ed.), *Children on playgrounds; Research perspectives and applications* (pp. 271–313). Albany: State University of New York Press.

Hartup, W. W. (1989). Social relationships and their developmental significance. *American Psychologist, 44,* 120–126.

Hazen, N. L., & Black, B. (1989). Preschool peer communication skills: The role of social status and interaction context. *Child Development, 60,* 867–876.

Howes, C. (1987). Social competence with peers in young children: Developmental sequences. *Developmental Review, 7,* 252–272.

Howes, C. (1988). Peer interaction of young children. *Monographs of the Society for Research in Child Development, 53,* 1–78.

Isabella, R. A., & Belsky, J. (1991). Interactional synchrony and the origins of infant-mother attachment: A replication study. *Child Development, 63,* 373–384.

Kupersmidt, J. B., & Coie, J. D. (1990). Preadolescent peer status, aggression, and school adjustment as predictors of externalizing problems in adolescence. *Child Development, 61,* 1350–1362.

Ladd, G. W., & Crick, N. R. (1989). Probing the psychological environment: Children's cognitions, perceptions, and feelings in the peer culture. In M. L.

Maehr and C. Ames (Eds.), *Advances in motivation and achievement, Vol. 6* (pp. 1–44). Greenwich, CT: JAI Press.

Ladd, G. W., & Golter, B. S. (1988). Parents' management of preschoolers' peer relations: Is it related to children's social competence? *Developmental Psychology, 24*, 109–117.

Ladd, G. W., LeSieur, K. D., & Profilet, S. M. (1993). Direct parental influences on young children's peer relations. In S. Duck (Ed.), *Learning about relationships [Understanding relationship processes 2]*. (pp. 152-183). Newbury Park, CA: Sage.

Ladd, G. W., & Price, J. M. (1987). Predicting children's social and school adjustment following the transition from preschool to kindergarten. *Child Development, 58*, 1168–1189.

Ladd, G. W., Profilet, S. M., & Hart, C. H. (1992). Parents' management of children's peer relations: Facilitating and supervising children's activities in the peer culture. In R. D. Parke & G. W. Ladd (Eds.), *Family-peer relations: Modes of linkage*. Hillsdale, NJ: Erlbaum.

Lamb, M. E., & Nash, A. (1989). Infant-mother attachment, sociability, and peer competence. In T. J. Berndt & G. W. Ladd (Eds.), *Peer relationships in child development* (pp. 219–245). New York: Wiley.

Lindsey, E., Mize, J., & Pettit, G. S. (1993). *Children's play with fathers and peers: Parallels in content and style*. Unpublished manuscript, Auburn University.

Maccoby, E. E., & Martin, J. A. (1983). Socialization in the context of the family: Parent-child interaction. In E. M. Hetherington (Ed.), *Handbook of Child Psychology. Vol. 4: Socialization, Personality, and Social Development* (pp. 1–101). New York: Wiley.

MacDonald, K. (1987). Parent-child physical play with rejected, neglected, and popular boys. *Developmental Psychology, 23*, 705–711.

MacDonald, K. (1993). *Parent-child play: Descriptions and implications*. New York: State University of New York Press.

MacDonald, K., & Parke, R. D. (1984). Bridging the gap: Parent-child play interaction and peer interactive competence. *Child Development, 55*, 1265–1277.

Meese, D. R., Mize, J., & Pettit, G. S. (1993). *Assessing social cognitive skills in preschool children: Measures development and initial validation*. Unpublished manuscript, Auburn University.

Miller, L. C., Lechner, R. E., & Rugs, D. (1985). Development of conversational responsiveness: Preschoolers' use of responsive listener cues and relevant comments. *Developmental Psychology, 21*, 473–480.

Mills, R. S. L., & Rubin, K. H. (1992). A longitudinal study of maternal beliefs about children's social behavior. *Merrill-Palmer Quarterly, 38*, 494–512.

Mize, J. (1994). Coaching preschool children in social skills: A cognitive-social learning curriculum. In G. Cartledge & J. F. Milburn (Eds.), *Teaching social skills to children: Innovative approaches* (3rd ed.). New York: Pergamon.

Mize, J., & Ladd, G. W. (1988). Predicting preschoolers' peer behavior and status from their interpersonal strategies: A comparison of verbal and enactive responses to hypothetical social dilemmas. *Developmental Psychology, 24*, 782–788.

Mize, J., & Ladd, G. W. (1990). A cognitive-social learning approach to social skill training with low-status preschool children. *Developmental Psychology, 26,* 388–397.

Mize, J., Pettit, G. S., & Brown, E. G. (in press). Determinants of mothers' active supervision of their children's peer relations: The interactive roles of beliefs, knowledge, and perceptions. *Developmental Psychology.*

Mize, J., Pettit, G. S., Lindsey, E., & Laird, R. (1993). *Mothers' coaching of social skills and children's peer competence: Independent contributions of content and style.* Paper presented as part of the symposium "Learning lessons about peer relationships: How parents intentionally teach their children social skills" at the biennial meeting of the Society for Research in Child Development, New Orleans.

Parke, R. D. (1992). Epilogue: Remaining issues and future trends in the study of family-peer relationships. In R. D. Parke & G. W. Ladd (Eds.), *Family-peer relationships: Modes of linkage* (pp. 255-281). Hillsdale, NJ: Erlbaum.

Parke, R. D., & Bhavnagri, N. P. (1989). Parents as managers of children's peer relationships. In D. Belle (Ed.), *Children's social networks and social supports* (pp. 241–259). New York: Wiley.

Parke, R. D., & Ladd, G. W. (1992). *Family-peer relationships: Modes of linkage.* Hillsdale, NJ: Lawrence Erlbaum.

Parke, R. D., MacDonald, K. B., Beitel, A., & Bhavnagri, N. (1988). The role of the family in the development of peer relationships. In R. Peters & R. J. McMahon (Eds.), *Social learning and systems approaches to marriage and family* (pp. 17–44). New York: Bruner/Mazel.

Parker, J. G., & Gottman, J. M. (1989). Social and emotional development in a relational context: Friendship interaction from early childhood to adolescence. In T. J. Berndt & G. W. Ladd (Eds.), *Peer relationships in child development* (pp. 95–131). New York: Wiley.

Patterson, C. J., Cohn, D. A., & Kao, B. T. (1989). Maternal warmth as a protective factor against risks associated with peer rejection among children. *Development and Psychopathology, 1,* 21–38.

Patterson, C. J., Kupersmidt, J. S., & Vaden, N. A. (1990). Income level, gender, ethnicity, and household composition as predictors of children's school based competence. *Child Development, 61,* 485–494.

Patterson, G. R. (1982). *Coercive family process.* Eugene, OR: Castalia.

Perry, D. G., Perry, L. C., & Rasmussen, P. (1986). Cognitive social learning mediators of aggression. *Child Development, 57,* 700–711.

Pettit, G. S., Dodge, K. A., & Brown, M. (1988). Early family experience, social problem solving patterns, and children's social competence. *Child Development, 59,* 107–120.

Pettit, G. S., & Harrist, A. W. (1993). Children's aggressive and socially unskilled playground behavior with peers: Origins in early family relations. In C. H. Hart (Ed.), *Children on playgrounds: Research perspectives and applications* (pp. 240–270). Albany: State University of New York Press.

Pettit, G. S., Harrist, A. W., Bates, J. E., & Dodge, K. A. (1991). Family interaction, social cognition, and children's subsequent relations with peers at kindergarten. *Journal of Social and Personal Relationships, 8,* 383–402.

Pettit, G. S., & Mize, J. (1993). Substance and style: Understanding the ways in which parents teach children about social relationships. In S. W. Duck (Ed.), *Learning about relationships* [*Understanding relationship processes 2*]. (pp. 118–151). Newbury Park, CA: Sage.

Putallaz, M. (1987). Maternal behavior and children's sociometric status. *Child Development, 58,* 324–340.

Putallaz, M., Costanzo, P. R., & Klein, T. P. (1993). Parental childhood social experiences and their effects on children's relationships. In S. W. Duck (Ed.), *Learning about relationships* [*Understanding relationship processes 2*]. (pp. 63–97). Newbury Park, CA: Sage.

Putallaz, M., Costanzo, P. R., & Smith, R. B. (1991). Maternal recollections of childhood peer relationships: Implications for their children's social competence. *Journal of Social and Personal Relationships, 8,* 403–422.

Putallaz, M., & Heflin, A. H. (1990). Parent-child interaction. In S. R. Asher & J. D. Coie (Eds.), *Peer rejection in childhood* (pp. 189–216). New York: Cambridge University Press.

Rubin, Z. (1980). *Children's friendships.* Cambridge, MA: Harvard University Press.

Rubin, Z., & Sloman, J. (1984). How parents influence their children's relationships. In M. Lewis (Ed.), *Beyond the dyad* (pp. 223–250). New York: Plenum.

Russell, A., & Finnie, V. (1990). Preschool children's social status and maternal instructions to assist group entry. *Developmental Psychology, 26,* 603–611.

Russell, G., & Russell, A. (1987). Mother-child and father-child relationships in middle childhood. *Child Development, 58,* 1573–1585.

Sinclair, J. J., Pettit, G. S., Harrist, A. W., Dodge, K. A., & Bates, J. E. (in press). Encounters with aggressive peers in early childhood: Frequency, age differences, and correlates of risk for behavior problems. *International Journal of Behavioral Development.*

Wahler, R. G. (1993). *Child conduct problems: Disorders in conduct or social continuity.* Unpublished manuscript, University of Tennessee.

Weiss, B., Dodge, K. A., Bates, J. E., & Pettit, G. S. (1992). Some consequences of early harsh discipline: Child aggression and a maladaptive social information processing style. *Child Development, 63,* 1321–1335.

Glossary

Aggression   Intentional physical or verbal behaviors directed toward another person or object with the intent to inflict damage

Attachment   An enduring emotional tie (for instance, between infant and caregiver) that is established through repeated interaction over time

Authoritarian   A parenting style characterized by parents' harsh, controlling behavior and a lack of responsiveness to their children's wishes

Authoritative   A parenting style characterized by parents' being firm in setting limits yet flexible in their attitudes, encouraging independence and high levels of communication

Circumspection   Awareness of and sensitivity to environmental and social cues

Coaching   Parental instruction and advice given to children about issues related to peers and peer relationships

Cognitive-social learning theory   A theory associated with A. Bandura that stresses the role of cognitive processes in social behavior

Internal working model   A set of generalized expectations about self and others that is carried forward into later childhood

Neglectful   A parenting style characterized by parental indifference

Orchestration   A form of parental management in which parents specifically set out to arrange and supervise their children's peer activities

Permissive   A parenting style characterized by parents' failure to set firm limits or require appropriately mature behavior of their children

Prosocial behavior   Giving or sharing objects, time, or goods with others

Protective factor   A characteristic or condition that promotes or maintains healthy development, even in the face of adverse circumstances

Social-cognitive processes   Underlying knowledge, thoughts, and feelings that guide children's behavior in social situations

Socialization   The acquisition by the child of the rules and values of society

Socially competent   Characterized by the ability to function at a high level within the give and take of peer interaction; socially competent children are generally highly regarded by their peers

Social transmission   The process by which parents convey messages to their children about what to expect and how to behave in interpersonal relationships

Sociometric assessment   Evaluation procedure in which children's judgments of each other are sought

Synchrony   The degree to which interactive partners are sensitive to one another's social cues and engage in smooth and reciprocated exchanges

Temperament   The individual mix of dispositional characteristics, such as activity level, moods, and emotional responsiveness, that characterize a person's behavioral style

Turnabout   A form of dyadic play in which one partner accepts or redirects the other's play suggestion

7

Peer Relations During Middle Childhood

Doran C. French
Lewis and Clark College

Marion K. Underwood
Reed College

*A*s you saw in Chapter 6, parents play an important role in shaping a child's early peer interactions. As the growing child spends more time outside the home
in the company of peers, however, playground and classroom
experiences, memberships in large groups, and other peer-group
influences become increasingly important. This chapter explores
some of the interpersonal factors that shape our social lives in
middle childhood: friend networks, social status, and peer acceptance or rejection.

NV & SD

Chapter Outline

- Friends and Networks
- Peer Social Status
- Summary

Upon entering elementary school, children are brought together with
a larger number of same-age peers than they ordinarily encountered in day
care or preschool. The exposure to this peer culture is an important developmental step in the movement from parent-child relations to the independently selected friendships of adulthood. Within this peer culture, children are very concerned with their friendships, the social networks within
which they are involved, and their status within the peer group. We will
focus on these aspects of peer relationships.

In this chapter, the term *friendship* refers to ongoing, close, mutual,
and dyadic (paired) relationships. Children interact with a number of
other peers who are playmates or acquaintances but not necessarily friends.
Their behavior with these individuals differs in important respects from
that seen with friends. Children have different degrees of involvement
with peers in their social environment—with friends, playmates, acquaintances, and perhaps enemies. We will use the term **peer network** to describe this larger group of peers.

FRIENDS AND NETWORKS

Characteristics of Childhood Friendships and Peer Networks

As Chapter 6 showed, children develop friendship relations as early as the third year of life. The amount of time that is spent interacting with peers increases during the childhood years, moving to over 40% between ages 7 and 11 (Hartup, 1983). Furthermore, friendships during childhood are quite stable. Berndt and Hoyle (1985) found that over 50% of 7-year-olds' friendships and over 70% of 10-year-olds' friendships were stable from the fall to the next spring of an academic year. When there are disruptions that may be caused by school moves and other such events, it takes time for children to develop new friendships (Berndt, 1987), but the patterns of choice are predictable. Children most often establish friendships with others of the same sex. Preference for same-sex interaction begins during preschool and becomes even more intense during middle childhood (Maccoby, 1990). Children are likely to hide the opposite-sex friendships that they have because of peer pressure (Gottman, 1986). Those opposite-sex friendships that they do have are more likely to occur in the neighborhood and in youth organizations than in school.

Peer networks are also segregated by sex. This gender segregation is sufficiently extreme during the elementary age years to lead Thorne (1986) to argue that girls and boys live in separate social worlds. As above, the mechanism that maintains the separation of these worlds is peer pressure (Thorne, 1986):

> In the lunchroom, when the two second grade tables were filling, a high status boy walked by the inside table, which had a scattering of both boys and girls, and said loudly, "Ooooo, too many girls," as he headed for a seat at the far table. The boys at the inside table picked up their trays and moved, and no other boy sat at the inside table, which the pronouncement had effectively made taboo. (p. 171)

Although close friendships between boys and girls during middle childhood are rare, children talk about the other sex with intense interest and play a variety of chasing or "cootie" games, which Thorne (1986) has called "rituals of pollution." Gottman and Mettetal (1986, p. 196) observed a pair of newly acquainted 10-year-old girls discussing chasing boys:

A: We chase boys.

B: We don't play shadow tag when it's sunny, which it rarely is.

A: We do. Except for chasing boys and playing chicken fights. Sometimes we play Kill the Guy.

B: Last year at our school they played Kill the Guy and one kid almost *did* get killed. He was knocked down and broke both of his legs and a hip and was out of school for almost half the year.

A: Oh well, we don't play Kill the Guy as rough. You know we don't use guns and ropes and sledgehammers.

B: They weren't using them neither.

A: We keep it down to hammers and chains.

The play groups of boys and girls also frequently differ in size. Girls are more likely to play in groups of two or three, whereas boys are more likely to be in larger groups (Waldrop & Halverson, 1975). The groups of boys are also likely to be easier to enter and less exclusive than those of girls (Eder & Hallinan, 1978). Boys' groups are more likely than those of girls to be organized around the task of completing a structured game with rules and clear winners and losers. Lever (1976) found that 65% of the play activities of fifth-grade boys and 35% of those of fifth-grade girls in a school setting involved such structured activity. Boys' and girls' friendships and social networks differ on other dimensions as well: Boys exhibit more concern with issues of dominance (Maccoby 1990), which is expressed through verbal as well as physical means; and boys are more likely to play in public areas, whereas girls are more likely to interact in the home.

In addition to choosing playmates of the same sex, children most frequently establish friendships with individuals of their approximate age. However, in certain contexts, children do interact extensively with peers who are older or younger than themselves (French, 1987). Mixed-age interaction is particularly likely to occur in neighborhood settings where there is a low density of same-age peers and where children are not separated into groups based on age (Ellis, Rogoff, & Cromer, 1981). Age segregation also appears to be more extreme in modern industrial societies. In cultures in which people depend on hunting animals and gathering plants for subsistence, it is more typical for children to play in multi-age groups, which often include both sexes (Konner, 1991). When children of our culture do participate in multi-age groups, however, children of different ages typically fulfill different social roles. Children usually expect to receive leadership from older children and are most likely to see younger children as targets of altruism or perhaps manipulation. Friendship relations are expected to occur between age-mates (French, 1984).

Although children typically establish friendships with age-mates, there are notable exceptions. Children who are socially incompetent (Ladd, 1983) and children

Boys' play activities are often athletic games that are played in public, with clear rules and winners and losers.

who are mentally retarded (Strain, 1984) are likely to develop friendships with individuals younger in chronological age than themselves. This phenomenon suggests that similarity of developmental level and social skill may be more important than similarity of chronological age in determining friendships.

Functions of Friendship

Peers provide children with experiences different from those derived from relationships with adults. In many respects, children participate unequally in adult-child relationships. The adult frequently controls the interaction, being largely responsible for negotiating the initiation, conduct, and termination of the interaction and resolving any conflicts that arise. Peers, on the other hand, approach interactions as equals, and the parties make roughly similar contributions. Because neither child holds more formal power than the other, decisions require negotiation, and conflicts must be resolved. Peer relationships are thus more symmetrical and less hierarchically organized than are adult-child relationships (Youniss, 1980).

Developmental theorists such as Jean Piaget (1932) and the neo-psychoanalytic theorist Harry Stack Sullivan (1953) argued that children derive benefits from interactions with peers that they do not gain from their relationships with adults. Piaget highlighted the equal nature of peer interaction, which he thought of as essential for the child's developing sense of morality. Sullivan emphasized the importance of friendships for the child's sense of self, for understanding the perspectives of others, and for establishing a foundation for the development of intimacy. These points are illustrated in the following often cited quotation (Sullivan, 1953, pp. 245–246):

> If you look very closely at one of your children when he finally finds a chum—sometime between eight and a half and ten—you will discover something very different in the relationship—namely, that your child begins to develop a real sensitivity to what matters to another person. Preadolescence is marked by the coming of the integrating tendencies which, when they are completely developed, we call love, or, to say it another way, by the manifestation of the need for interpersonal intimacy.

Recent researchers have continued to emphasize the unique importance of children's friendships. Hartup (1992) outlined four major functions of children's friendship:

1. Friendships serve as *emotional resources,* to the extent that they provide children with support for meeting challenges and coping with adversity. In extreme cases of stress or deprivation, attachment to

peers can partially compensate for inadequate attachment to parents.

2. Friendships can serve as *cognitive resources*. Children can be effective peer tutors and participate well in cooperative learning activities. In nonschool settings, peers provide information and instruction in social skills and appropriate behavior.

3. Peer relationships serve as *contexts* within which important social competencies emerge, including anger control, conflict management, sexual roles and behavior, and development of cooperation and intimacy.

4. Building upon the ideas of Sullivan discussed above, friendships are *precursors of later relationships*. The development of successful childhood friendships foreshadows success in subsequent relationships with friends, siblings, and romantic partners.

Development of Friendships

How do friendships develop during the childhood years? Do they develop as a result of changes in children's *understanding* as they get older? Researchers have attempted to answer this question in two ways. In one approach, children are asked to describe their friends. Their descriptions are categorized to assess the basis of friendship at different ages. A second approach has been to observe children and compare the interactions of friends and of acquaintances.

Children's Conceptions of Friendships   Bigelow (1977) asked Canadian and Scottish children between the ages of 6 and 14 to write essays about what they expect from their best friends. Raters coded the major themes presented in these essays by children of different ages. The youngest children tended to focus on proximity and common activities (for example, "We live in the same neighborhood and we like art"). Children in the middle age group focused on admiration of the character of another child (for example, "She is someone who is nice and honest"). Finally, those in the oldest group discussed friendships in terms of empathy, understanding, and self-disclosure (for example, "We are both introverted, have the same perverted sense of humor, and have long conversations about life"). Thus as children get older, their descriptions of friendships move from a focus on observable characteristics to a focus on internalized psychological features.

Other researchers have found similar developmental changes in children's beliefs about friends. For example, Berndt (1981b) conducted open-ended interviews with children of different ages, asking them, "How do you know someone is your friend?" and "What would make you decide not to be friends with someone anymore?" Five-year-old children responded with answers such as "He calls me" or "She plays with me," suggesting that they base friendship primarily on association and participation in common activity. Children of this age also focus on positive actions as well as the absence of negative behavior. Thus friends are expected to be nice to each other and not fight. The focus on friends' behavior becomes even more salient for older children. Twelve-year-olds expect friends to demonstrate intimacy, trust, and loyalty, whereas six-year-olds rarely mention these qualities.

Similar developmental changes occur in the child's understanding of reciprocity. Youniss (1980) explored the development of reciprocity in relationships by interviewing children aged 6 to 8, 9 to 11, and 12 to 14 regarding kindness, unkindness, friendship, initiating friendships, and reactions to unkind actions of friends. The youngest children appear to use a principle of direct reciprocity whereby friends share and help each other to an equivalent extent ("He gives me cookies and I give him some candy"). Children reported that unkindness means refusal to share, playing unfairly, or aggression. In contrast to the younger children's endorsement of direct reciprocity, children ages 9 to 11 are more likely to modify the extent to which they would share or help as a function of the needs of the other participant ("I give her part of my sandwich if she forgets her lunch"). Children of this age are concerned with removing inequalities between themselves and friends and with developing cooperative behavior in which they coordinate their actions to achieve some purpose. Finally, children aged 12 to 14 expand this notion of equality to include shared personalities and intimacy: "When someone found out they were adopted . . . try to cheer them up. Make them feel better." "He's a loner . . . help him to make friendships [and] learn to get along" (Youniss, 1980, pp. 70–71).

Findings from these and other studies of children's understanding of friendships and reciprocity (for example, Selman, 1981) suggest that children develop increasingly complex and differentiated views of friendship. This development in social understanding corresponds to the increasingly complex way they view the physical world, as well as their increased capacity to understand the perspectives of others (Flavell, Miller, & Miller, 1993).

Behavior with Friends   Changes in children's understanding of social relationships are paralleled by changes in their social behavior. Friendship relationships throughout childhood feature cooperation and engagement in activities. As children move into adolescence, their interactions are focused to a greater extent on achievement of intimacy (Gottman & Mettetal, 1986). Throughout, we see that children's behavior with friends is strongly dependent upon the social context.

In general, friends are more socially responsive to each other than are nonfriends. Foot, Chapman, and Smith (1977) compared the reactions of friends and acquaintances as they watched humorous cartoons. Friends laughed more frequently and intensely, smiled more, and gazed more at each other than did acquaintances. Newcomb, Brady, and Hartup (1979) obtained similar results from their observation of 6- and 9-year-old friends and acquaintances building towers with wooden blocks. Friends talked, laughed, and teased more than did acquaintances.

Under some circumstances, however, childhood friends may be less cooperative than nonfriends. Berndt, Hawkins, and Hoyle (1986) asked pairs of 9-year-old children to jointly complete a task requiring the coloring of geometric shapes. Some of these children were stable friends, whereas the friendship of others had dissolved. To establish competition, the child who completed the most figures obtained two nickels whereas the other child received one. Under these competitive conditions, 9-year-old friends shared less than nonfriends. Thus under competitive conditions in which sharing would be disadvantageous to maintenance of equity, friends may be even more competitive than nonfriends.

Friends also exhibit conflicts. Selman (1981, p. 242) observed an example of conflict in a school cafeteria at a day school for troubled children.

> Throughout lunch, Marvin, age eight, has been playing with a new Battlestar Galactica rocket. Joey, age nine, is manifesting an intense interest in using Marvin's rocket.

> *Joey:* Marvin, let me play with your rocket and I'll do anything you want.
> *Marvin:* Get me another dessert.
> *Joey:* (*Returning with a second orange*) Now can I play with your rocket?
> *Marvin:* Nope.
> *Joey:* If you let me use your rocket, I'll be your . . . Let me use it because I *am* your friend.
> *Marvin:* (*Matter-of-factly*) You're not my friend.
> *Joey:* (*Losing control, screaming until red in the face*) Yes, I am. I *am* your friend! Yes, I *am*! I'll *blast* you if you say I'm not your friend!

Because conflicts such as this are a part of most childhood relationships, the ability to deal with conflict is an important component of successful friendships (Gottman & Parker, 1986). In some contexts, friends are more likely to have conflicts than are acquaintances.

Hartup, French, Laursen, Johnston, and Ogawa (1993) developed a paradigm to observe conflicts in children. Two 9- to 10-year-old children (either friends or acquaintances) came to a research trailer and were taken to different rooms by researchers. Each was then taught rules to "Snake Pit," a board game devised by the experimenters, but each was taught a different set of rules. For example, whereas one member of the pair was taught that the rules provided for an extra turn upon landing on another player, the other member was taught that the player landed upon was sent back to the beginning. After being taught these rules, the children were placed together and asked to play the game. As expected, numerous conflicts arose. Many of these were caused by the rule discrepancies, but others arose from misunderstandings of aspects of the game or confusion about turn taking. Friends had more frequent, intense, and longer conflicts than acquaintances.

Perhaps friends have more intense disagreements because conflicts provide opportunity to resolve issues and strengthen their relationship. Nelson and Aboud (1985) found that the greater duration and intensity of conflicts among friends paid off in successful resolution. When issues over which conflicts had arisen emerged again, friends were less likely to argue about them than were nonfriends, which suggests that the friends had resolved the issues during their initial conflict.

Conflict among friends also depends upon context. In the study by Hartup and his colleagues (1993) described above, children were in a sense trapped in the same room with a task (that is, the game) to complete. In many other naturalistic contexts (such as on a playground or in a neighborhood), however, there is freedom to engage or disengage. Under these conditions, friends appear less likely than acquaintances to engage in conflict, often temporarily leaving the interaction when potential conflicts arise (Hartup, Laursen, Stewart, & Eastenson, 1988). This suggests that friends manage their behavior to minimize conflict when they are able to do so.

Researchers have also explored the developmental changes in children's understanding of the role of conflict within relationships. Young children see sharing and arguing as incompatible, whereas adolescents understand that relationships simultaneously include both cooperative and conflictual elements (Berndt & Perry, 1986).

Gottman and Mettetal (1986) provide the most comprehensive developmental theory of childhood friendships. They argue that different social processes are central to relationships at particular points in the life span. Preschoolers value developing and maintaining elaborate fantasy play. Fantasy play declines from preschool to middle childhood and becomes less important in promoting relationships.

During the elementary school period, children value inclusion in the same-sex peer group. Children affirm this sense of belonging by gossiping about those who violate group norms. Gottman and Mettetal (1986, p. 215) observed two girls who were becoming acquainted discussing a boy.

> *A:* Is Chip Buckley still short?
> *B:* Yes, he is very short.
> *A:* *(Giggle.)*
> *B:* Everybody says he comes out of a jar.
> *A:* Oh.
> *B:* It's because . . .
> *A:* We used to call him Cookie Buckley. Don't tell him this, but I kinda miss him.

B: You, did you used to like him?
A: No, but you know it's boring without him.
B: Hmm.

Gossip appears to serve several purposes, including promotion of information exchange about rules and expectations, social comparison, and limited self-disclosure. Additional self-disclosure displayed by children of this age is conveyed through discussion of embarrassing situations. Discussions of intimacy and direct self-disclosure are seen infrequently during this childhood period, however. Conversations such as the one below rarely occur until adolescence (Gottman & Mettetal, 1986, p. 218).

A: I feel kinda icky about the past two weeks. . . .
B: What? What in the past two weeks do you feel icky about?
A: It was like "Hi, Jane," "Hi, Suzie," *(giggle)* you know *(giggle).*
B: Yeah.
A: "Hi, Jane," "Hi, Suzie."
B: We didn't communicate. I haven't been communicating with much of anybody. . . .
A: I understand that, but I felt like, you know, Janet was . . .
B: Janet had taken your place.
A: Yeah, that's what I felt like.
B: Janet's not gonna take your place, kiddo *(sigh)*. How many times do I have to tell you that?
A: I'm insecure, you know.
B: I know.

Development in the way that children behave with peers roughly parallels their conceptions of relationships. The interaction of young children largely focuses on maintaining connectedness and managing the conflict that could potentially disrupt play. As children become older, their social interaction concerns understanding rules and defining their place in the peer group (through gossip and limited self-disclosure), although engagement in mutually enjoyable activity continues to be important. As children move toward adolescence, self-exploration through self-disclosure and feedback becomes increasingly important; this process builds upon the activity aspects of younger children's relationships.

PEER SOCIAL STATUS

Social Status Classification

In addition to valuing having friends and belonging to social networks, children are also concerned about their level of acceptance by the larger peer groups within which they participate (such as classrooms, athletic teams, youth groups, and the like). To assess acceptance, many researchers

---

Box 1　　　　**The Ethics of Sociometric Testing**

Several investigators have questioned whether the administration of sociometric measures, particularly those involving negative nominations, might be harmful for children (Asher & Hymel, 1981). Some worry that asking children who they like least might lead to even more negative behavior toward children with low peer acceptance. To guard against this possibility, researchers who collect sociometric measures typically gain children's informed consent to participate and make it easy for children to decline, schedule sociometric data collection to immediately precede a structured academic activity so that children will have less opportunity to discuss their nominations, and stress the importance of children's keeping their votes confidential (Bell-Dolan & Wessler, 1993).

The effects of sociometric status assessment have been assessed directly in several studies. Bell-Dolan, Foster, and Sikora (1989) observed the subsequent peer interactions of two groups of children: one who completed a positive and negative nomination sociometric procedure and a control group who gave positive and negative nominations for school activities. There was no evidence of negative effects of participating in the sociometric testing; negative behavior toward disliked peers did not increase, and children did not report feeling more lonely or unhappy after taking part in the testing. Although these results are encouraging, it is important that researchers using these procedures remain sensitive to potential risk and take all steps possible to minimize harm.

---

have relied on information obtained from members of the peer group. This choice reflects the fact that teachers and parents are only partially aware of the degree to which a particular child is liked by other children (Coie & Dodge, 1988). **Sociometric status** refers to the degree of a child's social acceptance by a group, as determined by nominations or ratings from other group members. (See Chapter 6 for details.)

To assess sociometric status, researchers ask individuals in some defined group, generally a classroom, to nominate individuals who fit specific descriptions. The children in a classroom may be asked to specify the classmates they most like to play with or who are their best friends; children thus named obtain **positive nominations.** The children may then be asked to specify the classmates they *least* like to play with; those children obtain **negative nominations.** (Asking children to provide negative nominations raises some ethical concerns; see Box 1 for a discussion of the issue.) Researchers may also ask children to nominate peers for a variety of items to assess specific behaviors: aggressive behavior ("Starts fights") and prosocial behavior ("Good leader" or "Cooperative"), for instance. Although one might expect that positive and negative sentiments are opposite each other, this is not the case. Positive and negative sociometric dimensions are only moderately correlated.

Researchers determine children's peer status by tabulating numbers of positive and negative nominations and assigning children to status groups. In the most commonly used classification system (Coie, Dodge, & Coppotelli, 1982), children are designated as having five types of peer status: *popular, rejected, neglected, controversial*, and *average*. Children in the **popular** group receive a high number of positive nominations and a low number of negative nominations. Children in the **rejected** group obtain an above average number of negative nominations and very few positive nominations. **Neglected** children receive very few nominations, positive or negative. Children classified as **controversial** receive above average numbers of both positive and negative nominations. Children in the average group have average numbers of positive and negative nominations. Using the Coie et al. (1982) system, most children (approximately 52%) are of average status or are unclassified. Other peer status groups include much smaller proportions of subjects: popular, around 12%; rejected, about 13%; neglected, 13%; and controversial, 7%.

Behavior of Children in Different Status Groups

It is important to remember that sociometric status refers to the child's status in the group and is not an observable characteristic of an individual child. There is substantial evidence, however, that children of different status groups tend to exhibit particular types of behaviors (Coie et al., 1982; Coie, Dodge, & Kupersmidt, 1990; Coie & Kupersmidt, 1983; Dodge, 1983). Researchers have focused on the relation between peer status and several types of behaviors: prosocial, aggressive, social-cognition, and group-entry behaviors.

Children classified as popular tend to be competent in a variety of ways; peers report that they are leaders, they help others, they are viewed as cooperative in group interactions, they have above average academic achievement, and they are good at sports (Bukowski & Newcomb, 1984; Coie et al., 1982). Popularity with peers does not appear to be strongly related to aggressive behavior; popular children receive average numbers of votes for "Starts fights" (Coie and Dodge, 1988). Overall, popular children appear to conform to social rules: They stay on task in the classroom, they know how to size up groups and enter them gracefully, and they refrain from highly aggressive behavior. As children move through elementary school, academic and athletic competence gain in importance as determinants of status, perhaps because older children engage in more social comparison related to achievement in these domains (Ruble, Boggiana, Feldman, & Loebl, 1980).

Peers identify two types of children who are actively disliked. Coie and Cillessen (1993) provided the following examples of these different types of rejected children. The first type of child we would label as *aggressive-rejected*, whereas the second type would be labeled *nonaggressive-rejected*.

> Consider Michael, for instance, an 8-year-old boy whose parents and school teacher have become very concerned about his frequent anger and aggression in interactions with other children. Michael tends to be bossy, dominating, and disruptive. He also frequently starts fights with other children. Often, he gets angry and upset with other children without adequate reason.
>
> A second example is Sean, another 8-year-old boy in Michael's school class. When other children come to school in an irritable mood, Sean is an easy victim for them to pick on. Other children do not seem to be very concerned when this happens. In fact, the other children often tease Sean and exclude him from their play. When Sean is around other children, he appears anxious and often says embarrassing things that make them uncomfortable being with him. (p. 89)

Approximately 50% of rejected children are aggressive and disruptive (French, 1988, 1990). These descriptions appear to be most typical of boys who are aggressive and rejected. It is important to note, however, that not all rejected children are aggressive and not all aggressive children are rejected (Coie, Belding, & Underwood, 1988).

Aggressive-rejected girls may engage in more subtle forms of aggression, such as facial sneers and manipulation of friendships (Crick & Grotpeter, 1993). Some theorists have argued that girls are more relationship oriented than boys (Gilligan, 1982), which suggests that girls will express anger and contempt toward one another by disrupting relationships (through such behaviors as gossiping and ostracism) and also that girls who do not interact much will not be well liked. Indeed, social withdrawal appears to be more strongly related to rejected status for girls in the later elementary years than for boys (Cantrell & Prinz, 1985; Ladd, 1983).

Children in the other rejected subgroup—those who are not aggressive—are quite different. Although they are disliked as much as aggressive-rejected children, they display few behavior problems. In fact, they appear to be quite compliant and they obey rules and

Children who are rejected by their peers can be either aggressive and bossy or compliant and quiet.

do well in school (French & Conrad, 1994). Researchers are currently trying to assess the reasons for their extreme unpopularity. A few of these children may be shy or withdrawn (Cillessen, van Ijzendoorn, van Lieshout, & Hartup, 1992); the rejection of others may be explained by a combination of their odd mannerisms, low physical attractiveness, and low interest or skill in athletics or childhood activities.

Children classified as neglected tend to have a very low social profile and interact infrequently with unfamiliar peers in initial encounters. Although it might make intuitive sense to assume that children in this group are shy, this does not appear to be the case (Coie et al., 1982). These children are also not seen by either parents or teachers as having serious discipline or mental health problems (French & Waas, 1986). The only consistent finding related to neglected status is that this group is consistently rated as below average on aggression. In a study of second- and fifth-graders, Carlson, Lahey, and Neeper (1984) found that peers rated neglected children as very unlikely to say that they could beat up everybody.

Developmental researchers have only limited information on the characteristics of controversial status children, in part because relatively few children fall into this category. These children are likely to have an extremely high social profile in that they talk frequently with peers and teachers and engage in humorous behavior that makes peers laugh (Dodge, 1983). Peers report that controversial children display a blend of some of the characteristics shown by popular and by rejected children (Coie et al., 1982). Like rejected children, they engage in aggressive and disruptive behavior, often seek help from teachers, and are frequently reprimanded by adults. Like popular children, they are viewed as good leaders.

Children in different status groups exhibit differences in social skill and competence. One approach to investigating these differences has been to observe children attempting to solve a complex social task, such as gaining entrance to an ongoing social interaction. This research is described in Box 2.

Social Cognition of Children in Different Status Groups

Popular children are skilled in determining the social intentions of others. Dodge, Murphy, and Buchsbaum (1984) showed children videotapes that depicted provoking situations such as a peer spilling paint on a picture; popular children were much better able to determine whether the provocation was intentional or accidental.

Aggressive-rejected children, on the other hand, seem to have trouble understanding the behavior of others. Dodge et al. (1984) found that these children have difficulty interpreting ambiguous social cues. When shown videotapes of anger-provoking situations, boys were less accurate in discriminating accidental and prosocial motives from hostile intentions. Aydin and Markova (1979) demonstrated that children with low peer ac-

Box 2

Children's Entry into Different Status Groups

One of the most useful approaches to studying the social skills of children in different status groups has been to observe them as they attempt to solve a difficult social problem. Martha Putallaz and her colleagues (Putallaz & Wasserman, 1990) conducted an ingenious set of studies exploring how children attempt to gain access to an ongoing interaction of other children. This is a problematic task for adults as well; consider the social competence and sensitivity required to merge into a group conversation at a party.

Putallaz and Gottman (1981a, 1981b) observed two children playing a game in a laboratory and the behavior of a third child who came into the play room after the game had been under way for 10 minutes. Popular children were more likely to be included and less likely to be ignored as they attempted to join groups. They entered groups by determining the interests and concerns of the dyad and then establishing themselves as sharing these concerns. In one example (Putallaz & Gottman, 1981b, p. 142), Matt, a popular child, joins the group by commenting on aspects of a word-naming board game in which children select words that begin with the indicated letter in one of three categories (animals, names, or jobs). The outcome of the interaction is that the other children include Matt in their play, eventually telling him it is his turn.

In contrast, socially rejected children appeared to have difficulty joining groups. These children waited longer to try to join and engaged in a type of anxious, hovering behavior. When they did try to make contact with the group, they were likely to talk about themselves, ask informational questions, and argue or disagree with group members. In the following example, Eric, an unpopular child, is ignored by the two group members as he talks about an incident that he was involved in during recess (Putallaz & Gottman, 1981, p.141).

> *Tom:*   Um . . . um . . .
> *Eric:*   Oh, you know . . . *(David makes a face and they laugh)* . . . you know I was playing with Glen. I hope you don't get mad at me. We're playing out there and Glen, he started to wrestle. I told him no so . . .
> *Tom:*   Monkey. Monkey. Hey, um monkey. Um, move ahead three spaces. It's your turn dumdum.
> *David:*   Hey, um M. Monkey.
> *Eric:*   Uh, Glen . . . poked, I poked his eye. I accidently poked Glen's eye and then he . . . he said he wouldn't take my apology, so Brian started getting mad at me so . . . and there I . . . Glen can see now . . . he said he couldn't see. Now he could see.

Box 2 continues

Box 2
(continued)

> David: I like this game.
> Tom: Okay. Okay.
>
> As occurred in the above example, rejected children are more likely than popular status children to be ignored by peer dyads they try to join. These studies illustrate status group differences in social skills. As might be expected, children with neglected peer status also tend to have difficulty joining peer social groups, waiting and engaging in hovering behavior prior to attempting to join (Putallaz & Gottman, 1981a).

ceptance tend to over-attribute hostility to peers. Dodge and colleagues have demonstrated repeatedly that children who are both rejected and aggressive show a strong bias toward hostile attributions. In summary, rejected children seem to have difficulty recognizing and abiding by norms for peer interaction—they behave aggressively, are disruptive in the classroom, misinterpret social cues, and have difficulty joining ongoing interactions among peers. Interestingly, neglected and rejected children are equally inaccurate in distinguishing hostile, accidental, and prosocial motives of peers (Dodge et al., 1984). Whereas in rejected children this misattribution often leads to aggressive behavior toward the provocateur, in neglected children the response can often be passivity and withdrawal (Dodge & Feldman, 1990).

A More Complicated Picture of Sociometric Status

The preceding discussion might appear to suggest that members of particular sociometric groups inevitably share certain characteristics—for instance, that rejected children are all very much like one another. Although individuals in status groups tend to exhibit some common behavior, peer status is not a trait and is not in and of itself a measure of behavior. More recent research has reinforced the idea that sociometric methods serve as valid measures of important social processes among peers, but it has also reminded us that the relation between social behavior and peer social status is complicated.

Although we organized the previous discussion by social status groups for convenience, we acknowledge that research should primarily focus on processes of relationships among children. Children of all status groups develop social relationships. Parker and Asher (1993) examined the relation between children's acceptance by the larger peer group and their quality of friendships and experience of loneliness. Many rejected children had best friends and were reasonably satisfied with the quality of their relationships, although their ratings of friendship quality were somewhat lower than those of other children. Other evidence suggests that rejected children are likely to affiliate with other rejected children (Ladd, 1983).

Causal Relation Between Status and Behavior   It is reasonable to look at the above characteristics of children in different status groups and assume that these characteristics are the cause of the peer acceptance and rejection. Thus it is possible that children become popular because they behave prosocially and rejected because they fight or exhibit inappropriate behavior. It is also possible, however, that assignment of social status by peers leads to differences in behavior. Perhaps the experience of social rejection is sufficiently frustrating and demoralizing to cause the child to behave aggressively. To disentangle cause and effect requires that researchers look at the development of relationships among individuals who have no previous history of interaction together.

In 1983, Coie and Kupersmidt examined the development of peer relationships in groups composed of four unacquainted fourth-grade boys. Sociometric status was assessed through nomination procedures in the boys' home school. They were assigned to groups made up of one member of each different status: rejected, popular, neglected, and average. They were driven separately to a laboratory play room for one play session per week for six weeks. Play sessions were videotaped, and the boys' social behaviors were observed and coded. On the way home from each play session, each boy was interviewed by his driver, including being asked whom he liked most in the group. In this way, the researchers were able to explore which behaviors were related to each boy's peer status at his home school as well as which characteristics were associated with his emerging social status in the new group.

Most boys reestablished their status position within the new group within three sessions. Furthermore, predictable differences were seen in the behavior of children in different status groups. For example, popular boys took leadership roles in reminding the other boys of rules and suggesting activities in times of indecision. Popular boys engaged in very little aggression and were very unlikely to be the targets of provocation. Popular and average boys engaged in similar amounts of talking and prosocial behavior. Rejected boys were highly talkative and active, were unlikely to stay on task or interact with group members, and frequently engaged in both physical and verbal abusive behavior. Neglected boys were the least talkative and interactive and the least likely to engage in physical or verbal aggressive behavior, and they were much more likely to respond to provocation by ignoring the other child or leaving the encounter.

Interestingly, the behavior of neglected boys depended heavily on whether the boys in the group were acquainted or not. (Several groups of boys who were familiar with one another were included in the study.)

Neglected boys in unfamiliar play groups were more talkative and interactive and engaged in more prosocial behavior than those in familiar groups. Coie and Kupersmidt (1983) propose that the fact that neglected children demonstrate skills in new social contexts explains why children in this status group are at less risk for later negative adjustment.

The finding that boys quickly reestablished their status in a new group suggests that they bring to new social situations a characteristic set of behaviors, skills, and interpersonal qualities that leads others to react to them in predictable fashion. It is important, however, to remember that social status is a product of opinions that are held by group members. Children may find greater social acceptance in some groups than in others. They may also find themselves locked into particular status positions based on their reputation and regardless of changes in their behavior.

Children's Reputational Biases   Hymel, Wagner, and Butler (1990) suggested that children make decisions about peers they like and dislike based not only on social behaviors they actually observe but also on their knowledge of a particular child's previous reputation. Once a child is socially rejected, this negative reputation may color perceptions of subsequent behavior. Reputational effects may become particularly pronounced in small communities or in contexts such as elementary schools, where children come to know one another over time. Research on children's emerging social status has confirmed that children respond to similar behaviors differently, depending on whether they are displayed by popular or rejected children. For example, Coie and Kupersmidt (1983) found that popular boys were the targets of less aversive behavior than were rejected or average boys. Dodge (1983) found that peers reacted more positively to the behavior of popular boys than they did to that of rejected boys, even when the behavior they engaged in was similar.

Hymel (1986) studied the effects of reputational biases by asking second-, fifth-, and tenth-grade children to make judgments about the behavior of familiar peers in hypothetical situations. She found that children judged popular children to be responsible for positive behaviors and minimized their responsibility for negative behavior. The reverse was true when the story protagonists were peers who were not well liked; children viewed rejected peers as much more blameworthy for negative behavior. This adds to the growing body of research evidence suggesting that peer social status is determined not only by social behavior but by social reputation: "It is not only *what* you do but *who* you are that counts" (Hymel, Wagner, & Butler, 1990, p. 174).

Behavioral Correlates of Sociometric Status Across Cultures
The great majority of investigators using sociometric measures have been working in North America, but a few cross-cultural studies are beginning to appear in the literature. Chen, Rubin, and Sun (1992) explored the re-

lationship between peer ratings of behavior and sociometric status in samples of Chinese and Canadian children. For the most part, similar behaviors were associated with peer status labels for the two samples; leadership was related to peer acceptance and aggressive-disruptive behavior was associated with social rejection. Interestingly, there was a difference between the Chinese and Canadian samples in the relation between nominations for shyness-sensitivity and sociometric status. In the Western sample, shyness-sensitivity was associated with social isolation, whereas for Chinese children, shyness-sensitivity was positively related to leadership and peer acceptance.

Although this research suggests that correlates of sociometric status may be somewhat similar across cultures, research on children in South America suggests that behaviors associated with peer status might differ with cultural context. Schaughency, Vannatta, Langinrichsen, Lally, and Seeley (1992) found that rejected children in second grade through fifth grade who lived in Buenos Aires, Argentina, differed from popular children in that they were described by peers and teachers as having more language and information-processing difficulties, poorer attention spans, and sluggish temperaments. Interestingly, teachers and peers did not describe rejected children as more aggressive and hyperactive. Although there are only a few cross-cultural studies, the evidence at hand suggests that we must use caution in generalizing results from North American samples to children from other cultures.

Implications of Social Status for Later Adjustment   A growing body of evidence has confirmed that social rejection by peers in childhood is predictive of adjustment difficulties in adolescence and adulthood. In a comprehensive review of over a hundred investigations, Parker and Asher (1987) concluded that low peer acceptance in childhood predicts dropping out of school, criminality, and some forms of psychopathology.

Kupersmidt and Coie (1990) demonstrated that rejected peer status in fifth grade predicted a variety of negative outcomes (including truancy, grade retention, dropping out of school, and police contacts) seven years later. Ollendick, Weist, Borden, and Greene (1992) followed up five years later on children classified as rejected in the fourth grade. In addition to continuing to be poorly liked by peers, the children also exhibited conduct problems, substance abuse, school failure, delinquency, and a tendency to drop out of school.

It should be noted that only a percentage of rejected children come to exhibit serious problems; in particular, it appears that those who are both rejected and aggressive are at most risk. Furthermore, peer relationship difficulties in childhood appear to be nonspecific indicators of later problem behavior. This means that there is no clear relation between peer rejection and the specific type of problem behavior manifested later. Instead, rejected children are at risk for developing a variety of problems.

Although previous work has clearly established that low peer status in childhood predicts later difficulties, we do not know the specific processes by which children who are socially rejected come to engage in problem behavior. Perhaps peers are sensitive to interpersonal problems in their very preliminary form, and these interpersonal difficulties evolve into more serious problem behavior in adolescence and adulthood. There is also evidence that rejected children sometimes group together to form deviant peer groups and thus facilitate one another's participation in delinquent and antisocial behavior (Dishion, Patterson, Stoolmiller, & Skinner, 1991).

Summary

Although we have focused on relationships between peers during the school years, it is important to recognize that peer relationships shape and are shaped by other relationships, particularly those with parents and siblings. For example, there is intriguing evidence that peer competence in childhood is predicted in part by parent and child attachment during infancy (Elicker, Englund, & Sroufe, 1992). Several parental characteristics also appear to foster social competence in children: warmth, moderate control, sensitivity, and use of democratic child-rearing practices (Putallaz & Heflin, 1990).

It is likely that peer interactions also influence family interaction patterns (Parke, 1992). Children acquire behavioral competencies and attitudes in the peer group that can affect parent-child relationships. In addition, as children begin to spend more time with peers, their relationships with parents may be transformed.

Friendships may also shape and be shaped by sibling relations. Kramer and Gottman (1992) demonstrated that the extent to which children engage in fantasy play and resolve conflicts with peers is a significant predictor of the quality of these children's interactions with their younger siblings. Siblings are also likely to introduce each other to other children and thus expose each other to different relationship contexts.

The peer relationship context overlaps considerably with the other relationship contexts discussed in other chapters. The best understanding of children's social competence will require a complete exploration of the concurrent and predictive connections between the domains of peer interactions and relationships with other significant figures: parents, siblings, and romantic partners.

Class Discussion Questions

1. How might boys' and girls' friendships differ during the elementary school years?
2. Children's social networks shape their values and their choices about

social behaviors. How might this influence be positive? How might it be negative?

3. How does rejection by the larger peer group feel for a child? How might this experience of rejection contribute to later problems such as delinquency or depression?
4. How much influence can adults (parents and teachers) have, and how much influence *should* they have, over the social relationships of children?

Homework Assignments

1. Find a setting where large numbers of preadolescent children gather (such as a mall or a skating rink). Observe the extent to which girls and boys interact together, the size of boys' and girls' groups, and the activities in which various groups are engaged. You might also focus on the frequency and types of interactions between the boys and the girls. How much chasing or teasing goes on between boys' and girls' groups?
2. Interview several children of a number of different ages about their conceptions of friendship. Ask them such questions as "What is a friend?" and "How can you tell if someone is your friend?" Ask them as well "What would make you decide not to be friends with someone anymore?" Determine the extent to which the responses you receive correspond to research findings on developmental changes in ideas about friendship.

Additional Readings

Coie, J. D., & Cillessen, A. H. N. (1993). Peer rejection: Origins and effects on children's development. *Current Directions in Psychological Science, 2*(3), 89–92.

Gottman, J. M., & Parker, J. G. (Eds.). (1986). *Conversations of friends.* New York: Cambridge University Press.

Maccoby, E. E. (1990). Gender and relationships: A developmental perspective. *American Psychologist, 45*, 513–520.

Selman, R. L. (1981). The child as friendship philosopher. In S. R. Asher & J. M. Gottman (Eds.), *The development of children's friendships.* Cambridge, England: Cambridge University Press.

Thorne, B. (1986). Girls and boys together . . . but mostly apart: Gender arrangements in elementary schools. In W. W. Hartup & Z. Rubin (Eds.), *Relationships and development* (pp. 167–184). Hillsdale, NJ: Lawrence Erlbaum.

References

Aydin, O., & Markova, I. (1979). Attribution tendencies of popular and unpopular children. *British Journal of Social and Clinical Psychology, 18*, 291–298.

Asher, S. R., & Hymel, S. (1981). Children's social competence in peer relations:

Sociometric and behavioral assessment. In J. D. Wine & M. D. Smye (Eds.), *Social competence* (pp. 52–77). New York: Guilford.

Bell-Dolan, D. J., Foster, S. L., & Sikora, D. M. (1989). Effects of sociometric testing on children's behavior and loneliness at school. *Developmental Psychology, 25*, 306–311.

Bell-Dolan, D. J., & Wessler, A. (1993, April). *Ethical administration of sociometric measures*. Paper presented at the Biennial Meeting of the Society for Research in Child Development, New Orleans.

Berndt, T. J. (1981a). The effects of friendship on prosocial intentions and behavior between friends. *Developmental Psychology, 17*, 408–416.

Berndt, T. J. (1981b). Relations between social cognition, nonsocial cognition, and social behavior: The case of friendship. In J. H. Flavell & L. Ross (Eds.), *Social cognitive development* (pp. 176–199). Cambridge, England: Cambridge University Press.

Berndt, T. J. (1987, April). Changes in friendship and school adjustment after the transition to junior high school. Paper presented at the Biennial Meeting of the Society for Research in Child Development, Baltimore.

Berndt, T. J., Hawkins, J. A., & Hoyle, S. G. (1986). Changes in friendship during a school year: Effects on children's and adolescents' impressions of friendship and sharing with friends. *Child Development, 57*, 1284–1297.

Berndt, T. J., & Hoyle, S. G. (1985). Stability and change in childhood and adolescent friendships. *Developmental Psychology, 21*, 1007–1015.

Berndt, T. J., & Perry, T. B. (1986). Children's perceptions of friendships as supportive relationships. *Developmental Psychology, 22*, 1007–1015.

Bigelow, B. J. (1977). Children's friendship expectations: A cognitive developmental study. *Child Development, 48*, 246–253.

Bukowski, W. M., & Newcomb, A. F. (1984). Stability and determinants of sociometric status and friendship choice: A longitudinal perspective. *Developmental Psychology, 20*, 941–952.

Cantrell, V. L., & Prinz, R. J. (1985). Multiple perspectives of rejected, neglected, and accepted children: Relation between sociometric status and behavioral characteristics. *Journal of Consulting and Clinical Psychology, 53*, 884–889.

Carlson, C. L., Lahey, B. B., & Neeper, R. (1984). Peer assessment of the social behavior of accepted, rejected, and neglected children. *Journal of Abnormal Child Psychology, 12*, 189–198.

Carlson-Jones, D. (1985). Persuasive appeals and responses to appeals among friends and acquaintances. *Child Development, 56*, 757–763.

Chen, X., Rubin, K. H., & Sun, Y. (1992). Social reputation and peer relationships in Chinese and Canadian children: A cross-cultural study. *Child Development, 63*, 1336–1343.

Cillessen, A. H. N., van Ijzendoorn, H. W., van Lieshout, C. F. M., & Hartup, W. W. (1992). Heterogeneity among peer rejected boys: Subtypes and stabilities. *Child Development, 63*, 893–905.

Coie, J. D., Belding, M., & Underwood, M. K. (1988). Aggression and peer rejection in childhood. In B. B. Lahey and A. Kazdin (Eds.), *Advances in clinical child psychology, Vol. 11* (pp. 125–157). New York: Plenum.

Coie, J. D., & Cillessen, A. H. N. (1993). Peer rejection: Origins and effects on children's development. *Current directions in psychological science, 2*(3), 89–92.

Coie, J. D. & Dodge, K. A. (1988). Multiple sources of data on social behavior and social status in school: A cross-age comparison. *Child Development, 59,* 815–829.

Coie, J. D., Dodge, K. A., & Coppotelli, H. (1982). Dimensions and types of social status. *Developmental Psychology, 18,* 557–570.

Coie, J. D., Dodge, K. A., & Kupersmidt, J. B. (1990). Peer group behavior and social status. In S. R. Asher & J. D. Coie (Eds.), *Peer rejection in childhood* (pp. 17–59). New York: Cambridge University Press.

Coie, J. D., & Kupersmidt, J. B. (1983). A behavioral analysis of emerging social status in boys' groups. *Child Development, 54,* 1400–1416.

Crick, N. R., & Grotpeter, J. K. (in press). Relational aggression, gender, and social-psychological adjustment. *Child Development.*

DeLawyer, D. D., & Foster, S. L. (1986). The effects of peer relationship on the functions of interpersonal behaviors of children. *Journal of Clinical Child Psychology, 15,* 127–133.

Dishion, T. J., Patterson, G. R., Stoolmiller, M., & Skinner, M. L. (1991). Family, school, and behavioral antecedents to early adolescent involvement with antisocial peers. *Developmental Psychology, 27,* 172–180.

Dodge, K. A. (1983). Behavioral antecedents of peer social status. *Child Development, 54,* 1386–1399.

Dodge, K. A., & Feldman, E. (1990). Issues in social cognition and sociometric status. In S. R. Asher & J. D. Coie (Eds.), *Peer rejection in childhood* (pp. 119–155). New York: Cambridge University Press.

Dodge, K. A., Murphy, R. M., & Buchsbaum, K. (1984). The assessment of intention-cue detection skills in children: Implications for developmental psychopathology. *Child Development, 55,* 163–173.

Eder, D., & Hallinan, M. T. (1978). Sex differences in children's friendships. *American Sociological Review, 43,* 237–250.

Elicker, J., Englund, M., & Sroufe, L. A. (1992). Predicting peer competence and peer relationships in childhood from early parent-child relationships. In R. D. Parke & G. W. Ladd (Eds.), *Family-peer relationships: Modes of linkage* (pp. 77–106). Hillsdale, NJ: Erlbaum.

Ellis, S., Rogoff, B., & Cromer, C. C. (1981). Age segregation in children's social interaction. *Developmental Psychology, 17,* 399–407.

Flavell, J. H., Miller, P. H., & Miller, S. A. (1993). *Cognitive development* (3rd ed.). Englewood Cliffs, NJ: Prentice-Hall.

Foot, H. C., Chapman, A. J., & Smith, J. R. (1977). Friendship and social responsiveness in boys and girls. *Journal of Personality and Social Psychology, 35,* 401–411.

French, D. C. (1984). Children's knowledge of the social functions of younger, older, and same-age peers. *Child Development, 55,* 1429–1433.

French, D. C. (1987). Children's social interaction with older, younger, and same-age peers. *Journal of Social and Personal Relationships, 4,* 63–86.

French, D. C. (1988). Heterogeneity of peer-rejected boys: Aggressive and non-aggressive sub-types. *Child Development, 59,* 976–985.

French, D. C. (1990). Heterogeneity of peer-rejected girls. *Child Development, 61,* 2028–2031.

French, D. C., Conrad, J., & Turner, T. M. (1994). Adjustment of antisocial and non-antisocial rejected adolescents. Manuscript submitted for publication.

French, D. C., & Waas, G. A. (1986). Behavior problems of peer-neglected and peer-rejected elementary-age children: Parent and teacher perspectives. *Child Development, 56,* 246–252.

Gilligan, C. (1982). *In a different voice: Psychological theory and women's development.* Cambridge, MA: Harvard University Press.

Gottman, J. (1986). The world of coordinated play: Same- and cross-sex friendship in young children. In J. M. Gottman & J. G. Parker, *Conversations of friends* (pp. 139–191). New York: Cambridge University Press.

Gottman, J., & Mettetal, G. (1986). Speculations about social and affective development: Friendship and acquaintanceship through adolescence. In J. M. Gottman & J. G. Parker, *Conversations of friends* (pp. 192–237). New York: Cambridge University Press.

Gottman, J. M., & Parker, J. G., (Eds). (1986). *Conversations of friends.* New York: Cambridge University Press.

Hartup, W. W. (1983). Peer relations. In P. H. Mussen (Ed.), *Handbook of child psychology, Vol. 4: Socialization, social development, and personality* (pp. 103–196), New York: Wiley.

Hartup, W. W. (1992, April). *Friendships and their developmental significance.* Paper presented at the Annual Meeting of the American Psychological Association.

Hartup, W. W., French, D. C., Laursen, B., Johnston, M. K., & Ogawa, J. R. (1993). Conflict and friendship relations in middle childhood: Behavior in a closed-field situation. *Child Development, 64,* 445–454.

Hartup, W. W., Laursen, B., Stewart, M. A., & Eastenson, A. (1988). Conflict and friendship relations of young children. *Child Development, 59,* 1590–1600.

Hymel, S. (1986). Interpretations of peer behavior: Affective bias in childhood and adolescence. *Child Development, 57,* 431–445.

Hymel, S., Wagner, E., & Butler, L. J. (1990). Reputational bias: View from the peer group. In S. R. Asher & J. D. Coie (Eds.), *Peer rejection in childhood* (pp. 156–186). New York: Cambridge University Press.

Konner, M. (1991). *Childhood: A multicultural view.* Boston: Little, Brown & Co.

Kramer, L., & Gottman, J. M. (1992). Becoming a sibling: "With a little help from my friends." *Developmental Psychology, 28,* 685–689.

Kupersmidt, J. B., & Coie, J. D. (1990). Preadolescent peer status, aggression, and school adjustment as predictors of externalizing problems in adolescence. *Child Development, 61*, 1350–1362.

Ladd, G. W. (1983). Social networks of popular, average, and rejected children in school settings. *Merrill-Palmer Quarterly, 29*, 283–308.

Lever, J. (1976). Sex differences in the games children play. *Social Problems, 23*, 479–487.

Maccoby, E. E. (1990). Gender and relationships: A developmental perspective. *American Psychologist, 45*, 513–520.

Nelson, J., & Aboud, F. E. (1985). The resolution of social conflict between friends. *Child Development, 56*, 1009–1017.

Newcomb, A. F., Brady, J. E., & Hartup, W. W. (1979). Friendship and incentive condition as determinants of children's task-oriented social behavior. *Child Development, 50*, 878–881.

Ollendick, T. H., Weist, M. D., Borden, C. M., & Greene, R. W. (1992). Sociometric status and academic, behavioral, and psychological adjustment. *Journal of Consulting and Clinical Psychology, 41*(3), 438–446.

Parke, R. D. (1992). Epilogue: Remaining issues and future trends in the study of family-peer relationships. In R. D. Parke & G. W. Ladd (Eds.), *Family-peer relationships: Modes of linkage*. Hillsdale, NJ: Erlbaum.

Parker, J. G., & Asher, S. R. (1987). Peer relations and later personal adjustment: Are low-accepted children at greater risk? *Psychological Bulletin, 102*, 357–389.

Parker, J. G., & Asher, S. R. (1993). Friendship and friendship quality in middle childhood: Links with peer group acceptance and feelings of loneliness and social dissatisfaction. *Developmental Psychology, 29*, 611–621.

Piaget, J. (1932). *The moral judgment of the child*. Glencoe, IL: Free Press.

Putallaz, M., & Gottman, J. M. (1981a). An interactional model of children's entry into peer groups. *Child Development, 52*, 986–994.

Putallaz, M., & Gottman, J. M. (1981b). Social skills and group acceptance. In S. R. Asher & J. M. Gottman (Eds.), *The development of children's friendships* (pp. 116–149). Cambridge, England: Cambridge University Press.

Putallaz, M., & Heflin, A. H. (1990). Parent-child interaction. In S. R. Asher & J. D. Coie (Eds.), *Peer rejection in childhood* (pp. 189–216). New York: Cambridge University Press.

Putallaz, M., & Wasserman, A. (1990). Children's entry behavior. In S. R. Asher & J. D. Coie (Eds.), *Peer rejection in childhood* (pp. 60–89). New York: Cambridge University Press.

Ruble, D. N., Boggiana, A. K., Feldman, N. S., & Loebl, J. H. (1980). Developmental analysis of the role of social comparison in self-evaluation. *Developmental Psychology, 16*, 105–115.

Schaughency, E. A., Vannatta, K., Langinrichsen, J., Lally, C., & Seeley, J. (1992). Correlates of sociometric status in school children in Buenos Aires. *Journal of Abnormal Child Psychology, 20*, 317–326.

Selman, R. L. (1981). The child as friendship philosopher. In S. R. Asher & J. M.

Gottman (Eds.), *The development of children's friendships*. Cambridge, England: Cambridge University Press.

Strain, P. S. (1984). Social behavior patterns of non-handicapped and developmentally disabled friend pairs in mainstream preschools. *Analysis and Intervention in Developmental Disabilities, 4,* 15–28.

Sullivan, H. S. (1953). *The interpersonal theory of psychiatry*. New York: Norton.

Thorne, B. (1986). Girls and boys together . . . but mostly apart: Gender arrangements in elementary schools. In W. W. Hartup & Z. Rubin (Eds.), *Relationships and development* (pp. 167–184). Hillsdale, NJ: Lawrence Erlbaum.

Waldrop, M. F., & Halverson, C. F. (1975). Intensive and extensive peer behavior: Longitudinal and cross-sectional analyses. *Child Development, 46,* 19–26.

Youniss, J. (1980). *Parents and peers in social development: A Sullivan-Piaget perspective*. Chicago: University of Chicago Press.

Glossary

Controversial   Sociometric status group defined by high positive and high negative nominations

Negative nominations   Peers' votes for a child as being disliked or as someone they least like to play with

Neglected   Sociometric status group defined by low positive and low negative nominations

Peer network   The sum of a child's peer contacts, including friends, enemies, acquaintances, and playmates

Popular   Sociometric status group characterized by high positive and low negative nominations

Positive nominations   Peers' votes for a child as a preferred companion

Rejected   Sociometric status group defined by low positive and high negative nominations

Sociometric status   An index of the extent to which a child is socially accepted in a specified group

8

Friendships in Adolescence

Thomas J. Berndt
Purdue University

*A*dolescence is a time when peer relationships become particularly important. Typically, an adolescent spends more time with friends than with family and develops a powerful identification with his or her peer group that shapes current and future life experiences. This chapter explores the specific functions of friendships in adolescence and takes a look at the myths and realities of "peer pressure."

NV & SD

Chapter Outline

- A Definition of Adolescence
- The Adolescent Agenda and the Functions of Friendship
- The Place of Friendships in the World of Peers
- Qualities of Friendship: Support and Conflicts
- Myths of Peer Pressure and the Reality
  of Friends' Influence
- Summary

Adolescents in the United States spend more time interacting with friends than with parents or other adults (Csikszentmihalyi & Larson, 1984). Adolescents also enjoy their interactions with friends more than they enjoy interactions with other people (Larson & Richards, 1991). These observations suggest the importance of friendships *to* adolescents themselves. They also imply that friendships are likely to be important *for* adolescent development. Yet before you can understand the friendships of adolescents, you need some information about adolescence itself.

A DEFINITION OF ADOLESCENCE

Adolescence is commonly defined as the developmental period from the onset of puberty to maturity. An adolescent is no longer a child but is not yet an adult. Specifying the exact age when adolescence begins is somewhat arbitrary, because individuals go through puberty at different ages. Moreover, the onset of puberty is typically earlier for girls than for boys. For girls it is usually around age 12; for boys, around age 14. The psychological experience of adolescence is also different for boys and for girls (Hill & Lynch, 1983). Developmental periods are rarely defined differently for the two sexes, however, so in this chapter age 12 will be taken as the beginning of adolescence for boys and for girls.

Specifying the age when adolescence ends is also difficult, because maturity is an abstract concept. Most often, **maturity** is defined by the age at which an individual in a particular society is assumed to be fully developed and thus is given the basic rights of an adult. In most Western societies, this is around age 18, when individuals receive the right to vote. Therefore, in this chapter age 18 will be taken as the endpoint of adolescence.

Of course, the average 12-year-old differs greatly from the average 18-year-old. The friendships of 12-year-olds also differ from those of 18-year-olds. Developments in friendship styles between these two ages are usually gradual and subtle rather than abrupt and dramatic. Nevertheless, the developments are important in showing how adolescents first move away from the patterns of childhood friendships and then move toward the patterns of adult friendships. Developmental changes in adolescents' friendships are discussed in each section of this chapter. Each section begins with a general characterization of adolescent friendships; then, differences between adolescents' friendships and those of children and adults are considered. When evidence is available, changes in friendship during the adolescent years are also described.

THE ADOLESCENT AGENDA AND THE FUNCTIONS OF FRIENDSHIP

Each developmental period has its own agenda, that is, its own list of tasks that a person must accomplish. On the adolescent agenda are four items that partly explain the functions of friendships during this period. First, adolescents gradually move out of the family circle and become more independent (Csikszentmihalyi & Larson, 1984). They do not want to become solitary individuals, however. They enjoy having companions who like the same activities. Friends partly replace parents and siblings as companions for adolescents. Stated differently, companionship is an important function of adolescents' friendships.

Second, as adolescents become more independent of their families, they need to find a place for themselves in a new and complex social world (Berndt & Perry, 1990). This new world is largely populated with **peers**—other adolescents who are the same or similar in age. Thus a second function of friendships is to give adolescents a sense of belonging in the social world and allies in navigating through that world. For example, friends can provide support for each other by giving each other help and advice. Intimate conversations with friends can also increase adolescents' self-esteem and self-confidence.

Third, adolescents begin to form their own **identity**—a set of ideas about who they are and what they can do with their lives (Erikson, 1963). Interactions with friends can play a major role in identity formation: On the one hand, support from friends can help adolescents form a positive identity; on the other hand, friends can challenge an adolescent's emerging identity. Adolescents often compare their performance in school, sports, or other activities to that of their friends. These comparisons can lead to rivalry and competition. The intensity of this rivalry and competition can affect adolescents' self-concepts and their social behavior.

Fourth, adolescents need to learn not only about themselves but also about the larger society. Adolescents gradually develop ideas and opinions about other people, social organizations, and legal and political systems (Keating, 1990; Torney-Purta, 1990). Their ideas and opinions are shaped by discussions with friends. Their behavior is also influenced by their friends' behavior. Influences of these types define yet another function of friendships in adolescents' lives.

Throughout this chapter you will see comments about the adolescent agenda and the functions of friendship. However, some questions about adolescents' friendships are not closely linked to the items on the agenda, and other questions are linked to multiple items. Therefore, this chapter is not divided into sections that deal with specific agenda items. Instead, the three sections deal with distinct sets of issues concerning friendship itself. The first section focuses on the place of friendships in the peer social world. We will discuss not only friendships between pairs of adolescents but also how these pairs link to form groups of friends. The second section focuses on both the positive and the negative qualities of friendships. Special emphasis is given to **intimacy**—a feeling of closeness and understanding that makes adolescents willing to reveal personal information to friends; but, as mentioned earlier, friends may also engage in competition and rivalry that leads to conflicts. The third section focuses on the processes and outcomes of friends' influence on each other. A central issue in this section is the popular belief—more a myth than a reality—that peer pressure often contributes to undesirable behavior by adolescents.

THE PLACE OF FRIENDSHIPS IN THE WORLD OF PEERS

Adolescents interact with peers during classes at school, when playing sports and other games, and even when working at after-school jobs. They feel most comfortable in these various settings when they have formed close relationships with a few peers whom they view as best friends. You can begin to understand the peer social world by learning how many best friends adolescents typically have, how these friendships form, and how stable they are.

Best Friends: One, Some, or Many?

In Mark Twain's novels, Huck Finn was Tom Sawyer's best friend. In an Old Testament story, Jonathan was David's best friend. These and other examples from literature portray each adolescent as having one best friend and suggest that these pairs of friends travel through their social world together.

In real life, however, when adolescents are asked to name their best friends, they often name several peers (Savin-Williams & Berndt, 1990). The number that they name varies depending on what, exactly, they are asked, but most adolescents asked a general question will name four or five best friends (Hartup, 1993a). Sex differences in the number of best-friend nominations are seldom significant—boys and girls name about the same number.

Not all the best friendships named by adolescents are equally close. Adolescents usually interact significantly more often with one best friend than with their other best friends (Berndt & Keefe, 1993). They also distinguish between their group of best friends and other peers whom they consider just friends (Hallinan & Williams, 1987). In other words, adolescents limit the number of peers they label as best friends, but they normally have a few best friends rather than only one.

Why do most adolescents have more than one best friend? This question can be answered in several ways. One answer is that an adolescent's very closest friend usually has other friends. When the adolescent and the closest friend get together with the other friends, a friendship group emerges (Brown, 1990; Hirsch & Renders, 1986). Often, all adolescents in the group will consider one another best friends.

Another answer focuses on the benefits of having a few best friends. An adolescent with only one best friend will not have a companion for activities if the best friend has a doctor's appointment or a big assignment to finish. Moreover, suppose that the adolescent and his or her friend have a serious argument and stop speaking to each other for a while. If they have no other friends, they will not have a companion for activities until they settle their argument. Adolescents who have a few best friends are not as likely to be socially isolated in these circumstances (Davies, 1982). In short, a friendship group fulfills one major function of friendship better than does a single best friend.

A third answer to the question states the same points more abstractly. Pairs of friends are the smallest units in the social structure of the peer world, which also includes larger and more complex units. Pairs link into groups as friendships form between adolescents and their friends' friends. Groups of best friends are then linked by weaker ties to other groups, giving the entire structure cohesiveness and stability. Such a structure provides a place for each adolescent and gives each adolescent a sense of belonging.

Making Friends: The Role of Similarity

The division of the peer social world into friendship groups is far from random. Most often, adolescents become friends with peers similar to themselves. Friendships usually form between adolescents who are similar in age, sex, race or ethnicity, and social class (Kandel, 1978; Savin-Williams & Berndt, 1990). Friends' similarity in these characteristics partly reflects the structure of their social world. Friendships can form only between adolescents who have opportunities for social interaction. School and neighborhoods are often segregated by age, race or ethnicity, and social class, so adolescents can most easily interact with peers like themselves on those characteristics.

Of course, schools and neighborhoods are not usually segregated by sex, so the predominance of same-sex friendships has other causes. As mentioned earlier, adolescents prefer friends with whom they can enjoy activities, and girls and boys differ in their activity preferences. For example, boys enjoy sports more than girls do, and girls enjoy talking on the phone more than boys do (Zarbatany, Hartmann, & Rankin, 1990). In addition, boys' style of interaction is rougher and less polite than that of girls, which lessens girls' eagerness to spend time with boys (Maccoby, 1988). Opposite-sex friendships become more common near the end of adolescence, during the senior high years (Epstein, 1983). However, these friendships are seldom like the same-sex friendships of younger adolescents. Instead, opposite-sex friendships often seem to represent a stage in the development of romantic relationships.

Most adolescents have a few best friends who are similar in how they dress, how they behave, and how well they do in school. However, friends are not as alike as peas in a pod.

Activity preferences also affect choices of same-sex friends. For example, adolescents who are in a youth organization such as the Boy Scouts often become friends with other adolescents in that organization, and adolescents who belong to athletic teams often become friends with other players on their team. The possible bases for friends' similarity in activities are as diverse as the activities of adolescents themselves.

One particularly important basis for forming friendships is similarity in academic achievement (Epstein, 1983). Friends' similarity in achievement has multiple sources. Students similar in achievement often have the same classes, so they have more opportunities for social interaction. They also tend to be similar in their preferences for activities. They are likely to agree, for example, on whether to spend a weekend doing a school project or hanging out at the mall. Therefore, they are likely to be more dependable companions for each other. A third source of friends' similarity in achievement is adolescents' concern with equality. In an early book on moral development, Piaget (1932/1965) argued that peer relationships are based on equality. Peers have no authority over each other, so they are assumed to respect each other as equals. Friends, in particular, think of themselves as equal in all important respects, including academic achievement. One junior high girl described a best friend by saying, "She's in the middle-level math class and I am too, so I know that she's not smarter than I am and I'm not smarter than she is." To this girl—and to many other adolescents—equality in academic achievement is a sign of equality between peers and is a requirement for friendship.

The emphasis on equality between friends adds further structure to the peer social world. An adolescent's position in the social world partly depends on the activity preferences, athletic ability, and academic achievement of his or her friends. In other words, adolescents' reputations are affected by the groups to which they belong (Brown, 1990). Moreover, their reputation affects the formation of their own identity. Having a definite position in the social world also eases the task of making friends with similar adolescents. On the other hand, belonging to a specific group can limit an adolescent's ability to make friends with adolescents in different groups.

Some adolescents deliberately set out to make friends with peers who are different from themselves. These adolescents recognize the structure of the peer social world and want to change their own place in that structure. Some try to make friends with the most popular peers in the school and become part of their group (Hirsch & Renders, 1986). But not all adolescents seeking to change their position in the structure are social climbers or status seekers. Some avoid the popular group, because they consider it snobbish, and make friends with peers who care less about the outward signs of social success (Eder, 1985).

Even adolescents who are not so calculating usually prefer that their friends be well liked by other adolescents rather than disliked. They also prefer that their friends do well at school rather than be low achievers (Cauce, 1986). Thus when adolescents make friends they strike a balance between seeking friends similar to themselves and seeking friends whom they perceive as different from themselves in desirable ways. How they strike this balance is critical to their social lives, because it determines their position in the social world. It is also critical to their self-concept and, therefore, to their personality development.

Friendship Stability

Most friendships among adolescents last not for a few days or weeks, but for months or even years (Savin-Williams & Berndt, 1990). This high degree of stability is characteristic of both boys' and girls' friendships. Apparently, the same conditions that affect the formation of friendships also increase their stability.

For example, opportunities for social interactions with peers tend to remain stable. Adolescent friends typically have a similar schedule of classes, ride the same school bus, or live in the same neighborhood for a year or more. In addition, their preferences for activities and their levels of academic achievement are fairly stable across months or years. Thus the same conditions that initially bring friends together often keep them together. These conditions give friends many opportunities for interaction with each other and fewer opportunities for interactions with other peers. Stated more generally, once adolescents have a place in the peer social world, they tend to keep that place. One part of keeping a place is keeping the same group of friends.

Some writers have suggested that adolescents benefit if they lack stable friendships and, instead, change their friends regularly (see Savin-Williams & Berndt, 1990). These writers assume that adolescents can get "stuck" with a group of friends, even as their own characteristics change. Under these circumstances, the argument goes, adolescents who stick with their old friends will miss opportunities to become friends with people whose interests more closely match their own.

There is some truth to this argument. Adolescents need to be able to make new friends as they meet new people and choose new activities. Frequent changes in friends, however, are typical not of socially successful adolescents but of adolescents who have social and psychological problems (Hartup, 1983, 1993a). Adolescents with less stable friendships are generally less well liked by their peers, are viewed less positively by teachers, and more often suffer from emotional disorders. These adolescents do not get along well with their friends and so cannot find a secure place for themselves in the peer world. The instability of their friendships is not a sign of their psychological growth; on the contrary, it reflects their inability to find a friendship group that they consider acceptable and that welcomes them.

Developmental Changes in the Peer Social World

Children generally name more best friends than adolescents name, and adolescents name more than adults name. One reason is that children differentiate little between types of relationships—young children sometimes say that all their classmates are their best friends. As children grow older, they begin to contrast friendships that are especially important with those that are less important. As children move into adolescence, they distinguish even more sharply between best friendships and other friendships.

Adolescents begin to reserve the label of *best friend* for the few peers with whom they have a particularly close relationship (Berndt & Hoyle, 1985).

The differentiation among social relationships continues into adulthood. Adults typically make very fine distinctions among social relationships (Duck, 1991; Matthews, 1986). To exaggerate a bit, adults place the people they know into categories like best friend (singular), close friends, good friends, "just" friends, coworkers, neighbors, acquaintances, and strangers. Consequently, many adults assume that adolescents can *really* have only one best friend. When adults make this assumption, they are using a definition of best friendship that holds for them but not for most adolescents. As adolescents move toward adulthood, however, their definitions of friendship become more adultlike.

Similarity is important for friendship formation not only in adolescence, but also in childhood and adulthood. Changes occur, however, in the type of similarity that most affects friendship formation. During early adolescence, friends are most similar in objective characteristics such as where they go to school. During middle and late adolescence, similarity in psychological characteristics is more strongly related to the formation of friendships (Duck, 1975).

Friendships may also be affected by developmental changes in the social structure of the larger peer group. Friendship groups with well-defined identities first emerge in early adolescence (Crockett, Losoff, & Petersen, 1984). During those years, the social structure of the world of peers may be most rigid. In late adolescence, near the end of high school, the social structure seems to become more flexible (Brown, 1990). Adolescents change their groups more freely and form friendships with peers in very different groups. Perhaps old boundaries between groups seem unimportant because high school seniors realize that graduation will bring an end to a social world that has defined their lives for years. Unfortunately, too little is known about this phase of adolescence to make this hypothesis more than a guess.

Finally, best friendships seem about as stable during adolescence as they were during the elementary school years (Berndt & Hoyle, 1985). However, it is impossible to draw definite conclusions until changes in adolescents' friendships are studied more carefully.

QUALITIES OF FRIENDSHIP: SUPPORT AND CONFLICTS

The qualities of adolescents' friendships may have stronger effects on their psychological development than the number of friendships they have or the stability of these friendships. When adolescents describe their friendships, they mention many positive qualities (Berndt, 1986; Youniss & Smollar, 1985). For example, they say that friends help them when they have problems and make them feel better when they are upset. In more general terms, friends provide support for one another. Adolescents also mention negative qualities of friendship, however. For example, they say that their friends sometimes annoy them and boss them around. These behaviors are often the source of conflicts between friends. Both positive and negative qualities, or support and conflict, are important for a complete description of friendships. We will consider positive qualities first because they have received more emphasis in major theories.

Intimate Friendships as Supportive Relationships

As mentioned earlier, one function of friendships is to support adolescents as they adjust to the many changes in their lives. Most theorists agree that the central element of a supportive friendship is its intimacy (Berndt, 1989; East & Rook, 1992; Sullivan, 1953; Youniss, 1980). During intimate conversations, best friends provide practical advice and emotional support for each other. Friends' support enhances adolescents' self-esteem and improves their ability to cope with stressful events. Intimate conversations in which a friend shares personal information also give adolescents a better understanding of other people and a broadened perspective on the world.

The benefits of intimate conversations are suggested by an eighth-grade girl's comments about her friendship with Sally, another eighth-grader:

> Sally is my best friend because she never tells my secrets. She understands what I'm going through, because she has the same problems that I do. Her parents are divorced and my parents were divorced, and now they're back together but they're not married. She understands what I mean when I talk about that.

The comments about Sally illustrate some facets of an intimate friendship. Most important, intimacy involves self-disclosure. Adolescents can tell their best friends all their secrets and problems. Intimacy also involves trust. Adolescents can tell secrets to friends without worrying that the friend will tell others. In addition, intimacy involves understanding and emotional support. Adolescents know that their best friends can appreciate how they feel and give them good advice about how to solve their problems. This girl's comments also suggest that her conversations with Sally have helped her cope with her parents' divorce and its aftermath.

Intimacy first becomes an important feature of friendships in adolescence (Douvan & Adelson, 1966; Savin-Williams & Berndt, 1990). To assess developments in the intimacy of friendships, researchers have used measures like the one described in Box 1; children and adolescents rate one of their best friendships on the items listed. Adolescents typically rate their friendships higher on the items measuring intimacy than do children. In addition, when adolescents describe their friendships in response to open-ended questions, they mention intimate conversations with friends more often than children do.

Box 1

Measuring the Quality of Adolescents' Friendships

Imagine that you are an adolescent who has agreed to participate in a study of best friendships. The researcher asks you to think of your best friend and then to answer the following questions about your friendship with that person.

	Never	Once in a while	Once a week	A few times a week	Every day
1. How often do you talk to your friend on the phone?	___	___	___	___	___
2. If you needed help with something, how often could you count on your friend to help you?	___	___	___	___	___
3. How often does your friend annoy or bug you?	___	___	___	___	___
4. How often does your friend "show off" or brag about doing something better than you?	___	___	___	___	___
5. How often does your friend help you when you can't do something by yourself?	___	___	___	___	___
6. How often do you and your friend get together on weekends or after school?	___	___	___	___	___
7. How often do you tell your friend something important that you want him or her to keep a secret?	___	___	___	___	___
8. How often do you feel as if it's hard to get along with your friend?	___	___	___	___	___
9. When you are playing games or sports, how often does your friend try to prove that he or she is better than you?	___	___	___	___	___
10. When you think you are not doing very well in school, sports, or something else, how often does your friend make you feel more confident in yourself?	___	___	___	___	___

Box 1 continues

Box 1
(continued)

	Never	Once in a while	Once a week	A few times a week	Every day
11. How often do you and your friend go places together, such as to a movie, skating, shopping, or a sports event?	___	___	___	___	___
12. When something is bothering you, how often do you talk to your friend about it?	___	___	___	___	___
13. How often do you tell your friend things about yourself that you wouldn't tell most kids?	___	___	___	___	___
14. How often do you get into arguments with your friend?	___	___	___	___	___
15. How often do you and your friend go over to each other's houses?	___	___	___	___	___
16. How often does your friend try to boss you around?	___	___	___	___	___
17. When you do a good job on something, how often does your friend praise or con-gratulate you?	___	___	___	___	___
18. How often do you and your friend borrow things from each other, like money, class notes, clothes, or other things?	___	___	___	___	___
19. How often do you and your friend just sit around and talk about school, sports, or any-thing else?	___	___	___	___	___
20. How often does your friend make you feel that your ideas and opinions are important and valuable?	___	___	___	___	___
21. When you feel really good about something that happened to you, how often do you tell your friend about it?	___	___	___	___	___
22. How often does your friend tease you about things that you do?	___	___	___	___	___
23. If you asked your friend to do a favor for you, how often would he or she agree to do it?	___	___	___	___	___

24. How often does your friend
    give you the confidence to do
    something you thought you
    couldn't do?   ____ ____ ____ ____ ____

25. When your friend disagrees
    with you, how often does he or
    she make you feel as if your ideas
    aren't as good as his or hers? ____ ____ ____ ____ ____

26. How often do you spend time
    with your friend when you have
    free time during the school day? ____ ____ ____ ____ ____

This questionnaire was used to examine the effects of adolescents' friendships on their behavior and achievement in school (Berndt & Keefe, 1993). Similar questions have often been used to examine the features and effects of friendships in childhood, adolescence, and adulthood (for example, Furman, in press). The questions focus on several features of friendship.

Question 1, about talking on the phone, assesses the frequency of interaction between friends. Questions 6, 11, 15, 19, and 26 assess the frequency of different types of interactions. Frequency of interaction provides a rough index of the importance of a friendship but tells little about its quality. Therefore, interaction frequency is not emphasized in theories of friendship or in this chapter because frequency is a poor proxy for closeness and tells little about the quality of friendship.

Question 7, which asks about telling secrets to the friend, measures a person's willingness to disclose intimate information. Questions 12, 13, and 21 also assess intimate self-disclosure or related behaviors. As stated in the text, intimacy is a central feature of adolescents' friendships, and it remains important throughout adulthood.

Question 2, about asking for help from the friend, assesses another positive feature of friendship: prosocial behavior, which includes positive social behaviors such as sharing, helping, and comforting another. The other questions on prosocial behavior are numbers 5, 18, and 23.

Question 10, about the friend's helping the person feel better, assesses support for self-esteem and positive feelings. Self-esteem support is one kind of support that intimate relationships provide (Cohen & Wills, 1985). One reason for measuring self-esteem support directly is that many writers have argued that good friendships bolster adolescents' self-esteem. Self-esteem support is also assessed by questions 17, 20, and 24.

Question 3, about annoying behavior by the friend, shifts the focus from positive features to negative features of friendship. Historically,

Box 1 continues

Box 1
(continued)

researchers looked exclusively at the positive features of friendship, but they gradually realized that friendships are not ideal relationships and that conflicts with friends can also affect adolescents' development. Questions 8, 14, and 22 also concern conflicts.

Question 4, about the friend's showing off or bragging, assesses another negative feature of friendship: unpleasant competition, rivalry, and other interactions in which the friend asserts his or her superiority. Additional questions assessing this feature are numbers 9, 16, and 25.

As noted in the text, female adolescents usually report a higher level of support, or more positive features, in their friendships than do male adolescents. The gender difference continues into adulthood (Berndt, in press). By contrast, male and female adolescents do not differ in their reports about the negative features of their friendships.

The emergence of intimate friendships during adolescence has also been documented in other cultures. Adolescents in the former Soviet Union, Ijo adolescents in Nigeria, and adolescents from the Inuit tribe in the Canadian Arctic all described intimate conversations as central to their friendships (Condon, 1987; Hollos & Leis, 1989; Kon, 1981).

During adolescence girls have more intimate friendships than boys do, both in the United States and in other cultures (Berndt, in press; Youniss & Smollar, 1985). Several kinds of evidence have shown this sex difference: When adolescents describe their ideas about friendship, girls refer to intimacy more often than boys do; when describing their own friendships, girls give higher ratings for intimacy than boys do. In addition, more boys than girls say they would not share intimate information with friends because they think the friends might tease or laugh at them. You should *not* conclude from these findings that adolescent girls have intimate friendships and adolescent boys lack them. Rather, you should assume that the level of intimacy in friendships is higher, on the average, for girls than for boys.

Both the functions of intimate friendships and the benefits of intimate conversations are easier to appreciate when you know the usual topics of these conversations (Hollos & Leis, 1989; Gottman & Mettetal, 1986; Raffaeli & Duckett, 1989; Rawlins & Holl, 1987). Many of these conversations can be described as gossip. Adolescents talk with friends about the appearance, activities, and personalities of their peers. They talk about the peers they like, the peers they dislike, and the reasons for their feelings. These conversations are valuable in helping adolescents understand their social world and judge the standards for behavior in that world. Gossip about peers is more common in girls' conversations than in boys' conversations. Boys, by contrast, spend more time than girls talking about sports. Boys and girls also talk about their experiences at school and their leisure activities. These conversations help adolescents make decisions about how to spend their time both in work and in play.

Some conversations between friends, like those of the eighth-grade girl with her friend Sally, are about family relationships. Others are about sexuality, and others are about life plans or other decisions. These conversations are less frequent than gossip or most of the other topics mentioned earlier. However, their frequency is probably not a good indication of their importance. Frequent or not, such conversations may be critical to adolescents for understanding the peer social world, forming an identity, and shaping beliefs about the larger society.

Other Features of Supportive Friendships

Intimacy is not the only important feature of a supportive friendship. Another feature mentioned in Box 1 is prosocial behavior. Prosocial behavior includes helping, sharing, and comforting another. Also part of a good friendship is self-esteem support. Friends bolster adolescents' self-esteem by praising them for their accomplishments or encouraging them when they feel bad about something. These features may be especially important to adolescents as they form an identity and develop a distinct self-concept.

One feature of a supportive friendship that is not mentioned specifically in Box 1 is loyalty (Berndt, 1986). Stated informally, adolescents expect their friends to act like friends when they are around other people. Loyal friends stick up for you in a fight with other kids, don't talk about you behind your back, and don't leave you for somebody else. Remember that adolescents live in a complex social world composed of loosely connected friendship groups. Adolescents need friends who will stand by them when they have quarrels with peers from another group. They don't want their friends to abandon them and join other groups.

The features of supportive friendships explain why these friendships are so valuable to adolescents. Adolescents' development must be enhanced by having friends who talk with them about their joys and sorrows, who help them when they are in need, who encourage them, and who are loyal. Adolescents whose friendships have these supportive features also have better psychological health than those whose friendships lack them (Berndt & Savin-Williams, 1993; Cauce, 1986; Kurdek & Sinclair, 1988). Adolescents who have supportive friendships have higher self-esteem and suffer less often from loneliness, anxiety, and emotional problems. When interacting with other people, these adolescents are more generous and helpful than other adolescents. They also have more positive attitudes toward school and higher levels of academic achievement. The relation of supportive friendships to psychological health has been found for both white and African-American adolescents in the United States and for adolescents in several other countries.

Although the evidence from research is impressive, it leaves one question open: Do supportive friendships actually improve psychological health, or do psychologically healthy adolescents form more supportive friendships? Perhaps adolescents with emotional problems and low self-esteem are so self-absorbed or so timid that they have difficulty developing supportive friendships. By tracking changes in friendships and psychological health over time, researchers have obtained a tentative answer to this question (Berndt, 1989; House, Umberson, & Landis, 1988). Adolescents' psychological health does affect their ability to form supportive friendships. But having supportive friendships also affects psychological health. That is, the direction of effects goes both ways—support from friends has an impact on adolescents' psychological adjustment and vice versa.

Developmental Changes in Friends' Support

You know already that intimacy emerges as an important feature of friendship in early adolescence. Many years ago Sullivan (1953) suggested that intimate friendships first appear in the preadolescent years, the years just before puberty. Later research has not confirmed this hypothesis. Although children can rate their friendships on intimacy items like those in Box 1, they rarely make comments that suggest they have an intimate friendship. For example, children rarely say that they share secrets with friends or that they talk about their worries and fears with friends. By contrast, sixth- and seventh-graders often mention their ability to share intimate information with friends and their friends' understanding of them.

After intimacy emerges as a feature of friendships, its level does not change consistently with age. Some evidence suggests that intimacy in friendships increases during adolescence (Blyth & Traeger, 1988), but other evidence suggests that it does not (Furman & Buhrmester, 1992). Evidence on any changes in friends' prosocial behavior and loyalty is equally mixed (Berndt & Perry, 1990). During adulthood, intimacy continues to be the most central feature of close friendships (Clark & Reis, 1988; Matthews, 1986). Prosocial behavior, self-esteem support, and loyalty are other features of supportive friendships among adults. We can conclude, therefore, that adolescence is the period in which friendships first develop all the features of supportive social relationships (Berndt, 1989).

Conflicts in Friendship

Of course, friendships are not always supportive. Friends have arguments with each other and sometimes even fight with each other. Despite their many similarities, friends often have different ideas, opinions, and preferences. These differences can lead to disagreements and then to conflicts. Under some conditions, conflicts may be more frequent between friends than between other peers because friends feel more free to state their views openly. In other words, friends are less concerned with behaving in a polite way (Hartup, 1993b).

The special nature of friendship can also contribute to interactions between friends that can sometimes have negative overtones. Remember that Piaget (1932/1965) assumed that equality and mutual respect are the hallmarks of peer relationships. Friends, in particular, are expected to view one another as equals. Yet Piaget was mistaken when he assumed that all peer relationships, and all friendships, are based on equality. As noted earlier, the motive for equality is opposed by strong motives to prove one's own competence through competition with others. Because friends often compare their performance, competition with close friends can be especially intense, although not always negative (Duck & Wood, 1995). This intensity is illustrated by the following comments of an eighth-grade boy about his friend Matt:

> We both play the drums, but I'm the lead drummer. We had a parade and I had a solo part on the drums. Matt wanted to do my solo halfway through the parade but I told him no. We're rivals on that, and on other things. In sports, Matt says he's better than I am, but how good he does in schoolwork doesn't count to him—he admits defeat at schoolwork.

This boy and his friend Matt compete in many areas. They constantly compete in playing the drum and in sports. Apparently, they once competed in academics, but this competition ended when Matt conceded that he isn't as good a student as his friend is. Friends may compete on other things too. One friend may claim to be more popular than the other. One friend may come from a wealthier family or have more expensive and stylish clothes than the other does.

Abraham Tesser (1984), a social psychologist, has suggested that competition and the conflicts that it provokes are common in all close relationships. Competition exists because people in close relationships often engage in social comparison: They compare their own performance in important domains with the performance of their relationship partner. If their performance is inferior to that of the partner, they are upset. In response, they may compete more intensely as they try to equal their partner. Or they may reduce the closeness of their relationship with their partner or even end the relationship.

Competition between friends is less intense when the friends have a strong motive to avoid interpersonal conflicts. In studies done a few years ago, Mexican-American children were found to be less competitive and more cooperative with their friends than were

Friends' competition is often enjoyable. But if one person begins to act superior to the others, the friendship may be threatened.

Anglo-American children (Kagan & Madsen, 1972). Competition is often discouraged in small, closely knit human groups, such as the Mexican-American population, because serious conflicts could threaten the survival of the entire group.

One anthropologist observed groups of adolescents among the Inuit people in the Canadian Arctic (Condon, 1987). He found that even during athletics these adolescents restrained their competition, trying to assure that neither team lost badly. Three years after doing these observations, the anthropologist returned to observe Inuit adolescents again. During the intervening time, the Inuit had started receiving television programs, and the adolescents had become avid fans of televised sports. When Condon observed adolescents' athletic contests this time, he found that they showed much more competitive behavior than they had before. Apparently, the adolescents' exposure to the competitiveness of the mainstream culture through televised sports had made them more willing to compete with their friends.

Of course, not all competition with friends is undesirable; but when competition is intense and leads to enduring conflicts and negative feelings, its effects are likely to be negative. Adolescents who have frequent conflicts with friends also have frequent conflicts with teachers and classmates because of their annoying and disruptive behavior. In addition, adolescents who have frequent conflicts with friends at the beginning of a school year often exhibit an increase in disruptive behavior at school during the year (Berndt & Keefe, 1993). Apparently, negative interactions with friends spill over and contribute to a generally negative interaction style.

Conflicts between friends can be reduced by focusing on their origins. Conflicts that arise from intense competition and rivalry can be discouraged by giving adolescents a different way of thinking about social comparison. In particular, adolescents can be invited to think about themselves and their friends as having complementary strengths and weaknesses (Tesser, 1984). An adolescent may be better than her or his friend at playing the drum, but the friend may be better at playing basketball. On balance, then, they are equal. Their self-esteem does not depend on proving themselves equal to each other in every arena. In other words, adolescents can be encouraged to think positively about themselves even while recognizing that they are not superior to their peers in all arenas.

Differences of opinion are another source of conflicts between friends. Rather than trying to eliminate all conflicts—an impossible task—adults can train adolescents in the skills needed to resolve conflicts successfully (Laursen, in press). For starters, adolescents need to control their anger during conflicts. They also need to rely on negotiation, rather than coercion, as a strategy for resolving conflicts. Finally, they need to view conflicts not as battles that they must win but as potentially positive events that could increase their understanding of one another. That is, conflicts can be viewed as opportunities to learn about the differences in people's attitudes and ideas. Learning about these differences will give adolescents a more accurate picture of social reality. Thus training in conflict-resolution skills could lead to both harmony between friends and better understanding of other people and society.

Developmental Changes in Friends' Conflicts

Because most theories of friendships have focused on their positive or supportive features, developments in conflicts with friends have received little attention. The friendship measure described in Box 1 includes items on quarrels with friends. It also includes items on competition and rivalry between friends. The two types of items, taken together, assess people's perceptions of the negative features of their friendships.

Judging from children's and adolescents' reports, the frequency of negative interactions with friends changes little with age. When responding to items like those in Box 1, adolescents report about as many negative interactions with friends as children do (Berndt & Perry, 1986). Apparently, the greater social maturity of adolescents does not indicate a greater ability to avoid conflicts with friends. But avoiding the conflicts may not be terribly important, because adolescents also say that these conflicts rarely weaken their friendships and may even strengthen them (Laursen & Collins, in press).

Under certain conditions, conflicts with friends do decrease between childhood and adolescence. For one study (Berndt, Hawkins, & Hoyle, 1986), fourth- and eighth-graders were paired in the fall of the school year with a classmate who was a close friend. The pairs of students then worked on a task that gave them opportunities to share with each other and to earn rewards for their performance. They usually did less well and received fewer rewards when they shared more with the friend. Under these conditions the students had two basic choices: They could compete and try to get the most rewards for themselves, or they could share with the friend and perhaps get fewer rewards than the friend did. In the spring, the students did the same task again with the same partners. By then some students were still close friends with their partners, and some were no longer close friends. How these pairs behaved on the task varied greatly with their age. Fourth-graders who were still close friends shared with each other less than did fourth-graders who were no longer close friends. Fourth-graders who were paired with close friends were so concerned about getting fewer rewards than the friends that they competed rather than sharing. Eighth-graders, on the other hand, shared more and competed less when they were still close friends with their partners than when they were no longer close friends. The pairs of friends said that their goal in the game was to achieve equality in rewards by sharing. The pairs who were no longer friends treated the task as a contest that they could win by competing. The eighth-graders' generosity toward close friends and desire for equality suggest that they placed sensitivity to a friend's feelings above competition (Youniss, 1980).

So, does competition with friends disappear as children move into adolescence? Of course not. The comments from the eighth-grade boy about his rivalry with Matt are anecdotal evidence that adolescents' friendships are not always cooperative, harmonious relationships. Under certain conditions, friends' competition may be more restrained in adolescence than in childhood, but competition and rivalry are significant features of many adolescent friendships. Remember that adolescents must begin to form their own identity. As they do so, they often want to test themselves in competition with friends.

MYTHS OF PEER PRESSURE AND THE REALITY OF FRIENDS' INFLUENCE

The qualities of adolescents' friendships have been virtually ignored by some writers (e.g., Bronfenbrenner, 1970; Steinberg & Silverberg, 1986). Instead, these writers have emphasized the presumed influence of friends' pressure. In both popular and scholarly writings, the prevailing opinion about such "peer pressure" is entirely negative.

More than three decades ago, Coleman (1961) wrote, "Our society has within its midst a set of small teen-age societies, which focus teen-age interests and attitudes on things far removed from adult responsibilities and which develop standards that lead away from those goals established by the larger society" (p. 9). A few years later, Bronfenbrenner (1970) wrote, "Where the peer group is to a large extent autonomous—as it often is in the United States—it can exert influence in opposition to values held by the adult society" (p. 189). Popular writers echoed this refrain then, and they continue to do so. They argue that peer pressure is a big problem, leading to sexual behavior, delinquency, and drug and alcohol abuse (Ansley & McCleary, 1992).

This view of friends' influence is so misleading that it might be called a myth. The usual assertions about peer pressure are inaccurate in their assumptions about both the direction and the strength of friends' influence. The following narrative by an eighth-grade girl suggests a starting point for drawing a more accurate picture of friends' influence.

> Right now the group that Michelle hangs around with is one that I used to hang around with. They smoke pot but I don't and Michelle doesn't either. The people in the group are nice, but I don't want to get into doing drugs. I'm starting to be friends with other people who are more popular and are not into drugs. Some people call them the Squares but they're not really that way—they like to have fun. But Michelle's starting to hang around with

Janice and her group. They smoke a lot of pot and they get in a
lot of trouble.

On a quick reading, this anecdote might seem like a perfect illustration of
the negative influence of peer pressure—the speaker suggests that her
friend Michelle is going to start using drugs because she is becoming
friends with a group of drug users. Yet when examined more closely, the
comments suggest a more complex picture of friends' influence. A careful
analysis of research data also suggests different conclusions about how
friends influence each other.

Processes and Outcomes of Friends' Influence

Rather than always being negative, the outcome of friends' influence is
variable. One researcher in England spent years observing adolescents' interactions with their classmates at school (Ball, 1981). He observed some
classrooms in which friends had a negative influence on one another's behavior and achievement. In these classrooms, friends encouraged one another to disrupt the class and not to study for tests. Friends also reinforced
one another's negative attitudes toward school. In other classrooms, however, friends had a positive influence on one another's behavior and
achievement. They discouraged disruptive behavior that reduced the
teachers' ability to conduct class. They encouraged academic achievement
by telling one another to study for tests and giving social approval to students who received high grades.

The critical difference between the two groups of classrooms was the
initial level of achievement of the students. Friends had a negative influence in classrooms where most students were low in achievement. Friends
had a positive influence in classrooms where most students were high in
achievement. Students with high levels of achievement also had positive
attitudes toward school. When most students were high in achievement,
the few students with negative attitudes did not form a cohesive friendship
group; instead they made friends with pro-school classmates and were
positively influenced by their friends.

Some adolescents in the United States have friends who are more interested in using drugs or acting tough than in doing well in school
(Brown, Clasen, & Eicher, 1986). Other adolescents have friends like the
Squares mentioned by the eighth-grader quoted earlier. These students do
not use drugs or make trouble in school. Still other adolescents—the
"brains"—have friends who value high academic achievement (Brown,
Mounts, Lamborn, & Steinberg, 1993). The differences between these
groups illustrate that friends' influence is not always negative. For many
adolescents the influence of friends is entirely positive. The outcomes of
friends' influence depend largely on the attitudes and behaviors of a particular adolescent's friends.

For most adolescents the direction of friends' influence is probably more positive than negative. Most adolescents report that their friends encourage them to study for tests and try for high grades rather than to neglect their school work (Brown et al., 1986). Most adolescents report that their friends discourage cigarette smoking and drinking of alcoholic beverages more than they encourage them (Keefe, 1994; Urberg, Shyu, & Liang, 1990). The behavior of these adolescents might be improved if they were *more* influenced by their friends, rather than less.

Ideas about peer pressure also convey the wrong image of the sources and the processes of peer influence. Some writings about peer pressure suggest the image of a gang of toughs telling a young adolescent, "You be at the fight with the Jets tonight, or else!" This image may sell movie tickets, but it does not describe the usual source of influence on adolescents. Even in gangs most decisions are made by consensus. The group discusses various activities in a casual way until everyone agrees on what to do (Suttles, 1971). In less-organized groups decision-making is even more informal. Adolescents not only are influenced by their friends; they also influence their friends, as they discuss their ideas, attitudes, and possible activities (Downs, 1987). Mutual influence during group discussions better characterizes how friendship groups operate than the image of one adolescent conforming to a group majority.

The processes of influence during group discussions are varied (Berndt & Savin-Williams, 1993). Friends sometimes offer rewards to others—for example, saying, "Let's go to the movies. I'll pay for the gas." One common reward is companionship; a friend might say, "Let's go the mall first, and then I'll play tennis like you want to." In other cases, friends use reasoning to persuade each other—for example, a friend might say, "You'd better study for your test because you'll get grounded if you flunk." In addition, friends use mild forms of punishment to change behavior. Teasing is the most common form. Suppose that an adolescent wears a new shirt to school, and one of his friends jokingly says, "Say, I didn't know they *made* shirts like that anymore! Did you get that from your Dad?" After this bit of teasing, there's a good chance the boy won't wear that shirt to school again!

Contrary to popular opinion, friends rarely use stronger forms of pressure when trying to change friends' behavior. They avoid the use of coercive pressure for at least two reasons. First, friendship is a voluntary relationship that can be ended by either partner. If a friend puts unwanted pressure on an adolescent, the adolescent can choose to end the friendship and not to interact with the other person anymore. Second, many adolescents believe that coercive pressure is incompatible with the mutual respect that is expected in a good friendship (Berndt, Miller, & Park, 1989). Adolescents often say that they are not influenced by their friends because they and their friends don't *try* to influence each other. For example, one adolescent said, "My friend has his ideas and I have mine, and we don't try to change each other's ideas."

Sometimes adolescents directly resist pressure from friends and act independently. Remember what the eighth-grade girl said about Michelle and her group of friends? She said that she had decided not to hang around with that group of friends anymore because she did not want to get into drugs. She made this decision even though her best friend Michelle remained close to the group. In other words, the girl decided that she would rather change her friends than change her behavior and start using drugs.

Adolescents are more independent than stereotypes imply. In one survey (Sebald, 1986) adolescents were asked if they considered their parents' opinions or their friends' opinions more important in making decisions such as how often to date and whether to go to college. About 30% of the adolescents wrote in answers like, "I'd figure it out myself," although that option was not printed on the questionnaire. These adolescents were, in a small way, making a declaration of their independence.

These statements about adolescents' independence do *not* mean that friends have little influence on adolescents' behavior. Many studies confirm that friends influence adolescents' use of drugs like tobacco, alcohol, and marijuana (Chassin, Presson, Montello, Sherman, & McGrew, 1986; Urberg, Cheng, & Shyu, 1991), as well as their sexual behavior and many other behaviors (Berndt & Savin-Williams, 1993). Friends also influence adolescents' attitudes toward school, their achievement in school, and their college plans (Epstein, 1983). In short, friends have a significant influence not only on relatively trivial matters such as what clothes adolescents buy and what music they listen to, but also on attitudes and behaviors that affect adolescents' physical and mental health and their future lives.

Individual Differences in Friends' Influence

Some adolescents are more susceptible to friends' influence than other adolescents. Girls seem to be more influenced by their closest friends than boys are (Billy & Udry, 1985; Davies & Kandel, 1981). As we discussed earlier, girls typically have more intimate relationships with their best friends than boys do. A highly intimate friendship is likely to be more influential than a less intimate one. However, when researchers have examined the influence of the several friends who comprise a friendship group, they have seldom found gender differences (e.g., Graham, Marks, & Hansen, 1991). It seems, then, that girls are not generally more susceptible to friends' influence but that they have a special relationship with their closest friend which gives that friend unusual influence.

Personality traits also affect an adolescent's susceptibility to friends' influence. Adolescents who lack self-confidence or have low self-esteem are most willing to follow friends rather than to assert their independence (Savin-Williams & Berndt, 1990). Conversely, adolescents who are high in self-esteem, intelligent, popular, and athletic are likely to have more influence on their friends than vice versa. Adolescents with these character-istics are likely to be the leaders rather than the followers in their friend-ship groups.

Finally, the influence of friends is affected by adolescents' relationships with parents (Dishion, 1990; Steinberg & Silverberg, 1986). Adolescents with permissive parents, parents who are unwilling or unable to monitor their adolescent's behavior, are especially responsive to negative influences of friends. Responsiveness to friends' influence is also high among adolescents with rejecting parents. Such parents rarely praise or show a positive interest in their adolescents. These adolescents, in turn, look to the friendship group as a source of security and self-worth. They care a great deal about maintaining good relationships with friends and so are easily persuaded by them.

Developmental Changes in Friends' Influence

As adolescents move out of the family and into the world of peers, you might expect their susceptibility to friends' influence to increase. Most research data show that friends do have more influence on adolescents than on young children, but friends' influence varies during adolescence (Berndt, 1979; Chassin et al., 1986; Urberg et al., 1991). Friends have the most influence in middle adolescence, or around age 15, for several reasons. Between early and middle adolescence, friends' interactions increase in frequency, and friendship groups become more cohesive. Therefore, friends become more influential. Between middle and late adolescence, romantic relationships become more important. Also, adolescents' capacity for truly independent decision-making increases (Berndt, 1979; Steinberg & Silverberg, 1986). These changes reduce the influence of same-sex friends.

Although the changes in friends' influence with age are noticeable, they are modest in size. Children, adolescents, and adults are influenced by all the people with whom they have formed close relationships, and, throughout life, those people include best friends. People use many techniques to influence one another, and all these techniques are used by adolescents and their friends. You should recognize that most writings about peer pressure exaggerate the influence of friends, but you should not err in the opposite direction. In rejecting the myth of peer pressure, remember the reality that friends can and often do have a powerful influence on the attitudes and behavior of adolescents.

SUMMARY

Adolescence begins with puberty and ends with maturity. In Western societies, adolescence normally includes the period between about 12 and 18 years of age.

Friendships are especially important during adolescence, because friends help adolescents accomplish critical life tasks. The adolescent agenda—the tasks for this period of development—includes gaining more independence from the family, finding a place in a social world of peers, forming an identity, and learning about the larger society. Friends provide various kinds of support for adolescents as they work on these tasks.

One important function of friendships is to give adolescents a stable and valued position in the peer social world. Most adolescents name several best friends who make up their friendship group. Adolescents usually select friends similar to themselves in age, sex, race, social class, preferences for activities, and academic achievement. During adolescence most friendships last for several months or even years. Adolescents with friendships that are more stable are better adjusted socially and psychologically.

Adolescents differentiate between best friends and other friends more sharply than children do but less sharply than adults do. During adolescence, similarity in psychological characteristics becomes more important for friendship formation. Friendship stability, however, seems to change little during the adolescent years.

Adolescents' friendships have both positive and negative qualities. The most significant positive quality of a friendship is its psychological intimacy—usually narrowly defined as the feeling of closeness and understanding that leads to self-disclosure. Wood (1993) suggests that this is a "feminized" view of intimacy that fails to give adequate weight to the other ways in which intimacy can be expressed—for example, by doing things together or for each other. Intimacy first becomes an important element of friendships during adolescence and remains important during adulthood. Other features of good friendships include prosocial behavior, self-esteem support, and loyalty. On the negative side, friends sometimes disagree about what they should do or what they should believe, and these disagreements can lead to conflicts. Conflicts can also arise because of friends' competition and rivalry. Adolescents who have frequent conflicts with friends tend to interact more negatively with other people. These conflicts can be reduced by encouraging friends to recognize their complementary strengths and weaknesses and by teaching adolescents conflict-resolution strategies.

Adolescents report about as many conflicts with friends as children do. However, when given a choice between competing and sharing with friends, adolescents compete less and share more than children do. Apparently, adolescents are more sensitive than children to a friend's hurt feelings about losing a competition.

Both popular and scholarly writers have assumed that peer pressure is a major cause of undesirable behavior in adolescence, but research data suggest that this assumption is more a myth than a reality. Peer influence can be either positive or negative, depending on the attitudes and behavior of an adolescent's friends. For most adolescents, friends' influence is more positive than negative.

Coercive pressure is not the primary means by which friends influence each other. Friends often discuss issues freely until they reach a consensus. They use reasoning, offers of rewards, or teasing to persuade each other.

Susceptibility to friends' influence is greater when adolescents are low in self-esteem and when they have neglecting or rejecting parents. Adolescents are more influenced by their best friends than are children, but friends' influence peaks around age 15. The changes in friends' influence with age are modest, however. Adolescents' desires to make their own decisions limit their friends' influence on them.

Class Discussion Questions

1. Is the typical level of friendship stability among adolescents high enough? What would be the advantages and disadvantages of trying to change schools in ways that might increase the stability of adolescents' friendships?
2. Reflections on one's own experiences can often be a useful source of ideas about development. What do you remember about the changes in your friendships as you matured from early adolescence through mid-adolescence and into early adulthood (the college years)?
3. Some adolescents have highly supportive friendships. Other adolescents have friendships high in conflict. What do you think is the most important cause of variations in the quality of friendships: adolescents' personality traits, the conditions of their social environments, or luck (chance)?
4. One point made in the chapter is that popular writings about peer pressure are inaccurate. What were your experiences with peer pressure in adolescence? How would you define peer pressure? If you experienced it, how did you react to this pressure?
5. Some writers assume that their friends, by themselves, lack the maturity necessary to be a positive influence on adolescents' development. Do you agree or disagree with this assumption? Do you think adults can intervene to enhance the positive influence of adolescents' friends? If so, how?

Homework Assignments

1. Watch a TV show or movie about adolescent life. Compare its portrayal of adolescents' friendships with the information in the chapter.
2. Find a newspaper or magazine article that deals with problem behaviors in adolescence, such as drug abuse or gang violence. See what the writers say about peer pressure. Summarize both the correct conclusions and the misconceptions in the article.
3. Describe your best friendship in adolescence, or interview an adolescent who is 12 to 16 years old about her or his best friendship. Then

answer the following questions. (1) What makes this relationship a best friendship? (2) What things did your interviewee not like about being friends with the other person? (3) What things does the interviewee do with the friend? (4) What do the interviewee and the friend do for each other? (5) How did they become friends? (6) How long have they been friends? (7) What might end the friendship?

Additional Readings

Berndt, T. J., & Ladd, G. W. (Eds.). (1989). *Peer relationships in child development.* New York: Wiley.

Brown, B. B. (1990). Peer groups and peer cultures. In S. S. Feldman & G. R. Elliott (Eds.), *At the threshold: The developing adolescent* (pp. 171–196). Cambridge, MA: Harvard University Press.

Hartup, W. W. (1993). Conflict and friendship relations. In C. U. Shantz & W. W. Hartup (Eds.), *Conflict in child and adolescent development* (pp. 186–215). Cambridge, England: Cambridge University Press.

Larson, R., & Richards, M. H. (1991). Daily companionship in late childhood and early adolescence: Changing developmental contexts. *Child Development, 62,* 284–300.

Youniss, J., & Smollar, J. (1985). *Adolescent relations with mothers, fathers, and friends.* Chicago: University of Chicago Press.

References

Ansley, L., & McCleary, K. (1992, August 21–23). Do the right thing. *USA Weekend,* pp. 4–7.

Ball, S. J. (1981). *Beachside Comprehensive.* Cambridge, England: Cambridge University Press.

Berndt, T. J. (1979). Developmental changes in conformity to peers and parents. *Developmental Psychology, 15,* 608–616.

Berndt, T. J. (1986). Children's comments about their friendships. In M. Perlmutter (Ed.), *Minnesota Symposium on Child Psychology: Vol. 18: Cognitive perspectives on children's social and behavioral development* (pp. 189–212). Hillsdale, NJ: Erlbaum.

Berndt, T. J. (1989). Obtaining support from friends during childhood and adolescence. In D. Belle (Ed.), *Children's social networks and social supports* (pp. 308–331). New York: John Wiley & Sons.

Berndt, T. J. (in press). Intimacy and competition in the friendships of adolescent boys and girls. In M. Stevenson (Ed.), *Gender roles across the life span.* Madison, WI: University of Wisconsin Press.

Berndt, T. J., Hawkins, J. A., & Hoyle, S. G. (1986). Changes in friendship during a school year: Effects on children's and adolescents' impressions of friendship and sharing with friends. *Child Development, 57,* 1284–1297.

Berndt, T. J., & Hoyle, S. G. (1985). Stability and change in childhood and adolescent friendships. *Developmental Psychology*, *21*, 1007–1015.

Berndt, T. J., & Keefe, K. (1993). Influences of friends' characteristics and friendship features on adolescents' adjustment to school. Unpublished manuscript, Purdue University.

Berndt, T. J., Miller, K. E., & Park, K. (1989). Adolescents' perceptions of friends' and parents' influence on aspects of their school adjustment. *Journal of Early Adolescence*, *9*, 419–435.

Berndt, T. J., & Perry, T. B. (1986). Children's perceptions of friendships as supportive relationships. *Developmental Psychology*, *22*, 640–648.

Berndt, T. J., & Perry, T. B. (1990). Distinctive features and effects of early adolescent friendships. In R. Montemayer, G. R. Adams, & T. P. Gullotta (Eds.), *From childhood to adolescence: A transitional period?* (pp. 269–287). Newbury Park, CA: Sage.

Berndt, T. J., & Savin-Williams, R. C. (1993). Peer relations and friendships. In P. H. Tolan & B. J. Cohler (Eds.), *Handbook of clinical research and practice with adolescents* (pp. 203–219). New York: Wiley & Sons.

Billy, J. O. G., & Udry, J. R. (1985). Patterns of adolescent friendship and effects on sexual behavior. *Social Psychology Quarterly*, *48*, 27–41.

Blyth, D. A., & Traeger, C. (1988). Adolescent self-esteem and perceived relationships with parents and peers. In S. Salzinger, J. Antrobus, & M. Hammer (Eds.), *Social networks of children, adolescents, and college students* (pp. 171–194). Hillsdale, NJ: Erlbaum.

Bronfenbrenner, U. (1970). Reaction to social pressure from adults versus peers among Soviet day school and boarding school pupils in the perspective of an American sample. *Journal of Personality and Social Psychology*, *15*, 179–189.

Brown, B. B. (1990). Peer groups and peer cultures. In S. S. Feldman & G. R. Elliott (Eds.), *At the threshold: The developing adolescent* (pp. 171–196). Cambridge, MA: Harvard University Press.

Brown, B. B., Clasen, D. R., & Eicher, S. A. (1986). Perceptions of peer pressure, peer conformity dispositions, and self-reported behavior among adolescents. *Developmental Psychology*, *22*, 521–530.

Brown, B. B., Mounts, N., Lamborn, S. D., & Steinberg, L. (1993). Parenting practices and peer group affiliation in adolescence. *Child Development*, *64*, 467–482.

Cauce, A. M. (1986). Social networks and social competence: Exploring the effects of early adolescent friendships. *American Journal of Community Psychology*, *14*, 607–628.

Chassin, L., Presson, C. C., Montello, D., Sherman, S. J., & McGrew, J. (1986). Changes in peer and parent influence during adolescence: Longitudinal versus cross-sectional perspectives on smoking initiation. *Developmental Psychology*, *22*, 327–334.

Clark, M. S., & Reis, H. T. (1988). Interpersonal process in close relationships. *Annual Review of Psychology*, *39*, 609–672.

Cohen, S., & Wills, T. A. (1985). Stress, social support, and the buffering hypothesis. *Psychological Bulletin, 98,* 310–357.

Coleman, J. S. (1961). *The adolescent society.* New York: Free Press.

Condon, R. G. (1987). *Inuit youth: Growth and change in the Canadian Arctic.* New Brunswick, NJ: Rutgers University Press.

Crockett, L., Losoff, M., & Petersen, A. C. (1984). Perceptions of the peer group and friendship in early adolescence. *Journal of Early Adolescence, 4,* 155–181.

Csikszentmihalyi, M., & Larson, R. (1984). *Being adolescent.* New York: Basic Books.

Davies, B. (1982). *Life in the classroom and playground.* London: Routledge & Kegan Paul.

Davies, M., & Kandel, D. B. (1981). Parental and peer influences on adolescents' educational plans: Some further evidence. *American Journal of Sociology, 87,* 363–387.

Dishion, T. J. (1990). The family ecology of boys' peer relations in middle childhood. *Child Development, 61,* 874–892.

Douvan, E., & Adelson, J. (1966). *The adolescent experience.* New York: Wiley.

Downs, W. R. (1987). A panel study of normative structure, adolescent alcohol use and peer alcohol use. *Journal of Studies on Alcohol, 48,* 167–175.

Duck, S. W. (1975). Personality similarity and friendship choices by adolescents. *European Journal of Social Psychology, 5,* 351–365.

Duck, S. W. (1991). *Understanding relationships.* New York: Guilford.

Duck, S. W., & Wood, J. T. (1995). For better, for worse, for richer, for poorer: The rough and the smooth of relationships. In S. W. Duck & J. T. Wood (Eds.), *Confronting relationship challenges* [*Understanding relationship processes 5*] (pp. 1–21). Thousand Oaks, CA: Sage.

East, P. L., & Rook, K. S. (1992). Compensatory patterns of support among children's peer relationships: A test using school friends, nonschool friends, and siblings. *Developmental Psychology, 28,* 163–172.

Eder, D. (1985). The cycle of popularity: Interpersonal relations among female adolescents. *Sociology of Education, 58,* 154–165.

Epstein, J. L. (1983). The influence of friends on achievement and affective outcomes. In J. L. Epstein & N. Karweit (Eds.), *Friends in school: Patterns of selection and influence in secondary schools* (pp. 177–200). New York: Academic.

Erickson, E. H. (1963). *Childhood and society* (2nd ed.). New York: W.W. Norton.

Furman, W. (in press). The measurement of children's and adolescents' perceptions of friendships: Conceptual and methodological issues. In W. M. Bukowski, A. F. Newcomb, & W. W. Hartup (Eds.), *The company they keep: Friendships in childhood and adolescence.* Cambridge, England: Cambridge University Press.

Furman, W., & Buhrmester, D. (1992). Age and sex differences in perceptions of networks of personal relationships. *Child Development, 63,* 103–115.

Gottman, J. M., & Mettetal, G. (1986). Speculations about social and affective development: Friendship and acquaintanceship through adolescence. In J. M. Gottman & J. G. Parker (Eds.), *Conversations of friends* (pp. 192–237). Cambridge, England: Cambridge University Press.

Graham, J. W., Marks, G., & Hansen, W. B. (1991). Social influence processes affecting adolescent substance use. *Journal of Applied Psychology, 76,* 291–298.

Hallinan, M. T., & Williams, R. A. (1987). The stability of students' interracial friendships. *American Sociological Review, 52,* 653–664.

Hartup, W. W. (1983). Peer relations. In P. H. Mussen (Series Ed.) & E. M. Hetherington (Vol. Ed.), *Handbook of child psychology: Vol. 4. Socialization, personality, and social development* (pp. 103–196). New York: Wiley.

Hartup, W. W. (1993a). Adolescents and their friends. In B. Laursen (Ed.), *New directions for child development: Close friendships in adolescence* (pp. 3–22). San Francisco: Jossey-Bass.

Hartup, W. W. (1993b). Conflict and friendship relations. In C. U. Shantz & W. W. Hartup (Eds.), *Conflict in child and adolescent development* (pp. 186–215). Cambridge, England: Cambridge University Press.

Hill, J. P., & Lynch, M. E. (1983). The intensification of gender-related role expectations during early adolescence. In J. Brooks-Gunn & A. C. Petersen (Eds.), *Girls at puberty* (pp. 201–228). New York: Plenum.

Hirsch, B. J., & Renders, R. J. (1986). The challenge of adolescent friendships: A study of Lisa and her friends. In S. E. Hobfoll (Ed.), *Stress, social support, and women* (pp. 17–27). Washington, DC: Hemisphere.

Hollos, M., & Leis, P. E. (1989). *Becoming Nigerian in Ijo society.* New Brunswick, NJ: Rutgers University Press.

House, J. S., Umberson, D., & Landis, K. K. (1988). Structures and processes of social support. *Annual Review of Sociology, 14,* 293–318.

Kagan, S., & Madsen, M. C. (1972). Rivalry in Anglo-American and Mexican-American children of two ages. *Journal of Personality and Social Psychology, 24,* 214–220.

Kandel, D. B. (1978). Homophily, selection, and socialization in adolescent friendships. *American Journal of Sociology, 84,* 427–436.

Keating, D. P. (1990). Adolescent thinking. In S. S. Feldman & G. Elliott (Eds.), *At the threshold: The developing adolescent* (pp. 54–89). Cambridge, MA: Harvard University Press.

Keefe, K. (1994). Perceptions of normative social pressure and attitudes toward alcohol use: Changes during adolescence. *Journal of Studies on Alcohol, 55,* 46–54.

Kon, I. (1981). Adolescent friendship: Some unanswered questions for future research. In S. W. Duck & R. Gilmour (Eds.), *Personal relationships 2: Developing personal relationships* (pp. 187–203). New York: Academic Press.

Kurdek, L. A., & Sinclair, R. J. (1988). Adjustment of young adolescents in two-parent nuclear, stepfather, and mother-custody families. *Journal of Consulting and Clinical Psychology, 56,* 91–96.

Larson, R., & Richards, M. H. (1991). Daily companionship in late childhood and early adolescence: Changing developmental contexts. *Child Development, 62,* 284–300.

Laursen, B. (in press). Closeness and conflict in adolescent peer relationships: Interdependence among friends and romantic partners. In W. M. Bukowski, A. F. Newcomb, & W. W. Hartup (Eds.), *The company they keep*. Cambridge, England: Cambridge University Press.

Laursen, B., & Collins, W. A. (in press). Interpersonal conflict during adolescence. *Psychological Bulletin*.

Maccoby, E. E. (1988). Gender as a social category. *Developmental Psychology, 24*, 755–765.

Matthews, S. H. (1986). *Friendships through the life course*. Beverly Hills, CA: Sage.

Piaget, J. (1965). *The moral judgment of the child*. New York: Free Press. (Originally published 1932.)

Raffaelli, M., & Duckett, E. (1989). "We were just talking . . .": Conversations in early adolescence. *Journal of Youth and Adolescence, 18*, 567–582.

Savin-Williams, R. C., & Berndt, T. J. (1990). Friendships and peer relations during adolescence. In S. S. Feldman & G. Elliott (Eds.), *At the threshold: The developing adolescent* (pp. 277–307). Cambridge, MA: Harvard University Press.

Sebald, H. (1986). Adolescents' shifting orientation toward parents and peers: A curvilinear trend over recent decades. *Journal of Marriage and the Family, 48*, 5–13.

Steinberg, L., & Silverberg, S. B. (1986). The vicissitudes of autonomy in early adolescence. *Child Development, 57*, 841–851.

Sullivan, H. S. (1953). *The interpersonal theory of psychiatry*. New York: Norton.

Suttles, G. D. (1971). *The social order of the slum*. Chicago: University of Chicago Press.

Tesser, A. (1984). Self-evaluation maintenance processes: Implications for relationships and for development. In J. C. Masters & K. Yarkin-Levin (Eds.), *Boundary areas in social and developmental psychology* (pp. 271–299). New York: Academic.

Torney-Purta, J. (1990). Youth in relation to social institutions. In S. S. Feldman & G. Elliott (Eds.), *At the threshold: The developing adolescent* (pp. 457–477). Cambridge, MA: Harvard University Press.

Urberg, K. A., Cheng, C.-H., & Shyu, S.-J. (1991). Grade changes in peer influence on adolescent cigarette smoking: A comparison of two measures. *Addictive Behaviors, 16*, 21–28.

Urberg, K. A., Shyu, S.-J., & Liang, J. (1990). Peer influence in adolescent cigarette smoking. *Addictive Behaviors, 15*, 247–255.

Wood, J. T. (1993). Engendered relations: Interaction, caring, power, and responsibility in intimacy. In S. W. Duck (Ed.), *Understanding relationship processes 3: Social contexts of relationships* (pp. 26–54). Newbury Park, CA: Sage.

Youniss, J. (1980). *Parents and peers in social development*. Chicago: University of Chicago Press.

Youniss, J., & Smollar, J. (1985). *Adolescent relations with mothers, fathers, and friends*. Chicago: University of Chicago Press.

Zarbatany, L., Hartmann, D. P., & Rankin, D. B. (1990). The psychological functions of preadolescent peer activities. *Child Development, 61*, 1067–1080.

Glossary

Adolescence   The developmental period from the onset of puberty to maturity

Identity   Ideas about one's characteristics and the roles one could adopt as an adult

Intimacy   A feeling of closeness and understanding that makes adolescents willing to reveal personal information to friends

Maturity   The age at which an individual in a particular society is assumed to be fully developed and thus is given the basic rights of an adult

Peers   For adolescents, this term refers to other adolescents who are of the same or similar age

9 Adolescent Sexuality: Trying to Explain the Magic and the Mystery

F. Scott Christopher

Arizona State University

The author would like to thank Fonda Christopher and Kami Knoell for their insightful comments on an earlier draft of this chapter.

Although some children may manifest an interest in sex earlier than adolescence, this stage of life witnesses the emergence of mature sexuality. Today more than ever, the issues that accompany this emergence are of interest to adolescents, their parents, educators, and just about everyone else. This chapter explores some of the important issues surrounding teenage dating and sexuality.

NV & SD

Chapter Outline

- Early Adolescent Sexuality
- Older Adolescent and Young Adult Sexuality
- The Dangers of Dating and Sex
- Summary

We had been going out almost ten months, and during that time had done everything possible without actual intercourse. We started to mean something to one another. After a while it got so that when we played around it seemed like unfinished business, intercourse seemed to be the natural completion to the activity. (Male, age 18)

I had been hinting strongly to her for a month that I would like to have sex with her. I had known her for six months. A close girl friend of hers had sex for the first time and they talked about [it]. She then had sex with me approximately two weeks later. (Male, age 19)

I didn't know him that well so it was more physical attraction that attracted me [to intercourse]. (Female, age 24)

These three anecdotes capture many of the important dynamics of adolescent sexual decision-making. The first male tells us that the *meaning* of his relationship to his partner is important. His statement that intercourse was a natural completion suggests the presence of unstated *norms* about when **coitus** (sexual intercourse) should occur. Compare his account to that of the second male. This person reveals that he had been trying to *influence* his partner to engage in intercourse for a month. For his partner, the sexual behavior of a friend tips the balance toward greater sexual involvement. Both of these accounts stand in sharp contrast to the last one, in which the decision to engage in coitus is based not on the qualities of the relationship but on the *physical attraction* of the partner. Taken together, these accounts demonstrate that multiple factors influence adolescent sexual decision-making.

This chapter will discuss these and other factors as it reviews what science has told us about adolescent sexuality. The chapter is divided into three parts: The first focuses on early adolescent sexuality; the second, on later adolescent and young adult sexuality; and the third, on some of the dangers of dating and sexuality.

EARLY ADOLESCENT SEXUALITY

What Role Does Family Play?

Examining the role of family in early adolescent sexual behavior (before the age of 18) is a natural place to begin, because adolescents' parents are often considered the primary socializers of their children with regard to sexual behavior and attitudes (Goldman & Goldman, 1982). This parental role probably forms the foundation for the popular belief that close-knit family relations and good communication buffer teens from peer pressures and influence them to resist engaging in sexual intercourse. It is necessary to point out, however, that even in close-knit families, adolescents are faced with the **developmental tasks** of beginning to become independent of family, developing their own identity, and considering a wider range of values.

One of the family's most basic qualities—its configuration—has been found to be related to the probability of early adolescents' engaging in coitus. Living with a single parent, rather than both biological parents, puts adolescents at risk for early coital activity (Newcomer & Udry, 1987; Rosenbaum & Kendal, 1990). This is especially true for daughters (Miller & Bingham, 1989). The dynamics behind this phenomenon have not been researched, but it has been suggested that single parents may not be as able to supervise, **monitor,** or control their offspring as well as two parents in the same household could (Miller & Moore, 1990). Adolescent **modeling** of parental dating behavior may provide a better explanation.

When compared with daughters from two-parent families, daughters of single mothers who do not date are no more likely to engage in coitus at an early age, whereas daughters of single mothers who date are at greater risk (Peterson, Moore, Furstenberg, & Morgan, 1985, as cited in Miller & Moore, 1990).

A more crucial question is whether the *quality* of parent-adolescent relationships is related to adolescent sexual behavior. Parent-adolescent relationships are multidimensional, so this question does not lend itself to a simple answer. Adolescents who have a **close relationship** with their parents are less likely to engage in sexual activity; again, this is especially true for daughters (Inazu & Fox, 1980; Weinstein & Thornton, 1989). Daughters who feel **support** from their parents are also at lower risk for early coitus (Jessor, Costa, Jessor, & Donovan, 1983), although not all investigators have found this to be true (Christopher, Johnson, & Roosa, 1993). **Parental control** attempts are also associated with teen sexual activities (Hogan & Kitagawa, 1985), but this appears to be a **curvilinear relationship** (Jessor et al., 1983; Miller, McCoy, Olson, & Wallace, 1986)—that is, too much or too little parental control results in greater risk of coitus in early adolescents, whereas a moderate amount of control results in a lower risk. Taken together, these findings show that early adolescents, and especially daughters, are least likely to engage in sexual intercourse when they have a close, trusting relationship with their parents who provide moderate control.

Research into parent-adolescent communication and its relationship to sons' and daughters' sexual activity has shown that high levels of communication about sexual matters are linked to similarity in parent-adolescent sexual *attitudes* (Fisher, 1986), but links between communication and teen sexual *behavior* are tenuous. Although mothers' reports of early communication about sex are associated with a lower likelihood of coitus in daughters, this association does not hold when daughters are asked about the same communication (Newcomer & Udry, 1985). Moreover, several researchers have failed to find a relationship between sexual involvement and family communication on either sexual or nonsexual topics (Christopher et al., 1993; Furstenberg, Herceg-Baron, Shea, & Webb, 1984). Other researchers report greater sexual communication for **nonvirgins** than **virgins** (Fox & Inazu, 1980). Moore, Peterson, and Furstenberg's (1986) investigation may shed some light. These researchers found that communication and parental attitudes are connected: Daughters of traditional parents who communicate about sex with them are less likely to engage in sexual intercourse, but the sons of these same parents are more likely to experience coitus. They found, however, that sons whose parents listen to them and discuss important life decisions with them are less likely to engage in coitus than sons whose parents do not do this, regardless of the parents' values.

The inconsistency in the above findings may be attributed to how studies have been conducted. Few researchers ask about the communication that took place before teens engaged in coitus. This means that higher levels of communication with nonvirgin children may be the result of parents' guesses about their children's sexual activity—parents may talk more in an attempt to ensure that their children protect themselves against the possible negative consequences of sexual explorations (Fox & Inazu, 1980). Furthermore, parents' willingness to talk to their adolescents about sex is linked to their comfort with doing so (Russo, Barnes, & Wright, 1991). Few parents are comfortable in this role, so most parents are far more likely to use analogies and generalities than solid factual information when they do discuss sex (Goldman & Goldman, 1982).

Peer Influences

The fact that families appear to have only a moderate influence on adolescent sexual behavior raises questions about peer influences. Peer influences have been measured in two ways. In the first, adolescents are asked how sexually involved they think their best friends are. These perceptions of a friend's sexual activity are associated with adolescent sexual behavior for white (Cvetkovich & Grote, 1980; Jessor et al., 1983) and Latino (Christopher et al., 1993) males and females. This approach gives an indirect indication of peer influences, but it does not measure the best friend's *actual behavior.* Furthermore, this approach measures perceptions at a single point in time, as opposed to a **longitudinal study,** which would take measures across time. Longitudinal designs have the advantage of showing whether peers influence adolescents' sexual behavior or whether adolescents' sexual behavior influences their choice of friends.

Billy and Udry (1985) examined best friends' actual coital behavior using a longitudinal approach. They found that only white females are susceptible to the influence of their friends' behavior. Virgins in this group are more likely to become nonvirgins if they have a best friend who is not a virgin. White males and females are more likely than nonwhites to choose friends whose actions are similar to their own. For both white males and white females, those who become nonvirgins are likely to choose friends who are also nonvirgins. Neither process operated for African-American males and females in the study, and in none of the ethnic and gender subgroups were friendship bonds broken because of changes in coital status.

Taken as a whole, the friendship findings suggest that peer influences work only for white female adolescents, and that one's own sexual behavior guides friendship choices for white teens as a group. Choosing friends who are also coitally experienced probably provides social reinforcement for this sexual exploration. These findings fly in the face of adolescents' claims that peer pressure is a critical reason for not waiting until they are older before trying coitus (Louis Harris & Associates, 1986)! Peer pressure may come from the more generalized peer context teens encounter daily rather than from their best friend's sexual activity.

As will be shown shortly, African-Americans have a higher level of sexual activity overall, and they may be more accepting of teen sexual involvement than whites. If, however, a general type of peer pressure operates in teens' daily lives, we would expect that coital rates among African-Americans in integrated school settings would differ from rates among African-Americans in mostly black schools. This has been found to be true: African-American teens attending all-black schools have much higher coital rates than those who are in school settings that include both white and African-American students (Furstenberg, Morgan, Moore, & Peterson, 1987). Moreover, white male and female adolescents are more likely to experience coitus as the percentage of African-Americans in their school settings increases (Day, 1992). These findings are *robust;* that is, they hold even when the effects of these teens' economic status and parental education are taken into consideration. Thus teens' sexual exploration is influenced by their immediate peer context.

Dating Dynamics

Although early adolescent sexual exploration takes place in a **dyad**—a two-partner relationship—researchers have tended simply to note the dyadic relationships but to ignore the dynamics that operate within a dyad. Existing findings indicate that the earlier dating begins, the earlier sexual intercourse takes place for African-American and white teens (Furstenberg et al., 1987; Leigh, Weddle, & Loewen, 1988). Most female teens also report that they were in a steady dating relationship with their first coital partner, whereas males are more likely to indicate that their first coitus occurred while casually dating (Zelnick & Shah, 1983).

Engaging in coitus at this developmental stage is tied to certain dyadic dynamics. African-American and white adolescent females' sexual activity is related to their wanting to please their partners, to an inability to say no, and to the feeling that coitus is expected of them (Cvetkovich & Grote, 1980). Adolescent females' coital frequency is also higher when the male decides whether coitus should occur and what type of birth control should be used (Jorgensen, King, & Torrey, 1980). These findings imply that young females may be particularly vulnerable when they are fulfilling the traditional female role demands of a steady dating relationship with a partner who fails to consider their wishes.

Hormones and Pubertal Development: Social Cues versus Biological Influences

One of the hallmarks of adolescence is the onset of **puberty.** Increases in **hormone** production result in an array of physical changes with different effects for males and females. Both male and female teens experience increases in *testosterone, estrogens,* and *progesterone,* as well as other hormones, but there are differences in the concentration levels that are related to gender. For instance, before puberty, **testosterone** levels in both sexes do not differ; with puberty, male levels increase ten- to twenty-fold, whereas female levels merely double (Udry, 1988).

Although heightened hormone production triggers physical changes that are fairly consistent in their sequential, physiological effects, the age at which these changes begin is not consistent. Some adolescents mature early, others mature late. Different aspects of sexual behavior are related to these physiological changes, but social scientists have questioned what factors cause this relationship. One possible cause is the response by others to the adolescent's physical changes. Parents may become more restrictive of a daughter's opposite-sex interactions when her breasts begin to develop or she begins to menstruate. Similarly, both male and female adolescents could be considered more worthy as dating partners by their peers because they are more physically mature. An alternative explanation is that the relationship between sexual behavior and pubertal changes is solely biological.

Some researchers who have examined pubertal changes and early sexual behavior have failed to find a relationship between when puberty begins and the onset of sexual activity (Dornbusch et al., 1981; Leigh et al., 1988); other researchers have found a link between the two. When a relation is found, it appears that African-American and white teenage girls who have their first menstrual cycle earlier than their age **cohorts** are more likely to experience early coitus (Rosenbaum & Kandel, 1990; Udry, 1979). African-American males who have wet dreams at earlier ages than their peers are also more likely to engage in intercourse at an earlier age (Zabin, Smith, Hirsch, & Hardy, 1986).

Udry (1988) and his colleagues provide possible explanations of why researchers have arrived at conflicting results. Few investigators have included *actual* measures of hormone levels. Without these biological **indicators** it is unclear whether findings are the result of responses by others to those who mature early or whether they are related to actual physiological changes in the adolescents. Udry and his colleagues used blood samples to establish hormone levels for a group of male and female teens. He also asked these adolescents about possible social influences on their sexual behavior, including those originating with peers and with parents, and about different aspects of sexual development, such as intercourse, thinking about sex, and arousal experienced in a variety of situations. Udry's results indicate that biological influences are different for males and females and that testosterone has the greatest hormonal effect (Udry, 1988). For males, increases in testosterone are related to increases in kissing and fondling and a greater likelihood of engaging in intercourse. This is not to say that social influences do not have an effect on males' sexual behavior. They do, but they are separate from biological influences. For girls, measures of sexual motivations, such as intentions to have sex and how much they would like and enjoy having sex, increase with increases in testosterone, but acts of sexual intercourse do not. Udry concluded that for females, social controls filter, or mediate, biological effects on coital behavior. It seems that biological and social factors play a role, but that biological influences are stronger and more direct for males than for females.

These findings become especially meaningful if we compare when puberty begins among today's adolescents compared to adolescents in the past. Over the course of 150 years the average age of females at their first menstrual cycle has gradually shifted from 17 to 12.8 years (Dyk, 1993). Males have experienced a comparable shift toward earlier physical maturation. Parallel changes in cognitive, social, and emotional development, however, have *not* occurred. This means that today's adolescents are apt to experience biological and social pressures to engage in sexual activity before they are cognitively capable of fully estimating the consequences of their actions and emotionally prepared to cope with potential outcomes.

What Type of Adolescent Is Sexually Active? The Role of Individual Factors

Several individual traits have been identified as related to early sexual involvement. For instance, early adolescents who attend church frequently, a common indicator of religiosity, are more likely to refrain from engaging in intercourse when compared with those who do not attend or who are irregular in their attendance (Miller & Moore, 1990). This holds true across ethnic groups; it has been found for white (Forste & Heaton, 1988), African-American (Leigh et al., 1988), and Latino youth (Day, 1992). Religious participation also seems more important than belonging to any particular denomination, although those who belong to fundamentalist denominations are somewhat less likely to engage in coitus (Leigh et al., 1988; Thornton & Camburn, 1987). Adolescents' church attendance is most likely the result of their parents' influence; one longitudinal study showed that mothers' religious participation brought about their adolescents' participation (Thornton & Camburn, 1989).

Adolescents' sexual attitudes are related to their sexual behavior. In general it can be said that teens with more permissive attitudes are more likely to have engaged in coitus (Bingham, Miller, & Adams, 1990; Udry & Billy, 1987). However, this may be overstating what actually occurs. For some teens it is undoubtedly true that having more accepting attitudes leads to early coital involvement; but for other teens it may be that early coital experiences lead to changes in their attitudes, with the attitudes becoming either more conservative or liberal. Support for this idea comes from a

Today's teens are likely to experience biological and social pressures to engage in sexual activity far sooner than previous generations did.

study that found that half of the nonvirgin females asked, and about a third of the males, believed that they were not yet old enough to have experienced sexual intercourse (Zabin, Hirsch, Smith, & Hardy, 1984).

Early experience of sexual intercourse may not be an isolated behavior. Jessor et al. (1983) hold that early coital behavior is a "problem" only because of **age-graded norms** in our society. In other words, the same behavior at a later age (for instance, young adulthood or adulthood) would not be as likely to be viewed as deviant. They, and others, support this position by showing that sexually experienced teens are more accepting of and more likely to engage in other deviant acts such as smoking, drinking, and drug use (Rosenbaum & Kandel, 1990). These behaviors are considered unacceptable for adolescents in American society, even though moderate forms of all three of these behaviors are often acceptable, if not normative, in adulthood.

Three additional individual factors have received the attention of researchers. The first focuses on the coital decision-making process. It has been found that African-American and white teens weigh potential positive and negative outcomes when they are considering whether to engage in coitus (Bauman & Udry, 1981), but that females, and especially African-American females, are more likely to do so than males (Udry & Billy, 1987). This finding is not surprising, as females are at greater risk for negative consequences from sexual activity. The second and third factors are **locus of control** and **self-esteem.** It is commonly believed that youth who see themselves as controlled by fate or others and who have low feelings of self-worth are more likely to engage in coitus. These adolescents are often seen as bowing to peer pressure or using sexual intercourse to become valued by others. Although there has been some support for these popular views (Day, 1992), not all investigators have found this to be true (Christopher et al., 1993; Rosenbaum & Kandel, 1990). Furthermore, when the popular views have been supported by research, the strength of the association between locus of control and self-esteem and sexual activity has not been strong (Miller, Christensen, & Olson, 1987; Rosenbaum & Kandel, 1990)—nor has it always been in the expected direction. In some instances sexual activity has been related to both positive and negative self-esteem, depending on individuals' sexual attitudes (Miller et al., 1987). Overall, the popular hypothesis about the important role of self-esteem and locus of control in adolescent sexuality is not strongly supported.

Looking at the Numbers

National surveys indicate that about 50% of adolescent males and females have experienced sexual intercourse by the time they are 16 years old (Sonenstein, Pleck, & Leighton, 1991; Zelnick & Shah, 1983), with males reporting average age for first intercourse about a half-year younger compared with females. This statistic does not tell the entire story, however. Rates of coital activity among teens have changed over time. Dramatic increases in sexual intercourse rates were evident during the 1970s. These rates leveled off in the 1980s (Hoefferth, Kahn, & Baldwin, 1987), and there are some indications of slight declines at the end of this decade, especially among African-American teens (Hoefferth et al., 1987; Sonenstein et al., 1991). At the same time, however, a greater number of adolescents are experiencing intercourse at younger ages (see Figure 9-1). Zelnick and Shah (1983) found that 22.7% of females and 37.3% of males reported they had experienced coitus by age 14.

Researchers have found ethnic and racial differences in rate and first experience of coitus. Compared to other ethnic and racial groups, African-American teens have consistently higher coital rates, and they begin sexual activity at an earlier age (Hoefferth et al., 1987; Sonenstein et al., 1991). Latino teens have typically been ignored in national surveys until recently (Day, 1992). When they have been included, it is evident that not all Latino subgroups behave the same. Day (1992) found that although Latinos did not differ from Anglos in their age at first coitus, Mexican-American males reported a one-year-older age than other Latino males.

These figures should not give the impression that adolescents engage in regular or frequent coital activities after their first experience of sexual

Figure 9-1
Mean Number of Sexual Partners since First Intercourse for Males in 1988 (*Source:* Sonenstein, Pleck, & Leighton, 1991)

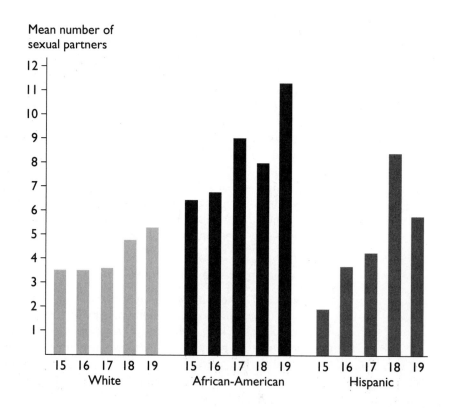

intercourse. Teen males report that they average slightly less than six months between acts of intercourse (Sonenstein et al., 1991). Younger males have longer intervals between sexual encounters than older males, and Latino males experience longer intervals than African-American or white males. Still, two-thirds of teens have sex again six months after their first experience (Miller & Moore, 1990).

One of the more noticeable outcomes of this sexual activity is adolescent pregnancies. Although the coital rates for teens in the United States are comparable to those for teens in other Western countries, the United States has the unfortunate distinction of having the highest adolescent pregnancy rate of all the developed countries in the world (Hayes, 1987). Although few teens in our country want or plan to become pregnant, more than 10% of whites and 20% of African-American teens say that they did not think or care about pregnancy when they first had sex (Moore & Peterson, 1989). The actual percentage of adolescents who have become pregnant remained fairly stable through the 1980s at about 11%, with African-American adolescents more likely to become pregnant than white adolescents (Miller & Moore, 1990).

Pregnant teens can deal with their pregnancies in different ways. Some teens choose to marry—36% of female adolescents who gave birth to a child in 1987 were married (Moore, 1989). The majority who carry the baby to term, however, give birth without getting married—347,880 girls in 1988. Most of these babies are kept by their single mothers rather than offered for adoption (Miller & Moore, 1990), and whites are more likely to choose adoption than African-Americans. Abortion is chosen by many—42% of all teen pregnancies among girls aged 15 to 19 ended in abortion in 1985, with white and African-American teens equally likely to choose this option (Henshaw & Van Vort, 1984). The individual and societal implications of this phenomenon have spurred different interventions with varying degrees of success (see Box 1).

The statistics offered to this point provide an overview of **heterosexual** involvement during early adolescence, but not all sexual activity is heterosexual. Estimates of **homosexual** activity at this stage are difficult to calculate for a number of reasons. First, contrary to popular beliefs, heterosexuality and homosexuality are not exclusive categories but are better thought of as existing along a continuum. It is not unusual for self-identified heterosexuals and homosexuals to have had both opposite-sex and same-sex sexual partners in their past (Peplau & Cochran, 1981; Remafedi, Resnick, Blum, & Harris, 1992). Second, calling oneself **gay** or **lesbian** occurs after a prolonged process, and few young teens have had the life experiences necessary to achieve this self-definition (Troiden, 1989). Finally, our society is extremely **homophobic.** This may not only result in an underreporting of homosexuality in surveys but also make it difficult for early adolescents to accept sexual attraction to someone of the same sex.

With these cautions as a starting point, the results of a study by Re-

Box 1

What Can We Do about Teen Pregnancy?

The high teen pregnancy rate has motivated policy makers, educators, and researchers to implement a variety of interventions. Initially, sex education in the classroom was used. Simply providing knowledge failed to change sexual behavior, however. In fact, a consistent finding across investigations has been that sex education has no effect on sexual behavior (Allgeier, 1992).

Another form of intervention has been abstinence-only programs. These programs emphasize "saying no" to sex and avoid providing factual information on **contraceptive practices** (Allgeier, 1992). Congress has funded abstinence-only programs since 1981. This form of intervention has also become increasingly popular with state legislators and those who establish curriculum in public schools. But ten years of evaluations of this strategy have failed to establish its viability (Roosa & Christopher, 1992), and many have begun to question the wisdom of policy makers who support an approach that has yet to demonstrate its effectiveness (Christopher & Roosa, 1990; Roosa & Christopher, 1990).

Two approaches have shown promise. Kirby, Barth, Leland, and Fetro (1991) evaluated a program that recognizes the cognitive functioning level of the teens and acknowledges the important role peers can play. Pressures to have sex from the media and peers and abstinence and contraceptive issues are discussed by instructors and adolescents in a manner that takes the cognitive development of the teens into consideration. The importance of avoiding unprotected coitus is stressed, and students role-play different interactions, including how to obtain contraceptives. Evaluation indicates that this approach may be most effective for virgins. Virgins who went through the program (the **intervention group**) were less likely to have engaged in intercourse and more likely to use contraception if they did become coitally active by the time of a follow-up assessment compared to virgins in a **control group.**

The most dramatic results, however, have come from programs that pair education with free and ready access to contraception (Zabin, Hirsch, Smith, Streett, & Hardy, 1986). Zabin and her colleagues targeted a group at high risk for teen pregnancy: very low-income African-American adolescents. They paired an in-school program, consisting of presentations, discussion groups, and counseling, with an after-school clinic that provided free educational information, medical examinations, and contraceptives. Comparison of participants to similar teens in a control group (who did not participate in either the in-school program or the after-school program) showed dramatic differences. The pregnancy rate among participants dropped by 30%, whereas the rate among controls increased by 57%. Those who participated were also older at first coitus and more likely to use effective contraception earlier in their sexual activity.

mafedi and colleagues (1992) are enlightening. They surveyed over 36,000 public school students in Minnesota. The majority of the students, 88.2%, identified themselves as heterosexuals, whereas 1.1% saw themselves as **bisexual** or homosexual. Just over 10% were unsure of their sexual orientation. Those who were unsure were less likely than the majority of their peers to have experienced only heterosexual interactions; they were more likely to report bisexual experiences and bisexual and homosexual fantasies. Understandably, the number of adolescents who were unsure decreased as they got older and their sexual identities became more fully developed.

OLDER ADOLESCENT AND YOUNG ADULT SEXUALITY

Around the age of 18, adolescents experience a new developmental status. They characteristically graduate from high school and either get a full-time job or further their education. This is a time for exploring the adult world. Many will move away from home and direct parental supervision. Changes in types of employment or college majors are not unusual. Heterosexuals may date several partners before deciding whom—or if—they want to marry. Dating provides the context for experiencing one's evolving sexuality. Although the sexual behaviors may be the same as those engaged in during early adolescence, the interpersonal context and developmental status of the individuals becomes more adultlike. Hence, new meanings are given to sexual behaviors by individuals, dating partners, peers, and society.

Dating and Sexuality for Older Adolescents and Young Adults

To understand the dynamics of dating relationships, it is necessary to step back and examine male-female differences in dating and sexuality. Single males are more sexually oriented than single females at this developmental stage. These young men are likely to see women in friendship interactions as sending sexual cues, even when these women do not see themselves as giving such cues (Abbey & Melby, 1986). Thus males may have a lower threshold for perceiving *sexual intent* (Shotland & Craig, 1988). This can result in misunderstandings about the sexual wishes of a dating partner. Males are also more accepting of casual sexual interactions than are women, who want an emotional investment by both partners (Carroll, Volk, & Hyde, 1985). It is not surprising, therefore, that men want sex after fewer dates when compared with women (see Figure 9-2). Furthermore, although women's roles have changed in other areas, males are still predominately the initiators of sexual interaction (O'Sullivan & Byers, 1992). These differences can create a sexual tension in dating relationships

Figure 9-2
Percent of Males and
Females Who Believe
Sexual Intercourse Is
Proper, by Stage of
Dating
(*Source:* Adapted from
Roche, 1986)

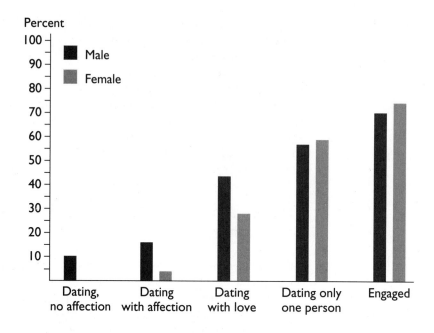

that is most easily resolved by direct communication, but dating couples rarely talk in depth about their sexual interactions (Cupach & Metts, 1991).

Given these differences, it is surprising that dating couples find enough common ground to want to engage in sexual intercourse! Which raises the question, What initially influences couples to engage in coitus? In one study single individuals were asked to focus on the *first time* they engaged in sexual intercourse with their most recent dating partner and to report on what influenced this interaction (Christopher & Cate, 1984). The most important influence was the loving, liking, and commitment the couple had achieved; predictably, this was more of an influence for females than for males. The second influence was how sexually aroused the individuals were, whether this arousal was conveyed to their partners, and how receptive the partner was to their sexual advances. The third factor focused on feelings of pressure and obligation, which originated in part from the partners' interactions and in part from perceiving friends as sexually active. Males were more influenced by this aspect, possibly indicating that males gain status among their peers when they engage in coitus in a dating relationship. Finally, males and females were equally likely to be influenced by circumstances such as alcohol use or whether the date was a special occasion (for example, was it a study break for pizza or a date for the spring formal dance?).

These findings should not be construed to mean that relationship intimacy is important in sexual decision-making only for women. Many men see emotional involvement as a prerequisite for intercourse (Carroll et al.,

1985), and love and intimacy are strongly related to sexual involvement in dating for both men and women (DeLamater & MacCorquodale, 1979). Thus gender differences exist, but relationship experiences are still important to men.

Other relationship experiences besides love and intimacy are related to sexual involvement. One of the most important is **commitment,** but commitment plays a different role in sexual involvement for different couples (see Box 2). Besides commitment, **equity** is related to engaging in sexual intercourse. The concept of equity addresses the balance of *rewards* and *costs* in dating. Relationships are equitable when partners perceive a balance between them of rewards and costs received. Inequity occurs when the rewards/costs "scale" tilts in the direction of one partner who receives relatively more rewards and is therefore overbenefited or who receives relatively greater costs and is therefore underbenefited. When compared with inequitable couples, equitable couples are more likely to engage in coitus because both partners (as opposed to only one) wish to and tend to be more sexually involved (Walster, Walster, & Traupmann, 1978).

Dyadic conflict is also related to sexual intimacy, but not in an expected direction. All of the four types of couples Christopher and Cate delineated in their 1985 study (see Box 2) experienced increases in conflict either when they first engaged in coitus or, in the case of *low involvement couples,* when they came close to engaging in coitus. Furthermore, conflict was positively related to engaging in sexual behaviors during the early stages of dating for the couples in this study (Christopher & Cate, 1988). In other words, increases in conflict are associated with increases in sexual involvement. It is unclear which comes first, conflict or sexual involvement. Couples may experience conflict because of gender-based differences in sexual expectations, and the conflict is settled by increasing sexual intimacy. Alternatively, couples may engage in sexual activity and afterward question what meaning to assign to their interaction. The ensuing conflict may help the couple to define the parameters of their relationship.

Two other relationship dimensions are related to sexual involvement at a precommitment stage of dating (Christopher & Cate, 1988). The first dimension consists of a group of behaviors used to maintain relationships, including verbal self-disclosure and changing one's behaviors to meet a partner's needs. These behaviors are used to develop intimacy at this stage of dating (Braiker & Kelley, 1979), which increases sexual involvement by itself. The relationship between sexual involvement and relationship maintenance activities is therefore understandable. The second dimension is ambivalence about the future of the relationship: questions about the future are linked to increases in sexual intimacy. Again, it is necessary to be cautious about cause-effect assumptions. Greater sexual intimacy during early dating may produce more ambivalence about a relationship's future; however, some individuals may resolve questions of future commitment by becoming more sexually involved.

Box 2   ## Commitment and Sex in Dating

Simply stating that commitment is strongly related to sexual involvement does not tell the complete story. Two groups of researchers have
examined *how* these variables are related to one another. Peplau, Rubin,
and Hill (1977) used a longitudinal design; Christopher and Cate (1985)
used a retrospective approach. Even with these design differences, their
findings are remarkably similar—giving the results additional impact.

Both teams found that some couples limited sexual involvement
to noncoital behaviors such as kissing and fondling. Peplau and her colleagues called them *sexually traditional couples,* and Christopher and
Cate called them *low involvement couples.* These couples held conservative sexual attitudes, had limited lifetime sexual experiences, and felt
that being in love was not a strong enough reason to engage in coitus.

At the other end of the spectrum, both teams found couples who engaged in sexual intercourse with little commitment—possibly on the first
date. *Sexually liberated couples* (Peplau et al., 1977), or *rapid involvement couples* (Christopher & Cate, 1985), were motivated by feelings of arousal
and saw love as desirable, but not necessary, for sexual intercourse.

Peplau and her fellow researchers found only one other type, *sexually moderate couples,* who believed that coitus was acceptable if they
were in love but a long-term commitment was not necessary. Christopher and Cate found two other types. For *gradual involvement couples,*
coitus was part of their commitment decision process. *Delayed involvement couples* were very different. They experienced low levels of sexual
involvement until they made a monogamous commitment. The commitment was especially important for these individuals, as it allowed them
to engage in a wide range of sexual experimentation as a couple.

Gender differences in approaches to sexuality, paired with the findings
that show a relationship between conflict, ambivalence, and sexual involvement, illuminate the fact that dating partners do not always agree
about how sexually involved they should become with each other. Even
when they are in agreement, the rules of dating seem to keep partners
from communicating their shared desire directly to each other (Cupach &
Metts, 1991). This means that single individuals must find ways to **influence** their partners either to become more sexually involved or to limit
sexual involvement. Early research into sexual influence in dating identified a number of different tactics men and women use, including rewards,
coercion, logic, manipulation, avoidance, and ignoring a partner's cues
(McCormick, 1979; Perper & Weis, 1987). More recent work shows that
young adults who are dating tend to use more than one tactic at a time, in
an overall *sexual influence strategy* (Christopher & Frandsen, 1990).

Christopher and Frandsen (1990) identified four sexual influence strategies used in dating. The tactics in the first strategy include statements of loving and liking, doing something special for a partner, and using non-verbal clues such as physical closeness and touching to convey sexual wishes. This strategy has been called *emotional and physical closeness* and increases the sexual involvement of couples. A second influence strategy, *logic and reason,* is used by those who want to limit their sexual intimacy, and it includes the tactics of making a rational argument, insisting on a level of involvement, and compromising with a partner. The final two strategies include *antisocial acts* (involving threats, force, and guilt induction) and *pressure and manipulation* (involving pressure, ignoring a partner's actions, using alcohol, and deception). Both are forms of sexual aggression, in which one partner's sexual wishes are imposed on the other partner without consideration of what that partner wants. Sexual aggression will be discussed later.

Parents and Peers Revisited

Healthy development during this stage of older adolescence and young adulthood requires individuals to become independent of their parents while still maintaining emotional closeness (see Chapter 15). People of this age have a concurrent need to become socially integrated with their peers. Furthermore, their peers may be alternative sources of rewards for behaviors and attitudes that their parents would not support, including sexual involvement. Does this mean that parents have little impact on the sexual involvement of older adolescents?

Parents' ability to influence may depend upon whom the older adolescent chooses for **referents.** Referents are individuals the adolescent identifies with and uses as models when making decisions about what constitutes correct behavior. Those who choose peers and see peers as sexually active are likely to be sexually experienced. On the other hand, older adolescents who choose parents as their primary referents are less likely to engage in sexual intercourse (Lewis, 1973; Walsh, Ferrell, & Tolone, 1976)—possibly because of the close parent-adolescent relationship. Fisher (1987) found that the higher the incidence of general, non-sexual communication between college students and their parents, the lower the likelihood of coital involvement of the students. This relationship was stronger for sons than for daughters.

Parents also play a role in adolescent gays' and lesbians' adjustment to their sexual orientation (Savin-Williams, 1989). Parental acceptance of their sexual status, and adolescents' feelings that parental acceptance is important for self-worth, are related to gays' and lesbians' self-esteem and feelings of comfort with their homosexuality.

Overall, however, a consistent finding across studies has been that heterosexual individuals at this stage of development are influenced by their perceptions of peers' sexual involvement (Daugherty & Burger, 1984; Reed & Weinberg, 1984). Furthermore, this influence is strong. DeLamater and MacCorquodale (1979) conducted research that included a wide array of variables, representing individual, dyadic, parental, and peer influences. Perception of peer coital behavior still had a sizable relationship to sexual behavior after controlling for all other influences. Although young adults' sexual involvement is commonly seen as an outcome of interacting relationship and individual factors, social factors need to be considered important as well.

Individual Influences

Older adolescents' sexual behavior is influenced by some of the same individual factors associated with sexual behavior during early adolescence. For example, older adolescents and young adults who attend church frequently or have strong religious beliefs are less likely than their peers to be sexually experienced (Herold & Goodwin, 1981; Reed & Weinberg, 1984). Similarly, attitudes about sexual conduct are related to sexual activity in the same way as they are in early adolescence (DeLamater & MacCorquodale, 1979).

A broader collection of individual traits, however, has been explored for older adolescents and young adults. Work on attitudes has expanded into examining *sexual values* that are based on individuals' moral and relationship reasoning. Virgins appear to hold to one of three different standards (D'Augelli & D'Augelli, 1977): Some have had little or no experience with any form of sexual interaction (including kissing, petting, and so on), some are adamant about remaining virgins until marriage, and some would engage in coitus if they encountered the "right" person. Similarly, nonvirgins typically hold to one of three standards: Some need commitment to a relationship to engage in coitus, some feel that commitment is not necessary as long as a mutual understanding with a coital partner is reached, and some engage in coitus but are confused about where their sexual behavior fits into their lives.

Sexual guilt is another individual trait that has been investigated. Feeling guilty about sex not only inhibits sexual behavior (Mosher, 1973) but represses sexual desires (Kutner, 1971) and is associated with a moral stand against premarital sexual involvement (Mosher & Cross, 1971). Still, not all single women who feel guilty about sex stop their coital activity (Lewis, Gibbons, & Gerrard, 1986). These women, however, are likely to become upset because their actions and their standards do not correspond, so they search for reasons for this inconsistency in their lives. They may thus become susceptible to exploitation by dating partners who provide reasons to be coitally active.

Self-monitoring, another individual trait, is a personality con-

Older adolescents' sexual behavior is influenced by some of the same individual factors associated with sexual behavior among early adolescents.

struct that focuses on how individuals decide what constitutes correct behavior (Snyder, Simpson, & Gangestad, 1986). Individuals who base their behavior on their own attitudes and internal states are low self-monitors. Alternatively, high self-monitors look for social and situational cues when deciding what action is appropriate. These two types of individuals differ in their sexual and dating practices. High self-monitors believe that casual sex is acceptable, and their behavior corresponds to this belief. They have more sexual partners and one-night stands than low self-monitors (Snyder et al., 1986). Low self-monitors, on the other hand, develop deeper commitments to their dating partners (Snyder & Simpson, 1984) and are not as sexually experienced (Snyder et al., 1986).

THE DANGERS OF DATING AND SEX

The Risk of AIDS

Adolescents who engage in certain sexual practices place themselves at risk of infection with the Human Immunodeficiency Virus (HIV), which usually develops into Acquired Immune Deficiency Syndrome (AIDS) and eventually results in death. These practices include unprotected oral-genital, anal, and vaginal interaction with any partner infected with HIV. This risk is present whether an adolescent is homosexual or heterosexual, as heterosexual transmission may play an even greater role in the spread of AIDS among adolescents than homosexual transmission does (DiClemente, 1992). Moreover, adolescents may not realize that they are infected with HIV—they can become HIV positive, or seropositive, during their teens and not show AIDS symptoms until they reach their twenties.

HIV infection rates are similar to those of other sexually transmitted diseases within certain populations. Rates are higher among males than among females (DiClemente, 1992), and they are higher among African-Americans and Latinos—especially those living in poverty—than among whites (Aral & Holmes, 1991). What makes this pattern particularly sobering is that adolescents accounted for 25% of new sexually transmitted disease infections in 1989 (Moore, 1989).

Given its consequences, it is surprising that the threat of AIDS does not seem to have any effect on the sexual activity of adolescents (Caroll, 1988). Although adolescents indicate that they consider AIDS in their sexual decision-making, actual sexual behavior remains unrelated to adolescents' stated concerns. Perhaps the problem is that youth still see AIDS as a homosexual disease as opposed to a disease that results from risky behavior.

Sexual Aggression in Dating

In recent years **sexual aggression** in dating has received increased attention by researchers and the popular press. Even with this scrutiny, it is difficult to say how many adolescents fall victim to sexual aggression, as a national survey has yet to be conducted. Smaller-scale studies provide an indication of this problem's scope. Koss, Gidycz, and Wisniewski (1987) report that 27.5% of the over 6000 college women they surveyed had been raped at least once since they were 14. Men may also experience unwanted sexual activity, but investigations of sexual aggression against dating men are scarce. Muehlenhard and Cook (1988) report that 6.5% of the men in their study had experienced coitus because of physical coercion, and 13.4%, because of a partner's verbal coercion. When single men and women who date are compared, however, it is very clear that men are more likely than women to be aggressive (Christopher, Owens, & Stecker, 1993a).

Some of the features of normal dating relationships may be related to sexual aggression (Burt, 1980). These include differences between male and female sexual expectations, males' lower threshold for perceiving sexual intent, and the misperceptions of sexual wishes that are possible because sexual interchanges in dating are predominately nonverbal (Burkhart & Stanton, 1988).

A number of characteristics of individuals who are sexually aggressive while dating have been identified. Male aggressors possess a set of attitudes that they use to justify their actions (Christopher, Owens, & Stecker, 1993b; Malamuth, Sockloskie, Koss, & Tanaka, 1991). Belief in such **rape myths** as "A woman can prevent a rape if she really wants to" and "All women secretly want to be raped" allows these men to assign blame for sexual activity to the women they assault. These men are sexually focused and active—they have a high number of sexual partners over their dating careers (Christopher et al., 1993b) and take a predatory view of dating (Kanin, 1969). Researchers have found that such men experience specific emotional states. Sexually aggressive single men harbor **hostility** toward women (Christopher et al., 1993b; Malamuth et al., 1991) and nurse a long-standing anger that is turned inward and is characterized by brooding (Christopher et al., 1993b). Furthermore, these men have low levels of **empathy** (Christopher et al., 1993b), which may explain why they engage in other forms of antisocial behavior (Burkhart & Stanton, 1988).

A similar set of characteristics has been found to be associated with women who are sexually aggressive (Christopher et al., 1993a). These women have attitudes that support their actions, and they experience high numbers of coital partners. Additionally, they feel hostile toward men and possess a brooding anger.

Both sexually aggressive men and sexually aggressive women have dating relationships punctuated by problems (Christopher et al., 1993a, 1993b). Their interactions with their dating partners are marked by conflict and by ambivalence about the future of the relationship. It is unclear whether these experiences are an outcome of the sexual aggression, or whether the aggression is prompted by poor dyadic interaction. If the latter is true, aggression may be used as a way to gain control of the relationship (Stets & Pirog-Good, 1989).

Finally, there are two forms of social support for male sexual aggression in dating. The first originates among their peers. These men have male friends who are similarly sexually aggressive and female friends who are likely to have been victims of sexual aggression (Gwartney-Gibbs & Stockard, 1989). The second comes from our culture, which is supportive of violence toward women (Burt, 1980) and prescribes dating role behavior that contributes to aggressive acts. Specifically, men's dating role calls for them to be "in control" and to be the sexual initiators; women's dating role demands that they passively accept a male partner's wishes and repair their relationships when things go wrong. Extreme forms of these role expectations lay the foundation for sexual aggression (Lloyd, 1991).

SUMMARY

The sexual activity of adolescents and young adults is popularly viewed as either an outcome of their personalities or the influence of their peers. The research findings reviewed in this chapter reveal that this is a simplistic view, however. In fact, a partial inventory of individual factors involved in adolescent sexual expression could include hormones, attitudes, church attendance, and values. A parallel listing of social factors should include ethnicity or race, parents' marital status, attempts at parental control, and actual and perceived peer sexual behavior. Finally, a catalog of relationship influences would not be complete without mentioning the role of commitment, love, conflict, and sexual influence strategies. The unmistakable conclusion that can be reached from this review is that adolescent sexuality is an important part of adolescents' and young adults' lives. Hence, many of the normal events, processes, and experiences that make up these individuals' daily existence also become intertwined in and part of their sexual development.

Class Discussion Questions

1. The class should divide into same-sex groups of about six students each. Each group lists what the opposite sex wants in a date and in a relationship. The groups then share their lists with the rest of class.
2. After reading the chapter, list what you see as the top ten influences on

adolescent sexual activity, in order from most important to least important. Then discuss with the class the reasoning behind your ordering.

3. Unintended pregnancy, AIDS, and sexual aggression are all negative outcomes of sexual involvement. In a small group, pick one of these topics and generate ideas about what you as individuals are willing, and not willing, to do to intervene in these problems on a personal and a societal level.

Homework Assignments

1. Create a brief, open-ended questionnaire about what influences sexual involvement. Distribute them to adolescents of different ages, being sure to protect confidentiality. Compare the responses you get to the chapter material.

2. Write a letter to your genitals about your past, present, and future sex life as a single individual. Hand in your letter, but do not sign it. Your instructor will share the letters with the class. Discuss what the experience of writing such a letter was like.

Additional Readings

Gullotta, T. P., Adams, G. R., & Montemayor, R. (Eds.). (1993). *Adolescent sexuality: Advances in adolescent development* (vol. 5). Newbury Park, CA: Sage.

Hayes, C. D. (Ed.). (1987). *Risking the future: Adolescent sexuality, pregnancy, and childbearing* (vols. 1 & 2). Washington, DC: National Academy Press.

Pirog-Good, M. A., & Stets, J. E. (Eds.). (1989). *Violence in dating relationships: Emerging social issues*. New York: Praeger.

McKinney, K., & Sprecher, S. (Eds.). (1991). *Sexuality in close relationships*. Hillsdale, NJ: Lawrence Erlbaum.

References

Abbey, A., & Melby, C. (1986). The effects of nonverbal cues on gender differences in perceptions of sexual intent. *Sex Roles, 15,* 283–298.

Allgeier, E. R. (1992). School-based sex education. Paper commissioned by the World Health Organization, Geneva, Switzerland.

Aral, S. O., & Holmes, K. K. (1991). Sexually transmitted diseases in the AIDS era. *Scientific American, 264*(2), 62–69.

Bauman, K. E., & Udry, J. R. (1981). Subjective expected utility and adolescent sexual behavior. *Adolescence, 63,* 527–534.

Billy, J. O. G., & Udry, J. R. (1985). Patterns of adolescent friendship and effects on sexual behavior. *Social Psychology Quarterly, 48,* 27–41.

Bingham, C. R., Miller, B. C., & Adams, G. R. (1990). Correlates of age at first sexual intercourse in a national sample of young women. *Journal of Adolescent Research, 5,* 18–33.

Braiker, H. B., & Kelley, H. H. (1979). Conflict in the development of close relationships. In R. L. Burgess & T. L. Huston (Eds.), *Social exchange in developing relationships*. New York: Academic Press.

Burkhart, B. R., & Stanton, A. L. (1988). Sexual aggression in acquaintance relationships. In G. W. Russel (Ed.), *Violence in intimate relationships* (pp. 43–65). New York: PMA.

Burt, M. R. (1980). Cultural myths and supports for rape. *Journal of Personality and Social Psychology, 38,* 217–230.

Caroll, L. (1988). Concern with AIDS and the sexual behavior of college students. *Journal of Marriage and the Family, 50,* 405–411.

Carroll, J. L., Volk, D. K., & Hyde, S. J. (1985). Differences between males and females in motives for engaging in sexual intercourse. *Archives of Sexual Behavior, 14,* 131–139.

Christopher, F. S., & Cate, R. M. (1984). Factors involved in premarital sexual decision-making. *Journal of Sex Research, 20,* 363–376.

Christopher, F. S., & Cate, R. M. (1985). Premarital sexual pathways and relationship development. *Journal of Social and Personal Relationships, 2,* 271–288.

Christopher, F. S., & Cate, R. M. (1988). Premarital sexual involvement: A developmental investigation of relational correlates. *Adolescence, 23,* 793–803.

Christopher, F. S., & Frandsen, M. M. (1990). Strategies of influence in sex and dating. *Journal of Social and Personal Relationships, 7,* 89–105.

Christopher, F. S., Johnson, D. C., & Roosa, M. W. (1993). Family, individual, and social correlates of early Hispanic adolescent sexual expression. *Journal of Sex Research, 30,* 45–52.

Christopher, F. S., Owens, L. A., & Stecker, H. L. (1993a). An examination of single men and women's sexual aggressiveness in dating. *Journal of Social and Personal Relationships, 10,* 511–527.

Christopher, F. S., Owens, L. A., & Stecker, H. L. (1993b). Exploring the dark side of courtship: A test of a model of male premarital sexual aggressiveness. *Journal of Marriage and the Family, 55,* 469–479.

Christopher, F. S., & Roosa, M. W. (1990). An evaluation of an adolescent pregnancy prevention program: Is "just say no" enough? *Family Relations, 39,* 68–72.

Cupach, W. R., & Metts, S. (1991). Sexuality and communication in close relationships. In K. McKinney and S. Sprecher (Eds.), *Sexuality in close relationships* (pp. 93–110). Hillsdale, NJ: Lawrence Erlbaum.

Cvetkovich, G., & Grote, B. (1980). Psychosocial development and the social problem of teenage illegitimacy. In C. Chilman (Ed.), *Adolescent pregnancy and childbearing: Findings from research* (pp. 15–41). Washington, DC: U.S. Department of Health and Human Services.

D'Augelli, J. F., & D'Augelli, A. R. (1977). Moral reasoning and premarital sexual behavior: Toward reasoning about relationships. *Journal of Social Issues, 33*(2), 46–66.

Daugherty, L. R., & Burger, J. M. (1984). The influence of parents, church, and peers on the sexual attitudes and behaviors of college students. *Archives of Sexual Behavior, 13,* 351–359.

Day, R. D. (1992). The transition to first intercourse among racially and culturally diverse youth. *Journal of Marriage and the Family, 54,* 749–762.

DeLamater, J. D., & MacCorquodale, P. (1979). *Premarital sexuality: Attitudes, relationships, behavior.* Madison: The University of Wisconsin Press.

DiClemente, R. J. (1992). Epidemiology of AIDS, HIV prevalence, and HIV incidence among adolescents. *Journal of School Health, 62,* 325–330.

Dornbusch, S. M., Carlsmith, J. M., Gross, R. T., Martin, J. A., Jennings, D., Rosenberg, A., & Duke, P. (1981). Sexual development, age, and dating: A comparison of biological and social influences upon one set of behaviors. *Child Development, 52,* 179–185.

Dyk, P. H. (1993). Anatomy, physiology, and gender issues in adolescence. In T. P. Gullotta, G. R. Adams, & R. Montemayor (Eds.), *Adolescent sexuality: Advances in adolescent development* (vol. 5) (pp. 35–56). Newbury Park, CA: Sage.

Fisher, T. D. (1986). An exploratory study of parent-child communication about sex and the sexual attitudes of early, middle, and late adolescents. *Journal of Genetic Psychology, 147,* 543–557.

Fisher, T. D. (1987). Family communication and the sexual behavior and attitudes of college students. *Journal of Youth and Adolescence, 16,* 481–495.

Forste, R. T., & Heaton, T. B. (1988). Initiation of sexual activity among female adolescents. *Youth and Society, 19,* 250–268.

Fox, G. L., & Inazu, J. K. (1980). Patterns and outcomes of mother-daughter communication about sexuality. *Journal of Social Issues, 36,* 7–29.

Furstenberg, F. F., Herceg-Baron, R., Shea, J., & Webb, D. (1984). Family communication and teenagers' contraceptive use. *Family Planning Perspectives, 16,* 163–170.

Furstenberg, F. F., Jr., Morgan, S. P., Moore, K. A., & Peterson, J. L. (1987). Race differences in the timing of adolescent intercourse. *American Sociological Review, 52,* 511–518.

Goldman, R., & Goldman, J. (1982). *Children's sexual thinking.* London: Routledge & Kegan Paul.

Gwartney-Gibbs, P., & Stockard, J. (1989). Courtship aggression and mixed-sex groups. In M. Pirog-Good & J. Stets (Eds.), *Violence in dating relationships: Emerging social issues* (pp. 185–204). New York: Praeger.

Hayes, C. D. (Ed.). (1987). *Risking the future: Adolescent sexuality, pregnancy, and childbearing,* Washington, DC: National Research Council.

Henshaw, S. K., & Van Vort, J. (1984). Teenage abortion, birth, pregnancy statistics: An update. *Family Planning Perspectives, 21,* 85–88.

Herold, E. S., & Goodwin, M. S. (1981). Adamant virgins, potential nonvirgins, and nonvirgins. *Journal of Sex Research, 17,* 97–113.

Hofferth, S. L., Kahn, J. R., & Baldwin, W. (1987). Premarital sexual activity among U.S. teenage women over the past three decades. *Family Planning Perspectives, 19,* 46–53.

Hogan, D., & Kitagawa, E. (1985). The impact of social status, family structure, and neighborhood on the fertility of black adolescents. *American Journal of Sociology, 90,* 825–836.

Inazu, J. K., & Fox, G. L. (1980). Maternal influence on the sexual behavior of teenage daughters. *Journal of Family Issues, 1,* 81–102.

Jessor, R., Costa, F., Jessor, L., & Donovan, J. E. (1983). Time of first intercourse: A prospective study. *Journal of Personality and Social Psychology, 44,* 608–626.

Jorgensen, S. R., King, S. L., & Torrey, B. A. (1980). Dyadic and social network influences on adolescent exposure to pregnancy risk. *Journal of Marriage and the Family, 42,* 141–155.

Kanin, E. J. (1969). Selected dyadic aspects of male sex aggression. *Journal of Sex Research, 5,* 12–28.

Kirby, D., Barth, R. P., Leland, N., & Fetro, J. V. (1991). Reducing the risk: Impact of a new curriculum on sexual risk-taking. *Family Planning Perspectives, 23,* 253–263.

Koss, M. P., Gidycz, C. A., & Wisniewski, N. (1987). The scope of rape: Incidence and prevalence of sexual aggression and victimization in a national sample of higher education students. *Journal of Consulting and Clinical Psychology, 55,* 162–170.

Kutner, S. J. (1971). Sex guilt and sex behavior sequence. *Journal of Sex Research, 7,* 107–115.

Leigh, G. K., Weddle, K. D., & Loewen, I. R. (1988). Analysis of the timing of transition to sexual intercourse for black adolescent females. *Journal of Adolescent Research, 3,* 333–344.

Lewis, R. A. (1973). Parents and peers: Socialization agents in the coital behavior of young adults. *Journal of Sex Research, 9,* 156–170.

Lewis, R. J., Gibbons, F. X., & Gerrard, M. (1986). Sexual experience and recall of sexual vs. nonsexual information. *Journal of Personality, 54,* 676–693.

Lloyd, S. A. (1991). The dark side of courtship: Violence and sexual exploitation. *Family Relations, 40,* 14–20.

Louis Harris & Associates. (1986). *American teens speak: Sex, myths, TV, and birth control* (Harris Poll). New York: Louis Harris & Associates.

Malamuth, N. M., Sockloskie, R. J., Koss, M. P., & Tanaka, J. S. (1991). Characteristics of aggressors against women: Testing a model using a national sample of college students. *Journal of Consulting and Clinical Psychology, 59,* 670–681.

McCormick, N. B. (1979). Come-ons and put-offs: Unmarried students' strategies for having and avoiding sexual intercourse. *Psychology of Women Quarterly, 42,* 194–211.

Miller, B. C., & Bingham, C. R. (1989). Family configuration in relation to the sexual behavior of female adolescents. *Journal of Marriage and the Family, 51,* 499–506.

Miller, B. C., Christensen, R. B., & Olson, T. D. (1987). Adolescent self-esteem in relation to sexual attitudes and behaviors. *Youth & Society, 19,* 93–111.

Miller, B. C., McCoy, J. K., Olson, T. D., & Wallace, C. M. (1986). Parental discipline and control attempts in relation to adolescent sexual attitudes and behavior. *Journal of Marriage and the Family, 48,* 503–512.

Miller, B. C., & Moore, K. A. (1990). Adolescent sexual behavior, pregnancy, and parenting: Research through the 1980s. *Journal of Marriage and the Family, 52,* 1025–1044.

Moore, K. A. (1989). *Facts at a glance 1989* (Fact sheet). Washington, DC: Child Trends, Inc.

Moore, K., & Peterson, J. (1989). *The consequences of teenage pregnancy: Final report.* Washington, DC: Child Trends, Inc.

Moore, K. A., Peterson, J. L., & Furstenberg, F. F. (1986). Parental attitudes and the occurrence of early sexual activity. *Journal of Marriage and the Family, 48,* 777–782.

Mosher, D. L. (1973). Sex differences, sex experiences, sex guilt, and explicitly sexual films. *Journal of Social Issues, 29,* 95–112.

Mosher, D. L., & Cross, H. J. (1971). Sex guilt and premarital sexual experiences of college students. *Journal of Consulting and Clinical Psychology, 36,* 27–32.

Muehlenhard, C. L., & Cook, S. W. (1988). Men's self-report of unwanted sexual activity. *Journal of Sex Research, 24,* 58–72.

Newcomer, S. F., & Udry, J. R. (1985). Parent-child communication and adolescent sexual behavior. *Family Planning Perspectives, 17,* 169–174.

Newcomer, S. F., & Udry, J. R. (1987). Parental marital status effects on adolescent sexual behavior. *Journal of Marriage and the Family, 49,* 235–240.

O'Sullivan, L. F., & Byers, E. S. (1992). College students' incorporations of initiator and restrictor roles in sexual dating interactions. *Journal of Sex Research, 29,* 435–446.

Peplau, L. A., & Cochran, S. D. (1981). Value orientation in the intimate relationships of gay men. *Journal of Homosexuality, 6,* 1–19.

Peplau, L. A., Rubin, Z., & Hill, C. T. (1977). Sexual intimacy in dating relationships. *Journal of Social Issues, 33,* 86–109.

Perper, T., & Weis, D. L. (1987). Proceptive and rejective strategies of U.S. and Canadian college women. *Journal of Sex Research, 23,* 455–480.

Reed, D. & Weinberg, M. S. (1984). Premarital coitus: Developing and reestablishing sexual scripts. *Social Psychology Quarterly, 47,* 129–138.

Remafedi, G., Resnick, M., Blum, R., & Harris, L. (1992). Demography of sexual orientation in adolescents. *Pediatrics, 89,* 714–721.

Roche, J. P. (1986). Premarital sex: Attitudes and behavior by dating stage. *Adolescence, 21,* 107–121.

Roosa, M. W., & Christopher, F. S. (1990). Evaluation of an abstinence-only adolescent pregnancy prevention program: A replication. *Family Relations, 39,* 363–367.

Roosa, M. W., & Christopher, F. S. (1992). Response to McBride & Thiel: Scientific criticism or obscurantism? *Family Relations, 41,* 468–469.

Rosenbaum, E., & Kandel, D. B. (1990). Early onset of sexual behavior and drug involvement. *Journal of Marriage and the Family, 52,* 783–798.

Russo, T. J., Barnes, H. L., & Wright, D. W. (1991). Parental factors influencing parent-child communication about general and specific human sexuality topics. Paper presented at the annual conference of the National Council on Family Relations, Denver.

Savin-Williams, R. C. (1989). Parental influences on the self-esteem of gay and lesbian youths: A reflected appraisals model. *Journal of Homosexuality, 14,* 93–109.

Shotland, R. L., & Craig, J. M. (1988). Can men and women differentiate between friendly and sexually interested behavior? *Social Psychology Quarterly, 51,* 66–73.

Snyder, M., & Simpson, J. A. (1984). Self-monitoring and dating relationships. *Journal of Personality and Social Psychology, 47,* 1281–1291.

Snyder, M., Simpson, J. A., & Gangestad, S. (1986). Personality and sexual relations. *Journal of Personality and Social Psychology, 51,* 181–190.

Sonenstein, F. L., Pleck, J. H., & Leighton, C. K. (1991). Levels of sexual activity among adolescent males in the United States. *Family Planning Perspectives, 23,* 162–167.

Stets, J. E., & Pirog-Good, M. A. (1989). Sexual aggression and control in dating relationships. *Journal of Applied Social Psychology, 19,* 1392–1412.

Thornton, A. D., & Camburn, D. (1987). The influences of the family on premarital sexual attitudes and behavior. *Demography, 24,* 323–340.

Thornton, A. D., & Camburn, D. (1989). Religious participation and adolescent sexual behavior. *Journal of Marriage and the Family, 51,* 641–653.

Troiden, R. R. (1989). The formation of homosexual identities. *Journal of Homosexuality, 14,* 43–73.

Udry, J. R. (1979). Age at menarche, at first intercourse, and at first pregnancy. *Journal of Biosocial Science, 11,* 433–441.

Udry, J. R. (1988). Biological predispositions and social controls in adolescent sexual behavior. *American Sociological Review, 53,* 709–722.

Udry, J. R., & Billy, J. O. G. (1987). Initiation of coitus in early adolescence. *American Sociological Review, 52,* 841–855.

Walsh, R. H., Ferrell, M. Z., & Tolone, W. L. (1976). Selection of reference group, perceived reference group permissiveness, and personal permissiveness attitudes and behavior: A study of two consecutive panels (1967–1971; 1970–1974). *Journal of Marriage and the Family, 38,* 495–508.

Walster, E., Walster, G. W., & Traupmann, J. (1978). Equity and premarital sex. *Journal of Personality and Social Psychology, 36,* 82–92.

Weinstein, M., & Thornton, A. (1989). Mother-child relations and adolescent sexual attitudes and behavior. *Demography, 26,* 563–577.

Zabin, L. S., Hirsch, M. B., Smith, E. A., & Hardy, J. B. (1984). Adolescent sexual attitudes and behavior: Are they consistent? *Family Planning Perspectives, 16*(4), 181–185.

Zabin, L. S., Hirsch, M. B., Smith, E. A., Streett, R., & Hardy, J. B. (1986). Evaluation of a pregnancy prevention program for urban teenagers. *Family Planning Perspectives, 18,* 119–126.

Zabin, L. S., Smith, E. A., Hirsch, M. B., & Hardy, J. B. (1986). Ages of physical maturation and first intercourse in black teenage males and females. *Demography, 23,* 595–605.

Zelnik, M., & Shah, F. K. (1983). First intercourse among young Americans. *Family Planning Perspectives, 15,* 64–72.

Glossary

Age-graded norms   Norms (averages, or standards) for behavior for a particular age or developmental stage

Bisexual   An individual who chooses sexual partners who are of the same and opposite sex

Close relationship   A relationship characterized by self-disclosure and feelings of attachment in which the partners influence each other

Cohort   A group of individuals who were born in the same historical period

Coitus   Sexual intercourse

Commitment   Personal feelings of obligation to remain in a relationship

Contraceptive practices   Use of birth control to prevent pregnancies

Control group   In a testing situation, the group that does not receive an intervention or treatment and is compared to the group that does (see *Intervention group*)

Curvilinear relationship   A relationship between two variables in which increases in the level of one variable are associated with both increases and decreases in the level of the second variable; represented graphically by either an upright or an inverted U

Developmental tasks   Objectives that need to be mastered at a particular stage of development in order to achieve a healthy outcome for that stage

Dyad   A two-partner relationship

Dyadic conflict   Disagreement between two partners over the resources, outcomes, or goals of a relationship

Empathy   The ability of one individual to take the perspective of another or to perceive what another person is feeling

Equity   One partner's perception of a balance of her or his rewards and costs relative to the rewards and costs of the other partner

Gay   A male homosexual

Heterosexual   An individual who chooses a sexual partner of the opposite sex

Homophobic   Characterized by irrational fear or hatred of homosexuals

Homosexual   An individual who chooses a sexual partner of the same sex

Hormone   A chemical substance produced by an endocrine gland that affects other body organs

Hostility   An emotional state that predisposes an individual to act aggressively

Indicator   A measure of a variable

Influence   Assertion of one's power in a relationship

Intervention group   In a testing situation, the group that receives an intervention or a treatment and is compared to a control group (see *Control group*)

Lesbian   A female homosexual

Locus of control   A personality construct that indicates whether individuals see themselves as controlling their own destiny (internal locus) or see their destiny controlled by fate, circumstances, and the actions of others (external locus)

Longitudinal study   A study designed to measure variables at different points across time, using the same sample

Modeling   Imitating

Monitor   To oversee another's activities

Nonvirgin   Someone who has engaged in sexual intercourse

Parental control   When parents dominate and assert their power over an adolescent's activities

Puberty   Developmental stage characterized by increases in hormone production and bodily changes; often used as an indicator of the beginning of adolescence

Rape myths   False attitudes or beliefs about rape, rapists, or victims of rape

Referent   An individual with whom one identifies and uses as a model when making decisions about what constitutes correct behavior

Self-esteem   The positive or negative evaluation of one's self

Self-monitoring   Personality construct used to indicate whether individuals judge the correctness of a behavior using their own standards (low self-monitors) or social and situational cues (high self-monitors)

Sexual aggression   Use of physical or verbal coercion with the goal of increasing sexual involvement

Sexual guilt   Feelings of guilt that are the result of sexual thoughts, feelings, or behaviors

Support   Positive regard by a parent or peer for an adolescent's activities

Testosterone   A hormone produced in the testes (also called the male sex hormone)

Virgin   Someone who has not engaged in sexual intercourse

10 Courtship and Marriage: Choosing a Primary Relationship

Tamara Goldman Sher
Illinois Institute of Technology

The author gratefully acknowledges the assistance of Keith Hersh for his research, thoughts, and comments on this chapter.

For most people, choosing a mate is a high priority task during the adolescent and young adult years, and the outcome of this task represents an important milestone in our lives—one that determines the outcomes of many other efforts, in relationships and otherwise. This chapter begins with a discussion of how we go about selecting our partners and then proceeds to examine the state of marriage (and alternatives to marriage) in the modern world.

NV & SD

Chapter Outline

- Courtship and Mate Selection
- Marriage
- Alternatives to Marriage
- Summary

In most Western countries today children are raised to believe that anything is possible for them. They can grow up to work in any profession, live in any neighborhood, pursue any leisure activities that interest them, and fall in love and marry whomever they choose. Reality, however, tells us differently. Certain professions are open only to people who have attained a certain educational level, and education in many countries is still largely a function of socioeconomic status. Neighborhoods remain segregated by race. Some people have more leisure time than others, and some cannot afford certain leisure time pursuits or time away from work. And finally, our choice of partners or spouses is often determined for us—by where we live, where we go to school, what work we do, what we do in our free time, and whom we know. Therefore, whom we meet, love, and settle down with is not as much a matter of free choice as we were raised to believe. In fact, the decisions we make and those that are made for us throughout our lives determine our eventual long-term partners.

This chapter will explore human mate selection throughout the life-cycle. *Mate selection* is a very unromantic term to explain how we choose our romantic partners for both the long and short terms. The first section will focus on the courtship process and how we come to choose the partners we do, in Western societies and in non-Western societies. The second section will focus on long-term relationships, including marriage, same-sex unions, and alternatives to such relationships.

COURTSHIP AND MATE SELECTION

Courtship is the term used to describe the dating process, or "dating game." Courtship, as traditionally defined, was the notion that one "courted" in order to get another to agree to a marriage proposal. Of course, today people date for many reasons and not necessarily to achieve the outcome of marriage or a long-term relationship. In fact, the term *courting* is no longer commonly used because its implication of traditional wooing of the woman by the man conflicts with today's notions of dating without stereotypic rules and carrying on a variety of relationships for a variety of reasons.

Dating

The practice of dating is the primary means of finding a long-term relationship, or mate selection, in most Western cultures. Finding the right partner is not the only function of dating in our society, however, although the other functions of dating are often overlooked. Some other reasons that people, especially adolescents and young adults, date are discussed below (from McCammon, Knox, & Schacht, 1993, pp. 354–355).

Development of Self-Concept   The "looking glass self" was a term coined by sociologist Charles Horton Cooley (1964) to refer to the self-concept that results from interactions with others. Dating allows us to develop aspects of our self-concept by observing how others perceive us in a one-to-one relationship.

Recreation   Adolescents often look to dating to provide an opportunity to be with peers, away from their parents. Adults often look to dating to provide a break from the stresses of their everyday lives, even though dating often is accompanied by stress, albeit a different type than that found on the job.

Companionship, Intimacy, and Sex   Over 70% of men and 75% of women in a national sample report having gone steady at least one time by age 18. What this tells us is that people often date for steady companionship, intimacy, and the potential for sexual involvement. It has been shown that the steadier and more involved the relationship, the greater the sexual involvement (Thornton, 1990).

Socialization   Dating, especially in the adolescent years, provides the opportunity to develop social skills such as conversing, listening, and expressing empathy. Dating also allows people to "try on" different roles in relation to others and to assess their comfort with each. People who are slower to begin dating are often slower to develop these skills. Unfortunately, such a situation can evolve into a vicious cycle, whereby these people need to be socially skillful in order to be attractive to others but cannot hope to be so until they have had the opportunity to practice with people who are attracted to them.

Status, Achievement, and Sorting   According to Rice (1990), dating is used at least partly to achieve, prove, or maintain social status. That is, dating can mean access to a particular desired social group. It has been noted that sex role stereotyping in dating still exists, especially for girls and women, in that they put more emphasis on attracting a high-status mate (Bascow, 1992). Also—for both sexes—dating helps people conform to socially accepted sex role expectations. One study describes how gay high school and college students often faked the heterosexual dating ritual in order to maintain an acceptable appearance (McNaught, 1983).

Choosing a Partner   Finally, dating may serve to pair two people for marriage or for a long-term committed relationship. One study (Woll & Young, 1989) looked at mate selection by asking clients of a video dating service (choosing a date by watching videotapes of others enrolled in the service) what they were interested in in a partner. Of those who responded, 89% said that they were seeking a serious, permanent relationship, rather than a casual one.

Almost all of the studies on the functions of dating have been conducted with young adults and adolescents. The nature of dating in later life is different, as shown in a series of studies by Bulcroft. These studies found that although younger people often date to explore and experiment with marital role arrangements, most older couples are not dating for purposes of mate selection (Bulcroft & O'Conner, 1986). Rather than romantic love, sexuality, or a potential future spouse, the primary reason mentioned for dating by both older men and women was companionship (Bulcroft & Bulcroft, 1991).

In addition to studying reasons for dating, researchers have examined who is likely to date. Gender was one of the strongest predictors of dating, with men much more likely to date and much more likely to date multiple partners. This greater likelihood may be explained by the lack of a sufficient number of eligible single men in the dating pool and the subsequent increase in value of less attractive men as dating partners (Bulcroft & Bulcroft, 1991). Gender differences exist as well with regard to who will date in later life. Men are more likely to date if they are younger, live in a single-family residence, are involved with organizations, and have contact with siblings. Women, on the other hand, are more strongly influenced by health and mobility (Bulcroft & Bulcroft, 1991).

Mate Selection

Historically, the ways that people found and selected partners have been as far from a random process as possible (Buss, 1985). There are many theories of why people want to date, how they choose to get to know some people over other people, and why they eventually choose one person to be a more intimate partner (see also Chapter 1).

The theory that has gained the most scientific scrutiny and support is the theory of **assortative mating,** which asserts that people find partners based on their similarity to each other in one or more characteristics—or the "birds of a feather flock together" theory. This phenomenon is also known as **homogamy.** This non-random pairing is thought to be most common in Western societies (Buss, 1985).

Assortative mating has been examined with respect to a wide variety of characteristics, ranging from purely physical traits, such as age, through neighborhood, religion, socioeconomic status (SES), and appearance, to more cognitive traits, such as intellectual abilities, preferences, voting records, and political ideologies. In other words, researchers have attempted to predict who will marry whom, based on a multitude of characteristics. The results of some of their findings are presented in Box 1.

A lot of the assortative mating that takes place results from the fact that people in Western cultures who eventually will pair off or marry must, with rare exception, meet each other first.[1] People are exposed to a very limited sample of possible partners: other people in their neighborhoods, in their schools, in their workplaces, and participating in their recreational activities. This limiting factor is known as **propinquity,** and it suggests that often people live near each other before they become partners or mates. In the late 1960s, research (Eckland, 1968) showed that, at that time, the chances of a person

Birds of a feather flock together: We tend to find partners who are similar to us in some important ways.

[1] Historically, there have been exceptions. In addition to mail-order brides, young orphaned women, juvenile delinquents, and inmates of poorhouses were sent to overseas colonies as wives for early settlers.

Box 1   ## Assortative Mating Trends

Following is a list of ways in which husbands and wives are found to be similar. The statistics explain how closely husbands and wives are *correlated* on the various characteristics. Note that a correlation of zero indicates that there is no consistent pattern between couples on this trait and that a correlation of 1.0 indicates that the patterns within couples are highly consistent on this trait.

Characteristic	Correlation*
Religious orientation	.65
Liking for children	.52
Intelligence	.39
Socially exciting	.37
Political conservatism	.36
Easygoing	.35

*These correlations come from Buss (1985), who gathered data on 93 couples. All the correlations are significant.

---

choosing as a partner someone who lived within walking distance of his or her childhood home was about 50%. Although American society has become increasingly mobile since the late 1960s, it is probably still true that we mate with people who live near us (or at least live near us when we meet them). Furthermore, people are not distributed throughout the country in a random way. Where people live, work, and play corresponds very closely with their social class. Therefore, it has often been asked whether propinquity, as a factor in mate selection, is not simply a function of class similarity or, vice versa, whether class similarity is not merely a function of propinquity.

The question of how physical appearance affects attraction has also been researched. Although physical attractiveness is an elusive and subjective concept, physically attractive people are regarded more favorably than their less physically appealing peers. This is true across the life span, from nursery school age through older adulthood (see Snyder, Berscheid, & Glick, 1985, for a review). More physically attractive people are seen as more competent, their evaluations of others have more impact, and their performances are more highly valued than those of less attractive people. Attractive persons may be appreciated for aesthetic reasons, as is good art;

people may believe that there is more to physical beauty than outward attractiveness; or people may want to associate with physically attractive people to enhance their own social standing (Huston & Levinger, 1978). It also appears that physical attractiveness is more important in males' evaluations of females than vice versa. Females' physical attractiveness has a strong influence on their dating frequency, whereas for males the connection is weak (see Huston & Levinger, 1978, for a review).

In general, however, everyone wants to date the most attractive person, and there is little tendency for people to be attracted to partners whose desirability matches their own (Skolnick, 1978). In fact, this aspect of dating has been labeled the "Groucho Marx effect." Just as Groucho Marx stated that he would not want to join any club that would have him for a member, people often do not want to date anyone who would be interested in them. However, people do not always pursue relationships with people they find most attractive. One reason might be that the cost of pursuing an unlikely relationship is to forgo alternative, and perhaps more promising, relationship possibilities (Snyder et al., 1985).

It therefore appears that people do not choose partners based on physical characteristics alone. The choice of a partner is often based, however, on a combination of (a) the degree to which we find the other person's attributes to be attractive and (b) the degree to which we assume the other would find us attractive (Huston & Levinger, 1978).

Exchange theory explains mate selection on the basis of an exchange of the assets and liabilities each person brings to a relationship (see also Chapter 1). Therefore, if Denise, a middle-class graduate student, marries Jamal, an upper-middle-class college graduate, both may "benefit" from the marriage, in different ways. Denise might benefit socially by moving upward from the middle class to the upper middle class; Jamal might benefit materially from his wife's higher earning potential, based on her more advanced degree.

We all know many people who have similar backgrounds or other points in common with us. To explain how we narrow down our choices of a partner, researchers have devised several theories about why people choose certain others to be their partners. These will be discussed briefly.

Some of the earliest, most controversial, and perhaps most romantic theories of mate selection suggest that it is pure instinct that attracts us to certain individuals. In other words, it was believed that for every man there existed a particular woman who in some predetermined way corresponded almost perfectly with him. This is known as an **unconscious archetype** (Eckland, 1968). This theory is most typified by expressions such as "Mr. Right" or the notion of "chemistry" between two people. Despite such common expressions, however, this theory has never been scientifically upheld.

Sigmund Freud's theory of mate selection, based on the Oedipus complex, suggests that in terms of temperament and physical attributes, one's ideal mate is a parent substitute. Therefore, a man seeks to "marry his mother," or someone like his mother, and a woman seeks to "marry her father," or someone like her father. Again, although the **parent image theory** is common in folklore and it seems reasonable that what we were exposed to while growing up is what we would seek to imitate in our marriages, this theory has not been upheld. That is, people are no more likely to choose partners who are similar to their opposite-sex parent than they are to find partners who are different from that parent.

The opposite of the assortative mating theory is the **principle of complementary needs,** or the idea that "opposites attract." This theory has been used to explain why a dominant person would choose a submissive one, why sadists choose masochists, and so forth. This theory is popular in folklore and has gained a scientific following. Winch's theory of complementary needs hypothesizes that each individual seeks another who will provide him or her with maximum need gratification and that the specific need pattern and personality of each partner will complement the needs and personality of the other (Winch, 1958). This theory has also been used to explain why the research on assortative mating based on similar *personality* variables has generally produced low correlations. However, studies generally do not support Winch's theory (see Murstein, 1980, for a review). These investigations again emphasize that people choose partners who are most like themselves on traits that they or society value (such as attractiveness, educational level, social status, or earning potential).

So Where Is Love?

We all have heard about love. Some of us have experienced romantic love; most of us hope to experience it at some time in our lifetimes. How do we define love? Poets, lyricists, philosophers, and novelists, among innumerable others, have attempted to define love. Love is many different things to many different people:

> There is making love and being in love, which are quite dissimilar ideas; there is love of God, of mankind, of art, and of pet cats; there is motherly love, brotherly love, the love of money, and the love of one's comfortable old shoes. (Hunt, 1969, p. 5)

Research generally does not support the idea that love happens suddenly (love at first sight) or that love is blind. There is evidence that falling in love is a gradual process. Recent research has advocated that love has three component processes: intimacy, passion, and commitment. Intimacy refers to feelings that promote closeness; passion deals with arousal, both sexual and motivational; and commitment consists of a short-term decision to love another person and a long-term commitment to maintain that love (Sternberg, 1986; see also Clark & Reis, 1988).

There is a difference in how men and women view love. Contrary to what many people may believe, research demonstrates that men are more *romantic* in relationships than women are: They tend to stay in love longer in premarital relationships, and they feel more grief and despair following a breakup than women do (Rubin, 1973). Interestingly, in a study done in the 1960s (Kephart, 1967), women—much more often than men—reported that the absence of romantic love would not necessarily deter them from a marriage. However, perhaps both men and women are becoming more romantic. An investigation conducted nearly two decades after Kephart's demonstrates that the clear consensus among both men and women appears to be that no matter how ideal a prospective partner might be on all other dimensions, one does not entertain the thought of marriage unless one is "in love" (Simpson, Campbell, & Berscheid, 1986). This shift toward more of the U.S. population at least believing in love as a prerequisite to marriage has been explained by decreasing societal pressure to marry at a young age, the media's increased emphasis on family life, and the social, economic, and legal independence of many women, which would change the reasons for marriage (Simpson et al., 1986). Nevertheless, though most of us strive for a love relationship, it is important to remember that love does not equal commitment and in many cases is not even a prerequisite for it.

Cross-Cultural Perspectives

The idea of marrying for love is a relatively new one and not a universal one, even now. A marriage in which the partners have chosen each other freely is sometimes referred to as a "love marriage," although, cross-culturally, love is not invariably the goal of marriage. For instance, although data from Africa, India, Israel, and Malaya indicate some freedom of choice in a marriage—such as choosing to marry later, choosing a partner with a higher educational level, and choosing to marry for higher socioeconomic status (Murstein, 1980)—love is seldom a factor. Although the world as a whole seems to be moving toward the idea of love marriages, the rate of change is slow and seems to be related to the rate of industrialization (see Murstein, 1980, for a review). In Turkey, for example, three-quarters of the marriages are still arranged by parents (Fox, 1975). In India a number of issues have impeded the change, such as a belief that there is only one predestined mate for each person (the unconscious archetype theory). According to this belief, parental supervision is essential to avoid mistakes—thus there are an increasing number of semiarranged marriages. In Africa there has been a movement away from traditional polygamy (multiple wives) by the more educated, but they constitute only a minority of the population (Harrell-Bond, 1976), and polygamy is often a symbol of wealth and prestige. In China the age at which individuals marry has risen, but marriages continue to be arranged by parents to some degree.

Similarly, in Japan, many still prefer the "nakode," or matchmaker, to play a role, even if only a ceremonial one. More women in Japan are working, however, in order to gain independence and to avoid arranged marriages.

As Murstein (1980) concludes, it can be speculated that the absence of economic means for women leads to early marriage and less marital freedom. The opportunity to work allows women to avoid arranged marriages, enhances the possibility of love marriages, and perhaps slightly diminishes the marriage rate.

Pathways to Marriage

A study of 50 newly married couples was conducted to determine various pathways to marriage (Cate, Huston, & Nesselroade, 1986). After interviewing each spouse about the progression of the relationship from casual dating through serious dating to making a commitment to marriage, the investigators found four distinct pathways toward marriage. The first was a slow progression toward marriage, with a number of ups and downs throughout the relationship. The second was a rapid move toward the commitment stage, with no downturns along the way. The third pathway included a courtship period of medium length, with an initial hesitation just before marriage, followed by a sharp rise to commitment. Finally, along the fourth pathway all three periods were equally important, with a pattern of a relatively long road toward commitment and a number of ups and downs along the way. Each pathway also revealed a different level of importance and pattern of conflict throughout the relationship. The first and third pathways, for example, revealed increased levels of conflict throughout the premarital period, whereas the pattern of the second pathway showed decreased conflict at the serious level of involvement.

MARRIAGE

The United States is considered to be a marrying country: 96.3% of U.S. men have married at least once by age 75, and 94.5% of women in the United States marry at least once by age 75 (Statistical Abstract of the United States, 1992, reported in McCammon et al., 1993, p. 362). Furthermore, 96% of college students in one recent study reported an intention to marry (Rubinson & De Rubertis, 1991).

That is the good news about marriage. The bad news is that, as we all know, marriage does not necessarily mean "forever" anymore. The divorce rate in the United States in 1992 was 4.7 per 1000. This means that approximately 2% of all married couples in this country divorce annually (National Center for Health Statistics, 1993) and that your chances of getting a divorce approach 50%. It is generally recognized that the divorce rate has stabilized since its peak in 1981, but it has not declined (see Figure 10-1). As one writer noted, "Just as God has been pronounced dead quite often, but has this sneaky way of resurrecting Himself, so everyone debunks marriage, yet ends up married" (Firestone, 1970, p. 251).

People marry for a variety of reasons (McCammon et al., 1993):

1. *Personal fulfillment.* Many people, for a variety of reasons, believe that marriage is a goal to achieve in adulthood. Achieving this goal therefore brings a sense of personal fulfillment.
2. *Companionship.* Companionship is considered to be the greatest expected benefit of marriage and may include intimate, personal, and informal types of companionship.
3. *Parenthood.* 95% of college students report that they intend to have children (Rubinson & De Rubertis, 1991). Although some people are willing to have children outside of marriage, most societies, and therefore most individuals, want to have and raise children within the context of marriage.
4. *Security.* People frequently marry for both the emotional and the financial security they believe a marriage can provide. However, marriage no longer guarantees either type of security: Because of divorce laws, divorces are easy to obtain, and many women are financially devastated as a consequence of divorce (Weitzman, 1990).

Figure 10-1
Marriage and Divorce Rates: United States, 1950–1991
(*Source:* U.S. National Center for Health Statistics)

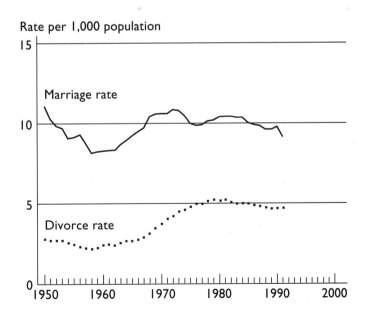

Rate per 1,000 population

Why People Marry

Equity Theory   Just as there are various theories of mating and court-ship, there are theories of marriage. An **equity theory of marriage** posits that people want the same proportion of rewards to costs as they be-lieve their partner has. The costs and rewards in a relationship can be both *physical* (such as effort, money, and gifts) and *psychological* (such as compli-ments, love, and respect) (Duck, 1991). In essence, people want fairness in their relationships, and relationships endure when people believe that they are being treated fairly. It should also be noted that as relationships de-velop, the time span between a cost and a reward tends to grow. So the more committed the relationship, the more willing the partners are to ac-cept a longer time before they receive a "payback" for their efforts. It has been noted that one sign of a relationship's progressing, or doing well, is when the partners no longer feel pressured or obliged to reciprocate every favor or reward that they receive (Duck, 1991). However, people still want fairness in the long run, and once a relationship begins to feel out of balance, people will again pay attention to the exchange.

Results of some recent studies based on equity theory demonstrate that people who hold global impressions that their relationships are equi-table, as opposed to those who do not, are more confident of staying to-gether in the future, are more content in their relationships, are less likely to have extramarital affairs, and report more positive affect and less nega-tive affect in their relationships (see Clark & Reis, 1988, for a review). However, other researchers have found that absolute reward levels predict relationship satisfaction much better than either equity or equality (Cate, Lloyd, Henton, & Larson, 1982). These investigations suggest that part-ners are highly committed to relationships as long as their rewards are high and exceed those available from their best alternative relationship, or ex-ceed their idea of what they deserve (Surra, 1990).

Role Complementarity   A committed relationship is complex and ideally involves not only mutual affection and a fair exchange of rewards and costs, but also some degree of **role, or behavior, complementar-ity.** This means that behaviors of both partners have to mesh together so that responsibilities are shared and domestic tasks get accomplished. Mar-riages based on traditional values, where one partner works to earn a liv-ing while the other partner works at home taking care of the house and children, revolve around the notion of complementarity: The wage-earner knows that he or she is responsible for earning money, and the homemaker understands that he or she is responsible for the house and the children. One does not have to worry about making money, and the other does not have to worry about cleaning the house or watching the children. However, there are many heterosexual and homosexual rela-tionships in which role responsibility and division of duties are not so clearly defined. With less clearly defined roles, couples must negotiate who is responsible for what and who receives what in return, often on an ongoing basis. Additionally, because they have chosen different roles than those of their same-sex parents or relatives, these couples may have few or no role models. Negotiating "new rules" takes time and adds pressure to a relationship. Many people, however, prefer this negotiation and the pressure that it entails to accepting a role that is not right for them. (See Box 2.)

Many marital problems are the result of a discrepancy between what the partners expect and their own beliefs about their marital roles (Newcomb & Bentler, 1980). When there is little overlap between the various roles and duties of the partners, marital happiness is generally low. On the other hand, marriages with equitable roles are usually more satisfying to the partners than those where either partner has more power than the other. As Duck (1991) notes, these issues cannot be left to chance. Partners must discuss their expectations and their desires so that an agreement can be reached on how best to distribute responsibilities in any long-term relationship.

His Marriage, Her Marriage

It has been noted that men benefit more from marriage than women do. Compared to single men, married men have superior mental health, lower suicide rates, greater career prospects, and longer lives (Bernard, 1973). Married women, on the other hand, have more psychological symptoms, are more depressed, have lower self-esteem, and are less happy than their unmarried counterparts; they also are less satisfied than their husbands are with their marriages (Bernard, 1973). There are many reasons offered for these differences in the ways that marriage affects men and women. For example, a woman in a traditional marriage must make many more changes than her husband if she is to adopt the traditional wife role. Furthermore, she loses power in both her relationship and her life, she lacks support on a day-to-day basis, and she probably faces a certain amount of tedium in a housekeeper role. It is what Bernard has termed the "Pygmalion Effect": Women make more adjustments in marriage than men do because they see themselves as having more at stake—that is, they have more to lose than their husbands do if the marriage ends.

This finding, as well as those from cross-cultural investigations, suggests that one factor that can significantly contribute to a woman's psychological well-being within marriage is work. Married women's participation in the U.S. workforce has been described as one of the most striking changes in the demography of the post–World War II American family (Greenstein, 1990). The large increase in the percentage of women in the labor force, from 27.9% in 1940 to 53.7% in 1984, corresponds to a series of changes in the age, marital status, and child-care responsibilities of working women in the United States (Menaghan & Parcel, 1990). The most striking change is in the greater employment of mothers of young

Box 2   Types of Marriage Relationships

According to Cuber and Harroff (1965), who interviewed 211 spouses, there are five different types of marital relationships:

1. *Conflict-habituated:* The spouses are basically incompatible; their relationship is characterized by conflict.
2. *Devitalized:* The spouses don't argue but are merely bored with each other; their relationship is characterized by lifeless and apathetic interactions.
3. *Passive-Congenial:* The relationship between these spouses is polite and superficial and always has been. The spouses in these relationships have interests in things and people separate from each other.
4. *Vital:* The spouses share an emotional closeness and enjoy each other's company; their central satisfaction is their relationship.
5. *Total:* This relationship is like the vital one, but it is more multifaceted. The spouses anticipate every opportunity to be together and schedule their day around each other.

It is not unusual for couples to start off with a total relationship and to drift downward into a conflict-habituated relationship—over a number of years the partners lose the interest they once had in making their marriage a priority.

Another *typology* of marriage is proposed by Fitzpatrick (1988). On the basis of 700 couples' responses to a questionnaire, she determined that partners hold basically three different perspectives about themselves in their marriage: traditional, independent, and separate. From these three individual perspectives, nine relational types can be constructed. The Pure type of relationship is one in which the husband and wife independently agree on a definition of their relationship; these couples are traditional, independent, or separate. Spouses who differ in their individual perspectives are categorized in one of the six Mixed types of relationship—for example, an independent husband married to a traditional wife, in which the husband and wife describe their relationship differently. Interestingly, of the 700 couples who were classified, 60% were classified into one of the three Pure types, suggesting that most husbands and wives do not define their marriages differently. Specifically, approximately 20% of the couples were traditionals, 22% independents, and 17% separates. Approximately 30% of the remaining Mixed marriages involved a separate partner or one who was emotionally divorced from the marriage. No Mixed type occurred with any greater frequency than the others (see Fitzpatrick, 1988, for more information).

children—the percentage of working married women with children under age 6 had risen to 59.9% by 1992 (U.S. Bureau of Labor Statistics, Bulletin 2340). Thus the traditional American ideal of marriage, in which the husband has an occupation outside the home and the wife has primary responsibility for the home and children, is no longer the norm.

There have been numerous studies of the effects of the employment of wives outside the home (see Menaghan & Parcel, 1990, for a review). In general, studies of the impact of employment on adult well-being report positive effects for both men and women; earned income appears to enhance self-esteem and a sense of mastery, which in turn increase overall well-being (see Mirowsky & Ross, 1986; Pearlin, Lieberman, Menaghan, & Mullan, 1981). One study found that among dual-career couples, marriages were high in both strains and satisfactions, with time an especially scarce commodity (Rappoport & Rappoport, 1971). Two variables, however, appear to be important in qualifying the effects of married mothers' employment: the extent of husbands' participation in family tasks and the match between wives' employment status and their own as well as their husbands' preferences (Menaghan & Parcel, 1990). Interestingly, though, one study found that for all wives (regardless of previously expressed preferences), movement from homemaking to full-time, or close to full-time, employment had positive effects; whereas the reverse movement, from full-time employment to homemaking, had a negative impact (Wethington & Kessler, 1989).

ALTERNATIVES TO MARRIAGE

The Gay Relationship

The term **homosexuality,** or **homoeroticism,** has been defined as the predominance of cognitive, emotional, and sexual attraction to those of the same sex (McCammon et al., 1993). The word *homosexual* may refer to either males or females who have a same-sex orientation. More often, however, the term **gay men** is used to refer to male homosexuals and the term **lesbians** to refer to homosexual women (Committee on Lesbian and Gay Concerns, 1991). It is estimated that between 5% and 10% of adults in the United States are predominantly homosexual (Smith, 1991), although most experts consider a person's sexuality to lie on a continuum between exclusively homosexual and exclusively heterosexual, with most people falling somewhere in the middle.

Despite a common stereotype, committed relationships are not the exception in the gay community. A study of 560 gay male relationships found that the average relationship lasted 7 years, and 76% of the respondents said that they were "committed for life" (National Survey Results, 1990, p. 1). Although gay male relationships often are not monogamous, the AIDS crisis has started to change the way gay men think of their rela-

Long-term commit-
ted relationships are
not solely the prov-
ince of heterosexual
individuals.

tionships. Of 92 couples in an organization devoted to supporting the gay relationship, 96.4%
reported that they were monogamous, and
most acknowledged that the AIDS crisis has
had a significant impact on their decision to be
sexually exclusive (Berger, 1990).

Long-term and committed relationships
exist among lesbian couples as well. Of the 706
lesbian couples surveyed, 18% reported that
they had been together 11 years or more, the
average relationship lasted 5 years, and 91% reported that they were sexually exclusive (National Survey Results, 1990). One reason that
lesbians might have longer commitments than
gay males is that women are typically taught to
value romantic and emotional relationships over
purely physical ones. Therefore, it is not surpris-
ing that in contrast to gay men, lesbians report that they developed an
emotional and loving relationship with their partner before the relationship became a sexual one. In fact, 93% of gay women in one study said
their first homosexual experience was an emotional one and that sex came
later (Corbett & Morgan, 1983).

Because, unlike heterosexual couples, homosexual couples receive
little societal support for their relationships, they are necessarily different
from opposite-sex romantic relationships (Huston & Schwartz, in press).
Homosexual people must often make an effort to arrange their lives so
that they meet other homosexual people, by choice of place to live
(propinquity), what they do for entertainment, and with whom they associate. Many often lead "double lives"—living in a heterosexual society
by day (that is, at work) and a homosexual society at night. Additionally,
once two homosexual people do meet and choose to become partners, a
lack of societal support may lead to instability in their relationship. For
example, gay male and lesbian couples cannot marry and do not have
the legal rights and responsibilities that accompany marriage.[2] Furthermore, family members often do not support such unions, which often
strains the relationship at best and forces a choice between family and a
lover at worst. Some couples or partners choose not to disclose their relationship to their parents, and the concealment further strains the relationship.

There are ways that gay men and lesbians can document their commitment to their partners, or lovers, that are legally binding. For instance,

---

[2] At the time of this writing the state of Hawaii was considering the legalization
of homosexual unions but had not yet passed such a law.

they can use wills to leave their property to a partner following their death. They can also draw up a power of attorney document that allows a lover to make health care decisions for them should they become incapacitated, rather than letting this responsibility fall to a member of a family from whom they may be estranged. This option is especially important to some gay couples in the age of AIDS. Finally, there are relationship contracts, which have no legal validity but are often used to specify the roles and responsibilities of each partner in a relationship. What is interesting to note, therefore, is that the law is more understanding of nontraditional relationships in death and ill health than it is of those relationships when the partners are healthy!

Cohabitation

Research on cohabitation, or living together in nonmarital unions, indicates that despite the postponement of marriage, people who live together have no less of an interest in a close or committed relationship than couples who marry. In 1988, in the United States alone, there were 2.6 million unmarried-couple households—a 63% increase since 1980 (U.S. Bureau of the Census, 1989). Another recent study showed that almost half of the 13,000 people interviewed had cohabited at some time and that 4% were currently cohabiting (Bumpass & Sweet, 1989). Cohabitation is not just a young adult phenomenon; 4 out of 10 couples had children. Although some research had demonstrated that marital quality was similar for couples who cohabited before marriage and those who did not (Macklin, 1983), more recent research on a larger sample found that, in fact, cohabitation is negatively related to marital stability, as evidenced by marital dissolution and propensity to divorce (Bumpass & Sweet, 1989).

Choosing to Remain Single

Various images of the single person are presented through the media. These images range from the "swinging single" bachelor (for example, Sam Malone on "Cheers") and the independent and single-by-choice woman (personified in Murphy Brown) to the lonely men and women who cannot find partners and spend all of their free time wishing they were married and feeling bad that they are not (as does the comic strip character "Cathy"). As with any broad grouping, there is enormous variety in the types of people who are of marrying age but are single, including the young unmarried and the divorced and widowed of all ages. The decision to postpone marriage has risen dramatically in popularity over the last decade. For example, in the United States the proportion of men ages 20 to 24 who had not yet wed was 78% in 1988, as opposed to 55% in 1970; for women in this age group, the proportion who never married increased from 36% in 1970 to 61% in 1988 (Surra, 1990). Age at marriage and length of marriage are of course related. Because delaying marriage increases the chance that it will never occur, an overall increase in age at first marriage is apt to result in an increase in the proportion of people who never marry (Surra, 1990). And the age of first marriage has been rising dramatically in most Western societies in the last 30 years. For example, in 1988, the estimated median age at first marriage for women in the United States was 23.6 years, and for men the comparable figure was 25.9 years—both the highest since the turn of the century at least (Surra, 1990).

SUMMARY

Finding a partner with whom you may spend a significant part of the rest of your life is no easy task. It is probably a quest that begins in early childhood, when socialization first begins. As you grow and mature, you discover your preferences, your personality traits become more set, and your needs become delineated. You make decisions, such as where you live, that affect who will be in your pool of possible partner choices. Love and the desire to be with someone are important in many cultures as determinants of partner choice. But, as noted in this and other chapters, they are not the determining factors. Society limits our choices or makes some decisions more comfortable than others. There is no "right" path to a life partner, no "right" person to fill that role—it is not even necessary to have a partner. And although our choices are numerous, they are certainly not infinite.

Class Discussion Questions

1. How do you think that your current or past romantic relationships have been "preselected" by (a) propinquity, (b) cultural norms, or (c) assortative issues (that is, similarity of traits)?
2. How is it functional for a society to endorse only heterosexual marriage? How is it dysfunctional?
3. If you have children now or are planning to have them in the future, how do you believe that you will shape your children's choice of a partner? How do you think you will react if your children go against your wishes in choosing a partner?
4. How does society make it difficult for people who go against mainstream thinking in their partner choices, either by choosing a same-sex partner, by not choosing a partner, or by marrying outside their subgroup?
5. How do mainstream opinions on mate selection ensure that certain people (such as women) or groups (gays, African-Americans) continue to have less social power?

Homework Assignments

1. Listen to a few popular songs and write notes on how the lyrics (a) support or (b) disprove the idea of assortative mating in our culture.
2. List some popular television shows and characters that promote our myths about what marriage means to both men and women, and describe how they do so.
3. Compose a classified ad for your ideal mate. Do the qualities you seek support or disprove an assortative mating theory? If they disprove it, what theory best supports how you choose a partner? Is there anyone in your class who seems like the perfect mate?

Additional Readings

Clark, M. S., & Reis, H. T. (1988). Interpersonal processes in close relationships. *Annual Review of Psychology, 39,* 609–672.

Duck, S. W. (1991). *Understanding relationships.* New York: Guilford.

Eckland, B. K. (1968). Theories of mate selection. *Eugenics Quarterly, 15,* 1–84.

Skolnick, A. (1978). *Exploring the intimate environment.* Boston: Little, Brown.

References

Bascow, S. A. (1992). *Gender stereotypes and roles* (3rd ed.). Pacific Grove, CA: Brooks/Cole.

Berger, R. M. (1990). Men together: Understanding the gay couple. *Journal of Homosexuality, 19,* 31–49.

Bernard, J. (1973). *The future of marriage.* New York: World.

Bulcroft, R. A., & Bulcroft, K. A. (1991). The nature and functions of dating in later life. *Research on Aging, 13,* 244–260.

Bulcroft, K. A., & O'Conner, M. (1986). The importance of dating relationships on quality of life for older persons. *Family Relations, 35,* 397–401.

Bumpass, L. L., & Sweet, J. A. (1989). National estimates of cohabitation. *Demography, 26,* 615–625.

Buss, D. (1985). Human mate selection. *American Scientist, 73,* 47–51.

Cate, R. M., Huston, T. L., & Nesselroade, J. R. (1986). Premarital relationships: Toward the identification of alternative pathways to marriage. *Journal of Social and Clinical Psychology, 4,* 3–22.

Cate, R. M., Lloyd, S. A., Henton, J. M., & Larson, J. H. (1982). Fairness and reward level as predictors of relationship satisfaction. *Social Psychology Quarterly, 45,* 171–181.

Clark, M. S., & Reis, H. T. (1988). Interpersonal processes in close relationships. *Annual Review of Psychology, 39,* 609–672.

Committee on Lesbian and Gay Concerns, American Psychological Association. (1991). Avoiding heterosexual bias in language. *American Psychologist, 46,* 973–974.

Cooley, C. H. (1964). *Human nature and the social order.* New York: Schocken.

Corbett, S. L., & Morgan, K. D. (1983). The process of lesbian identification. *Free Inquiry in Creative Sociology, 11,* 81–83.

Cuber, J. F., & Harroff, P. B. (1965). *Sex and the significant Americans.* Baltimore: Penguin Books.

Duck, S. W. (1991). *Understanding relationships.* New York: Guilford.

Eckland, B. K. (1968). Theories of mate selection. *Eugenics Quarterly, 15,* 1–84.

Firestone, S. (1970). *The dialectic of sex: The case for feminist revolution.* New York: Morrow.

Fitzpatrick, M. A. (1988). *Between husbands and wives: Communication in marriage.* London: Sage.

Fox, G. L. (1975). Love match and arranged marriage in a modernizing nation: Mate selection in Ankara, Turkey. *Journal of Marriage and the Family, 37,* 180–193.

Greenstein, T. N. (1990). Marital disruption and the employment of married women. *Journal of Marriage and the Family, 52,* 657–676.

Harrell-Bond, B. E. (1976). Stereotypes of Western and African patterns of marriage and family life. *Journal of Marriage and the Family, 38,* 387–396.

Hunt, M. (1969). *The affair.* New York: World.

Huston, T. L., & Levinger, G. (1978). Interpersonal attraction and relationships. *Annual Review of Psychology, 29,* 115–156.

Huston, M., & Schwartz, P. (1995). The relationships of lesbians and gay men. In S. W. Duck & J. T. Wood (Eds.), Understudied relationships: Off the beaten track [Understanding relationship processes 6]. Thousand Oaks, CA: Sage.

Kephart, W. M. (1967). Some correlates of romantic love. *Journal of Marriage and the Family, 29,* 470–474.

Macklin, E. D. (1983). Nonmarital heterosexual cohabitation: An overview. In E. D. Macklin & R. H. Rubin (Eds.), *Contemporary families and alternative lifestyles.* Beverly Hills, CA: Sage.

McCammon, S. L., Knox, D., & Schacht, C. (1993). *Choices in sexuality.* New York: West.

McNaught, B. R. (1983). Overcoming self-hate through education: Achieving self-love among gay people. In G. Albee, S. Gordon, & H. Leitenberg (Eds.), *Promoting sexual responsibility and preventing sexual problems* (pp. 133–145). Hanover, NH: University Press of New England.

Menaghan, E. G., & Parcel, T. L. (1990). Parental employment and family life: Research in the 1980s. *Journal of Marriage and the Family, 52,* 1079–1098.

Mirowsky, J., & Ross, C. E. (1986). Social patterns of distress. *Annual Review of Sociology, 12,* 23–45.

Murstein, B. I. (1980). Mate selection in the 1970's. *Journal of Marriage and the Family, 42,* 777–792.

National Center for Health Statistics. (1993). Births, marriages, divorces, and deaths for 1992. *Monthly Vital Statistics Report 41* (no. 12) (DHHS Publication No. PHS 83-1120). Hyattsville, MD: Public Health Service.

National survey results of gay couples in long-lasting relationships. (1990). *Partners: Newsletter for Gay and Lesbian Couples,* pp. 1–16.

Newcomb, M. D., & Bentler, P. M. (1980). Cohabitation before marriage: A comparison of couples who did and did not cohabit before marrying. *Alternative Lifestyles, 3,* 65–85.

Pearlin, L. I., Lieberman, M. A., Menaghan, E. G., & Mullan, J. T. (1981). The stress process. *Journal of Health and Social Behavior, 22,* 337–356.

Rappoport, R., & Rappoport, R. (1971). *Dual-career families.* Baltimore: Penguin.

Rice, F. P. (1990). *The adolescent* (6th ed.). Boston: Allyn & Bacon.

Rubin, Z. (1973). *Liking and loving: An invitation to social psychology.* New York: Holt, Rinehart and Winston.

Rubinson, L., & De Rubertis, L. (1991). Trends in sexual attitudes and behaviors of a college population over a 15 year period. *Journal of Sex Education and Therapy, 17,* 32–42.

Simpson, J. A., Campbell, B., & Berscheid, E. (1986). The association between romantic love and marriage: Kephart (1967) twice revisited. *Personality and Social Psychology Bulletin, 12,* 363–372.

Skolnick, A. (1978). *Exploring the intimate environment.* Boston: Little, Brown.

Smith, T. W. (1991). Adult sexual behavior in 1989: Number of partners, frequency of intercourse and risk of AIDS. *Family Planning Perspectives, 23,* 102–107.

Snyder, M., Berscheid, E., & Glick, P. (1985). Focusing on the exterior and the interior: Two investigations of the initiation of personal relationships. *Journal of Personality and Social Psychology, 30,* 526–537.

Sternberg, R. J. (1986). A triangular theory of love. *Psychology Review, 93,* 119–135.

Surra, C. A. (1990). Research and theory on mate selection and premarital relationships in the 1980's. *Journal of Marriage and the Family, 52,* 844–865.

Thornton, A. (1990). The courtship process and adolescent sexuality. *Journal of Family Issues, 11,* 239–273.

U.S. Bureau of the Census. (1989). Marital status and living arrangements: March 1988. *Current Population Reports* (Series P-20, No. 433). Washington, DC: U.S. Government Printing Office.

Weitzman, L. J. (1990). Women and children last: The social and economic consequences of divorce law reforms. In S. Ruth (Ed.), *Issues in feminism: An introduction to women's studies* (pp. 312–335). Mountain View, CA: Mayfield.

Wethington, E., & Kessler, R. C. (1989). Employment, parental responsibility, and psychological distress: A longitudinal study of married women. *Journal of Family Issues, 10,* 527–546.

Winch, R. (1958). *Mate selection.* New York: Harper and Row.

Woll, S. B., & Young, P. (1989). Looking for Mr. or Ms. Right: Self-presentation in videodating. *Journal of Marriage and the Family, 51,* 483–488.

Glossary

Assortative mating   A theory of mating that asserts that individuals find partners or mates based on their similarity on one or more characteristics

Equity theory of marriage   A theory that posits that a marriage will endure as long as the partners believe that their efforts are matched or exceeded by their rewards from the relationship or the other person

Exchange theory   A mate selection theory that states that people choose others on the basis of an exchange of the assets and liabilities that each person brings to the relationship

Gay men   Male homosexuals

Homogamy   The principle that people are attracted to others who are most like themselves

Homosexuality or **homoeroticism**   Cognitive, emotional, and sexual attraction predominantly directed to those of the same sex

Lesbians   Homosexual women

Parent image theory   The idea that a man seeks to "marry his mother," or someone like his mother, and a woman seeks to "marry her father," or someone like her father

Principle of complementary needs   The theory that opposites attract

Propinquity   A theory related to that of assortative mating that suggests that people will pair off or marry those geographically closest to them, based on the potential for familiarity

Role, or behavior, complementarity   The idea that behaviors of both partners have to mesh so that responsibilities are shared and domestic tasks get accomplished

Unconscious archetype   An early theory that for every man a particular woman exists who in some predetermined way corresponds most perfectly with him (and vice versa)

11

Marriage: Will I Be Happy or Will I Be Sad?

Clifford I. Notarius

Catholic University of America

We saw in Chapter 10 that most of us still choose to marry or enter lifelong partnerships, but that many of our unions end well before "death do us part." This chapter focuses on the role of communication in marital success and failure. First, it outlines trends in marriage and marriage failure and the effects of failures on experiences of family life, emphasizing the big consequences of little words and emotions. The chapter goes on to define good communication, to describe what gets in the way when things go wrong, and to suggest what couples can do to build a solid foundation for a successful marriage.

NV & SD

Chapter Outline

- A Lifetime Search for Intimacy
- The Foundations of Marriage
- Building a Good Foundation
- Conclusion

In these days of serial marriages, with celebrities and others joking that they are in their fifth, sixth, or seventh (and beyond) relationship, too little is said about the joys of a happy and stable marriage. National surveys show that happily married individuals are healthier (both physically and mentally) and consequently make less use of hospitals and outpatient clinics (Verbrugge, 1979). Married men and women report greater life satisfaction (Glenn & Weaver, 1988) and live longer than individuals who are divorced, separated, single, or widowed (Ross, Mirowsky, & Goldstein, 1990). When a marriage is troubled, many lives can go into turmoil. Separating and divorcing partners report a high incidence of physical and emotional problems and make correspondingly greater use of medical resources to treat their complaints (Kitson & Morgan, 1990). Among unhappy couples seeking marital therapy, about one-quarter report severe husband-to-wife physical violence and about one-third report mild physical violence (O'Leary & Vivian, 1990).

266

Celebrities are often as well known for their many marriages, divorces, or romances as they are for their professional achievements.

Spouses do not suffer alone. About one in three white children and three in five African-American children will experience the dissolution of their parents' marriage by the time they are 16 years old (Cherlin, 1992). Although there is some debate about the long-term consequences for children of their parents' divorce, there is general agreement that marital dissolution has at least a short-term negative impact upon children (Hetherington, 1989). Long-term effects are less clear, and children who experience their parents' divorce don't seem to be at greater risk in their own marriages (Bentler & Newcomb, 1978).

Given the number of couples who will divorce in any given year, the percentage of our population touched by relationship breakup and distress is huge. In 1992 there were 1,215,000 divorces in the United States. This amounts to a yearly divorce rate of 4.7 per 1000 population—the rate it has been for about the last three years. (See Chapter 10 for a further discussion of divorce rates.) Looked at another way, about one-quarter of those recently married will be divorced by the time of their seventh anniversary (Cherlin, 1992). Over a lifetime, almost one-half of all marriages will end in divorce.

A LIFETIME SEARCH FOR INTIMACY

Despite all the statistics on divorce and the breakdown of the American family, married life remains the preferred life-style. Just about every heterosexual adult in the United States will eventually get married in the search for intimacy with a life partner, although the timing of the wedding bells has fluctuated over the last 100 years, In recent years the median age of first marriage was estimated at 23.6 years for women and 25.9 years for men (U.S. Bureau of the Census, 1988). These ages of first marriage are closer to the norms that characterized the early 1900s than to those of the 1950s and 1960s, when partners married younger.

Because more people are choosing to live together, more couples marry at a later point in their lives. For many people in their twenties, a family celebration surrounding the news "We're getting married" has been replaced with a lively family discussion following the declaration "We've decided to move in together." To avoid the discussion altogether, some couples neglect to tell either set of parents about the arrangement. Although the reasons for a rise in cohabitation are many, you may be surprised to learn that living together before marriage isn't associated with an increased chance of relationship success (Thomson & Colella, 1992) and may be related to an increased probability of divorce (Newcomb, 1986). However, researchers are careful to caution that cohabitation by itself is not responsible for the increased chance of divorce. The association might be due to some other factor that is related to both the likelihood of cohabitating and marital instability, such as sexual adventurism. As you have probably been warned, correlation does not imply causation.

No matter when couples marry, certain necessary steps toward creating intimacy and making a relationship thrive must be taken. Weiss (1978) offers a valuable model of the tasks that need to be accomplished to achieve marital success. Weiss identifies 12 areas that all couples must deal with in their relationship. These are listed in Box 1 in the form of true-false questions, which can be used to assess where a couple stands on these tasks. The relative importance of each relationship area will rise and fall throughout the natural life course of a marriage, and we would expect couples to vary on how important each area is to them. For example, most newlyweds will not have to deal with parenting issues and can spend time having fun together as an extension of the courtship. On the other hand, a couple married 30 years will be rediscovering what it is like to be together again without children, and they may be struggling with family finances, as bills come in for college tuition and care of aging parents.

When an area is difficult for a couple (that is, when the answer to a question in Box 1 is "false"), then four additional questions can be asked. Each of these questions, also listed in Box 1, is related to a particular relationship skill that is necessary to cope with any current disappointment. In order to work toward a mutually satisfactory solution to a problem, partners must identify exactly what the problem is, they must feel supported and understood, they must be able to use problem-solving skills to work out their differences, and they must be able to change their behavior or accept the status quo without resentment. Together, these skills allow a couple to resolve their particular differences and the disagreements that will emerge, or reemerge, during their journey through the family life-cycle.

Given this framework, it is easy to see why communication between partners is so important. Without good communication, partners will have a difficult time figuring out what ails the relationship, they won't be able to show each other support and understanding, and they won't be able to figure out what each person will do to address the problem. Not surprisingly, the way partners communicate is the biggest difference between happy and unhappy couples (Gottman, 1979). In this chapter, you will learn about the precise communication patterns that contribute to marital happiness and marital misery and examine how thoughts and emotions interact with the spoken word to shape the ongoing communication process between husbands and wives. With a good understanding of what makes a marriage happy or sad, we should be able to construct programs to help couples achieve lasting relationship happiness. At the end of the chapter, we will take a look at current programs that are available to help couples.

Box 1	**Assessing Satisfaction in the Twelve Marital Tasks**

True   False

___   ___   1. We are good friends.
___   ___   2. We agree on demonstrations of affection.
___   ___   3. We are considerate of each other.
___   ___   4. Our sex life is good.
___   ___   5. We communicate well.
___   ___   6. We enjoy doing things together.
___   ___   7. We are good parents.
___   ___   8. We agree on household chores.
___   ___   9. We manage our finances well.
___   ___   10. We don't argue about each other's careers or work habits.
___   ___   11. We don't argue about each other's personal habits, including dress.
___   ___   12. We each can do things with friends or family without causing an argument.

For each statement answered false, answer the following four questions.

True   False

___   ___   1. We have a common understanding of our disagreements.
___   ___   2. I feel my partner is supportive of my wants and desires in this area.
___   ___   3. I feel we know how to resolve our disagreements in this area.
___   ___   4. I feel we've taken good steps toward resolving our disagreements in this area.

THE FOUNDATIONS OF MARRIAGE

There are three essential components that shape the communication process within a marriage: words, thoughts, and emotions. These three elements, in constant interaction with one another, determine whether a marriage will be happy or sad. The first element, words (and deeds), refers to the actual exchange process that occurs between husbands and wives. In the course of day-to-day interactions, partners say things to each other and do things that affect each other in often predictable ways. The second two elements, thoughts and emotions, lie within each individual partner and are the source of the often automatic words and deeds that shape the interactions. However, relationship partners need not operate like slaves to their thoughts and emotions, so there is always the potential for one's words and deeds *not* to follow directly from one's thoughts and emotions. The ability to maintain independence of thought, emotion, and action is in fact explicitly acknowledged as an important component of healthy relationship adaptation by some family scholars (for example, Bowen, 1978).

In developing our model of relationship functioning, it is important to keep in mind that a marriage is actually a system made up of two people. Whatever I say and do will have an effect upon my partner's emotions and thoughts and, consequently, upon her words and deeds. Her words and deeds will then affect my thoughts and emotions and, in short order, *my* words and deeds. Where we choose to break into this interlocking system between two people is somewhat arbitrary, and we must keep this point in mind as we develop our analysis.

Let's look in on a couple confronting a relationship challenge. Jason and Rebecca have been married about 18 months. One evening Rebecca comes home from a long day and wants to talk with Jason about something that made her angry at work: She tells him about an obnoxious interaction with her boss. Jason thinks, "Rebecca's boss is a creep, always has been. She's gotta learn to let the stuff he does roll off her back." He then replies, "Why didn't you just tell him to get lost?" Rebecca can feel a knot in her stomach grow tighter, and she thinks, "Why can't Jason ever side with me? What I need is a friend, not a lecture on what I should have done." She then replies, "That's not the point. I was so mad I couldn't get any work done the rest of the day." Jason continues, "You shouldn't let these things bother you." Rebecca retaliates, "You should learn how to be more supportive." Pretty soon Jason and Rebecca are in a heated argument, not about what happened to Rebecca at work, but about Rebecca's feeling that Jason "is always critical and unsympathetic" and Jason's feeling that "no matter what I do, it's always wrong." The couple's argument developed out of Jason's *and* Rebecca's words, emotions, and thoughts, and to zero in on just one aspect of the interaction is to miss the interdependence among all three elements in the model of relationship functioning that we are developing here.

Recent research has taught us much about the words, thoughts, and emotions that help determine whether a relationship will be happy or sad.

Words

Survey studies have consistently shown a strong relationship between marital happiness and communication (see, for example, Navran, 1967). Communication difficulties between spouses permit an accumulation of unresolved conflicts and the eventual erosion of marital happiness (Schaap, Buunk, & Kerkstra, 1988). Thus it is not surprising to find that a problem with communication is the top complaint of couples seeking marital therapy (Geiss & O'Leary, 1981).

Early in the study of marriage, researchers discovered that when they asked husbands and wives the same "objective" question, they received different answers. For example, in one study partners were separately interviewed on the telephone about specific behaviors that occurred in the past 24 hours. Husbands and wives were not in complete agreement even about behaviors as specific as sexual intercourse. Asked about less specific behaviors, spouses were much less in accord (Christensen & King, 1982).

It is perhaps not surprising that husbands and wives will see, interpret, and report on the events in their relationships according to their own perspectives and perhaps produce very different portraits of the same scene. What is seen as a "nice discussion over breakfast" by one partner might be described by the other as "another tension-filled meal where I was walking on eggshells and couldn't say anything." Obviously, both partners' views are crucial to understanding the marriage, and the precise way that partners differ from each other may tell us something important about the marriage. For example, the interpretations given to a simple act can dramatically alter its impact—did one partner cook dinner "to be romantic and do something sweet" or "to be nice so I'd agree to spend the holidays away from my parents"?

In taking a closer look at the words exchanged between husbands and wives, observers position themselves on the outside of the relationship looking in on the couple's communication process. Ideally, from their perspective on the outside of the relationship, each observer will see the partners' communication with unbiased eyes. Thus all outside observers should agree on what is going on between the partners. Even though the partners themselves may have very different views of their communication process, we want the outside observers to agree as much as possible. In practice, it turns out, observers do not necessarily agree with one another unless they receive extensive training and learn to use a common language system for describing the ongoing interaction.

In a typical study of the words exchanged in marriage, happy and unhappy couples come to a research laboratory that is furnished like a living room. Each couple is asked to fill out questionnaires, they're interviewed, and then they're videotaped as they discuss a current and unresolved issue in their relationship. Most couples planning marriage talk about money, relatives, and jealousy, whereas most newlywed couples wind up talking about money, careers, and communication. By the second year of marriage and from then on, the top three problem areas are money, sex, and communication (in Dickson-Markman & Markman, 1988).

No matter what topic the couple chooses to discuss, they are asked to take about 15 to 20 minutes to work toward a mutually satisfactory solution to the identified problem. These videotaped conversations are then meticulously analyzed by a team of trained coders. Each complete thought that each partner utters will be assigned 1 of 30 or more unique codes. A typical 15-minute conversation may have anywhere from 3 to 600 or more of these "thought units," and each one will get a separate code.

Although several codebooks have been developed by different researchers (for example, Gottman, 1979; Hahlweg et al., 1984; Notarius & Markman, 1981; Weiss & Summers, 1983), the following codes generally appear in each of the codebooks:

Agreement: Any statement of direct agreement ("Yeah, that's what I was saying") or assent ("Uhm hm")

Disagreement: Any statement of direct disagreement ("I don't think that's right") or yes-but ("Okay, but you're not looking at it correctly")

Positive Problem Solution: Any statement that offers a constructive solution to the problem ("I'll come home a half-hour earlier")

Negative Problem Solution: Any statement that offers an unrealistic solution to the problem ("I'll never leave the kitchen dirty again") or a refusal to change ("I'm not going to change because I didn't do anything wrong")

Criticism: Any statement in which the speaker expresses dislike of the partner's behavior in a way that is critical of the partner's behavior ("You're not doing your share around the house") or person ("You're an inconsiderate s.o.b.")

Problem Description: Any statement that gives information about a problem in a nonblaming fashion ("I think we've overspent our budget")

Mind Reading: Any statement that assumes the speaker knows what the thoughts, feelings, or attitudes of the partner are without asking ("You never like doing what I like to do")

In general, disagreements, criticisms, negative problem solutions, and mind-reading statements that are accompanied by a negative tone of voice or a negative facial expression are likely to have more impact on the listener than these same messages delivered with neutral or even positive nonverbal cues. On the other hand, agreements, positive problem solutions, and mind-reading statements delivered with positive nonverbal cues (such as a warm tone of voice or a smile) are likely to have a more heart-warming affect on the partner than these same messages delivered with neutral or negative nonverbal cues (such as a rude hand gesture or a sneer).

Take special note that these studies of communication always include a group of happy couples to serve as the comparison for the unhappy couples. If only unhappy couples were studied, as might happen if researchers relied on studying couples in therapy, it would be impossible to know whether the presence or absence of identified communication patterns was unique to the unhappy couples or if some of these patterns were also present among happy couples. As it turns out, many of the findings are quite surprising.

Let's see how good you are at guessing what the interactional differences are between happy and unhappy couples. Imagine watching an unhappy couple talk about an unresolved issue in their relationship and getting a count of how much agreement the partners show to each other, how much disagreement, how much criticism, and so on. Now imagine watching a happy couple have a similar discussion about one of their unresolved issues. Here's a hint about the findings: Unhappy couples have more disagreements, have fewer agreements, and exchange more criticism than happy couples. But how large are the differences between the group of happy couples and the group of unhappy couples? Make your guesses below by estimating the ratio of distressed to nondistressed interaction. For example, if you guess that happy couples have 50 agreements in their conversation and unhappy couples have 25 agreements, you would estimate that happy couples have 2 times the number of agreements of unhappy couples.

Agreements: Happy couples show _____ times the number of agreements of unhappy couples.

Disagreements: Unhappy couples show _____ times the number of disagreements of happy couples.

Problem Descriptions: Happy couples show _____ times the number of problem descriptions of unhappy couples.

Criticisms: Unhappy couples show _____ times the number of criticisms of happy couples.

Overall Positive Behavior: Happy couples show _____ times the number of overall positive behaviors of unhappy couples.

Overall Negative Behavior: Unhappy couples show _____ times the number of overall negative behaviors of happy couples.

Although there are some differences across the various studies, the ratios of the behaviors you've just estimated average out close to the following:

Agreements: Happy couples show approximately <u>1.75</u> times the number of agreements of unhappy couples.

Disagreements: Unhappy couples show approximately <u>2.0</u> times the number of disagreements of happy couples.

Problem Descriptions: Happy couples show approximately <u>1.25</u> times the number of problem descriptions of unhappy couples.

Criticisms: Unhappy couples show approximately <u>2.75</u> times the number of criticisms of happy couples.

Overall Positive Behavior: Happy couples show approximately <u>2.0</u> times the number of overall positive behaviors of unhappy couples.

Overall Negative Behavior: Unhappy couples show approximately <u>2.5</u> times the number of overall negative behaviors of happy couples.

These findings show that observers were able to detect some subtle differences in the interactions of happy and unhappy couples. The conversations of happy couples are not all good and the conversations of unhappy couples are not all bad. The problem-solving conversations of happy couples contain some disagreement, criticism, and negative behavior—but less than those of unhappy couples. Similarly, the problem-solving conversations of unhappy couples contain some agreement, problem description, and positive behavior—but less than those of happy couples. Note as well that the two groups of couples tend to differ more on the exchange of negative behaviors (criticism, disagreements, overall negative) than they do on the exchange of positive behaviors.

These findings give a good picture of what observers see in the conversations of distressed and nondistressed marriages. But do these differences mean anything? Even if observers agree on what words are exchanged between husbands and wives during a problem-solving discussion, does this really capture something fundamentally important about a relationship? Can scrutiny of one conversation actually reveal something about the marriage that will have lasting consequence? To answer these questions we need to see whether the communication patterns observed today predict how the relationship will be doing several years down the road. In essence we are asking, Can a detailed analysis of a couple's 30-minute problem-solving conversation today predict the future satisfaction of the couple three or more years later?

Is this couple happy or unhappy? Research has shown that the conversations of happy couples are not all good and that the conversations of unhappy couples are not all bad.

In 1980 Markman (1990) began studying a group of 135 couples planning marriage, and the couples have been reporting in about their marriages ever since. Markman found that the amount of disagreement that the wives displayed in 1980 was a good predictor of *future* distress. In the planning marriage stage, wives in couples who went on to have happy relationships disagreed with their husbands an average of 2.8% of the time. Wives in couples who went on to have unhappy relationships disagreed with their husbands an average of 4.9% of the time. Can it be that uttering disagreements just 1.75 (4.9 divided by 2.8) times more often is related to future relationship happiness? Small behavioral differences that presumably are repeated day after day in conversation after conversation do seem to have long-term consequences for couples.

Markman (1990) also found that the amount of overall negative *nonverbal* behavior was a good predictor of future satisfaction. Partners who went on to have unhappy relationships averaged about 1.8 times more negative nonverbal behavior than did partners who went on to have happy relationships. Again we see that these relatively small differences in the ways couples communicate can translate into rather large differences in the lives of the couples.

Other investigators have found that the behaviors exchanged in one problem-solving conversation predict changes in relationship satisfaction over time (Gottman & Krokoff, 1989). In that study, 25 couples were followed over a 3-year period. Relationships in which husbands showed more disagreement and criticism showed *less* decline in relationship satisfaction. Relationships in which wives showed more agreement and approval showed *more* decline in relationship satisfaction. It appears that some behaviors associated with current marital happiness and distress are related in an opposite manner to long-term satisfaction.

With these findings we can put together the following portrait of a marriage headed for difficulties over time. The partners do not have a way to handle conflict and disagreement so as to create solutions, support, and mutual understanding—so they do one of two things. Either they avoid discussing their problems, and resentments build up, or they constantly argue about their problems but never reach a resolution, usually feeling worse for having had the discussion or argument. Husbands and wives in relationships headed for difficulties may each contribute their own ingredients to the marital stew. The behavior of husbands that is associated with long-term relationship distress appears to be *withdrawal* from the relationship, whereas the problematic behavior of wives appears to be *compliance* (Gottman & Krokoff, 1989; Markman, 1990). Husbands who avoid conflict by withdrawing and wives who avoid conflict by simply agreeing with their partners seem to create fragile relationships that are vulnerable to increased difficulties over time. For example, when a couple becomes a family, many new demands are placed on the couple, and partners who lack adequate resources to meet these challenges head-on may be faced with a decline in relationship satisfaction and eventual distress (Benson, 1988; Cowan & Cowan, 1992).

Thus far we have learned about the words that go along with marital happiness and unhappiness. This is the domain with the strongest research foundation. Although less is known about thoughts and emotions, particularly about the longitudinal consequences of specific ones, let's examine what is known.

Thoughts

Searching for the Cause of Behavior   Happy and unhappy couples not only talk differently about the problems in their relationships, they think differently as well. No doubt talking is one outlet for these different thoughts. Each of us tries to make sense of our world by explaining events that we find significant. Nothing serious will happen if we fail to take note of a pleasant event. However, failure to take note of a potentially threatening event can have dire consequences. If you are out walking late at night and you see a threatening shape in the distance, it may be a matter of life and limb for you to determine whether the shape is the harmless shadow of a tree or the ominous outline of a suspicious character. Determining the threat of danger can allow you to cross the street quickly and reduce the risk of harm.

In relationships we continually make similar assessments (see Holtzworth-Munroe & Jacobson, 1985). Threats in relationships, however, are more likely to affect us on a psychological than on a physical level. Thus when we feel put-down, not respected, incompetent, or controlled by our partners, we often come up with an explanation to deal with this psychological threat to our well-being. These explanations, even if not necessarily accurate or objective, help make our world more predictable.

All explanations, however, are not created equal in terms of how they make us feel about our relationships. Some explanations for a partner's behavior will act to intensify the likelihood of conflict and discord, whereas other explanations will reduce the probability of conflict and increase the chance of maintaining marital harmony. The function of these explanations, or **causal attributions** (as they are sometimes called), will vary, depending on whether the actions in question are positive or negative.

For example, Mary is studying for an important test when Tim turns on the TV to watch the evening news. Mary thinks the volume is way too loud, and she would like to have quiet in the apartment. At this moment Mary is likely to come up with an explanation for Tim's annoying behavior (that is, his turning on the TV). She will become more upset if she interprets Tim's action as one of the following:

> Part of a long-standing pattern of his ("He always thinks first about what he wants and never about what I need.")
>
> A personal flaw ("He's selfish and inconsiderate.")
>
> A pattern of his that occurs in many settings ("This is just like the time we were having company and he messed up the house after I cleaned it.")
>
> Intentional ("He's trying to annoy me.")

Thinking these thoughts, what is Mary most likely to say to Tim? Put yourself in Mary's shoes for a minute, think what Mary is thinking, and come up with something Mary is likely to say. For instance, she might say, "Can't you ever think of anyone but yourself? I can't study with the TV going. Just once can you do something nice for me?" Or perhaps Mary will just think these things and, rather than saying anything, slap her books shut, storm into the bedroom, and slam the door. If either of these scenarios is a typical encounter, more than likely Tim and Mary will be having relationship difficulties. Thinking affects how we react to our partners and these reactions affect relationship quality.

Alternatively, Mary's reactions might be different if she follows a different line of thought—that is, if she interprets Tim's actions as one of the following:

An infrequent event ("Usually he's sensitive to my needs.")

Caused by situational circumstances ("Something must have happened today that he wants to see on the news.")

Limited to the here-and-now ("He let me study all afternoon.")

Unintentional ("He doesn't realize how loud the TV is.")

If Mary has these thoughts, what might she say to Tim when he turns on the TV? More than likely, it will be easier for her to ask Tim to change his behavior in a way that increases the likelihood of behavior change and decreases the likelihood of an argument: "I've got this big test tomorrow, Tim, and I'd really appreciate it if you'd turn off the TV or use the earphones. Thanks."

Spouses in distressed marriages tend to explain their partners' behavior in the worst possible light. If one partner does something the other one doesn't like, the distressed spouse blames the partner for a willful misdeed that is believed characteristic of the partner in many situations and many occasions. If her or his partner does something pleasing, the distressed spouse thinks it is an accident, unlikely to repeat itself and very uncharacteristic of the partner ("She's just being nice to me because her parents are visiting and she doesn't want them to see what's happening here"). Spouses in a nondistressed marriage tend to do just the opposite—they maximize the impact of positive behaviors and minimize the impact of negative behaviors (Fincham, Bradbury, & Scott, 1990).

You may be thinking that reactions happen automatically and follow directly from another's actions. Tim turns on the TV—Mary reacts automatically. However, this idea doesn't fit the reality of our lives. More than likely you can recall an event (such as getting stuck in a traffic jam) that bothered you greatly one day (you started pounding on the steering wheel and tried to weave in and out of traffic) but that you barely took notice of another day (you turned on the radio and sat back to enjoy the music). If events automatically caused our thoughts, the same event would produce the same thoughts and reactions each time it occurred. However, we know that isn't the case. The same event can cause a myriad of different reactions, depending on how we interpret events on any particular day. Our ability to take control of our thoughts, not be controlled by them, can be a wellspring of change for individuals and their personal relationships.

Hoping for the Best   There is another category of thought that also affects relationships. When we are confronted with a challenging task, we naturally have some belief in or expectation of our ability to carry out the task. One of the most important tasks for relationships is the resolution of disagreements. **Relational efficacy** (Notarius & Vanzetti, 1983) reflects the expectation that couples have of being able to reach a mutually satisfactory resolution of disagreements.

Box 2   **Capturing Your Thoughts**

To get a feel for how each of us makes sense out of important relationship events, think back to the last time you had a significant encounter, either positive or negative, with someone you are emotionally involved with. It could be a family member, a best friend, or a relationship partner. Next, take a minute or two to describe the encounter. Now, write down all the thoughts running through your mind to explain the behavior of the other person. You can also write down any explanations you have for your own behavior. For each explanation you've written down, use the guidelines in the section of the chapter entitled "Searching for the Cause of Behavior" to determine whether the explanation is general (She's always inconsiderate) or specific (He was late because he got a phone call), personal (She always forgets my birthday) or impersonal (He had so much on his mind from work that he forgot my birthday this year), and whether it implies the possibility of change (She wants to be with her family for the holidays this year) or is set in stone (He never wants to be with my family). What kinds of explanations did you tend to come up with? Notice how your thoughts are likely to affect your feelings about the events you are explaining. You might try experimenting with some alternative explanations for the event and see whether these alternative ways of viewing the event lead you to feel differently about what happened.

Happy couples expect to reach satisfying resolutions of their relationship disagreements more often than unhappy couples do; the happy couples have higher relational efficacy than unhappy couples. This expectation is in turn related to the explanations partners find for each other's behavior (Vanzetti, Notarius, & NeeSmith, 1992) and to their actual interactional behavior (Irwin, 1991). Vanzetti et al. (1992) compared partners who believed in their ability to resolve a relationship disagreement to partners who were less sure of their ability to reach a resolution. The partners with low relational efficacy were much more likely to hold their spouses responsible for behavior they considered negative and to "write off" their partners' positive behaviors. Partners with high relational efficacy did just the opposite: They gave their partners credit for behaving positively and excused any negative behavior.

It is therefore not surprising that these expectations are in fact related to the words exchanged during a problem-solving conversation. Researchers have found quite a strong association between the confidence partners have that disagreements in their relationship can be resolved and the words they actually use during the conversation (Irwin, 1991). For example, husbands and wives who expected to reach an agreement during a problem discussion had conversations in which the wives sent more positive messages (such as positive problem solutions and agreements) and fewer negative messages (such as negative problem solutions and criticisms) to their husbands than wives who didn't expect to reach an agreement. Thus the expectations husbands and wives have for being able to resolve their disagreements are significantly related to how they talk with each other when discussing a problem area.

There has not been much research yet into the long-term significance of relational efficacy, although preliminary findings show that efficacy predicted satisfaction 12 months later (Fincham et al., 1990). Efficacy expectancies have also proved to be very important predictors of relationship satisfaction across the transition to parenthood (Benson, 1988). New parents often experience a decline in marital satisfaction during the initial months following the birth of the first child. Even after taking into account how happy couples were prior to the birth of the first child, Benson found that relational efficacy was the best predictor of marital satisfaction 3 months after the birth of the child. Partners need confidence in their abilities to work out the problems caused by increased demands on their time and resources. This confidence is translated into the way partners speak to each other when conflicts occur (Irwin, 1991), and thus we see the delicate interplay between words and thoughts.

Belief in our abilities to carry out certain behaviors, or concern about our inability to reach satisfactory outcomes, has broad effects on us and our relationships (Bandura, 1986). If a conflict develops between partners and there is an immediate expectation that the conflict will deepen because "we never get anywhere when we talk about problems," it is very likely that there will be corresponding increases in physiological arousal, such as an increase in heart rate and sweating. Individuals who believe themselves capable of carrying out a specific task are less aroused when they approach the task than individuals who are worried that the task will get the better of them (Bandura, Reese, & Adams, 1982). Let us turn now from thoughts to emotional arousal.

Emotional Arousal

Words and thoughts are energized by the emotional reactions they elicit, and these together contribute to our actions. As noted above, our bodies are finely tuned to deal with threatening situations that require our arousal to effectively fight or flee. In close personal relationships neither fight nor flight is very helpful in settling conflicts, and yet we must somehow deal with the arousal that will accompany experienced threat. There is evidence that the more aroused we are—the more accelerated our heart rate, the more we sweat, and the faster our breathing—the more likely it is that there will be relationship difficulties.

In 1980 Levenson and Gottman (1985) studied a group of 19 couples by asking husband and wife to come to a laboratory suite after spending at least 8 hours apart. When the couple met at the laboratory, they didn't speak with each other. While they waited to have a conversation about the events of the day spent apart and a second conversation about an unresolved relationship problem, various physiological processes (for example, heart rate and sweating) were measured. After a 5-minute waiting period, the couple's conversations began, and physiological monitoring continued.

Three years later, Levenson and Gottman went back to the couples and measured their marital satisfaction. One of the central questions they were interested in answering was: Can partners' physiological reactions to each other (in 1980) predict changes in satisfaction over a three-year period (1980 to 1983)? The answer was a surprising yes! The couples who were most aroused while waiting to share the events of the day in conversation experienced the greatest decline in marital satisfaction over the next three years. Similarly, physiological arousal during each of the actual conversations also was associated with a decline in satisfaction over the next three years.

Looking further at the interactions in 1980 of these couples, Levenson and Gottman (1983) examined the moment-to-moment relations between a husband's and a wife's physiological arousal. They developed an index to measure how much the two partners' arousal increased and decreased simultaneously—as if there were some linkage connecting husband and wife. In a marriage with high physiological linkage, when one partner's heart rate accelerated, so did the other's. The least satisfied couples were found to have the greatest level of physiological linkage. Levenson and Gottman reasoned that partners in less satisfied relationships have discussions that are filled with more negative problem talk (which is consistent with the literature reviewed above) and that these negative interactions lead to the linked arousal of the partners.

We are now in position to weave together the various findings on words, thoughts, and emotional arousal in marriage.

A Circle Game: Words, Thoughts, and Emotions

In an intimate relationship, husband and wife glide between the roles of speaker and listener whenever one person stops talking and the other starts. The speaker's words and actions become the stimulus for the listener's thoughts and emotions. The listener's visible reactions become cues for the speaker's thoughts and emotions and begin to influence the ongoing stream of words. As soon as the partners trade speaker and listener roles, the processes continue, with a new player in each role. Over the course of a 30-minute conversation, the roles can change 100 or more times. The interdependence among the spoken word, hidden thoughts, and charged emotion influences both partners.

Since words, thoughts, and emotions feed off each other in a never-ending cycle, it doesn't much matter where we break into the circle. During conflict, the angry exchange of criticism, disagreements, and unflattering causal attributions is likely to increase physiological arousal (emotions). Conversations that start with partners harboring low expectations for reaching a satisfactory agreement (that is, interactions with low relational efficacy) are likely to begin with partners' being highly aroused and to be marked with an exchange of words that deepen conflict. A spouse who reasons that a flaw in his or her partner's character is to blame for a current difficulty is likely to feel hopeless, be more aroused, and use words that leave the partner feeling attacked.

But That's Not All . . .

To the circle-game portrait of marital interaction described above, we can add two psychological processes that will also affect how conflict develops, evolves, and becomes resolved. First, we know that we brew some of our most powerful thoughts about the words, thoughts, emotions, and actions pertaining to our relationship in the absence of our partner. After a good time, we reflect on the meaning of the encounter; after a conflict, we conduct an interactional "autopsy" to figure out what went wrong. The consequences of these private analyses will ultimately affect the interactions we have. Thus it is important to realize that significant relational processes also develop outside of the immediate context of partners' interactions with each other. Second, it is important to keep in mind that we are rapid learners—particularly when strong emotions are involved. How many of you can remember something you had always enjoyed eating until one day it was associated with becoming ill? We often lose our taste for such foods, even if the association we have formed between the food and our illness is faulty. In relationships we learn to associate certain cues with certain outcomes, and, once made, these linkages guide our behavior. If Bill believes that he and Kate always wind up in a bitter argument whenever the topic of money is discussed, what will happen when Kate says, "How much do you want to spend on vacation this year?" What might be a neutral question for some couples or an enjoyable question for others triggers in Bill the full-blown emotional reaction of the last ten discussions they had about money, which had left each of them hurt, disappointed, lonely, and hopeless. Often the past is as good a predictor of the future as we have, so Bill and Kate's predicament is understandable.

Nevertheless, we need not allow marital conflict to operate as a runaway train, racing out of control to an inevitable crash and burn. The train

Box 3   **Slowing Down a Conversation**

The circle game among words, thoughts, and emotions happens quite rapidly. When you discuss an important disagreement with someone you care about, the conversation can turn into an argument before either of you knows what is happening. One way of slowing down the process to examine the relations among words, thoughts, and emotions is to do an exercise in which the listener gives the speaker immediate feedback about every message spoken. To do this exercise you will need three index cards and a marker. On one index card make a big +, on another a big −, and on the third a big 0. These cards will stand for how a message makes the listener feel—positive, negative, or neutral. The next time you have a disagreement with someone you care about, use the feedback cards as follows. Agree on who is to speak first; the listener should hold the three feedback cards. As the speaker says whatever is on her or his mind, the listener will hold up one of the feedback cards, changing the card as often as necessary to show the speaker what the impact of each message is. Once the speaker is done and ready to become the listener, the listener gives the speaker the feedback cards, and they switch roles. The goal of this exercise is to heighten awareness of what kinds of messages have what kinds of impact upon each person.

can be stopped; however, it will take the concerted efforts of both partners to manage the words, thoughts, and emotions that power relationship conflict. Just as Bill and Kate learned that talk about money led to hopeless arguments, they can learn new ways of dealing with their disagreements that are mutually satisfying. As each step toward more rewarding outcomes is accomplished, there should be a corresponding increase in relational efficacy and decrease in disorienting physiological arousal. This is the essence of programs that help couples maintain their marital happiness or repair a troubled union (Notarius & Markman, 1993).

BUILDING A GOOD FOUNDATION

Keeping a Marriage Happy

As noted earlier, interactional studies of happy and unhappy couples show that both groups exchange both positive and negative communications. Happy couples, however, have a somewhat greater proportion of positive behaviors than unhappy couples do; and unhappy couples have a somewhat greater proportion of negative behaviors than happy couples do. This suggests that happy couples seem capable of changing the course of marital conflict so that the words, thoughts, and emotions don't escalate out of control.

Although there have been no further studies on linked physiological arousal, there are several studies pointing to the role of tit-for-tat negative exchanges in marital distress (that is, negative reciprocity). Interactional researchers have in fact shown that the conflict conversations of unhappy couples are much more predictable than the conversations of happy couples (Gottman, 1979). The predictability lies in the exchange of negative behaviors—one good zinger seems to beget another in return. Happier couples seem able to exit these exchanges by the introduction of more positive talk, which effectively breaks the chain of negative reciprocity.

In Markman's (1990) study of 135 couples planning marriage, he looked at each listener's likelihood of speaking a negative message immediately after receiving a negative message from the speaker. For example, suppose Jim complains, "I don't want to discuss the house. I don't see any reason why we need to clean it every week." What will be Janet's immediate reply? Will she meet the complaint with a complaint of her own—"You don't want to talk about anything, but this time you will." Or will she try to exit the negative cycle—"So you're saying that you'd prefer that we don't talk about cleaning the house now. Okay. It's important for me that we do, though, so when would be a good time to have the discussion?"

Analyzing the conversations between couples who were planning marriage, Markman found a different pattern in the conversations of couples who went on to be dissatisfied six years later than among the couples who maintained their relationship satisfaction. In couples who became dissatisfied over the six-year period, both husbands and wives (in the planning marriage stage) tended to send back a negative message if they received one. In couples who remained satisfied over the next six years, the partners were much less likely to reciprocally trade negative messages. In effect, these couples were able to break out of the escalating circle of thoughts, words, and emotion.

One question that surfaces from these findings is, Do the partners hear the negative messages and choose not to respond in kind, or are the partners actually oblivious to the fact that their partner said something negative? In a study designed to address this question (Notarius, Benson, Sloane, Vanzetti, & Hornyak, 1989) researchers observed both happy and unhappy couples having a conversation and then compared how the spouses themselves viewed the conversation with how trained observers viewed the same conversation. These researchers found that when wives in distressed relationships received negative messages from their husbands, they responded in kind 83% of the time and broke the negative-for-negative link with a positive behavior only 1% of the time. Among nondistressed couples, when wives received negative messages from their husbands, they responded in kind 76% of the time and broke the link with a positive reply 13% of the time. We can see that the vast majority of the time, happy and unhappy wives behaved similarly. However, the ability to deflect the escalation cycle may be a critical skill—one that doesn't have to be used frequently in order to bring a conversation back on track. Just when the conversation starts heating up, when doubts arise about getting anywhere, when arousal starts to boil, it may take but one positive re-direction to steer the discussion to a satisfactory solution. If three-quarters of the time you get back a negative comment after sending one to your partner, your partner's suddenly changing course with a positive redirection can catch your attention and rewrite the script for the rest of the talk.

Breaking the negative exchange cycle 13% versus 1% of the time may therefore carry more significance than the fact that among *all* couples the tendency is to reply to negative behavior with more negative behavior. Distressed and nondistressed husbands responded similarly. They both met a negative with a negative 78% of the time and responded to a negative with a positive 15% of the time. It may be that men and women have different roles to play in the interactions of happy and of unhappy couples (Baucom, Notarius, Burnett, & Haefner, 1990).

Advice on Preventing Marital Unhappiness

From magazines on the stands at grocery store checkouts to talk shows on TV to racks of self-help books at the neighborhood book store—there is no shortage of advice for the couple getting married. Few question the need for programs to improve the likelihood that a marriage will truly endure until "death do us part." For individuals trying to improve or repair their relationships, there is advice on all sorts of issues—how to fight fair, finding lovers to love and lovers to leave, the ten rules of everlasting love, the five secrets of sexual bliss—and on and on.

There are also organized programs that try to help couples build the foundation for marital harmony. Unfortunately, many of these programs have met with only modest success. The divorce rates themselves are a testimony to the limitations of these programs, and a review of prevention efforts up to 1979 revealed that the programs were not successful in preventing divorce or separation, nor were they effective in helping couples maintain their relationship satisfaction (Bagarozzi & Rauen, 1981).

More recent efforts, though, provide a basis for a more optimistic outlook on preventing marital distress. A careful survey of premarital prevention programs showed that most couples who participated in programs were better off than control couples not receiving the intervention (Giblin, Sprenkle, & Sheehan, 1985). Recently, Markman and his colleagues have evaluated the long-term effectiveness of their Premarital Relationship Enhancement Program (PREP) (Markman, Renick, Floyd, Stanley, & Clements, 1993). The work of this group is especially noteworthy because the couples have been consistently followed over a long period of time.

PREP is delivered in five 2- to 3-hour sessions, designed to increase couples' communication skills, enhance their problem-solving and negotiation skills, help them examine their expectations about marriage, and offer sexual education and strategies for relationship enhancement (Markman, Floyd, Stanley, & Lewis, 1986). Markman et al. (1993) reported a 4- to 5-year follow-up on couples who participated in PREP and those randomly assigned to a control group. Husbands in the PREP group reported significantly greater marital happiness than husbands in the control group; wives in the control group and the PREP group were equally satisfied with their marriages. On another important outcome variable, the PREP couples reported significantly less physical violence in the marriage than the control couples. The control couples were experiencing an average of about 1.5 acts of physical violence a year, compared to an average of less than .4 act per year among the couples who received PREP before marriage. Keep in mind that the PREP program involved only about 15 hours and took place before marriage, yet it seemed to have lasting effects upon marital partners. These effects may have been even more enduring with booster sessions, offered periodically or in times of need, such as when a couple was facing a new challenge (for example, a major relocation, the birth of their first child, illness in the family, or unemployment).

Treatment and prevention programs for couples are likely to become more effective as family researchers continue to study the bases of long-term relationship happiness. Perhaps contemporary advances in our understanding of relationship success and distress are contributing to the increased effectiveness of these programs.

CONCLUSION

In breaking down marriage into words, thoughts, and emotions, we are essentially defining sets of relationship skills that lead to marital happiness. The absence of these skills leads to marital conflict and, eventually, to marital discord and perhaps to divorce. Studies of happy and unhappy couples over time are beginning to pinpoint the precise skills that can keep a marriage happy today and tomorrow. As our understanding of the words, thoughts, and emotions of marital happiness and discord continues to grow, intervention and prevention programs will become more effective in helping couples develop and maintain relationships that are happy, not sad.

Class Discussion Questions

1. What factors do you think account for relationship happiness or difficulties? How do your ideas match or conflict with the empirical evidence reviewed in this chapter?
2. What words, thoughts, and emotions are associated with relationship satisfaction and with relationship break-up over time?
3. Discuss your experience completing the exercise in Box 2 (Capturing Your Thoughts).
4. Discuss your experience completing the exercise described in Box 3 (Slowing Down a Conversation). A procedure similar to that exercise was used in several research studies. How did the use of feedback cards affect your communication? Was the change positive or negative?

Homework Assignments

1. Collect several current magazines and look through them for advice on making a relationship happy. How does the advice compare with the information presented in this book?
2. Watch (or videotape, if possible) a soap opera that contains dialogue between a couple. Using the material in this chapter, analyze the words, apparent thoughts, and emotions of the couple, and offer a judgment on the strengths and weaknesses of the couple's communication.
3. Compare and contrast the portrait of happy and unhappy couples that emerges from the arts (song lyrics, fiction, paintings) with the portrait that emerges from the scientific study of relationships.

Additional Readings

Baucom, D., & Epstein, N. (1990). *Cognitive-behavioral marital therapy.* New York: Brunner/Mazel.

Fincham, F., & Bradbury, T. (1990). *The Psychology of Marriage.* New York: Guilford.

Gottman, J. (1976). Behavior exchange theory and marital decision making. *Journal of Personality and Social Psychology, 34,* 14–23.

Markman, H. (1981). Prediction of marital distress: A 5-year follow-up. *Journal of Consulting and Clinical Psychology, 49,* 760–762.

Notarius, C., & Markman, H. (1993). *We can work it out: Making sense of marital conflict.* New York: Putnam.

References

Bagarozzi, D., & Rauen, P. (1981). Premarital counseling: Appraisal and status. *American Journal of Family Therapy, 9,* 13–30.

Bandura, A. (1986). *Social foundations of thought and action: A social cognitive theory.* Englewood Cliffs, NJ: Prentice-Hall.

Bandura, A., Reese, L., & Adams, N. (1982). Microanalysis of action and fear arousal as a function of differential levels of perceived self-efficacy. *Journal of Personality and Social Psychology, 43,* 5–21.

Baucom, D., Notarius, C., Burnett, C., & Haefner, P. (1990). Gender differences and sex-role identity in marriage. In F. Fincham & T. Bradbury (Eds.), *The psychology of marriage: Basic issues and applications* (pp. 150–171). New York: Guilford.

Benson, P. (1988). Predicting relationship adaptation among new parents (Doctoral dissertation, Catholic University of America). *Dissertation Abstracts International, 49,* 4527.

Bentler, P., & Newcomb, M. (1978). Longitudinal study of marital success and failure. *Journal of Consulting and Clinical Psychology, 46,* 1053–1070.

Bowen, M. (1978). *Family therapy in clinical practice.* New York: Aronson.

Cherlin, A. (1992). *Marriage, divorce, remarriage.* Cambridge, MA: Harvard University Press.

Christensen, A., & King, C. E. (1982). Telephone survey of daily marital behavior. *Behavioral Assessment, 4,* 327–338.

Cowan, C., & Cowan, P. (1992). *When partners become parents: The big life change for couples.* New York: Basic Books.

Dickson-Markman, F., & Markman, H. (1988). The effects of others on marriage: Do they help or hurt? In P. Noller & M. A. Fitzpatrick (Eds.), *Perspectives on marital interaction* (pp. 294–322). Philadelphia: Multilingual Matters.

Fincham, F., Bradbury, T., & Scott, C. (1990). Cognition in marriage. In F. Fincham and T. Bradbury (Eds.), *The psychology of marriage: Basic issues and applications* (pp. 118–149). New York: Guilford.

Geiss, S., & O'Leary, K. D. (1981). Therapist ratings of frequency and severity of marital problems: Implications for research. *Journal of Marital and Family Therapy, 7,* 515–520.

Giblin, P., Sprenkle, D., & Sheehan, R. (1985). Enrichment outcome research: A meta-analysis of premarital, marital, and family interventions. *Journal of Marital and Family Therapy, 11,* 257–271.

Glenn, N., & Weaver, C. (1988). The changing relationship of marital status to reported happiness. *Journal of Marriage and the Family, 50,* 317–324.

Gottman, J. (1979). *Marital interaction: Experimental investigations.* New York: Academic.

Gottman, J., & Krokoff, L. (1989). Marital interaction and satisfaction: A longitudinal view. *Journal of Consulting and Clinical Psychology, 57,* 47–52.

Hahlweg, K., Reisner, L., Kohli, G., Vollmer, M., Schindler, L., & Revenstorf, D. (1984). Development and validity of a new system to analyze interpersonal communication: Kategorien-system fur Partnerschafliche Interaktion (pp. 182–198). In K. Hahlweg & N. Jacobson (Eds.), *Marital interaction: Analysis and modification.* New York: Guilford.

Hetherington, E. M. (1989). Coping with family transitions: Winners, losers, and survivors. *Child Development, 60,* 1–14.

Holtzworth-Munroe, A., & Jacobson, N. (1985). Causal attributions of married couples: When do they search for causes? What do they conclude when they do? *Journal of Personality and Social Psychology, 48,* 1398–1412.

Irwin, R. A. (1991). Cognitive and behavioral predictors of relationship change (Doctoral dissertation, Catholic University of America). *Dissertation Abstracts International, 52,* 1722.

Kitson, G., & Morgan, L. (1990). The multiple consequences of divorce: A decade review. *Journal of Marriage and the Family, 52,* 913–924.

Levenson, R., & Gottman, J. (1983). Marital interaction: Physiological linkage and affective exchange. *Journal of Personality and Social Psychology, 45,* 587–597.

Levenson, R., & Gottman, J. (1985). Physiological and affective predictors of change in relationship satisfaction. *Journal of Personality and Social Psychology, 49,* 85–94.

Markman, H. J. (1990). *Advances in understanding marital distress.* Unpublished manuscript. University of Denver.

Markman, H., Floyd, F., Stanley, S., & Lewis, H. (1986). Prevention. In N. Jacobson & A. Gurman (Eds.), *Clinical handbook of marital therapy* (pp. 173–196). New York: Guilford.

Markman, H., Renick, M. J., Floyd, F., Stanley, S., & Clements, M. (1993). Preventing marital distress through communication and conflict management training: A 4- and 5-year follow-up. *Journal of Consulting and Clinical Psychology, 61,* 70–77.

Navran, L. (1967). Communication and adjustment in marriage. *Family Process, 6,* 173–180.

Newcomb, M. (1986). Cohabitation, marriage and divorce among adolescents and young adults. *Journal of Social and Personal Relationships, 3,* 473–494.

Notarius, C., Benson, S., Sloane, D., Vanzetti, N., & Hornyak, L. (1989). Exploring the interface between perception and behavior: An analysis of marital interaction in distressed and nondistressed couples. *Behavioral Assessment, 11,* 39–64.

Notarius, C. I., & Markman, H. J. (1981). Couples Interaction Scoring System. In E. Filsinger & R. Lewis (Eds.), *Observing marriage: New behavioral approaches.* Beverly Hills, CA: Sage.

Notarius, C., & Markman, H. (1993). *We can work it out: Making sense of marital conflict.* New York: Putnam.

Notarius, C., & Vanzetti, N. (1983). The marital agenda protocol. In E. Filsinger (Ed.), *Marriage and family assessment* (pp. 209–227). Beverly Hills, CA: Sage.

O'Leary, K. D., & Vivian, D. (1990). Physical aggression in marriage. In F. Fincham & T. Bradbury (Eds.), *The psychology of marriage: Basic issues and applications* (pp. 323–348). New York: Guilford.

Ross, C., Mirowsky, J., & Goldstein, K. (1990). Impact of family on health: The decade in review. *Journal of Marriage and the Family, 52,* 1059–1078.

Schaap, C., Buunk, B., & Kerkstra, A. (1988). Marital conflict resolution. In P. Noller & M. A. Fitzpatrick (Eds.), *Perspectives on marital interaction* (pp. 203–244). Philadelphia: Multilingual Matters.

Thomson, E., & Colella, U. (1992). Cohabitation and marital stability: Quality or commitment? *Journal of Marriage and the Family, 54,* 259–267.

U.S. Bureau of the Census. (1988). Households, families, marital status, and living arrangements. (Current Population Reports, Series P-20, No. 412.) Washington, DC: U.S. Government Printing Office.

Vanzetti, N., Notarius, C., & NeeSmith, D. (1992). Specific and generalized expectancies in marital interaction. *Journal of Family Psychology, 6,* 171–183.

Verbrugge, L. (1979). Marital status and health. *Journal of Marriage and the Family, 41,* 267–285.

Weiss, R. L. (1978). The conceptualization of marriage from a behavioral perspective. In T. J. Paolino & B. S. McCrady (Eds.), *Marriage and marital therapy: Psychoanalytic, behavioral and systems theory perspectives* (pp. 165–239). New York: Brunner/Mazel.

Weiss, R., & Summers, K. (1983). Marital Interaction Coding System-III. In E. Filsinger (Ed.), *A sourcebook of marriage and family assessment* (pp. 85–115). Beverly Hills, CA: Sage.

Glossary

Causal attributions Explanations for events or others' behavior

Relational efficacy The expectation a person has of the likelihood of resolving a disagreement with a relationship partner

Survey studies A research strategy in which people are asked to answer questions designed to get at their thoughts and feelings about a phenomenon of interest to the researcher; the questions may be asked by an interviewer or appear on a written questionnaire

12

The Transition to Parenthood: Is Having Children Hazardous to Marriage?

Mari Clements
Penn State University

Howard J. Markman
University of Denver

One of the most important life changes we experience—though it is often taken for granted—is the transition to parenthood. The impact of this life event on the individual and the couple is the focus of this chapter. It examines the shift from beginning to end—from the decision to have children through the controversy regarding the often documented negative effects of the birth of their first child.

NV & SD

Chapter Outline

- The Decision to Have Children
- Transitions within the Transition to Parenthood
- Bundle of Joy versus Home Wrecker
- Conclusion

First comes love, then comes marriage
Then comes Johnny pushing a baby carriage.

For about 90% of American couples, this familiar nursery school rhyme accurately captures their developmental course (Houseknecht, 1978). Although it is certainly not the only family pattern, the thing that most married couples eventually have in common, besides a marriage license, is that they have children.

Given that this is the most common scenario for married couples in this culture, it is perhaps not surprising that researchers, the media, and the public seem to have focused so much attention on what happens to couples and marriages after the birth of children or, specifically, after the birth of their first child. Articles in magazines and newspapers offer advice to new parents not only about child care tasks, but also about what changes to *expect* in the marital relationship as a result of the birth of a child and how to combat those changes. Typically, couples are told to expect lower levels of romance, less time together, and less marital satisfaction, as well as higher levels of marital conflict and more problems in the relationship. In short, almost everything positive is predicted to decrease and everything negative is predicted to increase. All the reported difficulties implied in having children raise the question, Is having children hazardous to marriage?

On the other hand, the positive feelings and thoughts associated with having a child are evident in some of our most common expressions: A baby is referred to as "a bundle of joy"; birth is commonly called "a blessed event." Often couples actively plan for and eagerly anticipate the births of their children. When a baby is born, the new parents are far more likely to be congratulated than offered condolences.

So why is the birth of a child portrayed in such opposing terms? In this chapter we will examine both sides of this issue.

THE DECISION TO HAVE CHILDREN

There are almost as many reasons for having children as there are couples who have them. People have children not only because they want children, per se, but also in some instances because they are responding to societal expectations, they wish to perpetuate their family line, they want to have someone to love them, they want to express their love for the partner, or they failed to use birth control methods or the methods they used failed.

A "bundle of joy"

Armando and Maria, a young couple expecting their first child, spoke of their desire to have children as a fulfillment of both their love for each other and their religion. Maria said, "The time felt right to add another member to our family and to share the relationship that Armando and I have with each other. I think often babies seem to be a reflection of your love. I think they take your focus off yourself and allow you to see parts of your life that you didn't see before. I think God has given me a gift, and it's exciting to see the miracle created from the love Armando and I share. That's very much the heart of our relationship, and I feel that this is a new phase for us."

Armando concurs and adds his desire that the mistakes of the previous generation not be repeated with his child: "In my family there was a lot of abuse. I think that pattern will be broken in our generation due to conscious efforts on our part, which then alters the course of our whole family, and that's a change I'm really excited about."

The previous generation may have other effects on the decision to have children. For Emily and

Daniel, a couple who have chosen not to have children yet, the expectations of **families of origin** play an important role. As Emily says, "There are definitely family expectations. Since my husband is the only married male in his family who doesn't have children, there is a lot of pressure on him and on me to have children. And it's not only pressure to have a child, it's pressure to have a boy child to carry on the family name."

A different sort of pressure may be felt when the child is unplanned by one or both partners. As Sven states, "I didn't want children, but I guess my wife did, so she got pregnant. After I got used to the idea, I was happy about it and I really love my son, but it was a tough time for a while."

Some parents may see their child as someone to love and to love them. Michelle explains, "I wasn't really planning on having children when I got pregnant with Aaron, but he's mine, and I loved him before he was even born."

Gretchen relates her desire to have her own children to her experiences with other family members' children: "I always wanted to have children because I loved them. Any time there was a family gathering and there were children, they all gathered around me. I thought they were neat little people. When I was pregnant with my daughter, I would think forward to having my baby and holding her and taking care of her. I would get so excited I could barely stand it."

As is obvious from the above examples, couples have very different motivations and expectations when having children. There are numerous other reasons for having children, and each couple negotiates this decision in their own way.

TRANSITIONS WITHIN THE TRANSITION TO PARENTHOOD

Regardless of the motivation for having children, couples have a number of adjustments to make when children are born. When asked what changed when her son was born, Michelle responded, "What didn't change?"

Faced with the reality of midnight and early-morning feedings, dirty diapers, day care decisions, and childhood illnesses, not to mention the mother's physical recovery and the medical bills associated with the birth, new parents may feel as if their lives have been turned upside down by their baby. As Sven explained, "We made a number of life-style changes that hit our house, our cars, and our hobbies. Our messy house has become our destroyed house. Two-door cars and car seats don't match, so my two door with the killer stereo was sold, and we bought a family sedan instead. My fishing after work has turned into watching kids after work. It takes forever to do anything or go anywhere because you have to find the stuff for the kid so you can leave. You have to find the diapers and the wipes and the food and the extra clothes and the toys. And we didn't sleep at night anymore although I guess that's more my wife than me. I can't go to the movies anymore without a baby sitter, can't go skiing, can't do anything on the spur of the moment."

The reality of having a child who is totally dependent upon the parent for food, clothing, and shelter and who needs around-the-clock care is sometimes vastly different from what the parents had envisioned. Michelle reflected, "I knew it would be hard, but I didn't realize how life-changing it would be. You don't get to go out when you want to; you don't get to come and go as you want to. Your life revolves around your child."

The demands of an infant can place a strain on the marital relationship. In addition to inhibiting a couple's spontaneity, a child and a child's schedule can affect the relationship in other ways. The sexual relationship may be hampered by the couple's lack of sleep or by the child's inopportune awakenings. Some recreational activities that the couple previously enjoyed, such as swimming or mountain climbing, may be difficult or impossible to do with the infant. Quiet time alone may be limited to during the infant's napping.

The reality of parenthood is often different —and more exhausting—than we expect.

Further complicating this picture are possible changes in the way the partners relate to each other. Armando commented, "The way we relate to each other has already changed during Maria's pregnancy. After the baby comes, I think talking will change to become somewhat more task oriented. Some of our time will be taken up with tasks and children. I think I have a deeper sense of responsibility. Also, we have made a point of reexamining our values. In our view if you want a child to be generous, you have to be generous. We have been thinking about values and what we want to teach our child through our relationship."

Other changes can occur in the way partners feel about each other. Naomi said, "I had always heard that marriages change after having kids, but I didn't believe that would happen to Isaac and me. But after Rachel was born, things really did change. All the special 'sparks' and loving feelings that used to be just Isaac's were directed to the baby. I just loved being with her—she was so special. I think he felt really hurt and left out for a while."

Despite these changes, some couples find their lives greatly enriched by the birth of a child. As Elena commented, "It meant a lot of changes and a lot of work, but I can't imagine not having my son Enrique around, because I love him so much."

Couples must negotiate the changes that having a baby brings, but the long-term effects on marital satisfaction and adjustment are not clear. Is the long-term effect on marriage of having a child positive, negative, or neutral? Once the physical and relational adjustments have been negotiated, does the presence of a child enhance or detract from the marital relationship?

BUNDLE OF JOY VERSUS HOME WRECKER

Studies have examined the impact of having a child on marriage, but the question of what happens to marriages as a result of the birth of children has been asked and answered very differently by two distinct types of studies. The first type is studies conducted as part of projects that are designed explicitly to examine couples before, during, and shortly after the birth of their first child. The second type is studies carried out as part of projects designed to assess marital functioning over the early years of marriage, which may or may not include the birth of children. The first type of project will be referred to as a *transition-to-parenthood project.* The benefits and limitations of this type of study are outlined in Box 1. The second type of project will be referred to as a *parenthood-as-a-stage-of-marriage project.* The advantages and disadvantages of this type of approach are outlined later in the chapter in Box 2.

Transition-to-Parenthood Projects

Most transition-to-parenthood studies have documented declines in marital satisfaction and increases in marital conflict over the **transition to parenthood** (Belsky, 1985; Belsky, Lang, & Rovine, 1985; Belsky & Rovine, 1990; Cowan et al., 1985; Cowan, Cowan, Heming, & Miller, 1991; Wallace & Gotlib, 1990; Wilkie & Ames, 1986), though some recent work also shows that up to 50% of couples show no change or an increase in satisfaction (Belsky & Rovine, 1990). The results of two of the most influential projects in this area, the Pennsylvania Infant and Family Development Project and the Becoming a Family Project, will be discussed in detail as representative of most work in this field. (See Box 1 for a fuller explanation of the design of such projects.)

The Pennsylvania Infant and Family Development Project   This project, headed by Jay Belsky at Penn State University, has used multiple **cohorts** of **primiparous** couples over several years. Results have been **replicated** across cohorts. In each group, marked declines in self-reported measures of romantic love and marital satisfaction were evident. Belsky and colleagues found that several dimensions of marital satisfaction and personal adjustment declined after the birth of the child (Belsky, 1985; Belsky et al., 1985).

Belsky (1985) found declines in the overall marital relationship from the last trimester of pregnancy to nine months **postpartum.** The overall marital relationship was examined using a 12-item questionnaire assessing

Box 1

Design Elements of Transition-to-Parenthood Projects

Most transition-to-parenthood projects share several design elements. First, couples are recruited during their first pregnancy, generally from **obstetrical** offices or clinics, from university subject pools, or through newsletters. Second, the initial research session occurs while the woman is in the third **trimester** of pregnancy. Third, any subsequent research sessions are usually conducted shortly after the birth of the child. In some short-term studies, research sessions are conducted only shortly before and/or shortly after the birth of the child. Some longer-term transition-to-parenthood studies continue to follow couples into the child's second year, but a more common approach is to examine marital functioning into the child's sixth or ninth month. The fourth major commonality among most of these studies is their failure to include a childless comparison group, or **control group.**

These study designs have some inherent advantages and disadvantages. For instance, recruiting from medical settings may **bias** the sample toward middle- and upper-middle-class and/or older subjects. Couples from lower socioeconomic groups and very young couples may use fewer medical services. As a result, studies that recruit from obstetricians may not be able to address adequately what the transition to parenthood is like for these groups.

The second research design element, recruiting during pregnancy, may exert an effect as well. Pregnancy is commonly recognized as a time of increased emotional and physical arousal for the mother. Research conducted during this period may capture some aspects of this arousal, thus providing a clear picture of a more or less acute reaction to the pregnancy but not an accurate picture of overall marital functioning to date.

The third design element, research sessions conducted generally within the first year of the child's life, creates a weakness similar to that of recruiting during pregnancy. An enormous number of adjustments are made in the first year of a child's life. For instance, most children are physiologically incapable of sleeping through the night until sometime between their third and sixth month (Schmitt, 1991). Although most of us can tolerate an occasional late night, getting up one or more times in the middle of the night for three to six months—or even longer for some families—can prove to be a strain. In this case, short-term research designs are capable of measuring the acute reactions to the birth of a first child extremely well, but follow ups continued into the child's second year may be necessary in order to evaluate overall adjustment to parenthood.

The fourth design strategy, that of examining only parents, has the clearest disadvantage. If couples are studied before and after the birth of their first child and changes are observed, it makes sense to attribute these changes to the transition to parenthood; however, without a childless comparison group, this attribution cannot be made with certainty. Some changes may occur as a function of time. As an example, suppose a drug company wanted to conduct an experiment to prove that its new product was a wonder pill. Researchers might find 100 people with headaches and give them the pill. If they asked the subjects to rate their level of pain 6 hours later, they might document that 85%, or even 95%, of the sample reported less pain. But is this change due to the pill or to the nature of headaches? Do headaches remain constant over 6 hours? The only way to know this would be to have two groups of headache sufferers whose headaches, in some way, were determined to be roughly comparable—maybe they had endured their headaches for no more than 30 minutes, or maybe they all rated their headaches as moderately bad. One of these groups of headache sufferers would then be given the pill and the other group would not. If between 85% and 95% of the pill group reported less pain in 6 hours and between 85% and 95% of the no-pill group also reported less pain in 6 hours, what would that mean for the drug company? It might well mean that the headache pill had no effect. It could also be that 6 hours after giving the pill was a bad time at which to measure. Perhaps after 1 hour 85% of the pill group had no headache but only 20% of the no-pill group were feeling better.

Similarly, examining the transition to parenthood without a childless comparison group cannot answer questions about what caused the observed changes and how they fit into overall marital development. Both a control group and well-timed measurements are critical when addressing the effects of a change—whether it be taking a pill or having a child.

In summary, the transition-to-parenthood projects tend to provide very good assessment of couples' experience just before and shortly after the birth of a child, thus providing potentially revealing insights into the acute reactions brought on by the transition to parenthood. These projects tend to be limited in that they fail to include childless comparison groups and thus cannot untangle the effects of the transition to parenthood from effects of other causes.

such areas as the partner's sensitivity, respect for the partner, pleasure in sexual relations, expressions of love, and fun activities.

Similarly, Belsky and colleagues (1985) found modest declines in marital satisfaction as measured in the last trimester and one, three, and nine months postpartum. In this study, marital satisfaction was defined as reported overall satisfaction, frequencies of positive behaviors and of maintenance behaviors, and expressions of love. These findings showed the largest declines between the last trimester and the third month postpartum. Further, the effects were strongest for wives. The authors explained this gender difference as a function of changes in the marital relationship toward greater **instrumentality** and less emotional expression following the birth of the child. In other words, in the early months of the child's life the couple becomes more focused on doing things and has less time for expressing feelings. The authors supposed that this change would be more traumatic for the wife than the husband.

This conclusion, however, may not be adequate to explain the results. As the authors noted, the declines were greatest when measured from the last trimester to the third month postpartum. A less obvious result was that several measures of marital functioning seemed to stabilize or even recover between three and nine months postpartum. Perhaps most damaging to the authors' explanation is the observed rise in reported romance in the marriage over this period. From their report, it is not clear if this increase is significant. Nonetheless, it is curious that in marriages with supposed decreased emotional expression, spouses report increased romance.

An alternative explanation could be that having children may represent an acute event to which couples must adjust, rather than an event with a lasting negative effect on marriages. The observed larger declines in marital satisfaction from the last trimester to three months postpartum may simply reflect this adjustment, not a permanent change. This would explain the differential pattern of results obtained: The first three months of a child's life require a parent to make more adjustments than the next six months. Going from having no child to having a child almost certainly requires a greater degree of adjustment than going from having a small infant to having an older infant.

In a longer-term study from this project that assessed marriages after the first postpartum year, Belsky & Rovine (1990) found four patterns of marital change following the birth of the child. Only two of the four patterns represent declines in marital satisfaction; the other two show stable or even increased levels of marital satisfaction after the birth of the child.

The possibility that observed declines in marital satisfaction may be dips in response to an acute event rather than lasting declines is given further merit by the fact that the observed declines were found to be influenced by several factors. Child variables and individual expectations affected the postpartum adjustment of parents.

In a study of 34 men, Hawkins and Belsky (1989) found that paternal involvement with an infant was associated with declines in father's self-esteem. The authors speculated that the decline in self-esteem might have been due to the father's belief that involvement with babies was not masculine. Although the authors did not report measuring fathers' masculinity, they reasoned that feeling masculine was important to males' self-esteem and that highly involved fathers may have felt that their behavior was "unmasculine." This explanation did not make full use of their reported findings.

Although in general greater involvement with infants was associated with lower self-esteem for fathers, the sex of the child affected both paternal self-esteem and paternal involvement. The authors reported that fathers tended to be more involved with sons than with daughters. Also, greater involvement with sons was correlated with decreased self-esteem for fathers, but greater involvement with daughters was associated with increased self-esteem for fathers. That is, highly involved fathers of sons felt worse about themselves after the child's birth than they did before, whereas highly involved fathers of daughters felt better about themselves.

Hawkins and Belsky (1989) did not control for sex of the child in analyzing the association between involvement and self-esteem, but they did report controlling for fathers' educational and income levels. Because the variables of father's involvement, father's self-esteem, and child's sex were all related, it would be important to control for the effects of one variable while looking at the other two. The reported relationship between father's involvement and father's self-esteem did not take into account the relationships between child's sex and both paternal involvement and paternal self-esteem.

Controlling for the effect of one variable on another is very important, because the presence of a related and uncontrolled variable can distort the relationship between the remaining variables. For example, Denver Bronco fans are known for being extremely loyal to their team. Yet, every time the Broncos make it to the Super Bowl, Denver fans tend to become very sad. At first glance, this relationship seems paradoxical. Why would their team's going to the Super Bowl make the fans sad? There is another variable to be considered if this situation is to make sense. To _____ Broncos have lost all four of their Super Bowl games. Taking _____ his piece of information clearly changes the conclusions one _____ rst case we observe that the Broncos' fans are sad and we _____ that they are sad because the team makes it to the Super _____ ond case we observe that the fans are sad but we can con-_____ because the Broncos get beaten in the Super Bowl. In _____ ed behavior of the fans is the same. However, the in-_____ g variable, the fact that the Broncos keep losing, is _____ d the end result. The effects of the Broncos' losing _____ controlled, for.

_____ volvement and self-esteem, Hawkins and Belsky _____ l for sex of child in their overall analysis. When _____ f sons and fathers of daughters separately, they got _____ r the two groups: Fathers of sons felt worse about _____ children's births, whereas fathers of daughters felt _____ es. Their explanation that fathers' sense of masculin-_____ n self-esteem in highly involved fathers should be re-_____ on. It is unclear why involvement with daughters would _____ uline" than involvement with sons.

_____ nanges in marital adjustment were also not entirely a function of the transition to parenthood. Parents whose postnatal experiences were more negative than anticipated experienced more negative change in the marriage (Belsky, 1985). Violated expectations were especially important in predicting the satisfaction of mothers. This may be because many did not expect to experience traditional divisions of labor after the birth of the baby, and thus mothers had more responsibilities for caring for the child than they expected.

In summary, Belsky and colleagues have established an important research project examining the effects on marriage of the transition to parenthood. From the Pennsylvania Infant and Family Development Project have come a number of studies that have been pivotal to the current understanding of the transition to parenthood. Belsky and colleagues have demonstrated across measures and across cohorts that most positive indexes of marriage (such as marital satisfaction, romance, and love) decrease following the birth of the first child. Similarly, they have shown that most negative indexes of marriage (marital conflict and marital problems) increase over the same period. However, this project has been seriously compromised by the failure to include a childless control group and by the short-term nature of the majority of the studies.

Becoming a Family Project   This project, headed by Philip and Carolyn Cowan at the University of California at Berkeley, followed 72 primiparous couples from the last trimester of pregnancy to one year after the birth of the child. The project is particularly noteworthy in that the researchers have also included a group of 24 childless comparison couples. The inclusion of a control group is a critical step forward and is essential for attributing cause.

Studies from this project have also documented declines in marital satisfaction over the transition to parenthood. Furthermore, the marital satisfaction of parents decreases significantly more than that of childless couples.

To explain their data, Cowan and colleagues (Cowan et al., 1985; Cowan et al., 1991) developed a model of family structure that includes five domains. The first domain encompasses the individual within the family, and measurement of this domain includes indexes of self-esteem, self-concept, levels of emotional distress, and symptoms of depression. The second domain comprises the marital relationship, including the division of labor and marital communication patterns. The third domain captures the relationship between each parent and the child. The fourth domain describes the intergenerational relationships between children, parents, and grandparents. The fifth and final domain is the relationship between the nuclear family members and outside agencies, institutions, and people; this domain places special emphasis on the parents' work or school and the balance between social supports and stressors.

In reviewing their findings, Cowan and colleagues (1991) noted that "the childless couples showed change in several of the five domains, but *the new parents showed change in all of them"* (p. 83, italics theirs). This finding seemed quite remarkable until the five domains were reviewed. Two of the domains required the presence of a child. It is unclear how the third domain, relationship between parents and children, could have changed for members of the control group since they had no children. Similarly, three of the four sets of relationships in the fourth domain require children. Although relationships between adults and their parents might have changed for those in the childless group, it is unclear how the relationships among grandparents and grandchildren, parents and children, and grandparents, parents, and children could have changed, since there were no children. It appears that the domains were much more sensitive to changes that were a result of having children.

In summary, this project has also been crucial to the current understanding of the transition to parenthood and its effects on new parents. It embodies significant improvements in research design, both in longer-term follow up and in the inclusion of a childless control group. Despite these advantages, though, improvements could still be made. First, this project begins with couples who are already pregnant, so nothing is known about their prepregnancy marital functioning. Second, the control group could be improved. The **cell sizes** are very unequal, especially as complete data were available on only 15 childless couples (Cowan et al., 1991). The unequal cell sizes are problematic for many traditional statistical analyses (Keppel & Zedeck, 1989). A further problem with the control group is that they are "couples who had not yet decided whether to become parents" (Cowan et al., 1991, p. 81). It could be argued that because 90% of married couples *do* become parents (Houseknecht, 1987), a sample of couples who had decided *not* to become parents would not be representative of the general population. However, an ambivalent sample also might not provide the clearest picture of the effects of the transition to parenthood. It is possible that members of ambivalent and parent groups might differ in levels of commitment to their relationships. One might argue that the parent group may also be ambivalent about having children. But in one study of 99 married couples, Clements (1994) found that less than 2% of the sample had children despite intending to remain childless. In other words, very few couples who had intended to remain childless had children.

Parenthood-as-a-Stage-of-Marriage Projects

General marriage development studies have tended to find that relationship satisfaction is highest at the premarital stage and declines over time (Huston, McHale, & Crouter, 1986; MacDermid, Huston, & McHale, 1990; McHale & Huston, 1985; Markman, Clements, & Wright, 1991; Markman & Hahlweg, 1993). These studies have typically not found these declines to be worse for couples who have children. Two such projects, the Process of Adaptation in Intimate Relationships Project and the Denver Family Development Project, will be discussed below. (See Box 2 for an explanation of the design of such projects.)

The Process of Adaptation in Intimate Relationships (PAIR) Project   This is a longitudinal project designed to study couples from shortly before marriage to $2^{1}/_{2}$ years after marriage (Huston, McHale, & Crouter, 1986). A number of studies examining the effects of the transition to parenthood on marriage have ensued from this project.

MacDermid, Huston, & McHale (1990) studied 52 couples with children and 46 childless couples. They found that marital satisfaction and love decreased for both groups over time. Parents and childless couples did not differ in the extent or timing of these declines; however, reports of declines in romantic love and increases in marital conflict had different correlates for parents and childless couples. For parents, declines in love and increases in conflict were predicted by discrepancies between parents' sex roles and changes in the division of labor. Fathers who held more traditional gender role views but engaged in less traditional behaviors reported more marital negativity and less love for their wives. For instance, fathers who were engaged in child care activities even though they thought taking care of the child was the mother's job reported less love for the mother and more marital negativity. A similar pattern surrounding household tasks was not found for childless couples.

Similar results were also found in an earlier study by McHale & Huston (1985). In this study the authors found no differences between the declines in marital satisfaction reported by parents before and after the birth of their child and those reported by childless couples measured at the same times. In fact, the authors argued, declines in marital satisfaction due to the transition to parenthood cannot be separated from those due to time.

In summary, this project is a general study of adaptation in marriage. As such, it gives access to both a parent group and a childless control group. This is a major contribution of the work of Huston, McHale, and colleagues. A second contribution of this line of research has been Huston and McHale's relatively long-term data collection, following couples from before marriage through as many as $2^{1}/_{2}$ years of marriage. The majority of studies in this field have extended over 1 year or less.

With both a control group and a longer period for data collection, McHale and Huston have been able to take initial steps toward separating the effects on marriage attributable to the transition to parenthood from those that can be attributed to other potential causes (for example, normal changes in levels of marital satisfaction due to the passage of time). McHale and Huston's use of a control group was a necessary first step toward making such determinations, but their use of a longitudinal perspective was also critical. Without examining the marriages longitudinally before children, it would not have been possible to determine the course of

Box 2

Design Elements of Parenthood-as-a-Stage-of-Marriage Projects

In recent years researchers have used longitudinal projects to answer questions about marital change. Longitudinal studies follow couples over time and thus can examine changes throughout the development of the marriage. Some of these projects that began as studies of marital interaction and development have started to address issues of *family* interaction and development as well.

As previously noted, most couples in the United States do have children at some point in their marriage. Studies of marital development, then, may have access to a wealth of data about interaction patterns and satisfaction of couples before and after the birth of their first child.

This strategy for researching the effects of the transition to parenthood is less common than the transition-to-parenthood study, but as with those projects, parenthood-as-a-stage-of-marriage projects contain certain common design elements that lend them strengths and weaknesses. First, by definition, these are studies of marriages, not of couples becoming parents; thus couples become eligible to enter the projects based on their marital status, not their pregnancy. Couples are generally recruited either early in their marriage or during the formal or informal engagement period. Second, couples have children on their own time schedule, not that of the researchers, so research sessions typically are not conducted at regular intervals around the birth of the child. For instance, research sessions may be scheduled yearly; a child may be born just after or just before a scheduled research session. For this reason, such projects typically cannot measure acute reactions to the birth of the child. Third, couples do not have children at the same time. Thus in a given project, 10% of the couples might become parents in the first, 30% in the next year, and so on, so that comparisons across different research sessions must be undertaken. Fourth, questionnaires and tasks for couples to complete are based on the researchers' questions about marriage, so some questions about the transition to parenthood may well not be addressed. Finally, barring infertility and accidental pregnancies, the subjects decide for themselves who will fall into which group—couples are not assigned to parent groups and childless control groups. Also, because of this, cell sizes may be very uneven.

the marriages thus far. If marital satisfaction has not been assessed before pregnancy, can a significant decline in marital satisfaction after the arrival of children be thoroughly understood? It is possible, perhaps even likely, that significant declines in marital satisfaction have occurred throughout the relationship (that is, before and after marriage).

Although the work of Huston, McHale, and colleagues represents a significant step forward in assessing the effects of the transition to parenthood on marital functioning, there are several problems with their work. First, all couples had been married 2½ years or less. It may be that observed declines in marital satisfaction for parents and childless couples represent the end of the honeymoon phase. The pattern of results for couples married a longer period of time may well be different.

Second, the **sample size** in one of their studies (McHale & Huston, 1985) is small. It is unclear how stable the results obtained from this study with relatively few subjects would be, although it is encouraging that their later work tends to replicate their early findings.

Denver Family Development Project   This project, headed by Howard Markman at the University of Denver, began in 1980 with 135 couples who were planning a first marriage. Couples were recruited through communitywide advertising about the research project. Couples have been followed since 1980 at approximately yearly intervals. In each session, couples are interviewed, complete questionnaires, and participate in two 10- to 15-minute videotaped problem-solving interaction tasks that involve discussing two of their top three relationship problem areas. Thus a variety of observational and self-report data about these couples are available from both before and after the birth of the first child. These data have been used to examine the effects of the transition to parenthood as well as to address the questions posed in the larger longitudinal project (Duncan & Markman, 1988; Markman, Clements, & Wright, 1991).

For this larger project, couples who had children were matched with couples who did not have children but who had been married for the same length of time. Couples were matched on premarital relationship satisfaction, relationship status (formally engaged versus planning marriage), and several communication variables. A total of 28 childless couples and 30 parent couples were examined at four points: in a research session preceding marriage, in a first session after the marriage, in a session preceding the birth of the first child, and in a session after the birth of the first child. For each couple in the childless comparison group, the third and fourth sessions were scheduled to correspond to the third and fourth sessions of the couple with whom they were matched in the parent group.

Over time the transition-to-parent group did not differ from the childless control group in marital satisfaction, relationship problems, or levels of positive or negative communication. Both groups showed declines in marital satisfaction from before marriage to the second, third, and fourth assessment points, but these declines did not differ for parents and childless couples. Relationship problems increased for both groups from the third assessment point to the fourth assessment point, but this increase was the same for childless couples as for parent couples.

Both parents and childless couples evidence declines in marital satisfaction and increases in relationship problems over the same period in marriage. This suggests that declines in marital functioning may be attributed to the passage of time and accompanying developmental changes, as opposed to being the result of having a child.

This project is important in that it follows couples from before marriage to well after the birth of the first child, thus allowing examination of the marriage over time. As with all longitudinal studies, however, this strength may also be a liability. The average time from the research session preceding the marriage to the research session after the birth of the first child was over four years. Couples who are able to maintain their commitment to a research project, and who attend all four research sessions, are likely to be higher functioning than most couples (Rubin & Mitchell, 1976). Thus this group may not provide the clearest picture of the effects of the transition to parenthood on less stable or satisfied couples.

Reconciling the Differences

The pictures presented by projects designed to examine the transition to parenthood, exclusively, versus the transition to parenthood as a stage of marriage are significantly different. Projects designed specifically as transition-to-parenthood projects find significant declines in marital satisfaction from before to after the birth of the first child, whether or not a childless control group is included. Projects designed as general marriage projects also find declines in marital satisfaction over the same periods, but do not find these differences in parent and childless comparison groups. What accounts for these different findings?

The difference in **methodology** between the two types of projects almost certainly plays a role in the differing patterns of results. As previously noted, transition-to-parenthood projects schedule research sessions around the birth of a child. Sessions may occur in the third trimester and in first, third, sixth, and/or ninth month postpartum. In contrast, general marital projects that examine the transition to parenthood tend to schedule research sessions much less frequently and based on the demands of the project without reference to pregnancy. For this reason, transition-to-parenthood projects may capture the acute upheaval that the birth of a child may bring, whereas general marriage projects may provide a picture of the average functioning of the marriage.

It may also be that measures that have been developed for transition-to-parenthood projects are more sensitive to the potential changes that having a child brings. That is, areas of marital functioning that are more sensitive to the addition of a child may be measured more directly with some of these recently developed measures that are not widely used.

On the other hand, it may be that the observed declines in marital satisfaction are simply changes in marriage that would occur with or without the birth of a child. These changes may be more obvious to the couple and the researchers because of this event, but declines in marital satisfaction may occur as part of a developmental continuum rather than in response to the birth of a child. The couple and the researchers may compare marital functioning before and after the birth of the first child and determine that marital satisfaction is lower after the child was born, but the birth of the child may be more of a marker of change than a cause of change.

Just as the 21st birthday is a cultural marker of adulthood and graduation is a marker of education, the birth of the first child may serve as a marker in the developmental course of marriage. Each of these markers may be used to segment developmental trajectories, but the markers themselves do not cause changes. People do not change from children to adults because they have reached the age of 21; this change has occurred gradually. An individual is not uneducated the day before receiving a diploma and educated the day after. Even so, these markers serve as reference points for society and for the individual.

When such markers exist, people tend to use them as reference points. It may be that marital satisfaction follows a general course, starting high before marriage and declining after marriage. The birth of a child may be a marker on this trajectory that allows couples and researchers alike to see that marital satisfaction was higher before and lower after the marker; but just as being an adult is the result of a developmental progression, not a 21st birthday, so being less happy in marriage may be the result of a developmental course, not of having a child.

CONCLUSION

The transition to parenthood influences couples' marital relationships in ways that are not necessarily clear. There may be declines in marital satisfaction that are associated with having a child, but over the long term, these declines may not differ from those experienced by childless couples who have been married the same length of time.

It may be that having children requires couples to make adjustments that are similar to other adjustments made in married life. To the extent that couples are successful in negotiating these adjustments, through communicating and problem solving, marital satisfaction is likely to remain high. Conversely, if couples encounter difficulties in communication about children or other potential problem areas, it is likely that marital satisfaction will decline.

The effects on marriage of becoming parents are still undetermined. Further research, combining the best elements of both transition-to-parenthood projects and parenthood-as-a-stage-of-marriage projects, is needed. Specifically, more careful assessment of marriage before children are born, or even conceived, is important for understanding the level of marital satisfaction and the couple's ability to negotiate periods of adjustment. In addition, information gathered at specific times around the birth of the child is critical in assessing any sort of acute reaction to the child; data about couples' desire for children, parenting styles, and expectations of parenthood are important in order to assess the effects of violated expectations and parental disagreements. Longer-term follow up of parents and childless couples is also necessary to understand the lasting effects of children on marriage.

Further, although this chapter has focused on the effects of a child on marriage, it is important to note that there are numerous couples who desire children but are unable to have them. The effects of this situation on marriage are largely unknown and should be explored.

Couples who have children choose to do so for a number of reasons and experience a number of changes in their relationship. Despite the common assumption that having children causes less romance and happiness in marriage, it has not been clearly demonstrated that these changes have lasting effects on the overall level of marital satisfaction.

Class Discussion Questions

1. Take a position on the transition-to-parenthood debate. Is a child more accurately thought of as a "bundle of joy" or a "little marriage wrecker"? Support your position.

2. What obstacles does a single parent face? Are there cases in which facing these obstacles might be preferable to having a two-parent home? If so, what might these be?

3. Some researchers have argued that declines in marital satisfaction measured before and after the birth of the child can be understood as *changes* in the marital relationship and not as declines in quality, per se. For instance, a parenting role becomes part of the spouse's identity, and satisfaction with this aspect of the marital and family relationship may be high, even while satisfaction with the romantic partner role declines somewhat. This realignment of roles could yield no change in overall satisfaction. What do you think of this argument?

4. What do you think is the single most difficult aspect of becoming a parent? What might be the most rewarding? Why?

5. Would studies of the transition to parenthood conducted before the prevalence of dual wage-earner families have yielded different results? Why or why not? How about studies of families where both parents tend to work at home (such as in farming communities)?

6. Most attention has been focused on the changes that take place in marriage as a result of the birth of a *first* child. What effects, if any, would you expect to find as a result of the birth of the second child? A third child?

7. How are babies portrayed in the entertainment media? How does this portrayal perpetuate or challenge existing stereotypes?

Homework Assignments

1. You are advising a couple expecting their first child. Write a paragraph describing what you would say or do to prepare them. Are there readings that you would suggest? Are there articles or types of articles you would have them avoid?

2. Write a one-page description of the changes new parents usually encounter as a result of having a child. What are the potential consequences of those changes? Consider physical, emotional, and social domains in your response.

3. Interview one or both parents of a small child about their transition-to-parenthood experience. If you choose to interview a couple with older children (such as your own parents), ask them in what ways their perspective on the transition to parenthood has changed over the years.

4. Observe an infant. Write up your observations, paying particular attention to the demands the child places on the care-giver.

5. Watch a television show or movie that features a family with an infant. Based on what you know, would you say that this portrayal is accurate? Which member of the triad seems to have the most distorted role? What changes would you suggest to increase the realism while maintaining the entertainment value?

Additional Readings

Belsky, J., & Rovine, M. (1990). Patterns of marital change across the transition to parenthood: Pregnancy to three years postpartum. *Journal of Marriage and the Family, 52,* 5–19.

Cowan, C. P., & Cowan, P. A. (1992). *When partners become parents: The big life change for couples.* New York: Basic Books.

Cowan, P. A., & Hetherington, M. (1991). *Family transitions.* Hillsdale, NJ: Lawrence Erlbaum.

MacDermid, S. M., Huston, T. L., & McHale, S. M. (1990). Changes in marriage associated with the transition to parenthood: Individual differences as a function of sex-role attitudes and changes in the division of household labor. *Journal of Marriage and the Family, 52,* 475–486.

Notarius, C. I., & Markman, H. J. (1993). *We can work it out: Making sense of marital conflict.* New York: Putnam.

References

Belsky, J. (1985). Exploring individual differences in marital change across the transition to parenthood: The role of violated expectations. *Journal of Marriage and the Family, 47,* 1037–1044.

Belsky, J., Lang, M. E., & Rovine, M. (1985). Stability and change in marriage across the transition to parenthood: A second study. *Journal of Marriage and the Family, 47,* 855–865.

Belsky, J., & Rovine, M. (1990). Patterns of marital change across the transition to parenthood: Pregnancy to three years postpartum. *Journal of Marriage and the Family, 52,* 5–19.

Clements, M. L. (1994). *Declines in marital functioning over the transition to parenthood: Can we blame the marriage and not the child?* Unpublished doctoral dissertation, University of Denver, Denver, CO.

Cowan, C. P., Cowan, P. A., Heming, G., Garrett, E., Coysh, W. S., Curtis-Boles, H., & Boles, A. J. (1985). Transitions to parenthood: His, hers, theirs. *Journal of Family Issues, 6,* 451–481.

Cowan, C. P., Cowan, P. A., Heming, G., & Miller, N. B. (1991). Becoming a family: Marriage, parenting, and child development. In P. A. Cowan & M. Hetherington (Eds.), *Family transitions* (pp. 79–109). Hillsdale, NJ: Lawrence Erlbaum.

Duncan, S. W., & Markman, H. J. (1988). Intervention programs and the transition to parenthood. In G. Y. Michaels and W. A. Goldberg (Eds.), *The transition to parenthood: Current theory and research.* Cambridge, England: Cambridge University Press.

Hawkins, A. J., & Belsky, J. (1989). The role of father involvement in personality change in men across the transition to parenthood. *Family Relations, 38,* 378–384.

Houseknecht, S. K. (1987). Voluntary childlessness. In M. B. Sussman & S. K. Steinmetz (Eds.), *Handbook of marriage and the family* (pp. 369–395). New York: Plenum.

Huston, T. L., McHale, S., & Crouter, A. (1986). When the honeymoon's over: Changes in the marital relationship over the first year. In R. Gilmour & S. W. Duck (Eds.), *The emerging field of personal relationships* (pp. 109–132). Hillsdale, NJ: Erlbaum.

Keppel, G., & Zedeck, S. (1989). *Data analysis for research designs: Analysis-of-variance and multiple regression/correlation approaches.* New York: W. H. Freeman.

MacDermid, S. M., Huston, T. L., & McHale, S. M. (1990). Changes in marriage associated with the transition to parenthood: Individual differences as a function of sex-role attitudes and changes in the division of household labor. *Journal of Marriage and the Family, 52,* 475–486.

McHale, S., & Huston, T. L. (1985). A longitudinal study of the transition to parenthood and its effects on the marital relationship. *Journal of Family Issues, 6,* 409–433.

Markman, H. J., Clements, M., & Wright, R. (1991, April). *Why father's pre-birth negativity and a first-born daughter predict marital problems: Results from a ten-year investigation.* Symposium conducted at the biennial meeting of the Society for Research in Child Development, Seattle.

Markman, H. J., & Hahlweg, K. (1993). The prediction and prevention of marital distress: An international perspective. *Clinical Psychology Review, 13,* 29–43.

Rubin, Z., & Mitchell, C. (1976). Couples research as couples counselling: Some unintended effects of studying close relationships. *American Psychologist, 31,* 36–46.

Schmitt, B. D. (1991). *Your child's health.* New York: Bantam.

Wallace, P. M., & Gotlib, I. H. (1990). Marital adjustment during the transition to parenthood: Stability and predictors of change. *Journal of Marriage and the Family, 52,* 21–29.

Wilkie, C. F., & Ames, E. W. (1986). The relationship of infant crying to parental stress in the transition to parenthood. *Journal of Marriage and the Family, 48,* 545–550.

Glossary

Bias   To slant the results or properties of a study in a given direction

Cell size   The number of subjects in each experimental condition

Cohort   A group of subjects entering a study at a particular time

Control group   A group of comparable subjects who have not received the intervention of interest in a study

Families of origin   The families in which marital partners grew up

Instrumentality   The accomplishment of activities or fulfilling of roles, as opposed to interacting and sharing emotions

Methodology   The manner in which a study is conducted, including how subjects are selected, what measures are used, when research sessions are scheduled, and what statistical methods are employed

Obstetrical   Of or having to do with pregnancy and childbirth

Postpartum   After birth

Primiparous   Pregnant with the first child

Replicated   Found the same pattern of results in different studies or in different groups of subjects in the same study

Sample size   The number of subjects in a study

Transition to parenthood   The developmental stage in a couple's or individual's life during which the first child is born

Trimester   One third of a pregnancy; approximately 13 weeks

13

The Family and the Individual: Reciprocal Influences

Susan Witenberg Fisher
Albany Medical College

uring our adult years, most of us will become a part of a family group that is different from our families of origin. We will select a mate, marry, and have children, thus creating our own "family of procreation." In the modern world, people also create other sorts of families, but, in general, during this time in our lives we define some group of people other than (or perhaps in addition to) our families of origin that we are close to, spend time with, and are committed to. This chapter explores what exactly a family is, what functions it serves, and some important ways in which the family and the individual influence each other.

NV & SD

Chapter Outline

• What Is a Family?
• The Functions of the Family
• The Individual and the Family: Family Systems Theory
• Do We Recreate Our Family of Origin?
• Summary

In the preceding chapter you learned about the development of a couple as they evolve from a twosome to a threesome. With the birth of the first child, a couple becomes a family. Whether that couple decides to have only one child or a dozen children, that social group will always be a "family." Families with young children consist not only of parents plus their children but also of a complex set of interlocking psychological and social relationships that span generations and include many other people— grandparents, siblings, aunts, uncles, cousins, friends, and parents. A multi-generational perspective that includes vertical family expansion (parents, children, grandchildren) as well as horizontal family expansion (siblings, cousins, aunts, uncles) is the focus of this chapter.

The important issue to keep in mind is that our identity and evolving beliefs are not just a function of our own character at any given point in time, but are associated with a network of relationships among generations that have been transmitted over time. How a family functions has a great deal to do with how prior generations function(ed) and how each member of the present generation interacts with current family members and with those in previous generations.

WHAT IS A FAMILY?

Each of us probably has her or his own idea of what is meant by "my family." Maybe it includes our parents and brothers and sisters; everyone else is considered "a relative." Another possibility is that we think of our family as including all the people living who are related to us by blood. Still another possibility is to consider our family as those blood relatives and close friends of our parents who can be called upon whenever some assistance is needed. In different families and in different cultural groups, the word *family* means many different things (Harris, 1990). Just as the United States has a diverse population, with people originating from many parts of the world, so too it has many diverse forms of family organizations. Let's examine some of these different forms.

Nuclear Family

A **nuclear family** is generally defined as a married couple and their children (including biologically related children, adopted children, and, perhaps, foster children). Members of the nuclear family live in the same place, tend to eat meals together, and are a unit of economic consumption. This has been the predominant organization of the 20th-century family among Americans of European descent, even though earlier centuries were characterized by somewhat different family patterns.

Single-Parent Family

The **single-parent family** is a common variation of the nuclear family and consists of one parent and his or her children. A one-parent family may be formed through divorce, separation, or widowhood, or when an unmarried woman raises children on her own, which has become increasingly common in the United States. According to the 1990 report from the U.S. Census Bureau, 25% of children were living in homes headed by single parents. The greatest proportion lived with their mothers. Compare this with 1970, when only 12% of America's children were living in homes with just one parent present. This situation is even more striking when we look at the living situation of African-American children: In

1990 55% lived with one parent, as compared to 1970, when 33% lived with a single parent (cited in the *World Almanac*, 1992).

Extended Family

Another type of family organization is the **extended family**, in which, generally, three generations may be present (parents, children, and grandparents) but which may include brothers and sisters and their families. In Western Europe and in the United States before the 20th century, though nuclear family organization was predominant, it was not uncommon for members of an extended family to be living together, and grown children often remained in the homes of their parents with their grandchildren (Goody, 1983; Shorter, 1976; Stone, 1984). Although this kind of situation may still occur in the United States among families of European descent, it is more common for grown children (parents) and the elderly (grandparents) to live apart. In many non-Western cultures the extended family remains the most common pattern of organization. As an example, family ties are extremely strong among the Muslim Arabs, and many related families may live near one another.

The extended family is also central to the organization of the traditional Asian-Pacific family. Members who share blood ties to the father's ancestors and his extended family are of primary importance, and it is not uncommon for three generations to live together in one household (Ho, 1987; Shon and Ja, 1982). The teachings of Confucius, who lived from 551 to 449 B.C., greatly influenced the values governing traditional Asian-Pacific families. Of extreme importance is the emphasis placed upon filial piety, the respectful love for parents. Children are taught that parents are their greatest obligation and that regardless of what parents may do, children are still duty-bound to show respect and obedience. Closely related to obligation is the concept of shame and shaming. If a family member does something improper, it brings shame not only upon the individual but also upon the living blood relations as well as the deceased ancestors.

Extended families offer many advantages, including shared responsibility for child care, support of the elderly, and a sense of unity.

Kin Network

According to a number of scholars, African-American families in this country tend to organize themselves around large informal networks of blood relatives and community members who may be long-term friends but who are considered family members—what has been called a **kin network** (Boyd-Franklin, 1989; Hines & Boyd-Franklin,

1982; Stack, 1974). The responsibility for child care may be shared by any adult, and it is not uncommon for a child to be informally adopted and reared by family members or close friends. Elderly people also tend to be supported by a group effort of family members. The involvement of the group or community in caring for its members has its roots in the African tribal tradition that stressed a sense of collective unity (Nobles, 1980). As Hines and Boyd-Franklin stated (1982), "In contrast to the European premise of 'I think, therefore I am,' the African philosophy is, 'We are, therefore, I am.'" (p. 87).

The kin network has also been explained as being necessitated by the institution of slavery in the United States. Slavery disrupted families—when slaves were bought and sold, the nuclear or extended (slave) families were broken apart (Boyd-Franklin, 1989; Hill, 1972; Hines & Boyd-Franklin, 1982; McAdoo, 1981; Royse & Turner, 1980). Kinship ties, not necessarily drawn along blood lines, "remained a major mode of coping with the pressures of an oppressive society" (Boyd-Franklin, 1989, p. 87). The bonds of the extended family and the inclusion of non-blood relatives are critical to understanding the lives of African-Americans (see Box 1).

Blended Family

Also to be considered is the **blended family**, formed when a single parent joins households with another adult, whether a parent or childless. The joining together of two families reorganizes both families, who then have to adjust to functioning as a new household. Each member of the family has to adapt to the new "unit" that is making decisions about the household and about raising children. The children have to adapt to the other children in the household. Additionally, the children's other parents and their grandparents, who are not part of this household, may remain part of the children's family. If the children's biological parent remarries, or in some way joins with another family, then the complexities multiply. Blended families have grown increasingly common in the past two decades (Nichols & Schwartz, 1991).

Other Family Organizations

Not everybody chooses to marry and live in a nuclear family. Some married couples may decide not to have children. Some couples live together without marrying. People of the same sex may live together and consider themselves a family. Groups of people may live together as communal families that may include married and unmarried couples, single adults, and children. Whether or not these groups are recognized legally as families, the individuals in them may consider these relationships as family relationships.

Box 1   **Different Family Constellations**

Fictive Kin Networks

In African-American families, individuals who are not related by blood but who are considered part of the family are important in terms of involvement and function served. These family members, referred to by Stack (1974) as "fictive kin," might include numerous people who are "mamas," "papas," "aunts," "uncles," godmothers, babysitters, and neighbors.

The Nayars

The Nayars were a group in Southwestern India in whose culture the birth of a child did not obligate the man in any way to the mother and child. The man's strong ties were to the family in which he grew up; his obligation was to his female relatives—his mother, his mother's mother, and his mother's siblings. As far as children were concerned, his responsibility was not to his own but to his *sister's* children. The woman with whom he conceived a child might have a series of relationships with men. All this was part of the cultural norm (Fuller, 1976).

Israeli Kibbutz

A kibbutz is an agricultural collective in Israel. Among its other features is the rearing of children by the community as a whole rather than by their parents alone. In many kibbutzim (plural of *kibbutz*) children are raised by nurses and teachers, and they eat and sleep in areas away from their biological parents. The children often experience one another as brothers and sisters and when older tend to form sexual bonds with individuals outside their kibbutz (Spiro, 1975).

The persons responsible for raising children differ in American society and elsewhere, depending upon family circumstances, the economic and cultural setting, marital status of the parents, and a variety of other factors that may be as unique as each family. Some dramatic examples of different ways to construe family are provided in Box 1.

THE FUNCTIONS OF THE FAMILY

Historical Context

In the modern-day United States, marrying and forming a family generally follow a period of romantic love between two people who believe that

A nontraditional family at home

they will be happy and successful as a couple and, if they choose, as parents. (See the discussion in Chapter 10 of the role of love in mate selection.) It is only relatively recently, however, that love has been considered an important criterion for choosing a marriage partner. In Europe and America, up until about 100 years ago, the family was formed and maintained to assure the continuation of lineage (descendants from a common ancestor) and the transference of property. The family was viewed as a mechanism by which property was handed down from generation to generation. Spouses and children were valued for the work they performed and the goods they provided. In rural society the whole family worked to clear land, plant, cultivate, and harvest crops. Girls learned to cook, sew, spin, and weave; boys learned farming or a trade from either their father or another skilled worker. The elderly or infirm were cared for in the home. In many parts of the world children continue to be valued for providing support to the family, and the family is viewed from an economic perspective. This contrasts with modern-day United States and Europe, where families are considered from a **sentimental perspective** that emphasizes the emotional bonds and affection among members (Segalen, 1986; Shorter, 1975).

The Functions of Modern-Day Euro-American Families

The family is the social unit into which children are born, and it provides protection and training for the children. Adult family members provide income for the family from either jobs, investments, public assistance, or other sources. In some instances the family may function as a group working together to make a living—farm families are an example of this situation.

According to Parsons and Bales (1955), the function of the family is raising children and socializing them to succeed in their culture. Obviously, then, values will differ along cultural lines, and certain behaviors will be met with approval or disapproval, depending on the culture. For example, dominant American values teach children to become independent and think for themselves, to achieve, and to compete for higher social and economic status (Ho, 1987; McGoldrick, 1982). In traditional Asian-Pacific society, children are taught that the major consideration governing any action is the impact that action would have on their parents or family. Extremely close family ties and respect for elders persist throughout life.

Let's examine a common situation occurring in all families with young children to see how cultural differences and values might influence behavior. A young couple has a new baby who wakes up crying at night. Among middle-class Americans, much energy is expended by parents, professionals, and extended family members in trying to figure out how to stop the child's crying without bringing the child into the adult's bed. The belief is that if the child comes into the parental bed (and stops crying) then she or he will become too dependent upon the adults and persist in this behavior. This dependence is frowned upon in a culture that places great value on a child's achieving independence from the adults. Among Japanese families, however, it is quite common for babies and children to sleep with their parents. There is not such great emphasis on becoming independent from the family and/or the group; in fact, maintaining connection is emphasized. Therefore, because becoming independent from parents is not a goal, there is no urgency experienced by parents and society about children's learning to sleep by themselves.

From the brief discussion above you can see that the values and rules of the dominant culture influence behavior, as do the values and rules of any one group. There are both the overt (explicit) rules that govern social behavior and the covert (unspoken) rules that determine behaviors within the family. The overt rules are those that are the most easily described: proper etiquette, what is good and bad, what is valued and not valued. It is usually the parents and elders who instruct the younger generation about these codes of behavior (Scarf, 1987). Although the media and peers certainly influence behavior, the family is still the most powerful influence.

You may be questioning whether families are needed to transmit cultural values to the young. After all, can't schools do this? Much of the socialization of Western children occurs in schools and among peers. Hospitals and nursing homes care for the sick and the elderly. Goods and services are purchased with money acquired away from home. In the Western world sex outside of marriage is common, and it is no longer unusual for a woman to elect to have children outside of marriage. So what is the function of the family? Some would say that what is most valuable in families is the relationships, regardless of the presence or absence of children (Carter & McGoldrick, 1989). Members of a family provide affection, emotional support, and a sense of belonging, and this is the important function of the family today. No doubt you can think of other functions of today's family. What might these be?

THE INDIVIDUAL AND THE FAMILY: FAMILY SYSTEMS THEORY

Regardless of your cultural circumstance, no matter how you analyze the function of today's family, and despite the form your family of origin happened to take, your identity as an individual is greatly influenced by your family. Like it or not, we are shaped by our relationships in our family.

How the behaviors and relationships among family members are interpreted depends on the theoretical perspective of the observer. Numerous theoreticians have proposed different ways to examine family relationships. One of these perspectives is based on **systems theory**.

The fundamental premise of *family systems theory* is that people are part of a social context, and in order to understand them one must understand the family context, or system, as a whole. The family system includes not only the personalities and behavior of the individuals in the family but also their complex interactions. A system is a group of interrelated parts and the way they function together. If this definition seems a little abstract, consider the functioning of an ordinary wristwatch—imagine trying to appreciate how it works by simply examining the nature of the individual parts when they are spread out on a table. What makes the watch work is the interaction of the parts. This is analogous to a systems theorist's view that the family is greater than the individual members' personalities (Nichols & Schwartz, 1991). Viewing the family as a system is the hallmark of **family therapy**, which is based on an approach that considers human behavior as being fundamentally shaped by its social context.

Family Structure

Salvador Minuchin is an internationally renowned systems theorist who has provided a theoretical model, called **structural family theory**, to be used in understanding the behaviors that occur in families (Minuchin, 1974; Minuchin & Fishman, 1981). Minuchin devised his theory after working with numerous families in a variety of settings where therapy was provided to help manage problems: Children weren't eating, a boy was committing crimes, a parent was depressed, somebody was using drugs, and so forth.

Anyone who works with families (let alone lives in a family) can tell you that a family often appears to be a group of individuals, obviously influencing each other in powerful ways. Minuchin saw consistent, repetitive, and predictable patterns of behavior within families, associated with the way they were organized, or structured. To describe the **structure** of the family entails observing repeated patterns of behavior among members. For instance, if each evening the mother tells the child to wash before dinner and the child doesn't do it until the father tells him to do so, the interactions form a pattern. If this pattern is repeated over time and in other circumstances—say, the mother tells the child it is time to leave the playground and he doesn't do so (and even acts as if he hasn't heard her) until the father comes along and says, "Time to go!"—then the pattern reveals the structure: Mother doesn't get children to do as they are told, Father does. Time and again the father is perceived as the competent disciplinarian.

There are a myriad of possible interactions among family members, but according to Minuchin, over time and in a number of situations, a fairly predictable structure occurs that is characteristic of that particular family. In a family with school-age children, perhaps the mother does most of the interacting with the children at home. Perhaps she is still dressing and feeding a school-age child—actually putting the spoon in the mouth of her youngest child who is a third-grader. If, rather than resisting, the child snuggles on the mother's lap and asks for help getting dressed, and the mother complies, this pattern is noteworthy. If the mother is constantly doing things for other members of the family that they could easily do by themselves, a pattern emerges wherein the mother is the "doer" and the others behave in incompetent or lazy ways. This is how the family is structured, how it is organized. It is a function of all the individuals and their interactions.

Minuchin taught, and most family therapists believe (Nichols, 1988, 1992; Haley, 1976), that all families need to have an effective **hierarchical structure** in order to function well. In hierarchical arrangements there is a clear leader in charge (the military is a good example of this). Families need to have parents who are in charge of their children. If there is not an adoptive or biological parent available, then there needs to be a designated adult who is in charge. Moreover, parents or parent substitutes need to work together to raise the children, lest differences among the adults undermine their authority.

It is common in certain households and cultures for the eldest child to assist the parents with the younger children. For example, if the adults are working when the children are home, the eldest may be placed in charge and in a parental role. In African-American and white families this child can be either male or female; in Latino families this role is generally filled by the oldest female child (Boyd-Franklin, 1989). A child who fulfills this role is called a **parental child**. When a parent delegates responsibility to the oldest child, the parent remains in charge if the child is instructed to report to him or her. When the parental child is assisting the parent, the hierarchical structure is retained, and assuming responsibility is not thought to be problematic. Problems may arise, however, if the parental child has to be a parent to a parent who has abdicated responsibility. This burden can prevent the child from interacting with peers, and such children sometimes appear to be overburdened, depressed, or anxious (Boyd-Franklin, 1989; Minuchin, 1974).

Subsystems   Within the family there are subgroups of people, called **subsystems**, that may be determined by the generation, sex, or interests of the individuals (Parsons & Bales, 1955; Minuchin, 1974; Minuchin & Fishman, 1981). Children are obvious subsystems; the married couple is a subsystem. If there are a number of children, the child subsystems may break down by age: Teenagers are one system, grade-school children another. The girls may be one subsystem, the boys another. Sometimes, however, the subsystems are less obvious, though no less important to understanding how a family operates. Perhaps father and daughter enjoy the same activities and always agree with each other, whereas mother and son generally tend to spend time together. Father and daughter are one subsystem, mother and son another.

Subsystems are made up of family members who join together to serve a function. An individual can be a member of a number of different subsystems, and, of course, most of us are. A woman, for example, can simultaneously be a daughter, a mother, a sister, an aunt, and a wife. An individual has different roles in different subsystems. For instance, a woman acts (or should act) differently as a mother to her child than as a sister to her brother. You might tell your son to take off his shoes before coming into your house, but when you are at your brother's home you probably wouldn't tell your brother what to do. The mother who has been a caregiver may gradually become a care receiver as aging proceeds. As the caregiver she had an **executive function**, in that she made decisions for other family members and decided about the use of resources. If she later is in the position of having to be cared for, she may have to give up the executive role—she is then no longer in that subsystem but in another.

Interpersonal Boundaries   People, subsystems, and families all have *interpersonal boundaries*, invisible barriers that regulate the amount of contact with others. **Boundaries** serve to protect the separateness and autonomy of a family, its subsystems, and the individual.

Boundaries may range from rigid to diffuse. A rigid boundary is a very strong, restrictive boundary, permitting little contact with other people. You may know someone who interacts very little with others, someone you might feel uncomfortable approaching because he or she seems unreceptive, stand-offish, and cold. People draw rigid boundaries around themselves for various reasons, including religious or ethnic beliefs. When a family puts a rigid boundary around itself and does not permit contact with others, it is considered an **isolated family**.

You may remember a news account in 1992 about two little girls left at home in a Chicago suburb while their parents vacationed in Mexico. When neighbors were interviewed, it seemed that nobody knew the family because the family kept to themselves. Neighbors reported never having even seen the children. That family had a rigid boundary between itself and the outside world; one might imagine that the parents also had a rigid boundary between themselves and their children. Recall the situation in 1993 regarding the Branch Davidian headquarters in Waco, Texas. Cult leaders often insist on a rigid boundary between cult members and outsiders. The two cases just cited are extreme and unusual examples of people who maintain rigid interpersonal boundaries; however, everyone has her or his own level of comfort with closeness to and distance from others that is both culturally determined and a function of experience in the **family of origin** (the family one is born into and grew up in).

People and subsystems that have rigid boundaries between themselves and others or other subsystems are said to be *disengaged*. In **disengagement,** the individual is relatively isolated from others in the system or family. Beginning in the 1950s, family therapists in America described nuclear families in which the father worked long hours and was uninvolved with the goings-on of family life (Nichols & Schwartz, 1991). These fathers were characterized as being disengaged. In families where the parents (or the single parent) must work full-time jobs, there is the possibility that both parents are disengaged from the children and have relatively little involvement with them. On one hand, having a disengaged parent may force a child to become independent and competent, with many opportunities to make discoveries and solve problems for himself or herself. On the other hand, too little involvement and guidance may be associated with problem behaviors and negative feelings. Too little involvement (too much disengagement) between parent and child may be associated with the child's feeling unsupported or even unloved. Sometimes a disengaged parent may not react or act when the situation calls for it. The children may even resort to self-destructive activities, such as suicidal or dangerous pursuits, hoping an adult will respond. A tragic situation can occur when the caregiving adult responds to these desperate acts with nonchalance, believing the child is "only looking for attention." Mental health professionals stress that in these instances it is necessary for parents to become involved with and responsive to the child. Caregivers have to express their concern and demonstrate their availability to the child. Children need guidance and support; disengaged parents may not recognize when their child needs them.

At the other end of the boundary continuum are people with diffuse boundaries who are said to be *enmeshed*. In **enmeshment,** people behave with one another in a rather stereotyped fashion. Caregivers who are enmeshed with their children are overprotective and typically do not let the children take age-appropriate risks. Although they may be loving and kind, such parents spend excessive amounts of time with their children and do a lot for them. The children then tend to rely on their parents and may be quite dependent on them. The hovering and worried mother who refuses to let her preschooler run in the playground for fear he will skin his knee, who won't let him ride a bike for fear he'll fall, and who jumps in to resolve every disagreement he has with playmates, bears all of the signs of overinvolvement and enmeshment. (See Figure 13-1 for a diagrammatic representation of boundaries.)

Interpersonal boundaries, family structure, and subsystems are three key concepts that systems theorists employ when describing relationships within the family. Another important concept is that of the triangle.

Figure 13-1
Interpersonal
Boundaries.
Boundaries vary from
being rigid to diffuse.
Rigid boundaries are
overly restrictive and
permit little contact
with systems; diffuse
boundaries lead to
overdependence and
little sense of self-
competence.

Rigid (disengaged)	Clear	Diffuse (enmeshed)

Triangles   Like Minuchin, Murray Bowen (1978) considered the family as a network of interconnected relationships. He believed all families had the same fundamental relationships that could be consistently defined in every family, regardless of the large psychological differences between families. Even with differing values, attitudes, and personalities, certain fundamental relationships hold.

It is difficult to manage the intensity that occurs in relationships, and, according to Bowen, any time the emotional intensity between two persons cannot be managed, a third person becomes involved. Bowen called this three-person system a **triangle** and said it occurs whenever there is tension or anxiety (Kerr & Bowen, 1988). As Bowen (1978) put it, "the twosome might reach out and pull in the other person, the emotions might overflow to the other person, or the third person might be emotionally programmed to initiate the involvement. With the involvement of the third person, the anxiety level decreases" (p. 400). Bowen believed that the formation of triangles is a natural human tendency. He also believed that children's problems in a family are often related to the parents' relationship to each other and to their own parents. Triangles are forces in the family, and they are probably influenced by the preceding generation and the triangles that occurred there, and they will no doubt influence succeeding generations.

In their work with families with psychosomatic children, Minuchin, Rosman, and Baker (1978) elucidated the ways in which the symptomatic child is part of a triangle and is used (and puts himself or herself in the position to be used) to regulate the stress and conflict between the parents. This type of triangle may be represented as in Figure 13-2. For example, the symptoms of anorexia, Minuchin and his followers theorized, developed within a family system in which the child was part of a triangle involving the parents, and therefore the whole family was treated as symptomatic. The successful treatment of these families, using a structural family therapy approach, is one of the striking examples of the applicability of systems theory to understanding family relationships and helping solve problems.

DO WE RECREATE OUR FAMILY OF ORIGIN?

The answer proposed in this chapter to the above question is yes. The families we create through marriage and parenthood will, to a large extent, reflect our families of origin. We all bring to our relationships certain loyalties and certain myths, ideas, and fantasies about how to be in close

Figure 13-2
Triangle with Parents and Child.
Triangles are three-person systems wherein the conflict between two people is managed by involving a third. For example, parents may avoid conflict with each other by focusing on their anorexic child. (*Note:* Circles represent female family members; squares, males. Arrows point to the person who is triangulated.)

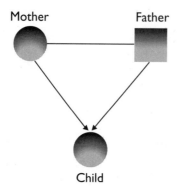

Mother   Father

Child

relationships. These internalized guidelines influence how we act with our romantic partners, our children, our siblings, and our parents. These guidelines influence whom we fall in love with and what leads each partner to be special to the other.

Theorists with different perspectives have proposed a variety of ways to understand these topics. Psychoanalytic theorists, specifically those who subscribe to **object relations theory**, would say that we relate to people in the present partly on the basis of expectations formed by early experience. There are also unconscious reasons for our actions (memories, feelings, and impulses of which a person is unaware) (Ackerman, 1958; Kernberg, 1976; Scharff & Scharff, 1987). In contrast to the psychoanalytic theorists' emphasis on the unconscious basis for our actions, is the emphasis by those who subscribe to **social learning theory** on our learning how to be parents from emulating our own parents, who serve as models of behavior (Bandura & Walters, 1963). Learning theory, which evolved from laboratory experiments on how animals and people learn, teaches that behavior is maintained by its consequences (Bandura, 1969) and that one person's behavior causes another's (Gordon & Davidson, 1981). Unlike object relations theorists, learning theorists view these processes not as unconscious mechanisms, but as occurring when we see and experience our parents and thus learn how to be a member of a family.

We may do things as we saw them done or in reaction to what we saw—we may, in fact, react in reverse ways. As an example, suppose Dominique grows up with a harsh, angry, and demanding mother. She vows that when *she* becomes a mother she will never show anger, will never criticize, and will always be gentle with her child. Dominique's daughter may come to expect others always to respond quickly to her demands and become more and more demanding as she grows up. She may someday become critical and tyrannical—like her grandmother. Dominique's antithetical behavior has inadvertently created a child in her own mother's image. Many theories, including learning theory, psychoanalytic theory, and systems theory, may provide explanations for why and how this occurred, but the fact remains that the granddaughter is like the grandmother—that history has repeated itself in the family. Systems theorists call this occurrence the **multigenerational transmission process**, to denote that families tend to repeat in the present what happened in the past (Bowen, 1978; Brown, 1991; Kerr & Bowen, 1988; McGoldrick & Carter, 1989). This repetition is accomplished in both direct and indirect ways, ways that we sometimes choose and sometimes do not. For example, we are taught by our caregivers what is good and bad, what is important and unimportant, what is to be valued and what is not. We choose the traditions we want to keep, the food we want to cook, and so forth. But other processes that we carry on, such as our involvement in triangles, are not taught; we experience them and do not necessarily understand them. The alliances we form in the family, the boundaries between ourselves and others, the triangles that occur in the families we create—all of these may initially have been experienced in our family of origin and may reemerge in one form or another in successive generations.

Family therapists and family physicians often use a drawing called a **genogram** to record information about family members and their relationships over at least three generations (McGoldrick & Gerson, 1985). Genograms provide a way to graph connections among family members and perhaps provide insight into how a given behavior fits within the family context. Use of genograms is rooted in the belief that patterns recur over generations—that there is a multigenerational transmission process. It also reflects the view that family interactions and relationships tend to be systemic and repetitive. Information about family composition, living situation, births, deaths, life changes, transitions, and traumas might all be recorded on a genogram. The facts and information may be used to understand the family structure and the triangles and the boundaries between members who are typically included in the genogram. Certain issues that are unique to a particular family may be highlighted. For example, suppose that in one family, historically, everyone worked as a laborer; in another, everyone worked in a profession. Suppose offspring from these two families marry. Certain issues that arise may be related to these aspects of their backgrounds. The genogram would clearly demonstrate these differences. Can you think of some issues that might arise, given the backgrounds of this hypothetical couple?

Although similar issues are relevant from one generation to another, the behavior of individuals may vary quite a bit from generation to generation, as in the example of Dominique, her mother, and her daughter. (The issue of how to handle anger and aggression was a problem for all three generations.) Let us now turn to a hypothetical family, the Rivera-Coles (described in Box 2), and examine how some of the above described concepts may be used to understand a family and its problems.

Juanita and Matthew appear to fall at different points on the continuum of interpersonal boundaries maintained with others. Juanita is open,

Box 2 Family Patterns: A Fictional Illustration

Juanita Rivera and Matthew Cole were laboratory partners in their sophomore biology laboratory class in college. Juanita admired Matthew's seriousness and methodical approach to problems. He seemed to know what he was talking about. Besides, he was tall and handsome and seemed like the strong, silent type she was always attracted to. Matthew liked his lab partner, who was friendly to everyone, warm, outgoing, and funny. Although Juanita seemed kind of giggly and silly, Matthew nonetheless felt at ease when with her. He looked forward to labs. When he noticed that she was a little extra friendly to him, he gathered up his courage to ask her if she wanted to study with him. She said yes, and they began a series of study dates that led to other dates. They began spending more time together. Matthew basked in Juanita's warmth and enjoyed all the attention she gave him. Juanita enjoyed how easy it was to please Matthew and noticed she felt safe and secure with him. With his very reserved manner, he seemed the voice of reason when her temper flared or she became upset by things.

Juanita grew up in a large family. Mealtimes had always been characterized by lots of people talking at once and lots of discussion and gossip. As she was growing up, Juanita was her mother's sounding board. Her mother used to confide in Juanita about her disappointments with Juanita's father's work history and how she had expected a grander lifestyle. Juanita's father was aloof from Juanita, who idealized him and wanted more from him. Juanita's mother was affectionate and very involved in Juanita's life. Juanita suffered headaches as a little girl and would lie in her mother's lap for hours while her mother rubbed her head.

Matthew had been the only child in his home. His mother was lonely because his father was deeply involved in work. People in the family did not talk about feelings much, nor was there much overt demonstration of affection. Every now and then his mother would complain about how lonely she was; Matthew used to hate these sessions and would try to get away from his mother.

Juanita was intrigued when visiting Matthew's mother but noticed she seemed a bit cold. Matthew enjoyed visiting Juanita's family, where everyone seemed warm and accepting—though he thought it unusual that everyone talked at once and always seemed so excited.

Juanita and Matthew decided to marry, and after the first few years they began to notice things about each other they hadn't seen before. Matthew found himself growing impatient with Juanita's talkativeness and demands for conversation. She seemed intrusive and a bit too open with others about their lives. Whereas he had once enjoyed the contact with her family, he began to dread going to gatherings of her family, where everyone talked about everyone else. Juanita found herself increasingly resentful that Matthew didn't want to talk and open up with her as much as she would have liked him to. He seemed to have begun drifting away. Gradually, his being a strong, silent type grew less appealing to her. She felt a bit sad and lonely. He felt resentful. She found herself talking with her mother every day as she awaited the birth of their first child.

The child was born and a second soon thereafter, and Juanita became very involved in caring for them and managing her job. Matthew became increasingly involved with his work. As with many couples at this stage, they had little time for each other, given all the demands on them. Now, however, they are faced with a family crisis. Their second child, Maria, who is 6 years old, is refusing to go to school. She vomits each morning and cries and says she wants to stay at home. Matthew thinks Juanita is too lenient and yells at his daughter to "get going and stop crying like a baby." Juanita tells Matthew that he is being too harsh, and she tries to coax their daughter to school. Despite their efforts, neither is able to get Maria to go to school.

friendly, warm and effusive; she showers others with affection and loves to talk and share things about herself with others. Matthew tends to be reserved and distant. At the beginning of their courtship these different styles seem mutually appealing: Juanita warms Matthew, and he experiences her attentiveness as caring. For her part, Juanita feels protected by what she perceives as Matthew's strength and his ability to stay out of the heat of a situation, particularly when her temper flares. She characterizes Matthew's reserve as "typically male" and doesn't think too much about it.

As their relationship continues, Juanita begins to feel lonely because Matthew won't converse and gossip with her as much as she would like. He seems quieter and less responsive than he did before. Both of them focus on the birth of their first child.

When the baby is born, the family structure changes. The couple have become parents, and the child is another person in the system they have to contend with. The second child is born, and the four of them are a family with, theoretically, two subsystems: children and parents. Juanita becomes a rather indulgent parent and she and the children now form a subsystem; Matthew is relatively uninvolved with the goings-on at home. An observer might say that the mother and children are enmeshed with one another and that the father is disengaged. Figure 13-3 provides a diagrammatic representation of this situation.

Juanita and Matthew are spending less time as a couple (a problem for

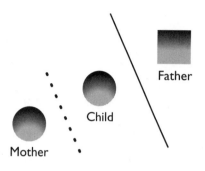

Figure 13-3
Mother and Children Enmeshed, Father Disengaged.
The enmeshment of mother and children is associated with father's disengagement; his disengagement is associated with the overinvolvement of mother with children.

all couples with young children) and are having difficulty being comfortable with each other. Matthew may be thinking "If only she showed me attention like in the old days" and "She's so permissive with the kids"; her thoughts may run to "Why doesn't he show he cares?" and "How come he doesn't respond to me as much as he used to?" Juanita pursues Matthew with her complaints and requests (or demands) that he be more involved. The more she pursues him, the more he resists. The more he resists, the more she pursues. A cycle of behavior has evolved that is associated with the tendency for one person (Juanita, the pursuer) to have more open boundaries than the other (Matthew, the distancer). During their courtship these issues didn't surface to the same degree as they do once there are the increasing pressures of changing roles (couple to parents), changing family structure (childless to family), keeping jobs, and rearing a family while trying to manage everything else in their lives. Family therapists are typically consulted at such times of transition, or change, in the family life cycle, because these are particularly stressful times for families (Carter & McGoldrick, 1989; McGoldrick & Gerson, 1985; Minuchin & Nichols, 1992; Nichols & Schwartz, 1991).

People who work with families have come to recognize that a problem can arise when parents have not resolved differences between themselves. Sometimes the problem becomes expressed through the children. In the Rivera-Cole's situation, Matthew's complaint is that Juanita is too indulgent with their children, and Juanita's complaint is that Matthew is too strict and doesn't know how to handle them. He grows angry and withdraws, while Juanita attends to the children with increasing indulgence and concern. Juanita and the children align together to form a **coalition**, excluding Matthew and increasing his disengagement. Diagrammatically, a coalition would be represented as in Figure 13-4.

What can happen to children in such a situation? Juanita, warm and loving as she is, remains as much involved in the children's lives when they are school age as she was when they were infants and preschoolers. All babies and children thrive on love and attention, but as they grow they need increased opportunities to take risks and become more involved with the outside world. When school begins, Maria, the younger child, says she

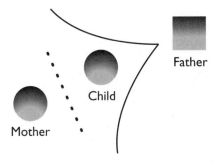

Figure 13-4
Coalition of Mother and Children. Mother is overly involved with children and responds to them with excessive concern and devotion. Mother and children form a coalition, aligning themselves against father. Father is nonreacting, even when a response may be necessary.

is afraid to go to school and cries every morning. Juanita permits Maria to stay at home with her, all the while worrying about her not attending school. Maria screams when Matthew yells at her to "stop acting like a baby." Juanita comforts the child. Maria is labeled by an individual counselor as having a phobia about school. A *family therapist*, however, might understand Maria's school refusal as a function of Juanita's enmeshment with Maria, Matthew's relative disengagement, and the parents' difficulties with each other. According to this view, Maria's refusal to attend school has less to do with her fear, per se, and more to do with **triangulation**—the spouses' involving her in their conflict. (It is interesting to note that in some cases when children refuse to attend school, the children themselves volunteer that they want to be home because they are worried about one of their parents.)

In the case of the Rivera-Cole family, a professional who follows systems theory might interpret Maria's not going to school as a function of Juanita's and Matthew's tensions associated with regulating their interpersonal boundaries (closeness and togetherness). Maria refuses school, which (1) provides Juanita with closeness and company, while she becomes anxiously involved with helping the child attend school; and (2) allows Juanita and Matthew to stop focusing on dissatisfactions having to do with their relationship and instead focus on issues surrounding Maria's refusal to attend school.

Triangles exist not only among members of the nuclear family but also among members of different generations. Juanita may talk with her own mother about difficulties with Matthew each time she and Matthew have a disagreement—creating the triangle illustrated in Figure 13-5. Tension between Matthew and Juanita may be temporarily reduced as Juanita turns to her mother instead of pursuing Matthew, who therefore no longer has to distance himself. Obviously, though, Matthew and Juanita have not figured out how to manage the tensions between them without the involvement of another generation (Juanita's mother or their children). If Juanita's mother rebuffs her daughter's attempts to talk with her about her marital problems, then the mother has not become triangulated (part of a triangle), and any number of outcomes between Juanita and Matthew might be possible.

Figure 13-5
Triangle with Couple
and Parent.
Juanita and Matthew
avoid conflict when
Juanita turns to her
mother to complain
about Matthew.

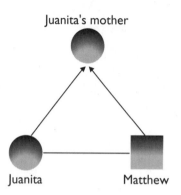

Juanita's mother

Juanita   Matthew

Given the history of Juanita's relationship with her mother, however, it is unlikely that her mother will stay out of Juanita's marital relationship. The situation in Juanita's own childhood, when conflicts between her mother and father were not addressed but detoured into a triangle with the child Juanita, is repeated by the adult Juanita, her husband, and children. The child Juanita suffered headaches in the context of enmeshment with her mother. Is this pattern being repeated in her own child's refusal to attend school and enmeshment with Juanita?

History also repeated itself in Juanita's choice of a marital partner: She chose to marry someone who tends to be distant—someone like her father. Growing lonely, she turned to the children (like her mother turned to her) and also to her mother (who herself turned to Juanita during periods of tension with Juanita's father). So, Juanita has remained within a triangle that existed when she lived in her family of origin. Her children also become part of a triangle. In two generations we see the pattern of the mother aligned with her child with the father on the outside. A genogram of this situation is shown in Figure 13-6.

The hypothetical Rivera-Cole family has illustrated some of the systems concepts that have been employed to describe families. Although the explanations are simplified, the example illustrates how the concepts of family structure, subsystems, interpersonal boundaries, and triangles can help us understand the workings of a family. You are now on your way to thinking systemically and understanding how one person's behavior not only is related to another person's behavior within a system but also is a function of relationships among other family members. Employing a systemic perspective is a way to examine a group of related elements that interact as a whole entity. We can see how this approach applies to a family, which is a group of people who are connected to each other in many ways. The connections span generations and may include blood relatives and others to whom one is socially connected and "like family."

Figure 13-6
Genogram: Three
Generations.
This genogram
represents three
generations in both
Matthew's and Juanita's
families. Family
therapists would add
information about the
families to help
understand current
problems.

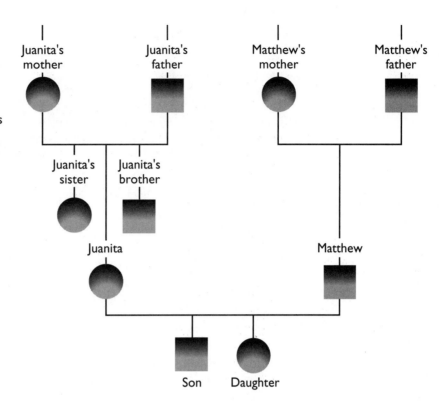

The systemic explanation of the Rivera-Cole family and its difficulties represents merely one way of explaining family relations. It is neither the only way nor necessarily the most useful way of thinking about families. And the Rivera-Coles are only one example of a nuclear family with children; there are of course other kinds of family organizations. Nonetheless, the concepts described above apply, regardless of the makeup of the family group.

SUMMARY

The important points made in this chapter are that, regardless of the form of the family, there are rules guiding family members' behavior—rules that are overt and rules that are covert. The concepts of family organization, subsystems, interpersonal boundaries, and triangles may all be used to describe family relationships. Families often function in consistent and repetitive patterns that may recur from one generation to the next. It is these patterns that reveal the structure of the family. When a new family is formed, the complex relationships and structures of preceding generations may still influence individual family members, and this is why the new family is thought to be influenced by old rules.

Class Discussion Questions

1. In the book *Very Old Bones*, by William Kennedy, the narrator comments that "We are never without the overcoats, however lice ridden, of our ancestors." What do you think the narrator meant by this comment? How does it tie into the concepts studied in this chapter?
2. Can you think of some instances when you were part of a triangle? How did you get pulled in? Did you pull in another person? What impact do you think these interactions had on you? On others in the triangle?

Homework Assignments

1. Construct a genogram of your family, considering three generations. Use Figure 13-6 (page 331) as a model.
2. Watch a television show about a family, and see whether you can describe the kinds of interpersonal boundaries the characters have and any triangles among the characters. Describe the structure of the family.
3. In the 1992 U. S. Presidential election there was a great deal of discussion of "family values." What would you say were the values in your family? What might politicians have meant when they echoed Vice President Quayle's cry that there be a return to family values?

Additional Readings

Katz, D. (1992). *Home fires*. New York: HarperCollins.

Kennedy, W. (1992). *Very old bones*. New York: Viking.

Minuchin, S., & Nichols, M. (1992). *Family healing: Tales of hope and renewal from family therapy*. New York: Free Press.

Nichols, M. (1992). *The power of family therapy*. New York: W.W. Norton.

References

Ackerman, N. W. (1958). *The psychodynamics of family life*. New York: Basic.

Bandura, A. (1969). *Principles of behavior modification*. New York: Holt, Rinehart & Winston.

Bandura, A., & Walters, R. (1963). Social learning and personality development. New York: Holt, Rinehart & Winston.

Bowen, M. (1978). *Family therapy in clinical practice*. New York: Jason Aronson.

Boyd-Franklin, N. (1989). *Black families in therapy*. New York: Guilford.

Brown, F. H. (1991). *Reweaving the family tapestry: A multigenerational approach to families*. New York: W. W. Norton.

Carter, E., & McGoldrick, M. (Eds.). (1989). *The changing family life cycle: A framework for family therapy* (2nd ed.). Boston: Allyn and Bacon.

Fuller, C. J. (1976). *The Nayars today*. New York: Cambridge University Press.

Goody, J. (1983). *The development of the family and marriage in Europe*. New York: Cambridge University Press.

Gordon, S. B., & Davidson, N. (1981). Behavioral parent training. In A. S. Gurman & D. P. Kniskern (Eds.), *Handbook of family therapy*. New York: Brunner/Mazel.

Haley, J. (1976). Development of a theory: A history of a research project. In C. E. Sluzki and D. Ransom (Eds.), *Double-bind: The foundation of a communications approach to the family*. New York: Grune & Stratton.

Harris, C. C. (1990). *Kinship*. Minneapolis: University of Minnesota Press.

Hill, R. (1972). *The strengths of black families*. New York: Emerson Hall.

Hines, P., & Boyd-Franklin, N. (1982). Black families. In M. McGoldrick, J. Pearce, & N. Giordano (Eds.), *Ethnicity and family therapy*. New York: Guilford.

Ho, M. K. (1987). *Family therapy with ethnic minorities*. New York: Sage.

Kernberg, O. F. (1976). *Object-relations theory and clinical psychoanalysis*. New York: Jason Aronson.

Kerr, M., & Bowen, M. (1988). *Family evaluation. An approach based on Bowen theory*. New York: W. W. Norton.

McAdoo, H. (1981). *Black families*. Beverly Hills: Sage.

McGoldrick, M. (1982). Overview. In M. McGoldrick, J. K. Pearce, and J. Giordano (Eds.), *Ethnicity and family therapy* (pp. 3–28). New York: Guilford Press.

McGoldrick, M., & Gerson, R. (1985). *Genograms in family assessment*. New York: W. W. Norton.

Minuchin, S. (1974). *Families and family therapy*. Cambridge, MA: Harvard University Press.

Minuchin, S., & Fishman, H. C. (1981). *Family therapy techniques*. Cambridge, MA: Harvard University Press.

Minuchin, S., & Nichols, M. (1992). *Family healing: Tales of hope and renewal in family therapy*. New York: Free Press.

Minuchin, S., Rosman, B., & Baker, L. (1978). *Psychosomatic families: Anorexia nervosa in context*. Cambridge, MA: Harvard University Press.

Nichols, M. (1988). *The power of the family*. New York: Fireside/Simon and Schuster.

Nichols, M. (1992). *The power of family therapy*. New York: Gardner.

Nichols, M., & Schwartz, R. (1991). *Family therapy: Concepts and methods*. Boston: Allyn and Bacon.

Nobles, W. (1980). *African psychology: Toward its reclamation, reascension and revitalization*. Oakland, CA: Black Family Institute.

Parsons, T., & Bales, F. (1955). *Family socialization and interaction*. Glencoe, IL: Free Press.

Royse, D., & Turner, G. (1980). Strengths of black families: A black community's perspective. *Social Work, 25* (5), 407–409.

Scarf, M. (1987). *Intimate partners: Patterns in love and marriage.* New York: Random House.

Scharff, D., & Scharff, J. (1987). *Object-relations family therapy.* New York: Jason Aronson.

Segalen, M. (1986). *Historical anthropology of the family.* New York: Cambridge University Press.

Shon, S., & Ja, D. (1982). Asian families. In M. McGoldrick, J. Pearce, & J. Giordano (Eds.), *Ethnicity and family therapy.* New York: Guilford.

Shorter, E. (1975). *The making of the modern family.* New York: Basic.

Spiro, M. (1975). *Children of the kibbutz: A study in child training and personality.* Cambridge, MA: Harvard University Press.

Stack, C. B. (1974). *All our kin: Strategies for survival in a black community.* New York: Harper.

Stone, L. (1983). *The family, sex and marriage in England, 1500–1800.* New York: HarperCollins.

The World Almanac. (1992). (pp. 944–945). New York: Pharos.

Glossary

Blended family   A stepfamily; a family united by marriage

Boundaries   Concept in structural family theory to describe emotional barriers around an individual, subsystem, and/or family

Coalition   Alliance between members of a family directed against another member of the family; inappropriate in that it is usually a parent and child who side against a third member of a family

Disengagement   Minuchin's term for emotional isolation in an individual, subsystem, or family

Enmeshment   Minuchin's term for one person's emotional over-involvement with another (usually among family members)

Executive function   Pertaining to being in charge of an organization; in this case, the family

Extended family   Family members, other than parent and child, who are related through blood ties; an informal extended kinship network includes non-blood relatives who are important and are like family

Family of origin   The family you are born into

Family structure   The way a family is organized, according to Minuchin; discovered by observing repeated patterns of behavior

Family therapy   A systems approach to therapy that considers the behavior of all family members as interdependent and sees the family operating as a unit

Genogram   Diagram of a family, usually including at least three generations

Hierarchical structure   Family structure with clear boundaries between generations and a clear "leader" (usually parents or a parent substitute)

Isolated family   A family that has rigid boundaries around itself and that interacts rarely with the outside community

Kin network   Large informal network of blood relatives and community members who are considered family

Multigenerational transmission process   Bowen's idea that ways of functioning in a family (or families) may be repeated in successive generations (new families/old rules)

Nuclear family   A parent or parents and their children

Object relations theory   A psychoanalytic theory emphasizing the effects of external experience on our emotional and cognitive functioning

Parental child   Child who takes on the responsibility for younger siblings or even for a parent

Sentimental perspective   Approach to considering families that emphasizes the emotional bonds and affection among members

Single-parent family   A family that consists of one parent and his or her children

Social learning theory   An approach to understanding behavior using principles derived from social and developmental psychology as well as from learning theory

Structure   Recurrent patterns of interactions

Structural family therapy   Minuchin's brand of family therapy

Subsystems   In a family, groups joined by commonality (for example, parents are a subsystem, children another)

Systems theory   A way of understanding how families (and organizations) work that emphasizes the whole rather than each individual (a watch is more than merely all the parts, it is how all the parts operate together that makes it a watch)

Triangle   Bowen's term for a three-person system that is formed whenever there is tension or anxiety in a relationship

Triangulation   Process whereby tension between two people is managed by involving a third person

14

Midlife Friendship Patterns

Rebecca G. Adams
University of North Carolina at Greensboro

Rosemary Blieszner
Virginia Polytechnic Institute and State University

*L*ike our family members, friends play important social and emotional roles during our adult years. The days of adolescent peer identification are by now well in the past, but friendships nevertheless fulfill needs that are not generally met by family members. Adult roles and responsibilities usually result in decreased leisure time, however, and necessarily lead to changes in friendship patterns. This chapter closely examines the importance of adult friendships, as well as the elements of and influences on the friendship patterns we establish in adulthood.

NV & SD

Chapter Outline

- The Importance of Studying Adult Friendship
- Conducting Research on Adult Friendships
- Influences on Friendship Patterns
- Elements of Friendship Patterns
- Summary

Today I woke up late. A message awaited me on my phone machine. It was from a former student, now a friend, who lives in New York and is planning a visit to my area. I noticed an unanswered letter on my desk from a high school friend who now lives in Colorado. The letter reminded me that it is my turn to call him.

I arrived at my office and checked my mailbox. Buried among advertisements and official mail was a letter announcing the upcoming wedding of one of my graduate school friends. Then I checked my e-mail messages. A friend I met while doing research wrote that his wife had had a miscarriage. A professional colleague wrote about his personal struggles in understanding spirituality. Then I called my collaborator on this chapter, who is also my close friend. We discussed our joint professional agenda and a weekend trip we are planning to take together. I had lunch with my sociology department friends—the same group of people I eat with almost every week day. And then I sat down to work on this chapter.

THE IMPORTANCE OF STUDYING ADULT FRIENDSHIP

Although all midlife adults might not report such a high level of daily friendship interaction, there is no doubt that in today's world, people are incessantly involved in social relationships in person, by telephone and letter, and even electronically. According to Gergen (1991), an adult's self-definition, or sense of identity, is in fact a relational one, in which "individual autonomy gives way to a reality of immersed interdependence" (p. 147). Understanding patterns of relating with friends thus becomes centrally important for interpreting contemporary adult lives. In this chapter we discuss influences on midlife friendship patterns, specific elements of friendship patterns, and connections among these elements. We set the stage for this discussion by first examining the functions of friends for middle-aged people and some of the limitations of existing research on midlife friendship.

Friendships serve many important functions in adulthood, providing affection and enjoyment, understanding and social support, companionship and counsel—and thus contributing to physical health and psychological well-being (Hobfoll & Stokes, 1988). Friendships might also affect an individual's status, power, wealth, attitudes, behaviors, and values. O'Connor (1992) observed that, besides affecting individuals, friendship affects society, such as by reinforcing the class structure and upholding the institution of marriage.

As we age from birth through our last years our opportunities for and constraints on friendships change, and, because we mature, we approach friendship with different attitudes, skills, and dispositions. Midlife friendship patterns are thus different from those exhibited by younger and older people. Furthermore, midlife friendships are affected not only by current sociological and developmental forces, but by prior experiences as well. Typically, the person in midlife has both long-term friends and far-off friends. Both of these types of friends are an important part of many adults' friendship networks (Rohlfing, 1995). By middle age, then, individual lives and friendship patterns are more varied than they are during earlier periods.

Although different people experience the middle years in many different ways, midlife is the stage of life with the potential for the most responsibilities. Not all middle-aged people are in committed relationships (a marriage or some other type of partnership), have children, or have steady jobs, but these circumstances typically have occurred by midlife if they are going to happen at all—and they can affect friendship. For example, involvement in a serious romantic relationship sometimes means a change in social network—cooling off friendships with people one's partner does not like, adding some of a partner's friends to one's network, and beginning to spend more social time with couples. Children both reduce the social time parents have at their disposal and provide a bridge to other adults at the same stage of the life course (those who have children around the ages of one's own). Similarly, work both absorbs time that could be spent socializing and provides new opportunities for friendship with co-workers.

Midlife adult friendships are also likely to differ from those of younger or older persons because changes in personality, interests, values, and goals occur in tandem with the heightened responsibilities mentioned above. For example, according to Erikson's (1963) theory of psychosocial development, successful resolution of the young-adult challenge of establishing satisfactory intimate relationships enables midlife adults to focus on expressing concern for the welfare of future generations, a concern that Erikson termed **generativity**. This phase in turn gives way to the life review and evaluation process of old age. Studies have confirmed Erikson's hypotheses, revealing that many midlife adults seem to be less concerned about themselves and more concerned about the world around them than young adults are (Midlarsky & Hannah, 1989; Neugarten, 1968). Midlife adults also tend to become more introspective than before—perhaps beginning to weigh their accomplishments against their goals—and many feel at the peak of competence and self-awareness (Neugarten, 1968). Often they are challenged to be dependable for their aging parents and to assist them in new ways (Blenkner, 1965).

Thus topics of conversation and shared activities of midlife adults and their friends might be different than at earlier or later stages of life. Midlife adults might express generativity by participating in community volunteer activities with their friends. They might seek advice and support from those of their friends who are experiencing similar developmental transitions and challenges (see Oliker, 1989). Feelings of competence might enable them to be more open to their friends than they had been in the past (Weick, 1989). Because of time constraints, they might be more selective in the friendships they initiate and maintain than they were before. If they understand themselves better than ever (Neugarten, 1968), they might also have deeper insights into their friends' personalities and concerns. From these examples we see, then, that both stage of the life course and level of maturity are likely to affect the friendships of midlife adults.

CONDUCTING RESEARCH ON ADULT FRIENDSHIP

Quality of Existing Studies

Most research on adult friendship has been conducted in the last 20 or 25 years, with a notable increase in the quantity and quality of studies in the past 10 years or so (see reviews in Blieszner & Adams, 1992; Nardi, 1992;

O'Connor, 1992; Rawlins, 1992). Unfortunately, most studies of midlife friendship have not been very sophisticated. Many investigations were small-scale studies or included friendship only as a secondary focus. Most researchers have examined the friendships of Caucasian, middle-class adults virtually to the exclusion of adults from other ethnic and socioeconomic backgrounds. Rather than defining midlife in terms of the responsibilities facing people (committed relationship, children, and/or a steady job) or in terms of their maturity (approach to generativity, depth of personal insights, feelings of competence), researchers of midlife friendship have arbitrarily focused on people of a certain age, typically 18 through 64 years old. This vast age span includes young adults and those in the early stages of old age as well as middle-aged ones, who are likely to have differing responsibilities and developmental characteristics.

Another problem is that researchers usually have not studied midlife friendship in terms of differences across the life course (by comparing friendships of people of different ages concurrently) or in terms of changes over time (by comparing people's friendships at one age to their friendships when they are older, in a longitudinal design). Because of these shortcomings, knowledge about midlife friendship is suggestive rather than conclusive. Doing research on adult friendship is further complicated by the elusiveness of the concept of friendship itself, as we discuss next.

Definition of Friendship

What does friendship mean to you? If you were to ask that question of a group of adults, you would receive almost as many answers as there were people in the group. Of course, you would be able to categorize the responses: Sharing, caring, helping, and the permanence of the relationship would be mentioned (see Chapter 1). You would also be able to discern patterns in your "data": The men would tend to mention the importance of doing things with their friends, and the women would remark on the importance of intimacy. People without college degrees would be less likely to have close friends of the opposite sex than those who had completed higher education. Rather than the loose clustering of responses in these patterns, however, what would be most obvious would be the tremendous variation in emphasis across individuals.

Why is there such a lack of agreement on the definition of friendship? If you were to ask the same adults to define relative or neighbor, almost total consensus would result: Relatives are determined by blood ties and neighbors by residence. These types of relationships are structurally defined: Relatives are identified by kin structure and neighbors by geographic location. Furthermore, the relationships are institutionalized: Families gather at holidays to affirm their solidarity, and neighbors form associations and have parties to assert their connection. Families and neighborhoods have names. In some societies friendships are also institutionalized. For example, in rural Thai society special friendships are formally initiated by a ritual in which the participants pledge mutual devotion and unconditional loyalty. Sacred power can be invoked whenever a party violates the vows (Piker, 1968). In contrast, in Western society, friendship is voluntary and is not institutionalized (Allan & Adams, 1989; Suttles, 1970). Friendship is not celebrated formally. We are free to define friendship as we prefer and to be friends with whomever we desire.

Or are we? If friendship is voluntary, why do adults choose friends of the same sex, age, race, religion, geographic area, and status level (Booth & Hess, 1974; Laumann, 1973)? If friendship is not institutionalized, how do we know when we are being a good friend? Allan (1989; Allan & Adams, 1989) recently reminded us that freedom regarding friendship in Western societies is not as great as it initially appears. Society provides norms for whom we choose as friends, how we treat them, and what is acceptable to expect of them. Although American friendships are not as structured or as institutionalized as other types of social relationships, they are not entirely voluntary.

INFLUENCES ON FRIENDSHIP PATTERNS

Friendship patterns are complex and vary tremendously across individuals. Think about why your parents or other middle-aged adults you know have the types of friendships they do. If you attribute their friendship patterns to their personalities, you have something in common with the scholars who view friendship as voluntary; they often emphasize the role of **psychological disposition** in determining friendship patterns. To the person wishing to improve her or his friendships, a dispositional theorist would suggest modifying attitudes or other personality characteristics. For example, many lonely people have poor self-esteem or problematic social skills; they might benefit from therapy aimed at changing dysfunctional beliefs or from social skills training (Rook, 1984).

If you credit friendship patterns to influences that are largely outside the realm of individual control, such as opportunities for and constraints on social interaction, you have a structural perspective. **Social structure** encompasses the interconnections among **social positions**. Different social positions offer access to differing levels of power, prestige, and wealth and thus provide different opportunities for friendship and varying constraints on behaviors that might lead to friendship. Structural effects on behavior include cultural expectations about how people should act (for instance, how much friends are expected to do for one another), role demands (such as expectations regarding work and family), and the availability, accessibility, or appropriateness of activities in various contexts (such as work, religious or volunteer organizations, or school). For example, wealthy people might be expected to entertain friends and spend money on activities shared with them. In contrast, working-class friends might expect more help from one another (see Rubin, 1976). Structural opportunities for and constraints on friendship-related behavior vary by context and by the social position of the individual in the context. Because it is usually difficult or impossible for an individual to change his or her social structure position (that is, to change age group, sex, race, or class), a structural theorist would most likely advise changing contexts—for example, moving to a new neighborhood or job—in order to improve friendship options or lessen constraints (Weiss, 1973).

In this chapter we treat friendship as having both voluntary and involuntary facets: It is influenced by the individual's psychological disposition and social structure position as well as by the characteristics of the contexts in which friendships can be formed and maintained. Together, the social and psychological aspects of an individual's characteristics and the properties of the contexts the individual inhabits shape her or his **behavioral motif**, which becomes the foundation for the person's friendship patterns. A behavioral motif consists of both the routine (Duck, 1994) and the unpredictable aspects of an individual's daily activities and his or her responses to them. An individual's behavioral motif would include the following:

The activities in which he or she engages

Whether participation in each of them is regular and scheduled

If participation is regular, what the schedule is

If participation is not regular, how long he or she typically pursues each activity

The extent to which each of the activities provides social opportunities

How the individual feels about her or his involvement in the activities

So people's structural and contextual opportunities for and constraints on participation in various activities and their psychological predisposition toward involvement in them determine what they actually do—the pattern of their daily lives. It is this process, the process of living from day to day, that shapes friendship patterns. Some friendships are thus based on routine, repeated, predictable interactions, and others are formed after chance meetings. The constellation of an individual's social and psychological characteristics and of contexts in which the individual participates sets the stage for the types of relationships that he or she has.

As we discussed earlier, age is one of the factors that affects this constellation of social and psychological characteristics and contexts. We would thus expect the behavioral motifs and the resulting friendship patterns of midlife adults to be different from those of younger and older people. In the next section we describe some of the aspects of friendship that researchers have found interesting and important enough to study, and we summarize what they have discovered about midlife friendships and the forces that shape them.

ELEMENTS OF FRIENDSHIP PATTERNS

Think about your best friend. How would you describe your relationship with this person? You might describe how connected you feel to your friend, the amount of respect you have for one another, which one of you is most likely to make decisions affecting both of you, and the sociological characteristics (age group, gender, race, class) you share in common. Researchers refer to these aspects of friendship as **internal structure**. You might also mention how you feel about your friend, what you think about him or her, or what you do when you are together. Researchers refer to these feelings, thoughts, and behaviors as the **interactive processes** of friendship. Or, you might focus on how long you have known the person, whether you want the friendship to become closer, to become less close, or to stay the same, and what you will do to change it or keep it as you want it to be. We use the term **phases** when referring to the beginning, **maintenance**, and ending stages of friendship.

Thus far we have focused on your thoughts about only one friendship (which researchers refer to as a **dyad**—a two-person group), but you can think about your entire collection of friends, your friendship **network**, in much the same way. It is possible to analyze the internal structure of networks, their characteristic interactive processes, and their phases. In the rest of this section, we will discuss each of these elements of friendship patterns, illustrate the importance of each aspect with examples, and summarize what we know about each element of the friendships of middle-aged people and how their friendships differ from those of people at other stages of the life course. When possible, we will discuss how gender and class shape midlife friendship patterns; as we noted earlier, though, most research has focused on white, middle-class adults, and the effects of race and ethnicity on friendship patterns of midlife adults remain unexplored.

Internal Structure

Dyadic Structure   Figure 14-1 graphically depicts four dimensions of dyadic friendship structure: power and status hierarchies, solidarity, and homogeneity. The power and status hierarchies are the vertical dimensions of relationships, the friends' relative positions on power and status. **Power** is the "probability that one actor within a social relationship will be in a position to carry out [her or] his own will despite resistance" from another (Weber, 1947, p. 152). For example, imagine two middle-aged men on a fishing trip. Each of them has previously been to the lake where they are headed, but each drove a different route. The more powerful of the two decides which route to follow, despite any disagreement posed by the other friend.

Status reflects the distance between actors in terms of stature, prestige, or moral worth (McWilliams & Blumstein, 1991). Imagine two

Figure 14-1
Examples of Dyadic Structure
(*Source:* Adapted from Blieszner & Adams, 1994)

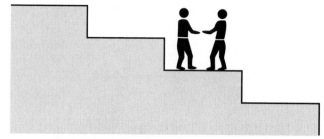

a. Low hierarchy (equality), high solidarity (emotional closeness), homogeneity (in terms of gender)

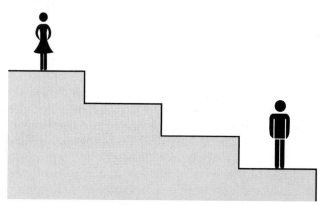

b. High hierarchy (inequality), low solidarity (emotional distance), heterogeneity (in terms of gender)

women working in a factory, one earning more money per hour than the other. If the lower-paid friend admires people who earn more than she does, her friend might have more status within their relationship. Of course, this example is a bit simplistic, because relative status in a relationship is based on many factors, not just a single one such as relative income.

In Figure 14-1 the hierarchical dimensions of friendship (power and status) are illustrated by the placement of the two friends on the staircase. In part a the friends are equal, and in part b one friend has more status or power than the other. But these examples are somewhat misleading, because they depict only one vertical hierarchy for each friendship pair, implying that a partner with relatively more power also has relatively more status. As McWilliams and Blumstein (1991) observed, however, these two vertical dimensions are independent. In some cases the powerful person does not have greater status because the exercise of power might violate norms and make the powerful partner less desirable. For example, the less powerful of the two men on the fishing trip might resent the way his friend ignored his opinion about which route to take. As a result, he might think that the friend is of lesser moral worth than he himself is (that

Although it might not always be obvious, even relationships among peers are characterized by power and status hierarchies.

is, of lower status). But in other cases the powerful person has greater stature in the eyes of the other. For example, imagine a middle-aged woman with breast cancer whose more powerful friend arranges for visiting nurses or home health care for her without having to be asked to. The cancer victim respects her powerful friend because she acts with resolve and helps with a problem.

Solidarity is the horizontal dimension, or the degree of intimacy or closeness between the people involved. In Figure 14-1 the people in a relationship high in solidarity are facing one another (part a). The authors of this chapter have a friendship high in solidarity: Little social distance separates us, we joke about people's getting us confused, and we are bound together both professionally and personally. The people in a relationship low in solidarity are not facing one another (part b). Sometimes professional colleagues have relationships low in solidarity. They spend time together, but they really do not feel that special connection that exists between close friends. In fact, some people purposefully keep their work relationships separate from their friendships.

Friendships are typically thought to be intimate (high in solidarity) and egalitarian (low in hierarchy). For this reason researchers have not explored these potentially varying dimensions of the internal structure of adult friendship, but studies of power and status in friendship might reveal fascinating differences among at least some people's friendships.

Homogeneity is the similarity of the friends in terms of their positions in the social structure external to the relationship, as evidenced by such characteristics as their gender, race, ethnicity, class, and age. Part a of Figure 14-1 depicts a gender-homogeneous pair, and part b depicts a gender-heterogeneous pair—a friendship between a man and a woman.

Adult friendship networks tend to be homogeneous in terms of occupational status, ethnicity, age, marital status, income, education, gender, and religion (see, for example, Fischer, 1982; Laumann, 1973; Verbrugge, 1977). Some scant evidence suggests that midlife is the stage during which people are most likely to select friends similar to themselves (Nahemow & Lawton, 1975). This tendency increases when the contexts in which adults form friendships—for example, religious, work, volunteer, or fraternal organizations—are homogeneous (Feld, 1982; Fischer, 1982; McPherson & Smith-Lovin, 1987). Furthermore, higher-status adults have more homogeneous networks than other middle-aged people, presumably because they have more control over where and how they spend their time (Laumann, 1973; Schutte & Light, 1978; Verbrugge, 1977). The effect of gender on the homogeneity of adult networks has not been explored systematically, but some evidence suggests that men report having more friends of the opposite sex than women do (that is, men have less gender-homogeneous networks than women do) (Booth & Hess, 1974).

Network Structure   Thus far we have only discussed the structure of dyads, but networks also have structure. Think about the Tinker Toys that you played with when you were a child or the kit you used for building molecules in your high school chemistry class. If we were to draw a friendship network, it would look like a structure you might have created with those molecule kits. Each of the sticks represents a link between friends, and each node represents a person in the network. The central node, to which all other nodes are connected, is the person whose friendship network is represented.

Networks have many structural dimensions. One dimension is hierarchy, that is, a network's vertical dimension. Picture a model of a friendship network, made out of Tinker Toys and resting on a table. The table top represents low power or status. The higher above the table top a node is, the more status or power it carries. In addition to degree of hierarchy, homogeneity (the proportion of nodes that are similar to the central node), and solidarity (the average length of the sticks connecting nodes), other aspects of network structure are the number of participants (network size, or the number of nodes) and the proportion of all possible friendships that exist among members (network **density**, calculated by dividing the number of sticks used by the total number of sticks that would be needed to connect each node to every other node).

The most basic structural variable in a network is size. Claiming a small number of friends and a large number of friends have very different consequences. Imagine, for example, a middle-aged man who is looking for a job: If he has a small circle of friends, he will not have as many possible sources of information about openings as will a man with a large circle of friends. Although many studies of adult friendship include measures of the size of the network, researchers generally report average number of friends by subgroup rather than an overall mean for the general adult population. Needless to say, these averages vary—from 4.7 to 7.8 (Fisher, 1982; Weiss & Lowenthal, 1975)—not only because of the differences in study populations, but also because of the differences in the definition of *friend* used.

The number of friends does not appear to vary much over the life course, and the findings on the effect of gender on network size are mixed (Blieszner & Adams, 1992). Some studies show that adult men have more friends than adult women have (for example, Fischer & Oliker, 1983); others show the opposite (for example, Weiss & Lowenthal, 1975). Some data indicate that among white-collar adults men have more friends than women have (Booth & Hess, 1974) and that among blue-collar adults women have more friends than men have (Weiss & Lowenthal, 1975).

Network density is a measure of "the extent to which links which

---

Box 1   **A Friendship Budget**

Helen Gouldner and Mary Symons Strong (1987) studied the friendships of 75 middle- and upper-middle-class U.S. women, aged 30 to 65 years. They discovered that each woman had her own personal "friendship budget." That is, the circumstances facing each woman affected the size and composition of her friendship network, as follows.

1. Some of the women had larger pools of potential friends than others did.
2. The women considered different proportions of their "pools" as acceptable friendship candidates.
3. Some of the women had greater needs for sociability or intimacy than others.
4. The women varied in how much time and energy they were able to devote to friendship.
5. Some of the women had better social skills than others.

---

could exist among persons do in fact exist" (Mitchell, 1969, p. 18) and is expressed in terms of a percentage. Investigators obtain the data necessary to compute the measure by asking respondents to answer a question about each pair of friends they name. The question varies across studies; a researcher might ask whether the network members know one another, are friends with one another, or see one another frequently. An affirmative answer constitutes a link (that is, a stick connecting nodes).

Figure 14-2 depicts three networks. Network a is 0% dense—none of

Figure 14-2
Examples of Network Density

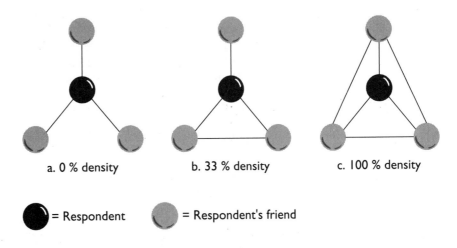

a. 0 % density   b. 33 % density   c. 100 % density

● = Respondent   ◐ = Respondent's friend

In a dense friendship network, each member knows the other members.

the respondent's friends know one another. Network b is 33% dense—only a third of the possible connections among the respondent's friends exist. Finally, network c is 100% dense—all of the respondent's friends know one another.

Dense networks have very different consequences than loosely knit networks. Imagine, for example, that a pregnant college professor entered labor the night before a teaching day. If she had a dense network of professional friends, she could contact one of her friends and ask that person to find someone to conduct the lecture the next day. The friend, by virtue of being part of this dense network, would know lots of the pregnant woman's friends and thus have a fairly high probability of being able to find someone who both cared about the pregnant woman and had the time and expertise to take over her class. If the pregnant woman had a network of friends who did not know one another, however, she might feel obligated to call each of them herself until she found someone willing to teach for her. So in this instance, a dense network would be more efficient and useful. On the other hand, imagine a middle-aged man whose wife leaves him for another man. He wants to confide in someone, but, because he has a dense network, if he tells one friend what has happened, all of his friends are likely to hear about it. Keeping this news confidential would be easier if he had a loosely knit network or at least one confidant whom none of his other friends knew.

Only a couple of investigators have examined the density of adult friendship networks, but neither one has studied the whole friendship network and excluded other types of relationships. Laumann (1973) found that the three closest friends of 27% of the Detroit-area men he studied knew one another (that is, the networks were 100% dense, like network c in Figure 14-2). About a third (31%) of the respondents had networks in which none of their three closest friends knew one another (network a), and 42% had networks in which one or two of their three closest friends knew one another (network b). Fischer (1982) reported that the average density of the network of associates, including both friends and relatives, was 44%.

Although gender differences in friendship network density have not been studied, the effects of age and class have been. Friendship network density apparently does not vary much across the life course (Blieszner & Adams, 1992). Fischer (1982) found that the associate networks of less-affluent and less-educated adults tended to be denser than those of wealthier or better-educated persons. In other words, the friends of lower-class people were more likely to know one another than the friends of more affluent people were.

Midlife Friendship Structure   As we discussed in the introduction, the forces affecting the lives of midlife adults are different from those affecting younger and older people, and thus it follows that their friendships are different as well. Compared to adults of other ages, midlife adults appear to have more homogeneous networks. Scant research suggests that network size and density do not vary systematically across the adult life course. Researchers have not examined the relative power and status of midlife friends or their solidarity. Future research will reveal more about the internal structure of midlife friendships and the circumstances that affect them.

Interactive Processes

Friendship processes are diverse and complex. For the sake of discussion, they are divided into three types: cognitive (thoughts), affective (feelings), and behavioral (actions). These processes occur both between members of friend dyads and within friendship networks. The three types of friendship processes affect one another, such that behaviors can affect thoughts and emotions, cognitive processes can result in affective reactions, they in turn influence future actions, and so on. For example, the friend who lectures for the woman in labor (a supportive behavior) will earn gratitude and affection (affective responses) from the pregnant woman, who will probably be inclined to return the favor in the future. Each friendship process can have a strengthening or a weakening effect on the friendship or network. Individuals differ both in the extent to which they employ processes strategically, versus assuming a more passive stance in the relationship, and in the extent to which their dispositions are oriented more toward one type of process than others. Also, people either express thoughts, feelings, and actions so their friends are aware of them or keep them hidden from their friends. The man on the fishing trip might never tell his friend how annoyed he was that the friend ignored his advice about which route to take. Moreover, people do not necessarily interact with all friends in their networks in the same manner. The woman with cancer who appreciates her friend's health care interventions might resent another friend's attempt to give her financial advice.

Before we discuss each type of process it should be pointed out that very little research has been conducted on specific processes in adult friendship. Many researchers have used indirect measures of interaction, such as frequency of contact or length of acquaintance, which indicate that socializing has taken place but reveal nothing about the nature of the interactions. Apparently, investigators who rely solely on indirect indicators assume that more quantity and variety of process is better than less—an assumption with questionable validity. A direct measurement of specific processes would be preferable (Blieszner & Adams, 1992).

Cognitive Processes   Each partner in a friendship has thoughts about herself or himself, the friend, and the friendship. Friends evaluate their own performance and the partner's performance of the role of friend, assess the stability of the friendship, explain events that occur in the friendship, interpret their own behavior as well as the partner's intentions or needs, and so on. These are **cognitive processes**. A shy person who engages in negative self-assessment ("I can never think of anything to say to start a conversation with a stranger") is using a cognitive process to undermine friendship possibilities. Cognitive processes also include the evaluations and judgments that one person makes of another's attractiveness, character, similarity to the self, and other important qualities. For example, the less powerful man on the fishing trip used a cognitive process in deciding that his fishing buddy was morally inferior to himself.

Research shows that middle-aged adults, like younger and older ones, consider similarity of values and interests to be important in friendship. People find it easy to get along with those whom they perceive as having the same type of personality as they have. Similarities contribute to ease of communication and shared experiences (Weiss & Lowenthal, 1975). Midlife adults also evaluate potential friends on the basis of politeness, friendliness, and similarity of background (Johnson, 1989).

Perceptions of real versus ideal friends reflect other cognitive processes. Weiss and Lowenthal (1975) found that descriptions of real friends did not differ much among teenagers, young adults, middle-aged adults, and older adults, suggesting that the functions of friends are established early in life and remain fairly constant throughout. When describing ideal friends, similarity to oneself was less important to the adults than to the high school seniors, indicating that adults are no longer as concerned with identity formation as teens are. Differences in descriptions of real and ideal friends were lowest for the middle-aged respondents, perhaps signifying increased selectivity of friends during midlife such that actual friends possess characteristics seen as ideal. Looking at sex differences, women provided more detailed descriptions of attributes of both real and ideal friends than men gave. Men emphasized similarity and women focused on reciprocity across all four life stages. The middle-aged persons had the simplest descriptions, perhaps because of family demands that competed with friendship. Taken together, these results show that differences in important friend characteristics reflect the stage of personal and family development of members in each age group.

Affective Processes   People have emotional reactions to friends and friendship. Empathy, trust, loyalty, and satisfaction are all positive emotions.

Indifference, anger, hostility, and jealousy are examples of negative or unpleasant emotions that friends can experience. These **affective processes** might or might not occur in a given relationship, and, if they do, they can vary in the frequency or strength of the feeling (Berscheid, 1983).

Investigators have studied several affective processes in midlife adult friendship. For example, predictors of friendship satisfaction were instrumental reward (for example, working on a joint task, respecting privacy, giving advice), emotional support, and shared interests. Emotional support and shared interests were especially important. Opposite-sex friends had lower satisfaction ratings than same-sex friends, but both groups showed a similar pattern of ratings (Argyle & Furnham, 1983).

Another emotion is trust. Contrary to expectations based on the fact that women reveal more about themselves to their friends than men do, the men in Davidson and Duberman's (1982) study had higher levels of trust for their best friends than the women had. But the men talked about impersonal, less risky topics more often than the women did (see below). Consider again the case of the man whose wife left him: Lack of trust might explain his hesitancy to confide in certain of his friends. Thus results of research on trust must be interpreted in light of the fact that, although the men perceived themselves as being open and trusting, this trust was on a superficial level because they actually invested little in the personal and interactional aspects of the friendship.

Oliker (1989) provided examples of another network-level affective process: friends helping each other manage their feelings. Women reported that they were able to talk about their feelings with friends, who, by allowing the expression of volatile emotions, helped them diffuse their reactions in a safe and effective manner. For example, a woman could express anger about someone in another relationship to a friend without escalating the conflict or damaging the other relationship. Best friends helped women manage their emotional reactions while acknowledging and affirming the reality of the feelings, thus reducing stress.

Behavioral Processes The action components of friendship, known as **behavioral processes**, include communication, such as disclosure of one's thoughts, feelings, and actions; displays of affection; social support or resource exchange; cooperation; accommodation to a friend's desires; joint activities; betrayal; manipulation; conflict; competition; and the like. Below we discuss some research results on various behavioral processes in adult friendships.

Talk cements friendships in adulthood, as least for women. When Johnson and Aries (1983) asked women about the most important benefit of their friendships, respondents highlighted the value of conversation, either by itself or along with other shared activities. Female friends were valued for listening noncritically, providing support that enhanced feelings of self-esteem, validating experiences, offering comfort, and contributing to personal growth.

Several researchers have compared women's and men's friendship communication patterns for various age groups. In terms of the content of conversations, women discussed topical, relational, and personal material with friends, but men focused mainly on topical material such as sports, business, and politics (Davidson & Duberman, 1982; Fox, Gibbs, & Auerbach, 1985). Women were more likely than men to speak with their friends on the phone for 10 minutes or more, talk in depth about personal problems, reveal doubts and fears, and discuss intimate relationships (Aries & Johnson, 1983). This pattern seems to occur throughout adulthood. Indeed, Dickson-Markman (1986) found that adults from 19 to 91 years old were quite similar on various dimensions of self-disclosure when length of friendship was taken into account. These results suggest that sex-role patterns influence conversational subjects and depth in adult friendship but that age has little effect on friendship communication.

Scholars have also examined relational conflict, which can be divided into emotional conflict (such as disagreements over beliefs and values) and criticism of another person's habits and lifestyle. Within same-sex friendships, conflict was fairly low in terms of criticism but higher in emotional terms. Conflict was slightly lower with opposite-sex friends than with same-sex friends (Argyle & Furnham, 1983). Another study found low levels of conflict between friends for both men and women. Overall, however, men reported more conflict in their relationships than women did, which supports the assumption that women have been socialized to suppress or avoid conflict (Davidson & Duberman, 1982). Looking at the connection between age and conflict with friends, a study showed that middle-aged and older people made more efforts to reduce disagreements with their friends than younger respondents did (Fox, Gibbs, & Auerbach, 1985).

Midlife Friendship Processes   People in the middle years of adulthood tend to be friends with those who share their values and interests. They spend time with friends they can trust and whose company they enjoy. A particularly important feature of women's closest friendships at this stage of life is the emotional support they provide.

Phases

Friendships are dynamic relationships that develop and evolve over time. They have beginnings, when partners become acquainted; middles, when solidarity and other features increase, decrease, fluctuate, or remain stable; and, sometimes, endings, for any of a variety of reasons. Change from one phase to another—from first impression to closest friendship, for example—can occur slowly or rapidly. The length of each friendship phase— building, sustaining, declining—varies across people and circumstances.

Movement from one friendship phase to another is sometimes delib-

---

Box 2

Women's Best-Friend Relationships

Stacey Oliker (1989) interviewed 21 working- and middle-class U.S. women, 20 to 59 years of age, about their best-friend relationships. She compared these friendships to marriage and found some interesting contrasts. For example, all but two of the women were able to think of benefits they received from their friends but not from their spouses. The intimacy between best friends was characterized by talking, understanding, and feeling. It is not that the women did not ever talk with their husbands or feel understood by them; rather, their common experiences with their best friends provided a depth of conversation, a level of sympathetic knowledge, and a degree of empathy that they did not typically experience with their husbands or anyone else.

---

erate and sometimes occurs by happenstance. Although the language used to describe friendship development suggests that friends proceed from one phase to another via planned, conscious mechanisms, individuals differ on the extent to which they consciously employ friendship strategies. Some friendships and changes in them "just happen," without overt effort on the part of either friend.

Friendship phases in the adult years are affected by the differential opportunities of adults—compared to college students, for instance—to meet potential friends and promote friendships. Also, developmental maturity and roles can distinguish the phases of friendship of midlife adults from those of younger or older people. Unfortunately, however, the literature on phases of friendship in adulthood is extremely limited. Although studies of the middle years of adulthood include descriptions of desired characteristics of friends, activities with friends, and other data that imply that individuals strive to build and sustain friendships during these years, few studies have asked middle-aged persons explicitly about the strategies they used to do so. This is a serious oversight, especially in light of research that shows the importance of support from friends for dealing with critical life events. Given the major life review and evaluation processes that begin in the middle years and the possibilities of demanding family responsibilities in rearing teenagers or caring for elderly parents, it seems crucial to understand the connection between the need for social support and friendship patterns at this stage of the life cycle.

Initiation Friendship forms when two people move from being strangers to being acquaintances to being friends; at the network level, the formation phase involves the emergence of new networks and the integration of individuals and pairs into existing networks. The beginning phase of friendship includes processes such as identification of or attraction to a potential friend, initial meetings with the potential friend (if a stranger), and getting to know the other and letting the other know oneself.

One source of friendship in the middle years is groups to which the individual belongs. Stein (1986) described the evolution of friendship in men's consciousness-raising groups. These friendships developed slowly, based on shared trust, exchange of information, and a growing sense of commitment between partners. On the other hand, lack of time to get together, feelings of competitiveness, greater achievement drives, and fears of getting too close were obstacles to friendship initiation within the men's groups.

A comparison of young adult and middle-aged men revealed that stage of life might have an effect on friendship initiation. In both groups, men emphasized the importance of current activities at work and in the neighborhood for promoting friendship initiation. But when the researchers looked at inhibitors of friendship initiation they found that midlife men were concerned about lack of time, whereas younger men focused on personality differences (Wall, Pickert, & Paradise, 1984).

Maintenance   The maintenance phase of friendship is perhaps the most variable period, in terms of both the processes that occur and the degree to which partners consciously attend to the relationship. Friends have many different ways of sustaining their interest in, affection toward, and involvement with each other. From time to time they might consciously or unconsciously evaluate each other, other friendships, friendship opportunities, and relevant social circumstances. Friends decide, for example, whether to retain the friendship at its current level of solidarity, change to a higher or lower level of involvement, engage in different activities together, dissolve the friendship, display indifference to it, or carry out a host of other possibilities. The maintenance phase can last for a very long time. Networks also have a maintenance phase: Individuals, dyads, and larger groups can either sustain a network as it is or attempt to change it in some manner.

Communication strategies are important in friendship maintenance. Rawlins (1983a, 1983b) analyzed people's feelings of independence and dependence in friendship and the expressive and protective functions of communication in friendship. Friends pursue individual goals or interests but depend on each other in times of need—contradictory aspects of friendship that require ongoing negotiations to keep the friendship in balance. Friends must also balance expressiveness (self-disclosure, directness, honesty, candor) with protectiveness (avoiding hurtful remarks or touchy subjects). Successful management of these communication dilemmas contributes to the maintenance of friendship.

Changes in life circumstances can have an effect on friendship maintenance, as Suitor (1987) found in her study of adult women who enrolled in college. Of course, full-time students had less time to interact with friends, but relationships with less-educated friends were more difficult to sustain than those with better-educated friends, because the former group did not approve of the return to school. Part-time students, however, were able to maintain friendships with their less-educated friends even as the ones with their better-educated friends declined. The status of "student" was less central to the identity of the part-time students, so they were better able than the full-time students to tolerate their friends' negative attitudes about the return to school.

Do the rules of friendship maintenance differ across age groups? Argyle and Henderson (1984) hypothesized that the rules endorsed by younger adults would emphasize help and availability more than those endorsed by middle-aged adults. This hypothesis was not confirmed; the two age groups did not differ in the rules they emphasized. But in another study, with young adults aged 17 to 34 years, older respondents were more likely to attribute the end of a friendship to lack of respect for privacy and too many requests for personal advice, whereas younger participants were more likely to attribute it to public criticism.

The strategies that contribute to retention of friendships vary for women and men and for same- and cross-sex friendships (Rose, 1985). Both women and men endorsed tactics related to acceptance, effort, time, communication, common interests, and affection as important for same-sex friendship maintenance. But women, more often than men, reported having no strategy for keeping cross-sex friendships and viewed time as unimportant in sustaining cross-sex friendships.

Dissolution   Some friendships enter a dissolution phase and others do not. Friendships might endure for decades, with the assumption of indefinite existence; they might end abruptly, as with serious disagreement or the death of one partner; or they might wither to a state of inactivity or to nonexistence from benign neglect. The causes of friendship dissolution might be involuntary (death, for instance) or voluntary (disagreement) and external (such as relocation) or internal (such as lack of support). Processes inherent in the dissolution phase range from direct and explicit declaration of the parting to more indirect ones, such as avoiding the friend or failing to initiate encounters. Network dissolution involves the elimination of one person or dyad, elimination of more than one dyad, or breaking up of all the friendship bonds in the network.

Neimeyer and Neimeyer (1986) studied midlife adults, initially unacquainted with one another, who participated in structured discussions and periodically rated all the group members on various characteristics. In pairs that did not become close during the 20-week session, at least one partner's level of attraction decreased over time, whereas in pairs that grew closer, the average level of attraction increased. As the people learned more about one another, the dyads that grew closer reached similar opinions of other group members fairly early and attained deep and extensive levels of agreement, but the deteriorating dyads took much longer to reach even a superficial level of consensus about other group members. The authors concluded that successful relationships must have a period of initial bonding after which dissimilarities are not very important, but extensive dissimilarities early on can lead to relationship deterioration.

Midlife Friendship Phases   People in middle adulthood strive to retain previously developed friendships, but they also take advantage of opportunities to make new friends in the neighborhood, at work, and through community and leisure activities. Effective communication is a crucial dimension of friendship maintenance. Changes in a person's life, such as attending college or becoming divorced, can interfere with existing friendships but might also provide chances to meet potential friends.

Connections Among the Elements of Friendship Patterns

Figure 14-3 is a graphic summary of the elements of friendship patterns we have discussed and of the interconnections among them. The diagram illustrates that at both the dyadic and network levels, structure and phases influence one another through interactive processes. For example, the two members of an egalitarian dyad might be more likely to confide in each other than the members of a hierarchical dyad and thus might be more likely to become friends. Or members of dense networks might spend more time doing things together, which might transform an acquaintanceship network into a friendship network.

Figure 14-3 also shows that dyads are imbedded in networks, and thus their characteristics act upon one another. The potential for processes at one level to affect structure and phases at the other level is indicated by the dotted box separating the two levels in the figure. For example, the members of dense friendship networks might share pleasant experiences more frequently than members of low-density networks. This might, in turn, reinforce the solidarity of member pairs. The structure of dyads can conversely

Figure 14-3
Friendship Patterns
(*Source:* Adapted from
Blieszner & Adams,
1994)

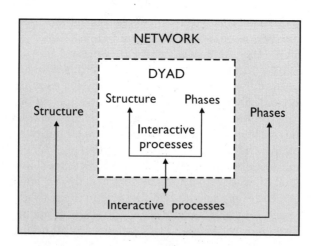

influence the structure of the overall network, though these effects are probably less likely to occur. But, for example, the members of egalitarian dyads might, through their attitudes, feelings, and behaviors, create an atmosphere in which network equality is preferred over hierarchy. Of course, the higher the proportion of the constituent dyads that share a given structural characteristic, the more effective their influence on network structure.

SUMMARY

The majority of middle-aged adults have friends and consider them to be important in their lives. People have more flexibility in choosing their friends than they do with regard to kin, co-workers, or neighbors. Throughout this chapter we have discussed unique features of middle age that can have an impact on friendships. Each person's particular life circumstances and developmental maturity affect the kinds of people who are available to become friends, the kinds of interactions friends have, and the level of emotional closeness that friends attain. At the same time, friendships in the middle years have many characteristics in common with friendships in earlier and later adulthood. Most people have friends who are similar to themselves and who enjoy similar interests and activities. Almost all agree that their friends provide valuable social and emotional support.

Opportunities for making, keeping, and interacting with friends are affected by characteristics such as age, gender, race, and class and by the everyday contexts in which people spend their time. To the extent that these factors vary for middle-aged persons compared to people of other life stages, they will have differential influences on midlife friendship.

Friendship patterns also vary across the population of midlife adults, in terms of internal structure of friend pairs and networks, interactive processes among friends, and phases of friendship. The internal structure of friendship networks and dyads affects the types of interactive processes that take place and thus the phases of friendships. Reciprocally, the phases of friendship affect cognitive, affective, and behavioral processes and thus aspects of internal structure such as hierarchy, solidarity, and density. To the extent that aspects of these dimensions are unique to midlife, they will lead to distinctive friendship patterns. Thus personal characteristics and development mesh with features of social structure to influence midlife friendship. More research, specifically examining these reciprocal influences, is required for a full understanding of friendship patterns in the middle years of life.

Class Discussion Questions

1. What are some of the functions of friendship in the lives of the middle-aged adults you know? When you reach middle age, what roles do you expect friendship to play in your life?

2. How is middle age different from other periods of life in terms of activities and responsibilities? How would these differences affect friendship patterns?

3. What does friendship mean to you? Which do you think affects friendship patterns more, psychological disposition or social structure position? What types of contexts are conducive to friendship formation and maintenance?

4. Think about your best friendship. Describe its internal structure, interactive processes, and phases.

5. Identify a circumstance that a midlife adult might face in which each of the following types of friendship networks would be useful: (a) high in density, (b) low in density, (c) high in hierarchy, (d) low in hierarchy, (e) high in homogeneity, (f) low in homogeneity, (g) small, (h) large, (i) high in solidarity, (j) low in solidarity.

6. Give an example of the ways in which the aspects of friendship in each of the following pairs might affect each other: (a) dyadic structure and dyadic processes, (b) dyadic phases and dyadic processes, (c) dyadic processes and network processes, (d) network processes and network structure, (e) network processes and network phases. For example, if a dyad is high in solidarity (an aspect of dyadic structure), what kind of affective processes might you expect to see? Would high solidarity lead to empathy, trust, loyalty, and satisfaction, or to indifference, anger, hostility, and jealousy?

Homework Assignments

1. Interview a middle-aged adult about her or his friendships. How does this person think that her or his age affects friendships? Have the person's friendships changed since earlier in life? If so, how and why? Does she or he expect current friendships to change in the future? If so, how and why?

2. Interview a middle-aged adult about the structure of his or her friendship network. Begin by asking your respondent to list the first names of all his or her close friends. (It is best to limit the list to close friends, because a list of general friends can be quite long.) Write the names both down the left-hand column of a piece of paper and across the top of the paper, making a grid. Start with the first friend listed, and ask whether this person knows each other friend in turn. In the row for the first friend's name, put a check mark under the name of the friend in question each time the answer is yes. Notice that the list of friends you need to ask about gets shorter as you move down the page. For example, when you get to the second friend, you will already know whether he or she is acquainted with the first person, so you don't need to ask about that pair again. Compute the density of the friendship network as follows:

   a. Count the checks (friendship links), and multiply the number by 100.

   b. Count the friends named (network size), and multiply the number
      by the number minus 1. Divide this product by 2.
   c. Divide the product you obtained in step (a) by the quotient you cal-
      culated in step (b). The result is the network density.
   In addition to density, you have already calculated network size. It is a
   fairly easy matter to calculate the percentage of the dyads in the network that are gender homogeneous (divide the number of people who
   are the same sex as your respondent by the network size).
3. Watch a TV show or video that involves midlife adults interacting
   with their friends. Note examples of affective and behavioral processes.
   See whether you can detect cognitive processes as well (this will probably require some interpretation or speculation on your part). Write a
   summary of one or more incidents that reveal the operation of the
   three types of processes, and speculate about the effects of the processes
   on the phase(s) of the friendship(s).

Additional Readings

Blieszner, R., & Adams, R. G. (1992). *Adult friendship*. Newbury Park, CA: Sage.

Fischer, C. S. (1982). *To dwell among friends*. Chicago: University of Chicago Press.

Nardi, P. M. (Ed.). (1992). *Men's friendships*. Newbury Park, CA: Sage.

O'Connor, P. (1992). *Friendships between women*. New York: Guilford.

Rawlins, W. K. (1992). *Friendship matters*. New York: Aldine de Gruyter.

Rubin, L. B. (1985). *Just friends*. New York: Harper & Row.

References

Allan, G. (1989). *Friendship*. New York: Harvester Wheatsheaf.

Allan, G., & Adams, R. G. (1989). Aging and the structure of friendship. In R. G. Adams & R. Blieszner (Eds.), *Older adult friendship* (pp. 45–64). Newbury Park, CA: Sage.

Argyle, M., & Furnham, A. (1983). Sources of satisfaction and conflict in long-term relationships. *Journal of Marriage and the Family, 45,* 481–493.

Argyle, M., & Henderson, M. (1984). The rules of friendship. *Journal of Social and Personal Relationships, 1,* 211–237.

Aries, E. J., & Johnson, F. L. (1983). Close friendship in adulthood: Conversational content between same-sex friends. *Sex Roles, 9,* 1183–1196.

Berscheid, E. (1983). Emotion. In H. H. Kelley, E. Berscheid, A. Christensen, J. Harvey, T. L. Huston, G. Levinger, D. McClintock, L. A. Peplau, & D. Peterson (Eds.), *Close relationships* (pp. 110–168). New York: Freeman.

Blenkner, M. (1965). Social work and family relationships in later life with some thoughts on filial maturity. In E. Shanas & G. F. Streib (Eds.), *Social structure and the family: Generational relations* (pp. 46–59). Englewood Cliffs, NJ: Prentice-Hall.

Blieszner, R., & Adams, R. G. (1992). *Adult friendship*. Newbury Park, CA: Sage.

Blieszner, R., & Adams, R. G. (1994). An integrative conceptual framework for friendship research. *Journal of Social and Personal Relationships, 11,* 163–184.

Booth, A., & Hess, E. (1974). Cross-sex friendship. *Journal of Marriage and the Family, 36,* 38–47.

Davidson, L. R., & Duberman, L. (1982). Friendship: Communication and interactional patterns in same-sex dyads. *Sex Roles, 8,* 809–822.

Dickson-Markman, F. (1986). Self-disclosure with friends across the life cycles. *Journal of Social and Personal Relationships, 3,* 259–264.

Duck, S. W. (1994). Steady as (s)he goes: Relational maintenance as a shared meaning system. In D. J. Canary & L. Stafford (Eds.), *Communication and relationship maintenance* (pp. 45–60). New York: Academic.

Erikson, E. H. (1963). *Childhood and society* (2nd ed.). New York: Norton.

Feld, S. L. (1982). Social structural determinants of similarity. *American Sociological Review, 45,* 797–801.

Fischer, C. S. (1982). *To dwell among friends*. Chicago: University of Chicago Press.

Fischer, C. S., & Oliker, S. J. (1983). A research note on friendship, gender, and the life cycle. *Social Forces, 62,* 124–133.

Fox, M., Gibbs, M., & Auerbach, D. (1985). Age and gender dimensions of friendship. *Psychology of Women Quarterly, 9,* 489–501.

Gergen, K. J. (1991). *The saturated self*. New York: Basic Books.

Gouldner, H., & Strong, M. S. (1987). *Speaking of friendship*. Westport, CT: Greenwood.

Hobfoll, S. E., & Stokes, J. P. (1988). The process and mechanics of social support. In S. W. Duck (Ed.), *Handbook of personal relationships* (pp. 497–517). Chichester, England: Wiley.

Johnson, F. L., & Aries, E. J. (1983). The talk of women friends. *Women's Studies International Forum, 6,* 353–361.

Johnson, M. A. (1989). Variables associated with friendship in an adult population. *The Journal of Social Psychology, 129,* 379–390.

Laumann, E. O. (1973). *Bonds of pluralism*. New York: Wiley.

McPherson, J. M., & Smith-Lovin, L. (1987). Homophily in voluntary organizations. *American Sociological Review, 52,* 370–379.

McWilliams, S., & Blumstein, P. (1991). Evaluative hierarchies in personal relationships. In E. Lawler, B. Markovsky, C. Ridgeway, & H. Walker (Eds.), *Advances in group processes* (Vol. 8, pp. 67–88). Greenwich, CT: JAI.

Midlarsky, E., & Hannah, M. E. (1989). The generous elderly: Naturalistic studies of donations across the life span. *Psychology and Aging, 4,* 346–351.

Mitchell, J. C. (1969). The concept and use of social networks. In J. C. Mitchell (Ed.), *Social networks in urban situations* (pp. 1–50). Manchester, England: Manchester University Press.

Nahemow, L., & Lawton, M. P. (1975). Similarity and propinquity in friendship formation. *Journal of Personality and Social Psychology, 32,* 205–213.

Nardi, P. M. (Ed.). (1992). *Men's friendships.* Newbury Park, CA: Sage.

Neimeyer, G. J., & Neimeyer, R. A. (1986). Personal constructs in relationship deterioration. *Social Behavior and Personality, 14,* 253–257.

Neugarten, B. L. (1968). Adult personality: Toward a psychology of the life cycle. In B. L. Neugarten (Ed.), *Middle age and aging* (pp. 137–147). Chicago: University of Chicago Press.

O'Connor, P. (1992). *Friendships between women.* New York: Guilford.

Oliker, S. J. (1989). *Best friends and marriage.* Berkeley, CA: University of California Press.

Piker, S. (1968). Friendship to the death in rural Thai society. *Human Organization, 27,* 200–204.

Rawlins, W. K. (1983a). Negotiating close friendship. *Human Communication Research, 9,* 255–266.

Rawlins, W. K. (1983b). Openness as a problematic in ongoing friendships. *Communication Monographs, 50,* 1–13.

Rawlins, W. K. (1992). *Friendship matters.* New York: Aldine de Gruyter.

Rohlfing, M. E. (1995). "Doesn't anybody stay in one place any more?": An exploration of the understudied phenomenon of long-distance relationships. In J. T. Wood & S. W. Duck (Eds.), *Understanding relationships: Off the beaten path* [*Understanding relationship processes 6*]. Thousand Oaks, CA: Sage.

Rook, K. S. (1984). Promoting social bonding. *American Psychologist, 39,* 1389–1407.

Rose, S. M. (1985). Same- and cross-sex friendships and the psychology of homosociality. *Sex Roles, 12,* 63–74.

Rubin, L. B. (1976). *Worlds of pain.* New York: Basic Books.

Schutte, J. G., & Light, J. M. (1978). The relative importance of proximity and status for friendship choices in social hierarchies. *Social Psychology, 41,* 260–264.

Stein, P. J. (1986). Men and their friendships. In R. A. Lewis & R. E. Salt (Eds.), *Men in families* (pp. 261–269). Beverly Hills, CA: Sage.

Suitor, J. J. (1987). Friendship networks in transition. *Journal of Social and Personal Relationships, 4,* 445–461.

Suttles, G. D. (1970). Friendship as a social institution. In G. McCall, M. McCall, N. Denzin, G. Shuttles, & S. Kurith (Eds.), *Social relationships* (pp. 95–135). Chicago: Aldine.

Verbrugge, L. M. (1977). The structure of adult friendship choices. *Social Forces, 56,* 576–597.

Wall, S. M., Pickert, S. M., & Paradise, L. V. (1984). American men's friendships. *The Journal of Psychology, 116,* 179–186.

Weber, M. (1947). *The theory of social and economic organization.* New York: Free Press.

Weick, A. (1989). Patterns of change and processes of power in adulthood. In S. Hunter & M. Sundel (Eds.), *Midlife myths* (pp. 235–252). Newbury Park, CA: Sage.

Weiss, L., & Lowenthal, M. F. (1975). Life-course perspectives on friendship. In M. F. Lowenthal and Associates (Eds.), *Four stages of life* (pp. 48–61). San Francisco: Jossey-Bass.

Weiss, R. S. (1973). *Loneliness.* Cambridge, MA: MIT Press.

Glossary

Affective processes   Emotional reactions to friends and friendship

Behavioral processes   Action components of friendship

Behavioral motif   Routine and unpredictable aspects of an individual's daily activities and the responses to them

Cognitive processes   Thoughts about oneself, one's friend, and the friendship

Density   Proportion of existing relationships to all possible relationships in a network

Dissolution   Ending phase of friendship

Dyad   A two-person group

Generativity   The concern midlife adults show for the welfare of future generations

Homogeneity   Similarity of people in a relationship in terms of social positions external to the relationship, such as gender, age, race, ethnicity, and class

Initiation   Beginning phase of friendship

Interactive processes   Feelings, thoughts, and behaviors through which friendship is expressed

Internal structure   The power hierarchy, status hierarchy, homogeneity, solidarity, and density of friendship dyads or networks

Maintenance   Sustaining (middle) phase of friendship

Network   A group of three or more people

Phases   Beginning (initiation), middle (maintenance), and ending (dissolution) periods of friendship

Power   Ability to carry out one's own will despite resistance from others

Psychological disposition   Personality and other individual characteristics that influence a person's typical behavior patterns

Solidarity   Degree of intimacy or closeness between people in a dyad or network

Social positions   Locations in society or smaller social groups that people can occupy; achieved through individual effort (such as level of education, occupation) or assigned by nature or society (such as race, gender)

Social structure   The interconnections among social positions that offer access to differing levels of power, prestige, and wealth

Status   Distance between people in terms of stature, prestige, or moral worth

15

Adults and Their Midlife Parents

Robert A. Lewis
Purdue University

Li-Wen Lin
Queens College

Even as we are busy accomplishing the tasks of adulthood (discussed in the previous chapters), most of us still sustain important relationships with our parents well into our adult years. These relationships necessarily change in nature and function as we get older, however, and this chapter explores in detail the effects of the child's maturation and progression into adulthood and the influences of the accompanying changes on the adult child–parent relationship.

NV & SD

Chapter Outline

• Attachment Theory
• Changes in Family Residences and Relationships
• Changes in Intimacy and Attachment
• Changes in Family Power
• Determinants of Resource Exchange
• Summary

After the kids leave home, some parents suffer from the empty-nest syndrome; others change the locks!
Anonymous (Strong & DeVault, 1993, p. 189)

Parenthood never ends! Relationships between parents and their children do not usually disappear during what are called the **launching years**, when children become adults and leave their parents' homes. This is true even for Americans of Western European origin. In fact, as has often been suggested, "Parenthood for many Americans may be more important and more enduring than many marriages" (Lewis, 1990).

Although there is evidence that the parent-child bond usually survives for decades, unfortunately there is no one systematic theory that explains very well the continuities and discontinuities over time in parent-child relationships, especially in the latter stages of family life (Troll & Bengtson, 1979). There is research evidence, however, that suggests that interdependence (both emotional and instrumental), involvement, love, affection, trust, and respect often continue for many decades between adult children and their parents. (See Chapter 1 for its discussion and definition of interdependence.)

Even though the parent-child bond usually survives over decades, the roles of parents and their children usually change dramatically over time and greatly shift in emphasis. The role of midlife parents typically shifts away from that of being providers and protectors of their now-maturing children and becomes a largely affectionate role. On the other hand, young adult children become more independent and/or interdependent and achieve more equal footing with their parents.

ATTACHMENT THEORY

One theory that may be extended to help explain why relationships between adult children and their parents survive over decades is attachment theory (Ainsworth & Bowlby, 1991). **Attachment** refers to the emotional bonding that usually occurs between a mother and her newborn baby; the bonding leads a child to seek to remain in contact and proximity with his or her parents (Ainsworth, 1972; see Chapter 4 for a more complete discussion of attachment theory). For most parents and their children, however, attachment does not end with childhood but extends over their lifetimes (Bowlby, 1979; 1980). Evidence that attachment continues for many midlife parents and their young adult children is seen in their behavior—both parents and children continue calling on the telephone and writing letters to retain psychological contact with one another, particularly if they are separated by great distance.

Some adult children never leave home, or they continue to live very close to their parents, sustaining strong relationships with various extended family members that may persist over lifetimes. This is especially true of members of some ethnic groups, such as Asian-Americans, who may live next door to or a short distance down the street from their parents throughout their entire adult lives. We will now continue to examine the wide variety of patterns of family residence that begin when (most) adult children leave their family homes.

CHANGES IN FAMILY RESIDENCES AND RELATIONSHIPS

What does it feel like to become a young adult, to leave home, and to have very different relationships evolve between you and your father and mother? What does it feel like to leave the homes of your parents and to enter the adult world of work or college?

Some writers, focusing on the young adult generation, have called this period between leaving one's home of orientation and the forming of one's own home the "between families time" (Meyer, 1980).

> The young adult has probably just completed one of the stormiest phases in the entire life cycle . . . [This period] . . . allows the adolescent to proceed toward becoming fully responsible for his or her life, launching a career, and being able to relate fully in an intimate way with a non–family member. (Meyer, 1980, p. 71)

Leaving Home

One of the prime events of this between families time—in fact, the major event that heralds in this time period—is the young adult's leaving home. Most parents remember the first time that they left home as young adults. This event is often remembered as being bittersweet, since it probably produced a feeling of finally being independent but maybe also a feeling of intense loneliness.

When young adults leave home, their relationships with their parents inevitably undergo some change.

Over time, however, many parents tend to forget the pleasure and the pain involved in becoming adults. Young adults may find leaving home at first to be ominous and scary, since they are leaving familiar people, places, and things. How can they go off to college and leave their dog Patches or their favorite cat, whom they saw being born? Surely, mom and dad won't take as good care of Patches as they did. Maybe they should go to a nearby junior college, instead, or get a job for a year before going off to that large state school. These and other imagined fears may loom large and prevent the young adult from leaving home . . . at least for a time.

Likewise, parents may begin to fear the loss of that child, especially the child who is last to leave home. They, too, may not yet be prepared for the eventual separation from their child, and so they may unknowingly raise obstacles to their child's separation from them and the family home.

Most of those who do leave home for college, a job, the armed forces, a living together relationship, marriage, or to have a child, eventually separate themselves successfully from their parents, while still maintaining some abiding emotional attachment to their parents and maybe even geographical proximity. A successful transition, however, often depends upon parents' willingness for children to become independent, not just financially, but emotionally as well. It depends also upon the young adult's willingness to become self-reliant and his or her achievement of self-reliance and a resulting interdependence between the two generations (Lewis, 1990). Interdependence between a midlife parent and an adult child may result from the sharing of "assistance or support given usually, but not necessarily, in times of need by other members of one's family of orientation . . . or mutual assistance when unexpected financial need arises and offering a 'shoulder to cry upon' during personal tragedy" (Lewis, 1990, p. 71).

The Cozy and Crowded Nests   Pittman (1987) describes three kinds of leaving home crises in which young adults either do not leave home or repeatedly fail to become emancipated. He calls these the **cozy nest**, when one or more children do not leave home but the parents are not too concerned; the **crowded nest**, when a child is chronologically grown up but has not yet left home and is therefore creating family stress; and the **fatal flight**, when kids do leave home but are unsuccessful in becoming emancipated.

In our larger society the "cozy nest" is perceived as pathologic (often characterized by alcoholism, mental illness, or disabilities) and often it arises in single parent families or when adult children are divorced or mothers are widowed. However, the cozy nest syndrome is not seen as pathologic by all ethnic groups. Instead, it may be particularly valued as an expression of family closeness and togetherness, in which case only the family's therapist may be uncomfortable (Pittman, 1987).

In the "crowded nest" one or more adult children have not successfully left home, a situation that may produce great stress for nearly all family members. This is the type of home described by Haley (1980) in his book *Leaving Home*; children feel unable to leave such a home and may turn to drug use or exhibit other symptomatology to divert attention away from their parents' conflictual marriage. In essence they mistakenly believe that their parents' marriage will certainly fail if they leave home.

Finally, in the "fatal flight" type of crisis, young adults eventually leave home only to develop psychiatric or drug problems, become imprisoned, or commit suicide; it is as if these young adults would rather die than return home. If their parents' marriage has subsequently ended in divorce or a parent's death, young adults suffering from fatal flight may need a substitute for their family home. They may be able to live with older siblings, grandparents, or other relatives for a period, until they can become more independent and self-reliant.

Robert Lewis and his graduate students have been researching adult children's leaving home and returning home for more than two decades. Overall, they have found that extensive changes usually occur during the launching years, not only in terms of leaving home, but also in terms of children's returning home.

Returning Home

Leaving home is not the only family event that may result in stress for launching parents. The unexpected return home of a young adult, once thought to be permanently launched, also appears to produce stress in some families (Lewis & Roberts, 1979; Lowenthal & Chiriboga, 1972). Families therefore may not only experience stress due to the loss of a member but also experience stress due to the addition of a member—that is, the unexpected return of an adult child due, perhaps, to the young adult's divorce or loss of employment.

According to a 1983 U.S. census study, there is a growing tendency for young adults to either remain in or return to the homes of their parents. For example, between 1970 and 1983, the number of young adults 18 to 34 years old who lived with their parents skyrocketed by 84.8% (Clemens & Axelson, 1985). Actually, U.S. census figures may be an underestimate, especially of the number of adult children who temporarily live with their parents following the child's divorce, separation, or widowhood (Bane, 1976).

The reasons that adult children return home are quite varied, as Lewis learned in his studies. Many of the reasons are economic, such as the loss of a job or an insufficient income (compared to the midlife parents' income). Other reasons are the adult children's completing their educational training, finishing military service, divorcing, and having new employment opportunities in their home town (Lewis, Volk, & Duncan, 1989).

Co-Residence

Most young married couples in Western society do not want to live with their parents after they are married. But, the younger they are when they are married, the greater the likelihood that they will do so, at least for awhile—especially when they cannot afford living quarters of their own. Skyrocketing housing costs, which amount to between 60% and 90% of a young person's income, have kept many a young adult, even married, at home. High unemployment and poor wages are also responsible for adult children's returning and staying home.

A Growing Group   As we have noted, the percentage of adult children continuing to live with parents has increased during the recent past. Therefore, for midlife parents it is not an atypical experience to still have an adult child sharing the household. For example, in 1984, 37% of people 18 to 29 years old still lived with their parents in their parents' household (Glick & Lin, 1986). According to a 1987–1988 National Survey of Families and Households, 45% of parents aged between 45 and 54 who had at least one unmarried adult child had one or more adult children living with them at home (Aquilino, 1990). This "not-so-empty-nest" phenomenon (Strong & DeVault, 1993) has created a new stage in the family life cycle—"adult children at home" (Aldous, 1990). This living arrangement is most likely to occur when the midlife parent is divorced but not remarried, when relationship quality between parents and their children is high, and when parents hold positive attitudes toward the continued support of their adult children (Aquilino, 1991; Goldscheider & Goldscheider, 1989).

Ethnic Differences   African-Americans have been described as highly involved in a network of family support, with parents and adult children often sharing the same roof. Similarly, co-residence is common among Latino families (Paz, 1993). These patterns may reflect some combination of economic need and preference related to family values and norms (Ward & Spitze, 1992).

Consequences   The outcomes of co-residence are also likely to vary with the characteristics of relations between parent and child. For example, the older the child, the less likely it is that parents will be happy with this living arrangement (Clemens & Axelson, 1985).

According to Aquilino and Supple (1991), parents may benefit from continued involvement with their adult children and often enjoy social interaction with co-resident children. This is especially true among mothers and daughters. In contrast, fathers reported that time spent with adult children who had definite plans to leave home was more enjoyable. In other words, fathers were less satisfied with co-resident living arrangements with their divorced or separated adult children than they were with similar arrangements with never-married children. Overall, however, the majority of parents were highly satisfied with the co-resident living arrangement and described mostly positive relationships with their adult children (Aquilino & Supple, 1991).

The Empty Nest

If one focuses not on the maturing child, but instead on the midlife parents after children have left home, there is usually some attention given to the **empty nest**. Pittman relates the joke that describes a priest, a minister, and a rabbi debating the point at which life begins.

> The priest and minister debated about whether life begins at the moment of conception or at birth. But the rabbi, older and wiser, said, "You're both too young to know this, but life doesn't really begin until the kids leave home and the dog dies." (Pittman, 1987, p. 205)

The terms *empty nest* and *postparental couples* have a rather negative sound, but they are symbolic of the ways that both social scientists and society at large have viewed the period that stretches from the departure of the last child from the home until the parents' retirement. In fact, until recently this time was viewed by social scientists as a "time of crisis" and a major family discontinuity, since it marked the children's "desertion" of the home or abandonment of their parents (Lewis & Roberts, 1979).

More recent social research, however, has found that the majority of parents do not experience stress and crisis after all their children have left home. Instead, the majority of both fathers and mothers view the empty nest as "a time of relief" or a "second honeymoon." When a minority of postparental mothers do experience crisis and great unhappiness, it can typically be attributed to their overinvolvement or overprotectiveness of a child, to poor timing (that is, an unanticipated life event such as the sudden departure of a child for military service), or to failure to reorganize family relationships (that is, the parent-child dyad remains "stuck" in ways of relating that were appropriate when the child was much younger) (Lewis & Roberts, 1979).

CHANGES IN INTIMACY AND ATTACHMENT

As noted earlier in this chapter, largely because of the emotional attachment between parent and child, the parent-child bond usually survives after young adult children leave the home of their parents. Although there may be some decrease in the level and intensity of intimacy and affection between midlife parents and their young adult children, the bond between them may even grow stronger as the young adults begin to have children of their own.

In a study of the changing nature of parent-child relationships from early to late adolescence, Newman (1989) found that 11-year-olds were more likely to be confident about their parents' love for them than were 17-year-olds. Increased family conflict may occur as teenagers begin to assert their autonomy and independence. Adolescents often want rights and privileges but may have difficulty accepting responsibility. Although the families of adolescents frequently are characterized by conflict and strained relations, parental bonds generally remain strong (Gecas & Seff, 1991). In addition, there is a significant increase in emotional closeness between the generations once the children are in their 20s (Rossi & Rossi, 1990).

Concepts of Intimacy

Various words have been used to describe the affectional quality of these parent-child relationships, including closeness, enjoyment, understanding, trust, fairness, respect, affection, liking, loving, approving, accepting, and attachment. However, there has been relatively little research investigating parent-child sentiment and emotional ties felt once a child reaches adult-hood.

Management of Intimacy

Sex   Research on parent-child closeness has shown that affective dimensions of relationships seem to vary greatly by sex. In their study of nearly 800 undergraduates, Hagestad and Fagan (1974) found that both men and women felt closer to their mothers than to their fathers. There is a more robust stability in the affectional ties between women and their children than between men and their children (Rossi & Rossi, 1990). Recent research, however, has indicated that boys and girls in high school perceive their parents as equal with regard to support provided, support received, and family intimacy (Windle & Miller-Tutzauer, 1992). Each parent may serve somewhat different emotional functions for their young adult children, though, with mothers generally playing a nurturing, supportive role and fathers serving as the source of security and the keeper of the authority of the family (Gooden & Toye, 1984).

Familial Structure   A review of the literature on remarriage and step-families indicates that emotional bonds between stepparents and stepchildren are generally less close than parent-child ties in intact families and are more likely to be characterized by conflict (Coleman & Ganong, 1990). Marital tension often involves a coalition between mothers and the children, with fathers receding to the sidelines of family affection. Furthermore, young adults report lower levels of closeness to their recently divorced fathers, whereas relations with mothers were not affected (Cooney, 1994).

Timing of Parenthood   It seems that the timing of parenthood and age differences confront parents and their children with developmental issues. Rossi (1980) found that mothers who have their children later in life have more problematic relations with them in midlife than do women who bear their children earlier. Similarly, a younger father is more energetic and able to participate in active sports and other masculine activities with a son than is an older father (Rossi & Rossi, 1990). These researchers also found, however, that the larger the age difference between fathers and daughters, the closer are their relationships.

Disruptions of Emotional Bonds

As we have already noted, child launching can produce disruptions even in well-established family relationships, even though most parents appear to enjoy their empty nest and do not believe that they have suffered any permanent loss. But a minority of both fathers and mothers report great

---

Box 1

On Golden Pond

An illustration of how one father and daughter managed their intimacy issues can be taken from the award-winning film *On Golden Pond*, adapted for the screen by Ernest Thompson from his 1979 play, which won three Golden Globe Awards. Most viewers of this film become entranced with a subplot that links an aging Norman Thayer (Henry Fonda) with his adult daughter, Chelsea (played by Jane Fonda).

Sometime before the film begins, Norman and Chelsea have become estranged from each other. Chelsea, an only child, has lived far from her parents and has visited them infrequently because she perceives that Norman has never respected her. Chelsea attributes her father's lack of pride in her accomplishments to the fact that she is a woman. She is therefore jealous of the attention Norman showers on her potential stepson, Billy, and assumes that this attention is due to male bonding.

Affection and emotional exchanges are restored between this adult child and her father, however, when Chelsea challenges herself to learn to do a backward flip off the diving board. Chelsea and Norman are reconciled, and Norman gives his daughter a diving medal he had won in his youth, now a symbol of his pride in her accomplishments.

It is interesting that, just like the characters they played in this, Henry Fonda's last film, the actors Henry and Jane Fonda were a father and daughter in real life who had become estranged to some degree and who experienced a reconciliation by working together on this film. It seems that sometimes life can imitate art.

---

unhappiness when, especially, their last child leaves the home. Such an unfavorable impact was once believed to be more common for mothers, especially those, as mentioned earlier, who had been overinvolved, overcommitted, or overprotective of their children. It may seem strange to learn, therefore, that recently a sizable minority of fathers also have reported experiencing negative impacts, such as being disturbed and unhappy, after their last child left home.

Some Fathers Suffer Too   Two decades ago Lewis and his associates studied young adults' leaving and returning home and found that just about as many fathers as mothers reported experiencing distress at the departure of their last child—23% and 22%, respectively (Roberts & Lewis, 1981). Nearly one-fourth of the fathers in a study in one Georgia county reported great unhappiness. Who were these fathers? They

Many fathers suffer just as much as mothers when their adult children leave home.

were those who tended to have had fewer children; who perceived themselves to be more nurturing fathers; and who, it was also found, had somewhat unhappy marriages (Lewis, Freneau, & Roberts, 1979). These fathers presented what became a common theme: They discovered that their marriages and few friendships had become empty shells at about the same time their loved children were leaving home. They had spent their earlier lives earning an income, which their older children and working wives now needed less, and they had become more nurturing at a time their wives and children had less need to be nurtured.

Nearly a decade later, the same researchers surveyed similar mothers and fathers in another area of the United States, only to discover even larger numbers of fathers who reported disruptions in their emotional lives when children left home. For instance, although only 7% to 10% of the fathers were extremely or very distressed, in a sample of 325 fathers in Indiana and Michigan, 41% of the fathers reported negative and disturbed reactions to any of their children's leaving home. Looking only at cases in which the youngest child had left home, the percentage of fathers reporting distress actually doubles. Reports of distress were especially common among fathers who were farmers, suggesting not only an emotional loss, but an economic one as well—the loss of another farm hand (Lewis & Duncan, 1991).

In summary, adult children's leaving home appears to have an important, negative impact upon a significant minority of fathers and mothers. Other clinical reports and observations corroborate these survey data. These reports suggest that, because of cultural changes in both men's and women's gender roles—especially the increase in nurturing behavior among fathers—the number of fathers distressed at their children's leaving home appears to be growing.

CHANGES IN FAMILY POWER

Growing Independence

Throughout childhood and adolescence almost all children depend on their parents for support and help. The late teens is a time of transition in which young adults become more concerned with establishing independence from the controls and influence of their parents. By the time adolescence is completed, most young adults may have fairly well-developed ideas of dependence and independence. They are becoming more compe-

---

Box 2   **A Case Study**

A composite case study, drawn from the stories of several distressed midlife fathers, paints the following picture of a grieving father (Lewis & Roberts, 1979).

> Mr. W., aged 52, referred himself [to a therapist] for treatment of his depression and alcohol dependency. He contacted the therapist after a business associate refused to ride home with him, following a friendly evening of food and spirits.
>
> Mr. W.'s depression was traced back two years to the three-month period in which his two daughters, now aged 21 and 25, were married. His compulsive drinking had begun shortly after his second daughter's marriage.
>
> Mr. W. had always been very close to his daughters, having long discussions with them and taking them to many school and social activities. He played a good deal with them when they were young and took them to parks and camping trips every summer. When the daughters began to date, they often sought their father's counsel.
>
> Mr. W. realized in therapy that his daughters were still very important to him and that he missed seeing them on a daily basis. He was a loving father to them and received a great shock when they left almost simultaneously. It was hard for him to admit that he must share them now with their husbands.
>
> The loss of his daughters was compounded by the realization that his marriage was less than meaningful. He had made few friends in spite of the many organizations in which he had worked. In actuality, he had no one at the beginning of therapy with whom he could share his life.
>
> [Eventually] Mr. W. began to explore possibilities for enriching his marriage and developing new friendships among male acquaintances. (p. 29)

tent and, therefore, more capable of meeting their own material and emotional needs.

On the other hand, from the parental perspective, the emphasis changes from actually providing safety, protection, and comfort for a child to worrying about the older child's safety, protection, and comfort (Newman, 1989). The young person's wish for independence and autonomy, together with a continued need for support and affirmation, does complicate the parent-child relationships of this period.

Handling Conflict

As might be expected, relationships that involve relative power or independence between midlife parents and their adult children are not without conflict. Conflict often arises because of parent-child misunderstandings or when adult children do not behave as the parents have taught them. For example, it is not unusual for parents to question their grown sons' and daughters' choices of vocation, friends, and dating partners, their use of time and money, and many other decisions that young adults feel they have a right to make on their own. If parents continue to share their homes with adult children, these relationships will probably be less conflictual and even enhanced if the parents relinquish some of their parental authority, recognizing that their children's attitudes and values differ from their own (Miller & Glass, 1989).

The usual teacher-student roles may become reversed as adult children teach their parents the "new" lifestyles they believe the parents should try hard to understand. Parents may have problems dealing with the stressful demands of accepting the behavior and living arrangements of their children, which may go against their own socialization, beliefs, and value systems. Some parents may feel that their own parenting goals—such as helping children achieve success in careers, live certain lifestyles, or achieve a certain quality of life—must be accepted by their young adult children.

DETERMINANTS OF RESOURCE EXCHANGE

Most middle-aged parents tend to provide continued economic support for their children, even when the children are young adults. For young people who are attending college, parents typically provide a major part of the funds needed for their tuition and living expenses. Young adults may also need financial help to cover the expenses of a wedding and setting up their own households. Many parents also provide financial support through gifts. One married woman in her late 20s recalled how much help her parents gave her and her husband when their first baby was born in their second year of graduate school (Gibson, 1983):

> Mom and Dad gave us a gift of the crib, carriage, high chair, and even a washing machine. Without those and other presents they brought whenever they came to visit, life would have been awfully barren . . . we were so proud that we were self-sufficient. And we weren't, really. (p. 183)

Parents typically have had more experience with solving problems and handling complex emotions than their adult children have had. A young adult can regain a sense of security by touching home base—either by calling or by visiting in person. Parents can also help to replenish self-confidence in their frustrated children by reminding them of their past successes and commenting on the strength and the skills they have developed (Haines & Neely, 1987).

Proximity

Geographic distance reduces the frequency of social interaction and the opportunity to reveal needs and problems and consequently reduces the incidence of all types of help flowing between the generations (Rossi & Rossi, 1990). When parents and children live far apart, they usually maintain some contact through the mail and by telephone. The older the children, the more likely they are to maintain a separate year-round residence and the less likely they are to get daily support from their parents (Shehan & Dwyer, 1989). Employed college students are also more likely to maintain a separate residence and to exchange less help and other support with their parents than do their unemployed peers (Shehan & Dwyer, 1989).

Financial Aid

Adult sons give more financially to their parents than daughters do (Goldscheider & Goldscheider, 1991). Individuals who have several siblings tend to give more money to their parents than do peers from smaller families (Goldscheider & Goldscheider, 1991). In contrast, the more children the parents have reared, the less help they give to any individual adult child (Rossi & Rossi, 1990).

Goldscheider and Goldscheider (1991) found that parents with higher incomes contribute more to their children's college educations. In contrast, they found adult children with higher incomes tended to receive less support for educational expenses from their parents. Rossi and Rossi (1990) also indicate that parents with higher incomes tend to give more general financial help to their young adult children, whereas children tend to give more help to low-income than to high-income parents.

Family Structure

Family structure (for example, two-parent families versus single parents) also affects the amount of support exchanged between the generations. For example, growing up in a two-parent family contributes to children's educational attainment, since two parents can provide each child with more attention, adult modeling, and interaction than can one parent (Rossi & Rossi, 1990). In contrast, families headed by mothers and step-parent families are found to contribute less to the educational expenses of their children (Goldscheider & Goldscheider, 1991).

SUMMARY

This chapter has shown that relationships between parents and their children do not usually disappear when children become adults and leave their parents' home. Instead, the parent-child bond endures for the lifetimes of those involved. One of the best theories to explain this continuity of relationships between parents and their children is attachment theory.

This does not mean, however, that the relationships between midlife parents and their adult children do not evolve over time. On the contrary, there are many changes—in family residence, in family intimacy and attachment, in family power patterns, and in resource exchanges.

Contact and exchanges (financial, emotional, and other help) often continue between parents and their children after the launching years. Middle-aged Americans from many ethnic backgrounds continue to provide economic support for their children over many decades. Even after adult children have left the family to go out on their own, relationships between many parents and children remain close and caring. The quality of their future contact depends on the type of parenting, proximity between the generations, and certain characteristics of individual family members, such as sex, age, employment, and income, as well as other familial configurations.

Class Discussion Questions

1. Discuss the authors' assumption that "parenthood never ends." Especially discuss your thoughts on *why* most parent-child bonds in the United States survive longer than most marriages. How is this different for different ethnic groups and different religious groups?
2. Discuss the social and personal factors involved in adult children's choosing co-residence. What are the advantages and disadvantages of co-residence?
3. Socialization (teaching/learning to be a social being) goes both ways. Parents socialize their children about family relationships, but children also socialize their parents. Discuss both sides of this process, bringing in illustrations from your own family, if possible.
4. Discuss how parent-child emotional closeness is affected by the sex of the parent and the sex of the child.
5. Discuss the main factors that affect the amount of resources exchanged between young adults and their midlife parents.

Homework Assignments

1. Watch a popular TV show—for example, a soap opera or a family situation comedy—and observe how adult children and their midlife parents interact. What are the indicators of closeness and conflicts? What

resources are exchanged? When parents and adult children live together, how do they deal with issues associated with living under the same roof?

2. For two or more weeks collect articles from a local newspaper that illustrate family members helping other family members. Count the number of articles that illustrate adult children giving something to their middle-aged parents and those that illustrate the reverse. Then, write up your own analysis of the kinds of help different family members provide for one another. Finally, try to determine whether the newspaper pays more attention to one generation than another or applauds some kinds of helping behavior and not others. If it does, why do you think this is the case?

3. Choose a videotape at your local video store that examines some important topics related to the two generations that we have examined, but within an ethnic group other than your own. After viewing the video, write a paper analyzing these topics, including some comparisons of the two-generation family in that ethnic group and your own family.

Additional Readings

Brubaker, T. H. (1990). Families in later life: A burgeoning research area. *Journal of Marriage and the Family, 52,* 959–981.

Cooney, T. M., & Uhlenberg, P. (1992). Support from parents over the life course: The adult child's perspective. *Social Forces, 71* (1), 63–84.

Keller, M. J., & McArdle, M. (1985). Establishing intergenerational exchange opportunities. *Activities, Adaptation & Aging, 7* (2), 31–43.

Lewis, O. (1965). *La Vida: A Puerto Rican family in the culture of poverty—San Juan and New York.* New York: Vintage Books.

Lewis, R. A. (1990). The adult child and older parents. In T. H. Brubaker (Ed.), *Family relationships in later life* (2nd ed.) (pp. 68–85). Newbury Park, CA: Sage.

References

Ainsworth, M. D. S. (1972). Attachment and dependency: A comparison. In J. L. Gewirtz (Ed.), *Attachment and dependency.* Washington, DC: B. H. Winston.

Ainsworth, M. D. S., & Bowlby, J. (1991). An ethnological approach to personality development. *American Psychologist, 46,* 331–341.

Aldous, J. (1990). Perspectives on family change. *Journal of Marriage and the Family, 52,* 571–583.

Aquilino, W. W. (1990). The likelihood of parent–adult child co-residence: Effects of family structure and parental characteristics. *Journal of Marriage and the Family, 52,* 405–419.

Aquilino, W. W. (1991). Predicting parents: Experiences with co-residence adult children. *Journal of Family Issues, 12,* 323–342.

Aquilino, W. W., & Supple, K. R. (1991). Parent-child relations and parents' satisfaction with living arrangements when adult children live at home. *Journal of Marriage and the Family, 53,* 13–27.

Bane, M. J. (1976). *Here to stay: American families in the twentieth century.* New York: Basic Books.

Bowlby, J. (1979). *The making and breaking of affectional bonds.* New York: Tavistock.

Bowlby, J. (1980). *Attachment and loss. Vol. III: Loss, sadness and depression.* New York: Basic Books.

Clemens, A. W., & Axelson, L. J. (1985). The not-so-empty-nest: The return of the fledgling adults. *Family Relations, 34,* 259–264.

Coleman, M., & Ganong, L. H. (1990). Remarriage and stepfamily research in the 1980's: Increased interest in an old family form. *Journal of Marriage and the Family, 52,* 925–940.

Cooney, T. M. (1994). Young adults' relations with parents: The influence of recent parental divorce. *Journal of Marriage and the Family, 56,* 45–56.

Gecas, V., & Seff, M. (1991). Families and adolescents. In A. Booth (Ed.), *Contemporary families: Looking forward, looking back.* Minneapolis/St. Paul: National Council on Family Relations.

Gibson, J. T. (1983). *Living: Human development through the lifespan.* New York: Random House.

Glick, P. C., & Lin, S. (1986). More young adults are living with their parents: Who are they? *Journal of Marriage and the Family, 48,* 105–112.

Goldscheider, F. K., & Goldscheider, C. (1989). Family structure and conflict: Nest-leaving expectations of young adults and their parents. *Journal of Marriage and the Family, 51,* 87–97.

Goldscheider, F. K., & Goldscheider, C. (1991). The intergenerational flow of income: Family structure and the status of black Americans. *Journal of Marriage and the Family, 53,* 499–508.

Gooden, W., & Toye, R. (1984). Occupational dream, relation to parents, and depression in the early adult transition. *Journal of Clinical Psychology, 40,* 945–954.

Hagestad, G. O., & Fagan, M. (1974, October). *Patterns of fathering in the middle years.* Paper presented at the annual meeting of the National Council on Family Relations, St. Louis, MO.

Haines, J., & Neely, M. (1987). *Parents' work is never done.* Far Hills, NJ: New Horizon.

Haley, J. (1980). *Leaving home.* New York: McGraw-Hill.

Lewis, R. A. (1990). The adult child and older parents. In T. H. Brubaker (Ed.), *Family relationships in later life* (2nd ed.) (pp. 68–85). Newbury Park, CA: Sage.

Lewis, R. A., & Duncan, S. F. (1991). How fathers respond when their youth leave and return home. In D. R. Powell & D. Unger (Eds.), *Prevention in the human services.* New York: Haworth Press.

Lewis, R. A., Freneau, P. J., & Roberts, C. L. (1979). Fathers and the post-parental transition. *The Family Coordinator, 28,* 514–520.

Lewis, R. A., & Roberts, C. L. (1979). Postparental fathers in distress. *Psychiatric Opinion,* Nov./Dec., 27–30.

Lewis, R. A., Volk, R. J., & Duncan, S. F. (1989). Stresses on fathers and family relationships related to rural youth leaving and returning home. *Family Relations, 38,* 174–181.

Lowenthal, M. F., & Chiriboga, D. (1972). Transition to the empty nest: Crisis, challenge, or relief? *Archives of General Psychiatry, 26,* 8–14.

Meyer, P. H. (1980). Between families: The unattached young adult. In E. A. Carter & M. McGoldrick (Eds.), *The family life cycle: A framework for family therapy.* New York: Gardner.

Miller, R. B., & Glass, J. (1989). Parent-child attitude similarity across the life course. *Journal of Marriage and the Family, 51,* 991–997.

Newman, B. M. (1989). The changing nature of the parent-adolescent relationship from early to late adolescence. *Adolescence, 24,* 915–924.

Paz, J. J. (1993). Support of Hispanic elderly. In H. P. McAdoo (Ed.), *Family ethnicity* (pp. 177–183), Newbury Park, CA: Sage.

Pittman, F. S., III. (1987). *Turning points: Treating families in transition and crisis.* New York: W. W. Norton.

Roberts, C. L., & Lewis, R. A. (1981). The empty nest syndrome. In J. G. Howells (Ed.), *Modern perspectives in the psychiatry of middle age.* New York: Brunner/Mazel.

Rossi, A. S. (1980). Aging parenthood in the middle years. In P. B. Baltes & O. G. Brim, Jr. (Eds.), *Life span development and behavior* (Vol. 3, pp. 138–207). New York: Academic.

Rossi, A. S., & Rossi, P. H. (1990). *Of human bonding: Parent-child relations across the life course.* New York: Aldine de Gruyter.

Shehan, C. L., & Dwyer, J. W. (1989). Parent-child exchanges in the middle years: Attachment and autonomy in the transition to adulthood. In J. A. Mancini (Ed.), *Aging parents and adult children* (pp. 99–116). Lexington, MA: Lexington Books.

Strong, B., & DeVault, C. (1993). *Essentials of the marriage and family experience.* Minneapolis/St. Paul: West.

Thompson, E. (Author). (1979). *On golden pond* [Film]. I. P. C. Pictures.

Troll, L., & Bengtson, V. (1979). Generations in the family. In W. R. Burr, R. Hill, F. I. Nye, & I. L. Reiss (Eds.), *Contemporary theories about the family: Vol. 1, Research-based theories* (pp. 127–161). New York: Free Press.

Ward, R. A., & Spitze, G. (1992). Consequences of parent–adult child co-residence. *Journal of Family Issues, 13,* 553–572.

Windle, M., & Miller-Tutzauer, C. (1992). Confirmatory factor analysis and concurrent validity of the perceived social support–family measure among adolescents. *Journal of Marriage and the Family, 54,* 777–787.

Glossary

Attachment   The emotional bonding that usually occurs between a mother and her newborn baby; a strong, intimate tie between two people that persists across time

Cozy nest   When one or more adult children do not leave home, but the parents are not too concerned

Crowded nest   When a child is chronologically grown up but has not yet left home and is therefore creating family stress

Empty nest   The period that stretches from the departure of the last child from the home until the parents' retirement

Fatal flight   When young adult children leave home but are unsuccessful in becoming emancipated

Launching years   The period of time during which children become adults and leave their parents' homes

16

Forty-Forever Years? Primary Relationships and Senior Citizens

Judy C. Pearson
Ohio University

The author wishes to express her appreciation to Jennifer Waldeck for her assistance in locating research literature for this chapter.

he later years of our lives are a time when we experience a multitude of physical, emotional, social, occupational, and relational changes. Virtually all of these changes require shifts in the ways that we conduct our personal relationships. In this chapter we will examine the challenges older individuals encounter in maintaining primary relationships during this time—often well past the fortieth year of marriage. Even though we all want our primary relationships to last forever, few of us are prepared for the special hurdles we will encounter if we are successful in finding someone with whom to grow old.

NV & SD

Chapter Outline

- The Challenges of Primary Relationships in Later Years
- Resolving the Challenges of Primary Relationships in Later Years
- Relational Satisfaction in Later Years
- Summary

How do primary relationships in later life compare with those we have already discussed? Do they operate in the same ways, or are there different elements to think about? That is, are they better or worse, easier or more difficult, more or less satisfactory than primary relationships at earlier points in the life cycle? Bill Cosby (1987) observes:

> The essential ingredients for a fulfilling life are the same for young and old. Older people need not undergo a prescribed disengagement from life. Love, friendship, a feeling of connectedness with others, and a sense of humor remain critical to our sense of well-being. (p. 23)

384

Romantic stories and poetry suggest that long-term relationships are better as they extend into the autumns of our lives. Elizabeth Barrett Browning, for example, wrote, "Grow old along with me, the best is yet to be." On the other hand, cartoons, jokes, and other popular artifacts suggest that aging consists of the decay of the body and the mind, which, in turn, create negative spirals in our relationships. In this chapter we will explore both the negative and positive features of primary relationships in later life.

THE CHALLENGES OF PRIMARY RELATIONSHIPS IN LATER YEARS

The challenges encountered over the marital life span test even the most hardy partner, and the demands of marriage are perhaps even more difficult for couples in later life. The romanticized view of the **golden years**, in which couples see themselves growing old side by side, is not always realized. In this first section of the chapter we will explore some of the complications of primary relationships among older individuals. The chapter will highlight changes in sexuality and sex roles, retirement, chronic illness, institutionalization of one spouse, and death—and will identify some coping strategies that couples may use.

Change

Couples of any sexual orientation who remain together through their later years will experience many changes. They may experience more marital satisfaction, more relational commitment, and more interdependence. But other changes may not be so positive. Often increasing age brings decreased health and vigor, and such changes can affect sexual relations and intimacy (among other things) and can increase dependence on others (see Chapter 19).

Sexual Relations and Intimacy   The sexuality of seniors has not been thoroughly explored. However, there are a number of studies that help us understand it better. Popular wisdom suggests that older people do not enjoy active sex lives, but we will see later in this chapter that, in fact, more systematic investigations show that they do.

Nonetheless, age does bring changes to the sexual relationship. For example, a woman may not produce enough lubricating secretions for intercourse to be comfortable, and a man needs more stimulation to reach erection and orgasm. Illness or medication can affect arousal and response.

Psychological problems and relational difficulties, which can occur at any age, may also hamper sex.

Some older couples report that their only sexual problem is having to hide the fact that they are sexually active from their friends and family. They feel passion and pleasure, but others disapprove. The couples' children and friends, and even some professionals, are shocked or critical.

Other older people report that they become bored over time with the same partner. The lack of variety and change results in viewing sex as monotonous. Finally, some individuals fear rejection by their partners because they are less attractive or active than they were earlier. Women may be particularly susceptible to these concerns.

Just as sexuality changes, so does psychological intimacy. If one's marriage has been good, it seems to get even better. If the marriage has been unsatisfying, it becomes unbearable. The change in intimacy may occur because most of us change our priorities sometime after midlife (Hochman, 1993).

Sex Roles   Sex roles change over the life span. During earlier years, particularly at times of the child-rearing years, distinctive sex roles are not uncommon. As couples age both husbands and wives tend to adopt a more **unisex** pattern, in which their behaviors cannot be distinguished on a sex role continuum. In general, men are likely to become more nurturing of small children, increasingly dependent on their spouses, and more eager to engage in conversations and friendships. At the same time, women are likely to be independent and assertive. Greater understanding between women and men becomes possible, but confusion over these new roles is also possible.

Retirement

Sex-role crossover can coincide with retirement. Adjustments become necessary for both people in this transition period. The effects of a wife's retirement are relatively unexplored because of the fact that women's retirement from paid work roles is a relatively recent development. Thus the effects of wives' retirement on marital satisfaction is not yet clear (Brubaker & Hennon, 1982; Scanzoni & Szinovacz, 1980).

The effect of the husband's retirement on marital satisfaction, although more widely studied, is not clear either (Ekerdt & Vinick, 1991; Lee & Shehan, 1989; Pearson, 1989). Some couples find that the husband's retirement allows them hours to enjoy each other and their shared hobbies. Other couples find that the husband's retirement interferes with the independent activities that the wife has developed as a home-making mother.

Retirement sometimes leads to sex-role crossover for husbands.

Some changes may result in more positive outcomes. Men who have retired sometimes participate more in household tasks as one way to cope with retirement (Keither & Brubaker, 1979). For example, Harry Nelson, in a 54-year marriage, did almost no housework while he was working; today he does all of the vacuuming and grocery shopping for the couple. Like Ferne Nelson, most wives appreciate their husbands' increased participation (Aldous, 1978; Hill & Dorfman, 1982).

Retirement might not be disruptive for older couples, but some strains do occur. Men may question their identity or be unsure of how they are to spend their time. Women may find it disconcerting to have their husbands home all day. As one wife of a newly retired man quipped, "I married you for better or worse, but not for lunch." Clearly, retirement changes the relationship between the couple.

Chronic Illness

Another challenge to long-term relationships is ill health. Poussaint (1987) observes, "The 'best years of our lives' are frequently marred by a slow but inevitable decline in our physical and, occasionally, mental abilities" (p. 2). Many diseases are relatively slow moving and yet seriously debilitating. Alzheimer's disease, various forms of cancer, and heart disease may be detected years before they prove fatal. However, the insidious nature of such a disease can "kill" an individual's primary relationships long before it kills the physical body. For example, the kindly husband who has Alzheimer's disease may begin to physically abuse his wife. The cheerful wife who learns she has a fatal form of cancer may become withdrawn and depressed.

An increasing number of people are living to very old ages, and chronic illness marks the later years for many (Hansson, Jones, & Fletcher, 1990). Marital partners and other family members are increasingly called on to provide long-term care. Some interpersonal behaviors may have detrimental effects on the ill person. Fiske, Coyne, and Smith (1991), for example, have shown that a hostile critical attitude on the part of the caretaker results in psychological distress for the patient and greater distancing between the partners.

Institutionalization

Chronic illness may lead to **institutionalization**. Couples may find that one partner may eventually need more care than can be provided at home (Locker, 1976). Although the likelihood of becoming institutionalized is greater for individuals without families, it occurs increasingly for individuals who have spouses (Tobin & Kulys, 1981).

What is it like for a spouse to remain in the community after the partner has been institutionalized? Until recently, little attention was paid to the person left at home (Locker, 1981; Schmidt, 1987). In many ways the spouse experiences the same physiological, physical, and sociological reactions as a widow or widower does following the death of a partner (Rollins, Waterman, & Esmay, 1985). McPherson (1983) notes the contradictions in this person's role: On one hand, he or she is still married and has a commitment to another person but is not allowed the companionship normally associated with marriage. On the other hand, she or he is, for all intents and purposes, single but is unable to start a new life with a new partner.

The change in caregiving may also create distress. The spouse may have been consumed in providing extensive and personal care for the ill partner at home. Strangers now care for the partner. Impersonal professional attention may replace the personal care from a loving spouse. Occasionally, conflict arises between the spouse and the staff of the institution, and the visits between the institutionalized partner and the spouse may be emotionally disruptive.

Spouses who remain in the community have few norms and role models. Role loss, role ambiguity, and role conflict create additional difficulties (Rollins, Waterman, & Esmay, 1985; Schmidt, 1987). **Role loss** refers to what occurs when one no longer can fulfill a certain role because of life changes. **Role ambiguity** is the uncertainty people may feel about their changed roles. **Role conflict** refers to a clash among one's roles, which may occur at a time like this because individuals are suddenly expected to play different roles. The spouse who remains in the community faces loneliness as he or she attempts to manage day-to-day life without the partner. Nonetheless, she or he is called upon to be loyal to the institutionalized partner. For example, Sophia, who lives in northern Minnesota, institutionalized her husband Darrel a year and a half ago. She has always enjoyed hunting and fishing and was unable to do so for the many years that she served as Darrel's primary caretaker. Now that Darrel is institutionalized, she has formed a friendship with Harold, who is her hunting and fishing partner. Although the two do not have an intimate relationship, neighbors disapprove of Sophia's conduct and feel that she is being disloyal to her spouse.

Death

More often than not, chronic illness and institutionalization are precursors of death. The death of one member of the couple has two victims: the individual who loses his or her life and the widow or widower. A spouse's death may be devastating to the survivor. Widowed individuals experience greater risks of health problems and economic hardship than their married counterparts (Bound, Duncan, Laren, & Olernick, in press; Smith, 1991; Zick & Smith, in press). The economic, mental, and physical well-being of the surviving spouse show dramatic declines (see, for example, Holden, Burkhauser, & Myers, 1986; Hurd & Wise, 1989; Lopata & Brehm, 1986; Smith & Zick, 1986; Zick & Smith, 1986, 1988). Depression is common for both women and men after the death of a spouse (Zisook & Shuchter, 1991).

Does one's sex affect adjustment to a spouse's death? The literature is mixed (Farnsworth, Pett, & Lund, 1989). No major differences between widowed men and women have been shown in several studies (see, for example, Clayton, Halikas, & Maurice, 1972; Lund, Caserta, & Dimond, 1986). Some research, though, has suggested that widowers are at greater risk than widows, especially in their health (Gerber, Rusalem, Hannon, Battin, & Arkin, 1975). However, Carey (1979) determined that widowers are better adjusted than widows, even when individuals are categorized by income, length of forewarning of the death, education, and age.

Whether the surviving spouse is male or female, he or she must reconcile the loss and rearrange his or her life without the partner. In all cases there are three kinds of loss to be dealt with, not just one:

1. Emotional ties with the lost partner must either be coped with or severed.
2. The role of husband or wife must be disbanded or reorganized.
3. Everyday routines must be revised. (Hagestad & Smyer, 1982).

Leroy, 85, lost his wife Natasha last year. He cries easily at the mention of her name. He still makes liver and onions every Wednesday night, even though it was Natasha, not he, who liked this meal. He continues to attend a couples group at his church, although as a "single" he is beginning to feel a little out of place. Leroy has yet to reconcile his loss in his behavior.

RESOLVING THE CHALLENGES OF PRIMARY RELATIONSHIPS IN LATER YEARS

Primary relationships in later years provide a summons to action. Older people may answer the questions that are posed by seeking and gaining social support, remarrying, renewing close relationships with family members, finding solace in religion, maintaining their health, developing relational competence, and relying on sexuality and intimacy.

Social Support

Social support is "support accessible to an individual through social ties to other individuals, groups, and the larger community" (Lin, Ensel, Simeone, & Kuo, 1979, p. 109). The function of social support is to facilitate coping in stressful situations. In general, the more social support an individual receives, the more she or he is protected from the stressors of

life. Older people, like their younger counterparts, need socially supportive networks.

Social support does not always function in a positive manner, however. Hansson, Jones, and Fletcher (1990) note that "negative interactions
within support networks may overshadow many positive effects of support" (p. 451). For example, some older persons may resent being helped
down stairs or be offended when they are offered help, which (to them)
suggests that they cannot help themselves. Social support may create problems rather than solutions when older adults are treated with stereotypic
responses, such as assuming that they are not interested in physical activities or that they are not excited by the prospects of dating. Stereotypic beliefs about age-related declines may blind network members to the particular needs of individual older people: Not every older person needs help
crossing the street! Similarly, social support may be more harmful than
helpful when individual differences in relational competence are not considered—for example, a newly single older person may be keenly aware of
strategies to initiate relationships, but individuals in the social network
may not know of the person's abilities. Finally, changes in the social network itself, and uncertainty about those changes, may create stressful,
rather than supportive, situations. For instance, the death of a life-long
close friend may make an older person feel suddenly very vulnerable and
alone.

Women and men are not provided with the same amount of social
support. Antonucci and Akiyama (1987) found that adult women of all
ages report larger social networks than do men. They are also more likely
than men to receive support from multiple sources. Men are more likely
to rely on their spouses exclusively. For both women and men, however,
the quality of support—rather than the quantity of support—is related to
feelings of well-being. For example, older people who have a number of
people calling them on the telephone and checking on them may be less
satisfied than older people who have just one or two phone calls from
someone very special to them each day. In general, positive perceptions of
social support are more important to the well-being of women than to
men. In other words, women are more likely to qualify their support than
are men, while men are more likely to accept all forms of social support as
relatively the same.

As we discussed earlier, when one member of the couple becomes less
capable, he or she may need to be institutionalized, and for many people,
placing a spouse in institutional care represents a crisis. At this point, the
spouse remaining in the community tends to stand alone, and she or he
may be in particular need of reassurance and connectedness with others
(Hansson, Jones, & Fletcher, 1990; Nathan, 1986). He or she also needs
assistance in dealing with the new circumstances and needs to learn about
available social services. Some communities offer specific support groups
for spouses remaining in the community. These groups work to allay any

guilt the spouse may feel. They share strategies that others have used to cope with their new situations. They also encourage the expression of feelings of loss and loneliness. Spouses remaining in the community are put in contact with others who are living through similar circumstances.

The death of one's spouse may represent another crisis in which swift social support is crucial. As time passes, and one is labeled a widow, different kinds of support may be appropriate. Morgan (1989) found that relationships with friends and family members were viewed as both positive and negative among widows. About 40% of these relationships were negative, with family members receiving more negative references than friends did. It seems, therefore, that friends, rather than family members, may be more valuable sources of support after the loss of one's spouse.

Remarriage

A new marriage may fill the void left by widowhood or divorce (Lopata & Brehm, 1986; Zick & Smith, 1988). Smith, Zick, and Duncan (1991) observe, "Remarriage is one of the most important determinants of physical and economic well-being among the widowed" (p. 361). The likelihood of remarriage fluctuates based on age, sex, race, and education. Cleveland and Gianturco (1976), for example, found that at all ages, widowers have a higher likelihood of remarriage; widows have a lower probability of ever remarrying at all ages, and the chances of remarriage declined substantially with increasing age. If the widow is African-American, she is even less likely to remarry (Spanier & Glick, 1980). Remarriage rates for women may be even lower if they have a college degree (Goldman, Westoff, & Hammerslough, 1984). Smith, Zick, and Duncan (1991) summarized their findings as follows:

Remarriage may improve older individuals' economic and physical conditions.

> Among middle-aged widows, blacks and those with dependent children in the home have lower rates of remarriage. For middle-aged widowers, living in urbanized areas limits the prospects of remarriage. For older widowers, education and, to some extent, economic status appear to have positive effects on the remarriage rates. Overall, age and time since widowhood have the strongest and most consistent effects on remarriage rates for different widowed groups. (p. 361)

Remarriage may serve to improve the economic and physical condition of the widowed, but it appears that widowed men are more likely than widowed women to reap the benefits. This trend may continue in the future, as women continue to live longer than men. At the same time, widowers who choose not to remarry or who cannot remarry also will have more to lose: Widowed men who do not remarry have higher rates of mortality following widowhood than do widowed women who do not remarry (Smith, Zick, & Duncan, 1991).

Relationships with Other Family Members

Most older people rely on, and appreciate, their familial relationships. Researchers have established that the importance and nature of interaction between parents and their children is different for women and men. Specifically, older women had higher life satisfaction when they were closer to their family and when their children agreed with them about such issues as child-rearing and management of money. Their self-esteem was higher when their children provided them with psychological support and emotional security and lower when the number of letters or gifts increased—older women may value human contact more than they do written or gratuitous evidence of relationships. The Castelluccios, for example, had a large family of six children. Today the children live all over the country, and one son lives in Europe. The children generally have successful careers, and they are very good about sending Christmas and birthday gifts. They also write fairly regularly, but they rarely have time to visit their parents. Mrs. Castelluccio laments the situation.

Older couples also value relationships with their grandchildren. The relationships between grandparents and grandchildren, in particular, have been shown to be extremely strong (Rosebud-Harris, 1982). About half of older grandparents in one study—those 65 years old or older—saw their grandchildren (some of whom are adults) every day or so; nearly 30% saw them every week or so (Kivett, 1980; Webb, 1985). About 43% of undergraduate college women in another study reported they felt quite close or extremely close to their grandparents (Hoffman, 1979–1980). Other young adults have explained that the motive for their visits with grandparents is to share quality time (Robertson, 1975). Shufen, a college sophomore, explained that her grandparents do not seem to make judgments about her to the same extent that her parents tend to, and she thus prefers to spend time with the grandparents when she goes home for a visit.

What do grandchildren and their grandparents talk about? Webb (1985) identified seven topics that were reported as being discussed by at least 30% of adult grandchildren. These topics are (in order of likelihood of being discussed) family, school and education, health (usually the grandparent's), dating and marriage, work (both the grandchild's and the grandparent's), travel, and food.

Religion

Religion has an increased importance for a large number of people as they grow older (Ainlay & Smith, 1984; Hunsberger, 1985). Does religion provide assistance to the older individual in dealing with life stresses? The jury is still out.

The importance of religion is unclear because the definition of *religion* that is often used is crude. Religion is sometimes simply equated with church attendance or activity (Herriott & Kiyak, 1981). Rosik (1989) suggests that better methods of assessing the importance of religion are available, particularly those based on intrinsic-extrinsic (I-E) religious orientation dimensions (Allport & Ross, 1967; Gorsuch, 1984). An **intrinsic religious orientation** is an orientation toward religion as a goal in itself; with an **extrinsic religious orientation**, religion is used as a means to another end, such as increasing participation in social events. In general, an extrinsic orientation is related to poorer adjustment. People who view religion as a goal in and of itself, rather than as a means to another end, seem to fare better (Rosik, 1989).

Health

Although it may be surprising, good health may be an outcome of satisfying relationships with others (see Chapter 3). Our physical, psychological, and relational health are highly correlated. Health is also a predictor of other positive features of the later years. Farnsworth, Pett, and Lund (1989) found that self-reported personal health was the major predictor of successful management of loss and well-being for both divorced and widowed individuals. People with good health reported more satisfactory outcomes. Elisha and Curtis were married nearly 60 years when Curtis died. Throughout their marriage the couple played golf, swam, and took long walks. Elisha affirms that she has coped with Curtis's death by maintaining her physical regimen after his death.

Relational Competence

Social support, remarriage, relationships with other family members, religion, and health are all important in general to positive outcomes for older people. However, we should keep in mind that the elderly are not a homogeneous group. Older people are as varied as their younger cohorts are.

One individual difference that sets the successful older person apart from less successful individuals in the same age range is relational competence. Researchers Hansson, Jones, and Fletcher (1990) identify the satisfied and successful older person as someone who is actively engaged in life. They hypothesize that some seasoned adults can assess their skills and dispositions, estimate their coping options, join supportive relationships, and resolve difficulties that arise within such relationships more competently than can others of similar chronological age. Hansson and associates refer to such people as **relationally competent**. They suggest that this term "encompasses a mix of temperamental, cognitive and emotional characteristics that facilitate meeting people and developing potentially useful relationships, but also help one to meet the needs of relational partners, strengthening and bolstering the relationships over long and perhaps stressful periods of time" (p. 454). Individuals who are relationally competent are probably more likely to have a variety of friendships and acquaintances. This network of social resources may better enable them to cope with difficulties and manage stressful situations (Hobfoll, 1988).

Sexuality and Intimacy

As we observed earlier, sexuality and intimacy are not the exclusive property of young people. Edward Brecher (1984) reported that the vast majority of men and women over 50 are still sexually active (by intercourse, masturbation, or other means). Two-thirds of unmarried individuals over the age of 70 remain sexually active. Couples may report a decreased frequency of intercourse, but they report a qualitative increase. Sex is less intense, but more satisfying.

Bretschneider and McCoy (1988) found similar results. They questioned 200 men and women from age 80 to 102. About half of these individuals said that sex was at least as interesting and important to them now as it had been in the past. Studies such as these support Janet Belsky's (1989) comment, "The 70s are far from a sexual death knell."

Marsiglio and Donnelly (1991) examined sexual behavior among married people who were 60 years of age and older. About 53% of the entire sample—and 24% of those 76 years of age and older—reported having had sexual relations at least once within the past month. Further, individuals who had been sexually active within the past month were active on an average of once a week.

Nonetheless, sexuality and intimacy change as couples become older. Some of these changes create problems. But they may also become part of the solution. The interpretation of the changes is critical in determining whether a person views sexuality and intimacy as a burden or a gift. Couples in lasting, loving relationships enjoy and describe highly satisfying sex lives. They agree that they often must adapt to physical limitations and become less "athletic" in their behavior and positions. They describe sexual activity as "sweeter" and say they take more "time to pleasure each other" (Pearson, 1992).

In some ways sexuality improves because of changes in hormonal levels and external pressures. Karlen (1992) addresses the positive side of seasoned sexuality:

> Nature sets young men and women at odds, victims of raging hormones and chaotic feelings. Young men want love, but their androgens (male hormones) drive them toward clocklike sexual release. . . . Young women feel desire, but society and their neuro-

hormonal systems focus them more on love and intimacy. . . . Slowly men learn that having regular sex demands emotional commitment. Women learn that keeping love means erotic commitment. They accommodate. . . . In fact, aging offers men and women a chance to understand each other as never before, and to find greater sensuality together. (pp. 52–53)

Women and men are better able to understand each other because of the changing nature of their sex roles. Women and men become more alike, as was noted earlier. Women become increasingly assertive and less inhibited, both in and out of bed. The fear of pregnancy is gone. The demands of child-rearing have lessened. Their levels of estrogens (female hormones) are lower, whereas the relative level of androgens (male hormones) is higher. Physical and psychological changes combine to make their desire more like men's. A woman can better understand a man's frank wish for pleasure and release—she herself may now feel and express it more openly.

Meanwhile, men learn that desire, arousal, and orgasm do not always occur simultaneously. Their drive for orgasm becomes less urgent and their interest in romance becomes more important. Their feelings mirror those of young women, who often do not separate sex from intimacy. Touching and foreplay become as meaningful as orgasm.

These sex role shifts may solve previous sexual problems. They may improve satisfactory sexual lives. They surely help explain one of the conclusions offered perennially by older couples that the quality of their sex lives has improved. Warmer and more rewarding sex lives may be a function of the greater understanding that is possible because of physical and psychological changes.

The qualitative improvement in sexuality over time may affect gay relationships as well as heterosexual ones, as Karlen (1992) observes:

Gay men may find that as sexual drive seems less imperious with age, the intimacy and stability of relationships increase. Older lesbians may find that a distance they once felt between romance and sex has shrunk. Thus for them, as for heterosexual couples, the quality of sex may actually be enriched by age. (p. 53)

Some physical changes may intrude on satisfying sexual relationships. Both women and men may experience some discomfort or difficulties in reaching orgasm because of normal changes. In addition, illness, medication, depression and conflict may hamper sex.

Most of these problems can be solved, however. Artificial lubricants and different foreplay and coital positions all reduce the effects of physical aging. Honesty and openness between partners as well as the development of a more positive sexual attitude can enhance one's sexual pleasure. Karlen (1992) concludes, "Discovering or rediscovering climax in maturity is not rare" (p. 54).

Psychological intimacy is often strengthened during this time, too. People become increasingly intimate with each other and even with themselves. Some people gain a deeper awareness of who they are after their fiftieth or sixtieth birthday. The later years become a time to explore previous behaviors, to risk new actions, and to grow in a variety of ways.

One characteristic that happily married older couples possess is their knack for **positive distortion** in their perceptions of their partners. The stories of older, happily married couples were documented in *Lasting Love: What Keeps Couples Together* (Pearson, 1992). Although the partner might look less than ordinary to an uninvolved observer, spouses routinely defined him or her as "handsome," "good looking," "sexiest man I know," and "the most beautiful woman in the world." This ability to positively distort has side benefits to one's sex life.

Most people are not physically perfect in their prime, and they are even more physically flawed in the later years. Sometimes people attempt to maintain their youthfulness by finding a younger partner. This solution has limited benefits, however, and may "boomerang," causing the older partner to feel even older by comparison.

People in satisfying relationships probably learn to overlook the signs of age in their partner. They may recall how their partners appeared to them in the early days of their relationship rather than how they have become over time. The wrinkles, the sags, and the scars are smoothed, lifted, and faded away. As one women in her 80s wrote: "People who have spent a lifetime together see each other not only as they are but also retain an image of how the other looked in the early days, like a double exposure that hides to a large extent the telltale signs of the passage of time" (Karlen, 1992, p. 54). If older lovers do not see each other through rose-colored glasses, they certainly evidence a strong astigmatism.

Long-term lovers have the advantages that life experiences offer. They share with younger couples the desire to be sexual and intimate with a partner. Karlen (1992) provides an apt observation.

> We never outgrow the need to be intimate, to give and re-
> ceive pleasure with the hands, the skin, the entire body. At any
> age physical love is a tonic, an affirmation, a tie to life and to
> other people. . . . And maturity can bring the ripeness to keep ex-
> panding and enriching sexuality. (p. 57)

RELATIONAL SATISFACTION IN LATER YEARS

Primary relationships in later years may be deeply satisfying or sadly disappointing. The happiness or unhappiness of earlier years may be exaggerated or exacerbated now. Hochman (1993) reminds us, "Most mental health experts agree that after children have left the house, good marriages get better; poor ones become unbearable or not fulfilling" (p. 17).

For most people, the later years are marked by increased companionship for each other. Spouses tend to provide less personal information to each other because they know each other "by heart." They have developed idiosyncratic ways of communicating with each other that are often not understood by outsiders. In general, communication becomes more implicit. Couples tend to be less analytic and more noncommittal. They exhibit a passive and congenial style (Zietlow & Sillars, 1988).

Marital satisfaction has been widely studied in relationships of all stages. Happiness in the later stages may be lowered because of some of the transitions and changes that occur during this period. Retirement, chronic illness, institutionalization, and other factors may mar the patina on the perfect relationship. Couples who are generally satisfied learn strategies of adjustment to these "slings and arrows of outrageous fortune." Galvin (1993) concludes, "For couples in good health, this stage may truly be the 'golden years of communication' " (p. 98).

For many decades, marital theorists and researchers have reported a curvilinear relationship in marital satisfaction. Married couples reported the greatest levels of happiness in their early married years and toward the end of their married lives (Glenn & McLanahan, 1982). Indeed, Pearson (1989) wrote this about the couple in their later years:

> The couple may be happier at this point than at any other time, except for the beginning of their marriage. Marital satisfaction and overall life satisfaction fluctuate in a consistent way throughout the adult's family life cycle. (p. 229)

A recent study throws sand in the gears of this marital theory, however. Vaillant and Vaillant (1993) examined marital satisfaction in two ways. Like other researchers, they asked couples in their later years to recall their happiest and unhappiest marital periods. As noted above, past research had shown that most couples reported their greatest happiness in the earliest years of their marriage and in the latest years; they reported less happiness in the middle years, with the lowest satisfaction at about 20 years of marriage. Vaillant and Vaillant found this same curvilinear pattern, although it was weak. However, because they studied the same couples over a period of 40 years, Vaillant and Vaillant were able to measure marital satisfaction in another way: by having couples in various life-stages describe their current marital happiness. When they studied marital happiness in this way, the U–curve disappeared. Marital satisfaction instead remained generally stable, especially in the middle and later years. Vaillant and Vaillant (1993) concluded:

> The couples did not differ in their assessment of the stability of their marriage, or in their closeness to separation or divorce, or in their mutual sexual satisfaction. The difference between the spouses came only in their assessment of the difficulty of solving

disagreements, which seemed for the wives to become more difficult over time. (p. 230)

This revolutionary study suggests that marital satisfaction may not fluctuate over the life-cycles as many earlier studies suggested. Earlier results may have been a function of the nature of the investigations. In other words, over time, couples remember happy and unhappy periods differently. When older couples are asked to reflect upon their past marital lives, they may report greatest happiness at the present and in the far distant past. The child-bearing years, the years when adolescent children are in the home, and the period of launching the children are reported to be less satisfactory in retrospect. When couples are asked about their marital satisfaction as they are living through each stage, however, their responses may show the levels of satisfaction to be comparable.

Couples who have remained together and are reasonably happy show a commitment to the relationship and a new level of interdependence based on years of interaction. Marital satisfaction in these later years is also related to some other factors—for example, life satisfaction, global well-being, mental health, and psychological well-being—for both women and men, but especially for elderly women (Glenn & Weaver, 1981; Thompson & Nussbaum, 1988). Similarly, marital satisfaction is positively related to morale; again, this is especially true for the females in the relationships (Lee, 1978, p. 131). Finally, the husbands' perception of the marriage, the positive dimension of well-being, and physical health all predict women's well-being but do not predict men's well-being (Quirouette & Gold, 1992). Such studies illustrate the notion that husbands and wives show different levels of responsiveness to other personal and relational qualities.

Marriage is clearly better for men than it is for women, using health, self-ratings, and reactions to family events as criteria. Married men are in better mental health than are married women, and unmarried women are in better mental health than are unmarried men (Gotlib & Hooley, 1988; Taillefer, 1987). Men also give their marriages higher marks than do women (Akiyama & Antonucci, in press; Depner & Ingersoll-Dayton, 1985; Weishaus & Field, 1988). "His" marriage is better than "her" marriage because traditional female roles are more difficult and demanding than are traditional male roles (Barnet & Baruch, 1987; Methorst, 1984). Women are put at greater risk for psychological distress—serving as a wife and mother entails greater emotional reactivity to family events compared to being a financial provider.

These difficulties are even more pronounced in older marriages. Quirouette and Gold (1992) observe, "In older cohorts in particular, women were expected, by virtue of their family caregiving role, to be attentive to their husbands' well-being and satisfaction and to respond physically and emotionally to their needs throughout marriage" (p. 258). Older women, compared to older men, receive fewer confidences and reassurances within their marriages (Depner & Ingersoll-Dayton, 1985). A recent study confirmed previous consistent evidence showing that "older married women are more responsive to their spouses' global, marital, and physical well-being than are older married men" (Quirouette & Gold, 1992, p. 268).

The older couple may also continue to have favorable relationships with others in their family. Older adults identified affection, assistance, respect, responsibility, and open communication as expectations they have of their adult children. Their desired relationships were marked by warmth, sharing, affection, and avoidance of direct interference in each others' lives (Blieszner & Mancini, 1987).

SUMMARY

An increasing number of people will find themselves in the same primary relationships, from youth into their later years. These relationships must endure a variety of changes. Retirement, chronic illness, institutionalization, and death are all summonses to action in the later years. How do couples resolve these problems? They find solutions in maintaining social support, entering into remarriage, establishing close relationships with other family members, finding solace in religion, maintaining their health, developing relational competence, and relying on sexuality and intimacy.

Class Discussion Questions

1. How do primary relationships in the later years compare with primary relationships at your age? Compare and contrast the advantages and disadvantages of relationships at each stage.
2. What would be the ideal relationship for you in your later years? Would you prefer to be married, cohabiting, living alone, or residing with relatives? What factors influence your decision? Do you know people in each of these situations? How do they cope with their lifestyle?

Homework Assignments

1. Interview an older couple. Try to determine the problems they experience and how they cope with those problems. What are their greatest sources of joy? What are their greatest concerns? When was their relationship happiest? Encourage them to tell stories describing their relationship.
2. List 10 or 15 weekly television programs. How many of them include people in their later years in primary relationships? How are those relationships depicted? What do the media tell people about relationships in later years? How many of these messages are based on stereotypes?

Additional Readings

Belsky, J. (1989). *Here tomorrow: Making the most of life after 50.* Baltimore: Johns Hopkins University Press.

Brubaker, T. (Ed.). (1990). *Family relationships in later life.* Newbury Park, CA: Sage.

Hunter, S., & Sundel, M. (Eds.). (1989). *Midlife myths: Issues, findings, and practical implications.* Newbury Park, CA: Sage.

Pearson, J. C. (1992). *Lasting love: What keeps couples together.* Dubuque, IA: William C. Brown.

Pearson, J. C. (1993). *Communication in the family: Seeking satisfaction in changing times* (2nd ed.). New York: HarperCollins.

References

Ainlay, S. C., & Smith, R. D. (1984). Aging and religious participation. *Journal of Gerontology, 39,* 357–363.

Akiyama, H., & Antonucci, T. C. (in press). An examination of sex differences in social support in mid and late life. *Sex Roles.*

Aldous, J. (1978). *Family careers: Developmental changes in families.* New York: Wiley.

Allport, G. W., & Ross, J. M. (1967). Personal religious orientation and prejudice. *Journal of Personality and Social Psychology, 5,* 432–443.

Antonucci, T. C., & Akiyama, H. (1987). Social networks in adult life and a preliminary examination of the convoy model. *Journal of Gerontology, 42,* 519–527.

Barnet, R. C., & Baruch, G. K. (1987). Social roles, gender, and psychological distress. In R. C. Barnet, L. Biener, & G. K. Baruch (Eds.), *Gender and stress* (pp. 122–143). New York: Free Press.

Belsky, J. (1989). *Here tomorrow: Making the most of life after 50.* Baltimore: Johns Hopkins University Press.

Blieszner, R., & Mancini, J. A. (1987). Enduring ties: Older adults' parental role and responsibilities. *Family Relations, 36,* 176–180.

Bound, J., Duncan, G. J., Laren, D. S., & Olernick, L. (in press). Poverty dynamics in widowhood. *Journal of Gerontology.*

Brecher, E. M. (1984). *Love, sex, and aging.* Boston: Little, Brown.

Bretschneider, J. G., & McCoy, N. L. (1988). Sexual interest and behavior in healthy 80- to 102-year-olds. *Archives of Sexual Behavior, 17,* 109–129.

Brubaker, T. H., & Hennon, C. B. (1982). Responsibility for household tasks: Comparing dual-earner and dual-retired marriages. In M. Szinovacz (Ed.), *Women's retirement: Policy implications of recent research* (pp. 205-219). Beverly Hills, CA: Sage.

Carey, R. G. (1979). Weathering widowhood: Problems and adjustment of the widowed during the first year. *Omega, 10,* 163–174.

Clayton, P. J., Halikas, J. A., & Maurice, W. L. (1972). The depression of widowhood. *British Journal of Psychiatry, 120,* 71–77.

Cleveland, W. P., & Gianturco, D. T. (1976). Remarriage after widowhood: A retrospective method. *Journal of Gerontology, 31,* 99–103.

Cosby, B. (1987). *Time flies.* New York: Doubleday.

Depner, C. E., & Ingersoll-Dayton, B. (1985). Conjugal social support: Patterns in later life. *Journal of Gerontology, 40,* 761–766.

Ekerdt, D. J., & Vinick, B. H. (1991). Marital complaints in husband-working and husband-retired couples. *Research on Aging, 13,* 364–382.

Farnsworth, J., Pett, M. A., & Lund, D. A. (1989). Predictors of loss management and well-being in later life widowhood and divorce. *Journal of Family Issues, 10,* 102–121.

Fiske, V., Coyne, J. C., & Smith, D. A. (1991). Couples coping with myocardial infarction: An empirical reconsideration of the role of overprotectiveness. *Journal of Family Psychology, 5*(1), 4–20.

Galvin, K. H. (1993). First marriage families: Gender and communication. In L. Arliss & D. Borisoff (Eds.), *Women and men communicating: Challenges and changes* (pp. 86–101). Fort Worth, TX: Harcourt Brace Jovanovich.

Gerber, I., Rusalem, R., Hannon, N., Battin, D., & Arkin, A. (1975). Anticipatory grief and aged widows and widowers. *Journal of Gerontology, 30,* 225–229.

Glenn, N. D., & McLanahan, S. (1982). Children and marital happiness: A further specification of the relationship. *Journal of Marriage and the Family, 44,* 63–72.

Glenn, N. D., & Weaver, C. N. (1981). The contribution of marital happiness to global happiness. *Journal of Marriage and the Family, 43,* 161–168.

Goldman, N., Westoff, C. F., & Hammerslough, C. (1984). Demography of the marriage market in the United States. *Population Index, 50,* 5–25.

Gorsuch, R. L. (1984). Measurement: The boom and bane of investigating religion. *American Psychologist, 39,* 228–236.

Gotlib, I. H., & Hooley, J. M. (1988). Depression and marital distress: Current status and future directions. In S. W. Duck (Ed.), *Handbook of personal relationships* (pp. 543–580). New York: Wiley.

Hagestad, G. O., & Smyer, M. A. (1982). Dissolving long-term relationships: Patterns of divorcing in middle age. In S. W. Duck (Ed.), *Personal relationships, Vol. 4: Dissolving personal relationships* (pp. 155–187). New York: Academic Press.

Hansson, R. O., Jones, W. H., & Fletcher, W. L. (1990). Troubled relationships in later life: Implications for support. *Journal of Social and Personal Relationships, 7,* 451–463.

Herriott, M., & Kiyak, H. A. (1981). Bereavement in old age: Implications for therapy and research. *Journal of Gerontological Social Work, 3,* 15–43.

Hill, E. A., & Dorfman, L. T. (1982). Reaction of housewives to the retirement of their husbands. *Family Relations, 31,* 195–200.

Hobfoll, S. E. (1988). *The ecology of stress.* Washington, DC: Hemisphere.

Hochman, G. (1993). Over-50s and the new intimacy. *New Choices for Retirement Living, 33,* 14–17.

Hoffman, E. (1979–1980). Young adults' relations with their grandparents: An exploratory study. *International Journal of Aging and Human Development, 10,* 299–309.

Holden, K. C., Burkhauser, R. B., & Myers, D. A. (1986). Income transitions at older stages of life: The dynamics of poverty. *The Gerontologist, 26,* 292–297.

Hunsberger, B. (1985). Religion, age, life satisfaction, and perceived sources of religiousness: A study of older persons. *Journal of Gerontology, 40,* 615–620.

Hurd, M. D., & Wise, D. A. (1989). The wealth and poverty of widows: Assets before and after the husband's death. In D. A. Wise (Ed.), *The economics of aging* (pp. 147–200). Chicago: University of Chicago Press.

Karlen, A. (1992, April/May). Appreciating the sexual you. *Modern Maturity,* 52–54.

Keither, P. M., & Brubaker, T. H. (1979). Male household roles in later life: A look at masculinity and marital relationships. *Family Coordinator, 28,* 497–502.

Kivett, V. R. (1980). The kinship network and the elderly. In J. E. Montgomery (Ed.), *Handbook of aging.* Washington, DC: Home Economics Association.

Lee, G. R. (1978). Marriage and morale in later life. *Journal of Marriage and the Family, 40,* 131–139.

Lee, G. R., & Shehan, C. L. (1989). Retirement and marital satisfaction. *Journal of Gerontology, 44,* 226–230.

Lin, N., Ensel, W., Simeone, R. S., & Kuo, W. (1979). Social support, stressful life events, and illness: A model and an empirical test. *Journal of Health and Social Behavior, 20,* 108–119.

Locker, R. (1976). Elderly couples and the institution. *Social Work, 21*(2), 149–150.

Locker, R. (1981). Institutionalized elderly: Understanding and helping couples. *Journal of Gerontological Social Work, 3,* 37–49.

Lopata, H. Z., & Brehm, H. P. (1986). *Widows and dependent wives: From social problem to federal program.* New York: Praeger.

Lund, D. A., Caserta, M. S., & Dimond, M. F. (1986). Gender differences through two years of bereavement among the elderly. *Gerontologist, 26,* 314–320.

Marsiglio, W., & Donnelly, D. (1991). Sexual relations in later life: A national study of married persons. *Journal of Gerontology, 46,* 338–343.

McPherson, B. D. (1983). *Aging as a social process.* Toronto: Butterworth.

Methorst, G. J. (1984). Partners of psychiatric outpatients: The difference between husbands and wives on psychological well-being and its implications for marital therapy. In K. Halweg & N. S. Jacobson (Eds.), *Marital interaction: Analysis and modification* (pp. 375–386). New York: Guilford.

Morgan, D. L. (1989). Adjusting to widowhood: Do social networks really make it easier? *The Gerontologist, 29*(1), 101–107.

Nathan, P. K. (1986). Helping wives of Alzheimer's patients through group therapy. *Social Work with Groups, 9*(2), 73–81.

Pearson, J. C. (1989). *Communication in the family: Seeking satisfaction in changing times.* Glenview, IL: Scott Foresman.

Pearson, J. C. (1992). *Lasting love: What keeps couples together.* Dubuque, IA: William C. Brown.

Poussaint, A. F. (1987). Introduction. In B. Cosby, *Time flies* (pp. 1–31). New York: Doubleday.

Quirouette, C., & Gold, D. (1992). Spousal characteristics as predictors of well-being in older couples. *International Journal of Aging and Human Development, 34,* 257–269.

Robertson, J. F. (1975). Interaction in three-generation families, parents as mediators: Toward a theoretical perspective. *International Journal of Aging and Human Development, 6,* 103–110.

Rollins, D., Waterman, D., & Esmay, D. (1985). Married widowhood. *Activities, Adaptation, and Aging, 7*(2), 67–71.

Rosebud-Harris, M. C. (1982). A description of the interactional and subjective characteristics of the relationships between black grandmothers and their grandchildren enrolled in the University of Louisville. *Dissertation Abstracts International, 43,* 2714A.

Rosik, C. H. (1989). The impact of religious orientation in conjugal bereavement among older adults. *International Journal of Aging and Human Development, 28,* 251–260.

Scanzoni, J. H., & Szinovacz, M. (1980). *Family decision making: A developmental sex role model.* Newbury Park, CA: Sage.

Schmidt, M. G. (1987). The patient's partner: The spouse in residential care. *Health and Social Work, 12,* 206–212.

Smith, K. R. (1991). *Risk of mortality following widowhood: Sex differences between men and women following sudden and expected widowhood in a national sample.* Unpublished manuscript.

Smith, K. R., & Zick, C. D. (1986). The incidence of poverty among the recently widowed: Mediating factors in the life course. *Journal of Marriage and the Family, 48,* 619–630.

Smith, K. R., Zick, C. D., & Duncan, G. J. (1991). Remarriage patterns among recent widows and widowers. *Demography, 28,* 361–374.

Spanier, G. B., & Glick, P. C. (1980). Paths to remarriage. *Journal of Divorce, 3,* 283–298.

Taillefer, S. S. (1987). *Etat civil, sexe et santé mentale au Quebec.* Unpublished master's thesis, University of Montreal, Canada.

Thompson, T., & Nussbaum, J. (1988). Interpersonal communications: Intimate relationships and aging. In C. W. Carmichael, C. H. Botan, & R. Hawkins (Eds.), *Human communication and the aging process* (pp. 95–110). Prospect Heights, IL: Waveland.

Tobin, S. S., & Kulys, R. (1981). The family in the institutionalization of the elderly. *Journal of Social Issues, 37*(3), 145–157.

Vaillant, C. O., & Vaillant, G. E. (1993). Is the U-curve of marital satisfaction an illusion? A 40-year study of marriage. *Journal of Marriage and the Family, 55,* 230–239.

Webb, L. (1985). Common topics of conversation between young adults and their grandparents. *Communication Research Reports, 2,* 156–163.

Weishaus, S., & Field, D. (1988). A half-century of marriage: Continuity or change? *Journal of Marriage and the Family, 50,* 763–774.

Zick, C. D., & Smith, K. R. (1986). Immediate and delayed effects of poverty among the recently widowed: Patterns from the 1970s. *The Gerontologist, 26,* 669–675.

Zick, C. D., & Smith, K. R. (1988). Recent widowhood, remarriage, and changes in economic well-being. *Journal of Marriage and the Family, 50,* 233–244.

Zick, C. D., & Smith, K. R. (in press). Patterns of economic change surrounding the death of a spouse. *Journal of Gerontology.*

Zietlow, P. H., & Sillars, A. L. (1988). Lifestage differences in communication during marital conflicts. *Journal of Social and Personal Relationships 5,* 233–245.

Zisook, S., & Shuchter, S. R. (1991). Depression through the first year after the death of a spouse. *American Journal of Psychiatry, 148,* 1346–1352.

Glossary

Extrinsic religious orientation   An orientation that views religion as a means to another end

Golden years   The romanticized view of later life in which spouses view themselves as growing old with their partner by their side in ideal circumstances

Institutionalization   The placement of an older individual, who has become unable to care for himself or herself (or whose partner is no longer able to care for him or her), in an institution for congregate care

Intrinsic religious orientation   An orientation that views religion as a goal in itself

Marital satisfaction   The degree of positive or negative assessment of one's marriage; this assessment tends to be a perceptual, rather than an objective, variable

Positive distortion   The knack that satisfied spouses have of viewing their partners in more complimentary terms than they might be seen by others outside the relationship

Relationally competent   Having the combination of temperamental, cognitive, and emotional characteristics that assist one in meeting people and developing and maintaining positive relationships

Role ambiguity   Uncertainty about one's role, which may occur when one is expected to play more than the accustomed role or when one's role changes

Role conflict   A clash in one's roles, which may occur when one is expected to play different roles over time or when one is expected to move in and out of different roles at the same time

Role loss   Loss of a role because of predicted or unpredicted life changes

Social support   Support available to people through social ties to other individuals, groups, and the larger community

Unisex   A pattern of similar, rather than dissimilar, sex roles, often seen as couples age; sex role behaviors become almost undistinguishable on a sex role continuum

17

Friendships in Old Age

Sarah H. Matthews
Cleveland State University

ontrary to some stereotypes about old people, the elderly are just as interested in initiating and maintaining friendships as their younger counterparts. However, the later years of life create unique obstacles for friendships—obstacles that must be overcome or adapted to in order for older individuals to be able to have satisfying friendships. This chapter examines some of these unique circumstances in detail and also discusses the effects of different enduring friendship patterns during this stage of life.

NV & SD

Chapter Outline

- Old Age as a Context for Friendships
- Summary
- Conclusion

This chapter focuses on friendships in old age. Although there is no agreement on precisely when "old age" begins, by the time people have lived for 60 years—and certainly by the time they have lived for 75—the issues raised in this chapter are likely to affect their friendships.

The chapter begins with a discussion of old age as a context different from earlier life stages. Elderly persons have developed friendships over the course of many decades in response to changing circumstances. Over the course of their lives, they have accumulated a network of relationships on which they draw as their life circumstances change in old age.

Interactions with others in daily life are structured so that those who become friends are likely to be of the same social class and race. Narrowing the circle of likely friends further are cultural expectations or rules that discourage friendships between persons of different ages and between a man and woman (at least in the culture of the United States). These expectations mean that elderly persons have fewer choices than younger persons, as death increasingly takes its toll on age peers, particularly for men.

Contrary to the conventional wisdom, friendships are just as important to elderly individuals as they are to younger people.

Even barring deaths, the friendships of elderly persons are likely to be affected by **sensory changes** and **frailty**. The former makes communication difficult; the latter challenges friends to maintain not only the relationship but reciprocity within it.

Three styles of friendship are introduced in the chapter—acquisitive, discerning, and independent—to capture the variety of ways in which individuals deal with friends over the course of their lives. Finally, three circumstances likely to be encountered in old age—retirement, migration, and widowhood—and the effects of each on friendships are discussed.

OLD AGE AS A CONTEXT FOR FRIENDSHIPS

People who are considered elderly in this society have lived through six, seven, eight, or even as many as nine decades of relationships. Each person has met many people throughout these years in a variety of situations. Some of these situations encouraged friendly relations and friendships to develop; some precluded their development. Some of the relationships were fleeting; some, long term. Some were maintained simply because people saw one another in the course of their daily lives—for example, friends at work. Others required effort to maintain because the friends' lives diverged—for example, one friend married while the other remained single. Compared to younger persons, the old have a much longer legacy of friendships and friendly relationships. Some of these are current ties, others have ended abruptly because of deaths or irreconcilable differences, and still others have merely faded away and may be reinstated if and when opportunity arises.

Each elderly person's legacy of friendships is different. There is a tendency to view the old as a uniform group, when in fact they are more different from one another than members of any other age category. Members of an age cohort were born at the same time, but after that their lives began to diverge so that by the time they are old, each has a unique history of relationships. When circumstances change in old age because of retirement, widowhood, changes in residence, deaths of friends, and changes in health status, this legacy of relationships and experiences with friendship is what the old draw on to adapt to new situations (Jerrome, 1981).

Old age is often depicted as a time of diminished activity and loss of relationships. More recently, however, researchers have found evidence to suggest that, just as in any other stage of life, relationships continue to be cultivated. Both the circumstances that individuals create in their lives and

Box 1

That Old Gang of Mine: Lifetime Bonds Reassure the Soul

Hilda Nyland's club of Sunday school chums has outlasted the near West Side church where they all met some 80 years ago. It has outlived all but one of their husbands.

She was a faithful member of this club when she married in 1928. Her club members have rejoiced and mourned with her as she passed many more milestones, becoming a grandmother, a great-grand-mother, and in 1973, a widow.

The members, all in their late 80s and early 90s now, "meet once a month in our homes or apartments, just to reminisce and talk," says Nyland. "It really is quite remarkable; we all know everything about each other."

In Cleveland, it's not uncommon for school friends to stay in touch and meet regularly for decades to follow. More than 15 such clubs have contacted "Everywoman" to let us know they exist. They aren't sororities or formal women's clubs—yet these informal groups provide emotional ballast through the ups and downs of life, members say.

Each club is different, but within each group, members share a certain sameness. These longtime friends who grew up in the same neighborhood tend to make similar decisions regarding marriage, mothering and careers. Members invariably live on the same side of the city.

For one group of friends who met in the 10th grade at West Tech High School, their life patterns are so similar that members couldn't even pass down baby clothes to each other. "Our children were all about the same age, so there wasn't much of that," recalls member Carol Kalina, 69, of Broadview Heights.

Perhaps it's the fact that they chose the same roads that makes these friendships so enduring.

Some clubs, like Kalina's group, are composed mainly of women who stayed home to raise their children. Other groups are filled with career women. When Cleveland Municipal Judge Mabel Jasper gets to-gether annually with longtime friends, the roster includes a former Ebony Fashion Fair model, a retired teacher and an executive assistant to a college president.

Jasper's club of five friends was started by three who attended Central High School in the 1940s. Jasper fell in with the group later, while attending Kent State University. All five now live in different cities: Jasper is the only one to remain in the Cleveland area. But they get together annually for a week-long extravaganza of a reunion hosted by a different member each year.

Box 1 continues

Box 1
(continued)

In August, they met in Cleveland and stayed for a week at Jasper's home. Jasper arranged for the women to take a ride on Lolly the Trolly, shop at Tower City and the Galleria, tour the Justice Center where she works, and party in the flats. The highlight of the week was a slumber party featuring a midnight talent show. "That was a riot," Jasper recalls.

Longtime friends "are like family. They're just tried and true," reflects Jasper, who says she prefers these week-long romps with friends to an exotic vacation. "We always discuss what's the most exciting thing that's happened to us that year, and our goals and aspirations. It's a lot of fun."

As telling as the front pages of a newspaper, the mementos of these clubs reflect the history of the years they span.

Joan Raddell's club dates to 1943, when members met in the sixth grade at Holy Cross Elementary School in Euclid. Activities have changed a lot over the years for this club, says Raddell, 61, of Richmond Heights. In the 1940s, members biked, swam in Lake Erie, had pajama parties and boy-girl parties, made rosaries for and wrote to World War II servicemen.

Now their activities consist of monthly meetings and attending the weddings of each other's children. Husbands are invited to summer barbecues, winter dinners and theater parties and cruises. They celebrated their 50th anniversary with a Mass last summer.

"We've shared our faith, our laughter and our tears over the years and it's still called 'The Club,'" says Raddell.

Most Cleveland clubs meet monthly, and meetings range from gourmet potlucks in someone's home to luncheons out on the town. Some groups are purely for socializing; others have chosen social service as their purpose.

For Betty Bickett-Botti, 62, of Gates Mills, her club of seven Shaker Heights High graduates has been together 25 years. "We have a gourmet club. We have cooked every nationality there is to cook," she says, laughing. "We've been together through births, deaths and marriages. And the older we are, the more dear we become to each other."

Members host bridal and baby showers for each other's children. Husbands get invited to two club events, a summer picnic and a Christmas party. At meetings, the talk is lively, revolving around current events, interesting recipes, and of course, grandchildren.

The chatter at these meetings isn't idle, members say. In fact, if membership has its privileges, good conversation ranks as the biggest one. More so than any other part of belonging to such a women's club, it's the regular talks that members say give them immeasurable emotional support.

"All we do is talk about things in the news or things that are bothering us. I think it's very healthy sort of a group," explains Carol

Kalina. During a typical meeting, her club members might share solutions for keeping kids still in church or other problems they face as parents and grandparents. They support each other through operations and the onset of physical limitations. "We really feel like we're more like sisters than just friends," she says.

For Mary Lou Drdek, 59, of Brooklyn, her club membership dates back to when she was a Bluebird, at age 5. She and her friends went through Bluebirds and Campfire Girls, and when they graduated out of those clubs, "we all decided to keep together even though we didn't have the organization any more."

"We decided to have some kind of purpose instead of gabbing all of the time," and so for decades members have contributed money to a Jesuit priest originally from the Cleveland area who does missionary work in India.

Like the other groups, Drdek and her friends have shared each other's joy and suffering. One friend is on dialysis; club members help out by picking her up from her dialysis appointment three times a week.

These lifetime bonds reassure the soul, says Drdek. "I know if there would be anything at all wrong with me, they would all be there for me," says Drdek. "What more could you want?" [Margaret Bernstein, *The* (Cleveland) *Plain Dealer*, September 21, 1993]

the situations in which they find themselves often lead to new friendships. David Unruh's work (1983) on the participation of the old in "social worlds," such as ballroom dancing and bicycling, shows the ingenious ways in which elderly persons pursue their interests while also making friends.

Rebecca Adams (1987) found that over the course of a three-year period some of the friendship networks of the elderly widows she interviewed had expanded. Research on retirement communities demonstrates that changes in circumstances almost require that newcomers establish at least initial friendships in a very short period of time. Arlie Hochschild (1978) described how a group of widows in a public housing project for the elderly built relationships with one another to form a community. Similarly, in her study of the residents of a larger French retirement community sponsored by a labor union, Jennie-Keith Ross (1977) documents how the residents sorted themselves into friendship groups.

Like their younger counterparts, then, the old are involved with friends. Their friendship networks are not static. Friendships continue to be maintained, lost, gained, and placed "on hold" for possible reactivation at a later time.

The only circumstance that apparently leads to loss of friends is becoming frail, dependent, and/or housebound. A consistent finding in the research literature is that friends who are old generally do not provide extensive care for one another in these circumstances and are not expected to do so. Instead, family members—spouses and children—provide care for their elderly relatives when and if they are no longer independent (Johnson, 1988). "Companionship" alone tends to characterize friendship in old age to a much greater degree than at younger ages (O'Connor, 1992).

It is not surprising, therefore, that researchers have found that the availability of friends is more important than family to the morale of elderly persons (Arling, 1976). Friends serve as a confirmation of independence and worth in a way that family members cannot: Friends spend time together and provide support of their own volition because they enjoy one another's company, whereas relatives are obliged by kinship norms to interact with and help one another.

In early stages of the life-cycle, people trust that their friends have a high regard for them and will "come through in a pinch," but they usually are able to avoid testing these assumptions. Young and middle-aged adults generally have relatively short-term crises—for example, divorces, injuries from which they recover, and periods of unemployment. When adults have long-term crises, they are put in the position of testing their friendships; they often become socially isolated, as friends gradually become less attentive (Charmaz, 1991). For the old it is often more difficult to avoid testing friendships because of the long-term nature of changing circumstances, particularly chronic health conditions and sensory changes from which there is no recovery. Widowhood may also take its toll when one's friends are still married. These issues are discussed in more detail below.

Structural and Cultural Effects on Friendships in Old Age

Structural Effects   In American society there are norms governing who should be friends with whom. As noted in Chapter 1, one of the components of the definition of friendship is that it is a voluntary relationship. If it were completely voluntary, however, members of friendship dyads might have very different characteristics. In fact, people are friends with those who are similar to themselves. Lois Verbrugge (1977) describes this as the **homogeneity bias**. It operates in old age no less than in other age groups. Typically, friends are the same social class and race. In most cases, they also are the same sex and age.

In their daily lives, individuals have the opportunity to meet, and get to know well enough to consider friendship with, primarily people who are similar to themselves with respect to social class. The CEO of General Motors is unlikely to spend much time with assembly-line workers. Secretaries in an organization take coffee and lunch breaks with one another, not with their bosses. Neighborhood schools bring together children of the same socioeconomic status. Members of the Junior League are rarely welfare recipients. Residents of retirement communities have similar incomes and similar backgrounds (Hochschild, 1978; Johnson, 1971; Ross, 1977; Smithers, 1985).

Each person occupies a social location within the society and, therefore, is likely to meet and have the opportunity to get to know as potential friends those who are in similar social locations. When elderly persons are placed together in nursing homes on the basis of their similarity in health status alone, it is not surprising that they rarely develop friendships with one another (Gubrium, 1975; Shield, 1988).

Cultural Expectations   At least in American society, friends also are expected to be age peers. The extent to which the society is age segregated often goes unnoticed. Some people do not approve of retirement communities because they separate the old from the young in "unnatural" settings; they see segregating children from all but a few adults in schools, however, as perfectly "natural." In work settings, people of varying ages may associate with one another, but those who become friends are likely to be close in age. Thus, not only are people likely to have disproportionate access to age peers, but, even when they interact with persons who are older or younger, they are encouraged to choose their friends from age peers. In fact, when friends differ widely in age the unusual nature of their relationship is often accounted for by referring to it in kinship terms—for example, "He's my other father" or "She's like a daughter to me." In this way, the age difference between the two friends is acknowledged as atypical.

Similarly, a friendship between a man and a woman requires explanation: Friends are expected to be the same sex. Hence, a woman with a male friend may explain to others, "He's only a friend." This qualification is necessary to indicate that the relationship is not what persons expect between two individuals of different sexes, that is, a sexual or potentially sexual one. Two women friends do not need to explain that they are "only" friends. Neither do two men.

The unspoken rules governing friendships, then, are that they are between age peers and between persons of the same sex, and studies indicate that they usually are (Laumann, 1966; Verbrugge, 1977). This holds true in old age as at any other age, but elderly persons pay a higher price than younger people for conforming to this rule, as you will see below.

Do the Elderly Conform to Cultural Expectations?   That friendships in old age are between people of the same age and sex is illustrated by findings from a study in which members of two different 1936 high school graduation classes were surveyed about their friendships in conjunction with their 50th high school reunion, when they were approximately 68 years of age (Matthews, 1988). The 168 respondents were asked to identify up to 6 of their closest friends.

Altogether, they identified 704 friends, if the 37 couples who were identified are counted as 1 friend. Of the 667 friends who were not couples, only 8.2% of those identified by men were women, and only 15.1% of those identified by women were men. Two-thirds of both the men and the women identified only same-sex friends. Even when the 37 couples who were identified by 17 people are added, the number of networks including cross-sex friends is not increased by very much.

The average age of the identified friends was 63.4 years, with the youngest friend being 21 and the oldest, 95. Using as an "index of homogeneity," ages within 2 years of the respondents' ages (66 to 70 inclusive), Stueve and Gerson (1977) found that 39.1% of the friendships were age homogeneous. Men reported a higher percentage of friends who were younger than 66—52.1%, compared to 41.4% for women. Only 12.2% of the friends, however, were age 50 or younger.

These findings show that these older respondents conformed to the homogeneity bias: Most men identified only men as friends, most women identified only women as friends. Although only two-fifths of the friends were the same, or almost the same, age as the respondents, most of the friends were not very much older or younger.

Effects of Cultural Expectations in Old Age   How do these cultural expectations affect friendships in old age? With respect to friends' being the same age, the high mortality rate among the old means that the pool of age peers from which to choose friends diminishes with time. Men are disproportionately affected by this phenomenon because their life expectancy is shorter than women's. This may explain why the men in the high school reunion study were more likely than the women to name friends who were younger than 60.

Furthermore, the age homogeneity bias means that deaths of friends become a regular occurrence in the lives of the old. One woman warned an interviewer, "This is what you are going to run into with us [elderly people], that we are missing people that we were close to, either because they have fallen apart or dropped dead" (Matthews, 1986, p. 117). Another woman in her late 80s finally responded impatiently to an interviewer's repeated probes about her current friends, "They all passed away, you know, I'm living this long" (Matthews, 1986, p. 115).

Effects of Sensory Change and Frailty   As one of the women above indicated, in addition to friends dying, the old are more likely than younger adults to have health problems. They also experience sensory changes, such as deafness or reduced vision, that make it difficult for them to continue to be involved in friendships.

One elderly woman explained to an interviewer (Matthews, 1986) that she had decided not to resume participation with a group of women friends who had met weekly for a number of years. She had been quite ill during the six months before the interview:

> And I think it can't be now because I don't hear. I'm all right when you and I are talking, but if I try to hear anybody's conversation, I just can't enter in. And I can't see very much. And my walking, my balance is affected, and then I get this bad ear. So you can see I have a lot of things against me. (p. 116)

Another woman described a friend who had died recently:

> She had been stone deaf and not seeing anyone much, and I haven't been able to get out since I don't drive. And since she's hard of hearing, I couldn't call her up. I had to relay a message and it wasn't very satisfactory. (p. 117)

This woman's difficulty maintaining contact with her friend illustrates the effects of both chronic, debilitating illness and sensory changes, each of which is much more likely to be experienced by elderly than by younger persons.

The Question of Reciprocity   These changes, however, do not mean that the individuals are no longer friends. Friends who have known one another for a long time may develop "faithfulness" to a relationship that "serves to maintain the relationship, even if the original reason for forming the relationship no longer remains" (Kurth, 1970, p. 159). The woman quoted above said of her deceased friend, "She's an old friend; someone I always loved dearly. I think she was a very gracious and lovely woman" (Matthews, 1986, p. 117). Another woman described the change in the quality of her relationships with two friends, one who had recently died and one who was very ill. She noted that the relationships had become one-sided, since neither was able to contribute anything to her (Matthews, 1986):

Often, elderly individuals who need more help from their friends than they can reciprocate do not want to become a burden, so they withdraw from these relationships.

> And the quality changed in that way and it just helped to bring out the fact of how deep our friendships were. Because there was no cutting off of the friendship, that being, "You're not all right, I'm finished." That just couldn't be done. (p. 118)

Nevertheless, as Graham Allan (1989) argues, when a friend becomes ill and the giving becomes one-sided, "the majority of friendships can be expected to fade slowly, notwithstanding the concern and goodwill expressed and genuinely felt within them" (p. 113). Even when two friends are still alive, they in fact may be alive for one another only in memory because their friendship can no longer be "active."

The woman cited above who decided not to resume meeting with a group of friends after having been ill for six months illustrates another important factor that makes reciprocity an issue in friendships in old age. Elderly persons who are the recipients of goodwill may discourage their friends from continuing to provide companionship. As noted in Chapter 1, friends manage their relationship so that it approaches as nearly as possible the ideal. When one friend becomes dependent on the goodwill of the other, he or she may act to limit interaction to avoid harming the relationship (Rawlins, 1992). In the journal she kept while residing in a nursing home because of severe arthritis, Joyce Horner (1982) recounted her ambivalent feelings about returning to live in the house she had shared with a friend:

> Yesterday I was home . . . I was home and felt I was a lot of trouble and perhaps not worth it. That it was lovely to be at home, with crocuses coming up and purple finches and a fire and *The Marriage of Figaro* and, most, being with friends. But I am a liability and a millstone and I feel I'll get to be more of one, always taking and always asking for things. I laugh more when I'm at home than I get any occasion for here, and cry more here—though I don't think anyone knows—than anywhere I've ever been in my life. (p. 6)

Although she was miserable in the nursing home, she felt that any additional "inconvenience" to her good friend Elizabeth would be asking too much. Throughout the journal she continued to view living in the nursing home as the only way to maintain a reciprocal relationship with Elizabeth and her other friends.

Frailty and increased dependency present strains to friendships that only the closest can survive and, even then, only through careful management on the part of the dependent, as well as the less dependent, friend. In a sample of very frail elderly clients of a Social Service Department who were living alone, O'Connor (1992) found that only 20% reported having a very close friend.

Although the elderly do not have a monopoly on frailty and dependency, these conditions are nevertheless more common in old age than at any other time in the life-cycle. Even when only one person in a friendship dyad is frail, each is challenged to participate in a relationship that is no longer reciprocal. One must be content to give more than she or he receives, and the other, to receive more than she or he is able give. Under these conditions both must rely on long-term reciprocity if they are to continue to see the relationship as balanced.

Friendship Styles

As noted earlier, each of us accumulates a legacy of relationships throughout his or her life. This legacy does depend on the opportunities each of us has to meet and get to know others, but it also depends on our view of the importance of friendships in our everyday lives. The significance of individual proclivities toward friendship became apparent in **life history interviews** with 63 elderly persons who participated in a study of friendship (Matthews, 1986). Three styles of friendship, developed over the life course, were identified. Each had different consequences in old age. Structural effects and cultural expectations, as well as sensory changes and frailty, are filtered through the style of friendship that each individual has developed over his or her life. The styles and some exemplary elderly persons who use each of them are discussed below.

Acquisitive Style   As the label implies, elderly persons who make use of the **acquisitive friendship style** acquired friends throughout their lives. Some of them added new friends to old ones as they moved through their lives. In old age they were likely to have friends from different periods of their lives—for example, from grade school, college, various places of employment, community activities, church, neighborhoods, and senior centers.

To illustrate the acquisitive style of friendship, Rawlins (1992), who used this typology in his work, cites a 73-year-old widow:

> I just made different friends. I kept some of the old ones, of course; I worked in Dayton—I'm originally from Dayton—and I keep up with them a lot—some of them. Some of them, you know it's just like when you marry too, you sort of drift away from other people. But I've made lots of new friends here. And I've been here permanently for 20 years. So I'm half Hoosier and half Buckeye. (p. 260)

From her perspective in old age this woman saw her life as divided into two parts, and she has friends from each one.

In all likelihood, this woman is using two broad definitions of friendship (Matthews, 1983). The first is a "friends as particular people" definition. Friends are viewed as irreplaceable and made early in life. By the time two friends reach old age, they share a history in which they have personally experienced the ups and downs of one another's lives (Adams, 1986; Brown, 1981). She also is using a "friends as relationships" definition. These are people who do the kinds of things friends do for one another—for example, talk about current experiences and problems and share various activities such as lunch, bridge games, golf, bingo, and concerts. This requires that friends be readily available to one another. This type of friend, unlike the former type, is replaceable if she or he dies, moves away, or becomes incapacitated. Although people in everyday life may use the word "friend" to describe both types, in fact, each type occupies a different niche in elderly persons' lives.

Some elderly persons who were classified as acquisitive did not maintain any friends from earlier in their lives but nevertheless continued to make friends throughout their lives, whenever their situation changed.

One elderly woman had acquired three friends in the ten years preceding the interview (Matthews, 1986), and she explained about one:

> Well, I would consider her my best friend. She lives just right across the boulevard from me. I met her when we were taking driving lessons together, about seven years ago. We had never known each other before but there again she's a very friendly person and when I got to class, we would talk, you know, quite a bit when we would see each other at school. And then later when I passed my test, she was one of the first persons that I called to tell her about it. And I think that since then we started to be friends together. Now we call each other every day.

Although this woman had not maintained friends from earlier in her life, she acquired new ones as her circumstances changed. In old age her friendships were of relatively short duration, and she used the "friends as relationships" definition. Nevertheless, she considered her relatively short-term friends to be close.

Discerning Style   Elderly persons who use the **discerning friendship style** have very few friends, but they are deeply committed to each of them (Matthews, 1986). One man, for example, indicated that there was only one person who qualified as "what I would call a true close friendship":

> Now this is a man who is seven years older. My brother and I were seven years apart; my brother was seven years older. And this man, we grew up together, so he's known me since I was knee high to a duck and, in fact, he and my brother would have to take care of me. There was just the two of us in the family, so when I was about the age of three or four, why they were saddled with me. And this friendship has maintained itself all through the years and that's quite a few years. Now at least a couple of times a year I go to visit him and his wife and they come by here and visit with me. (pp. 46–47)

This man was not socially isolated. In describing someone who was his "counterpart in the banking business," he explained:

> Now we've known each other a long time, but I don't consider him a friend. I guess there'd be lots of people you'd put in that category. Yes, you are glad to see each other and they know you, but you wouldn't just on the spur of the moment call them up or they call you; their social life might be in an entirely different arena. (p. 47)

This man exemplifies the discerning style of friendship because he draws a sharp distinction between close friends and mere acquaintances.

William Rawlins (1992) cites an 82-year-old woman to illustrate the discerning style:

I really don't have a lot of friends. I've had a lot of acquaintances, but I think I only have one friend, one and I really and truly love her. We've been friends since we were tots, tiny tots. . . . I like people and I like to talk with them, but I don't really go out of my way to really make friends. (p. 251)

Those who use a discerning style of friendship have put a very few eggs in one basket. They use only the "friends as particular people" definition of friendship (Matthews, 1983). Their friends are not replaceable.

Independent Style   Individuals who adopt the **independent friendship style** are content with friendly relations (Kurth, 1970). They use the circumstances of their lives—some of which they make—to interact with others on a friendly basis, without establishing friendships per se. To paraphrase a popular song, they are friends with the ones they are with. An elderly woman classified as independent was asked if there was one friend who stood out, about whom she and the interviewer could talk (Matthews, 1986):

No, I am a very private person. I always lived by the rule "no explain, no complain." When you say too much you are revealing too much about yourself. You should retain a little bit of your privacy and thereby you get pride and you get self-discipline. The very private things you keep to yourself. (p. 35)

Those who apply the independent style shy away from obligations associated with friendship and are content with friendly relations. They let the situations they are in provide people with whom to interact on a friendly basis. They use neither the "friends as particular people" definition nor the "friends as relationships" definition. They care only that there are people available with whom to engage in a friendly way.

These three distinct styles are intended to capture the different approaches to friendship that elderly people bring with them to old age. Those classified as "independent" do not feel that it is important to have close friends; they are content with "friendly relations." Those who are "discerning" feel that it is very unlikely they will meet people who might qualify as friends after adolescence or early adulthood. They are deeply committed to a handful of friends who are irreplaceable. Between these two extremes are the "acquisitive," who are open to forming friendships throughout their lives, including in old age. Some who use this style maintain old friendships while acquiring new ones, so in old age their current friends are drawn from different periods of their lives; others are content to let new friends replace the old, so their friendships in old age are of a relatively short duration. These three styles, developed over the course of a lifetime, have different consequences in old age.

Box 2   **Friendship Styles**

Make a list of your friends (up to six), and answer the following questions about each of them. (Material adapted from Matthews, 1988.)

1. What is your friend's age?
2. What is your friend's sex?
3. Where did you meet this friend?
4. How often do you see this friend?
5. How long have you known this friend?
6. How far from you does the friend live (in miles).
7. Which of the other friends you listed does this friend know?

Once you have answered the questions for all of the friends you listed, examine the information and answer the following questions.

1. *Homogeneity bias.* What proportion of your friends are your age, give or take two years? What proportion of your friends are the same age as you? What is the age range of your friends?
2. *Meeting.* What settings seem to be important for meeting potential friends? How much effort did you have to make to meet these friends?
3. *Interaction.* How often do you see your friends? Is there a relationship between how often you see someone and how long you have known him or her? Is there a relationship between how often you see someone and how far you live from one another?
4. *Long-term friends.* Do you have both short- and long-term friends? Judging from the number and duration of your friendships, do you think you use the independent, acquisitive, or discerning style of friendship?
5. *Friendship network.* Do your friends know one another? In other words, do you and your friends form a network of ties or are you friends with individuals?

Repeat this process, answering each question from the point of view of one of your parents and one of your grandparents. Once you have organized the data, answer the following questions. Are there any discernible differences in friendship patterns among the three of you? Do the differences appear to be related to age? Does style of friendship appear to be a family trait? Do you think your friendships will be similar to your parent's and your grandparent's when you reach their respective ages? Why or why not?

Changes in Status

Two predictable changes in status occur in old age for those who have been employed and those who have been married: retirement and widowhood. Both are likely to affect friendships. No longer embedded in formal relationships on the job or in a marriage, elderly persons must rely on informal relationships to a much greater degree than when they were younger (Jerrome, 1981; Rosow, 1976). A third change, voluntary migration, which is made possible by retirement and for which widowhood may be a catalyst, is less predictable but relatively common in old age. Each of these changes in status is discussed below. Friendship style affects the significance of each of these for friendships as well.

Retirement   Although mandatory **retirement** has been outlawed in the United States, most people still retire before their 65th birthday. They leave behind them not only a job, but also their co-workers, clients, and/or customers, who are no longer seen daily or even occasionally. Depending on the quality of the relationships that were experienced on the job, this may be seen as a blessing or a curse. Whichever, increased time and absence of built-in ties to people on the job may lead some people to seek other avenues for friendship or companionship. Graham Allan (1989) points out that people vary in their desire for additional contacts:

> Some people have little need for new friendships because the space they have for sociability is already "filled" sufficiently by existing relationships. The resources they have for friendship— and sociability does require time, and, to some extent, money— are, as it were, committed elsewhere. . . . Those who are already quite fully committed socially are likely to put less effort into initiating new friendships than those who are not. (p. 43)

Retirement may mean that someone is no longer as "socially committed" and now has room to acquire new friends.

Rather than new friends, recently retired persons may choose to draw on their legacy of relationships to deepen existing ties (Jerrome, 1981). Fate may also play a role. A visit to a senior center, for example, may bring together two people who once were friends but had lost contact. It may be easier for them to resume a friendship because, after all, they already know one another and have a shared past.

The desire for new contacts, as well as the strategies adopted to pursue them, depend on people's style of friendship. Those with a discerning style are not affected by retirement because their friendships are long-standing, committed relationships that are independent of other involvements. Those who are independent, and who therefore relied on their jobs to provide them with friendly relations, must seek new ways to be around others routinely; otherwise, they run the risk of becoming socially isolated. For the acquisitive, a desire to add new friends to their networks will depend on whether the "space they have for sociability" is sufficiently filled (Allan, 1989).

One woman explained why she went to the local senior citizens center on the first day after she retired (Matthews, 1986):

> I quit work the first of May last year and I thought, "I'm not going to stay in bed and I'm not going to get lazy." So I went

right down to the Senior Center on the second. And I said I was going to inquire because I wasn't going to get in a rut. (p. 140)

On her first day at the center she met a woman whom she described in the interview as a good friend. Altogether, she had acquired three friends with whom she was socializing, both at and away from the senior citizens center. In contrast, an elderly man classified as independent in this study used the same strategy, but he continued to frequent a number of senior centers to meet and talk with those who happened to be there. He made no attempt to cultivate close friendships but was content to "shoot the breeze" for a few hours a day with others who frequented the centers.

Retirement may also bring a drop in income. Reduced income affects friendships primarily when the difference between the two friends' incomes is great. One man, for example, received a relatively modest pension but had many friends who received more generous ones, even though their incomes while they had been employed were comparable. He reported that after three years of retirement the difference in the amounts of their respective pensions began to take its toll (Matthews, 1986):

> Our financial situations are farther and farther apart. They have more and more money and we have less and less. And, although our friendship remains strong, it still is not as much so, as when they say, "We want to go to Virginia Beach," or "We want to go here or there, why don't you join us?" We have to say "no" because we just can't afford it. That's the difference between public employees as I was and employees in industry, where their income doesn't decrease as much in retirement years. (p. 119)

Most friends are unlikely to face this situation because the homogeneity bias matches them on income level as well as on age, sex, and other characteristics.

The other issue with respect to decline in income after retirement, as Allan (1989) notes, is that friends simply may not have the financial resources to afford to get together. For example, two friends who worked in different cities but who saw one another during the summer when they traveled together may find that the size of their respective pensions precludes travel, and as a consequence their friendship may fade away.

Migration   Retirement also cuts people loose from the requirement that they live close to their jobs. This makes **migration** possible. In the last two decades states in the Sun Belt have swelled in population—in part because their climates are attractive to elderly persons. The decision to move after retirement, however, makes maintenance of friendships problematic. Both those who move and those who stay lose friends to distance. One elderly man recounted his feelings of being deserted (Matthews, 1986):

> One friend of ours, we shared medical offices for a number of
> years. . . . And that was a significant relationship. We're still close
> friends. . . . The thing is, they're away all winter. They're away
> about six months out of the year. That interferes in a close friend-
> ship. When they come back we pick it up again, but it's a handi-
> cap to a friendship. There are a number of our friends who go
> away for the winter. . . . So we always kid them that in winter
> we're here alone, which is not exactly true, but you feel aban-
> doned. (p. 120)

Persons who migrate after retirement, however, may be instrumental
in friends' decisions to follow them to new locales. Charles Longino
(1988) describes, for example, the experiences of Canadians who winter in
Florida:

> A common pattern for retirement migration is the establish-
> ment of a visiting routine with other family members and friends,
> especially if the migrants live near a resort. Visits often prelude a
> move to the area, after which the chain of visits begin anew with
> a new host.

Friends' relocation, then, may be an important factor in elderly individuals' choosing to move after retirement, but only for those using the acquisitive and discerning styles of friendship. For the independent, because
they rely exclusively on friendly relations, maintenance or loss of friendships is not germane to decisions about migration. Their absence of close
attachments in one locale, however, may make moving to another one
easier.

In old age, moves also occur because elderly parents and their adult
children simply would prefer to live near one another and now, because
of retirement, have the option to do so. Elderly parents may also move to
live near adult children as a precaution, in case the parents' health deterio-
rates or because one or both have become frail. Many of the elderly persons interviewed by David Unruh (1983) for his book on social worlds of
the old had moved to be near their children.

Being dependent on children, while it may not be desirable, is
nonetheless acceptable. Being dependent on friends is neither desirable
nor acceptable. Family members provide insurance that friends do not
(Johnson, 1988) or, perhaps more accurately, that friends cannot provide
because of problems associated with their advanced age. Even if elderly
friends are still self-reliant, continuing to rely on them may be viewed as
too much of a risk. Younger family members are better insurance than elderly friends.

Although moving close to family is deemed the wise alternative when
independence is challenged, for both the discerning and the acquisitive the
costs of moving away from friends may be very high. Social services that

assist elderly persons to live independently might make it possible for them to continue living where they want to and have the added benefit of preserving "active" friendships. Those who use the independent style of friendship cannot count on friends to see them through even short-term crises—they must rely exclusively on kin and social services.

Widowhood   Losing a spouse in old age (or at any age) moves the surviving spouse out of the world of couples into the world of single persons. Even for husbands and wives who maintained separate social lives and friends, the need to cope with loss of a spouse affects friendships (Matthews, 1986). Widowhood, like retirement, may also signal that it is time to move to smaller living quarters or to be nearer children, thereby disrupting established patterns of friendship.

Since women have a longer life expectancy than men and tend to marry men who are older than they, this transition is more likely to be required of women than of men. Anne Martin Matthews (1991) makes the following observation:

> Friendship ties are particularly vulnerable when widowhood
> occurs as an off-time life event, as when the person is widowed at
> a young age . . . and therefore lacks an appropriate reference
> group of others who have shared the experience and can express
> a "consciousness of kind." (p. 48)

Widows in their early 60s are in the minority. At that age the majority of women, and therefore most of their friends, are likely to be married. Widows in their 80s are in the majority and can more easily find others with whom they have a "consciousness of kind."

The issue, however, goes beyond widows' ability to empathize with the recently bereaved. For a wife, as both Jerrome (1984) and Oliker (1989) point out, any potential conflict between her husband and her friend is resolved in the husband's favor. For two women to continue to be friends, they must be willing to accept that a husband's wishes take priority and put their own friendship in second place. Women who have never been married have not faced this constraint and have had more freedom throughout their lives to pursue close friendships, especially with other single women. More single than married women may have had the opportunity to become committed to their friends and, in old age, to have developed "faithfulness" to a friendship (Kurth, 1970). Widowed women friends, perhaps for the first time since adolescence, are in a position to do things together and for each other without the constraints of their marriages, just as single women have been able to do throughout their lives.

On the other hand, elderly widowed men, who comprise a significantly smaller group and who are, on average, older, are more welcome in the world of coupled sociability. Although the proportion of widowed men who remarry is higher than it is for widowed women, it still is relatively low, especially for men over the age of 75 (Connidis, 1989). Widowed men, however, are likely to have women friends and to interact with others as part of a couple. Widowed women are much more likely to confine their friendships to women, viewing cross-sex friendships, at least between age peers, as courtship relationships, which many elderly women would prefer to avoid (Adams, 1985; Matthews, 1986; Rawlins, 1992).

SUMMARY

Elderly people have a long legacy of relationships that they have accumulated through many decades as circumstances in their lives have changed. Their style of friendship and their legacy of relationships combine to determine their experiences of friendships in old age. In this stage of the life-cycle, informal relationships become paramount.

There is a homogeneity bias operating in U.S. society such that friends tend to be not only the same social class and race but also the same sex and age. Elderly persons, therefore, are likely to lose friends to death, and their pool for replacements will shrink. This is particularly true for men because of their shorter life expectancy.

In addition to death, the primary obstacles to friendship maintenance and formation in old age are sensory changes and frailty. These interfere with people's abilities to meet and communicate with friends. They also challenge the reciprocal nature of ties. Two frail friends are unlikely to be of much assistance to one another; and when only one friend is frail, the relationship becomes unbalanced. Unless the friendship has been very close over many years, maintaining a sense of reciprocity often is nearly impossible.

Three styles of friendship capture the distinctions among the ways people deal with friends throughout their lives and in old age. Those who use the acquisitive style expect to make new friends in whatever circumstances they find themselves. As old friends die, move away, or become frail, they feel comfortable replacing them with new friends or strengthening existing relationships. They are likely to have friends who will supply emotional if not instrumental support if they become frail or dependent.

Those who use the discerning style rely on friendships that have endured for decades. They may be able to count on their friends' willingness to show strong commitment when circumstances require emotional and instrumental support, but they are also more likely to have lost them to death or circumstances that preclude easy sociability and the exchange of assistance.

Those who use the independent style, because they rely on situations to provide them with friendly relations, are able to take advantage of the many settings in which adults, including elderly people, congregate—for example, senior centers, churches, and adult education classes. When they require emotional and instrumental assistance because of frailty, however, people with independent friendship styles will be out of luck: Their associates are unlikely to have developed a commitment to them.

Retirement is likely to affect friendship ties. Not since adolescence have individuals had as much time to devote to informal activities with friends. For the acquisitive, more time may be spent with old and new friends. Retirement also means that people are no longer required to live near a job; they now may choose where to live. Migration may break up active friendships, but it also may be instrumental in people's reinstating them, as well as building new ones, in different locales.

Widowhood also affects friendships. Because of their shorter life expectancy, men are less likely to be required to cope with losing a spouse. Even if men are widowed, they are likely to continue to participate in a world of coupled friends because they are paired with single women. Elderly women, on the other hand, are very likely to become widowed and at relatively younger ages. Older widows have an advantage over younger ones in that there are more older widows. Their women friends may become more central in their lives, as they seek companionship to replace the conjugal bond.

CONCLUSION

Old age as a stage in the life-cycle brings both the potential for enhanced friendships and the threat of their loss. Enhancement stems from the increase in available time that retirement brings. For women, widowhood may mean the opportunity to invest in women friends without the competition of a marriage. Threat stems from death, as well as the intrusion of sensory decline and increased frailty, both of which make reciprocal relationships difficult to maintain. These gains and losses, however, are filtered through friendship style. Those elderly persons who use the acquisitive style are not as susceptible to these threats as those who use the discerning and the independent styles, and they are in a better position to take advantage of the opportunities presented.

Class Discussion Questions

1. Think about your grandparents and/or other elderly persons that you know. Do these elderly people have friends? How did they meet them—for example, when they were children? at work? at a senior center? Do they have life-long friends, only recently acquired friends, or both? What kinds of things do they do with their friends? Relative to family members, how important are these friends?
2. If you lived in a nursing home, would you view the other residents as potential friends? Why or why not?

3. Poll the class to discover whether anyone has a friend who is elderly. Discover how those students happened to acquire these older friends. Explore why other students do not have elderly friends.

Homework Assignments

1. Conduct a life history interview with an elderly person to find out about friendships throughout his or her life. What style of friendship does she or he appear to have: independent, discerning, acquisitive, or something else? What are the apparent consequences in old age for this person of having adopted this style of friendship?
2. Spend time with a group of elderly people, maybe at a bingo game, an ice skating rink, a ballroom dancing event, or an adult education class for senior citizens. Observe how they interact with one another. In what ways are their interactions similar to and in what ways different from your interactions with your friends in comparable situations?
3. Ask people your age whether they have close ties with elderly individuals who are not relatives. If they do, do they consider them friends? Why or why not? Ask them to compare how they feel about the elderly persons and how they feel about friends their own age. If they do not have any such close ties, ask them to explain why they do not. Draw conclusions about whether there is an age homogeneity bias operating in friendships among your age peers.
4. Watch the movie *Harold and Maude*. Based on the conceptual vocabulary in Chapter 1, were Harold and Maude lovers or just friends? Justify your assertion.
5. Survey some elderly people using the questions in Box 2. Tabulate your results, and draw conclusions about their patterns of friendship.

Additional Readings

Adams, R. G., & Blieszner, R. (Eds.). (1989). *Older adult friendships: Structure and process.* Newbury Park, CA: Sage.

Allan, G. (1989). *Friendship: Developing a sociological perspective.* New York: Harvester Wheatsheaf.

Chown, S. M. (1981). *Friendship in old age.* In S. W. Duck & R. Gilmour (Eds.), *Personal relationships, Vol. 2: Developing personal relationships* (pp. 231–246). New York: Academic.

Brown, B. B. (1981). A life-span approach to friendship: Age-related dimensions on an ageless relationship. In H. Z. Lopata & D. Maines (Eds.), *Research in the interweave of social roles: Friendship* (pp. 23–50). Greenwich, CT: JAI.

Hess, B. (1972). Friendship. In M. W. Riley, M. Johnson, & A. Foner (Eds.), *Aging and society, Vol. 3: A sociology of age stratification* (pp. 357–393). New York: Russell Sage Foundation.

Matthews, S. H. (1986). *Friendships through the life course: Oral biographies in old age.* Beverly Hills, CA: Sage.

O'Connor, P. (1992). *Friendships between women: A critical review.* New York: Guilford.

Rawlins, W. K. (1992). *Friendship matters: Communication, dialectics, and the life course.* New York: Aldine de Gruyter.

References

Adams, R. G. (1985). People would talk: Normative barriers to cross-sex friendships for elderly women. *The Gerontologist, 25,* 605–611.

Adams, R. G. (1986). Secondary friendship networks and psychological well-being among elderly women. *Activities, Adaptation and Aging, 8,* 59–72.

Adams, R. G. (1987). Patterns of network change: A longitudinal study of friendships of elderly women. *The Gerontologist, 27,* 222–227.

Allan, G. A. (1989). *Friendship: Developing a sociological perspective.* New York: Harvester Wheatsheaf.

Arling, G. (1976). The elderly widow and her family, neighbors, and friends. *Journal of Marriage and the Family, 38,* 757–768.

Brown, B. B. (1981). A life-span approach to friendship: Age-related dimensions on an ageless relationship. In H. Z. Lopata & D. Maines (Eds.), *Research in the interweave of social roles: Friendship* (pp. 23–50). Greenwich, CT: JAI.

Charmaz, K. (1991). *Good days, bad days: The self in chronic illness and time.* New Brunswick, NJ: Rutgers University Press.

Connidis, I. A. (1989). *Family ties and aging.* Toronto: Butterworths.

Gubrium, J. (1975). *Living and dying in Murray Manor.* New York: St. Martin's.

Hochschild, A. R. (1978). *The unexpected community.* Berkeley: University of California Press.

Horner, J. (1982). *That time of year: A chronicle of life in a nursing home.* Amherst: University of Massachusetts Press.

Jerrome, D. (1981). The significance of friendship for women in later life. *Aging and Society, 1,* 175–197.

Jerrome, D. (1984). Good company: The sociological implications of friendship. *Sociological Review, 32,* 606–715.

Johnson, C. L. (1988). Relationships among family members and friends in later life. In R. M. Milardo (Ed.), *Family and social networks* (pp. 168–189). Newbury Park, CA: Sage.

Johnson, S. K. (1971). *Idle haven: Community building among the working-class retired.* Berkeley: University of California Press.

Kurth, S. B. (1970). Friendships and friendly relations. In G. J. McCall (Ed.), *Social relationships* (pp. 136–170). Chicago: Aldine.

Laumann, E. O. (1966). *Prestige and association in an urban community.* New York: Bobbs-Merrill.

Longino, C. (1988). On the nesting of snowbirds: Canadian-born residents of the United States. In L. C. Mullins & R. D. Tucker (Eds.), *Snowbirds in the Sun Belt: Older Canadians in Florida* (pp. 17–36). Tampa: International Exchange Center on Gerontology, University of South Florida.

Matthews, A. Martin. (1991). *Widowhood in later life.* Toronto: Butterworths.

Matthews, S. H. (1983). Definitions of friendship and their consequences in old age. *Aging and Society, 3*, 144–155.

Matthews, S. H. (1986). *Friendships through the life course: Oral biographies in old age.* Beverly Hills, CA: Sage.

Matthews, S. H. (1988). Friendships and friendship networks of men and women in their late 60s. Paper presented at the annual meeting of the Midwest Sociological Association, Minneapolis, MN.

O'Connor, P. (1992). *Friendships between women: A critical review.* New York: Guilford.

Oliker, S. J. (1989). *Best friends and marriage.* Berkeley: University of California Press.

Rawlins, W. K. (1992). *Friendship matters: Communication, dialectics, and the life course.* New York: Aldine de Gruyter.

Rosow, I. (1976). Status and role change through the life span. In R. H. Binstock & E. Shanas (Eds.), *Handbook of aging and the social sciences* (pp. 457–482). New York: Van Nostrand Reinhold.

Ross, J.-K. (1977). *Old people, new lives.* Chicago: University of Chicago Press.

Shield, R. R. (1988). *Uneasy endings.* Ithaca, NY: Cornell University Press.

Smithers, J. A. (1985). *Determined survivors.* New Brunswick, NJ: Rutgers University Press.

Stueve, C. A., & Gerson, K. (1977). Personal relations across the life-cycle. In C. S. Fischer, R. M. Jackson, C. A. Stueve, K. Gerson, L. M. Jones, & M. Baldassare (Eds.), *Networks and places* (pp. 79–98). New York: Free Press.

Unruh, D. R. (1983). *Invisible lives.* Beverly Hills, CA: Sage.

Verbrugge, L. M. (1977). The structure of adult friendship choices. *Social Forces, 56*, 576–597.

Glossary

Acquisitive friendship style Continuing to acquire new friends throughout the life course

Discerning friendship style Considering just a very few persons, acquired early in life, as one's only friends

Frailty Physical weakness that decreases one's mobility and ability to react quickly

Homogeneity bias Tendency for friends to be of the same sex, age, race, and social class

Independent friendship style   Being content with friendly interaction with whomever one encounters rather than having specific friends

Life history interview   An interview in which someone is asked to recount his or her life story, guided, in some cases, by the researcher, who asks the person to speak about specific topics in depth

Migration   Changing one's place of residence from one part of a country to another

Retirement   Leaving the paid labor force and receiving income from pensions and other forms of transfer payments rather than wages

Sensory changes   Decreases in the sharpness of any of the five senses—taste, touch, smell, hearing, and sight

Widowhood   The state brought about by the death of one's spouse

18 Interpersonal Relationships in Multi-Generational Families

Mary Ann Parris Stephens
Kent State University

Sarah L. Clark
Kent State University

As our life expectancies get longer, we encounter new sorts of relational possibilities and challenges. Although some of our parents and grandparents may be elderly and frail, requiring care from family members or others, an increasing number of them will be active and vigorous. How does an adult child relate to a parent who is planning a trip to climb the Himalayas? Isn't Grandma supposed to be staying home, baking cookies and knitting afghans? This chapter explores the shifts in relationships that are taking place between adult children and their parents, as well as between grandchildren and their grandparents, as the older generation reaps the benefits of healthy lives well into "the golden years."

NV & SD

Chapter Outline

- Multi-Generational Families in Modern Life
- Relationships Between Parents
  and Their Adult Children
- Relationships Between Grandparents
  and Their Grandchildren
- Summary

Family relationships are important to each of us throughout our lives. Our families provide us with security, love, and a sense of belonging, and they help us know who we are and where we came from. When most of us think of families, we generally think of young to middle-aged parents and their children, who range from infants to adolescents. This chapter emphasizes a different kind of family, one in which there are at least three generations, at least two of which have reached adulthood. These families are composed of parents, their adult children, and their grandchildren. This chapter will explore the diversity and complexity of these multi-generational families.

Perhaps you are thinking that we will discuss kindly, gray-haired, sometimes forgetful old people who are not able to care for themselves very well. You may also be thinking that this chapter will show how their hard-working, middle-aged children and teen-aged grandchildren take care of them. However, when you are finished with this chapter you will have learned that although many multi-generational families fit these images, many also do not: Many parents continue to be important sources of help to their adult children and grandchildren, and many grandparents are far from being "old." We will look at relationships between parents, their adult children, and their grandchildren and see how these relationships are influenced by a variety of social factors, including ethnicity, gender, divorce, and drugs.

MULTI-GENERATIONAL FAMILIES IN MODERN LIFE

In most families children play a very important role in their parents' lives. Children extend their parents' social networks and link them with succeeding generations. However, not all people have children, and Box 1 describes the interpersonal relationships of adults who are childless in later life.

It is interesting to explore the reasons people have children in the first place. Historically, people had children for utilitarian reasons. In preindustrial times the family needed help with work around the farm and home, and children provided an important source of labor. Infant mortality rates were high, so families wanted to have many children to assure that there would be enough help for the work at hand (Thomas, 1992). Today, people in most developed countries usually do not mention these pragmatic reasons for having children. Instead they most often report wanting children in order to have close relationships with them (Neal, Groat, & Wicks, 1989). (See also the discussion of this issue in Chapter 12.)

There have been two major demographic shifts during the 20th century that are relevant to multi-generational families. First, there was a marked increase in births in the mid-1940s, and this trend was sustained for the next 20 years. This period is often called the Baby Boom. Children born during this time will contribute to the increase in the number of older adults in the next century. Second, because of improvements in medical care, there was a marked decrease in the rate of death over the past 100 years. Although the lower death rate can be mostly attributed to fewer infant deaths, there are also many more people living to old age.

Now let us review how much the older adult population has grown in this century. In 1900 about 4% of the U.S. population was people over

Box 1

Interpersonal Relationships of Childless Older Adults

Although most Americans believe that they will have adult children when they are over age 65, about 20% are childless when they reach this age. Among people who are aged 85 and older, the percentage without children jumps to over 30%. Many of these individuals may have chosen not to have children, perhaps because they were of childbearing age during the Great Depression or World War II, but many others are childless because they have outlived their children. Some researchers believe that childless older adults have fewer social and family ties and are more socially isolated than older adults with children (Brubaker, 1985). Thus older adults who do not have children or grandchildren may be missing out on important interpersonal relationships. Do these people have *any* close personal relationships at all? If so, with whom? The answer depends on whether people are childless because they have outlived their children or because they have never had children.

Recent research suggests that older adults who have outlived their children are indeed likely to have fewer social contacts than other older adults (Brubaker, 1985; Johnson & Troll, 1992). This may be true because a vital component of the parents' social networks ceases to exist with the loss of their children. To compensate, they may turn to other family and friends, but these relationships may have been neglected for many years, and it may be difficult to foster them in later life. Furthermore, many people who have outlived their children have also outlived most of their other family and friends. They may then have to build new relationships, at a time when they might find it difficult to meet new people.

A different picture emerges, however, for people who have never had children. It has been shown that people who remain childless throughout their lives are less isolated than those who once had children. Connidis and Davies (1990) found that these older adults have well-developed social networks, including relationships with friends and other family members, especially siblings. Rubinstein, Alexander, Goodman, and Luborsky (1991) found that relationships of women who have never had children fall into three categories: blood ties, friendships, and "constructed kin" ties. Relationships with family (blood ties) are most often with aged parents, siblings, and nieces and nephews. Throughout their lives, childless women also develop intense, long-term friendships. Constructed kin relationships are with people described as "like family" and have usually existed for many years. The women interviewed felt that they could count on their constructed kin as they could on family, and they characterized these relationships as having the same strong emotional ties that are often found in families. Apparently, people who remain childless foster strong social bonds throughout their lives, and these ties remain vital and important into old age.

Increasingly, people occupy intergenerational roles simultaneously and for longer periods of time.

the age of 65; by 1985 their representation had grown to about 12%. It is projected that by the year 2030 older adults will make up 21% of the U.S. population. What is even more remarkable is that the fastest growing segment of the population is individuals who are 85 and older (Gilford, 1988). Thus the population of older adults in the United States is not only growing larger, it is also growing much older.

The increase in the older portion of the population has been partly responsible for more multi-generational families than ever before. Another major factor affecting this trend is that in some subgroups, people are becoming parents at earlier ages. Some researchers have reported as many as six or seven generations represented within a single family (Burton, 1987). Although such families are unusual, it is still the case that typical parents today can expect to know not only their grandchildren, but their great-grandchildren as well. In addition, because people are living longer, they can expect to occupy intergenerational roles, such as parent and grandparent, for much longer periods of time than in the past (Bengtson, Marti, & Roberts, 1991).

Although the structure and size of multi-generational families in America differ greatly, there are also many similarities to be found. In the next section we explore some of the common features of parents' relationships with their children who have reached adulthood. In the final section we examine parents' relationships with the next generation, that is, the children of their own children.

RELATIONSHIPS BETWEEN PARENTS AND THEIR ADULT CHILDREN

Parents' relationships with their adult children are usually quite different from their relationships with these same children when the children were young. During their children's formative years, parents are responsible for providing the basic essentials of life, such as food, clothing, and shelter, as well as for shaping their children's intellectual, moral, and social development. Children's needs change as they mature into adulthood. They become more self-sufficient and do not have to rely on their parents for the same things they had to rely on them for when they were younger. In addition to these developmental changes, many adult children get married, and when they do, their attention and allegiances tend to shift away from their parents. Marriage also introduces new members to the family, through in-law relationships and possibly the birth of grandchildren.

There is ample evidence to suggest that the parent-child bond is important and meaningful to both parties, and there is usually a strong desire to maintain this relationship. Box 2 illustrates this point by describing the somewhat unusual situation of the parent-child bond being severed through the death of an adult child. Under more usual circumstances, however, children's developmental and social changes require parents and children to change their ways of interacting with one another in order to maintain their relationships. Researchers sometimes refer to these changes in patterns of interaction as **role transitions**.

It is probably obvious to you that no two families are exactly alike in the ways they resolve their parent-child role transitions. However, within a given culture there are many widely accepted beliefs and attitudes about how people should relate to one another, and these expectations are called **norms of behavior**. Johnson (1989) has identified several norms of behavior in American families that frequently shape the role transitions between parents and their adult children. When children reach adulthood—especially when they marry—a major change occurs in their relationships with their families of origin. In most cases loyalties are shifted away from their parents to other significant relationships. Most parents adhere to the **norm of noninterference**, which dictates that parents become less involved in their adult children's daily lives. Furthermore, by living in separate households parents and their children usually have fewer contacts with one another. When adult children marry, the contacts that do occur usually involve the children and their spouses jointly, rather than the children alone.

Another common characteristic of American family life is that women are the key persons who manage and coordinate family relationships. Thus women are the means through which generations within a family maintain close relationships. To reflect this norm, women are often referred to as **kin-keepers** (Johnson, 1989).

Johnson (1989) further points out that, compared to families in other cultures, American families are noted for being relatively unstructured regarding **norms of reciprocity** (beliefs about what one person should do in return for the help of another) and **norms of obligation** (beliefs about what one person should do for another, regardless of what that other person has done for him or her). As a result, there is a wide range of options available to American family members in the kinds of relationships they can have with one another. There is even the rarely chosen option to forgo kin relationships altogether.

In a survey of parents and their adult children, Hamon and Blieszner (1990) asked about both parties' expectations for what adult children should do for their parents. The parents and the adult children agreed that

---

Mothers Who Outlive Their Adult Children

Although many parents sometimes fear the death of their own children, most fully expect that they will die long before their children do. When an elderly person loses an adult child, fears of isolation and loneliness may be created as well as concerns about who will be there to offer assistance in times of need. This unexpected event may also leave the elderly person feeling robbed of a long-held and treasured identity as a parent, in addition to the pain associated with the loss of a child at any stage of life.

Goodman, Rubinstein, Alexander, and Luborsky (1991), researchers at the Philadelphia Geriatric Center, conducted a study of elderly women who had recently experienced the death of an adult child and were trying to cope with the loss. The researchers were particularly interested in cultural differences in the ways women cope with such an event, so they compared Jewish and Christian mothers. Although all the women expressed sadness over the loss, there were marked differences in the Jewish and Christian mothers' reactions. Overall, the Jewish women were more depressed and fixed in grief, with the loss remaining central to their lives. In contrast, the Christian women appeared to be more accepting of the death and seemed to think about it in a way that allowed them to get on with their lives. The reactions of the women in this study point out the importance of the mother-child bond even in later life and demonstrate how religious and cultural values can affect the ways that mothers cope when this bond is severed by their child's death.

---

children ought to provide their parents with a great deal of emotional support and should discuss important matters with them. They also agreed that children should not be expected to live close to their parents or to write to them often. Unlike the children, however, parents did *not* think that they should receive money from or live with their children. They also did not think that their children should change their work schedules to help them out. Overall, there was generally good agreement between parents' and children's expectations. Thus despite the flexibility in American families regarding the norms of obligation, there seems to be a general consensus across generations about adult children's roles in relation to their parents.

Theories about Adult Child–Parent Relationships

In an attempt to explain how parents and their adult children relate to each other, several theories have been proposed. One of these theories is called social exchange theory, and it focuses on the costs and rewards of family relationships. Another theory, called social structural theory, focuses on similarities and differences among family members on such factors as age and gender. We will briefly discuss both of these perspectives and some of the research associated with each, using Suitor and Pillemer's (1991) review as a guide.

As you may recall from Chapter 2, **social exchange theory** assumes that people attempt to maximize their rewards and minimize their costs in any interpersonal relationship. This theory also assumes that each partner in a relationship expects that the rewards she or he provides the other partner with will be returned or reciprocated. The theory does not assume, however, that return of the reward will necessarily be immediate or that the same kind of reward will be returned.

Relationships are thought to be most harmonious when partners believe they are getting at least as much out of a relationship as they are putting into it. The theory predicts that when there is an imbalance in a relationship such that one's costs outweigh one's rewards, the relationship will be troubled. In this situation, nonfamily relationships are likely to end. However, in families, where the ending of relationships is more difficult, conflict may arise.

There is substantial evidence in the gerontological literature to support this theory. Research has shown that when adult children believe that their relationships with their parents have become inequitable (for instance, when parents do not provide the support they once did), the children tend to feel less affection for and attachment to the parents, and conflict is likely to occur (Suitor & Pillemer, 1991). It should be noted, however, that independence is highly valued among parents and that dependence, especially on children, is feared. Therefore, maintaining balance, or equity, in parent-child relationships is of prime importance to both generations (Lee & Shehan, 1989).

In contrast to social exchange theory, **social structural theory** does not focus so much on interpersonal transactions as on the social positions and roles that partners in a relationship hold. The theory can include such social status factors as marriage, age, and gender. It is assumed that the more similar these roles and positions are for two partners, the better their relationship will be, because the partners will have more in common. For parents and adult children, therefore, the theory would predict that as the children acquire many of the social positions of their parents (for example, when the children get married and become parents themselves) the quality of the parent-child relationship will be enhanced (Suitor & Pillemer, 1991).

Suitor and Pillemer's (1991) review of age, marital status, and gender reveals that there is considerable evidence in the gerontological research to support this theory too. When children become older, both they and their parents report more harmonious relationships. In addition, children's transition from being single to being married is associated with an increase in positive feelings between them and their parents. However, with regard to gender, the theory is only partially supported. The strongest affectional ties are found between mothers and daughters (which is consistent with the social structural theory) and the weakest affectional ties are between fathers and sons (which is inconsistent with the theory). Research shows that in any parent-child relationship that includes a woman (either a mother or a daughter), affectional bonds are stronger. These findings provide more evidence for the idea that women are kin-keepers.

There is research that supports both theories' notions about parent–adult child relationships, and it may be impossible to determine which theory is more accurate because each looks at different aspects of personal relationships. It is probably best to view these theories less as being in competition and more as complementing each other. For example, mother-daughter relationships may be stronger not only because the partners are of the same gender but also because their relationships involve more equitable exchanges of valued resources such as emotional support.

Contact Between Parents and Their Adult Children

In preindustrial times, when children became adults they tended to live close to their parents. In some cases parents and their adult children continued to reside in the same household (even when the children had children of their own), and in other cases children moved away but continued to live in the same (or a nearby) community. Geographic mobility is much more common in modern life, and many adult children move to locations far from their parents. This trend raises questions about how increased physical distance between parents' and adult children's homes affects the amount of contact they have. In this section we will take a look at multi-generational households (where more than one generation lives in the same house) and the effects of physical distance on contact between parents and adult children who reside in separate households.

Multi-generational households have never been very common in American families, and their numbers have dropped significantly in the past two decades. In the early 1960s nearly one-third of older adults shared households with their adult children. By the mid-1970s this figure had declined to 18%, and it remained stable through the 1980s (Crimmins & Ingegneri, 1990). There is ample evidence to suggest that most older adults want to maintain their independence and live separately from their children. The resulting relationships between most parents and their adult children might best be described as **intimacy at a distance** (Streib, 1973).

Although most parents and their adult children do not want to share the same household, research has shown that many want to live relatively close to one another. Most families seem to be successful in accomplishing this goal (Bengtson, Rosenthal, & Burton, 1990). In a study of multi-generational families, Shanas (1979) found that three-fourths of older adults lived within a half hour's drive of at least one of their children. This is a classic study, because these findings ran counter to popular beliefs at that time, which suggested that modern older adults were isolated from their families because of their children's geographic mobility. It is interesting to note that the percentage of parents living within half an hour of their children did not change during the 1980s (Crimmins & Ingegneri, 1990).

Peterson (1989) reviewed research on the relation of physical proximity to contact between parents and their adult children and concluded that the amount of contact does not change as physical distance increases, but the types of contact do. When children live at greater distances, they and their parents tend to substitute telephone conversations and letters for visits with each other, and visits occur less often but are of longer duration. In addition, distance does not seem to alter the amount of affection in these relationships. In sum, this research indicates that families have been able to adjust to the changing demands of modern society, in that physical distance does not pose a major barrier to relationships between adult children and their parents.

What Adult Children Do for Their Parents

When children reach adulthood they encounter new opportunities to provide the kind of support to their parents that their parents once gave them. Let's examine how parents describe the relationships they have with their adult children. Of special interest are the kinds of emotional and tangible support that parents receive from these relationships.

Long and Mancini (1989) studied parent-child relationships, using Weiss's (1974) classification of the kinds of support that often characterize adult relationships. As noted in Chapter 1, Weiss's theory describes six kinds of support received from partners in these relationships: attachment (feelings of being connected and secure), social integration (a sense of belonging), reliable alliance (knowing that help can be counted on), guidance (advice and expertise), reassurance of worth (feelings of competence and esteem), and opportunity for nurturance (a sense of being needed).

Although all forms of support were mentioned by the parents in Long and Mancini's (1989) study, attachment, reliable alliance, and opportunities for nurturance were mentioned most often. Parents stated that their children provided them with an intimate, mutually respectful, and sharing relationship. Parents also indicated that their children often provided them with many forms of assistance such as transportation and help with home repairs. Although the children were more independent than they had been in earlier years, parents also valued the fact that the children allowed them to continue their nurturant parenting roles.

The findings of this study highlight the breadth of what parents receive in their relationships with their adult children. Throughout the interviews with the parents the themes of independence and reciprocity were common (Long & Mancini, 1989). Although it is clear that parents appreciate what they get from their children, it is also evident that they do not wish to become overly reliant on their children. Instead, they strongly insist that they want to maintain a high degree of reciprocity and mutual exchange.

What Parents Do for Their Adult Children

A popular belief is that as parents grow older they receive more from their children than they give. The fact is, however, that many older adults continue to be important resources to their adult children, especially when the children are undergoing stress. Many middle-aged and young adults experience stress associated with such social problems as divorce, chemical dependence, and unemployment. Research suggests that adult children do, in fact, turn to their parents for help during such stressful times.

Greenberg and Becker (1988) interviewed married couples about the life stressors that their adult children had experienced. Of special interest were how the children's stress affected these parents and what the parents did to help their children through the difficult times. Parents indicated that they provided help to all their children, but they gave most help to those children who had experienced major life problems.

The kinds of problems that were most distressing to parents were those that upset their children emotionally—having a major illness, going through marital difficulties, or experiencing alcohol and drug abuse problems. Regardless of their children's situations, parents frequently provided their adult children with many resources such as money, child care, and advice. When children were experiencing especially difficult problems, parents increased their efforts and provided even more of these same resources. Based on this study, it seems clear that parents often choose to continue nurturing and helping their children long after their children have become able to provide for themselves.

Parents with developmentally disabled children experience a somewhat different evolution in their relationships with these children. Many children with developmental disabilities are not likely to gain the crucial skills and resources that allow for self-sufficiency in adulthood. Thus their dependency often creates a state of **perpetual parenthood** for their parents (Jennings, 1987). The parents of developmentally disabled children frequently have little choice but to continue providing the same level of support when the children become adults as they did when the children were younger. Because individuals with these disabilities are living longer than ever before, caring for these children is becoming a significant issue for many older adults. These parents experience many worries such as the recognition of their own aging and what this means for their children's future care. In addition, the problems of social isolation and financial burdens that began with their children's birth are magnified as parents enter later life, when their health, social, and financial situations change.

In the next section we will discuss parents' relationships with their grandchildren. These relationships share many of the complexities that characterize parent–adult child relationships, but grandparent-grandchild relationships are often even more diverse.

RELATIONSHIPS BETWEEN GRANDPARENTS AND THEIR GRANDCHILDREN

Although it is obvious that in order to become a grandparent one must first be a parent, there are some implications of this truism for the grandparent-grandchild relationship that may not be so obvious. Achieving parenthood involves one's own choices and actions, but achieving grandparenthood is based on the decisions and actions of one's children. Grandparenthood is sometimes called a **countertransition** because it is dependent on the role transitions of others (Burton, 1987). In addition, the relationships that develop between parents and their children are mostly determined by those two parties, but the relationships that develop between grandparents and their grandchildren may be strongly influenced by the intervening generation of adult children (that is, the grandchildren's parents). Thus adult children are key players in the development and maintenance of the relationships between grandparents and grandchildren. They not only determine how and when their parents become grandparents, they also can affect the amount and kind of contact that is possible between their parents and their children. In this section we will see how the grandparent role has changed over time, the different types of grandparenting characteristic of modern American grandparents, and the meaning of the grandparent-grandchild relationship to those in each of these generations.

The Changing Nature of the Grandparent Role

The tenuousness of the grandparent role in modern American families is accompanied by a great deal of ambiguity about the norms of behavior for grandparents. Unlike parenthood, grandparenthood has no clearly defined legal or social obligations, and thus a wide range of options exist for how grandparents relate to their grandchildren (Johnson, 1983). The relatively undefined role of grandparents in today's society is in stark contrast to the prescriptive role they filled in the past.

In preindustrial American society grandparents usually had a great deal of authority and power over both their adult children and their grandchildren (Barranti, 1985). As a result their relationships with their grandchildren involved primarily discipline and guidance. American family structure has changed, though, and grandparents generally do not hold the same positions of authority that they once did. Accordingly, relationships between grandparents and their grandchildren have changed and now involve more warmth and indulgence than discipline and advice (Barranti, 1985).

When we think about grandparents, most of us probably conjure up stereotypes that include people who not only are indulging and warm but also have a variety of other characteristics. The "traditional" grandmother is often sentimentally described as gray haired and plump. She is thought to spend her days tirelessly baking cookies for her grandchildren and her evenings sitting by the fire wrapped in a shawl (Johnson, 1983; Thomas, 1992). The "traditional" grandfather, too, evokes many of the images associated with old age such as wearing glasses and being hard of hearing. He is also thought to take his grandchildren fishing, teach them carpentry skills, and tell them fascinating stories about the "good old days" (Thomas, 1992).

But as with many stereotypes, those pertaining to the traditional grandparents bear little resemblance to most modern grandmothers and grandfathers. Today people often become grandparents while in their 40s and 50s (Thomas, 1992), and many are actively involved in their careers. In addition, many grandparents still have living parents and grandparents of their own who need much of their attention. Thus although they are important to grandparents, grandchildren often represent only one part of the grandparents' very busy lives.

Given the ambiguity surrounding the grandparent role, grandparents have a variety of choices regarding how they interact with their grandchildren. The choices they make often reflect the competing demands of their own lives (such as work) as well as their own needs and personalities. Note, however, that these choices are usually made in the context of their adult children's life circumstances and wishes concerning the grandparent-grandchild relationship.

Divorce among adult children is one such life circumstance that raises a host of questions for the relationship between grandparents and their grandchildren. Although the problem of ambiguity about the grandparent role exists in intact families, it is magnified in divorcing families for at least two reasons. First, even though divorce is more prevalent now than in the past, society has not yet established norms for what family members (especially grandparents) should do when a divorce occurs. Second, because in many parts of the United States grandparents do not have full legal rights regarding their grandchildren, grandparents often cannot be sure that they will be able to maintain contact with their grandchildren after a divorce. The dilemma is especially great for grandparents whose adult children do not receive custody of the grandchildren. Because 90% of all divorcing mothers retain custody of their children and 50% of all fathers do not stay in contact with their children after the divorce, maternal grandparents are more likely than paternal grandparents to remain involved with their grandchildren (Johnson, 1989).

Given the wide range of options and circumstances of grandparenthood, it is no wonder that grandparent-grandchild relationships in American society are best characterized by their diversity. Despite this diversity, there seems to be a certain degree of consensus about what grandparents—in particular, grandmothers—should and should not do in their relationships with their grandchildren. In a study examining norms pertaining to grandmotherhood, Johnson (1983) found that grandmothers have more explicit beliefs about what they should not do than what they should do. Most believe that grandmothers should not interfere, in that they should not give advice or be judgmental; they should not be disciplinarians; and they should not overprotect or spoil their grandchildren. Grandmothers also believe that they should not try to buy their grandchildren's love and should not be disappointed if their grandchildren do not return favors.

In contrast to what they think they should not do, grandmothers' ideas about what they should do are somewhat less behaviorally specific. Most see themselves as advocates who are there to love their grandchildren and to give them feelings of security and self-esteem. Grandmothers also believe that they should provide a sense of continuity with the past and be a source of fun in their grandchildren's lives. Finally, in keeping with the tenuous and ambiguous nature of their roles, most grandmothers believe that they must define and earn their relationships with their grandchildren, not just expect that desirable relationships will automatically occur.

What type of grandparent do you think this man is? (See Box 3.)

Different Types of Grandparenting

Many researchers have attempted to describe and classify various types of grandparenting. Several typologies have been developed, and Box 3 describes one of the most enduring and frequently used classification systems. Before reading further, you may wish to read this box and see how one of your grandparents would be described in this classification scheme.

Although such typologies may offer rich descriptions of grandparenting, they are often limited by their assumptions. For example, most assume that a particular grandparent is best described by only one type of grandparenting strategy (for example, the "fun-seeking" or "formal" grandparent). This assumption fails to recognize that a given grandparent may use different kinds of strategies

---

Box 3   **What Kind of Grandparent Do You Have?**

Many researchers have tried to classify grandparents into various types. There is still disagreement about the best and most accurate classification system, but one proposed by Neugarten and Weinstein in 1964 is still widely used today. They classified grandparents into five types: Formal, Fun-Seeker, Distant Figure, Surrogate Parent, and Reservoir of Family Wisdom. Below are some questions based on their research. Answer yes or no to each of these questions regarding one of your grandparents (or an older adult who fulfills that role) to see where your grandparent fits in their system.

Yes   No

1. Does your grandparent make it clear that he or she is not your parent, and so will not do things that would go against your parents?
2. Is your grandparent playful; does your grandparent do things with you just for fun?
3. Was your grandparent involved in many decisions about how to raise you?
4. Does your grandparent have authority over both you and your parent?
5. Does your grandparent like to spoil you a little every once in a while?
6. Does your grandparent have parental authority over you?
7. Do you only see your grandparent on major holidays or at family functions?
8. Do you feel as if your grandparent is another parent for you?
9. Does your grandparent teach you special skills or family traditions?
10. When you were little, did your grandparent sometimes help out your parents by babysitting you?
11. Do you have a loving relationship with your grandparent, one that makes both of you happy?
12. Is your grandparent kind but generally emotionally distant?
13. Was your grandparent around more often than your parent as you were growing up?
14. Is your grandparent a powerful force in your family?

Classify your grandparent as one of the following types, based on your answers. If you answered Yes to questions 1, 5, and 10 and No to question 7, your grandparent is the Formal type. If you answered

Box 3 continues

Box 3
(continued)

Yes to questions 2 and 11 and No to question 6, your grandparent is the Fun Seeker type. If you answered Yes to questions 1, 5, 7, 10, and 12, your grandparent is a Distant Figure. If you answered Yes to questions 3, 6, 8, and 13 and No to question 1, your grandparent is a Surrogate Parent. Finally, if you answered Yes to questions 1, 9, and 14, your grandparent is a Reservoir of Family Wisdom.

You may find that your grandparent is described by more than one category. This is what most researchers have found. Based on experiences with your grandparents, do you have ideas about how to categorize grandparenting styles so that the categories describe grandparents better than this system?

with different grandchildren, that grandparenting strategies may change as grandparents age, and that different grandparenting strategies may be appropriate for children at different developmental stages. Another limitation of these typologies is that much of the research has been conducted with grandparents of very young children (see, for example, Neugarten & Weinstein, 1964).

Cherlin and Furstenberg (1985) studied grandparenting strategies among grandparents of teenagers. Their study revealed three major categories of grandparenting that reflected different kinds and amounts of involvement: active, passive, and detached. Active grandparents (those who have the most contact with their grandchildren and are most involved in their lives) are generally younger and live relatively close to their grandchildren. Passive grandparents (those who have less contact and are not very involved) are older and also tend to live close to their grandchildren. Detached grandparents (those who have the least contact and involvement with their grandchildren) are generally older and live at greater distances from their grandchildren. One striking difference between these findings and those reported by others is the failure to identify the more playful type of grandparent (such as the "fun-seeker," reported by Neugarten & Weinstein, 1964). This difference may be due, in part, to the different developmental needs of teenagers compared to young children.

Findings by Cherlin and Furstenberg (1985) suggest that grandparenting strategies may change as grandparents age and that physical distance may also be a major factor in relationships. Despite differences in grandparenting styles, a majority in each of Cherlin and Furstenberg's groups indicated that they felt very close to their grandchildren. However, feelings of closeness to grandchildren tended to increase with increases in grandparents' involvement.

Cherlin and Furstenberg (1985) also reported that grandparents tend to be more involved with some grandchildren than with others. They call this phenomenon **selective investment**. Reasons for differential investment in grandchildren include the physical proximity of the grandparents to their grandchildren, the grandchildren's personalities, and the quality of the relationships between the adult children and the grandparents. Therefore, deciding which grandchildren to invest in appears to be yet another option available to grandparents.

Ethnic and Racial Differences in Grandparenting   Most research on grandparenting has focused on white families, and little attention has been given to racial and ethnic minority families. Burton and Dilworth-Anderson (1991) have highlighted the importance of the grandparent role in African-American culture. Historically, African-American grandparents have served as surrogate parents or co-parents to their grandchildren, and many continue to do so today. During the post–Civil War "great migration" of African-Americans from the South to areas in the North and the West, many African-American grandparents cared for their grandchildren while their adult children established themselves in new communities. Today, many African-American grandparents, especially maternal grandmothers, still take on the parent role; but they do so for different reasons, including the teenage pregnancy and chemical dependence of their children. Box 4 discusses the concerns and rewards of grandparenting when adult children are unable to care for their own children.

The Cherlin and Furstenberg (1985) study found that many more African-American grandparents could be classified as active (63%) than white grandparents (26%) or other racial and ethnic minority grandparents (33%). These findings may be due, in part, to the co-parenting trends that Burton and Dilworth-Anderson (1991) describe. These researchers have suggested that because the typologies of grandparenting strategies were developed using white families, they may not be appropriate for describing grandparenting among African-American families. However, other research has shown that even among whites, there are systematic differences between ethnic groups (for example, Italians, Scandinavians, and the Irish) in their grandparenting styles. These sociocultural and racial differences in grandparenting styles indicate yet another limitation of grandparenting typologies.

Differences Between Young and Old Grandmothers   In every society there are social **age norms** that prescribe appropriate activities for a given stage of life. These norms operate as internalized clocks that inform us when to enter and exit important social roles. When people enter or exit roles "off time," they often have difficulty adjusting.

Burton (1987) studied "on-time" and "off-time" grandmothers. On-time grandmothers (those aged 42–57) felt that they were in the right role at the right time, and they were delighted to be involved with their grandchildren. Off-time grandmothers (those aged 25–38) felt that they

---

Box 4

Grandparents as Surrogate Parents in an Alcohol and Drug Epidemic

Alcoholism and drug addiction have been recognized as problems in American society for many years. Although it is widely known that these problems can also affect members of the addicted person's family, their impact on grandparents has only begun to receive attention from researchers. Burton (1992) studied grandparents who had assumed responsibility for raising their grandchildren as a result of their children's drug addiction. In these families, drug addiction had interfered with the young parents' abilities to provide the care and security their children required. In the inner-city neighborhoods where Burton's research was conducted, 30% to 50% of the children under the age of 12 were being raised by a grandparent. Some of the grandparents in Burton's study were raising as many as five to eight grandchildren at once. In some cases the grandchildren had mental or physical disabilities due to their parents' drug use and required special care. Most of the grandparents had serious health problems themselves, such as heart disease and diabetes. The grandparents experienced a great deal of stress in caring for their grandchildren. They often reported fears about the dangers in the neighborhoods where they were raising the children (for example, drug trafficking and drive-by shootings), and they organized their own and their grandchildren's activities around the high-crime times on the streets. They also discussed the difficulty of keeping up with their grandchildren's school and social activities (for instance, homework and birthday parties) and their beliefs that they would continue to serve as parents to their grandchildren for many years to come. Despite these stresses, the grandparents also found many rewards in their roles as surrogate parents, and many described the opportunity to raise a grandchild as a "blessing" and as "a reason for living."

---

were in the wrong role for this time in their lives, and they often resented being grandmothers. They saw grandparenthood as interfering with other on-time activities in their lives, such as education, work, and romantic relationships.

Burton (1987) found that in some families the young grandmother refused to take on any responsibility for her teenaged daughter and the daughter's baby. The result was that caretaking responsibilities shifted to the next older generation, and the great-grandmother took on parenting responsibilities for her teenaged granddaughter and new great-grandchild. Because these great-grandmothers were themselves only in middle-age (46–57 years), many were also caring for their own aging parents. The findings of Burton's study underscore the importance of on-time entry into the grandparent role for the successful adjustment of the grandparent and other family members.

The Meaning of Grandparenthood

Some researchers have focused on the *meanings* that grandparents assign to their roles as grandparents. It has been argued that "meaning" is an important component of any social role because it provides information on how individuals interpret the enactment of a role (Kivnick, 1985). Meaning may be especially important to the grandparent role because there are few social guidelines for how this role should be enacted. Consequently, the meanings that individual grandparents assign to their roles may be the strongest determinants of how they carry out their roles.

Kivnick (1982, 1985) has identified five dimensions of meaning that grandparents often assign to their roles: Centrality, Valued Elder, Immortality Through Clan, Reinvolvement with Personal Past, and Indulgence. *Centrality* refers to the extent to which the role is central to grandparents' activities, self-identity, and purpose in life. *Valued Elder* represents the desire to be an esteemed and wise resource to grandchildren. The hope for personal and family continuity through grandchildren is reflected in the dimension of *Immortality Through Clan*. The dimension of *Reinvolvement with Personal Past* emphasizes that experiences with grandchildren are ways for grandparents to recapture their own childhood experiences, especially those involving *their* grandparents. Finally, *Indulgence* refers to the extent to which grandparents view the grandparent role as one that involves giving, tolerance, and leniency toward grandchildren. Kivnick proposes that all grandparents hold each of these views to some degree but that the relative importance of each dimension differs. These individual differences in meaning may help to account for the wide variations in grandparents' relationships with their grandchildren.

Research has shown that relationships with grandchildren are highly valued by grandparents because they offer grandparents opportunities to maintain vital social connections and a sense of social identity (Kivett, 1991). Grandmothers in particular believe that grandchildren represent a way to extend themselves beyond their own lifetimes. Grandparenting also is a way to fulfill the need for stimulation and to feel competent and creative. In addition, the support grandparents provide their grandchildren adds structure to their own lives and allows them a way to act on their altruistic beliefs (Timberlake, 1980).

It is also clear that grandchildren value their relationships with their grandparents. Grandparents' personalities, the activities they share with their grandchildren, and the special attention they give to their grandchildren are among the most common reasons that grandchildren give for feeling close to their grandparents. Grandparents are also valued as role models, teachers of life skills, and sources of advice and inspiration. Some grandchildren also appreciate spending time visiting their grandparents in the grandparents' home, and some indicate that when their grandparents are frail, helping their grandparents is a way for them to act on *their* altruistic beliefs (Kennedy, 1991).

SUMMARY

In this chapter we have examined personal relationships in families where at least three generations are represented and at least two of these generations have reached adulthood. The focus was on two kinds of relationships: those between parents and their adult children and those between grandparents and their grandchildren. Demographic shifts have increased the prevalence of multi-generational families and have changed the nature of family relationships. Theories concerning relationships between adult children and their parents include social exchange theories and structural theories. The amount of contact between adult children and their parents as well as the living arrangements of these generations are affected by geographic mobility and physical proximity. We discussed the ways in which the two generations are involved with and support each other.

In this chapter we also looked at the changing nature of grandparent-grandchild relationships in modern American society, including changes in role expectations. There are several different types of grandparenting style, which are affected in part by ethnicity, race, and age.

In sum, this chapter has shown that most parents maintain strong social ties with their adult children and with their grandchildren. In addition, it has emphasized that parents remain important resources of support to the younger generations. Although some characteristics of multi-generational families have undergone transition, in keeping with changes in American society in general, the value placed on intergenerational family relationships has not diminished. Instead, these relationships continue to be important for the identity, adjustment, and well-being of parents, their adult children, and their grandchildren.

Class Discussion Questions

1. Compare the relationship you currently have with your parents with your relationship ten years ago. Discuss the changes that have taken place in this relationship in terms of the research on parent-child role transitions that was discussed in this chapter.
2. What do you do for your parents now that you are an adult? What do your parents do for their parents (your grandparents)? Which concept captures these relationships better, norms of reciprocity or norms of obligation? Why?

3. Why do you think women have been labeled "kin-keepers"? What biological, social, or cultural factors may have contributed to this phenomenon?
4. Compare and contrast the "traditional" grandparent to your own grandparents. Give reasons for any similarities and differences you find. Pay special attention to your grandparents' age, health, financial status, and ethnicity.

Homework Assignments

1. Watch a television program or movie or read a story or play depicting a relationship between a parent and an adult child. Analyze this relationship in terms of social structural theory and social exchange theory. Which describes the relationship better, and why? (Suggested television programs: *All in the Family*, *The Cosby Show*, and *Roseanne*; suggested movies: *On Golden Pond*, *Used People*, and *Nothing in Common*; suggested fiction: *Breathing Lessons* by Ann Tyler, *Death of a Salesman* by Arthur Miller, and *The Thorn Birds* by Colleen McCullough)
2. While spending time with your parents or grandparents, keep a log for a day or so in which you record things you do for one of them and things that person does for you. Remember to record the intangible things (such as expressions of caring and appreciation) as well as the tangible ones (help with homework, lending money). After you have finished recording this information, decide whether the social exchanges are balanced or imbalanced. Does this information reflect the quality of the relationship you share?
3. Make a list of the roles in your family and culture that are defined by age norms. What are the consequences when roles are entered or exited "off time"? Consider both family and societal consequences.

Additional Readings

Johnson, C. L. (1988). *Ex familia: Grandparents, parents, and children adjust to divorce.* New Brunswick, NJ: Rutgers University Press.

Minkler, M., & Roe, K. M. (1993). *Grandmothers as caregivers: Raising children of the crack cocaine epidemic.* Newbury Park, CA: Sage.

Roberto, K. A. (1993). *The elderly caregiver: Caring for adults with developmental disabilities.* Newbury Park, CA: Sage.

Stephens, M. A. P., Crowther, J. H., Hobfoll, S. E., & Tennenbaum, D. L. (Eds.). (1990). *Stress and coping in later life families.* New York: Hemisphere.

References

Barranti, C. C. R. (1985). The grandparent/grandchild relationship: Family resource in an era of voluntary bonds. *Family Relations, 34,* 343–352.

Bengtson, V. L., Marti, G., & Roberts, R. E. L. (1991). Age-group relationships: Generational equity and inequity. In K. Pillemer & K. McCartney (Eds.), *Parent-child relations throughout life* (pp. 253–278). Hillsdale, NJ: Erlbaum.

Bengston, V. L., Rosenthal, C., & Burton, L. (1990). Families and aging: Diversity and heterogeneity. In R. H. Binstock & L. K. George (Eds.), *Handbook of aging and the social sciences* (3rd ed.) (pp. 263–287). San Diego: Academic.

Brubaker, T. H. (1985). *Later life families*. Beverly Hills: Sage.

Burton, L. M. (1987). Young grandmothers: Are they ready? *Social Science, 72,* 191–194.

Burton, L. M. (1992). Black grandparents rearing children of drug-addicted parents: Stressors, outcomes, and social service needs. *The Gerontologist, 32,* 744–751.

Burton, L. M., & Dilworth-Anderson, P. (1991). The intergenerational family roles of aged black Americans. *Marriage and Family Review, 16*(3–4), 311–330.

Cherlin, A., & Furstenberg, F. F. (1985). Styles and strategies of grandparenting. In V. L. Bengston & J. F. Robertson (Eds.), *Grandparenthood* (pp. 97–116). Beverly Hills: Sage.

Connidis, I. A., & Davies, L. (1990). Confidants and companions in later life: The place of family and friends. *Journal of Gerontology: Social Sciences, 45,* S131–149.

Crimmins, E. M., & Ingegneri, D. G. (1990). Interaction and living arrangements of older parents and their children: Past trends, present determinants, and future implications. *Research on Aging, 12,* 3–35.

Gilford, D. M. (Ed.). (1988). *The aging population in the twenty-first century*. Washington, DC: National Academy.

Goodman, M., Rubinstein, R. L., Alexander, B. B., & Luborsky, M. (1991). Cultural differences among elderly women in coping with the death of an adult child. *Journal of Gerontology: Social Sciences, 46,* S321–329.

Greenberg, J. S., & Becker, M. (1988). Aging parents as family resources. *The Gerontologist, 28,* 786–791.

Hamon, R. R., & Blieszner, R. (1990). Filial responsibility expectations among adult child–older parent pairs. *Journal of Gerontology: Psychological Sciences, 45,* P110–112.

Jennings, J. (1987). Elderly parents as caregivers for their adult dependent children. *Social Work, 32,* 430–433.

Johnson, C. L. (1983). A cultural analysis of the grandmother. *Research on Aging, 5,* 547–567.

Johnson, C. L. (1989). Divorce-related changes in relationships: Parents, their adult children and children-in-law. In J. A. Mancini (Ed.), *Aging parents and adult children* (pp. 33–44). Lexington, MA: Lexington Books.

Johnson, C. L., & Troll, L. (1992). Family functioning in late late life. *Journal of Gerontology: Social Sciences, 47,* S66–72.

Kennedy, G. E. (1991). Grandchildren's reasons for closeness with grandparents. *Journal of Social Behavior and Personality, 6,* 697–712.

Kivett, V. R. (1991). The grandparent-grandchild connection. *Marriage and Family Review, 16*(3–4), 267–290.

Kivnick, H. Q. (1982). *The meaning of grandparenthood.* Ann Arbor, MI: UMI Research Press.

Kivnick, H. Q. (1985). Grandparenthood and mental health: Meaning, behavior, and satisfaction. In V. L. Bengston & J. F. Robertson (Eds.), *Grandparenthood* (pp. 151–158). Beverly Hills, CA: Sage.

Lee, G. R., & Shehan, C. L. (1989). Elderly parents and their children: Normative influences. In J. A. Mancini (Ed.), *Aging parents and adult children* (pp. 117–134). Lexington, MA: Lexington Books.

Long, J. K., & Mancini, J. A. (1989). The parental role and parent-child relationship provisions. In J. A. Mancini (Ed.), *Aging parents and adult children* (pp. 151–166). Lexington, MA: Lexington Books.

Neal, A. G., Groat, H. T., & Wicks, J. W. (1989). Attitudes about having children: A study of 600 couples in the early years of marriage. *Journal of Marriage and the Family, 51,* 313–328.

Neugarten, B. L., & Weinstein, K. K. (1964). The changing American grandparent. *Journal of Marriage and the Family, 26,* 199–204.

Peterson, E. T. (1989). Elderly parents and their offspring. In S. J. Bahr & E. T. Peterson (Eds.), *Aging and the family* (pp. 175–191). Lexington, MA: Lexington Books.

Rubinstein, R. L., Alexander, B. B., Goodman, M., & Luborsky, M. (1991). Key relationships of never married, childless older women: A cultural analysis. *Journal of Gerontology: Social Sciences, 46,* S270–277.

Shanas, E. (1979). Social myth as hypothesis: The case of the family relations of old people. *The Gerontologist, 19,* 3–9.

Streib, G. F. (1973). Facts and forecasts about the family and old age. In G. F. Streib (Ed.), *The changing family: Adaptation and diversity.* Palo Alto, CA: Addison-Wesley.

Suitor, J. J., & Pillemer, K. (1991). Family conflict when adult children and elderly parents share a home. In K. Pillemer & K. McCartney (Eds.), *Parent-child relations throughout life* (pp. 179–199). Hillsdale, NJ: Erlbaum.

Thomas, J. L. (1992). *Adulthood and aging.* Boston: Allyn and Bacon.

Timberlake, E. M. (1980). The value of grandchildren to grandmothers. *Journal of Gerontological Social Work, 3*(1), 63–76.

Weiss, R. S. (1974). The provisions of social relationships. In Z. Rubin (Ed.), *Doing unto others* (pp. 17–26). Englewood Cliffs, NJ: Prentice-Hall.

Glossary

Age norms   Cultural expectations about when in their lives people should enter and exit specific social roles

Countertransition   Role transitions that occur in one person's life based on transitions made by a role partner

Intimacy at a distance   The desire of parents and adult children to live separately from one another but to maintain close relationships

Kin-keepers   People who manage and coordinate family relationships; in traditional American culture, women usually fulfill this function

Norm of noninterference   Cultural expectation about parent–child relationships that says parents will become less involved in their children's daily lives as their children become adults

Norms of behavior   Cultural expectations about how people should relate to one another

Norms of obligation   Expectations about what one person should do for another, regardless of what that other person has done for him or her

Norms of reciprocity   Expectations about what one person should do in return for the help of another

Perpetual parenthood   Parenthood that is prolonged because of an adult child's inability to become self-sufficient and independent from the parents

Role transitions   Significant changes in patterns of interaction between role partners that are often based on developmental and social changes by one or the other partner

Selective investment   The decision to be more involved with some role partners than with others

Social exchange theory   The theory that people attempt to maximize their rewards and minimize their costs in any interpersonal relationship

Social structural theory   The theory that the more roles two people have in common, the better their relationship will be

19

The Caregiving Relationship

Jim L. Query, Jr.
Loyola University

Lyle J. Flint
Ball State University

heir healthy, vigorous counterparts aside, there will always be some percentage of elderly people who re- quire care because of physical or emotional difficulties. These indi- viduals, after several decades of assuming the caregiver role, are now thrust into the role of care recipient, and the shift to this new interpersonal role is often quite difficult to negotiate. It can be ac- companied by the loss of autonomy, pride, and dignity. If the caregiver is a family member, he or she also has the difficult task of adjusting to the shift in the relationship. This chapter exam- ines the challenges in negotiating this life-sustaining relationship.

NV & SD

Chapter Outline

- The Nature of Caregiving
- The Role of Communication in Caregiving Relationships
- The Caregiver's Perspective
- Uncertainty Reduction Theory in Reverse
- The Nature and Impact of Symbolic Crises
- Family Challenges in Caregiving
- Additional Forces Confronting Multi-Generational Families
- External Sources of Social Support
- Conclusion

Little definitive information is available concerning the specific com- ponents of caregiving that foster therapeutic interaction. Since a significant number of elderly individuals suffer from debilitating conditions such as strokes, fractured hips, cancer, and Alzheimer's disease (Guarasci, 1988;

Kreps, 1986; Query, 1989; Query & Smilowitz, 1988a, 1988b), an analysis of their communication with caregiving networks may provide some additional insight. Many of the stressors that these individuals confront—role reversal or shifts, increasing dependency, loss of companionship, and less shared meaning—will also challenge elderly individuals and their families who are not ill or debilitated. In order to illustrate the concepts discussed in this chapter, we will follow a hypothetical family in their efforts to care for an elderly and infirm grandmother. Meet the Robleza family.

Diego Robleza has just returned home from a difficult day of classes at college. He had two essay exams, and a term paper was due. His mood is one of impatience and fatigue. Diego just wants some quiet time for himself.

His older sister, Maria, has been home all day. In addition to feeding, dressing, reading to, and playing with their younger siblings, Jesus and Yanina, Maria has attempted to do household chores. Maria has also cared for her grandmother, Conchis, who has Alzheimer's disease. The head of the household is Cristabalita Robleza, Conchis's daughter, who works 12 hours a day to provide for this family.

Maria: Diego, I really could use some help. There is so much to do, and it never seems to end.

Diego: Look Maria, you have it easy. You're not being graded or pressured to earn a degree. I'm a man, and I shouldn't have to do housework or provide care!

Maria: Fine! Cook your own damned supper then. Also, tell Jesus, Yanina, and Conchis that their needs and well-being aren't your concern! Our home is just a resting place for you, huh? We might as well be strangers to you!

Diego: Oh Maria, why don't you just drop this martyr argument. How difficult can it be taking care of two little ones, the house, and grandmama?

Maria: You really have no idea, do you?

Diego: Yes, I do.

Maria: Let's just see about that. I'm going out for three hours and you're in charge.

Diego: Fine! I'll show you, hija.

Unfortunately, the preceding situation is not uncommon; it occurs all too frequently and across many cultures (Kreps & Kunimoto, 1994). Without some sustained assistance, the vitality of the Robleza's relationships, as well as their health status, will be lowered to some degree.

In this chapter we focus on the intergenerational relationships that are at risk for adverse psychological and relational outcomes when chronic illness or catastrophic disease strikes an elder family member. Some families also experience these stresses in the "horizontal" family relationships—when siblings, cousins, aunts, uncles, or other extended family members are called on to aid in caregiving. Examining a condition that ripples across generational lines (Alzheimer's disease) will show us the role of caregiving relationships in exacerbating or lessening the intensity of family health care crises.

After Maria slammed the front door on her way out, Diego entered Conchis's room. Conchis started talking with Diego.

Conchis:	You know Raul, I don't know about the way I am treated here.
Diego:	Grandmama, I'm Diego. My father, Raul, died over ten years ago. Did Maria put you up to this? She knows it's still painful for me to talk about his death.
Conchis:	Now Raul, I want you to get me out of here. These bad people want to hurt me.
Yanina:	Diego, I'm hungry.
Jesus:	Mano mio, I want you to read me a story.
Conchis:	My, supper is ready, yet no one is eating.
Yanina:	Where's my food, Diego?
Jesus:	Okay, I get the picture. Yanina is your favorite!
Diego:	Just a minute!
Conchis:	We need to call the police, Raul. There are several strangers in our house!
Yanina:	So, you're not feeding grandmama either!
Diego:	That's it! Yanina and Jesus, to your room now!
Conchis:	I am dialing 911, Raul. You're evil and trying to harm us!

THE NATURE OF CAREGIVING

When an older family member suffers from a debilitating illness, all members of the family are at risk for stress-related difficulties.

Diego initially believed that taking care of children, the house, and someone with Alzheimer's disease were easy tasks. As the dialogue reveals, however, **caregiving** involves much more than just being there. It also entails more than merely giving someone what he or she requests. To help us better appreciate the complexity of caregiving, let's first examine some definitions of caregiving.

Sommers and Shields (1987) note that defining *caregiver* is difficult, as the role "covers a wide spectrum of services, depending on the degree of disability, living arrangements, and economic circumstances" (p. 16). Biegel, Sales, and Schulz (1991) advance a view of caregiving that is closely linked to the care recipient's chronic illness and needs over a lengthy period of time; caregiving is thus seen as "the increment of extraordinary care that goes beyond the bounds of normal or usual care" (p. 17). Since Conchis has Alzheimer's disease, this increment of care can only be expected to increase dramatically. Individuals with Alzheimer's gradually lose their ability to communicate and have been known to live with the disease outside of nursing facilities for ten or more years. Cicirelli (1992) also advances an illness-and-need–driven view of caregiving: Caregiving serves primarily to manage the symptoms of frail elderly and satisfy their daily living needs (p. 3). As Alzheimer's disease unfolds, its victims can no longer attend to the daily living tasks that most of us take for granted. A caregiver, then, attempts to address the needs of the care recipient, so the role of caregiver is thus complex and dynamic.

Clarifying the Role of "Needs"

The "needs" of care recipients span at least four areas, including **activities of daily living (ADL)**, **instrumental activities of daily living (IADL)**, **skilled health care**, and **psychological care** (see Cicirelli, 1992; Yu et al., 1993). Assisting care recipients with ADL tasks involves helping with personal care such as bathing, dressing, eating, and grooming. Assisting care recipients with IADL tasks involves helping with shopping, handling money, transportation, and cooking. Skilled health care tasks include giving injections and monitoring vital signs. Psychological care tasks involve providing emotional support to care recipients.

It has only been an hour since Maria has left, and yet, to Diego, it seems like forever. He feels frustrated, confused, unsure of himself, and angry. He has yet to feed anyone, and he must also give Conchis a bath.

> *Diego:* Jesus and Yanina, look, I'm sorry I got angry. I just couldn't handle everything at once. I love you both very much. I have no favorite. I also need your help to get things done around here. If you'll just give me a chance, I know I can come through for us.
>
> *Yanina:* Okay, I guess. . . . All I wanted was supper, you know?
>
> *Jesus:* I should have been more patient too. I'm sorry.
>
> *Diego:* Okay! We're a family. Together we can make this situation work. While I fix supper, why don't you watch a video with Grandmama?
>
> *Jesus:* I like that idea.
>
> *Yanina:* Me too.

In only a short time Diego has begun to develop an appreciation for some of the daily challenges that Maria handles so well. He notices a book about caregivers sitting on the kitchen counter. Perhaps Maria's success is due in part to the information in it. Diego begins reading while he stirs the macaroni and cheese.

Types of Caregivers

To his surprise, Diego learns that there are at least four types of caregivers, ranging from primary to general and lay to professional (informal to formal). Initially, he is somewhat confused about these categories. Reading further, however, he notes that the primary criteria for these categories are the amount of time spent providing care and the amount of formal training received prior to providing care.

Concerning the level of involvement, there are two types of caregivers. A **primary caregiver** is an individual who provides the bulk of the care to the recipient on a regular and frequent basis, often ranging from 5 to 24 hours daily. Maria is an example of this caregiver type. A **general caregiver** is an individual who provides some care to the recipient on an irregular and occasional basis, often ranging from 4 or fewer hours daily (see Query, 1990). Diego falls into this class of caregivers.

There are also two types of caregivers with respect to background or training. A **lay** or **informal caregiver** is an individual who provides care without having received accredited training and/or certification. Typically, family members such as the Roblezas fit into this category. A **professional** or **formal caregiver** is an individual who provides care after receiving accredited training and/or certification. Health care providers such as nurses, physicians, social workers, and allied health personnel usually make up this category.

"Average" Caregiver Characteristics

As Diego reads further, he comes across a discussion of what the "average" caregiver of children and elderly relatives would look like. Although anyone might wind up as a caregiver, the authors identify several characteristics that provide a profile of the typical caregiver.

Sommers and Shields (1987), for example, report that at least 75% of caregivers are female. In sequential order, the most likely relationship of such a woman to the care recipient is spouse, daughter, sister, daughter-in-law, niece, granddaughter, and friend. Diego quickly notices that this list excludes males.

Diego asks himself why females are more likely to be caregivers. A possible explanation is that, traditionally, females have been socialized to be nurturing and supportive. That explanation sounds right to Diego, especially when he thinks about how many women are nurses and teachers. For males these "feminine" behaviors are atypical and involve role reversals (Sommers & Shields, 1987, p. 166). Traditionally, males are socialized to be rational and strict disciplinarians. Nurturing behaviors among males, then, have generally been viewed as taboo or "wimpy." This information helps Diego realize that it's not surprising he assumes Maria "should" be their grandmother's caregiver (and he feels a bit guilty for his inappropriate behavior with Maria).

Diego also begins to wonder about families who pro-

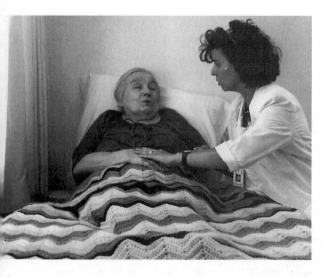

What type of caregiver do you think the woman on the right in this photo is?

vide care for an elderly relative with a disease such as Alzheimer's. By understanding their characteristics, Diego may better appreciate the dynamics of his own family's situation. He begins to uncover more bits and pieces in the book.

In terms of age, the average caregiver is about 57 years old (Biegel et al., 1991). However, a sizeable portion of the caregiver population is somewhat older. More than 35% of caregivers are 65 years of age or older, and more than 10% are 75 or older (Stone, Cafferata, & Sangl, 1987). Although Diego and Maria are only 18 and 19, their mother, Cristabalita, is 54 and a primary provider for Conchis.

Caregivers appear to be of moderate means. Only about 10% of caregivers reported an income in the high category (a yearly income of $40,000 or higher, in 1982 dollars) according to the 1982 National Long Term Care Survey (Stone et al., 1987). Nearly a third were classified as "poor" or "near poor." Diego knows that his family belongs in this category. Indeed, if it weren't for his mother's working so much and Conchis's small monthly disability payments, the family wouldn't make it.

The next caregiver characteristic that Diego reads about is that caregivers are less likely to be employed compared with people in similar age groups. Approximately one-third of caregivers are employed, and those who are typically face competing demands. For example, nearly 10% of caregivers interviewed in one study were forced to quit their jobs, and 20% reported that their caregiving responsibilities caused some form of job conflict (Stone et al., 1987). Diego shudders to think about what would happen if his mother couldn't depend on Maria to care for Conchis, the kids, and the house.

The final characteristic of caregivers that Diego reads about centers on their health status. Only a quarter of caregivers report themselves as possessing excellent health. A little over one-third report their health as only "fair" or "poor" (Stone et al., 1987). Although some of this decline in health status may be due to natural aging, a significant part could also be due to excessive and chronic stress levels.

The contexts within which caregivers of children and of persons with Alzheimer's function are especially traumatic, characterized by extreme and prolonged stress that is fueled by high levels of uncertainty. Unmitigated, these conditions often trigger debilitating emotions such as guilt, anger, frustration, and depression among caregivers, family members, and persons with Alzheimer's (Aronson, 1988; Gilhooly, 1984; Zarit, Orr, & Zarit, 1985). An additional outcome is that as the frequency and severity of the stressors increase, the potential for misunderstanding increases significantly (Query & Smilowitz, 1988a, 1988b).

As Diego readies the plates he thinks about all the long hours put in by Maria and their mother, Cristabalita. He cannot imagine how they so routinely juggle all the demands of caregiving, working, and everyday living. What could be the keys to their success? He recalls part of a conversation from yesterday:

Cristabalita:	Maria, you're such a godsend. You amaze me with your determination, dedication, and diligence. You also have a knack for keeping cool when things just seem out of control.
Maria:	Thank you mama, but I'm not really special. I'm just doing what needs to be done. Besides, I often feel so helpless around grandmama. I rarely know how she's going to react to us.
Cristabalita:	That's one of the toughest things about this disease. As it progresses grandmama will become highly unpredictable, and she may do unusual things. When this happens, it'll be all too easy to blame her. You know, she's acting up to get my attention; or, she's angry with me; or, she resents me acting like her parent. The truth is, though, grandmama can't control these disruptive behaviors.
Maria:	Ay, you're scaring me, mama.
Cristabalita:	I get frightened too, hija mia. I can only imagine how grandmama feels.
Maria:	I know what you mean. . . . I feel like my relationship with grandmama has been changed forever—and against my wishes. If only we could communicate with her like we used to.

As Diego muses over this exchange, he realizes he needs more information. He hopes the next section of the caregiver book will be helpful.

THE ROLE OF COMMUNICATION IN CAREGIVING RELATIONSHIPS

The nature and quality of relationships are forged, maintained, and dissolved through communication with others. Duck (1992), for example, notes that "talk is inextricably linked to human social interaction and underlies human relationships" (p. vii). Fisher (1987) has even argued that a "relationship" cannot exist without individuals' coordinating these behaviors to exchange meaning. A key implication of these views appears to be that the levels of "coordination" and "meaning" ultimately achieved in a relationship will be shaped by the communication skills or communication competence of those involved (see Kelly, 1982; Sanmiguel, 1992; Sarason, Sarason, Hacker, & Basham, 1985; Spitzberg & Cupach, 1984).

Although there are many opinions, often conflicting, on how to best define communication competence, scholars often agree that communication competence, or skills, can be categorized along three dimensions: cognitive, behavioral, and affective (Kreps & Query, 1990).

The cognitive area encompasses message encoding and decoding skills of individuals across contexts and relationships. In the case of communicating with a person with Alzheimer's, these cognitive skills are helpful, but only to a point. As we observed, Diego couldn't seem to convince his grandmother that he was not Raul, that it was unnecessary to call 911, or that supper was not ready.

The behavioral area encompasses communication skills that individuals use to implement goal-oriented strategies while maintaining the integrity of other people. For example, Diego knew he had been brusque with Jesus and Yanina because he was frustrated with Conchis. He had treated them like little children. Diego quickly realized, however, that he couldn't accomplish his objectives—fixing dinner and bathing Conchis—without their assistance. So he explained to them why he had lost his temper. He also offered an apology, and he sought their assistance in a timely and sensitive fashion.

The affective area of communication competence describes how locus of control shapes our relationships with others (Kreps & Query, 1990, p. 307). Rotter (1966) interprets locus of control along a continuum representing the degree to which individuals assume and enact responsibility for environmental consequences. The continuum ranges from **high locus of control** (internal) to **low locus of control** (external). According to Rotter (1966) "internals" see themselves as directly affecting the events and relationships that shape their lives (p. 1). In contrast, "externals" assume minimum responsibility for life events and relationships; they attribute outcomes to fate, chance, or luck (Rotter, 1966, p. 1). Both Diego and Maria could be characterized as internals. Although their communication was not totally smooth or calm, each is actively involved in seeking to maintain the stability of their family situation. Had they been externals, their reactions and messages would have most likely reflected a reluctance to act and a passive attitude.

The above-mentioned areas of communication competence—cognitive, behavioral, and affective—are not mutually exclusive. Thus it is frequently difficult to neatly separate complex communication skills according to these categories. Notwithstanding this difficulty, we can advance our definition of **communication competence**: the perceived tendency to seek out meaningful interaction with others, render support, be relaxed, appreciate others' plight, and take turns appropriately.

Relationship Quality

Another important dimension of relationships, with implications for caregivers, is how interaction characteristics shape relational outcomes. Fisher (1987) identifies four primary characteristics of interaction that determine relational quality. These characteristics describe interaction in terms of observable events. For example, **discontinuity** is the ability to pick up interaction where it left off, despite the time that has elapsed (hours, days, weeks) since the last interaction. **Synchrony** is the fitting together of interaction so that a recognizable pattern emerges that identifies the nature of the relationship. **Recurrence** is being "tuned in" to the synchrony of the interaction so as to recognize relational rituals and identify relational problems. Finally, **reciprocity** is the degree to which the participants agree on the definition of the relationship.

As he clears the table, Diego begins to understand better why he feels so distant from his grandmother. Their interaction reflects large deficits in the above characteristics. For instance, Conchis has great difficulty understanding the passage of time. She can only talk about her childhood with accuracy; the present seems very jumbled to her. Also, she does not understand how Diego can talk about the past, present, and future simultaneously. Diego further observes how his interaction with Conchis has no lasting pattern. It is as if he and she are strangers. These losses of discontinuity and synchrony affect recurrence and reciprocity levels. We can expect that these latter characteristics will also continue to decline as Conchis's disease advances.

THE CAREGIVER'S PERSPECTIVE

After storming out of the house and forcing Diego to take over, Maria goes to the nearby park. It has been too long since her last visit, and the surroundings provide a picturesque and tranquil haven from the tempest at home. The majestic trees, the gentle winds, the delightful pine aromas, and the bubbling creek are calming influences that help Maria rethink her situation. She knows that she lost her temper with Diego. What would she say to her mother now, especially after Cristabalita had called her a godsend? Of course, Maria could just explain that the stress finally caught up with her or that she is still just a teenager, or maybe she could say that it was all Diego's fault, or maybe she could blame Jesus and Yanina. None of these potential explanations, however, seems satisfactory.

As she continues to search for answers, Maria replays her interaction with Diego, and she immediately recalls his statement that males shouldn't have to provide care for children or elderly relatives. Although Maria is tempted to label Diego an insensitive brute, she knows that deep down her brother is very warm, caring, and responsible. So where did his sexist and irresponsible attitude come from? One likely answer could be American cultural values, which also appear in caregiving practices. Now some of the information in her caregiver book is really starting to make sense.

The gentle breezes blow, and Maria sobs inconsolably. It is as if the authors of the caregiver book had peered into her soul, they so aptly described her frustration, her pain, her sorrow, and her despair.

UNCERTAINTY REDUCTION THEORY IN REVERSE

Although it seems as if a lifetime has passed before her eyes, Maria glances at her watch and notices that only an hour has slipped by. She wipes her tear-stained face and tries hard to recall more of the authors' words. She remembers their discussion of uncertainty reduction theory (URT) and its later reversal when applied to caregiving relationships with individuals with Alzheimer's. When Maria had first come across the word *theory*, she had panicked. She had even wanted to stop reading right then, but something had urged her on. She had soon found out that a theory is an explanation of some happening or behavior that can be tested. For example, one theory suggests that individuals with Alzheimer's disease are more likely to become abusive or agitated if others communicate with them in a certain way. To test this theory, social scientists make an educated guess, or a hypothesis, and collect data from persons with Alzheimer's and their caregivers. A possible hypothesis could be that caregivers who use lengthy sentences to communicate with persons who have Alzheimer's will be more likely to observe a high state of agitation than caregivers who use short sentences.

URT seeks to explain how individuals can reduce levels of uncertainty during initial interactions and offers predictions about their communication behaviors (Berger, 1979; Berger & Calabrese, 1975; Heider, 1958). A key premise of this theory is that as individuals lessen their doubts about each other, they are able to better select appropriate communication behaviors and make more accurate predictions about each other's responses. A desirable outcome for the participants is thus enhanced control of the situation. Barclay (1971) drives home this point: "Relationships must be established on a firm and predictable basis. Individuals in a group cannot feel secure unless they know certain types of stimuli will elicit certain types of responses" (p. 48).

As Alzheimer's unfolds, family members will engage in a series of initial interactions. Unfortunately, though, their uncertainty levels will *rise* rather than fall, and their relationship with the relative who has Alzheimer's will undergo dramatic changes. A reversal of URT provides a useful conceptual framework for understanding and analyzing many of these changes.

Stages of Interaction

Maria recalls that initial interaction can be broken down into three stages: entry, personal, and exit. The entry phase typically involves the exchange of nonthreatening factual information such as age, home town, occupation, and so forth. Cultural rules, or norms, play a major role in determining the appropriate information to release. In the personal stage the exchange usually involves self-revealing information such as beliefs, attitudes, and values. Societal conventions are less forceful here. In the exit stage the exchange focuses on the likelihood of future interaction. The individuals express their desire to communicate with each other again or to terminate communications (Infante, Rancer, & Womack, 1990, p. 273). Norms may have little impact in this final stage.

Maria thinks back on many of her interactions with Conchis, and she realizes that URT is operating in reverse. For instance, her grandmother often decides that there is no need for interaction. She will quietly lie awake for hours. She refuses to or can't respond to Maria's conversation. These behaviors might usually occur during the exit stage.

At other times Conchis discloses information, such as intimate details surrounding her love affairs, to Jesus and Yanina. Although the young children do not ask for this information, grandmama supplies it repeatedly. This sort of communication would typically occur during the personal stage.

There are also instances when Conchis recites a litany of background information such as her family tree, all the places she has lived, and her varying ages; although grandmama is only 70 she tells people that she is 40, 25, 36, or 50, depending on her mood. This is usually entry stage communication.

What happens in the case of persons with Alzheimer's, then, is that others' ability to predict their behavior decreases markedly as the disease advances. This increasing unpredictability may also foster widespread sentiments of inadequacy, denial, anger, and/or guilt among caregivers and families (Aronson, 1988; Brown, Lyon, & Sellers, 1988; Query, Parry, & Flint, 1992). Because of these feelings, family members and caregivers often misrepresent the seriousness of the situation, making it more difficult for them to get the support they need as well as triggering a marked sense of chaos (Kreps, 1988).

THE NATURE AND IMPACT OF SYMBOLIC CRISES

Human beings' need to order and control their environment is essential, especially when the individuals confront a catastrophic disease such as Alzheimer's. In addition to severe physiological impacts, this type of disease often presents formidable **symbolic crises** (Query & Smilowitz, 1988a, 1988b; see also, Good, 1977; Good & Good, 1981; and Kreps, 1988). A symbolic crisis is triggered when the affected person and his or her significant others define the catastrophic health condition in ways that block informed understanding and exacerbate the harmful effects of the specific diagnosis. A good example of a symbolic crisis is reported by Kreps (1988) in his analysis of a man's reactions to the diagnosis of cancer:

> The man may even refuse treatment because he believes such
> health care to be futile in reversing the illness. This reaction may

be contrary to current medical information that indicates the viability of specialized treatment for this particular illness, but the man's reactions are consistent with his symbolic evaluation of the health condition. (p. 240)

In the case of the Robleza family, one symbolic crisis was avoided when Cristabalita described several possible, *faulty* interpretations of Conchis's behavior: She's acting up to get my attention; she's angry with me; she resents my acting like her parent. Had these tenuous judgments been allowed to stand, they would have had an adverse impact on the interactions between Conchis and her caregivers. For example, the urgency of Conchis's legitimate requests might have been discounted.

Symbolic crises triggered by catastrophic disease also have at least two other dimensions. The second part of these crises occurs when communication patterns among persons who have Alzheimer's, their families, and other caregivers are invariably altered and relationships subsequently redefined, often against the will of the participants (Guarasci, 1988). What often occurs is that the exchanges between persons with Alzheimer's and their caregivers deny existing relationships or create new, unacceptable ones. Diego experienced this dimension of a symbolic crisis when Conchis communicated with him as if he were her dead son-in-law, Raul. When she equated Diego with "bad people," he was again thrust into this type of symbolic crisis. Maria also felt the impact of this dimension when she complained to her mother, "I feel my relationship with grandmama has been changed forever, and against my wishes. If only we could communicate with her like we used to. . . ."

The adverse effects of this relational flux may be dramatically increased by the onset of the third dimension. Just as problematic as the faulty meaning assignment and forced alteration of relationships components is the involuntary redefinition or loss of symbolic self. For example, certain cancer treatments, such as chemotherapy or colostomies, can create pervasive feelings of disgust and/or self-hatred in patients and their families, or in patients and their primary and general caregivers (Wortman & Dunkel-Schetter, 1979). These powerful emotions frequently forge "new" identities in cancer clients that discourage meaningful interaction with their families and other caregivers.

A similar process occurs among persons who have Alzheimer's. As the disease progresses the individual with Alzheimer's loses her or his symbolic self through irreversible amnesia, and a loved one is thus transformed into a "walking shell" (Kapust, 1982; Kapust & Weintraub, 1984; Mace & Rabins, 1981; Query, 1989). In effect, the family loses its loved one twice. The first time is through symbolic death; the second time, which may be some 20 years later, is through physical death. It is not surprising, then, that family caregivers often shun their loved ones as a form of denial and self-preservation. The agony of looking into a loved one's blank eyes and being unable to communicate at even a basic level can overwhelm many caregivers.

Maria prepares to head home but is thankful for this brief time alone. The respite enabled her to organize her thoughts, recognize her shortcomings, and realize that she is not super woman or super caregiver. She also feels that she can now apologize to Diego, better understand his point of view, and explain what happened to grandmama.

FAMILY CHALLENGES IN CAREGIVING

While she's at work, Cristabalita worries constantly that she has placed too much responsibility on her daughter Maria. She's only 19 after all, and she should be able to go out more. If only Raul were still alive. He would know how to help. He would also support Cristabalita's decision to keep Conchis at home for as long as possible.

Cristabalita is further concerned about the toll of caregiving on Maria and the rest of the family. All of them have had to make so many adjustments. For instance, Cristabalita changed her work schedule to be home in the evenings; now she works from 5:00 A.M. to 5:00 P.M. instead of 8:00 A.M. to 8:00 P.M., which she preferred because it allowed her a few extra hours to sleep in the morning. So that Conchis could have her own room, Yanina moved in with Jesus. Maria gave up her part-time job at the library and has really become like a second parent. Diego rescheduled his night classes and now attends school during the day, and he no longer plays his stereo—any type of rock-and-roll music upsets Conchis greatly. The kids do not invite friends home any more because it is uncertain how Conchis will react, and their friends may not understand the situation.

Many families find themselves in the same position as the Robleza family. Large numbers of impaired, elderly individuals are cared for at home because of the emotional and financial costs of institutional care (Hay & Ernst, 1987; Office of Technology Assessment [OTA], 1990). Considering the increase in informal caregiving, researchers have examined the social and psychological benefits and costs of the caregiving process. The most obvious benefit of caregiving is the intrinsic value of the care as a demonstration of one's commitment and love. However, caregivers also face significant costs, including stress, career conflicts, and confusion in personal roles.

Pearlin, Mullan, Semple, and Skaff (1990) note that caregivers are vulnerable to varying degrees of stress emanating from two general sources—primary and secondary stressors. **Primary stressors** are hardships and difficulties directly related to caregiving. Primary stressors in turn produce **secondary stressors**, which are role-centered or intrapsychic. Specific primary stressors include the physical and mental status of the care recipient; the problematic behavior of the care recipient; the work overload, or burnout, of the caregiver; and the loss of what had been the usual interaction with the care recipient. Caregivers are vulnerable to potent secondary stressors, which may take the form of family conflicts, job conflicts, economic problems, the loss of their social life, and such intrapsychic stressors as negative self-concept, loss of self-identity, **role captivity** (feeling as if one is trapped in the caregiving situation), and a decreased sense of competence.

Cristabalita's family contends with these primary and secondary stressors daily. For instance, Maria has a high caregiving burden—the children, Conchis, and the house—whereas Diego usually has a low caregiving burden. Maria also experienced depression while at the park. Cristabalita also experiences high stress—she has changed her work schedule, works 12 hours daily, and feels very guilty that she can't be more of a daughter to her mother and parent to her own children. But caregivers are not the only family members who experience stress under these circumstances; being cared for can also be stressful. Conchis's behaviors—varying her age, calling 911 unnecessarily, believing that Diego is Raul, and being unable to remember things that just happened—are evidence that she is stressed, as well.

At least two conclusions about primary and secondary stressors can be drawn. First, although secondary stressors flow from primary stressors, they are no less potent than primary stressors. Second, as Pearlin et al. (1990) report, the outcomes of primary and secondary stressors are often depression, anxiety, irascibility, and poor physical health.

Within the Pearlin et al. (1990) model of caregiver stressors and outcomes, there are other caregiver costs or risks that merit further discussion. Caregivers, for example, often confront and grapple with conflicts between their careers and the demands of caregiving. As mentioned earlier, approximately one-third of all caregivers are employed, and nearly 10% of caregivers report having to quit their jobs to meet caregiving responsibilities (Stone et al., 1987).

In one study Pearlin et al. (1990) found that caregivers experienced a conflict between work and caregiving in a variety of ways: They worried about the care recipient while at work; they had less energy for work; they were interrupted at work by phone calls from or about the care recipient; they were dissatisfied with their quality of work; and they missed too many days of work. It appears, then, that caregivers face unique problems triggered by the conflicts between caregiving and employment.

The Challenge of Fluid Roles

Another serious problem many caregivers face is confusion over changing roles. Communication scholars stress that individuals define themselves in terms of interaction patterns (Fisher, 1987). As caregiving responsibilities increase, the caregiver becomes less able to participate in a variety of social interactions. Additionally, old friendships and established networks begin to diminish. What often occurs is that, as caregiving responsibilities take the place of recreational activities and social interaction, caregivers are forced to redefine "the self."

The process of redefinition of the self is made more difficult by the stress of caregiving. Research indicates that during times of enduring hardship the self-esteem of the caregiver may suffer (Pearlin, Lieberman, Menaghan, & Mullan, 1981). Related to the self-esteem problem is the notion of role captivity. Caregivers often struggle with the feeling of being captive in the caregiving role. They feel compelled to engage in the caregiving activity at the expense of other, more desirable activities. The obvious and understandable outcome of this role struggle is usually depression and other negative health conditions (Pearlin et al., 1990). In the Robleza family, Maria is experiencing role captivity and Cristabalita is at risk for the problem.

Within the family structure, caregivers often experience substantially changed roles. Pearlin et al. (1990) noted that the family is "a central arena for secondary role strains . . . and having a close relative who needs care can certainly reawaken old family grievances as well as create new ones" (p. 588). The researchers identified three areas of conflict between the primary caregiver and other family members. The first area concerns the impairment of the recipient; that is, the degree and seriousness of the disability and the means of dealing with it. The second area concerns the amount and quality of care provided by other members of the family. A third area concerns the attention and acknowledgment accorded to the primary caregiver by other members of the family.

Each of these areas plays a role in the interaction among the Roblezas. For instance, Diego did not really believe that it would be that difficult to care for Conchis and the children. He also believed that the bulk of caregiving should be provided by women. His whole attitude thus communicated to Maria that he did not value her efforts or her as a person.

It seems reasonable to conclude that, although there are benefits to caregiving, the costs are formidable. As the caregiving situation changes, it becomes a great challenge to maximize the benefits and minimize potential risks or negative outcomes.

ADDITIONAL FORCES CONFRONTING MULTI-GENERATIONAL FAMILIES

Although there has been little research conducted on multi-generational caregiving, one study has examined the extent to which third- and fourth-generation family members are involved in elderly caregiving. Baum and Page (1991) reported that even though greater resources (in terms of available caregivers) existed in multi-generational families, the caregiving responsibility still rested primarily with the adult daughter. For the Roblezas, the bulk of the caregiving burden is shouldered by granddaughter Maria because Conchis's daughter, Cristabalita, must work.

Baum and Page's (1991) finding that the adult daughter assumes the primary burden of caregiving does not necessarily imply that the third- and fourth-generation family members are unaffected by the caregiving process. Systems theory indicates that any change in the family system is going to affect the entire family to some degree (Littlejohn, 1989). For example, the higher level of stress experienced by the primary caregiver will certainly affect the way she interacts with her own offspring or her siblings. For example, when Maria had enough of Diego's insensitive remarks, she walked out and left him in charge.

Springer and Brubaker (1984) identify some of the difficulties faced by a multi-generational family as caregiving for an elderly relative becomes more intense. For instance, there are several issues that need to be addressed when an elderly care recipient moves into a multi-generational household—issues of space, household management, and friendships.

Space is limited in nearly all homes, and children and adults are very territorial. When an elderly relative moves into a home, usually a child must give up his or her room. This means not only that one child needs to move, but generally that a second child is impinged upon by having to share a bedroom. This inconvenience often triggers resentment on the part of the children toward the elderly care recipient. Within the Robleza family, Yanina and Jesus are most likely to experience and vent these negative feelings—Yanina had to give up her room to Conchis and move into Jesus's room.

Each caregiving family has to address several pressing household management questions: To what degree is the management hierarchy of the home upset by the arrival of the elderly care recipient? Who makes the decisions? Should the elder defer to the wishes of the caregiver because it is her home? Should the children defer to the wishes of the elderly recipient out of respect? Each of these questions presents a thorny dilemma that must be grappled with and resolved in order to facilitate a smooth transition. In the case of Conchis, most of these questions are moot because of her marked level of impairment. During the day, Maria is the chief decision maker; at night, Cristabalita takes over.

As both the care recipient and the members of the caregiver's family have existing friendships, several issues arise in this area when the elder moves into the home. For instance, to what degree should the caregiver entertain friends of the care recipient? Should the family curtail visits from various friends, and if so, to what degree? What levels of noise will now be appropriate? As with the other concerns, there are no quick and easy answers. Families must evaluate the needs of each member and negotiate mutually acceptable arrangements.

It is clear that when an elderly care recipient moves into a multi-generational home, there are a number of issues that must be addressed. Furthermore, the family will feel the effects of competing demands placed on the caregiver. The mother of a family, when placed in the caregiving role, will have less time for her family. Her children may feel neglected and begin to foster feelings of jealousy toward the care recipient. The caregiver may feel guilt and suffer from depression.

Possible Strategies to Ease Adaptation

Various scholars (Schmidt, 1980; Springer & Brubaker, 1984) have provided suggestions for controlling some of the disruption faced by multi-generational caregiving families.

1. There must be open and honest communication, which should include the care recipient if possible. Ideally, this interaction will help the children of the caregiver become more aware of the intensity of the burden that is placed on the caregiver. Their assistance should be sought to help alleviate the work load.
2. The caregiver should schedule specific times for uninterrupted interaction with her or his children and spouse.
3. If possible, the caregiver should establish a specific time devoted solely to the care recipient when it will be least disruptive to the family.
4. The caregiver should find some source of social support outside the home with whom to share feelings.

While not foolproof, these strategies and others can lessen the likelihood of potential conflicts.

EXTERNAL SOURCES OF SOCIAL SUPPORT

Cristabalita always looks forward to lunch time. In addition to the much needed break, she enjoys talking and visiting with her co-worker and friend Treva. She and Cristabalita are very close in age and work the same shift. Treva has always been an excellent listener and willing to help Cristabalita in any way she can. For example, when Conchis was first diagnosed with Alzheimer's disease, Treva donated a week's sick leave to Cristabalita. This generous gift allowed her to have paid days off in order to move Conchis and set up a caregiving routine.

> *Treva:* Cristabalita, how are you doing? You look like you're a million miles away.
>
> *Cristabalita:* Well . . . hi. I guess you're right. I'm just worried about Maria and Conchis.

Treva:	Yes, I know. Maria does such a wonderful job of taking care of everything, though.
Cristabalita:	That's just it. I feel like I should be doing more. I also worry about Maria's stamina and lack of social life.
Treva:	Well, you're right, you do want to give Maria some time off on a regular basis. But remember too, you're taking care of business by bringing home the bacon. You know, you need some relief too. You should look into the company's new assistance programs. I've heard they're very good.
Cristabalita:	Uh, well, uh, I don't know. So many people just don't understand about this disease.
Treva:	I agree, but these programs helped Angela Kay and her family. You know her grandfather has Parkinson's disease?
Cristabalita:	No, I didn't. Maybe I'll look into it after all.

Employee Assistance Programs

One significant source of both formal and informal support to caregivers is at the workplace. Many employers already provide an **employee assistance program** (EAP) for child care providers and employees with other special needs. Research indicates that loss of productivity and levels of stress are similar, if not greater, among caregivers of elderly individuals as among child care providers (Neal, Chapman, Ingersoll-Dayton, Emlen, & Boise, 1990). Employers are thus beginning to acknowledge and take appropriate action to address the need for EAPs for caregivers of elderly individuals. In a 1988 study, for instance, Hewitt Associates found that 77% of the U.S. companies surveyed anticipated significant and immediate increases in elder care benefits provided (cited in True & Wineman, 1989).

Ingersoll-Dayton, Chapman, and Neal (1990) examined three EAPs designed for caregivers. Each program provided a seminar series and then offered the following options: (1) care-planning meetings with a knowledgeable social worker; (2) formation of support groups; (3) the establishment of a "buddy system." None of the employees chose the buddy-system option, so the researchers assumed that employees felt that this was not a viable alternative. The researchers did find, however, that the seminar series coupled with either the care-planning option or the social-support option was positively evaluated by the employee participants. Questionnaires given to employees before and after the interventions showed that the employee participants were significantly more knowledgeable with respect to services and resources for the elderly after the seminar than before.

The employee participants who chose the care-planning option rated the following intervention activities as helpful: (1) receiving information regarding services and resources; (2) receiving information about providing care to the elderly; (3) addressing concerns about the future. Those who chose the support-group option rated the following intervention activities as helpful: (1) talking informally with other caregivers; (2) receiving emotional support; (3) addressing concerns regarding the future.

Two important changes appeared to have resulted from the EAP programs studied by Ingersoll-Dayton et al. First, employee participants reported they changed the way they communicated with the care recipient. They were now able to approach difficult and sensitive subjects without causing upsetting situations. Second, the caregivers realized the value of not making decisions for the care recipient or performing tasks of which the care recipient was still capable.

The study by Ingersoll-Dayton et al. (1990) not only provides evidence for the efficacy of EAPs but also provides a key point for further consideration: Over one-third of the employees responding to the EAP were not yet caregivers—they were anticipatory caregivers, or individuals who thought they would be caring for an elderly relative at some point in the future. This finding indicates the need for companywide programs that target all employee groups, not only current caregivers.

Cristabalita was glad that she had taken Treva's advice. After attending a "share the load" session at work she felt much better. It was comforting to know that others were experiencing similar situations with their elderly loved ones. Moreover, as co-workers shared some of their trials and tribulations, Cristabalita's feelings of guilt, helplessness, and isolation began to fade away. Now if she could only come up with some type of relief for Maria, Diego, Jesus, and Yanina.

Support Groups

A second strategy available for caregivers is joining a **support group**. These groups provide support to their members and help them improve mastery of their environments (Albrecht & Adelman, 1987; Gottlieb, 1988; Maguire, 1983). Support groups usually have the following characteristics in varying degrees: (1) a problem shared by all members; (2) a fluctuating helper-helpee relationship among members; (3) a consciously determined organizational structure; (4) an emphasis on internal decision-making or self-determination; and (5) the giving and receiving of affective and material assistance among members (Query & James, 1989).

Support groups can provide a forum through which individuals can reduce their uncertainty concerning diseases such as Alzheimer's. Glosser and Wexler (1985), for example, examined the impact of seven support groups meeting for a limited time of eight weeks. The goals of these support groups centered on information distribution about the medical and behavioral characteristics of the disease, coping skill instruction, venting of emotions, and reinforcement. The results indicated the following were the most helpful activities, in order:

1. Learning coping strategies from other caregivers
2. Having the opportunity to interact with other caregivers
3. Sharing intimate feelings with other caregivers
4. Obtaining accurate and comprehensible information about the medical aspects of the disease
5. Receiving support from other caregivers
6. Acquiring strategies for successfully dealing with daily client problems

Glosser and Wexler also noted that at least 60% of the caregivers rated the preceding activities as very helpful (p. 234).

A study conducted by Hartford and Parsons (1982) also illustrated that support groups can help their members better redefine and cope with dependency-laden conditions such as dementia. At a large gerontological research facility, a support group was developed to help meet the needs of caregivers seeking assistance and alleviate the workloads of staff social workers. These caregivers rendered assistance to frail, dependent, older adults on a regular basis. The guiding research objective was to identify common themes of concern about dependent loved ones, focusing especially on caregiving strategies and relationship quality. The chief pragmatic goal was to establish a low-risk and supportive communication environment among the group members to ease caregiving burdens.

Interpreting the results, the investigators concluded that the most important outcomes of the experience for the caregivers were improved functioning, enhanced understanding of the disorders, and a sense of relief triggered by sharing powerful and intimate feelings with peers.

In a similar study, Haber (1983) investigated the benefits of a support group designed to enhance the health status of its elderly members. The participants identified four advantages of belonging to the support group:

> 1) the availability of multifaceted support over an extended period of time without cost; 2) the sharing of personal experiences that engenders understanding, resource-sharing, and depth of feeling that may be unattainable with a professional worker; 3) decentralized services that are more accessible than centralized public service agencies and more reliable in a time of diminishing human service resources; and 4) the strengthening of community networks. (p. 251)

Taken together, these studies suggest that by pooling resources and sharing ego-threatening information, group members are empowered to reduce their environmental uncertainty, develop effective coping skills, and make informed decisions. In effect, group members are often able to acquire new and revitalized self-identities from effective support-group processes in a low-risk communication environment (Query, 1987; see also LaVorgna, 1979; Lazarus, Stafford, Cooper, Cohler, & Dysken, 1981).

Respite Care

A third strategy available to caregivers is **respite care**. Respite care is short-term care, ranging in duration from a few hours to a month, that allows family caregivers some "breathing room." Caregivers are then able to attend to personal matters, engage in social activities, and recoup some of their psychological and physical energies. Ample research clearly demonstrates the health-protective effects of respite care (Rheaume, Larkin, & Seltzer, 1988; Shelley, 1988; Zarit, Orr, & Zarit, 1985).

Respite care for elderly individuals and their family members is available through a variety of agencies in most communities. Some of these are social service agencies such as the local chapter of the Alzheimer's Association, the local area Agency on Aging, the local mental health association, and senior service organizations. Many communities also have day care centers for elderly individuals. At these sites elderly care recipients may receive meals and trained medical supervision and can usually participate in a variety of activities. Home health care services may provide respite through trained companion programs. Nursing facilities also often provide respite care facilities, where the family can entrust the care recipient to trained professionals for a brief time. The fees for respite care vary according to the nature of the services, facility, locality, and length of time the facility or service is utilized.

Through her company's EAP program, Cristabalita learned about some support groups and respite care programs. She decided she would definitely explore these options for her family. As she clocked out, she had a new sense that, together, her family could overcome many future challenges. Together, they could help lessen some of the pain, strife, and heartache and they could create some meaning out of this tragedy. The final result, of course, would still be the same—eventually, Conchis would die. Their journey along the way, however, would be marked by sharing and a loving bond.

SUMMARY

The caregiving challenges many of us will inevitably face are great. Until major health care reform can be accomplished, large-scale organizations such as the federal government, state health organizations, and local hospitals will have to stretch limited resources to deal with global-sized problems. Families will often find themselves in similar positions when an elderly loved one requires at-home care. Although informed understanding is not a panacea for all the problems such home care brings, it is a vital first step in preparing us for caregiving roles. Awareness, understanding, appreciation, and rehearsal of strategies can enhance our effectiveness as caregivers. We can then make a difference in the quality of life of our care recipients.

Class Discussion Questions

1. Has your family or a friend's family been involved in an extended caregiving role for an elderly relative? If so, in what ways was the experience similar to the Roblezas'?

2. Suggest some strategies for helping male family members to better appreciate and adopt the caregiving role.

3. What types of competing demands do primary caregivers experience? What types of strategies might be used to meet these competing demands?

4. Has your family or anyone you know experienced a "symbolic crisis"? If so, identify it and explain which of the three dimensions you experienced. Suggest some strategies to reduce its future occurrence and impact.

5. What kinds of similarities and differences do you think the Roblezas (as a multi-generational family) have with a single- or dual-generational family in the caregiving situation?

6. What kinds of relationships and communicative interactions are you likely to see between an elderly care recipient and an informal caregiver, as opposed to a formal caregiver?

7. Identify several characteristics of communication (for example, communication competence, relational qualities, locus of control), and provide specific examples of how the recipient-caregiver relationship is affected by these characteristics.

8. A caregiver can find a significant source of both formal and informal support in an employee assistant program (EAP) at work. What goals and strategies should be included in an EAP designed to help caregivers?

9. In caring for the terminally ill, why is it important to emphasize the "journey of caregiving" rather than the inevitable outcome?

Homework Assignments

1. Using your local phone book, identify two social service agencies that appear likely to provide assistance to caregivers of individuals with Alzheimer's disease. Contact these organizations to determine the following: (a) their address and hours of operation; (b) their mission(s); (c) the services provided; and (d) available resources such as quarterly newsletters, free educational literature, identity bracelet programs, respite care programs, support groups, lending libraries or video libraries. Describe the relationship between their mission(s) and their services.

2. Try to obtain one of the following video tapes: *Alzheimer's Disease: The Long Nightmare; Not Alone in the World; My Mother, My Father; OK to Be Old; Senior Support Systems* (or another video about Alzheimer's). After viewing a film, provide a brief overview of the key points. Having considered the content of the film, what specific advice would you

provide to the Roblezas? Would you recommend this film to Diego and/or Maria? If so, why? If not, why not?

3. Imagine that you are the human resources director of a large plant for a major auto manufacturer. The plant has existed at this location for several decades; many of the current employees are third-generation relatives of the original employees. Gail, the general manager of the plant, has indicated that she believes there is a problem within the current work force. In particular, there is a high degree of absenteeism among many of the workers who are the primary caregivers of their elderly parents. Many of the elderly care recipients are also retired employees from the plant. Gail believes that the company must assume some responsibility to help its employees.

    Your task is to prepare a proposal for an EAP that will convince the company's headquarters that the plant should sponsor such a program. Your proposal must (a) justify the establishment of an EAP, keeping in mind that the company's top management is likely to keep a sharp eye on "the bottom line"—how much it will cost; (b) list planned outcomes of the EAP, including benefits to the company as well as the employees; and (c) specify strategies, or procedures, to be used in the EAP. Keep in mind that this must be a professional quality proposal that will be evaluated by the top management of your company.

4. Contact a large local business and ask whether it offers an EAP. When you find a business that has an EAP program, compare and contrast the program's features with those described by Ingersoll-Dayton, Chapman, and Neal (1990). Write a paper that explains the similarities and differences. Close your paper by sharing your views concerning businesses that provide EAPs.

Additional Readings

Aronson, M. K. (Ed.). (1988). *Understanding Alzheimer's disease.* New York: Charles Scribner's Sons.

Kapust, L. R. (1982). Living with dementia: The ongoing funeral. *Social Work in Health Care, 7,* 79–91.

Kapust, L. R., & Weintraub, S. (1984). Living with a family member suffering from Alzheimer's disease. In H. B. Roback (Ed.), *Helping patients and their families cope with medical problems* (pp. 453–480). San Francisco, CA: Jossey-Bass.

Kreps, G. L., & Kunimoto, E. N. (1994). *Communicating effectively in multicultural health care settings.* Newbury Park, CA: Sage.

Mace, N., & Rabins, P. (1981). *The 36 hour day.* Baltimore: Johns Hopkins University Press.

References

Albrecht, T. L., & Adelman, M. B. (Eds.). (1987). *Communicating social support.* Newbury Park, CA: Sage.

Aronson, M. K. (Ed.). (1988). *Understanding Alzheimer's disease*. New York: Charles Scribner's Sons.

Barclay, J. (1971). *Foundations of counseling strategies*. New York: Wiley.

Baum, M., & Page, M. (1991). Caregiving and multigenerational families. *The Gerontologist, 31*, 762–769.

Berger, C. R. (1979). Beyond initial interaction: Uncertainty, understanding, and the development of interpersonal relationships. In H. Giles & R. N. St. Clair (Eds.), *Language and social psychology* (pp. 122–144). Oxford, England: Basil Blackwell.

Berger, C. R., & Calabrese, R. J. (1975). Some explorations in initial interaction and beyond: Toward a developmental theory of interpersonal communication. *Human Communication Research, 1*, 99–112.

Biegel, D. E., Sales, E., & Schulz, R. (1991). *Family caregiving in chronic illness*. Newbury Park, CA: Sage.

Brown, J., Lyon, P., & Sellers, T. D. (1988). Caring for the family caregivers. In L. Volicer, K. Fabsizewski, Y. Rheaume, & K. Lasch (Eds.), *Clinical management of Alzheimer's disease*, (pp. 29–42). Rockville, MD: Aspen.

Cicirelli, V. G. (1992). *Family caregiving: Autonomous and paternalistic decision-making*. Newbury Park, CA: Sage.

Duck, S. W. (1992). *Human relationships* (2nd ed.). Newbury Park, CA: Sage.

Fisher, B. A. (1987). *Interpersonal communication: Pragmatics of human communication*. New York: Random House.

Gilhooly, M. L. M. (1984). The impact of care-giving on care-givers: Factors associated with the psychological well-being of people supporting a dementing relative in the community. *British Journal of Medical Psychology, 145*, 172–177.

Glosser, G., & Wexler, D. (1985). Participants' evaluation of educational/support groups for families with Alzheimer's disease and other dementias. *The Gerontologist, 25*, 232–236.

Good, B. S. (1977). The heart of what's the matter: The semantics of illness in Iran. *Culture, Medicine, and Psychiatry, 1*, 25–29.

Good, B. S., & Good, M. D. (1981). The meaning of symptoms: A cultural hermeneutic model for clinical practice. In L. Eisenberg & A. Kleinman (Eds.), *The relevance of social science for medicine* (pp. 165–196). Dordrecht, Holland: D. Reidel.

Gottlieb, B. H. (1988). Marshaling social support: The state of the art in research and practice. In B. H. Gottlieb (Ed.), *Marshaling social support: Formats, processes, and effects* (pp. 11–51). Newbury Park, CA: Sage.

Guarasci, C. (1988). *Communication in the caregiving relationship: A theme analysis based on interviews with persons diagnosed with a life-limiting cancer and hospice team members*. Unpublished master's thesis, Ohio University, Athens, OH.

Haber, D. (1983). Promoting mutual help groups among older persons. *The Gerontologist, 23*, 251–253.

Hartford, M. E., & Parsons, R. (1982). Groups with relatives of dependent older adults. *The Gerontologist, 22*, 394–398.

Hay, J. W., & Ernst, R. E. (1987). The economic costs of Alzheimer's disease. *American Journal of Public Health, 77,* 1169–1175.

Heider, F. (1958). *The psychology of interpersonal relations.* New York: Wiley.

Infante, D. A., Rancer, A. S., & Womack, D. F. (1990). *Building communication theory.* Prospect Heights, IL: Waveland.

Ingersoll-Dayton, B., Chapman, N., & Neal, M. (1990). A program for caregivers in the workplace. *The Gerontologist, 30,* 126–130.

Kapust, L. R. (1982). Living with dementia: The ongoing funeral. *Social Work in Health Care, 7,* 79–91.

Kapust, L. R., & Weintraub, S. (1984). Living with a family member suffering from Alzheimer's disease. In H. B. Roback (Ed.), *Helping patients and their families cope with medical problems,* (pp. 453–480). San Francisco, CA: Jossey-Bass.

Kelly, J. A. (1982). *Social skills training: A practical guide for interventions.* New York: Springer.

Kreps, G. L. (1986). Health communication and the elderly. *World Communication, 15,* 55–70.

Kreps, G. L. (1988). The pervasive role of information in health and health care: Implications of health communication policy. In J. Anderson (Ed.), *Communication yearbook 11* (pp. 238–276). Newbury Park, CA: Sage.

Kreps, G. L., & Kunimoto, E. N. (1994). *Communicating effectively in multicultural health care settings.* Newbury Park, CA: Sage.

Kreps, G. L., & Query, J. L. (1990). Health communication and interpersonal competence. In G. M. Phillips & J. T. Wood (Eds.), *Essays commemorating the 75th anniversary of the Speech Communication Association* (pp. 293–323). Carbondale, IL: Southern Illinois University Press.

LaVorgna, D. (1979). Group treatment for wives of patients with Alzheimer's disease. *Social Work in Health Care, 5,* 219–223.

Lazarus, L. W., Stafford, B., Cooper, K., Cohler, B., & Dysken, M. (1981). A pilot study of an Alzheimer patients' relatives discussion group. *The Gerontologist, 4,* 353–357.

Littlejohn, S. W. (1989). *Theories of human communication* (3rd ed.). Belmont, CA: Wadsworth.

Mace, N., & Rabins, P. (1981). *The 36 hour day.* Baltimore: Johns Hopkins University Press.

Maguire, L. (1983). *Understanding social networks.* Beverly Hills, CA: Sage.

Neal, M. B., Chapman, N. J., Ingersoll-Dayton, B., Emlen, A. C., & Boise, L. (1990). Absenteeism and stress among the employed caregivers of the elderly, disabled adults, and children. In D. E. Biegel & A. Blum (Eds.), *Aging and caregiving: Theory, research, and policy* (pp. 160–183). Newbury Park, CA: Sage.

Office of Technology Assessment. (1990). *Confused minds, burdened families.* Washington, DC: U.S. Government Printing Office.

Pearlin, L. I., Lieberman, M. A., Menaghan, E. G., & Mullan, J. T. (1981). The stress process. *Journal of Health and Social Behavior, 22,* 337–356.

Pearlin, L. I., Mullan, J. T., Semple, S. J., & Skaff, M. M. (1990). Caregiving and the stress process: An overview of concepts and their measures. *The Gerontologist, 30,* 583–594.

Query, J. L. (1987). *A field test of the relationship between interpersonal communication competence, number of social supports, and satisfaction with the social support received by an elderly support group.* Unpublished master's thesis, Ohio University, Athens, OH.

Query, J. L. (1989). Alzheimer's disease and dementia. In B. B. Dreher & J. Alter (Eds.), *Interdisciplinary casebook in geriatric communication* (pp. 73–81). Danville, IL: Interstate.

Query, J. L. (1990). *A field assessment of the relationships among interpersonal communication competence, social support, and depression among caregivers for individuals with Alzheimer's disease.* Unpublished dissertation, Ohio University, Athens, OH.

Query, J. L., & James, A. C. (1989). The relationship between interpersonal communication competence and social support among elderly support groups in retirement communities. *Health Communication, 1*(3), 165–184.

Query, J. L., Parry, D., & Flint, L. J. (1992). The relationship among social support, communication competence, and cognitive depression for non-traditional students. *Journal of Applied Communication Research, 20*(1), 78–94.

Query, J. L., & Smilowitz, M. (1988a, September). *Caregiving within Alzheimer support groups: A preliminary examination.* Paper presented at the annual meeting of the Speech Communication Association of Ohio, Worthington, OH.

Query, J. L., & Smilowitz, M. (1988b, November). *Alzheimer support groups: A review of the relationships among perceived locus of control, communication strategies, and social support.* Paper presented at the annual meeting of the Speech Communication Association, New Orleans, LA.

Rheaume, Y. L., Larkin, J. P., & Seltzer, B. (1988). Institution-based respite care. In L. Volicer, K. Fabiszewski, Y. L. Rheaume, & K. Lasch (Eds.), *Clinical management of Alzheimer's disease* (pp. 75–86). Rockville, MD: Aspen.

Rotter, J. B. (1966). Generalized expectancies for internal versus external control of reinforcement. *Psychological Monographs, 80* (Whole No. 609).

Sanmiguel, L. M. (1992, November). *The gynecologist-patient context: A model and research agenda.* Paper presented at the annual meeting of the Speech Communication Association, Chicago.

Sarason, B. R., Sarason, I. G., Hacker, A., & Basham, R. B. (1985). Concomitants of social support: Social skills, physical attractiveness, and gender. *Journal of Personality and Social Psychology, 49,* 469–480.

Schmidt, M. G. (1980). Failing parents, aging children. *Journal of Gerontological Social Work, 2,* 259–268.

Shelley, F. D. (1988). *When your parents grow old* (2nd ed.). New York: Harper & Row.

Sommers, T., & Shields, L. (1987). *Women take care: The consequences of caregiving in today's society.* Gainesville, FL: Triad.

Spitzberg, B. H., & Cupach, W. R. (1984). *Interpersonal communication competence.* Beverly Hills, CA: Sage.

Springer, D., & Brubaker, T. H. (1984). *Family caregivers and dependent elderly: Minimizing stress and maximizing independence.* Beverly Hills, CA: Sage.

Stone, R., Cafferata, G. L., & Sangl, J. (1987). Caregivers of the frail elderly: A national profile. *The Gerontologist, 27,* 616–626.

True, N. B., & Wineman, J. (1989). Caregiving and retirement planning: A new partnership. *Compensation and Benefits Management, 5*(4), 283–286.

Wortman, C., & Dunkel-Schetter, D. (1979). Interpersonal relationships and cancer: A theoretical perspective. *Journal of Social Issues, 35,* 120–155.

Yu, E., Liu, W. T., Wang, Z. H., Levy, P. S., Katzman, R., Zhang, M. Y., Qu, G. Y., & Chen, F. F. (1993). Caregivers of the cognitively disabled in Shanghai, China. In S. Zarit, L. Pearlin, and & K. Schaie (Eds.), *Caregiving systems: Formal and informal helpers* (pp. 5–30). Hillsdale, NJ: Erlbaum.

Zarit, S. H., Orr, N. K., & Zarit, J. M. (1985). *The hidden victims of Alzheimer's disease.* New York: New York University Press.

Glossary

Activities of daily living (ADL)   Tasks that involve personal care such as bathing, dressing, eating, and grooming

Caregiving   A process in which an individual has to relate to a care recipient and provide various types of assistance

Communication competence   The tendency to seek out meaningful interaction with others, render support, be relaxed, appreciate others' plight, and take turns appropriately

Discontinuity   The ability to pick up an interaction where it left off, despite the time (hours, days, weeks) that has elapsed since the last interaction

Employee Assistance Program (EAP)   Formal and informal social support programs offered by employers to employees

General caregiver   An individual who provides some care to the recipient on an irregular and occasional basis, often for four or fewer hours daily

High locus of control   A psychological trait that characterizes people who have a strong sense of control of their own behavior and future

Instrumental activities of daily living (IADL)   Tasks that involve shopping, handling money, transportation, and cooking

Lay or **informal caregiver**   An individual who provides care without having received institutionalized training and/or certification

Low locus of control   A psychological trait that characterizes people who have a weak sense of control of their own behavior and future

Primary caregiver   An individual who provides the bulk of the care to the recipient on a regular and frequent basis, often for from five to twenty-four hours daily

Primary stressors   Hardships and difficulties directly related to caregiving

Professional or **formal caregiver**   An individual who provides care after having received institutionalized training and/or certification to do so

Psychological care   Behavior that provides emotional support to care recipients

Reciprocity   The degree to which the participants in a relationship agree on the definition of the relationship

Recurrence   Being "tuned in" to the synchrony of an interaction so as to recognize relational rituals and identify relational problems

Respite care   Respite care is short-term care, ranging in duration from a few hours to a month, which allows family caregivers some free time

Role captivity   The feeling of being trapped in the caregiving role

Secondary stressors   Role-centered or intrapsychic hardships or strains

Skilled health care   Care that includes such tasks as giving injections and monitoring vital signs

Support groups   Groups designed to provide support to their members and improve members' mastery of their environments

Symbolic crises   Traumatic and health-threatening situations that occur when a patient and his or her significant others define the health condition in ways that block understanding and health care delivery

Synchrony   The fitting together of interaction so that a recognizable pattern emerges that identifies the nature of a relationship

Part Three

The Next Millennium

20

The Future of Interpersonal Relationships

Nelly Vanzetti
Private Practice, Tulsa

Steve Duck
University of Iowa

We live in a time when social, medical, and technological changes are happening faster than ever before. While we struggle to keep up with these advances, we may be unaware of the ways in which they have already begun to exert a profound influence on the nature, structure, and function of our interpersonal relationships. This chapter provides a brief overview of the significant developments that have shaped this century, discusses a number of relationship trends that have already emerged and how our relationships have changed as a function of these trends, and offers some speculations about continued developments and their possible influences on our interpersonal lives.

NV & SD

Chapter Outline

• Demographic Trends
• Medical Trends
• Technological Trends
• The Other Side of the Debate
• Personal Relationships Reconsidered
• Conclusion

Since the beginning of this century the whole Western world has experienced unprecedented economic growth and a dizzying rate of technological progress. Contributing to the impact of all of these changes in the United States has been the rapid population growth known as the **baby boom**. In the 18 years between 1946 and 1964 the population of the United States increased by nearly 50 million people. Members of this baby boom generation have shaped social trends since they were born, and they will continue to do so for decades to come. When the baby boomers were children, the need for schools and teachers increased dramatically. When they reached college age, universities flourished. Now that they have graduated from college and entered the workforce, the employment market is tight and highly competitive. And in having their own families the baby boomers will continue to influence population growth until they are out of their childbearing years, around the turn of the century. Finally, as members of the baby boom generation age they will create strong markets for services and industries geared toward elderly individuals. The baby boom phenomenon is important in our consideration of current trends, since many of the changes we will discuss in the following sections can be traced directly to the developmental stages of the baby boom generation.

The astounding increase in the number of individuals working outside the home is a prime example of an important social phenomenon primarily due to the coming of age of the baby boom generation. Since 1940 the labor force has grown at a rate that is historically unequaled. The number of Americans employed outside the home has more than doubled in the last 50 years, growing from 53 million in 1940 to 116 million in 1990.[1] The lion's share of this growth is due to the increase in women's participation in the workforce, which rose from 27% in 1940 to 64% in 1980. That is, just over one-quarter of all women 14 and over worked in 1940, compared with almost two-thirds of women over 16 who worked in 1980. There are a number of reasons for the phenomenal increase in women's representation in the labor force during these years. During World War II many of the adult women in this country went to work outside the home, filling job vacancies left by men who went to war. Many of these women stayed in the workforce after the war ended. But this was only the beginning of a social trend that gained significant momentum during the next 30 years. Between 1950 and 1980 women's representation in the workforce grew even faster than it had before. The economy was growing, more jobs were being created, and dual–wage earner families were consuming more goods and services (which, in turn, resulted in more jobs, a stronger economy, and so on).

During the ten years between 1980 and 1990 this trend declined slightly. In 1990 women's participation rate was 57%, a decline of about 7% compared with the 1980 statistic. This decline is a good example of how developmental stages in the lives of baby boomers influence social trends. Women born between 1945 and 1960 were between 20 and 35 years old in 1980. These young adult years are generally the developmental period during which people enter the workforce and begin careers. By 1990, however, many of these women had reached the age when it was time to begin a family, so there was a slight decline in the labor force par-

[1]Unless otherwise noted, all statistics are taken from the *Statistical Abstract of the United States: 1992* (112th Edition), published by the U.S. Bureau of the Census, Washington, DC.

At the Nation's Call

Large numbers of women entered the workforce during World War II, starting a trend that continues today. The text of this Bell Telephone System ad from that time specifically mentions both men and women, describing them as "thoroughly trained, well equipped and eager to do whatever task may be set for them"—indicating that women were considered indispensable members of the workforce.

ticipation rate. The fact that the decline was small reflects the fact that many women continued to work while raising families. It seems reasonable to expect that the labor force participation rate for women will increase when the children of these baby boomers reach school age and the mothers who chose to stay home return once again to the workplace. Irrespective of this small fluctuation in women's participation in the workforce, since the Second World War women have consistently increased their representation in the world of work outside the home. In part, these changes in the labor force are reflective of economic growth; more people are working because there are more jobs. But other factors have played a role in this very important change.

Working outside the home has also become a more viable option for women because of the shrinking size of the American family. Many different family forms exist in the United States, as you learned in Chapter 13, but overall, the statistics show that the average American household—that is, people who live under the same roof—has gotten smaller over the years. The average number of people in an American household decreased from 4.76 people in 1900 to 2.75 people in 1980—a reduction of more than 40%. But it is not just our households that are getting smaller; the nuclear family is getting smaller also. The invention of effective, inexpensive, and accessible methods of birth control led to a decrease in the size of the average American family, from 3.67 individuals in 1960 to 3.18 individuals in 1991. Smaller families mean child care responsibilities are not as great or as long lasting. Even if a woman decides to stay home until her child is in school, with only one child that means staying home for a maximum of six years. Compare this with the length of time a mother would have to stay home until five children were all attending school, and it is clear that the mother of one child will be back out in the workforce far sooner than the mother of five. In addition, the possibilities for placing one's child in alternative care arrangements become more feasible if fewer children are involved. Imagine what a single parent would have to earn in order to place five children in daycare and break even!

Advances in travel and communication technologies have made the other side of the world nearly as accessible as the other side of town, and this too has had its effects. In 1989, 17% of Americans changed their place of residence, and more recent estimates indicate that 20% of Americans change their residence each year. It is no longer necessary to live in the same town as the rest of the family if we wish to see them or talk to them, and many of us don't. Our family relationships do not appear to be suffering as a result, however: A recent study on the extended family networks of older adults found no differences in the quality of relationships between aging parents whose adult children lived more than 60 miles away and parents whose children lived near them (Mercier, Paulson, & Morris, 1989). A similar finding has been reported for African-American families as well (Taylor & Chatters, 1991).

In addition, more workers are using increasingly sophisticated personal computing and communication resources to work at home rather than going to an office. This creates more possibilities for working mothers and fathers to combine work and parenting responsibilities.

The developmental changes of the baby boom generation, the growth of the workforce, an increasing number of women working outside the home, the shrinking of the American family, and the increasing sophistication of travel and communications technologies are all backdrops against which our relationships are played out. The rest of the chapter will examine some specific issues that have already had an impact on our relational lives, point out how relationships are changing, and speculate about what might happen in the future.

DEMOGRAPHIC TRENDS

Demography is the statistical study of human populations. The number of people who live in a place and the numbers of births, deaths, marriages, and divorces are all demographic indicators. Several important demographic trends have been discussed above. In this section we will examine other trends that are important for our relationships. Many of the changes that will be discussed focus on traditional marital and family constellations, because the time period during which these changes occurred was initially characterized by the prevalence of traditional families. Keep in mind, however, that nontraditional family forms have arisen in part as a direct result of these trends.

Increased Divorce Rates

The skyrocketing divorce rate has been in the headlines for many years. Currently, 50% of all first marriages end in divorce. Contrary to the popular belief that you marry the first time for children and the second time for life, the divorce rate for second and subsequent marriages is actually a bit higher than 50%! The ease of getting divorced, as well as the experience of divorce, have numerous effects on the forms of our relationships and the ways in which we think about and conduct ourselves in relationships.

Maybe you've seen reruns of television shows from the 1950s or

1960s that depict two-parent families with two or three children, where the father works to support the family and the mother stays home raising children, cooking, and cleaning. This type of family—the kind seen on "Leave It to Beaver" or "The Donna Reed Show"—has become increasingly unusual during the last 40 years, in part because of the rise in divorce. Divorces create single-parent families, in which there is only one parent heading the household. Often that one parent has primary responsibility for both raising the children and supporting the family. This family form is so common in modern society that we often forget it represents a fundamental change in what constitutes a family.

When single heads of households remarry they create **blended families**, or families in which the partners and their children from previous relationships combine to form a new family. If the new couple then has children of their own, the blended family consists of two parents with children from at least three different pairings of parents. The television show "The Brady Bunch" was about a blended family, and although it was a situation comedy, it dealt with many of the unique challenges of blended-family relationships.

Divorce, then, has a direct impact on the changing family structure. But the high divorce rate may also have more subtle influences on interpersonal relationships. Many people are choosing to remain single, partly because the odds against making a marriage work seem too high. Perhaps because of the ease of getting divorced, others seem to view marriage as a temporary situation rather than a permanent institution. Elizabeth Taylor's marital history (at last count, eight husbands, one of whom she married twice) exemplifies the concept of **serial monogamy**. Serial monogamy refers to the practice of having a number of primary relationships over time, while having only one partner at any given time. It might be interesting to think about how a marriage viewed as a temporary arrangement would be different from a marriage viewed in the more traditional "'til death do us part" way. Do you think the nature of the relationship would be fundamentally different? How might this difference manifest itself?

Increased Employment of Women

As we saw above, one of the most profound changes in the United States in recent decades has been the increase in the percentage of women who are employed outside the home. Women are more career oriented than they have been at any other time, and more career opportunities exist for women than ever before. More women are choosing not to marry, are getting married later, or are heading households, all of which result in more women working.

Some proportion of the increase in the number of working women can be considered an *effect of* changing relationship patterns. For example, the increase in the number of single working mothers is, at least in part, a direct result of the increase in divorce rates.

But this trend also has profound implications for relationships. Women who are self-sufficient (or who know they can be) seem to be more willing to terminate relationships they are unhappy with (Rankin & Maneker, 1987; Starkey, 1991). A woman who knows she can take care of herself is likely to conduct her relationships differently than a woman who feels she would not be able to make it on her own. For example, research shows that many abused women do not terminate abusive relationships in part because they feel financially dependent on their abusive spouses (Davis & Hagen, 1992). A modern woman's ability to feel capable of making it on her own also reflects, to some degree, relatively recent changes in the legal and social status of women. Prior to the 19th century women were seen as property, and as such they had very few rights as independent entities. The existence of conditions like these made it impossible for women to be self-sufficient, regardless of other circumstances. But the influence between these two conditions flows two ways; that is, changes in women's social and legal status are also influenced by women's participation in the workforce. A person who works receives compensation for doing so, usually in the form of money. Money, in a capitalistic economic system, means power. And the more power women have, the more they can influence the social and legal conditions of the system within which they function. Women's social and legal power, as indicated by economic independence, control of wealth, participation in labor unions, and representation in high-status occupations, the legal profession, and elected office, has increased steadily over the last 50 years (Caplow, Bahr, Modell, & Chadwick, 1991). These changes have been associated with an increase in cross-gender friendships—as distinct from affairs—that provide much emotional and instrumental support.

Another implication of being out in the workforce may surprise you. Increased opportunity—just being in situations where it is possible to meet people—has been cited as one reason for the increase in women's rates of extramarital sexual involvement (Small, 1992). It seems that more women working means more women having affairs. Affairs often lead to breakups, so women's increased participation in the workforce has coincided with an increase in the divorce rate.

Finally, more working women means that more children are being raised by primary caregivers other than their parents, a phenomenon that has wide-ranging implications not only for current family relationships but also for the children's relational futures. (See Chapter 4 for a discussion of the importance of the primary caregiver in the life of a child.)

Increased Rates of Teen Pregnancy

More teenagers than ever are having children (Vinovskis, 1988; see also Chapter 9 for a complete discussion of teenage sexuality). The number of babies born to 10- to 14-year-old girls *doubled* between 1940 and 1989. During that same time period, the birth rate for 15- to 19-year-olds increased 10%. Exactly what do these figures mean? They mean that almost 60 out of every 1000 girls between the ages of 10 and 19 in this country in 1989 had a baby.

The teen pregnancy rate has at least two implications for family structure. First, since people who marry younger are more likely to get divorced (see Chapter 10), young parents who marry contribute to the continuing rise in the number of single-parent families and, eventually, blended families. Pregnant teenagers who choose not to marry also create single-parent families. So sooner or later, the increase in teen pregnancies increases the number of single-parent households.

Second, there is a growing trend among young parents to enlist the aid of their own parents in raising their children. More grandparents are finding themselves raising a second family during their later years (Kennedy & Keeney, 1988; Werner, 1991), an experience that profoundly alters the relational course of both the children's and the grandparents' lives. When a teenage girl needs her own mother's help in raising her baby, the grandmother is probably still relatively young and may have spent several years building a career. If she is asked to care for an infant grandchild so that her own daughter can finish high school or go to college, instead of being an independent career woman, this grandmother is faced with the same sorts of career-versus-child care decisions that she confronted when she first had her own children. For the couple who find themselves raising a grandchild, the long-awaited freedom from raising small children, with its promise of time alone, travel, and other adult diversions, disappears as well. Some of these grandparents face the prospect of raising children well past the years when they felt they had the necessary energy, patience, or desire to take on such a task.

The Graying of Society

With the aging of the baby boom generation and improvements in public health, the proportion of the population made up of elderly people is growing. One important social change related to this fact is the increasing number of adult children, often married and raising families of their own, who are caring for an elderly parent or parents. (See Chapters 18 and 19 for more complete discussions of intergenerational family relationships.) According to the American Association of Retired Persons, over 7 million adult children are currently providing care in their homes for an elderly parent, and this number is sure to rise over the next several decades.

This type of arrangement can have a significant impact on all of the family relationships involved. Children raised in homes where grandparents are present will have very different relationships with them (and perhaps with elderly people in general) than children who only visit grandmother and grandfather. The complex negotiations and important changes that occur in the relationship between aging parents and their adult children (see Chapters 15, 18, and 19) will probably be intensified by living under the same roof, especially if the elderly parent requires physical care. The caregiving couple will have to juggle the demands of work, children, and their parents, leaving even less time than they previously had for attending to their own relationship. In the worst case, conflict resolution may take a back seat to just taking care of what must get done, leading to eventual dissatisfaction. On the other hand, such an arrangement could lead to closer families, in which children respect and value the elderly, adult children feel the satisfaction of returning the care their parents provided for them during their early years, and the aging parents live the last years of their lives surrounded by people who love them. Naturally, there is a whole range of options on a continuum between the worst-case scenario and the best-case scenario. Each family's experience will probably be slightly different, but it is safe to predict that none will remain unaffected.

Does this trend herald a return to the expanded household, with three or more generations of family members living together or in close proximity to one another? Multi-generational households, along with families who maintain close contact among extended family members, have become less apparent in modern American culture (although they were never as common in certain historical periods as we tend to think) but have always been the norm in many other cultures (de Vos, 1990; Domino, Affonso, & Slobin, 1987). (See Chapter 13 for a full discussion of alternative family constellations.) A return to extended families would be a dramatic shift away from the nuclear family that is now the norm in mainstream American culture.

The Increased Cost of Living

An economic trend that might also move American society in the direction of extended family living is the increasing cost of living. As a college student, you are probably painfully aware of how tough it is to make a living these days. Urban living in particular might seem prohibitively expensive on an entry-level salary, even for the new college graduate who has landed a good job.

Many young people are dealing with this fact of life by returning to their parents' homes to live while they build their careers, save for a house, or otherwise prepare to strike out on their own. The popular television program "The Cosby Show" lightheartedly portrayed parents who longed for an empty nest after years of childrearing, only to find their adult children bouncing back to the parental home to live. "The Cosby Show" made us laugh about the situation, but the developmental courses of the parent-child relationship and the marital relationship are necessarily altered when an adult child moves back home. In the parent-child relationship, the usual developmental task at this life stage is the establishment of a more egalitarian relationship between the parent and the child. This relational progression is made substantially more complicated by the adult child's return to the parental home. The parental roles of disciplinarian, protector, and authority are no longer appropriate because the child is now grown up, but an appropriate set of new rules is not clear. Can the parents impose a curfew on an adult child? Do they have the right to prohibit overnight stays by their child's romantic partner? These and a host of other questions arise that require different kinds of parent-child negotiations than individuals expect at this developmental stage. (See Chapter 15 for a more complete discussion of this subject.)

Changing Family Structures

All of the trends described above have direct implications for the evolution of the social institution we call the family. Recent decades have seen increases in certain types of family structures that already existed (such as the single-parent family) as well as the formal recognition of previously ignored family forms (such as the blended family and gay and lesbian families), and these changes are not going unnoticed. Some see these changes as the "breakdown" of the American family, and alarm over this purported breakdown has figured prominently in newspaper headlines and political campaigns in recent years. Others, however, see the changes as part of a natural process in which cultural norms evolve over time in response to a number of social, environmental, political, technological, and economic influences. It is clearly no longer possible to make generalizations about the American family. Part of American cultural ideology is that we are a highly resourceful and inventive people—if the old system doesn't work, we change it—and that is what is happening to our families today. We are reinventing them, and only time will really tell what they will look like 100 years from now. Perhaps a decade from now the societal norm will resemble an Israeli kibbutz, where the children live communally instead of in their parents' homes (see Chapter 13 for a description of this social organization). For now the only safe bet is that family forms will be increasingly diverse, as each individual and each family strives to create something that works.

MEDICAL TRENDS

In the futuristic society depicted in Aldous Huxley's *Brave New World* medical technology has advanced to the point that human reproduction is automated, and children are raised communally. Freed from worries about pregnancy and the need to raise and socialize children, individuals engage in promiscuous sex, which has become the societal norm. As a consequence, what we think of as "intimacy" between a man and a woman is virtually nonexistent. Concepts we consider important—such as fidelity, monogamy, and loyalty—have no meaning in relationships between individuals.

Although this example may seem extreme, changing attitudes toward birth control and the invention of modern methods of birth control in the 1950s and 1960s led to changes not totally unlike those in Aldous Huxley's fictional world. The sexual revolution of the 1960s, made possible by these fifties-era developments, ushered in a new set of values with respect to male-female relationships (including marriage) that persist today.

Thus we can see medical science's potential for influencing the nature and quality of our relationships. Let's review some of the medical developments that have already changed our relationships and will continue to do so in your lifetimes.

Extended Life Expectancies

In 1900 the average man could expect to live until he was 46 years old; the average woman could expect to live to the ripe old age of 48 (U.S. Bureau of the Census, 1975). Ninety years later, men can expect to live over 70 years, and women's life expectancy is approaching 80. With continuing advances in medicine there is no telling how long your own grandchildren might live. The relational implications of this phenomenon are legion. For years, when couples repeated the traditional marriage vow " 'til death do us part," they meant (depending on the ages of the individuals) 20 or, at most, 30 years. A young couple making this pledge today can anticipate 50, 60, or even more years together! Given that the social, legal, and economic barriers to divorce continue to drop, and that significant fluctuations in the quality of the marital relationship seem to characterize most long-term marriages (Pearson, 1992; also see Chapter 16), it is anyone's guess what can motivate couples to remain in a marriage of this length.

In addition to changing the life span of marital relationships, extended life expectancies mean a much larger proportion of the population will be made up of elderly individuals. This fact has the potential to require us to change the way we integrate (or, more accurately, don't integrate) elderly people into society. When wealthier, healthier, and more active elders make up a larger proportion of the population, they will become more influential politically and economically. It will no longer be possible to ignore their needs, push them aside, and forget about them. People of all ages will have to change the ways in which they relate to this important group of individuals.

AIDS and Other Sexually Transmitted Diseases

As discussed above, medical advances in birth control technology and attitude changes regarding birth control contributed to the social phenomenon that has been called the "free love" era, or sexual revolution, of the 1960s. During this time physical intimacy between individuals was seen as independent from the traditional prerequisites of love and marriage. Sex for pleasure became a legitimate activity in its own right, changing our notions of what "normal" relationship development consisted of. Couples generally had sex sooner in the relationship, often before there were any significant emotional ties between them. Cohabitation became a norm for couples who were considering making a commitment, and many couples adopted lifestyles in which extramarital relationships were acceptable. Since the early 1980s, however, it has become increasingly dangerous to engage in sex of any kind, but especially casual sex with many partners.

The most dramatic danger is the possibility of contracting the Human Immunodeficiency Virus, or HIV. As you are no doubt aware, HIV infection leads to a medical syndrome called Acquired Immune Deficiency Syndrome, or AIDS. There is no cure for AIDS; it is a terminal illness. The early victims of AIDS were mostly gay men and intravenous drug users, but today AIDS is an "equal-opportunity" killer. Male, female, gay, straight, teenagers, young adults, adults, white, Native American, African-American, Latino, Asian—all segments of the population are contracting HIV and dying. In addition to AIDS, there are other sexually transmitted diseases (STDs) for which there are no cures; some of these have been linked to life-threatening diseases such as cancer. Thus the rules for our relationships are beginning to change in a number of ways.

In spite of the evidence that, by and large, heterosexual individuals are not altering their sexual behavior in response to the threat of AIDS (Caroll, 1988), there is a strong movement advocating a return to **premarital celibacy**, or abstinence from sexual involvement prior to marriage. For the large majority of teens and young adults, adhering to a policy of premarital celibacy will mean they have to find new things to do on dates! Since dating is our society's main method of mate selection (see Chapter 10), a shift toward sexual abstinence has implications for the way we choose long-term partners.

Some people have suggested that these health threats may serve to decrease the divorce rate, since finding a new partner can entail so much risk, or at least inconvenience. According to this view, the knowledge that a relationship might not be perfect but it is "safe" outweighs the value of finding a more perfect relationship with someone else. Could the tragedy of AIDS lead to renewed commitment to "old fashioned" values such as celibacy, monogamy, and preserving our primary relationships? Perhaps, but only if a cure is not found; and the cost of this renewed commitment—failing to find a cure for AIDS—is probably too high a price to pay by anyone's standards.

The most extreme view of the potential consequences of the AIDS epidemic is a world in which sexual interactions increasingly take place over the telephone or at some other safe remove. Telephone and computer sex lines already exist in most communities, and their growth is astounding. For some, sex at a distance may be appealing, but others may question the point of such activity. Whatever your opinions on this issue, if, as in *Brave New World*, medical science can develop ways for humans to reproduce without having sex or carrying children (and the first of these is already possible), it is conceivable that sex could eventually evolve into a noncontact sport.

Decreasing Fecundity

If you find yourself thinking how preposterous the above ideas are, think again. **Fecundity**, the biological capacity to conceive and bear a child, is decreasing in modern society. In the language of demographics, fecundity is different from fertility, in that *fertility* refers to the birth rate of a population (the rate at which individuals within an identified group are choosing to have children) whereas *fecundity* refers to an individual's biological ability to bear children. Fertility, then, reflects people's *choices* regarding whether to have children; fecundity is not a matter of choice. Modern society's decreasing fecundity means that more people are unable to have children than ever before. Unlike the decrease in fertility rates demonstrated by most of the Western world, the decrease in fecundity is not considered voluntary or desired. Indeed, this decrease has created a booming business in infertility services of various sorts, from counseling to complex and futuristic medical interventions designed to help people have the children they want. Why is fecundity decreasing? There are no doubt a number of causes, including more women delaying having children until later in life, when fecundity decreases naturally. Some evidence exists that our ingestion of chemicals and other substances we have introduced into our daily lives may make us sterile (Flam, 1989; Schmidt, 1992; Shoop, 1991). Common household products, such as processed foods and cleaning and personal care products, contain long lists of chemicals that might have these effects. Reading the ingredients list of any of these items might make you think twice about what it could be doing to your body.

In her recent novel *The Children of Men*, fiction writer P. D. James powerfully depicts a future in which humans are no longer capable of reproducing at all and are therefore doomed to extinction. The story is set in the year 2021, and the book's protagonist recalls that decreases in the number of children born around the globe were noted in the early 1990s:

> We thought we knew the reasons, that the fall was deliberate, a result of more liberal attitudes to birth control and abortion, the postponement of pregnancy by professional women pursuing their careers, the wish of families for a higher standard of living. . . . We were polluting the planet with our numbers; if we were breeding less it was to be welcomed. . . . But as I remember

it, no one suggested that the [fecundity] of the human race was dramatically changing. . . . Overnight, it seemed, the human race had lost its power to breed. (pp. 10–11)

She goes on to describe the meaninglessness of a world in which there is no hope for future generations—a world in which there is such demoralization that those who do not commit suicide exhibit "lassitude, depression, ill-defined malaise, a readiness to give way to minor infections, [and] a perpetual disabling headache" (James, 1992, p. 12).

Regardless of the causes of present-day decreases in fecundity or of whether such an extreme future as is described in *The Children of Men* could actually come about, more and more people want children but cannot have them themselves. Many of these people also have substantial economic resources. In a capitalistic system, demand, combined with available resources, leads almost inevitably to the provision of goods, even if those goods can be provided only with substantial innovation. It is easy to imagine that medical science will, in response to a growing demand, eventually achieve the capacity to produce children in a way that does not rely on the inexact and low-probability processes of nature. Combine this achievement with the growing dangers of sex as we know it, and we begin to see how sex and childbearing could become obsolete.

TECHNOLOGICAL TRENDS

Advances in technology, like advances in medicine, have significant and lasting effects on the ways we conduct our interpersonal lives. The 20th century has seen the invention of radio, television, and video games, as well as a host of entertainment devices and work tools including personal computers, radios, cassette players, compact disc players, and televisions. These devices tend either to facilitate communication between people (for example, fax machines and electronic mail and bulletin boards) or, by creating highly individualized sensory experiences that involve a person with the technology rather than with other people (for example, a walkman or a video game), to inhibit interpersonal communication. The following sections look more closely at some technological trends that facilitate relationships as well as some that inhibit interpersonal interaction.

How Does Technology Facilitate Our Relationships?

In an era of rapid development and change, advances in the technology of communication have led the pack. At the turn of this century it was barely possible to telephone someone a few miles away, and few people had access to this technology. As we approach the turn of the next century, we can not only talk to anyone virtually anywhere on earth within seconds but also instantaneously send documents, data, and images around the world. Via electronic mail and our personal computers, with a few key-strokes we can "talk" to groups of like-minded individuals scattered around the globe. Electronic bulletin boards and interest groups make it possible for people who might never meet to form relationships based on mutual interests. E-mail friends are reminiscent of pen pals, although the frequency of exchange is probably far higher through the electronic medium. But this technology facilitates more than friendships. Recently, on-line dating services for singles have sprung up and are becoming increasingly popular (Catalfo, 1991; Queenan, 1990). Today there are married couples who met, courted, and fell in love, communicating only through computer mail.

How might these developments influence the nature of our relationships? As Chapter 10 (on mate selection) and Chapters 14 and 17 (on friendship) pointed out, a major factor determining our choices of friends and partners is proximity. In general, it has been true that two people can't get to know each other unless they live, work, or play in geographic proximity to one another. Furthermore, since geographic proximity usually means homogamy—that is, people who live, work, or play in the same place typically also share other attributes such as class, race, and socioeconomic status—people tend to have relationships with individuals who are more like them than unlike them. Technology-aided relationships suffer no such restrictions. A person in New York can get to know someone in Hawaii just as easily as she or he can get to know someone next door. Race, class, and socioeconomic characteristics are difficult if not impossible to determine from a computer screen. More important, perhaps, is that the interest-driven nature of many computer relationships de-emphasizes distinctions between people based on these factors. When you communicate with someone by computer about a mutual interest, you don't have to worry about running out of things to say or whether you've outstayed your welcome. Are we bound for a world in which proximity and homogamy have increasingly less influence on our relationships? If so, we can expect these developments in communication to contribute to increasing diversity in friendships, couples, and families in the next century.

How Does Technology Inhibit Our Relationships?

While many of us are busy building new relationships and maintaining old ones using the new technology, there are also technological treats that make individual isolation tempting. Television has evolved from a device designed to increase family interaction (remember those old shows in which the whole family gathered around the television set to watch a program together?) to a means of escape from interaction with others. As programming has become more diverse and viewing options have increased, the diversity in individual preferences has slowly but inevitably

Will our increasing dependence on and involvement with machines lead to decreasing ability and interest in interaction with each other?

led to the present norm of several televisions per household—ideally, one per person—so that each person can watch what he or she wants. Alone. Moreover, a host of individualized entertainment technologies make it possible to be in public places—even in crowds—and yet be in one's own isolated world. Virtual reality, perhaps the ultimate in isolationist entertainment technology, is currently available but as yet is too expensive for most people's pocketbooks. Via virtual reality the individual enters the world of the video game, where interpersonal communication is impossible and irrelevant.

A pessimistic view of this trend might lead to predictions of increasing isolation of individuals in society. Increased interpersonal isolation could then lead to decreased interpersonal skills, which in turn could lead to further isolation. A hundred years of this, and the vision becomes one of a society in which people live alone, play alone, and work alone as much as possible, since interacting with humans is so much more difficult than interacting with machines.

But there is a difference between getting what you need from a machine and getting it from another human being. Suppose that we could get all of Weiss's provisions of relationships (Weiss, 1974; see the discussion of these in Chapter 1) from machines. Would we be likely to do that? Consider the case of psychotherapy. Over the years many computer programs have been designed to replace therapists in carrying out psychotherapy. The client would type what she or he had to say, and the computer was programmed to respond the way a therapist would respond. Some of these programs were actually quite sophisticated, and therapists who tested the products agreed that the computers actually were "behaving" the way they themselves might act in a session with a client. Despite the level of sophistication of the program and the "insightfulness" of the computer's responses, however, none of these computer therapy programs ever achieved any popularity. It seems that there is something qualitatively different about a person-to-person interaction that makes it more satisfying than a person-to-machine exchange, even if the two objectively provide the same things.

Finally, there are still some provisions of relationships that technological devices cannot (yet?) provide, such as physical contact. Until your virtual reality teammate the cyborg can hug you, chances are you will turn to a real human eventually.

The isolationist scenario, then, seems unlikely. It is more likely that people will choose when they want to interact with other people and when they don't. Like so many other modern developments, technological advances contribute to the range of options available to us at any given time. An optimistic view might maintain that the quality of our interactions will be enhanced through these developments, since people will only interact with each other when they want to. In addition, the capacity for sharing technological experiences will probably also be developed. Like the double headset for the Walkman or the two-person video game, two or more people will eventually be able to participate together in virtual reality if they wish. In these ways individuals will have more choices than ever regarding when to be alone and when to be with other people. It is unlikely that most people will exclusively prefer to be alone.

THE OTHER SIDE OF THE DEBATE

Scientists discovered long ago that in nature every action generates an equal and opposite reaction, and human nature appears to be no different. In the face of dramatic demographic changes in the family, we have recently witnessed a strong resurgence of a rhetoric that extols "family values." Thus while all of the changes and developments discussed throughout this chapter push us toward change, there are also numerous social, personal, and political factors that push right back toward stability. For example, it would be difficult to move toward communal child-rearing without tearing down and rebuilding entire communities; our neighborhoods, towns, and cities are built to accommodate nuclear (or larger, but not smaller) families. Another strong force in the service of stability is organized religion, a powerful social institution that pushes toward the maintenance of relationships as we know them. Any kind of change happens slowly, and social change perhaps the most slowly of all.

PERSONAL RELATIONSHIPS RECONSIDERED

Our relationships are continuously evolving, and this chapter has explored the ways that they might continue to evolve in the future. What has not been discussed, however, is whether the needs that underlie social interaction remain the same over time. For example, a human body needs nourishment, and we normally get that nourishment by eating food and drinking water and maybe taking vitamin pills. But if in the future scientists develop lotions that we can rub on our bodies that provide all the nourishment we need, we might never eat a bite or drink a drop. In this example, the method of getting what we need has changed, but the need has remained the same, and it has been filled just as well by the new method. Like the body's need for nourishment, Weiss's (1974) provisions of relationships (see Chapter 1) appear quite basic, and all the changes we have discussed in this chapter appear to be alterations in the *forms* of need fulfillment rather than fundamental changes in the needs themselves.

If we define a personal relationship as something that fulfills interpersonal needs, then the alterations in the forms of need satisfaction that we have discussed imply alterations in our conceptions of relationships. Specifically, if a personal relationship is defined by what it provides, and machines supply us with some or all of the provisions of relationships, then are we having personal relationships with the machines? If not, then is there some other quality that actually defines the essence of a personal relationship? This book has presented many ideas about how we conduct relationships, what purposes they serve, and how they influence our lives. In your own life you have already experienced many of the personal relationships discussed in this text. What do you think truly defines a personal relationship?

Conclusion

This text has discussed the diversity of relationships that shape our interpersonal worlds. Throughout our lifetimes, who we are, what we think, and how we behave are strongly influenced—perhaps even determined—by our personal relationships. As you have seen, different relationships fulfill different needs at different points in the life-cycle. But one thing remains constant: Personal relationships are always important in our lives, from the moment we take our first breath to the moment we exhale our last.

As we look toward a new decade, a new century, and a new millennium, perhaps we can be certain of only one thing: Progress will continue to change the world as we know it. And when the world changes, so do we. Our interpersonal lives are intricately and inextricably interwoven with our political, medical, economic, and scientific lives in a process of reciprocal influence. The interdependence that characterizes our personal relationships also characterizes our societal relationships, and that is, ultimately, the point of this chapter. In making this point, we have explored some specific changes happening around us and the potential interpersonal effects of those changes. Predicting the future, however, is a risky business, and it is likely that none of these speculations will prove entirely accurate. It is certainly true, however, that changes in these areas (and others) will lead to the continuing evolution of our relational lives.

Class Discussion Questions

1. Do you think that Weiss's provisions of relationships still hold? What if, in the distant and murky future, all of our interpersonal needs can be filled by machines (including hugs from virtual reality cyborgs)? Do we then have relationships with those machines? In other words, is a relationship defined by the provision of interpersonal needs, or is it more than that?

2. Role-play relationships from a different era. Two students might role-play a married couple from the early part of this century, then two others might role-play a parent-child relationship from another time in history. After each role play, discuss the representation and how it differs from those relationships today. The "actors" should tell the class how it felt to enact those roles. In the role plays and the discussion pay attention to the following: the size and generational makeup of the households; the geographic location of the various family members; the roles of children, parents, and grandparents; and the roles of men and women.

3. Discuss how you conduct your courtships (or dating relationships). How do you find potential partners? What activities do you engage in together? What activities do you not engage in? How do you handle issues of physical intimacy? Compare and contrast your answers with norms that existed in the fifties, sixties, seventies, and eighties. Can you discern trends in courtship patterns? If so, how might these trends develop over the next 50 years?

4. Conduct an informal class survey on what technologies you own and use, both for entertainment and for work. Discuss what percentage of your leisure and work time is spent in solitary, person-machine interactions and how much is spent in interpersonal interaction. How do you feel about these percentages? Would you like to change them, and if so, how?

Homework Assignments

1. Interview a family member or a friend from another generation about his or her family of origin. Ask about the size of the household; the size of the family; the courtship and relationship development with her or his partner; the roles of men and women; and the roles of children, parents, and grandparents. In addition, ask your interviewee what his or her grandparents said about *their* relationships. Contrast these with the course of your own relational life and where there are differences, identify some societal change that has influenced this process.

2. Find an article in a magazine or newspaper that reports some new medical or technological development, and write a brief essay on how this development might affect interpersonal relationships in the future.

3. The cartoon family "The Jetsons" was an attempt to predict what the family of the future would be like. Based on how relationships have evolved already and how you think they might continue to evolve in the future, discuss what the creators of "The Jetsons" got right and what they missed. In what areas have we already changed more than they predicted, and in what areas have we not progressed as far?

4. Write a letter to your future great-grandchildren telling them what relationships were like in your day. Remember that what they need to

know is related to how things have changed since your time. That is, if children still live with their parents when they are growing up, you probably don't need to tell them that children lived with their parents in your day. On the other hand, if children in their era are raised communally, they will be amazed that children used to live with their parents "in the olden days."

Suggested Course Papers

1. Read *Brave New World* by Aldous Huxley,[2] *He, She, and It* by Marge Piercy, or *The Handmaid's Tale* by Margaret Atwood, and write a paper describing how the relationships depicted in those books are different from relationships today. Discuss how the form and function of the personal relationships in the novel have been influenced by political, environmental, technological, medical, and economic progress. Finally, comment on the similarities and differences between the developments described in the book and the changes occurring in society today.

2. Watch the movie *Ordinary People* and write a short paper using concepts from the text to analyze each of the following, as depicted in one or more scenes from the movie: the Jared family; Conrad's relationship with his therapist; Conrad's relationship with one of his friends; the relationship between Conrad's parents; and Conrad's relationship with his girlfriend.

Additional Readings

Atwood, M. (1986). *The handmaid's tale.* New York: Ballantine.

Gergen, K. J. (1991). *The saturated self: Dilemmas of identity in contemporary life.* New York: Basic.

Huxley, A. (1932). *Brave new world.* New York: Harper & Row.

James, P. D. (1992). *The children of men.* New York: Warner.

Pearson, J. C. (1992). *Lasting love: What keeps couples together.* Dubuque, IA: William C. Brown.

Piercy, M. (1991). *He, she, and it.* New York: Ballantine.

Skolnick, A. S., & Skolnick, J. H. (Comps.). (1992). *Family in transition: Rethinking marriage, sexuality, child rearing, and family organization* (7th Edition). New York: HarperCollins.

Smith, Q. K. (Ed.). (1991). *The psychology of grandparenthood: An international perspective.* London: Routledge.

Stockwell, E. G., & Groat, H. T. (1984). *World population: An introduction to demography.* New York: Franklin Watts.

---

[2]Instructors are cautioned that *Brave New World* contains sexist and racist material.

References

Caplow, T., Bahr, H., Modell, J., & Chadwick, B. (Eds.). (1991). *Recent social trends in the United States: 1960–1990*. Buffalo, NY: McGill-Queen's University Press.

Caroll, L. (1988). Concern with AIDS and the sexual behavior of college students. *Journal of Marriage and the Family, 50*, 405–411.

Catalfo, Q. (1991). America, on-line. *New Age Journal, 8*, 46.

Davis, L. V., & Hagen, J. L. (1992). The problem of wife abuse: The interrelationship of social policy and social work practice. *Social Work, 37*, 15–20.

de Vos, S. (1990). Extended family living among older people in six Latin American countries. *Journals of Gerontology, 45*, 87–94.

Domino, G., Affonso, D., & Slobin, M. (1987). Community psychology in the People's Republic of China. *Psychologia: An International Journal of Psychology, 30*, 1–11.

Flam, F. (1989). She who laughs gas conceives last. *Science News, 135*, 182.

Kennedy, J. F., & Keeney, V. T. (1988). The extended family revisited: Grandparents rearing grandchildren. *Child Psychiatry and Human Development, 19*, 26–35.

Mercier, J. M., Paulson, L., & Morris, E. W. (1989). Proximity as a mediating influence on the perceived aging parent–adult child relationship. *Gerontologist, 29*, 785–791.

Pearson, J. C. (1992). *Lasting love: What keeps couples together*. Dubuque, IA: William C. Brown.

Queenan, J. (1990). Terminal attraction. *Gentlemen's Quarterly, 60*, 120–121.

Rankin, R., & Maneker, J. S. (1987). Wives' employment status and marital duration in a population filing for divorce. *Journal of Divorce, 11*, 93–105.

Schmidt, K. F. (1992). The dark legacy of fatherhood. *U.S. News & World Report, 113*, 94–96.

Shelley, F. D. (1988). *When your parents grow old* (2nd ed.). New York: Harper & Row.

Shoop, J. G. (1991). Threats to reproduction, child development are poorly regulated. *Trial, 27*, 77–80.

Small, M. F. (1992). The evolution of female sexuality and mate selection in humans. *Human Nature, 3*, 133–156.

Starkey, J. L. (1991). Wives' earnings and marital instability: Another look at the independence effect. *Social Science Journal, 28*, 501–521.

Taylor, R. J., & Chatters, L. M. (1991). Extended family networks of older black adults. *Journals of Gerontology, 46*, 210–217.

U.S. Bureau of the Census. (1975). *Historical statistics of the United States, colonial times to 1970, Bicentennial edition, Part 2*. Washington, DC: Author.

U.S. Bureau of the Census. (1992). *Statistical abstract of the United States: 1992* (112th ed.). Washington, DC: Author.

Vinovskis, M. (1988). *An "epidemic" of adolescent pregnancy: Historical and policy considerations*. New York: Oxford University Press.

Weiss, R. S. (1974). The provisions of social relationships. In Z. Rubin (Ed.), *Doing unto others* (pp. 17–26). Englewood Cliffs, NJ: Prentice-Hall.

Werner, E. E. (1991). Grandparent-grandchild relationships among U.S. ethnic groups. In Peter K. Smith (Ed.), *The psychology of grandparenthood: An international perspective*. London: Routledge.

Glossary

Baby boom   The period of rapid population growth that occurred between 1946 and 1964, during which the population of the United States increased by 50 million people

Blended family   A family formed when individuals who have children from previous relationships get together

Demography   The statistical study of human populations

Fecundity   The biological capability to conceive and bear children

Premarital celibacy   The practice of refraining from interpersonal sexual activity before marriage

Serial monogamy   The practice of having only one primary relationship at a time but more than one primary relationship over time

Name Index

Subject Index

Credits

These pages constitute an extension of the copyright page. We have made every effort to trace the ownership of all copyrighted material and to secure permission from copyright holders. In the event of any question arising as to the use of any material, we will be pleased to make the necessary corrections in future printings. Thanks are due to the following authors, publishers, and agents for permission to use the material indicated.

Part One: 1, The Terry Wild Studio.

Chapter 1: 14, David Young-Wolff/PhotoEdit. **16,** Robert Brenner/PhotoEdit.

Chapter 2: 27, The Terry Wild Studio. **35,** Stephanie Rausser/FPG International.

Chapter 3: 50, John Terence Turner/FPG International. **60,** Emillio A. Mercado/The Picture Cube.

Part Two: 75, Kevin Laubacher/FPG International.

Chapter 4: 81, John Coletti/The Picture Cube. **88,** Michael Newman/PhotoEdit.

Chapter 5: 107, The Terry Wild Studio. **115,** Myrleen Ferguson/PhotoEdit. **119, Box 5-4** from *Manual for the Sibling Inventory of Differential Experience (SIDE),* by D. Daniels and R. Plomin, 1985. Reprinted with permission of the author.

Chapter 6: 132, Robert Finken/The Picture Cube. **139,** Myrleen Ferguson/PhotoEdit.

Chapter 7: 158, Larry Lawfer/The Picture Cube. **167,** Michael Newman/PhotoEdit.

Chapter 8: 186, Navaswan/FPG International. **197,** Robert Brenner/PhotoEdit.

Chapter 9: 220, Spencer Grant/The Picture Cube. **222, Figure 9-1** reproduced with the permission of the Alan Guttmacher Institute from Freya L. Sonenstein, Joseph H. Pleck, and C. Ku Leighton, "Levels of Sexual Activity among Adolescent Males in the United States," *Family Planning Perspectives, 23,* No. 4, July/Aug. 1991, pp.162-167. **226, Figure 9-2** adapted from "Premarital Sex: Attitudes and Behavior by Dating Stage," by J. P. Roche, 1986, *Adolescence, 21,* No. 81, Spring 1986, 107-121. Copyright © 1986 Libra Publishers, Inc. Adapted with permission. **231,** Emillio A. Mercado/The Picture Cube.

Chapter 10: 247, Jamila Mimouni/Liaison International. **253, Figure 10-1** from *Monthly Vital Statistics Report, 40*(13), September 30, 1992. **258,** The Terry Wild Studio.

Chapter 11: 267, Liaison International. **269, Box 11-1** based on "The Conceptualization of Marriage from a Behavioral Perspective," by R. L. Weiss. In T. J. Paolino and B. S. McCrady (Eds.), *Marriage and Marital Therapy: Psychoanalytic, Behavioral and Systems Theory Perspectives,* pp. 165-239. Copyright © 1978 Brunner/Mazel, Inc. Used with permission. **274,** Dennie Cody/FPG International.

Chapter 12: 292, Spencer Grant/The Picture Cube. **294,** The Terry Wild Studio.

Chapter 13: 314, Ellis Herwig/The Picture Cube. **317,** Mark Richards/PhotoEdit.

Chapter 14: 344, Figure 14-1 adapted from *Adult Friendship,* by R. Blieszner and R. G. Adams, p. 7. Copyright © 1992 Sage Publications, Inc. Adapted with permission of Sage Publications, Inc. **345,** Cleo Photography/PhotoEdit. **348,** FPG International. **356, Figure 14-3** from "An Integrative Conceptual Framework for Friendship Research," by R. Blieszner and R. G. Adams, 1994, *Journal of Social and Personal Relationships, 11,* p. 166. Copyright © 1994 Sage Publications, Ltd. Reprinted with permission.

Chapter 15: 367, Michael Newman/PhotoEdit. **374,** David S. Strickler/The Picture Cube. **375, Box 15-2** from "Postparental Fathers in Distress," by R. A. Lewis and C. L. Roberts, *Psychiatric Opinion, Nov./Dec. 1979,* 29-30. Copyright © 1979 Opinions Publications, Inc. Reprinted with permission.